Accessories of
DRESS
An Illustrated Encyclopedia

Mrs. George Lingen............................*Thomas Sully*

The fashionable leghorn of 1800 with its dark, rich, contrasting ties and trim appears to be worn over a little hood which marks with delicacy the oval of the face.

ACCESSORIES OF
DRESS
AN ILLUSTRATED ENCYCLOPEDIA

Katherine Morris Lester

and

Bess Viola Oerke

Drawings by
Helen Westermann

DOVER PUBLICATIONS, INC.
Mineola, New York

Bibliographical Note

This Dover edition, first published in 2004, is an unabridged republication of the work originally published in 1940 by The Manual Arts Press, Peoria (Illinois), under the title *Accessories of Dress: An Illustrated History of the Frills and Furbelows of Fashion.*

Library of Congress Cataloging-in-Publication Data

Lester, Katherine Morris.
    [Illustrated history of those frills and furbelows of fashion which have come to be known as : accessories of dress]
    Accessories of dress : an illustrated encyclopedia / Katherine Morris Lester and Bess Viola Oerke ; drawings by Helen Westermann.
        p. cm.
    Published in Peoria, Ill. in 1940 under the title: An illustrated history of those frills and furbelows of fashion which have come to be known as: accessories of dress.
    Includes bibliographical references and index.
    ISBN 0-486-43378-1 (pbk.)
    1. Dress accessories—History. I. Oerke, Bess Viola. II. Westermann, Helen. III. Title.

GT2050 .L4L47 2004
391.4'4—dc22

2004041349

Manufactured in the United States of America
Dover Publications, Inc., 31 East 2nd Street, Mineola, N.Y. 11501

Preface

THE subject, Accessories of Dress, carries one back to the very threshold of costume. Here accessories were born. They appeared for the first time when primitive man, finding his most satisfying expression in body painting and tattoo, added to this his desire for ornament—rings dangling from his ears, chains around his neck, girdles about his hips, bracelets strung on his arms and legs, and perhaps a feather or two in his hair.

The earliest articles of adornment were those used to ornament different parts of the body, and interesting to note, these were the very places where such objects seemed to fit naturally. The parts of the body destined to carry ornament are those contracted or narrower portions above large bony or muscular structure—the forehead and temples, the neck and shoulders, the waist and hips, above and below the knee, the ankles, the upper arm, the wrist, and in a lesser degree, the fingers. Primitive man made use of all these centers for adornment, using headbands, necklaces, girdles, bracelets, and ankle rings. Then, to keep evil forces from entering the body, he hung pendant ornaments at the ears, the lips, and the nose, thereby adding earrings, nose rings, and lip rings to the long list of objects used in personal adornment.

Later, as body covering or clothing came to be worn, various accessory articles appeared for the head, neck, shoulders, waist, legs, and arms. So it is that our modern hats, bonnets, shawls, belts, girdles, shoes, hose, etc., lead back over a long trail to the primitive urge for ornament.

In organizing the material for this work the authors have followed the old-time sequence—accessories for the head, accessories worn about the neck and shoulders, and those worn on the feet and legs and on the arms and hands. Added to these are other ornaments which the modern world inherits from a developing civilization, culture, and taste; i.e., accessories carried in the hand and those worn on the costume. Our fans, gloves, parasols, laces, handkerchiefs, ribbons, etc., are later refinements which, combined with the earlier body ornaments, cover a wide range of those accessories which Fashion has so happily ordained for the enrichment and beauty of modern raiment.

It is the earnest wish of the authors that within these pages teachers of home economics, homemakers, club women, students of the theater, students of costume, and all others historically minded may glean a new, a more complete appreciation of the various accessories of modern dress, so familiar in themselves and yet replete with meanings unsuspected by the uninitiated.

Much of the data offered is in nowise new. Rather has it been the plan of the authors to trace a consecutive story of each accessory, thus giving the student a comprehensive view of the particular ornament or detail of costume and its place in fashion history. It is apparent that copious illustration is both a vital and indispensable part of any text relating to costume. For this reason both drawings and photographs have been liberally used. The drawings have been carefully gathered from authentic sources, and the famous portraits may be seen in the various art collections of Europe and America.

For the generous use of photographs illustrating the text the authors take this opportunity to acknowledge the courtesies extended by Tiffany & Co., the Metropolitan Museum of Art, the Hispanic Society of America, the Lenox Library, the Brooklyn Museum of Fine Arts, the Boston Museum of Fine Arts, the Isabelle Stewart Gardner Museum, Boston; the Massachusetts Historical Society, the Fogg Art Museum, Harvard University; Pilgrim Hall, Plymouth; Essex Institute, Salem; Worcester Art Museum and the American Antiquarian Society, Worcester; Rhode Island School of Design; Gallery of Fine Arts, Yale University; Walker Gallery of Art, Bowdoin College; Pennsylvania Academy of Fine Arts, Independence Hall, Philadelphia; the John Herron Art Institute, Indianapolis; the Detroit Institute of Arts; the Toledo Museum; and the Art Institute of Chicago.

Permission to reproduce material from foreign galleries, the rights of which are copyrighted or reserved, has been extended by the Victoria and Albert Museum, the National Portrait Gallery, and the Wallace Collection, National Gallery, London; the Ashmolean Museum, Oxford; the National Gallery, Edinburgh; the Royal Irish Academy, Dublin; the Louvre, Versailles Gallery, Paris; the Hohenzollern Museum and the Staatliche Museum, Berlin; the National Gallery, Munich; the Dresden Gallery; Rijks Museum, Amsterdam; the Prado, Madrid; and the National Museum, Stockholm. Special acknowledgments of these are made in the text.

The authors would not forget all those who have so successfully written on the fascinating subject of costume. These scholars have provided much in the field of accessories, and a comprehensive list of their works is included in the General Bibliography.

THE AUTHORS

Contents

Part I

ACCESSORIES WORN ON THE HEAD

CHAPTER 1

The Hat

There came up a lass from a country town
intending to live in the city,
In a steeple-crown *hat* and a Paragon gown
who thought herself wondrous pretty:
Her Petticoat serge, her stockings were green,
her smock cut out of a sheet, Sir;
And under it all, was seldom yet seen
so fair a young maid for the street, Sir!
Roxburgh Ballads, 1685

THROUGH the centuries the hat has played a varied and, at times, an amusing role in the history of dress. Today it is regarded as an essential detail in the costume of both men and women. In the apparel of women the hat is comparatively modern, whereas in men's dress, as a simple cap or hood, it dates back to remote times. From this ancient and humble beginning, followed by constant changes through the centuries, it has emerged as the indispensable head covering of moderns.

All primitive peoples have worn the simple, close-fitting cap. Figure 1. Some form of the cap was worn by the Egyptians, the Greeks, the Romans, the Gauls, the Franks, and the Anglo-Saxons. It was used as early as 4000 B.C. From that distant period down to the fourteenth century it continued to be the accepted head covering for the great mass of the people. Though hats came at a much later date, both the words "hat" and "cap" seem to have had their origin in terms used to designate the primitive home. Long before these peoples gave much thought to clothes they built themselves shacks or huts which, according to Planché,* they called *haet* or *hutt*. Their head coverings imitating the ancient hut were probably given the same name, a term which through the centuries changed to the modern word *hat*. The word "cap" comes from the Anglo-Saxon *cappe;* however, Planché, an early authority writing on the subject of costume, points out that the Belgic Britons had in their language the word *cappan*, used by later peoples of the same region in describing their conical caps made of rushes and curiously resembling the ancient hut made of wattles tied together in a similar way and called *cab, cabban*, whence our modern word *cabin*. So it would appear that some relation

---

* Planché, J. R., *A Cyclopedia of Costume*, Vol. I.

seemed to exist, particularly in these early days, between the primitive home and the first head covering.

The ancient cap made of skins, often with the shaggy side out, of cloth, of woolen stuff, and later of leather, probably at first resembled a loose,

Figure 1. Early Caps Seen in Various Anglo-Saxon Manuscripts of the 9th, 10th, and 11th Centuries

hoodlike cap, then took on more or less of a conical shape. This was gradually followed by more fitted shapes. The first recorded use of a hat with a brim comes from ancient Greece, where the *petasus* and *pileus*, low-crowned, broad-brimmed hats of felt, sometimes likened to a "barber's basin," were worn by huntsmen and travelers. However, with rustics of this and later periods, the simple cap, sometimes conical, sometimes with side flaps, continued to be worn. By the fourteenth century the popularity of the cap gave way to the hood, which with its long peak lent itself to many interesting arrangements and so helped to prolong the fashion over a considerable period. Hoods were fashionable for both men and women. Previous to this women had been wearing enveloping veils, short coifs, and, later, chin straps and wimples with head veils. It was not until a much later date that both men and women adopted the hat as it is known today. Consequently, in tracing the development of the modern hat it is necessary to go back through the period of veils and hoods to the little cap which innocently enough started the fashion of hats.

COURTESY, MUSEUM OF FINE ARTS, BOSTON

Figure 2. Head of Rameses III, Showing Wig

In Egypt, as in other warm countries, the climate and manner of living had much to do with dress development. Though the hat had no place in the Egyptian wardrobe, the various types of headdress served as worthy substitutes. Persons of all classes occasionally wore caps, some of which were large, others close fitting. Men generally, however, preferred the wig. See page 84. Wigs had been adopted at an early date and were worn as a protective covering from the sun. They were usually constructed of human hair or sheep's wool. The hair was shaved or cut short and the wig, built upon a netlike foundation, allowed the heat of the head to escape. Figure 2. In fact, the wig far surpassed the modern turban which is worn for the same purpose.

Another very familiar head covering was the simple cloth or kerchief fitted about the brow in such a way that it fell to the shoulders, sometimes in two broad bands or lappets which framed the face. Figure 3. Dignitaries of Egypt are seen in a helmet cap, apparently of woolen stuff, rising high above the head. Figure 4. These are usually orna-

Figure 3. Egyptian Head Covering

mented with emblems symbolic of office or rank. Chief among the princely insignia were the asp, signifying kingly power; the lotus, the emblem of abundance; and the sacred feather, indicating sovereignty.

Figure 4. Alabaster Head,
Ptolemaic Period

Figure 5. Wigs of an Egyptian
King and Queen

Though hats for women came at a much later date and in an entirely different world, it is interesting to note the elaborate wigs, ornamental bands, wreaths, and ribbon which, in a measure, made up to these women of Egypt for the lack of a hat. During the Old Empire and down to the Eighteenth Dynasty (1583 B.C.), elaborate coiffures falling over the shoulders and entirely concealing the contour of the head were worn. Figure 5. These masses of long hair, either plaited or straight, hung at the

PLATE I. The Deceased Entertained by the Goddess Nut . . . . *From an Egyptian wall painting*

back, covering the shoulder blades, while two side pieces fell to the front of the shoulders. These side tresses were secured by combs or an ornamental headband. As stated by many authorities, these large constructions must have been wigs, for the same woman is frequently seen in different coiffures, some of which are long and elaborate, others short. In still others a little of the natural hair is seen under the wig. The wall painting "The Deceased Entertained by the Goddess Nut" gives a very definite idea of this coiffure of three thousand years ago. PLATE I. The most important ornamental head covering of the early period was the *vulture* headdress of the Egyptian queen. Both sculpture and painting show the royal lady wearing this emblem of the sacred bird whose plumage covers the head. Figure 6. In marked contrast with this ancient headdress is the tall cap or crown of a much later date worn by Nefertiti, queen of Amemophis IV,

COURTESY, METROPOLITAN MUSEUM OF ART

Figure 6. The Vulture Headdress of an Egyptian Queen, Ptolemaic Period

who reigned during the fourteenth century, B.C., and whose daughter was the wife of King Tutankhamen. PLATE II. During this later period the former heaviness was abandoned and various styles were accepted. A few examples of the prevailing mode show outstanding bobs; others are long

Figure 7. Headdresses of Egyptian Women

Figure 8. Egyptian, a Style Which Succeeded the Heavy Wig

front and back and short on the shoulders. Some show a more natural arrangement of the hair which reveals rather than conceals the contour of the head. Wreaths, ribbon, and the lotus flower turned about the head were used as ornament. Figure 8. It is said that the ribbon which the Egyptian woman tied about her brow, leaving two streamers hanging at the back, is the first sign of the modern hatband.

PLATE II. Queen Nefertiti . . . . *Bust, painted in limestone with eyes of rock crystal*

Nefertiti, meaning "The Beautiful one has come," was the queen of Amemophis IV, 1375-58 B. C.

One of the most familiar types of ancient cap came from Phrygia in Asia Minor. This has passed into history as the "Phrygian bonnet." Figure 9. Originally it resembled a hood with a pointed, extended crown.

Figure 9. Forms of the Phrygian Cap

bent forward, with flaps hanging to the shoulders. When made of pliant material, the crown lay in a soft fold; when made of leather, the crown supported itself, taking on the form of a helmet. It was later worn in Greece and Italy and, during the thirteenth and fourteenth centuries, was revived in a somewhat similar shape as the hood and worn as a fashionable head covering by both men and women. At this time the tippet or pointed crown assumed many and amusing styles. See page 11. The general shape of the Phrygian bonnet is seen in many later types of headgear. Even in modern times, an occasional molded hat form harks back to this little cap of long ago.

Figure 10. The Petasus

After a drawing by Winckelmann.

In Greece, coverings for the head were not generally worn. Here again the mild climate and the leisurely life of the people made no particular demands for head coverings. Among the peasant folk the little, close-fitting cap, sometimes with flaps fastened under the chin, was sufficient. Strange as it may seem, it was reserved for the men of Greece to introduce the hat with a brim. This was of felt, tied under the chin and known as the *petasus* and *pileus*. Figure 10. Such a hat was worn only by travelers and huntsmen as a protection from the sun. When not upon the head it was pushed back on the shoulders and supported by a string about the neck. The felt used for the petasus as well as for caps, cloaks, and shoes of this day was made by matting together hair or bits of wool while moist. In England, as late as the fourteenth century during the reign of Edward II, a type of felt hat similar to the petasus was worn.

Greek women are said to have been blessed with beautiful and abund-

ant hair. This is characteristic of southern races. No doubt the vanity of the feminine world of that day found complete satisfaction in the beautiful crowns, diadems, cauls, and tiaras which ornamented the head. At least there is no mention of hats. Instead, when a covering for the head was needed, the *himation* served the purpose, for it could be easily adjusted about the head and shoulders.

Figure 11. Large Caps That Came by Way of Byzantium and Rome

In Rome, the leaders of fashion followed the Greek custom. When necessary they adjusted the toga in such a way that it could be readily pulled over the head. Roman women had no need for hats. Their veils, nets, and adjustable wigs, however, received the same careful attention that a modern woman bestows upon her hat.

After the conquest of Gaul by Julius Caesar (55 A.D.), Roman civilization was gradually introduced into that corner of western Europe. Later there followed the invasion of the Franks from the north, bringing other influences. The mingling of the Romans, Franks, and Gauls naturally brought about many changes in dress. During the long period of the Middle Ages the cap with its many variations continued to be the favorite head covering for men. Women, too, wore the little cap. It was, however, reserved for

Figure 12. Headrail
After a drawing in Cotton ms., Claudius, B IV.

the feminine world to make new and interesting changes in this important matter of dressing the head.

Middle Ages

Throughout the long period of the Middle Ages, women of all classes favored head draperies of one sort or another. These were usually large, square, oblong, or circular pieces of linen or cotton material falling from the head to the shoulders or below, sometimes reaching the feet. When long, this drapery was known as the *palla*, a name no doubt taken over after the Roman occupation. Another popular headdress which came by way of Byzantium and Rome was the large, turbanlike cap edged with a roll or pad. Figure 11. Though the crown and roll were usually of different colors, both were decorated with narrow bands set at regular intervals. The hair was completely hidden, for the cap fitted close to the brow, coming well down over the ears so as to leave only the lobes visible. Soon

Figure 13. Fashionable Coifs of the Middle Ages

the large cap gave way to one smaller and more snug fitting. The decorative bands were reduced to five, and these were frequently edged with pearls. A jeweled crown or coronet was often worn just above the roll, and a beautiful veil added the finishing note. Though the caps appear to be a very charming headdress and must be considered as a type fashionable during this early period, they were by no means so generally popular as the simple drapery or veil, which has passed into history as the *couvrechef.*

By the tenth and eleventh centuries conditions were rapidly changing. The Romans had introduced weaving, needlework, and dyeing, and materials were becoming more varied. Trade had been established with Britain, and, naturally, various customs and manners were carried back and forth across the channel. In Britain the identical type of head covering had developed under the name *headrail.* Figure 12. This drapery is considered woman's characteristic headdress of the early Middle Ages. Under the modernized name it served the woman of the new age with the same degree of comfort and satisfaction as had the palla and veil of old. This drapery seems to have been sufficiently large to have covered the head and to be wrapped about the neck and passed over the shoulder. Head draperies were always in color, never white, and materials, as is evident from the folds, were varied. In some, the cloth falls in innumerable small folds; while in others only a few appear.

About the year 1100, these head draperies grew smaller and the long, flowing hair was much in evidence. Many early drawings show the hair arranged in two long plaits twined about with colored ribbon. Some-

times ribbon and false hair were braided in with the natural hair with the intention of suggesting long and abundant locks. Another fashion was that of covering the long braids with cases of gay-colored silk, usually finished off with tassels. This attractive coiffure was always completed by the addition of short veils of cotton or linen. Of course these little coifs varied with the distinction of the wearer. Many leaders of fashion adorned the head with transparent veils which sparkled with gold and silver spangles. When the veil was secured by a diadem, a very majestic appearance was given these women of long ago. Figure 13.

Figure 14. The Wimple

At this period men's caps, formed of rush and straw, began to take a definite shape. They resembled loose caps with crowns of various heights. A few of these were given brims and worn with a string attached so they could be pushed back off the head, to hang behind the shoulders. Soon these shapes were repeated in wool, felt, and other materials. The art of felt making is probably as old as that of weaving. It was practiced in both Greece and Rome. The story runs that St. Clement, fourth bishop of Rome, first discovered this property of wool by placing bits of it in his sandals. During his long travels, heat, moisture, and friction wore the wool into a compact mass, which

Figure 15. The Gorget

he afterward recognized as a very useful material. Felt hats have been in use to the present day, their rise and fall in popularity being affected only by new and temporarily more attractive materials.

One can readily understand how draping the head, adopted so generally by women of the Middle Ages, created the tendency to frame in the face and hide the hair. In the twelfth century (1154-1216) the flattering fashion of the *chin strap* was introduced. A band of white linen was passed under the chin, and brought up, and pinned at the top or side of the head; another band was bound about the forehead; and over this arrangement of bands was draped the veil. Thus the hair was entirely covered. Sometimes, after the chin strap had been adjusted, the stiffened band about the forehead was so placed that it resembled a little, low, broad-crowned cap. This framing of the face soon ushered in another mode which strongly appealed to the feminine heart. A shaped piece of fine, white or colored material was caught under the chin and, while its fulness draped the throat, was brought up tightly around the face and either pinned to the hair at the side or carried to the top of the head and fastened. Over the head was draped a veil which hung to the shoulders, framing the face. Thus the *wimple* was born. Figure 14. Sometimes the complete headdress, veil and wimple, is termed the wimple. Wimples are first mentioned in twelfth century records. A manuscript of that date mentions, "small gwimples for ladies' chyunes," and "gwimples dyed saffron," which leads one naturally to suppose that yellow was a popular color. Following the wimple came the *gorget* (1200 A.D.). Figure 15. This accessory was an ample piece of material carried about the neck several times, and frequently pinned high at the sides to the headdress. In many ways it answered the same purpose as the wimple. The gorget was always

Figure 16. The Development of the Medieval Hood

tucked in at the neck of the gown and therefore is distinct from the *guimpe*, which fell outside the neck opening. Though the exact shape of the gorget is not known, an inventory of the time of Henry VIII, listing the apparel of his queen, shows this entry, "A *gorget* of silver tissue, in length one yard and three quarters." This gives a definite idea of its size, and one's imagination can readily picture the appearance of this mass of material draped about the neck and shoulders.

During the twelfth century, men's head coverings seem limited to the little, close-fitting cap, often with a pointed crown. In this day caps were removed by catching hold of the point; consequently, peaks were a necessity. About 1300, a general revival of the pointed hood, the Phrygian cap of ancient days, set a new mode for both men and women. The medieval hood practically usurped the place of all other forms of headgear and was worn by both men and women. As worn by men, however, it shows an unusually interesting and novel development.

In its earliest form the hood resembled a long, pointed, open bag, with an oval opening in the side for the face. Figure 16. It was slipped over the head, with the opening adjusted to the face; the cape fell over the shoulders. The cape was sometimes lengthened and, when buttoned down the front, formed a kind of cloak. However, it is the peak of the hood, known in England as the *liripipe*, which was the unique feature of this new fashion. During the fourteenth century this appendage grew to an exaggerated length and was left hanging at the back. If, however, the fancy of the wearer dictated, it was twisted around the crown so that the shortened end, tucked through the coils, fell at one side of the head. These various adjustments of the hood introduced many and amusing styles. The "dagged edge," so fashionable for all garments about 1346, was also applied to the hood. The "dagges" were made by cutting the edges of material in the form of leaves and scallops. Sometimes the broad, lower edge of the cape with its dagged edge was rolled up around the crown, giving a coxcomb effect, and the long peak falling at the side or back

Figure 17. The Chaperon with Various Fanciful Arrangements of the Liripipe, about 1346

was tucked in at the girdle. Some of the dandies of the period ventured a more fanciful arrangement. After slipping on the hood, the portion intended to cover the shoulders was gathered up and pleated in the form of a fan, and the long peak was then twisted around it to keep the material in place. These arrangements came to be known as the *chaperon*, and gradually developed into an odd and picturesque "made-up" head covering. Figure 17. It took the form of a stuffed roll called a *roundlet*, which encircled the head and was worn over a close-fitting cap. Material resembling the loose skirt of the hood was gathered and draped over the pad,

PLATE III. *Detail*, Romance of the Rose

The roundlet with the vestige of the liripipe.

and a broad piece of cloth suggesting the liripipe, sometimes nine feet in length, was fitted at one side of the roundlet. This was usually twined about the shoulders like a scarf and then tucked in at the girdle. A detail from the tapestry "Romance of the Rose" shows the roundlet with its

mass of material inserted at the crown and the former liripipe, now a scarf, at the side. PLATE III. With this amusing fashion in men's hats the long peak of the medieval hood gradually passed from the scene. One sees, as a very last vestige of the liripipe, the little round hats of the late century with a scarf attached at one side, the end knotted and thrown over the shoulder. Figure 18.

Hoods as worn by women continued long in vogue. Figure 19. Women, too, must have worn the liripipe, for a chronicler in 1346, in describing the appearance of ladies riding to a tournament and affecting masculine dress, remarks, "They wore short hoods and liripipes wrapped around their head like cords." In later days (1400), ladies' hoods were made of silk and velvet, frequently slashed and lined with fur. During the reign of the parti-col-

Figure 18. The Last Sign of the Liripipe

ored gown, hoods as well as gowns were fashioned half one color, half another, as feminine fancy dictated. An interesting account written ten centuries later, after hats had been definitely accepted, compares the respective value of the hat and hood, much to the disadvantage of the hat:

Hoods are the most ancient covering for the head, and are far more elegant and useful than the modern fashion of hats, which present a useless elevation, and leave the neck and ears completely exposed.

PUGIN, *Glossary of Ecclesiastical Ornament and Costume*

1300-1500 A.D.

Over a long period hoods had proved a popular head covering for both men and women. At the same time there were, of course, hats and caps made of felt. For instance, about the close of the thirteenth century (1280), the crowns of men's felt hats were high and peaked, with brims turned up at the back and at the front drawn out in elongated form. Often a single feather was added at the side, front, or back. Many times this high-crowned hat was seen worn over the hood. See Figure 26, page 19.

While men of the late Middle Ages were disporting themselves in hoods and high-crowned hats, women, too, were initiating a change.

After a period of veiled and hooded heads, it is not surprising that a new fashion was about to step upon the scene. Women, however, were reluctant to give up the covering of the hair; consequently, the new mode devised only a new method for the same old practice. About the year 1300, hairdressing came to be a popular diversion, and in the course of several decades the art was destined to evolve new and surprising creations. In the new fashion the hair was first parted at the back, with the long strands brought forward, plaited, and arranged in either elongated or wheel-like forms at each side of the head. In the earlier stages of this new mode, the wimple and gorget were still frequently worn over the side extensions. Soon, however, the luxurious fashion of a golden network, formed into cylindrical, circular, or other shapes, led the way to the distinct mode of the

Figure 19. Hood and Wimple

"reticulated headdress," which continued in varied forms for nearly three hundred years (see the Hair Net, page 123). The early nets or cauls were formed of a fine, gold wire, often set at the intersections with pearls and

Figure 20. The reticulated Headdress, 1382

other gems. They were held firmly in place at the sides of the face by a golden headband with projecting sides which fitted over the upper edge of the cauls. In Figure 20, from the drawing of an effigy of 1382, the side cylinders fit over the hair, concealing the ears. The rigid piece across the forehead with extensions on either side caps the top edges of the cauls, holding them securely in position. Though the whole arrangement of net and band is known as the *crespine*, it was to the band in particular that this term was applied. At the back a net was fastened to the edge of the crespine and the sides brought forward and fastened to the cauls.

Frequently a veil, probably known as the *crispinette*, was added to this elaborate headdress. As the fashion for golden nets continued, from time to time various changes appeared. One of the most elaborate examples of net and veil is that seen in the effigy of Beatrice, Countess of Arundel, who died in 1439. Figure 21. Here the side ornaments are large, the coronet of unusual proportions, and the veil is stretched its full width and probably extended by wires.

In the latter part of the fourteenth century, about 1380, a new and striking fashion appeared. No doubt the heads of women veiled, hooded, and netted, prepared the way for this astonishing mode. In their effort to outdo anything that had previously existed, the fair leaders of that distant day fashioned head coverings of great height: towering peaked bonnets,

Figure 21. Headdress of Beatrice, Countess of Arundel, about 1400

Figure 22. The Towering Headdresses of the Late Middle Ages

Figure 23. The Hennin and Escoffion

great heart-shaped arrangements, and tall horn-shaped creations. These new styles in headdress usually fitted the head like a little cap, covering the ears and cheeks so that not a wisp of hair could be seen. At first the hair was hidden under a caul or fell loose under the back drape. Though several types of this exaggerated headdress were worn, the *hennin* and *escoffion* were the established leaders. Figures 22, 23. The great hennin was a towering, conical cap worn back on the head. To the tall peak a veil of various lengths was attached. In some instances this is known to

PLATE IV. Marie, Wife of Potinari

A very handsome costume of velvet enriched with fur. The hennin is secured by pins to the frontlet. The necklace is an unusual specimen of this early period.

17

have reached the extravagant length of ten and twelve feet. Women found the hennin set back on the head difficult to keep in position. This introduced the *frontlet*, which was made of a rigid wire netting fitted

over the head with an extension over the forehead to which the hennin was pinned. Usually frontlets were covered with black velvet or silk, though among the nobility frontlets of gold were often seen. PLATE IV. The escoffion was a kind of two-horned arrangement, each horn being sometimes even a yard in length. The horns were usually a network of gold webbing or a light material well stiffened with starch. Many times the tips of the horns were decorated with little flags, veils, or whisks of fringe, and over these was draped the large veil of fine silk or sheer gauze.

So ridiculous were these extravagances that they were denounced by preachers and condemned by lay moralists. One bishop preached a sermon against the outrageous fashion and directed the people, upon the approach of a woman so dressed, to cry, "Beware of the ram! Beware of the ram!" He promised ten days pardon to all who should in this way show their indignation. Other moralists started the cry, "War to the hennin! War to the hennin!" All these attacks,

Figure 24. The Tall Hennin

From late 14th century ms.

however, only led to greater extravagance on the part of the ladies. Hennins continued until lovely woman herself decreed the change. A detail from the impressive scene of "Joan of Arc at the Court of Chinon," by Boutet de Monvel, presents a group of court ladies wearing the tall headdress, each exquisitely lovely in its daintiness and charm. PLATE V.

In England the hennin was known as the "steeple headdress." Figure 24. About 1340 it changed somewhat to a less extravagant form and has passed into history as the "butterfly headdress." Figure 25. In this fashion the hair was drawn back from the face and covered with a close, high-crowned cap, or a netted case made of silk or velvet, sometimes em-

Figure 25.
The Butterfly
Headdress

After a drawing of the effigy of Isabella Cheyne, 1482.

broidered and ornamented with gems. The veil, measuring about two yards in length, and half as wide, was a stiffened gauze. It was creased in the proper way and pinned to the front hair. Being stiffened, it was easily supported over the gold wires which were attached to the front of the cap.

Keeping pace with the towering headdresses of women were the peaked bonnets worn by men. As early as the eleventh century the word "bonnet" had been applied to the little cap. No doubt this came about

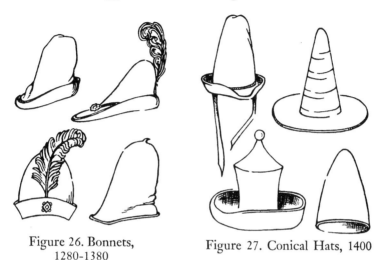

Figure 26. Bonnets, 1280-1380

Figure 27. Conical Hats, 1400

through the use of a woolen cloth called *bonnette*, which was at that time a new and popular material. Although the bonnet was at first a close-fitting cap, the crown was gradually raised until about 1380 it attained a peaklike form. Many of these sugar-loaf and elongated crowns had rolled brims of fur; others were without brims. Figure 26. A dandy of the period frequently carried his high hat on his walking stick, and it was considered smart for him to set it upon his head by a dexterous move of the stick. A second

Figure 28. Little Hat with Long Feathers Worn by Fashionable Beaux, 1485

detail from the painting by Boutet de Monvel pictures a group of courtiers in the headgear of this period. The variety of hats is interesting. The skullcap, several forms of the hood, and the tall, peaked caps, without brims, are pictured. PLATE VI. It was not long before the high, peaked caps became conical hats with circular brims. Figure 27. At the very end of the century, as if vying with the ladies in splendor, the dandies of the

PLATE V. *Detail*, Joan of Arc at the Court of Chinon . . *Boutet de Monvel*

Towering hennins with flowing veils, handsome fabrics, cut velvets and brocades, combined with ermine suggest the luxury of court life in the late 14th century.

PLATE VI. *Detail*, Joan of Arc at the Court of Chinon . . . *Boutet de Monvel*

Tall hats, caps, and the chaperon are much in evidence. Note other details: shoes, hose, and fabrics.

period in both England and France adopted a most singular hat. Over a close cap, usually scarlet in color and covering only the crown of the head, they wore atilt a low, rolling-brimmed hat of medium size decorated with outrageously high-standing feathers (see page 76). These feathers were of various colors, and the stem of each was usually ornamented with rows of pearls and other gems. The bunch of high feathers was set at the front or side of the little hat and, curving backward, presented a very imposing effect. Figure 28. When it was not worn on the head these dandies of long ago let this unusual hat hang behind the shoulders supported by a cord as was the petasus of old. So much for the beaux of the period. Gentlemen more sedate and dignified had adopted a little hat with a low, broad crown. This had originated in Italy and was

soon popular in France, Spain, and England, and so generally worn that it has become recognized as a distinct historical type. At this time the future Henry VIII was Prince of Wales, and the drawing, Figure 29, shows the young prince in the fashionable bonnet which subsequently became the popular "beret."

Figure 29. The Early Bonnets Which Merged into the Beret

1500-1600

With the opening years of the new century, women's fashions took a turn. The height of former years completely disappeared and milady contented herself with a nunlike hood. Hoods were fashionable in Italy, France, England, Spain, Flanders, and Germany. Each differed from the other according to the taste of the nation adopting it. In France, and the other countries as well, the simplest form of hood fell free to the shoulders. Soon variations began to appear. First, the hood was lined with bright, contrasting material, brocade or gold lace, and the front turned back about the face. Next, the sides were cut up some distance, forming long lappets which fell to the front of the shoulders, while the back curtain, termed a "fall," fell free. Figure 30. Very shortly the long lappets as well as the fall were turned up and pinned in various ways to the crown. Many were the ways of folding and pinning the lappets, and each presented a new form of hood! Figure 31. When made of linen they were often starched and, arranged in various ways, made a very imposing headdress. The novelty of the English headdress was the pointed or gabled effect given the front, probably by wiring. Though the hair is sometimes seen it is usually concealed in silken cases. The hood-and-veil was always black but the lining was either red or white. Under the hood a white or golden coif was usually worn. This was frequently frilled, and stiffened sides came forward on the cheeks and sometimes curved out and up at the neckline. In PLATE VII, the portrait of Lady Guilford, by Holbein, suggests the richness of material used in the headdress of the period. The hair is here covered with the silken cases and over this is placed the hood. The white lining suggests the coif, though it is not strictly so. The side lappets of a rich woven material are

Figure 30. Early Forms of Gable Headdress, 1500

Figure 31. Two Types of Lappet Arrangements

The lappets were arranged in various ways. In the left view one side of the hood is turned back and pinned to the crown, while the opposite side hangs free.

Over the frilled coif in the right view the lappets appear to be turned up and pinned; one side of the hood is then brought up and forward, forming a peak over the front, while the opposite side hangs free.

pinned up, and the back fall, which appears to be velvet, hangs free. The broad, low-cut neckline, the chains, pendant, and rings are all characteristic of the period. The costume of Lady Rich (also in PLATE VII) is more simple. Here the stiffened coif is lace edged. The brooch and ring are the only ornaments, and upon these Holbein, that master of detail, put much loving care. Fortunately this headdress of the early century has been preserved to future generations in a large number of portraits of famous women painted by Holbein, who at this time was court painter to the English King, Henry VIII.

Following this fashion of the gabled headdress came the smaller hoods commonly called French hoods. The bonnet of Lady Lee, PLATE VII, shows something of the transformation that had taken place. The hair is no longer covered but is plainly visible. It is parted in the middle and brought down over the ears. The back hair was always hidden in a black velvet bag known as the *cale*. This velvet bonnet with its pearl ornamentation is very handsome and in perfect harmony with the general richness of the costume. Lady Lee carries the fashionable pomander or scent box without which no toilet of the day was quite complete. By-and-by French hoods grew very, very small and were set back on the head. The portrait of Catherine Howard, PLATE VII, painted by Holbein, shows this version of the French hood and presents a head so charming that it is difficult to conceive of it having been cut off.

Figure 32. The "Marie Stuart" Coifs or Caps

In adjusting the French hood a little coif of white linen or gold net was usually first fitted over the head; over this a stiffened band of velvet or satin was set bonnetlike far back on the head. Sometimes the stiffened band of the hood was flat, or again it might be adjusted to stand at an angle. Strings were usually attached so it could be tied under the chin, and a veil invariably hung at the back. It is said that Anne of Cleves upon her arrival in England wore such a French hood. Henry VIII took possession of all her personal effects, and was graciously pleased to allow her six changes of apparel and "six French hoods with edgings of goldsmith's work, but without a diamond or pearl."

Presently the little hood was reduced still more. The sides and back were shortened, and the front, probably with the help of wiring, given a dip over the forehead, while the sides curved back to the head in the familiar heart-shaped effect. Mary, Queen of Scots, educated in France,

Lady Guilford . . . . *Holbein*

The gabled headdress is set over silken cases which confine the hair. The side lappets are turned up and pinned; the "fall" of velvet hangs free.

Lady Rich . . . . *Holbein*

The white, lace-edged coif is here still worn under the hood, but over the cases confining the hair. Side lappets are pinned up.

Lady Lee . . . . *Holbein*

This smaller hood without lappets followed the gabled headdress. The hair is no longer confined in cases.

Catherine Howard . . . . *Holbein*

The hood with veil is set back and tied under the chin. Note cuffs, probably "Spanish black work."

PLATE VII

had married Francis II. This little cap coming in during the period 1589-90 received the name "Marie Stuart" cap and, as such, has passed into history. Figure 32.

As for men's hats, the introduction at the end of the previous century of the low, wide-crowned beret literally drove all other hats and caps off the market. This little hat was made of the finest materials—silk, velvet, felt, and cloth. Color, too, played an important part. In a wardrobe account of Henry VIII one item reads, " . . . for making three *cappes* of velvette the one yalowe, the other orange colour and the thirde greene." Another mentions a "*hatte* of greene velvette embrowdered with grene silke and lined with grene sarcenette." In the earlier stages of this popular hat, the crown was low and of moderate width with a narrow brim. Gradually the crown grew so broad and flat that it resembled a plate turned down upon the head. Later, the form changed still more: the crown was raised and its fulness came to be supported upon a wire frame. In this form it gradually merged into the tall hat of 1600, Figures 33, 34.

Figure 33. Various Forms of the Toque

The earliest of these little berets were made in a very simple way. An oval or circular piece of material was used for the crown. This was sufficiently large so that the outer edge could be pleated in to fit the head. A narrow brim, about three inches deep and cut on the curve, was attached to this crown. Some drawings show the brim

Figure 34. Various Forms of the High Hat, Late 1600

turned down; generally, however, the preference falls to the turned-up brim. Many times the brim was cut in tabs held together by cords, or turned up and ornamented with a handsome, jeweled brooch. Often, as in France, the under part of the brim was of a different color. The drawing of Henry VIII as a youth, Figure 29, pictures the early fashion, while his portraits of mature years invariably show the low, platelike beret or the beret with the turned-up brim and the encircling feather.

Another variation of the early beret was made by gathering in a circular piece of material around the outside edge. The brim was then formed by turning in the edge the desired width and sewing it down. Figure 35. This made the headband, which was still further defined by a band of gold braid. Still another type was made of two circular pieces of material sewed together at the outer edge. The circular opening for the head was cut in the underpiece, which was fitted to the head and held in place by a band about the opening. It is possible that a wire set about the outer edge on the inside helped to maintain the circular form. Sometimes a low, padded crown was sewed to the center of the upper piece and a feather attached to this. The little beret passed through many changes. It was slashed, jeweled, feathered, and worn at a smart angle; standing plumes, tall and short, set at the back, side, or front, added the note of distinction. In England, the low, encircling feather was patronized by that royal arbiter of fashion, Henry VIII, this mode being continued until the time of Elizabeth.

COURTESY, METROPOLITAN MUSEUM OF ART

Figure 35. Portrait (believed to be that of Sir Thomas Wyatt) . . . . *Flinck*

A form of the early low beret, 1500-45.

By the latter half of the sixteenth century the low beret was relegated to the professions and the use of elderly men who made no effort to follow the fashion. The popular form of the high, soft crown known as the *toque* was now adorned with a standing plume and worn set well back on the head by both men and women. Figure 33. At the same time the "Marie Stuart" cap came in for its share of change. A crown was soon fitted to the little heart-shaped coif, giving it the appearance of a heart-shaped hat. Figure 37. All these popular types of the beret and heart-shaped hats have been made familiar by the portraits of both men and women who were conspicuous fashion leaders in this colorful sixteenth century.

In men's hats the outside band was, at this period, a very important feature of the hat. Sometimes it was beautifully embroidered, sometimes jeweled, or, again, it was simply a necklace of great value. The hatband is said to be a survival of the ancient fillet with which the women of Egypt bound the brow. In the old manuscripts of the Middle Ages it is shown with two streamers as part of the ecclesiastical headdress. In modern times it is seen in many hat shapes worn by children. The sailor with two ribbon streamers hanging over the brim and the Scotch cap with its ribbons are distinctly twentieth-century survivals of the early headband.

The inside band is a development from the early practice of drawing up the circular form to fit the head. Later the plain leather, inside band, without lacing, was fitted to the hat. A survival of the custom of draw-

Figure 36. The Little Beret with a Feather

Worn over a Handsome Caul

Figure 37. The "Marie Stuart" Cap Becomes a Hat

ing up and tying the hatband remains in the little bow which today finishes the modern inside band.

Toward the close of the sixteenth century, as crowns rose, brims began to widen and the felts of beaver were introduced. True, beaver hats had been worn before the sixteenth century, but it was at this particular period that they were especially prized by those who kept abreast of the fashion. The period in which the fur of the beaver was first used in the manufacture of hats is undecided. Such hats, however, were imported from Flanders before the end of the

Figure 38. High Hats of Puritan Days

fourteenth century. Chaucer, in the *Canterbury Tales*, describes the merchant as wearing:

On his head a Flaundrish *beaver* hat.

Among the effects of Sir John Faslog (1459) was "a hatte of *beaver* lined with damask."

1600-1700

During the early years of the seventeenth century the beaver hat became a choice and costly accessory of dress, although at first it was the simple, high-crowned beaver, so familiar in the dress of our Puritan forbears. Figure 38. It continued to hold an exclusive place for many years. Indeed, so prized was the beaver that it was frequently left as a bequest in the wills of those who were fortunate enough to possess one. As late as 1674 hatboxes, similar to those of today, were a strict necessity for protecting the valuable beaver. Hats were carefully packed in these when not in use. Philip Stubbes, that able chronicler of his day, has a word to say on the hats of the period:

Some are of silk, some of velvet, some of taffeta, some of sarcenet, some of wool, and what is more curious, some of a certain kind of fine hair; these they call *beaver* hats, of twenty, thirty, and forty shillings apiece, fetched from beyond the sea, whence a great sort of other varieties do come.

Reference is again made to the popular beaver in the diary of the matchless Pepys, under date of June 26, 1661, "This day Mr. Halder sent me a *beaver* which cost me 4£50s—an enormous price for a hat considering the value of the money at this period."

The beavers of this day were high in the crown—sometimes peaked, sometimes round, sometimes flat—with narrow brims. They resembled the later "stovepipe" hats of 1820-30. They were worn set back on the head, set high, or atilt. The hatband, too, came in for its share of display. This was very elegant, usually of ribbon encrusted with gems. Jeweled necklaces were frequently twined about the crown, and on one occasion the Duke of Buckingham is reported to have worn upon his hat the "Mirror of France"—a great diamond, the finest in England.

COURTESY, METROPOLITAN MUSEUM OF ART

Figure 39. Portrait of a Man . . . *Hals*

The high-crowned, wide-brimmed beaver and the falling lace-trimmed collar with cuffs to match are typical modes of the early 17th century.

The vogue for the beaver hat was of great commercial benefit to the colonies in America. Year after year great hogsheads of these pelts were sent to England and Holland, where they were used in the manufacture of the famous beaver hats. Figure 39.

It is interesting to note that at this time hats were worn within as well as out of doors. The custom of removing the hat when indoors is distinctly a modern idea, impossible to date. During the later cavalier days

when the great, plumed hats were fashionable, the measure of a gentleman was revealed in the ease and grace with which he doffed his hat.
No doubt this doffing of the hat gradually led to removing it altogether
when indoors. At any rate, in the seventeenth century hats were constantly worn at table, at church, and elsewhere. This custom undoubtedly was a silent reminder of the dignity and authority of the "man of
the house." Only on one occasion were hats removed—in the presence of
royalty. Again, Pepys writing on the subject says, "An hereditary honor

Figure 40. Cavalier Hats, 1600

and privilege granted to one of my ancestors was that he might wear his
hat before the king." Today, although hats are generally removed indoors, when visiting the British House of Commons one is surprised to see
the members wearing their hats while the house is in session.

During the same century, probably about 1625-1640, a new and distinct shape was given the beaver hat. It had come by way of Flanders, and
soon was accepted as the very acme of fashionable dress. The reigns of
Louis XIII of France and Charles I of England are always associated with
this high-crowned, rolling-brimmed hat set off with plumes. The tilted
brim was usually held in position by an ornamental clasp which also secured the feathers. Figure 40.

Gradually, with the passing of the years, this hat changed in form; the
crown became lower and rounder and the brim broader. Vary as it did,
however, its curves and flowing lines fitted admirably into the dashing
costume of this romantic period. PLATE VIII. The famous paintings of
the Dutch master Frans Hals and his Flemish contemporary, Sir Anthony
Van Dyck, preserve the grace and charm of this picturesque type of
gentleman's hat.

While the cavaliers of the early seventeenth century were disporting
themselves in plumed hats and other picturesque wearing apparel, the
ladies were busy keeping up with the changing fashions. They, too, ini-

PLATE VIII. Charles I . . . . *Van Dyck*

The royal costume illustrates the very height of the mode—high boots with spur leather, lace collar and cuffs, the wide-brimmed beaver, the sword, the walking stick, and the fashionable gloves.

tiated a change. No longer were the French berets, toques, and Marie Stuart caps the popular styles. Milady again gave her first thought to coiffure. Early in the century the hair was dressed low with little curls hanging at each side of the face. By-and-by the curls grew longer, and later, about 1660, distended on wire frames, were held out at each side of the head, and very appropriately known as "heart breakers." With this coiffure hats were impossible; consequently hoods were devised. Women's headdress of the third quarter of the century is distinctly that of the

Figure 41. Hoods, Late 1600

hood. Figure 41. The most simple form of this hood resembles a length of material thrown carelessly over the head, with the ends twisted loosely and tied under the chin. The portrait of Elizabeth Paddy Wensley, painted between 1670-75, gives a definite idea of one phase of the hood. Here it appears to be worn over a lace-frilled cap. Other details of the costume are characteristic of the fashionable dress of this early period. PLATE IX. Caps were made of various materials, often of one color faced with contrasting hue or fur. Silks and the finest of gauzelike materials were favored by the fashionable, while the less fastidious were content with more durable stuffs. As the coiffure became lower and gradually changed into a more natural arrangement of the hair close to the head, hoods grew smaller. This fashion is reflected in the early hoods worn by Puritan mothers in America.

It appears, however, that the hooded head was altogether too demure for our lady of fashion, for it was soon followed by an elaborate headdress which took its name from one of the favorites at the court of Louis XIV. As the story goes, and it has become a matter of history, the Duchess de Fontange was attending one of the royal hunting parties. While out upon a lively jaunt, a gust of wind carried off her hat. Undaunted, the duchess quickly twisted a ribbon around her disheveled locks in such a way that the hair fell over the brow and the loops stood up behind. So charmed was the king and so enchanted the company that the very next day all the ladies appeared with the headdress *à la Fontange!*

PLATE IX. Elizabeth Paddy Wensley

The early hood is here worn over the little cap. Note lace, earrings, necklace, rings.

33

In the fontange, however, formal pleatings of gauze, lace, and silk took the place of the disheveled locks. These were made to stand stiffly, raised from a large bow. On either side of this arrangement fell lappets of lawn and lace. Sometimes these were gathered in at the back, forming a little, baglike cap. Figure 42. The laces used in making the fontange were the

exquisite, handmade laces of Brussels and Mechlin, for no machines for lace making had yet been invented. Consequently, the cost of milady's fontange was a serious matter. Even so, the fontange continued. This unusual headdress was known in England as the *commode*, and though it remained fashionable for many years it fell from favor in England long before France could be persuaded to give it up. In time, Louis came to regret his first ad-

Figure 42. The Fontange

miration for this wily makeshift of the duchess. It reached such extravagance that he finally commanded it be laid aside. This edict was obeyed for a time but the fontange soon reappeared and flourished until one day a beautiful English lady, her hair dressed low, was presented at court. In an instant the fontange became extinct! The astonished King remarked, "I own that I am mortified when I think that all my voiced authority could not succeed in suppressing these extravagantly high headdresses. No person, even out of compliance to me, would reduce hers an inch. A stranger arrives, *'une guenille d'Angleterre,'* with a low headdress, and instantly the princesses rush from one extreme to another."

While women were wearing the high fontange, menfolk hesitated to give up the handsome beaver. Toward the latter half of the century during the reign of Charles II of England (1600-85) and Louis XIV of France (1643-1715), the brim of this cavalier hat grew still broader and, laden with plumes, was too wide to support itself. It began to droop, to hang down. This effect gave rise to the expression "slouched hats." It

Figure 43. Early Forms of the Tricorne

Figure 44. Later Forms of Tricorne

was very difficult to manage so inconvenient a form of headgear. This inconvenience led to turning it up or "cocking" it on one side, then on two sides, and finally on three sides. Thus the three-cornered hat, the *tricorne*, was formed. So popular was this style of hat and so continuous has been its favor that it has become a permanent feature in the history of the hat. Figures 43, 44.

Various were the types of tricorne. Many were elaborate with plumes and gold and silver braid.

COURTESY, METROPOLITAN MUSEUM OF ART

Figure 45. Black Velvet Hat with Feather Trimming

Venetian, early 19th century.

Others were trimmed with an edging of feathers, and still others were severe in line and trimmed with bands of braid. Figure 45. Everywhere the cocked hat was considered a mark of distinction. Sometimes the brim was rolled in the form of a spout, and again it was shaped "like the nose of a greyhound." But in whatever form it appeared it was always regarded as an indication of taste and style. It is related that one John Sly, an English haberdasher, sent forth an announcement to the effect that he was preparing "hats for several kinds of heads that made figures in

PLATE X. Clara Walker Allen . . . . *John Woolaston*

The costume exemplifies the popular mode for lace. Lace cap, lace fichu, and lace ruffles set in the short sleeves were the acme of fashionable dress.

the realm of Great Britain with cocks significant of their powers and faculties. His hats for men of the faculties and physic do just turn up to give a little lift to their sagacity; his military hats glare full in the face; and he has a familiar cock for all good companions between the above mentioned extremes."

The cocked hat continued to be the favorite for a century. Toward 1800 it assumed a rounded crown, and the cockade was the fashionable decoration. Figure 46. The cockade, at one time a badge of distinction worn only by royalty and those in the royal service, has in this twentieth century become a commonplace ornament designed for the many instead of the few. It has also shrunk in size from an imposing decoration to a small rosette of ribbon, feathers, or a button with ribbon pleatings. In France during the Revolution

Figure 46. The Cockade, Front View

Figure 47. Caps of Early 1700

it was worn as a symbol of allegiance to the old government. Later it was regarded as a convenient badge of social distinction. Today it is worn merely as a dictate of general fashion. It is said that the cockade is a vestige of the liripipe of the medieval hood. The long cape of the hood, when turned up about the head and laid in pleats, was bound with the long liripipe which was wrapped about the head holding the pleats in place. This

PLATE XI. Mrs. Elliot . . . . *Gainsborough*

A charming interpretation (English) of the high headdress of the late 18th century.

caused the pleated portion to fall in such a way as to resemble a cock's comb. When the edge of the cape was "dagged," as it frequently was, it suggested still more the jagged comb of a cock. The latter cockades often showed a bit of fluted ribbon with a dagged edge attached to a rosette of ribbon. Cockades worn with the tricorne were varied in both form and color and imparted an air of distinction to the wearer equal if not superior to the former lavish use of the plume.

1700-1800

Fashion never continues in the same path for long; consequently, after the high fontange and just before the towering "heads" of the next century, she paused. The low coiffure had now become the mode, and caps—lace caps, caps of gauze, linen, and lawn—were in the ascendency. Figure 47. This little cap apparently was only the earlier fontange minus the upstanding flutes of ribbon and lace; the lappets, however, remained. These were sometimes tied, or, if milady preferred, were left hanging at the back. At this period both young and old wore some kind of cap, in as well as out of doors. The very charming portrait of Clara Walker Allen, PLATE X, gives one a glimpse of early American costume at the time

COURTESY, NEW YORK HISTORICAL SOCIETY

Figure 48. Mrs. George Ogilvie

The mob cap with its ruchings and ribbon was the highly favored head-dress of the late 18th century.

when the little cap was in its heyday. The finest of laces were frequently used in making these dainty headdresses, and here our lady of the portrait wears her cap and fichu of the same pattern, which is likewise seen in the ruffles of the sleeves. Caps remained in fashion from the early days of the century (1700) until the hair began to rise in those amazing towerlike constructions ever associated with the name of the French queen, Marie Antoinette. The cap took many forms and ranged in size from the small lace cap to the great *mobs*, so conspicuous in the portraits of many American women of this early period. Figures 48, 49. The large mobs were a development of the small cap, for they kept pace with the heightening coiffure. They were often very elaborate, made of gauze and net adorned with bits of fluttering lace or lawn, and the final emphasis, a large ribbon bow, was placed at the center front.

Sometime during the seventies, probably about 1774, a most extraordinary contrivance for the head made its appearance. This was the *calash* (from the French *calèche*, meaning "carriage"). It was, indeed, a novel bonnet. Figure 50. It is said to have been introduced much earlier in England (1765) as the invention of the Duchess of Bedford. In France, however, a similar hood was in existence before this date. The recumbent effigies of the sixteenth and seventeenth centuries testify to the use of such a hood, and the calash may have been a revival of this older head covering, with some improvements, under a new name. The large and

Figure 49. Mr. and Mrs. Ralph Izard . . . . *Copley*

Shows fine faces and strikingly interesting examples of Colonial dress. Note the buttons of the coat, the stock, the short breeches, buttoned and buckled below the knee; in particular, note Mrs. Izard's mob, and the narrow, black velvet neckband.

novel bonnet was usually made of silk or fine linen, and resembled the extension top of a carriage. Whalebone run through shirrings which were about three inches apart sustained the extended frame. The neckline was drawn in and fitted. A ribbon or streamer was attached to the center of the front edge, and with this the bonnet could be coyly pulled down over the face or pushed back just as the fair wearer wished. Hence it was that the calash received its name, "bashful bonnet."

By-and-by, however, as if weary of caps, bonnets, and simple coiffures, the leaders of fashion cast about for something new. Instead of running to hats proper, these women of the late eighteenth century indulged their taste for the most elaborate headdress ever devised. This was the day of Marie Antoinette and her court. She and her court ladies introduced the

PLATE XII. Princess de Lamballe

This towering headdress represents the fashionable mode just previous to the Revolution. Note the use of artificial flowers.

new and extravagant headdresses which have passed into history as the monstrosities of the eighteenth century. PLATE XII. The hair was now frizzed, tangled, and raised to an amazing height over masses of false hair and pads of tow. It was then encircled with ribbon to keep it in

place and covered with a generous sprinkling of powder. Figure 51. Frequently tall plumes were added, tending to give greater height. "It was a fine sight," said a lady of the court, "to see that forest of plumes in the Versailles gallery moving with the least breath of air." So high were these scaffoldings of the period that the ladies of the day were compelled to remove the roofs of their sedan chairs in order to make room for the towering headdresses. Commenting on the extravagant taste of all women in the matter

Figure 50. The Calash

Figure 51. Forms of the Elaborate Headdress Worn During
the Late 18th Century

After a drawing from Racinet.

of hairdressing, Addison, in the *Spectator*, remarks, "There is not so variable a thing in nature as a lady's headdress. Within my memory I have known it to rise and fall above thirty degrees."

And now hats had to be invented to cover the coiffure! Figure 52. This was the period (1780) when hats for women became so important as an accessory in dress that the millinery industry started at once on its upward trend. At this time the growing complexity of life and its de-

PLATE XIII. The Honorable Mrs. Graham . . . . *Gainsborough*

The high headdress of the late 18th century is here graced with a little silk hat adorned with plumes. The costume is one of exquisite charm and interprets with unusual feeling the modes of the time.

PLATE XIV. Duchess of Devonshire . . . . *Gainsborough*

The beautiful Duchess wears the fashionable "Gainsborough," which, with its sweeping curves and ostrich plumes, is a most effective setting for the lovely face and mass of golden hair. Note the dainty fichu, a charming note in late 18th-century costume.

mands, particularly in dress, kept the great centers of manufacture busy. England, France, and Italy were keeping abreast of the time supplying the market with beautiful materials of every description. Then women's inventive genius reached new heights. Hats were as whimsical and varied as the minds that conceived them. At first, a little round hat was set atilt, right in front of the towering mass. Figure 53. Soon larger hats with brims appeared. These were designed to cover the elaborate headdress. They were very light in structure, usually a mixture of gauze, silk, lace, ribbon, and feathers. Though the brims were given a grace-

Figure 52. Fashions in Hats, Late 18th Century

ful curve, they were so out of proportion to the head that today they appear ridiculous. Figure 55. But about 1786 the taste of two leading portrait painters, Sir Joshua Reynolds and Thomas Gainsborough, began to show a marked influence on the mode. The high headdress began to lower and the hair fall in massive curls over the shoulders and down the back. Hats then showed low crowns and wide brims turned down back and front into sweeping half circles and adorned with handsome plumes. PLATE XIV.

Toward the end of the century, as if tiring of headdresses and hats, women began to drape the head with scarfs of gauze, silk, crepe, and ribbon. Sometimes these were arranged turban fashion; other times they were wrapped about the head and the hair was pulled up through the ribbon where it did not overlap. By the last quarter of

COURTESY, METROPOLITAN MUSEUM OF ART

Figure 53. Headdress, Pink Silk Heavily Embroidered in Gold Thread; French, Late 18th Century

the century the milliner's trade was rapidly becoming a source of great wealth. At this period immense bales of straw were being exported from Italy to other countries. Beautiful leghorns, black horsehair, and chip were among the favorites. Straw was the last word in material for hats.

One correspondent in reviewing the details of fashion in that day exclaimed, "Straw! Straw! Straw! Everything is ornamented with straw from the cap to the shoebuckles!" These straws were shaped by the deft fingers of the milliner into the most alluring and bewitching of bonnets. As used in the late eighteenth century the word "bonnet" applied to all types of head coverings worn by women—hats, turbans, and scarfs. Never before had the term "bonnet" been used generally for feminine headgear. True, "bonnet" had been familiar as far back as the Middle Ages. It had always referred, however, to the little, low cap worn by men, and the same cap with the high, sugar-loaf crown. The new use of the term coming in at this time makes the eighteenth century conspicuous as the period when bonnets for women first appeared. And an important period it was! By the end of

COURTESY, INDEPENDENCE HALL, PHILADELPHIA

Figure 54. Mrs. Robert Morris . . . . *Charles Wilson Peale*

Though the elaborate headgear of the late 18th century was *not* beautiful, it *was* fashionable, and American woman followed the mode with the same zeal as did her sisters in the fashion centers of Europe.

the century milliners everywhere were making bonnets.

During the same period, about 1790, there appeared for the first time the round, high hat for men. This later became known as the "stovepipe." It was destined to go through many changes. It gradually changed into the high silk hat which has persisted to this day as the conventional hat for men's formal wear.

Figure 55. Hat, 1787

After a drawing from Racinet.

1800-1900

For a short time just at the turn of the century, as men's hats began to ascend toward the high, cylindrical form, women too adopted the high, straight hats with narrow brims. These were decorated with flowers, ribbon, and lace. Figure 56. The fashion, however, was very short-lived, and soon the little turban, which was a development of the French toque, became a popular favorite, continuing well into the early part of the new century. Silk turbans adorned with a feather, muslin turbans covered with embroidery, and straw turbans trimmed with flowers and ribbon were the vogue. At the same time, wide-brimmed leghorns, straws, and chips, often tied down with a gay-colored handkerchief or veil, were equally popular (Frontispiece). Soon, however, all forms of woman's headgear succumbed to the little bonnet! But then the term "bonnet" was greatly restricted. No longer did it

Figure 56. Hats, 1790

After a drawing by Fairholt.

apply to all forms of feminine headgear. The word came to be used only in referring to that unique type of head covering which tied under the chin. From that day to this *bonnets* are distinct from *hats*, for *bonnets* tie under the chin.

Figure 57. Sign Hanging before Fashionable Millinery Shop, Early 19th Century

From Godey's Lady Book, 1859.

The high note in millinery of the nineteenth century is the alluring poke bonnet. *Godey's Lady's Book* of 1859 shows a quaint sign which is said to have hung before the shop of a fashionable milliner. Figure 57. It speaks for the popularity of the mode more eloquently than words. So many and varied were the changes played upon the popular theme of the bonnet that the fashion continued well past the middle of the nineteenth century. At first these little bonnets fitted the head, coming close to the sides and allowing scarcely any of the hair to be seen. Sometimes the poke was high, extending out from the head, and the intervening space was filled with lace, flowers, and ribbon. Plumes, also, added to height. Figure 58. No matter what type the bonnet, it always lent a piquant charm to the pretty face beneath it.

Figure 58. The Poke Bonnet, 1800-40

While the poke was enjoying its first season of popularity, the gentleman's tall hat introduced at the close of the last century began to find itself. Its shape varied from time to time. On the earliest hats, crowns

Figure 59. Early Forms of High Hat, 1800

were rounded and medium high; brims were broad and rolling. Gradually, however, as crowns began to ascend, brims became narrower. Usually they were rolled close to the crown at the sides with a decided dip front and back. The favorite tall hat of 1823 had a crown very wide at the top and tapering in a deep curve toward the brim, which was wide with an almost imperceptible dip front and back. Figure 59. Color, too, was important, for all fashion books from 1818 to 1835 show a decided vogue for fawn, gray, and white beavers. With their tall, light beavers, large cravats, and beautifully frilled shirts, our gentlemen of yesterday were a pleasing complement to the ladies in their winsome poke bonnets and full skirts.

In the feminine world the popularity of bonnets continued. Toward the fifties they appeared more quaint, with their little capes about the shoulders and frills of lace about the face. Figures 60, 61. For the bonnets of this period the hair was arranged low on the top, with masses of puffs, rolls, and braids falling about the neck. Frequently the loose back hair was held in a net made of braided chenille or ribbon.

During the sixties the little hat with a low crown made its appearance. Figure 62. This little hat was destined to become a great favorite and to continue with slight changes all through the seventies. In the early years it was set low on the head. Trimmings of ribbon and flowers gave a little accent to the front, and streamers of ribbon hung at the back. As the seasons passed, the styles in hairdressing be-

COURTESY, METROPOLITAN MUSEUM OF ART

Figure 60. Mrs. John Church
Cruger . . . . *Healy*

This winsome lady wears the flaring, open bonnet of 1842, with the filmy veil attached to the crown. The shoulder scarf or pelerine was later transformed into the dolman of the late 19th century.

Figure 61. Bonnets of 1850

came more elaborate. Fashion now called for the hair to be dressed high on the top, and for the back to be filled in with a chignon of braids and curls. Figure 63. Then the little hat became a pile of ribbon, lace, and flowers. It sat atilt well over the front, and the streamers of lace and vines fell over the huge chignon. Contemporary with this style of little

Figure 62. The Little Round Hat of 60's

hat the bonnet again appeared. Now, however, the style had changed. Instead of fitting the head closely, covering the ears, as did the earlier bonnets, these were set high over the elaborate hairdress. Streamers of ribbon attached at the crown were brought forward and tied under

Figure 63. Hats of the 70's

the chin. Usually the crowns were molded into form and the brim, if there was a brim, covered with folds of silk and velvet. Figure 64. At this date bonnets were made of leather, horsehair, felt, straw, and silk. They were trimmed with flowers, ribbon, lace, and plumes. Again bonnets were the last word in fashionable millinery! *Harper's Bazar* of March, 1873, gives the following fashion news about the popular bonnet:

Spring *bonnets* are larger than those of winter, the crowns are well-defined, square and high enough to hold a towering coiffure. Parisian ladies of any age from fifty years down now wear this jaunty sailor perched far back on the head. Most of the new shapes may be used either as a round hat or a bonnet, a pair of strings tied under the chin is all that is necessary.

Courtesy, *Harper's Bazaar*

In the following year these shapes were perched far back on the head. They were worn with or without ribbon ties as milady's fancy dictated.

Between the sixties and seventies the gentleman's high hat, having passed through various shapes, became established in a tall cylindrical form. Figure 65. This new type of gentleman's hat is said to have been fashioned by a London hatter named Hetherington. Wearing his newly created stovepipe, this ambitious Englishman walked from his shop into the street. A crowd soon gathered. So great was the curiosity that, in the excited jostle, a boy broke his arm, a woman screamed and fainted, and men shouted in amazement. Hetherington was arrested for "inciting a riot,"

Figure 64. Bonnets of the 70's

and was bound over to keep the peace. In describing the incident a London paper referred to the hat as a "tall structure designed to frighten timid folk."

Figure 65. Later Forms of the High Hat, 1855-1890

In some of these tall shapes one sees again slightly different combinations of crown and brim. In some, crowns were wide at the top and tapered very slightly toward the brim; in others, crowns were wide at the headline and narrowed a very little toward the top. Brims were narrow and straight, bound with ribbon; sometimes they were rolled at the sides and unbound. The great majority of these early high hats were made of the coveted beaver or silk plush. The first tall "silk" hat was made in Florence, Italy, and, because of the satinlike luster given the highly polished beaver, was called a "silk beaver." This undoubtedly brought in the silk plush hat, which began to take the place of the beaver. PLATE XV.

The form, or frame, of this gentleman's hat was first made of several layers of cotton fabric which had been sized and cemented together. The plush, after having been shaped on the block, was cemented to the fabric frame. Hot irons were used in the process, and not a sign of a crease was allowed to creep into the plush as it was pressed upon the form. When this was completed the plush, with the aid of hot irons and a vigorous brushing, was given a high polish. Next in importance was the roll of the brim. A heated process was used for this. The hat was placed on the press and remained there for a given length of time. The heat was then turned off, but the hat remained in the press until the temperature fell and the fabric cooled. Trimming and lining added the finishing note; then the silk hat was ready for the market. Though the black silk hat was the choice for dress and formal occasions, the tall gray or white beaver still continued a favorite with many until about 1890.

In this matter of hats, the nineteenth century is outstanding as a gentleman's century. During this period the changes and development in men's hats is most marked. Further, the styles introduced at this time have since remained permanent, their rise and fall in popularity being merely a matter of fashion. The unusual development in the hat business at this time was due, in great measure, to the invention in 1846 of a machine for making felt.

During the last quarter of the century the soft felt hat attained great popularity in America. In 1849 the famous Hungarian patriot, Louis Kossuth, had been brought as a guest to this country by the United States Government. He wore a great soft hat which seemed to express his own dauntless spirit and dynamic character. His hat made a great impression. It is not surprising that it was soon adopted. From that day to this the soft felt in various styles of crown and brim has been a general favorite for business and informal wear. Though black has always been accepted, the modern world finds grays, greens, browns, and blues increasingly popular. Caps, also, came in for recognition during this century. Though they had been worn previously, they had never been popular. Now they were adopted as a convenient, light form of headgear especially appropriate for traveling and sport. Figure 67a. Though every man had a cap and wore it, he also had his tall hat at hand for important occasions, especially for his Sunday walk to church.

Figure 66. Soft Felt

In 1871 the derby, with its stiff, molded crown and rolling brim, was the popular novelty in men's hats. The derby was designed in 1850 by an English hatter, William Bowler, and in England today the derby is still known as the *bowler*. It was first adopted by William Coke, an English sportsman, as a substitute for the tall hat usually worn with the fashion-

PLATE XV. Edouard Manet . . . . *Henri Fanton-Latour*

During the late 19th century the silk hat was the very height of fashionable dress. With slight changes in line it continues the choice for formal wear. Note gloves, stick, collar, and cravat.

able hunting outfit. When it came to climbing over and through hedges, the tall hat had proved itself very much of a nuisance, and then, too, it frequently was blown off, which was indeed a great embarrassment. For a long time the derby was known as the "billy-cock," after its staunch supporter, William (Billy) Coke. When first introduced it was looked upon with rather cool disdain, but gradually the low crown, narrow brim, and light weight brought it recognition. The height and contour of the derby changed from year to year as did also the manner of wearing it. Sometimes it was set straight on the head in a very dignified way; at others it was worn set back or at an angle. This was

Figure 67a. Caps, 1870-80; 1900

supposed to present a very smart appearance. Soon everybody was wearing the derby except judges, statesmen, and a few other pompous individuals who felt their dignity at stake unless supported by the tall silk hat.

Figure 67b.
The Derby

Figure 67c. Modern Panama
and Straw

The straw hat, though worn in tropical countries for many centuries, did not become fashionable in Europe until 1800. By the end of the century, sailor shapes, round hats, and others following the general lines of the soft felt, were worn extensively. It was in 1870 that the first straw hat was machine sewn. Since that time many machines for sewing the braid and hydraulic presses for fixing the shapes have been developed. The straws used in American hat factories of the twentieth century are brought mainly from Italy, China, and Japan. Among the various popular straws the *Panama* holds first place. The first Panama hat is said to have been made in Ecuador some 275 years ago. As Panama was, at that distant date, the only market for these hats, they became known as the "Panama," and as such have become famous. The making of straw hats is today one of the great straw industries of the world.

In woman's world the bonnet seemed destined to "go on forever," for all through the eighties it continued its way unmolested. It was now, however, smaller and not so elaborately covered with decoration. Then, as the style of coiffure changed to a more natural arrangement, hats began to take other, more varied shapes. The trimming now became secondary to the hat shape and tended to emphasize the lines of the hat rather than to conceal them. Near the close of the century, hats were both large and small, but the bonnet, in diminutive form, still remained a favorite. All through the eighties and nineties the use of birds, wings, and the aigrette flourished. Indeed, no hat was worthy the name unless adorned with some part of a bird! It is amazing to read that less than fifty years ago the forms of sea gulls, black birds, red birds, and humming birds contributed to the adornment of milady's fair head. One of the leading fashion magazines of the period seriously points to the fashions for the coming fall and names the natural birds to be

PHOTOGRAPH, GIRAUDON

Figure 68. The Lady with a Glove . . . . *Caralus Duran*

A typical figure of the late 19th century, when bonnets ruled the millinery world.

used—the blackbird with pointed wing and tail feathers; humming birds in clusters of three and four; sea gulls of natural color and dwarfed copies of these. Such decorations were to be placed on the back or brim of the hat with wings and tail pointing toward the front or back, as the shape of the hat suggested. The enviable and expensive aigrette was indicated as a very exclusive feature of the coming mode. Figure 69.

It is estimated that in the United States alone five million birds were killed each year for the purpose of trimming women's hats. Shortly, however, the Audubon Society of America instituted a crusade against this practice, prevailing upon women everywhere to discourage the wearing of any part of the bird upon the hat. The movement was highly successful. The Audubon Plumage Law prohibited in all the important millinery centers the sale of aigrettes and the feathers of other native birds. Soon the popular sentiment directed against the use of such decoration led to its swift abandonment. Milliners now gave their attention to the making of pom-poms, cockades, and other fanciful ornaments that did not necessitate the slaughter of birds. Very beautiful and charming effects were secured by the use of dyed goose and chicken feathers. These, together with ribbon, flowers, lace, and velvets, the sweeping plume, and ostrich tips continued to be the leading materials for trimmings.

Figure 69. Hat with Bird and Aigrette, 1890

Twentieth Century

By the twentieth century hats were as varied as the faces they framed. It is, indeed, an endless task to present the varieties in women's hats. It is of interest, however, in the history of hats that the pendulum swings from extreme to extreme. The high headdresses of the Middle Ages fell to the closely coiffed head and the Marie Stuart cap. The built-up "heads" of the eighteenth century succumbed to the little cap. The chignon of the seventies gave way in the eighties and nineties to a more natural arrangement of the hair, with smaller hats. With the beginning of the new century, Fashion again asserted herself and heads grew large. This time the hair was raised loosely over a false roll and dressed high. This was the popular *pompadour*. The hat then of necessity was set high, and was sometimes raised by a bandeau. Figure 70.

A popular version of this new headgear was the large black velvet hat, set high, and adorned with handsome ostrich plumes. This was the famed "Merry Widow." Figure 70. At this period, the light opera *The Merry Widow* by the Viennese composer Frans Lehar had taken the world by storm, and, as in times past, the popular name had attached itself to the hat. The fashion created a great demand for ostrich feathers, and with this a new form of uncurled plume known as the "willow" was exceedingly popular. Figure 71. With the passing of the seasons there were continual variations in the large hat. In 1910 it broadened to an exaggerated width, and the head band was enlarged so that the hat was set well down over the great mass of hair. Figure 72. Various fabrics—silk, velvet, satin, lace, and straw—were all used in making these hats. Of course, after a period of sufficient endurance on the part of the public, hats were reduced in size.

During these early years of the twentieth century the automobile revolutionized the headgear of women. First there was the large hat of 1908-10 with the enveloping veil approximately eighty-two inches in length by twenty-four in width. See Veils, page 69. At this period cars

Figure 70. The Large Hat Set High and The "Merry Widow"

were almost entirely open, and the veil protected milady's locks and general appearance. Open cars were followed by closed cars and gradually the large unwieldly hats of 1910 gave way to smaller hats. By 1912 the stiff fabric hats of the first decade of the twentieth century—both those that sat high over the raised pompadour and those that sat low—had passed from the fashion scene. With these vanished also the airy trimmings of lace, ribbon, and flowers. All these have become a thing of the past. From 1912 on, molded felts and straws in a multitude of styles for all occasions have taken the place of the elaborate headgear of thirty years ago.

Color and materials have always played an important part in the milliner's art. As the twentieth century wears on, materials vie with those of earlier years. Metallic cloth, velours, panne velvets, and molded felts in brightest colors, as well as black, appear in both large and small models. Sometimes crowns are tall to give milady an appearance of height. Six months later crowns are low!

Figure 71. The Willow Plume, 1908-10

During the twenties a new fashion in coiffure suddenly stepped upon the scene. Milady's locks were clipped, and the fashion of bobbed hair absorbed the feminine mind. This was a fashion new to the modern world, but reading back to the French Revolution one hears of the clipped locks, cut short to make the headsman's task less irksome. The French fashion, which was widely worn, was influenced by that gruesome practice. In the modern world bobbed hair has no such meaning. It is simply another expression of comfort and style sought by the feminine world. From the first, bobs were many. There was the "boyish bob," the "semibob," and the

Figure 72. Large Hats Set Low, 1909-10

bob that was "permanent-waved." With this very close coiffure it is not surprising that hats began to shrink. By 1929, 1930, and 1931, hats

Figure 73. Hats of 1931—The "Princess Eugénie"

could not be smaller! Following the small hat there came in 1931 a revival of the little, round hat of the sixties. It was hailed as the *Princess Eugénie*, because in that past period the Princess Eugénie had given a forward spurt to the mode by wearing it with great distinction. Figure 73. Season after season the small hat with variations in line and accent, continued in favor. Figure 74. Not until 1935 did a change come. At this time hints of the return of the wide-brimmed hats became a reality, and milady appeared in a very exaggerated width of brim and a low, almost flat crown. Figure 75. Thus fancy continued to play upon the hat, ever bringing forth new forms and new lines designed to enhance the beauty of the wearer and endow her with that enviable attribute of charm—*chic*. To this end Fashion constantly draws from every source, going far afield, if need be, for her modish ideas.

Far outside the range of our fashion world are other head coverings possessing a character and style distinctly individual. There are the colorful turbans of the East, the pith helmets of the tropics, the fez* of the Turk, the elaborate headdresses of the Chinese and Japanese, and nearer still the picturesque sombrero of the Mexican. These head coverings, with their unusual forms and interesting patterns, contribute much to the inventive skill of the modern designer of hats.

One can see that the "way of the hat" through the centuries has been long—doubly so, for from the beginning

Figure 74. Hats of the 1930's

Figure 75. The Low, Broad-brimmed Hat of 1936

milord appropriated to himself one form of head covering and milady quite another. With this continued practice two distinct lines of the hat naturally developed. Though in the early stages gentlemen captured the plumes, gold lace. and other finery, these, together with ribbon, lace, and flowers, were finally yielded to the feminine world. On the gentlemen's side are found the primitive cap, the medieval hood, the roundlet, the berets of 1500, the plain beavers and picturesque cavaliers of 1600, the tricorne of 1700, the stovepipe, derby, cap, soft felt, Panama, and various straws of 1800-1900. In the feminine world are the veils, coifs, hoods, toques, pokes, bonnets, hats—high and low, large and small, in endless variety. "Hats for men" and "hats for women" continue to hold the fashion stage. On they come year by year, moving in cycles of high and low,

* The fez was abolished as a part of the Turkish national dress, November 25, 1925.

large and small, repeating the general shapes of the past with simple changes in form, materials, and color to match the changing spirit of each new age. For at all times, Fashion sees to it that the hat is timed to the tempo of the world in which it moves.

REFERENCES*

Ashdown, Mrs. Charles H., *British Costume During Nineteen Centuries.*
Calthrop, Dion Clayton, *British Costume*, Vol. II; pp. 26, 104, 109.
Dooley, William H., *Clothing and Style.*
Erman, J. P. Adolph, *Life in Ancient Egypt.*
Fairholt, F. W., *Costume in England.*
Hughes, Talbot, *Dress Design.*
Lester, Katherine Morris, *Historic Costume*, pp. 57, 218.
Norris, Herbert, *Costume and Fashion*, Vols. I, II.
Planché, J. R., *Cyclopedia of Costume*, Vol. I — *Dictionary.*
Rhead, G. W., *Chats on Costume.*
Sage, Elizabeth, *A Study of Costume*, pp. 49, 215.
The Foundation Library, Vol. X; pp. 56-64.
Wilkinson, Sir John Gardiner, *A Popular Account of the Ancient Egyptians,*
    Vol. II.

* Given in full in Bibliography.

CHAPTER 2

The Veil

The beauteous queen advancing, next display'd
The shining *veil*, and thus endearing said:
"Accept, dear youth, this monument of love,
Long since in better days by Helen wove;
Safe in thy mother's care the vesture lay,
To deck thy bride, and grace thy nuptial day."

Odyssey XV

AMONG the most ancient and honored of costume accessories is the
veil. The story of the veil is as varied and interesting as the story
of woman herself. Through the centuries it has been in turn the badge of
bondage, of modesty, of religious zeal; the symbol of position, of mourning, of marriage; and yet again it has held its place in the feminine wardrobe merely as a dictate of Dame Fashion.

Special mention of the use of the veil in woman's dress is made in the
Bible. It was the romantic meeting of Rebekah and Isaac, who waited in
the field at eventide, that inspired the first biblical mention of the veil:

For she had said unto the servant, what man is this that walketh in the
field to meet us? And the servant had said, It is my master; therefore she took
a *veil* and covered herself.

Genesis 24:65

We are told that during Solomon's time the Hebrew women wore veils
of gauze, not primarily as a protection but as an indication of their social
position. In a letter to the Corinthians, Paul admonishes the women to
cover their heads in the house of worship in recognition of the presence
of the Lord. Even today many religious orders of sisterhood use the veil
as a badge of humility. At least one instance is on record of the wearing
of veils by men. St. Ambrose, writing in the fourth century, tells of
"silken garments and *veils* interwoven with gold" with which the bodies
of rich men were encompassed.

It is from that ancient cradle of civilization, the valley of the Euphrates
and Tigris, that the veil, the emblem of modesty and bondage from time
immemorial, has descended. Centuries before the beginning of Mohammedanism, the oriental woman had been compelled to hide her features
from the gaze of man. For the last 1200 years the Mohammedan woman

has been wearing the veil as a badge of her own subjection and her inferiority to man. This veil of the East, however, is far removed from that wisp of modern transparency worn by women of the western world. The purpose of the oriental veil was to conceal the features; that of the

Figure 76. Veiled Women of Egypt

Figure 77. Veiled Women of Turkey

Occident is designed to make the wearer more attractive. Ancient Egypt is not the land of the veil. Her women wore elaborate wigs and headdresses, painted and rouged their faces, and darkened their eyes with *kohl*. All this was done to be seen and admired, not to be covered with a veil! After contact with the East and more extended trade relations, the veil came into Egypt. It is not unlikely that the woman of the upper classes exhibited the same pride in fine transparent veils as did her sisters of the East. The luxury of sheer linens and exquisite tissues is characteristic of ancient Asiatic civilization, and these, no doubt through ever-widening trade relations, found their way into neighboring countries. After the coming of Mohammedanism, women of Egypt generally accepted the veil. As late as the early twentieth century the upper-class Egyptian woman, when out-of-doors, concealed her face to the eyes with a bit of white transparent cloth which hung in a short narrow panel, and protected her head and the sides of her face with a black veil or headdress. A woman of the less-favored classes fastened over her face just below the eyes a piece of somber-colored material, usually black, that fell in a long narrow panel. This veil was prevented from coming in contact with the mouth and nose by a cylinder of light metal which rested over the forehead between the eyes and was attached to the hair at the top of the head. The head and figure was then wrapped in the black shawl, leaving only the two dark eyes visible. Women of the Bedouin tribes cover their faces to the eyes and shroud their heads in a shawl. Figure 76. In all countries where Mohammedanism is still followed, whether it be in Egypt,

Morocco, or Algeria, the women of the Arab tribes still wear the veil of thousands of years ago. Figure 77.

In ancient Greece, women were accustomed to wear a thick and heavy veil which resembled a garment. It was hung from the back of the head and covered the shoulders just as a modern shawl is sometimes used. These early veils were of wool, and frequently of fine linen, the material being chosen to fit the occasion of its use. This garment, though called a veil, in no way resembled the dainty chiffons, nets, and gauzes of the modern world. Later, in the classic period, veils of fine linen were used as a head-dress, and these were frequently drawn across the face. Occasional mention is made of little white veils intended to cover the head and not similar to the general dress either in color or material. Figures 78, 79. Thus,

Figure 78. Greek Veils

Figure 79. Greek Veil
After Hope.

Apollonius speaks of the veil which Medea hung upon her head: "She threw the *veil* over her sweet head." These little white veils were small pieces of linen, very sheer and transparent, so fine, indeed, that they were often likened to spiders' webs. Stuffs were so transparent in texture that they were called "mists." The mantle which Iphigenia threw over her head was so fine she could see through it. All veils were undoubtedly made of the finest and most transparent fabric known to the ancients, probably similar to modern lace and cambric. The fineness of the Greek veil is distinctly suggested in the famous fresco, the *Aldobrandini Marriage*. The delicacy of the folds is plainly apparent; one is also led to believe that the veil of Greek brides was white. The frequent mention of white veils, however, does not preclude the use of other colors, for saffron was highly favored, and purple and other hues worn. The many references in the *Iliad* and *Odyssey* leave no doubt as to the beauty and importance of this article of apparel. Of Helen we read:

> O'er her fair face a snowy *veil* she threw,
> And softly sighing from the loom withdrew.
>
> *Iliad*, III

PLATE XVI. Livia "Pudicitia"

"In Livia was concentrated the quintessence of Roman aristocracy." *
Note the beauty of the face, the arrangement of the hair, the headdress.
The enveloping palla appears transparent as it passes over the left hand and
falls over the arms.

* Ferrero, Guglielmo, *The Women of the Caesars*. The Century Company, New York, 1912.

Penelope, when urged to choose between remaining with her aged father or following her husband, indicates her preference for the latter by drawing her veil over her blushing features:

A *veil* of richest texture wrought she wears.
Odyssey, XVIII

And again:

A *veil* translucent, O'er her brow displayed.
Odyssey, XVIII

Referring to the veil of Nausica we read:

The nympth's fair head a *veil* transparent graced.
Odyssey, V

The entire face of Grecian women was not usually covered except when in mourning. At such a time it was not a distinct veil but a part of the mantle, often a somber green or black, drawn over the head.

Her face wrapped in a *veil* declared her woes.
Odyssey, IV

Figure 80. The Hennin Veil, 14th Century

Figure 81. A 14th-Century Veil

After Viollet-le-Duc.

At a later period the use of the word veil was more comprehensive, referring to the many coifs and net caps worn.

In Rome the heads and faces of vestal virgins were covered while they walked in procession or during a sacrifice. The *Palliolum*, a veil of beauty, was the favorite of the women of Rome. Arranged over the hair and held in place by bands and wreaths, it fell in graceful folds to the shoulders. The *palla*, a shawl-like mantle, was often so arranged as to take the place of the veil. It was usually of lightly woven wool, silk, or linen, sometimes plain and sometimes decorated with bands of color. Though the manner of adjusting varied with the taste of the wearer it was usually wrapped about the figure in rather an intricate fashion, with one long end frequently brought over the head as a veil. PLATE XVI. The *flammeum* of pagan brides was a flame-colored veil whose tint was probably somewhere between yellow and orange, likely adopted from the Etruscans, to whom it was a festive color. Christian brides of Rome wore purple and white veils.

Middle Ages

During the Middle Ages large squares of material were draped over the head as a simple head covering. They were sufficiently ample to envelop the shoulders and, frequently, fall to the waist. They were of various materials and undoubtedly of many colors. This drapery which veiled the head and shoulders has passed into history, we have noted, as the *couvrechef*. In England the identical head covering was known as the *headrail* (see Figure 12, page 8). It too, was of various materials and colors, though never white. It persisted with variations through several centuries. Another form of head drapery was represented by squares

Figure 82. Mrs. Perez Morton....
Gilbert Stuart

The vigorous brush strokes only suggest the crisp, transparent veil. Note how the interest of the portrait centers in the beautiful face.

of fine linen and cotton, which were secured and held in place by a coronet or crown of gold or other metal about the brow. They were, indeed, a charming note in the costume of the period (see Figure 13, page 10). During the fourteenth and fifteenth centuries when the elaborate reticulated nets and wimples encumbered the head, veils were draped over the entire headdress, completely covering the hair, sides of the face, and neck (see Figure 14, page 11). The modern world sees the remains of these medieval headdresses in the various veiled orders of the sisterhoods.

Somewhat later, as was noted in the discussion of hats, came the extravagant headdresses of the fifteenth century, the great hennin, little hennin, escoffion, and their many and curious variations. Figure 80. These were frequently surmounted with dainty veils falling from the peak to various lengths. It is said that Isabelle of France, a famous fashion leader of that day, wore a sugar-loaf headdress of great height with a long veil falling from the tip to the floor.

1500-1700

Following the towering hennins there came first upon the fashion scene the nunlike hoods with their "falls" of materials at the back; then, in 1540, followed the small French hood. Suspended from the back of these little hoods, women of both France and England wore veils of fine tissue or gauze which fell below the waistline (see PLATE VII, page 23 [Catherine Howard]). During Elizabeth's reign the veil was an important item in fashionable dress. Portraits of Elizabeth; Mary, Queen of Scots; and others of the period show a very decorative veil which has the effect of a cape or wrap. Such veils were very fine in texture and, by means of wiring, the part which covered the head and shoulders assumed wide, winglike curves which gave a very picturesque effect, often greatly heightened by edgings of pearls and other jewels. Later, during the same period, the fashion for veils gradually abated and they soon became passé.

Figure 83. Veil to Be Drawn over Face at Will, 1830

In the American colonies, that intrepid and pious Welshman Roger Williams believed thoroughly in the tradition of the veil. He demanded that women of Salem wear veils when attending church meetings. This custom prevailed for a long time. When in mourning, colonial widows, regardless of age, wore heavy black veils.

The custom of wearing long, heavy black veils when in mourning is one that continued for many, many years. The fashion of the mourning veil has varied all the way from a short veil falling over the head and shoulders to one enveloping the figure. Fashions in mourning have been quite as exacting as fashions in general. For years, and indeed as late as the last quarter of the nineteenth century, heavy black crepe veils falling from the hat or bonnet were worn for a definite length of time known as the "period of mourning." In the modern world, however, the custom has almost vanished. It is now a strange sight, like an echo from the past, to see in this day a figure veiled in black.

The bridal veil made its appearance in England during the time of Shakespeare. It was not, however, original with the English; for centuries before, Roman and Hebrew brides had worn yellow veils symbolic of marriage. The origin of the English bride's veil is one of those disputed questions which will never be settled. Perhaps it is the same little coif once worn by medieval brides but now grown a bit more ample; or, as stated by one writer, it "may be nothing more than a milliner's substitute for the flowing tresses which in old times concealed not a few of the bride's personal attractions and covered her face as she knelt at the altar." Elizabeth Stuart, daughter of James I, possessed an abundance of flowing hair and for this reason was not thought to require a wedding veil.

Though the fashion of the wedding veil was long an established custom in the reign of George III (1760-1820), the use of both the wreath and veil declined and was soon looked upon as "old fashioned." In the early years of this reign, Horace Walpole, a social reformer in small matters,

greatly approved of the passing of the wedding veil. He speaks specifically of the beauty of his niece during her wedding ceremony when the alternate blushes and paleness of her face were not concealed by a wedding veil. He then concludes, "It was as sensible a wedding as ever was."

1700-1900

Throughout the reign of George III, veils of lace were a fashionable note in costume. They were frequently attached to the brims of hats, and fell free, sometimes reaching the knee. By 1806, hats and bonnets had become greatly varied in shape, and veils assumed new styles. The tall feathers and artificial flowers of that day were covered with veils that trailed

Figure 84. Drawn-back
Veil, 1873

Figure 85. Face Veil, 1890

Figure 86. Straight Veil, 1895

over the brims of hats. Sheer white veils and others made of costly lace were also worn without hats. These were draped over the head and fell in soft folds about the neck and shoulders. The Stuart portrait of Sarah Bowdoin Dearborn (the Walker Gallery of Art, Bowdoin College) shows a handsome veil of the period draped over the head and shoulders. PLATE XVII. Another admirable painting by Gilbert Stuart is that of Mrs. Perez Morton, which hangs in Worcester Art Museum. Figure 82. The manner in which the veil is painted and the transparency suggested could be interpreted only by the hand of a master painter.

About 1830 there came the vogue for long veils fitted with a drawstring at one end. These were tied about the bonnet crown (see Figure 60, page 49). The veil usually hung at the back and could be drawn over the face at will. Figure 83. These veils were often of net with Brussels or Honiton appliqué, or of a net known as Limerick lace. More simple veils were of plain net with a design in running stitch across the end. In 1860, when low hats were the vogue, a little veil reaching only the tip of the nose and called a "nose veil" was very popular. In 1863, veils were worn straight and close, without a fold, over the face. These were called "face veils." During the seventies, when little bonnets were the fashion, veils hung long and loose over the face, and the ends were caught and tucked in or pinned to the bonnet. Figure 84. Later they were crossed, brought forward, and tied under the chin. The last quarter of the century saw many new shapes in hats, both large and small. With the wide-brimmed hat the veil was frequently drawn up under the chin and fastened at the back. Figure 85. Or, if milady preferred, it was set around the edge of the wide brim and hung straight, the ends being caught up and tied at the back. Figure 86. Nose veils, face veils, dotted veils, and embroidered veils continued to be the fashionable addition to the hat.

Figure 87. Automobile Veil, 1908–12

Twentieth Century

In the early years of the twentieth century, as motoring gained more and more in popularity, large veils, approximately two-and-a-half yards in length, were worn over the large hats of the period. Figure 87. At this time motor cars were for the most part open, and the veil served the practical purpose of protecting the hat and hair against the wind and dust. On other occasions milady chose a veil of fine net covered with a scroll pattern in line embroidery. These were usually white or cream in color and invariably worn with the large hat. Figure 88. During these years the wedding veil, which had been intermittently popular, rose to new heights and the modern world began to note many different styles. These varied all the way from the short coifs draping the head to the elaborate veils of lace, embroidered net, and tulle, which, caught by the bridal wreath or little cap, fell in a sweeping, billowy train about the feet.

PLATE XVII. Sarah Bowdoin............................*Gilbert Stuart*

A handsome lace veil falls from the head, meeting the scarf about the shoulders. Note the double ruff, arrangement of the hair, and interesting face.

In the modern world, the veil as a symbol of service has become a recognized accessory of the Red Cross uniform. White is always the nurse's color. In later years, however, colored coifs have been adopted as part of the regulation Volunteer Service uniform. Permission to use the veil as part of the volunteer uniform was granted in 1917 by the Central Committee of the American Red Cross.

From 1910 to 1924, veils in the fashion world were of many sizes and weaves. Little veils fitting the face closely and therefore called face veils were worn with the small street hat. Veils for more formal wear were dec-

Figure 88. Embroidered Veil, 1908–10

orated with heavy, embroidered borders and hung free from the brims of the large hats popular at that time. By-and-by, as hats grew smaller and fitted the head closely, there was no special need for veils and they gradually disappeared. Ever and anon, however, a revival of the fashion is attempted. In 1934-35 stiff little veils were set at a flare about the hat brim, just shading the eyes. Figure 89. After all, the practical use of the veil is of small consequence; it is the beauty of the veil and the contribution it makes to effective dress that gives it charm.

Figure 89. A Popular Veil, 1935–36

Among Spanish women the veil vies with the fan in importance. Like the fan, it invites rather than repels masculine attention. The beautiful lace veil known as the *mantilla* is a part of that indefinable charm ever associated with the Spanish senorita. The mantilla must not be confused with the *velo*, a black lace scarf commonly worn by all classes of Andalusian women for morning shopping tours and attending mass. The mantilla is a very handsome and distinctly Spanish veil of lace. It is either white or black, usually a lace known as *blonde*. For dressy occasions, Easter Monday and the bull fights, white is always worn. During Holy Week and the fiestas black is imperative. The mantilla is always carefully arranged over the head and shoulders. The hair is dressed high, crowned with a handsome comb which acts as a support, and over this the lace mantilla is arranged to fall in easy folds about the head and shoulders. Sometimes a cluster of crimson carnations placed against the dark hair at one side adds a bit of alluring color. The white lace mantilla is always graceful and becoming, while the black often imparts a subtle fascination to the dark-skinned beauty. The mantilla is as old as Spanish history; it can be traced from the earliest of head coverings worn in Spain through its successive phases to its present captivating

Figure 90. Red-Cross Veil

form. The Spanish woman's mantilla is held sacred by law and can never be seized for debt.

Fashions may come and fashions may go, yet no event with reference to the veil is of more striking significance than that which has taken place in the modern world of the East. Until recently women of the East were still wearing that age-old badge of inferiority. The veil was still considered a protection to sex. Removing or turning it forcibly aside continued to be regarded as an insult of the first order. In this twentieth century, however, new ideas, shaking off the dust of tradition, come forward in rapid succession. In Turkey, in 1908, a movement to discard the veil was started. It gained strength until in 1925 the new and startling reforms instituted by Mustapha Kemel, then president of the Turkish Republic, made possible the complete emancipation of woman from her age-old bondage of which the veil was the symbol. Women of Turkey were not required by law to unveil, but every opportunity and encouragement was extended them to do so. By 1930 a veiled woman was seldom seen on the streets of Istanboul or Ankara.*

While this marvelous change was going on in Turkey, adjoining countries were keeping abreast of the times. In 1932, representative women from Persia, Syria, Palestine, Irak, and India met in Teheran to demand suffrage—equal rights with men. How did they do it? By removing the veil.

Today the "unveiling of women" has become a fact. In the large and more progressive centers women were ready for the change, and the transition came with ease. In the smaller and outlying districts women have been slow to adopt their new-found freedom, and many still cling to the ancient custom, going about with their faces veiled. Even so, the veil of the East is going. Time alone is needed for complete readjustment. The oriental mind, compared to the occidental, is slow to make changes; but,

---

* The new names given under the new Republic to Constantinople and Angora respectively.

in the end, the veil, that badge of bondage from time immemorial, will have passed. Upon this epochal transformation in the life of Eastern women future chroniclers of fashion may dwell, not on their bondage and backwardness, but, instead, on the alacrity and zeal with which new fashions in headgear, and particularly in veils, if you please, are sought by the fashion-bent leaders of the new East!

Few accessories of modern dress boast comparison with the strange and varied ancestry of the veil. From a symbol of bondage it has passed to the opposite extreme, a badge of the fashion-minded. Equally varied have been the materials which fashion the veil. From the somber stuffs of the ancients through linen, cotton, silk, lace, and the finest gauzes, it has emerged in the dainty chiffons and nets of our modern world. To achieve that enviable note of smartness so eagerly sought in present day modes, Fashion, ever and again calling upon the age-old veil in one form or another, continues to add both distinction and charm to her newest creations.

REFERENCES

Ashdown, Mrs. Charles H., *British Costume During Nineteen Centuries*.
Blanc, Charles, *Art in Ornament and Dress*, pp. 106, 112.
Calthrop, Dion Clayton, *English Costume*, Vol. I; pp. 9, 18.
Child, Theodore, *Wimples and Crisping Pins*, pp. 19, 41, 61, 86.
Earle, Alice Morse, *Two Centuries of Costume in America*, Vol. I, II.
Ellsworth, Evelyn Peters, *Textiles and Costume Design*, p. 19.
Evans, Mary, *Costume Throughout the Ages*, pp. 18, 34, 53, 106, 129.
Fales, Jane, *Dressmaking*, pp. 11, 16.
Hartley, Dorothy, *Medieval Costume and Life*.
Kelley and Schwabe, *Historic Costume*, p. 79.
Norris, Herbert, *Costume and Fashion*.
Peterson's Fashion Magazine, Volume of 1863.
Picken, Mary Brooks, *Secrets of Distinctive Dress*.
Rhead, C. W., *Chats on Costume*, p. 153.
Sage, Elizabeth, *A Study of Costume*, pp. 11, 215.

CHAPTER 3

Feathers

Appoint the feather-maker not to faille
To *plume* my head with his best estridge tail.

ROWLAND, *A Pair of Spy Knaves*

FEATHERS of birds have always formed a part of the decorative dress of races of a low order of civilization. Primitive peoples have as a rule an innate love of brilliant color and a keen sense of arrangement.

Figure 91. Figures of Libyans Wearing Feathers
From the tomb of Seti I.

Feathers need little preparation for man's use, and the system of mounting them is very simple. It is not surprising that they have been a favored means of decoration among various peoples in remote times, and again in the modern world have become a choice and distinctive accessory of dress.

Middle Ages

The bride of primitive days wore feathers on her wrist as a sign that she belonged to her husband. In ancient Egypt it was the sacred feather that denoted sovereignty. An important badge of royalty in the dress of the king was the royal apron, which hung from the girdle and was richly

PLATE XVIII. Francis I . . . . *Clouet*

The little hat with its white plume tipping the front edge and its jeweled ornament enriching the brim was the accepted fashion in hats of the period, 1515-47.

decorated with colored feathers. The priests of Egypt wore feathers in their hair to denote their ranks. Upon the walls of the tomb of Seti I, the Libyans are pictured wearing one or two upstanding feathers in their hair.

Figure 91. In Greece and Rome beautiful, long-handled fans were made of many, varicolored feathers.

During the long period of the Middle Ages feathers seem to have been utterly overlooked until the thirteenth century. At that time we read of *Genevieve, the Feather Seller.* This is the period when men found delight in the long, straight feather which, upstanding at the back of the hat, added a new and fashionable note to the headgear of this day. Figure 92. The feather of the peacock was one of the choice novelties for this decoration. By 1485, the vogue for feathers had

Figure 92. The Simple Feather
Decoration
From History of Thebes, *1461-83.*

greatly increased, and dandies of the day wore little, rolling-brimmed hats adorned with feathers of preposterous length. Figure 93. The unusual feature of this decoration, however, was not the feather but the fact that each was of a different color. Moreover, the stem of each feather was ornamented with pearls and other gems. With fashionable gentlemen arrayed in head coverings of such

Figure 93. Bonnets Worn by
Fashionable Gallants at Close
of 15th Century

From an old engraving.

elegance, it is not surprising that knights of the period, not to be outdone, added towering feathers to their helmets. The first use of feathers in military costume appeared about 1420, when only a single plume was worn fastened into a socket on the crown of the basinet. Figure 94. When more than one was worn the ornament was called a *panache*. The word "plume" came into use at a somewhat later period when feathers were worn at the sides or back of the headpiece. In 1606, it is recorded that knights wore "strange feathers of rich and great esteem which they called 'Birds of Paradise'."

1500-1600

During the early Renaissance the ostrich plume came more and more into use. With the round, flat hats fashionable at this time, long plumes attached at the side encircled the crown, tipping the front brim. PLATE XVIII. These characteristic hats of the sixteenth century have been made familiar through the many portraits by the immortal German master, Hans Holbein. Later, as

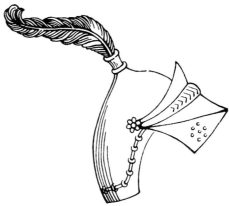

Figure 94. Early Use of the Feather in Military Dress, about 1420

crowns rose and were transformed into fashionable toques, little up-standing feathers or tips of the ostrich plume gave a touch of novelty to the hat. Speaking of the fashion for feathers, one is reminded of the words of that able if caustic chronicler of fashion, Philip Stubbes, whose patience was sorely tried by the sight of men wearing feathers in their hats:

Men are content with no kind of hat without a great bunch of *feathers* of divers and sundry colours. Many get good living dyeing and sellying them, not a few prove themselves fooles by wearing them.

It was during the reign of Henry VIII that women are said to have first worn feathers in the hair. Queen Elizabeth (1558-1603) lent her aid in promoting the fashion by insisting on wearing, as a decorative feature, little red wings just over the ears. Another royal lady, Mariana of Austria, whose portrait remains as a witness for the mode, adopted the long plume as a part of her very elaborate coiffure. Figure 95. Though the use of plumes as a fashionable note in hairdressing began at this time, the fashion was indeed modest when compared with the great extravagance of the mode during the last quarter of the eighteenth century, when Marie Antoinette ruled the fashion world.

It was in the period of Elizabeth, also, that the fan was taken up by leaders of the mode. With the passing of the years it came to be one of the most important and beautiful of dress accessories. In the early days fans were usually made of ostrich feathers dyed various colors, set in handsome handles of carved ivory or metal, and when not carried in the hand were suspended from the girdle.

1600-1800

The outstanding fashion in men's dress of the early seventeenth century was the picturesque hat with sweeping plumes. Many famous portraits of this day have been preserved in the works of Sir Anton Van Dyck, Peter Paul Rubens, and Frans Hals. In 1670 the tricorne appeared. In many instances it was trimmed with full plumes; at other times the up-

COURTESY, METROPOLITAN MUSEUM OF ART

Figure 95. Mariana of Austria............................... *Velasquez*

The formal and extravagant headdress with its numerous bows, rosette, and full white plume, is in strict keeping with the elaborate costume and the formal dignity of the princess herself.

turned brim was filled with curling feather tips. The popularity of the tricorne continued for approximately a hundred years. Though the same fashions were general in all countries, one or the other took the lead in certain extremes of the mode, especially in this use of the handsome plume. For instance, in France, in the early days of its popularity, the tricorne was more elaborately trimmed than elsewhere. During the last quarter of the eighteenth century when the "heads" of women were mounting higher and higher, elevated still more by the use of tall waving plumes, France again took the lead. It is said that the plumes worn in a single evening by Marie Antoinette were valued at 125 francs. We are told that in 1784 when milady's plumes were not upon her head they were carried in a swordcase in the back of her carriage.

PLATE XIX. Mrs. Seymour Thomas........*Whistler*

The long ostrich plume, curled and dyed in various hues, added the fashionable note to hats of the late 19th century.

Succeeding the towering headdresses of the late eighteenth century came the graceful, wide-brimmed hat laden with plumes. This has passed into history as the *Gainsborough* (see PLATE XIV, page 44). The portraits of many beautiful women painted by the English masters Thomas Gainsborough and Sir Joshua Reynolds testify to the popularity of plumes and the great charm they held for the period.

Apropos of feathers, and considering the extravagant taste of young men for fine clothes during the late eighteenth century, it is interesting to read the wholesome advice sent by George Washington, under date of January, 1783, to his nephew, Bushrod Washington:

Do not conceive that fine *feathers* make fine birds. A plain genteel dress is more to be admired and obtains more credit than lace and embroidery in the eyes of the sensible.

Nineteenth and Twentieth Centuries

In the early nineteenth century the plume was occasionally used as a trimming on the popular poke bonnet, but its place in the millinery field was gradually usurped by ribbon, lace, and flowers. By the sixties, dainty bonnets of organdie and taffeta trimmed with the curling tips were general favorites. Peacock feathers, and those of the pheasant as well, came in for their share of popularity. During this period the drooping plume, a popular and becoming style, was worn in England on the wide-brimmed beaver riding hat. Later, in America, particularly in the South, the ostrich-trimmed riding hat was a popular favorite. Again in the eighties the long plume was introduced as a decorative note for the evening coiffure. Many times these were of unusual length, falling from the back comb to the shoulders. By the nineties the hair was dressed high, and tiny ostrich tips in black, white, and delicate colors combined with the aigrette, tipped the high headdress, adding a further note of distinction to the wearer. Toward the end of the century the extravagant use of whole birds, wings, or the aigrette as a trimming for hats reached such proportions that public attention was called to the fashion. As has been pointed out in the chapter on hats, the demands of this mode were particularly objectionable because many of the most beautiful varieties could be obtained only at nesting time, when the parent birds were slain and the helpless young left to perish of starvation. The destruction of birds of plumage for these passing whims of fashion brought severe criticism from the thinking public, and in time the fashion was abandoned. This sentiment against the use of naturalistic trimmings of birds and feathers led to the development of a distinctly new and unique field. By the clever arrangement of various kinds of dyed feathers and plumes, such ornaments as cockades, pom-poms, tassels, and fringes were designed for the most fashionable millinery trade. No longer could it be said that woman

PLATE XX. The Green Bodice.............................*J. Alden Weir*

The long boa of curled ostrich feathers was a fashion of the late 19th and early 20th centuries.

was wearing upon her hat the wing and breast of a bird. No, indeed. These effects were only clever designs wrought by the artful milliner and her needle. Soon entire hats were made of goose feathers dyed in various tints of blue, green, or orchid. One form of arranging feathers gradually led to another, and soon goose feathers and ostrich plumes were being made into long boas to be worn about the neck and shoulders. PLATE XX. Shortly, evening scarfs and gowns were edged with feathery bands of colored and uncurled ostrich tips. Fans, too, come in for their share of feathery decoration. The floating delicacy of the feather imparted lightness and beauty to both large and small fans of various shapes. About 1900, large feather fans in which a number of full-length plumes were dyed in various colors and mounted in ivory handles added a charming note of color to the evening gown.

The fashion for feathers has waxed and waned through the centuries. Among all kinds of feather decoration the ostrich plume holds first place for beauty. For smartness and that unmistakable air of jauntiness, the straight upstanding feather has no rival. Plumes, tips, single or in groups, together with the various cockades, small designs, and trimmings constructed of feathers, have greatly enlarged the field of feather decoration. In the modern world this field has developed into an industry giving employment to thousands.

REFERENCES

Cole, George S., *A Dictionary of Dry Goods*, p. 132.
Earle, Alice Morse, *Two Centuries of Costume in America*, p. 55.
Elite Styles, October, 1921.
New International Encyclopedia, Vol. 8.
Planché, J. R., *Cyclopedia of Costume*, Vol. I.
Sage, Elizabeth, *A Study of Costume*, pp. 5, 140.
The Illustrated Milliner, June, 1818; February, March, June, 1919; September, 1921.

CHAPTER 4

The Wig

Three things are men most likely to be cheated in, a horse, a *wig*, and a wife.
BENJAMIN FRANKLIN, *Poor Richard*, 1736

AS is true of many accessories of dress, the wig dates from antiquity. While the modern revival of wigs in the eighteenth century was plainly a dictate of fashion, designed for only beauty and distinction, the wig of antiquity was worn chiefly for its practical value.

The ancient Egyptians were expert wigmakers. The fashion demanded wigs for both men and women. On first thought it seems an odd custom for people living in a hot climate to adopt a covering for the head. The wig of the Egyptians, however, was designed to keep the head cool, thus serving the same purpose as the modern turban. The hair was either cut short or the head was shaved. The wig was built upon a netlike surface that allowed the heat of the head to escape and at the same time served as a protection from the sun. Usually the top of the wig was made of curled hair and the sides composed of a succession of plaits. Others appear to have been made of wool or other stuffs, and were probably worn by those who could not afford real hair.

The earliest wigs worn by men seem to have been the short-haired wig which was adopted by all classes from shepherd to prince. The great lords, however, and other important persons wore both short- and long-haired wigs. The short-haired wigs show a construction of little curls arranged in horizontal rows lapping over each other like the tiles of a roof. Figure 96. The ears were covered as well as the back of the neck, and little of the forehead was visible. Though this was originally a noble headdress, as early as the Fifth Dynasty workmen were aping their masters by wearing the same. In the long-haired wig the hair was usually parted in the middle and fell in a thick mass to the shoulders. Sometimes it was curled across the forehead and slightly waved. Figure 97. Even at this early date the vanity of men in this matter of wigs is apparent. History records that during the Old Empire one Shepsere, who held a courtly office, caused four statues of himself to be prepared for his tomb. In two of these he wears the usual wig, in the third his hair is long and flowing, and in the fourth the long wig, which reaches down to the middle of his back, is made of innumerable little curls. The fashion of the short- and long-haired wig continued with minor changes down to the Eighteenth Dynasty, when the hair of both men and women was given a softer and more natural effect. By the Twentieth Dynasty, however, fashions reverted to the old custom of heavy wigs framing the face.

COURTESY, MUSEUM OF FINE ARTS, BOSTON

Figure 96. Wig, Egyptian, VI Dynasty

Paintings upon mummy cases and sculptures indicate that styles in women's wigs also varied with the periods. During the early dynasties, wigs were large structures reaching the shoulders. Gradually these grew longer and more massive until in the Twelfth Dynasty, and later, they are pictured with heavy lappets falling to the front of the shoulders. The sculptured likeness of the Lady Sennuwy, whose husband, Prince Hepzefa, was military governor of the province of Ethiopia about 2000 B.C., is an excellent example of this wig. Figure 98. Here the hair is parted over the forehead and falls in the usual fashion over the breast. Occasionally the ends of the wig were given a fringelike arrangement. In a few instances women of royal birth wore short-haired wigs extending only to the shoulders, and often under the wig in front one can catch a glimpse of the natural hair. In the statue of the Princess Nofret, the wig is secured by a richly ornamented band, and the heavy mass of hair falls to the shoulders. Figure 99. About the middle of the Eighteenth Dynasty, when many changes in clothing were made, fashions in wigs also changed. A more

COURTESY, MUSEUM OF FINE ARTS, BOSTON

Figure 97. Portrait of Head Showing Wig, Egyptian, XVIII Dynasty

natural and graceful arrangement of the hair was introduced. Figure 100. It now fell in soft ringlets or plaits without concealing the contour of the head (see Figure 7, page 5). Later, during the Twentieth Dynasty, the wheel of fashion turned and women again adopted the heavy coiffure, crimped and curled and extending not only to the shoulders but in some instances to the waist.

Among the ancient Assyrians and Persians large wigs, curled, plaited, and oiled, were not uncommon.

The Romans were very fastidious in this matter of dressing the head.

We read that several of the Roman emperors wore wigs. These were a kind of peruke called *capillamentum*. It was among Roman women, however, that the wig was especially popular. They are said to have preferred the fine, blonde hair of the Gauls and Germans rather than their own dark locks, and for this reason indulged their fancy by ordering blonde wigs. Juvenal describes the Empress Messalina, when about to venture forth on her nocturnal escapades, as covering her dark locks with a flaxen wig. These women of Rome were so fastidious in the matter of wigs that their care extended even to the sculptured portrait. Many of these were made with adjustable wigs, and in this way the portrait was always kept up to date. The sculptured portrait of Lucilla, wife of Lucius Verus, formerly in the Campidoglio, shows the wig of black marble made so that the piece may be easily removed and another substituted.

Though the people of antiquity were acquainted with the practical advantages of the wig, it remained for the eighteenth century to achieve its most picturesque development. The mere mention of wigs as a part of costume instantly

COURTESY, MUSEUM OF FINE ARTS, BOSTON

Figure 98. The Lady Sennuwy
Black granite, Old Kingdom.

carries the mind to this particular chapter in the history of dress. Indeed, it was in the wig that the art of dress of this period culminated.

1600-1800

Wigs had entered gradually upon the fashion scene. The long hair fashionable in 1600 no doubt furnished a part of the inspiration. There was, also, the famous "love lock," a curl longer than the rest of the hair and worn on the left side, that had been introduced by Charles I of England. Both this and the flowing hair did much to inspire the introduction and acceptance of the wig. Furthermore, the women of this period had shown a fondness for changing the color of their hair. This had been managed not always by dyeing but sometimes by a change of ready-made coiffures. The use of these brought no end of condemnation from the moralists, and women were called upon to repent and sacrifice these worldly vanities. Repentance, however, was at the most brief, for after a short interval women continued their ways with more "shamelessness" than before. Preparing the mind still further for the wig was the custom of wearing "false heads" which had been for decades a dis-

COURTESY, METROPOLITAN MUSEUM OF ART

Figure 99. Head of Nofret, Showing Natural Hair under Front of Wig, Egyptian, IV Dynasty

tinguishing feature of the court jester.

According to the English authority F. W. Fairholt, the earliest record of a wig in the modern world appears in the privy purse expenses of Henry VIII where, under date of December 1592, is an entry of twenty shillings "for a peruyke for Sexton, the king's fool." Toward the end of the sixteenth century wigs are known to have been worn to some extent. Both Queen Elizabeth and Mary, Queen of Scots, indulged their taste for numerous wigs. However, it remained for Louis XIII of France (1610-43) and Charles II of England (1660-85) to popularize the fashion so effectively that the whole world conformed to the pattern. The year 1660 is the accredited year for

COURTESY, METROPOLITAN MUSEUM OF ART

Figure 100. Hair Ornaments of the Lady Senebtisi; Gold Wire Circlet and Gold Rosettes, XII Dynasty (2000–1975 B.C.)

Wig modern; ornaments as on body when found.

the coming of the wig. Previously Louis XIII had introduced and worn at court a wonderful "false head" made of natural hair and reaching to the waist. This, and all the first wigs worn by the king, were meant to represent the natural hair. They were parted in the middle and hung in long curls framing the face. Following the death of Louis XIII the reins of government passed to Louis XIV, who was the proud possessor of beautiful, abundant hair. Consequently, wigs were given up for a time. During his father's reign, while Louis XIV was still a child and the wig was quickly taking the heart of the fashionable world, his beautiful and abundant hair was the delight of the French court. The courtiers, by way of compliment, had "heads" or wigs made to resemble the locks of the youthful Louis. Naturally he was greatly pleased and later, with the coming of his own baldness, the compliment of the courtiers became a personal necessity. Louis adopted the wig. As a result wigs again came into fashion, and continued with various extravagances into the following century.

Figure 101. The Campaign Wig

In England, the steadily graying hair of the King, Charles II, led him to adopt the wig. His Majesty was very dark; hence his first wig was big and black. It is recorded that one day as he looked at his wigged portrait he exclaimed: "'Od's fish! but I'm an ugly black fellow!" Following the King's example many of the most fashionable wigs were black. After a period of black wigs there followed the demand for fair and dark-brown hair. So great was the need for supplies of human hair that children, when on the streets alone, were approached and, before they were aware, had their locks clipped for the wigmaker's art. Since human hair was very expensive, both horse-hair and goat hair were used in the making of wigs.

The natural wig of the earlier days soon gave way to a more formal wig with curls hanging down the back and over the shoulders. These "heads" of curled hair were known as *perukes* and *periwigs*. The natural hair was shaved close for the proper wearing of the wig. The peruke usually refers to the formal and elaborately curled wig; the periwig was also a formal wig, not so elaborate, its name simply distinguishing it from wigs of a less formal type. The *campaign* wig was another type of formal wig which came to be popular in 1684. Figure 101. This wig had long sidepieces twisted at the ends. It is described by Randle Holme in his *Academy of Armoury* (printed in 1685) as one having, "Knots or bobs, a dildo or corkscrew on each side, with a curled forehead." In forming the curls the hair was wound tightly around small rollers of pipe clay while hot. Though this is the period when wigs were particularly the pride of gentlemen, they were also worn by women. By-and-by the wig reached a greatly exaggerated size. The front was raised in a double peak, and the long waving curls fell over and below the shoulders. Possibly it was the two-peaked arrangement of women's hair at this time that inspired this singular style in men's wigs. At any rate it is worthy of note that the type was contemporary in the hairdressing of men and women.

Figure 102. Peter Fanuel. . . .
John Smibert

The closely curled wig, the stock and jabot, the plaited frills at the wrist, and the many buttons on waistcoat and coat are strikingly characteristic of gentlemen's dress of the early 18th century.

It is well to observe that the wig was in no sense a camouflage for natural hair. No, indeed, a gentleman's wig was openly a matter of great personal pride. It was, in fact, so important, so essential to his affluence, that no gentleman would appear in public without it. Hair "in a state of nature" had become intolerable! It is not surprising that, with the ever-increasing popularity of wigs, attention, time, and money were turned to the selection, the making, and the maintenance of this important accessory. The greatest skill and finest artistry were necessary requirements in the proper making of a peruke. So great were the demands that a new fashion service was created—that of the *perruquiers*. These makers of wigs had their own academy and were considered artists. It is said that in 1776 there were thirty-two masters of the trade, and that St. Michael was the patron of their guild. In France, many leaders of fashion supported their own private perruquiers. Louis XV (1715-1774), in whose reign the fashion developed into a mania, is said to have required the services of forty court perruquiers. At the height of wig popularity pomades and powder were used with the greatest extravagance. Pomades were first touched over the hair to keep the powder in place. These were made from various fats and perfumed with popular scents. Powder is said to have been introduced about the year 1690. It is a historical fact, however, that in Roman days the Emperor Nero (54-68 A.D.) and others down to the year 268 indulged in the use of gold dust for powdering the hair. In still more ancient times the Assyrians and Persians dusted their

PLATE XXI. Elihu Yale...............................*Enoch Zeeman*

The magnificent wig, the handsome waistcoat with turned-back cuffs, the lace cravat, the ruffles at the hand, the buckled shoes and, in fact, every detail of dress, depicts the very height of fashion of this period in the late 18th century.

89

hair and beards with gold. When first introduced into the modern world, powder was white; later pink, gray, and blue were popular tints. The base of these powders was finely sifted starch combined with plaster of Paris. All powders were highly scented with ambergris, musk, orris root, jasmine, and bergamot. The powder was usually showered over the wig, frequently covering the shoulders. An early reference to the use of powder is found in an old account book of 1634. "Paid for a Quayle pipe for poudring the hair." The quail pipe was a simple tube blown through to attract quail. The inference is that a similar tube was used for blowing powder over the hair. During the process a glass cone was held over the mouth and nose. Powder went out of fashion about 1794, having been popular for one hundred years.

COURTESY, NEW YORK HISTORICAL SOCIETY

Figure 103. Johannes Schuyler. . . .
Pieter Vanderlyn

An unusual and very formal wig. The long, white cravat, also in formal style, is in full keeping with the dignity of the portrait.

With the fashion of the powdered and perfumed peruke came the custom of combing the hair in public. Combing the wig was a popular grace somewhat similar to twirling the mustache. Beautiful combs in handsome cases were carried by the beaux of the day. When assured of admiring spectators at the theater or in other public places, these little combs were brought forth and the dandy proceeded with elegant ease to comb his peruke.

Combing the peruke, at the time when men of fashion wore large wigs, was even in public places considered an act of gallantry.
From the Epilogue, *Wrangling Lovers,* 1677

An early writer of this interesting period, upon visiting England, somewhat contemptuously describes the young men who frequent public places as "creatures compounded of a *periwig;* and a coat laden with *powder* as white as a miller's; a face besmeared with snuff, and a few affected airs."

Though the exaggerated periwig continued through the reign of Louis XV, it gradually gave way to a smaller wig rolling back from the forehead and drawn into a loose queue behind where it was tied with a large, ribbon bow. From time to time the queue was treated in various ways. The great victory of the Duke of Marlborough on the field of

Ramilies, in May 1706, made the *Ramilie* wig the most popular of its day. Figure 104. The long queue was now tied at the nape of the neck with a black bow, plaited, and then tied again at the end. This was a very popular wig, though considered less formal than the periwig. An anecdote recounts that the favored Lord Bolingbrooke once presented himself wearing this informal wig before Queen Anne, who, much affronted, remarked that he would doubtless next appear in his nightcap. By-and-by the tail of the Ramilie was turned up, forming the "pigtail" wig. Figure 105. With the queued wig the top hair was dressed low, and the side locks were formed into one, two, or three horizontal curls. Figure 106. Sometimes one horizontal curl extended from above the ear on the right, around the head to the left. The queue, in one form or another, was worn by all classes of society, and was also adopted by the army and navy. The consumption of hair powder at this time was enormous. The queued wig is invariably seen with the little tricorne, the favorite hat of the century. At the same period bags and bows were introduced. Figures 107, 108. The falling back hair was now confined in a black sack or velvet bag and tied with a wide, black ribbon. (The bag wigs are said to have originated with French servants, who tied their hair up in leather bags to keep it out of the

Figure 104.
The Ramilie Wig

Figure 105.
The Pigtail Wig

way, for flowing curls were considered out of place in the dress of a serving man.) These fashionable silk and velvet bags were supplied with a hidden drawstring for pulling up the opening to fit the queue. Many of them were quite large and lay well across the shoulders. A writer of 1774 says: "At present such unmerciful ones are worn that a little man's shoulders are perfectly covered with black satin."

In England in 1772, the macaronies, who were the fashionable "bloods" of the day, adopted a high toupee, and with it wore their own hair in a knot or queue at the back. In a play of the period, *The Model Husband*, one character is made to remark: "I met with nothing but a parcel of toupee coxcombs who plaster up their brains under periwigs." The macaronies were the first to adopt the *catogan* or *club*, the unbraided queue folded back upon itself and tied. Figure 109. Many women also wore the macaroni wig. In this coiffure the hair was drawn upward over a high cushion of wire and the back hair arranged in a festoon of curls. A plume or group of feathers added the finishing touch to the structure. Following the many types of queued wigs came the bob wigs, intended to represent the natural hair.

COURTESY, METROPOLITAN MUSEUM OF ART

Figure 106. Don Sabestian Martinique....*Goya*

This distinctive personality wears the wig with the modish side rolls, the lace jabot, striped silk coat, and short breeches.

Contemporary with these fashions prevailing in France and England were the styles in the American colonies. Plymouth and Boston were settled early in the seventeenth century, and somewhat later the wig made fashionable by Louis XIV was worn by the leading colonists. By 1670 the "plain people" as well as governors, ministers, and magistrates were wearing this popular accessory. The portraits of this early American period picture the colonists in large, black, thickly curled wigs. In 1673, this extravagance led the Massachusetts legislature seriously to discuss the propriety of the colony's adopting such extraordinary fashions. The clergy also denounced, in general, extremes in dress, and condemned wigs, in particular. Further, the Puritans resolved that "ye wearing of extravagant, superfluous wigs is altogether contrary to truth." The Quakers, who adopted the dress of the period without trimmings of any kind, are said to have occasionally powdered the hair and worn the periwig. Finally the question of wig-wearing resolved itself into one that could not be settled for the simple reason that all the notables in the colony had adopted them! Wigmaking had, indeed, become an important business. Advertisements ran in the papers extolling this wigmaker and that. One such notice furnishes an illuminating example of the importance of the craft:

WILLIAM LANG,

WIG-MAKER AND HAIR DRESSER,

Hereby informs the Public, that he has hired a Person from Europe, by whose assistance he is now enabled, in the several Branches of his Business, to serve his good customers, with all others, in the most genteel and polite tastes that are at present in Fashion in England and America. In particular, *wigs* made in any Mode whatever, such as may grace and become the most important Heads, whether those of Judges, Divines, Lawyers or Physicians,

Figure 107. The Bag Wig   Figure 108. The Bag and Wig

together with those of an inferior kind, so as exactly to suit their Respective Occupations and Inclinations. *Hairdressing*, for Ladies and Gentlemen, performed in the most elegant and newest taste . . . . Ladies in a particular Manner, shall be attended to, in the nice, easy, genteel and polite Construction of Rolls, such as may tend to raise their Heads to any Pitch they may desire, also French curls made in the neatest Manner. He gives cash for hair.

Figure 109. The Club or Catogan

Indeed, wigs were now as magnificent as those at the French court, and the colonists likewise took as great a pride in their special barbers as did the French in their *perruquiers*. Barbers were employed for yearly service, calling from house to house, inspecting the family wigs, and keeping them all *a la mode*.

The handsome wig shown in the portrait of Elihu Yale, PLATE XXI, is, indeed, as superb as any worn at court. The front is raised in the fashionable double peak and the long, beautifully waved curls fall over the shoulders. Other details of the rich dress are worthy of note. The soft cravat of fine lace is lapped in front, the frills at the hands no doubt match the lace of the cravat, the coat carries its row of buttons down the front, the brocade waistcoat and large cuffs are especially handsome, and the shoes with large silver buckles are characteristic of the century. This portrait, painted in 1717, is a witness to the elegance in dress maintained at the time. The wig worn by Peter Faneuil, Figure 102, is very handsome, closely curled and long at the back. He favored many buttons on his coat and waistcoat, and the usual four buttons to support the cuffs. The fine lawn of the frilled jabot

PLATE XXII. Nicholas Boylston.................................*Copley*

The "smart" indoor turban protected the closely shaven head from draughts and cold. Note the handsome *banyan*, the fashionable negligee of the period.

is repeated in the frills at the hand. Somewhat later the full, short wig came to be adopted by many men of the professions. These were usually made of snow-white hair in varying degrees of bushiness. They are frequently seen in portraits of the New England clergy and are invariably accompanied by the familiar "bands," the two shortened tabs of white cambric which gave the correct emphasis to the collar band. Figure 110.

Wigs continued to hold their own for many years. In 1720 white wigs were so fashionable that white hair for their manufacture brought a tremendous price. In 1734 light-gray hair periwigs were selling to the colonists at about four guineas each, gray cue perukes something less, and bob perukes a trifle more. Gray at this time was a very fashionable hue.

With the continual wearing of wigs came the turbanlike cap worn indoors when the wig was removed. PLATE XXII. With this cap there is invariably seen a garment closely resembling a dressing gown and known as the *banyan*. This was usually fashioned of rich stuffs—brocades, figured metal silks, velvets—and was probably of East Indian origin. In the home the elaborate coats of the period were removed and this very comfortable and informal robe took its place. When the closely

COURTESY, NEW YORK HISTORICAL SOCIETY

Figure 110. Archibald Laidlie

The short, "busy," white wig was adopted by many of the distinguished members of the New England clergy, while the "band," two shortened strips of white lawn or cambric, was invariably worn.

shaven head was relieved of the hot wig it was protected from chills and draughts by the popular cap made of a gay-colored material and worn cocked at one side. The importance of the banyan and cap may be judged by the number of distinguished men who sat for their portraits wearing this becoming *negligée* and the equally informal cap.

In France by 1788 men were beginning to wear their own hair tied at the back in imitation of the wig. During the Revolution (1789), the general trend toward simplicity of dress influenced many to deny themselves even the suggestion of a wig, and short hair was commonly seen. Wigs did, however, continue their hold upon the professional classes. It is said that even as late as 1800 doctors were still clinging to their wigs. At this period wigs for women were in the ascendency. In fact, women are known to have had their beautiful and abundant hair cut short in order to wear the wig. It may be that the mountains of hair worn in the previous years, together with the frizzing, curling, and pomading practiced, had just about worn out women's heads, and short hair with a wig was now a welcome change. An interesting reference to the popularity of wigs worn by American women at this period is found in the letters written by the daughters of Thomas Jefferson. These two ladies, while preparing for their residence at the White House, wrote to Mrs. Madison, ordering wigs of the most fashionable shape to be ready for them upon their arrival. "They are universally worn," wrote Mrs. Randolph, "and will relieve us of the necessity of dressing our own hair, a business in which we are not adepts." The second daughter, Mrs. Eppes, possessed a glorious mass of auburn hair, but, though her father was well aware of her intention, he did not object to her sacrificing it to wear the fashionable wig.

COURTESY, NATIONAL MUSEUM, STOCKHOLM

Figure 111. George Washington. . . .
Wertmiller

The natural hair rolled at the sides, well powdered, and held in a queue tied with black silk ribbon, followed the elaborate wigs.

1800-1900

In America at this period, as in France, men were returning to the display of their own hair. Those who were fortunate enough to possess it wore their locks waved, curled, and tied in a queue. This was the final imitation of the wig. Powder was frequently added. Figure 111. By 1820 long hair was practically out and wigs were declared passé.

In this twentieth century wigs have passed into oblivion. A survival of the custom, however, still remains in the legal dress of England, where formal wigs are worn as part of the professional dress of the English court. The wig has flaps of formal curls hanging in front, and is said to resemble the wig worn by Queen Anne in the early years of her reign (1702-14).

Today, wigs, like patches and masks, are remembered with a kindly interest. We recognize the charm they held for people of the period in which they flourished. Life was literally a stage and "all the men and women merely actors." Running true to form, our modern world, when seized with the play spirit, brings forth its masks, patches, and wigs, and disports itself in masquerade, enjoying, if only for a moment, the irresistible charm of a most artificial, most extravagant, but withal most delightful period of fashion.

REFERENCES

Earle, Alice Morse, *Two Centuries of Costume in America.*
Erman, J. P. Adolf, *Life in Ancient Egypt,* pp. 219-225.
Evans, Mary, *Costume Throughout the Ages,* pp. 74-93, 156-178.
Fairholt, F. W., *Costume in England.*
Lester, Katherine Morris, *Historic Costume,* pp. 28, 29.
Planché, J. R., *Cyclopedia of Costume,* Vol. I—*Dictionary.*
New International Cyclopedia, Vol. 23.
Sage, Elizabeth, *A Study of Costume,* pp. 2, 5, 8, 106, 121-155.
Wilkinson, Sir John Gardiner, *A Popular Account of the Ancient Egyptians.*

CHAPTER 5

The Patch

Yonder's, my lord, your son with a *patch* of velvet on his face: whether there be
a scar under it, or no, the velvet knows.

All's Well That Ends Well. Act IV, sc. 5

A PATCH was a tiny bit of plaster given an advantageous position
upon the chin, near the mouth, or beside the eye. By its contrast
with the fairness of the skin the dark patch was believed to enhance one's
beauty.

Patches date from Roman times. Though adopted by Roman women
as an attractive novelty, the patch then was only a refinement of the
primitive practice of body painting. It is sometimes said that the idea of
the patch as a fashion in the seventeenth century did not come from early
Rome but originated with the use of plasters worn as a cure for headache.
Of course, it may be that the custom was indeed handed down from
Rome, where in the decadent period patches were worn by Roman senators as well as by women. The most likely theory of all, however, is that
it grew out of an interesting superstition associated with the location of
moles, which at this time were regarded as marks of great beauty. Something over two centuries ago fortunetellers enjoyed a wide patronage by
predicting future good and evil based upon the location of moles. Regardless of that, whatever may have been the origin of the patch, women of
the seventeenth century started a vogue for it which grew to such proportions that its reign fills a full page in the history of dress.

1600-1800

In France, patches of black taffeta were cut in various shapes—stars,
moons, crowns, and other eccentric forms—and given as many unusual
names. Figure 112. The "coquette" was placed on the lip, the "roguish"
on the nose, the "impassioned" at the corner of the eye. The proper placing of these patches required real judgment and was looked upon as an
art to be studied. A play of the period suggests that a patch too low on
the cheek "pulps the flesh too much"; when near the eye "she downright
squints"; and when placed near the temple it gives a "sedate air." The importance of placing the patch advantageously is vouched for in this line
from *The Wrangling Lovers,* "All the Passions in the features are, We

may show, or hide 'em, as we know how to affix these pretty artificial moles."

As usual with such innovations, sharp wrangling arose over the widespread fashion of the patch. Massillon, the distinguished French preacher, delivered sermon after sermon against the practice. Fashion, however, could not be controlled by this method, and beauty spots grew apace. Every lady carried her little patch box of silver, ivory, or tortoise shell. Figure 113. This was frequently supplied with a mirror. It was no uncommon sight to see milady adjust a patch or two in public places with the same careless ease the modern woman displays in powdering her nose or adjusting her hair.

All through the fashion world the same custom prevailed. In England as early as 1665, women were spotting their faces in affectation of a mole, "to set off their beauty such as Venus had." The *Spectator* furnishes a humorous account of the impression made by fashionable English women upon four visiting Indian kings:

Figure 112. The Patch at Its Worst

From Bulwer's Artificial Changeling.

The women look like angels, and would be more beautiful than the sun were it not for little black spots that are apt to break out in their faces and sometimes rise in very odd figures. I have observed that those little blemishes wear off very soon, but when they disappear in one part of the face, they are apt to break out in another, insomuch that I have seen a spot upon the forehead in the afternoon, which was upon the chin in the morning. *Spectator*, 54

As late as 1700 a lady of fashion was never without her patches, but in Queen Anne's day (1702-14), the fashion of patches took a queer turn. The spirit of party rivalry ran so high that even the women took sides. Some were Tories and some were Whigs, and the manner of patching proclaimed the party! Again Addison, that keen observer of his time, has a word to say:

About the middle of last winter I went to see an opera at the theatre in the Haymarket, where I could not help but take notice of two parties of very fine women who had placed themselves in kind of battle array against one another. After a short survey of them I noticed that they were patched differently; the faces on the one hand were spotted on the right side of the forehead, and those upon the other on the left. I quickly perceived that they cast hostile glances at one another; and that their patches were placed in these different situations as party signals to distinguish friends from foes. . . . Upon inquiry I found that the Amazons on my right were Whigs, and those on my left Tories.

Indeed, so enthusiastic were women in supporting their chosen party that marriage papers drawn up expressly stated that whatever the husband's political opinions might be the wife was at liberty to patch as she pleased!

Fashions in accessories of dress come and go, returning anon through the centuries. The fashion of patches, however, has never been revived. The nearest approach to a return of the custom was in 1919, when

COURTESY, METROPOLITAN MUSEUM OF ART

Figure 113. Patch Box, Blue Enamel with Ivory Lining
Trophies of love painted in green on gold, French, 1700.

women wore veils in which there were black dots similar to the spots of yesterday. The mesh veils with one or more black chenille dots were distinctly an adaptation of the patch period.

Looking back to the period of patches one is amused, and at the same time one wonders at the shifting standards of beauty. In the twentieth century the fashionable woman seeks expert advice and skillful methods for the removal of that mole which the women of earlier days admired in Venus, and cherished as a note of beauty in themselves.

REFERENCES

Calthrop, Dion Clayton, *English Costume*, Vol. II.
Fairholt, F. W., *Costume in England*.
Lester, Katherine Morris, *Historic Costume*, pp. 130, 140, 170, 171.
New York Times, January 26, 1930.
Parsons, Frank Alvah, *The Art in Dress*, p. 158.
Planché, J. R., *Cyclopedia of Costume*, Vol. I—*Dictionary*.
Sage, Elizabeth, *A Study of Costume*, pp. 123, 132, 140.

CHAPTER 6

The Mask

Her *mask* so hinders me,
I cannot see her beauty's dignity.
MARSTON, *Satires*, 1598

THE history of masks is one of surprising interest. Nearly every race, from most primitive times to periods of advanced civilization, has found some use for the mask. Perhaps the painted face of a primitive warrior inspired the first mask. At any rate, many of the early tribal masks suggest the abode of a fiendish and warring spirit. In tribal and religious ceremonies, in the dance, in the drama, in peace and war, the mask has played a unique part.

Masks in China have had greater variety of form than in any other country in the world. About the eighth century they were introduced into China from Japan, probably in connection with Buddhism. One of the oldest masked dances is the *sambasso*. This dance is said to have originated in a religious performance held in Japan in 807. It was believed that this masked dance exerted a magic influence in stopping the progress of fissures that frequently opened in the earth. In later centuries, the mask has been conspicuous in many of the dance dramas of Japan.

In the field of dramatic art and under the patronage of the Greek theater the mask was brought to a high state of development. In the large theaters of ancient Greece it was difficult for the audience seated at a distance to see facial details. Consequently, the actor had to be made more conspicuous. His stature was increased by thickening the soles of his buskins, his clothes were padded, and his face was covered by a vividly painted mask with enlarged features. To carry the voice a small device was set in the mouth opening. The various actors were fitted with masks which in their individual designs expressed the different characters portrayed. In contrast with this the Greek chorus, when appearing as a unit, wore masks of a uniform pattern. Archaeological discoveries, and literary evidence as well, indicate that masks were in use as early as 400 B.C.

As with all things artistic, so with masks; they passed on to Rome. As early as the first century they were in constant use in the Roman theater, in Roman secular festivals, and in religious fetes. One unusual use of the mask was peculiar to Rome. All families of prominence preserved waxen masks of their distinguished ancestors. These were not death masks, but are believed to have been modeled as a portrait from life. They were tinted in close imitation of nature, making them as nearly lifelike as possible. Many families possessed large collections and looked upon them with great pride. On the ocasion of a death in the family the masks were brought forth. During the elaborate funeral ceremonies certain men impersonated the long line of distinguished ancestors by wearing these lifelike masks.

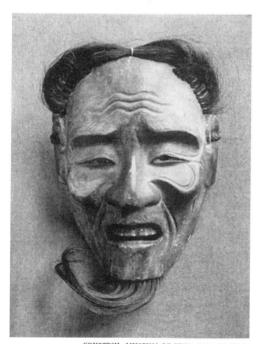

COURTESY, MUSEUM OF FINE ARTS, BOSTON

Figure 114. Japanese Mask, "The Spirit of the Pine Tree," Early 18th Century

Middle Ages-1600

During the thirteenth and fourteenth centuries, masks were worn in the miracle and mystery plays, which were the popular form of dramatic entertainment at that time. The actors were always supplied with masks and hooded capes. The collection of masks included those of women, bearded men, angels, and a number of fantastic heads representing animals.

Though the record of the mask is interesting and varied, not until the late sixteenth century was it seized upon by Fashion. Then masks became an important accessory of dress. These masks of the sixteenth century are demure and color-less trifles when compared with the galaxy of historical masks. Though Fashion urged them as a means for "protecting beauty," underneath this appeal there was the same age-old element of charm—the charm of mystery and illusion. These masks were made of odd forms of black velvet and were used at first to shield the eyes. They were short, shielding only the eyes and permitting the lower part of the face to be seen. In France, the mask was called the *loup*, meaning "wolf," because it had a tendency to frighten children. In England, this same mask was known as the *loo* mask. During the Elizabethan period (1558-1603), all leaders of fashion wore these little, black, velvet accessories. Indeed, no well-bred woman would venture upon the street without her mask. By-and-by white masks of fine cloth covering the entire face became fashionable. These were especially favored by ladies for use when riding. When not in use they were hung by a string to the girdle.

In the early days of mask wearing, the little accessory was carried in the hand, ready, upon the slightest provocation, to be placed before the eyes. Figure 116. Later, it was tied by strings about the head, or fastened otherwise by wires behind the ears. The long masks were kept in position by a velvet or glass button, fastened to a string or metal stay and held between the teeth. Frequently two strings or stays were used, and a bead or button was held in each corner of the mouth.

The purpose of the mask was similar to that of the veil, supposedly that of protection. At this time, the ladies of the French court and society, and the English as well, wore great quantities of powder and rouge. The mask served to protect the make-up from sun, wind, and dust. As a further protection, glass was frequently filled into the eye apertures.

1600-1700

The popularity of masks in Shakespeare's time may be judged by the frequent references to them in his plays of that day:

These happy *masks* that kiss fair ladies' brows.
Romeo and Juliet. Act I, sc. 1

With faces fit for *masks* or rather fairer.
Cymbeline. Act V, sc. 3

. . . these black *masks* proclaim and enshrine beauty.
Measure for Measure.
Act II, sc. 3

Figure 115. Terra-Cotta Mask, Greek, Hellenistic Period

In 1650 the popularity of masks greatly increased. Ostensibly they were now worn for either of two purposes—as a protection for the delicate skin or to conceal some unbecoming feature. It is said that when worn to conceal plainness of countenance they were called *cachelaid*, meaning "hide-ugly." Many of the black velvet masks were lined with white silk and folded over like a small purse. During the reign of Louis XIV, when troublous times were brewing, quite a fad for this little mask used as a disguise developed. Men adopted them, wearing at the same time the wide-sleeved domino with hooded cape. In this guise they were able to mingle with the crowds without fear of recognition. Ladies, too, began to meddle in politics, and they too found security behind their masks. Wearing them upon the street or in political gatherings they were able, thus protected, to gather information which could be used for or against popular movements. In commenting on this use of the mask, the distinguished French author Augustin Challamel says, "Conspiracies that had been hatched in boudoirs broke out in the streets, and women took up arms and placed themselves at the head of seditious parties."

Figure 116. Renaissance Figure with Mask

Whatever the political advantage of the mask may have been, it remains plainly evident that the element of mystery contributed much to its popularity and charm. By-and-by the wearing of the mask became a matter of etiquette and was governed by established laws. For instance, it was never worn when riding in a carriage. It was always removed when curtsying, especially when persons of distinction were gathered. In 1663, Pepys commented on the fashion, remarking that ladies attending plays put on "visards which hide the whole face and had become a fashion; and so to the exchange to buy a visard for my wife." He added that a French mask led Mrs. Pepys to some unpleasant encounters on the street with ill-bred courtiers.

1700-1800

In the early years of the eighteenth century the plays in London had become so bold and evil that lady patrons were compelled to wear masks to conceal their steady blushes. Despite their blushes, however, women are said to have attended the theater in ever-increasing numbers. When Queen Anne raised her voice against the theater and issued a royal command that plays must be reformed and refined the mask ceased to be in fashionable favor!

Contemporary with the fashion in France and England was the vogue for masks in America. Though the pioneers of Massachusetts were engaged in a severe struggle for existence and their wardrobes were limited, the mothers and daughters of these early days were guilty of indulging in the luxury of masks. In Salem and Boston, black velvet masks were selling at two shillings each. In other sections the mask was likewise having its day. The colonial dames of New York and the wives of Virginia and South Carolina planters were following the same fashion. When George Washington's stepdaughter was six years old, he sent to Europe for masks for both his wife and daughter. It is not uncommon to see children's masks listed in the bills of sale of this period. The "loo," or half mask, was a favorite, imported in all sizes. We are told that the custom of wearing half masks at costume balls originated in Italy. At these gatherings the *domino*, another name for the half mask, was always worn by women.

Figure 117. Mask, 1640

The modern world is chiefly concerned with masks in the form of "false faces," in which little of the historic craft remains. The element, however, which has been the controlling force behind the mask from the days of the primitives, to the Renaissance, to modern times, is the element of mystery. It was this element of mystery captured by capricious Fashion that brought the mask into costume, and made it the conspicuous feature of dress during one of the most remarkable periods of historic fashion.

REFERENCES

Havemeyer, Loomis, *Drama of Savage Peoples*.
Kniffen, Herbert Reynolds, *Masks*.
Lester, Katherine Morris, *Historic Costume*, pp. 116, 138.
Macgowan and Rosse, *Masks and Demons*.
Sage, Elizabeth, *A Study of Costume*, pp. 35, 107, 123, 132.
New International Encyclopedia, Vol. 15.

CHAPTER 7

Earrings

Superbus swaggers with a *ring* in's eare;
And likewise as the custom is, doth weare
About his neck a riband and a ring;
What makes me think that he's proud of a string.

HUTTON's *Epigrams*, 1619

THE love of ornament for personal decoration is a deeply rooted instinct which expresses itself freely in all primitive peoples. This same love of ornament finds expression in the higher civilizations as well,

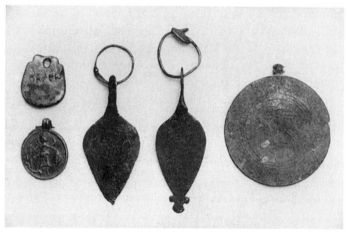

Figure 118. Pendant Earrings, Egyptian, Coptic Period

but it is here coupled with more or less restraint. The most barbarous ornaments are those fastened into the body by means of piercing or mutilating the flesh—nose rings, lip pieces, and earrings. So widespread has been the mutilation of the ears that it may be regarded as a common practice among primitive peoples. In some instances, ears with their pierced lobes and weight of ornament, sometimes as much as half a pound, have become so deformed as to hang down touching the shoulders. Even in modern times, the practice of ear piercing has survived.

The ancient Egyptians, whose history has been recorded from 4000 B.C., undoubtedly wore earrings through the pierced lobe of the ear.

Many such ornaments have been recovered. Their exact date, however, is uncertain, for it is difficult to say whether they belong to the most ancient Egyptian age or a somewhat later period. These simple earrings are large, round, single hoops from one and a half to two inches in diameter, and frequently of still greater size. Some of these earrings have been found constructed of as many as six open hoops soldered together to make one solid ring. Others, of silver and gold, about the size of an ordinary ring, show a small opening in one end into which the opposite end has been fitted after being passed through the ear. To some of these is added the pendant lotus flower and other drops. Figure 119. From numerous tomb pictures, one is led to believe that the ancient Egyptian woman was just as interested in these trinkets of fashion as is her modern sister. "Ladies at a Party, Talking about Their Earrings," Figure 120, after Wilkinson, is a vivid picture of the examination and animated conversation sometimes carried on over these fashionable ornaments. As commercial relations with the East and countries bordering the Mediterranean gradually widened, Egyptian jewelry naturally took on much of the elegance seen in the ornament of neighboring peoples.

Figure 119. Earrings, Egyptian

During the Ptolemaic period (beginning 30 B.C.) the characteristic earring was the swelling crescent of gold, a form popular in Grecian and later-day design. Figure 121.

The earliest home of the really artistic earring was Babylonia, then later Assyria, where men wore it as a symbol of rank. Kings and nobles as well as soldiers wore these ac-

Figure 120. Ladies at a Party Talking about Their Earrings

From an Egyptian wall painting, after Wilkinson.

cessories, usually pendants in the form of long, pear-shaped drops or cones attached to a heavy ring or crescent. During the reign of the later kings they were made in the form of a cross or a group of balls. The most popular materials used were gold and silver. The Persians, Phoenicians, and the pre-Hellenic peoples of the Aegian wore superb earrings.

Among the rare treasures uncovered during the excavations carried on in 1872-75 in the island of Cyprus, were large numbers of earrings, bracelets, finger rings, necklaces, and other ornaments.* A long while before the Trojan War, Cyprus had cities and commerce. Probably on account of the wide commercial activities carried on with neighboring countries and the East, her people advanced more rapidly in knowledge, art, and general civilization than any other Phoenician colony. The treasures found indicate that the artists of that day did exquisite work in gold; indeed their engravings on both stone and metal have scarcely been surpassed. In earrings, the crescent form was a favorite. The simplest type

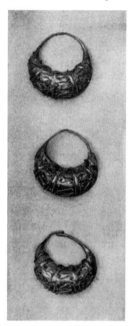

Figure 121. Egyptian,
Late Ptolemaic

Shows Greek Influence
in Gold Granular Work.

was the plain, flat crescent suspended from a ring. Also, the plain crescent was given a raised edge and a wire ornamentation over the surface. Enamel soon came into use, giving a richness of color. Lastly, the crescent was swelled into a solid gold form with charming surface decoration. Other examples show rosettes, bunches of fruit, and pendant ornaments which appear very modern. Figures 122, 123.

Definite records of the use of the earring by the ancient Hebrews are preserved in the Bible. Jacob obtained jewels of gold in the land to which he fled. Earrings also had been worn as charms or amulets by the idol worshipers taken into his household. They put their trust in these instead of relying upon Jehovah. And, during the trek to Canaan under Moses' leadership, the Hebrews gave their earrings to Aaron, who used them in making the famous golden calf.

Among the early Greeks, earrings were worn by both men and women, not only as ornament but as protection against evil spirits. The earliest form of earring was a swelling loop of bronze. Later it took on other forms, a single drop, a gold ball, or a vase-shaped pendant. Finally the pendant reached the exaggerated length of three inches. During the Golden Age, when civilization in Greece reached its highest development, women indulged their taste for two distinct types of earrings. One of these was worn against or close to the lobe of the ear, entirely covering it; the other hung as a pendant continuing the line of the ear instead of concealing it. "Nike Driving a Two-Horse Chariot," as shown in Figure 125, gives a very definite idea of the elaborate design of the period. Later there appeared the single pearl earring, and also those composed of many pieces of coin-shaped metal. They were usually sus-

* These treasures now make up the famous *Cesnola Collection* of The Metropolitan Museum of Art, New York City.

pended by a small ring from the main ornament. Every movement of the head produced a tinkling sound, very pleasing to the wearer. Ancient peoples seem to have liked tinkling ornaments, for they have been found over and over again in many sections of the ancient world. In Greece, another singular custom developed which, however, did not extend beyond the confines of that country. This was the popular fashion of wearing only one earring. Children as well as their fashionable mothers sometimes wore an earring in the right ear only.

Figure 122. Various Types of Gold Earrings

Cyprus, about 2000-2500 B.C.

In later days of the period earrings were occasionally worn by men. On a vase in the Vatican Library a figure of Achilles displays earrings; in his will Plato mentions "golden earrings," and a record states that Xenophon reproached one Apollonides because "his ears were bored." Among the famous marbles are several which, according to Winckelmann, undoubtedly had ear pendants.* The holes in the ears of the daughter of Niobe of the Medicêan Venus, and of two beautiful heads of green basalt formerly in the Villa Albani indi-

Figure 123. Earring, Cyprus   Figure 124. Greek Earrings

cate ear ornaments. Only two statues, however, are known in which these ornaments, round in shape, are formed from the marble itself. One of these is a caryatid formerly in the Villa Negroni, the other a Pallas, once at Frascati but later moved to England.†

---

* Winckelmann, *History of Ancient Art,* Vol. III, Chapter 2.
† Ibid.

The Etruscan tombs have yielded earrings of both Greek and Italian types. They furnish examples of styles used over a period of probably six hundred years, and form a continuous series illustrating this ancient form of decoration. Figure 126. These are remarkable in gold embossed with filigree and granulated work. Judging by the number of certain designs found, it is evident that the most popular Etruscan patterns were the handbag shape, the gondola, the ear plaque, and the ring pendant. Pendants were usually of white glass, representing birds and animals. They seem to have been blown over a network of gold wire. The ear plaques usually show long chains depending from them, often ending in gold tassels. With the Etruscans, stones were seldom used, the jeweler depending solely upon the artistry of minute granulations in goldwork. Pearls, however, were occasionally em-

COURTESY, MUSEUM OF FINE ARTS, BOSTON

Figure 125. Gold Earring, Greek 5th Century, "Nike Driving a Two-Horse Chariot"

ployed. Strange enamels often decorate the gold. Occasionally *cloisonné* enamels in opaque white, blue, and green have been recovered. During the Renaissance and in even more modern times the jewelers of Italy, reviving the beauty of Etruscan design, have furnished models of earrings for practically all of Europe.

The Romans naturally acquired a taste for these Etruscan-designed earrings. Pliny says that on no part of the dress was greater expense lavished than on the earrings. Indeed, they rank as one of the greatest extravagances of Roman times. Figure 127. Just before he died Seneca wrote that some earrings worn by women were so costly that a

Figure 126. Etruscan Earring

single pair was worth the revenue of a large estate, and Juvenal sneeringly remarks, "There is nothing a woman will not allow herself, nothing she holds disgraceful, when she has encircled her neck with emeralds, and inserted earrings of great price in her ears, stretched with their weight." A number of portrait busts of Roman matrons show pierced ears, among them that of Antonio, the wife of Drusus. The Roman goldsmiths were the first to popularize the use of precious stones set in earrings. Emeralds, rubies, sapphires, and garnets, all cut *en cabochon*—that is, polished but not faceted—were in demand. Pearls were always a favorite. Enormous sums were paid for them, especially for pearls of large size to be used as ear jewels. The Greeks valued their earrings for the delicate workmanship lavished upon them, the Romans for the material. As a result

Figure 127. Roman Pendant Earrings

Roman earrings became less artistic. Like the earlier Grecian men, some of the younger men of Rome attempted to adopt earrings, but Emperor Alexander Severus (222 A.D.) bitterly opposed it.

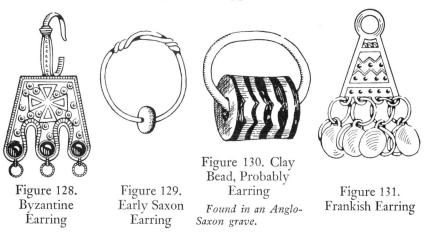

Figure 128. Byzantine Earring

Figure 129. Early Saxon Earring

Figure 130. Clay Bead, Probably Earring

Found in an Anglo-Saxon grave.

Figure 131. Frankish Earring

With the establishment in the third century of the imperial court in Byzantium, taste in ornamental details of dress grew even more luxurious. Women of fashion wore large earrings of various shapes—circles, squares, triangles, and crescents. Many of these were pierced with designs of different pattern; others were solid, engraved or decorated with enamels. Sometimes the entire large plaque was covered with *cloisonné* enamel. In this type of work the design to be filled in with enamel had to be outlined and hammered to a shallow depth; then delicate wires, to separate the different colors, were soldered in place. Birds in pairs was a favorite design with the Byzantine jeweler. The mosaics of this luxurious period picture men as well as women wearing large, elaborate earrings.

The Celts are believed to have been the first among northern nations to adopt the earring. The Anglo-Saxons sometimes wore a small earring, usually of plain wire orna-

Figure 132. Earrings, Merovingian Period

mented with a single bead. Figure 129. Large beads of variegated clay have been found in Anglo-Saxon graves and these too may have served as ear pendants. Figure 130. The early tombs of Belgium, Germany, and Austria have yielded very beautiful examples of German workmanship. Figure 131.

During the early Middle Ages when France was laying foundations for the future style center of the world, the people living there gradually took over the customs and fash-

COURTESY, NATIONAL PORTRAIT GALLERY, LONDON

Figure 133. Robert Carr, Earl of Somerset

Many portraits of the early 17th century show men of fashion wearing handsome earrings.

ions of their conquerors. Jewelry, particularly in the form of brooches and buckles, continued the luxurious note of Byzantium. Figure 132. The taste for elaborate earrings, however, declined. In fact, during the greater part of the Middle Ages, when heads were draped and veiled, the custom was so abandoned by leaders of fashion that practically no one wore earrings except the peasantry. This, however, was only the "lull before the storm," for with the coming of the Renaissance a vigorous revival of this alluring fashion laid siege to the hearts of women and no item of feminine ornament was more widely worn.

1500-1700

The new period was resplendent with dress and jewels. Earrings were large, long, and elaborate, hanging in some instances to the shoulders. Not to be outdone, the men of the period imitated the ladies and adopted the earring. In the National Portrait Gallery, London, are several portraits of distinguished men of old England wearing this attractive ornament. The handsome Earl of Somerset, Figure 133, wears his finely kept hair in the prevailing mode, covering all but the lobes of the ear, from which hang the jeweled earrings. Queen Elizabeth's favorite, Sir Walter Raleigh, wore handsome ear ornaments (see PLATE XLIX, Chapter 36). Later, the Duke of Buckingham is said to have worn diamond earrings.

Henry III of France, called the effeminate ruler, together with his court, delighted in these fashionable ear pendants. Charles I of England, as a leader of fashion, is known to have exercised the greatest care in the selection of these ornaments. In preparing for his walk to the scaffold, he took the same pride in the earrings as in other details of his dress. Arriving there he carefully removed and handed them over to a faithful follower. Since that time they have been preserved as a highly valued relic.

All through the century (1600-1700), pearls were the favorite jewels. Figures 134, 135. They were worn as necklaces and bracelets as well as earrings. The portrait of the charming Madame de Sevigne, fashion leader

Figure 134. Earrings from Portraits of Bianca Capella, Gabrielle d'Estres, and Ann of Denmark

Figure 135. Renaissance Earring

From a Portrait in the Castle of Gotha

of the late century, is a beautiful example of the lustrous pearl used as ornament. See page 189. French, English, Spanish, Portuguese, and German goldwork, although based on Italian originals, developed certain characteristics peculiarly national in style. Figure 136. Portraits of many distinguished men of this period show that the popularity of the earring continued.

A fashion far more unusual than that of the earring was the queer custom of wearing earstrings. It is difficult for us to understand the lure of the string tied into the punctured edge of the ear. Several portraits, however, testify to this strange fashion. Planché states that the custom may have traveled to England from Denmark with Anne, mother of Prince Henry. A portrait of Christian, King of Denmark, wearing the earstring hangs at Hampton Court palace. Frequent mention of ear-

COURTESY, METROPOLITAN MUSEUM OF ART

Figure 136. Earrings, Goldsmith's Work, Italian, 18th Century

See matching brooch, page 174.

COURTESY, METROPOLITAN MUSEUM OF ART

Figure 137. Earrings, Gold with Amethysts, French, 19th Century

strings is found in the old plays of Jonson, Beaumont, and Fletcher. The following lines appear in one of Marlowe's plays:

Figure 138. Jet Ear-rings, 1875

Yet for thy sake I will not bore mine eare
To hang thy durtie silken shoo-tires thru.

Finally both the earring and the earstring disappear from civilized men's dress, never to this day to return.

Famous portraits of women of the early eighteenth century show the continued favor of the pearl earring, although the hair at this time was worn fluffed over the ears and, in many instances, partly concealed any ornament that may have been worn. Old portraits likewise show a distinct preference for pearl necklaces, bracelets, and rings.

By the close of the century, brilliant-cut diamonds had come to stay. Since the middle of the previous century Dutch lapidaries had been experimenting, striving to perfect processes for producing the brilliant-cut stone. With their success jewelry became lighter, more attention being given to the beauty of the stone than, as in earlier centuries, to the elaborate setting. From this period forth, diamonds have held first place among jewels. Queen Marie Antoinette possessed handsome diamond earrings in which the stones were set in long vertical arrangement with one large, brilliant drop.

COURTESY, NEW YORK HISTORICAL SOCIETY, DE PEYSTER COLLECTION

Figure 139. Stone Cameo Earrings and Pendant, Early 19th Century

1800-Twentieth Century

The general fashion for earrings continued well into the nineteenth century. During the forties earrings were sold in "sets" including brooch and bracelets, all in similar pattern. Black onyx and jet earrings combined with gold and pearls were the "top of the mode." Figure 138. A little later cameos took first place. Figure 139. During the seventies women wore long gold-and-enamel earrings finished with gold fringe. These were succeeded by a single diamond, studding the ear—the enviable ornament which proclaimed wealth. Between 1880 and 1900 the popularity of the earring declined, and soon this ancient ornament passed from the fashion scene. The custom of piercing the ears was undoubtedly responsible for its disappearance. About 1900, however, popular interest suddenly was revived. The renewed interest and the rapidity of the recovery were due to the invention of a new, patented screw device which attached the earring to the ear without mutilating the flesh. Now earrings of every description could be easily fitted to the ear! This fact, together with the introduction of inexpensive "costume jewelry," which came into full swing with the twentieth century, made it possible for milady to possess many and varied types of jewelry (see page 173). In fact, jewelry appropriate for every costume could now be purchased for a nominal sum and was accepted in the most fashionable circles. Rare and precious jewels are now reserved for the most part for unusual formal occasions. Many of the antique designs popular in past centuries have been modernized with so much artistry that they find an acceptable place among the accessories of the most exacting leader of fashion.

The choice and wearing of jewelry, just as the arrangement of the veil, the tilting of the hat, or the adjustment of the wrap, have come to express in great measure the taste and culture of the wearer. Earrings continue to hold the favor of women the world over, not only those living in more backward countries, but those, as well, who dwell in the highly cultivated centers of civilization.

REFERENCES

Calthrop, Dion Clayton, *English Costume*, Vol. III.
Boehn, Max von, *Modes and Manners;* "*Ornaments,*" Chapter VI.
Child, Theodore, *Wimples and Crisping Pins.*
Dooley, William H., *Clothing and Style.*
Earle, Alice Morse, *Two Centuries of Costume in America.*
Guhl and Kohner, *Life of the Greeks and Romans.*
Lester, Katherine Morris, *Historic Costume*, pp. 34, 119.
Norris, Herbert, *Costume and Fashion.*
Parsons, Frank Alvah, *The Art in Dress*, pp. 38, 178.
Rhead, C. W., *Chats on Costume.*
Sage, Elizabeth, *A Study of Costume*, pp. 22, 168, 191.
Wilkinson, Sir John Gardiner, *A Popular Account of the Ancient Egyptians*, Vol. I.

CHAPTER 8

The Hairpin

They pinched her feet, they singed her hair,
They screwed it up with *pins*.

OLIVER WENDELL HOLMES, *My Aunt*

THE first known pins for confining the hair were the light spines and heavier thorns, always within easy reach of both primitive belles and their menfolk. Slender bones and strips of cane were probably found to be just as practicable for holding these early topknots in place. Ancient burial places have yielded pins of many types. Those of the Bronze Age show various sizes with ornamental heads, many of which were no doubt used as hairpins (see Chapter 14, Figure 195). The ancient Egyptians shaved their heads and wore wigs, but somewhat later bronze or gold bodkins were used in the elaborate headdress of Egyptian women. In Cleopatra's time bodkins or skewers of wood, bone, and ivory were employed for holding the plaits and curls of hair. Figures 140, 141. These were often seven or eight inches in length, frequently ornamented with beads of gold. Though these very early pins were useful and sometimes beautiful, they are far removed from the simple wire, bone, or rubber hair-

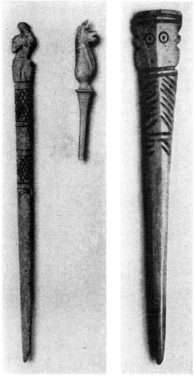

COURTESY, METROPOLITAN MUSEUM OF ART

Figures 140, 141. Early Egyptian Hairpins

pins of modern times. While the earlier pin was a single shaft the simplest form of the modern hair pin is shaped like the letter U elongated, with two prongs to the pin. However, despite new shapes and diversity of material, the hairpin is still useful rather than ornamental.

In the East, Japan and China have furnished various types of pins for the hair. Many of the early Japanese pins were ornamented with the iris, which was believed to be a protection against evil. In China during the T'ang Dynasty (618-906), when the art of engraving on wood made its first appearance, the new art was applied to the large wooden hairpins worn by Chinese women. Many of these were covered with a coating of silver. Figure 142. Later, during the Ming period (1368-1644), Figure 143, more elaborate and detailed carvings were done on silver, ivory, and jade, and the pearl was frequently used as a setting. Figures 144, 145. Hairpins of this period are far superior to later examples.

Women of classic Greece wore a variety of pins or bodkins. Figure 146. Usually the hair was gathered in a mass on the crown of the head where it was fastened, or it was twisted in the form of a knot and held in place by the bodkin. These pins were usually made of ivory or metal.

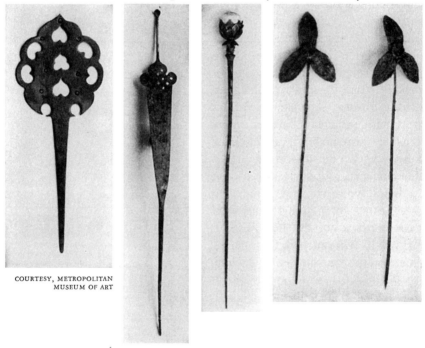

COURTESY, METROPOLITAN
MUSEUM OF ART

Figures 142–145: 142—Chinese Hairpin, Silver on Wood, T'ang Dynasty, 618–906. 143—Chinese Hairpin, Silver, Paddle Shaped, Ming Period, 1368–1644. 144—Chinese Hairpin, Silver Gilt with Pearl in Head, Ming Period. 145—Silver Hairpins with Floral Heads, Ming Period

One of the favored pins was topped with the form of the *cicada*. Occasionally pins were ornamented with figures in gold, or embellished with enamels and jewels. Many of these bodkins have been preserved, and, though they are trifles, they remain mute witnesses to that feeling for beauty which distinguishes this ancient civilization. Figures 147, 148.

Roman women wore a profusion of hair ornaments, among them the bodkin of gold, silver, or ivory. Some of these were supplied with aper-

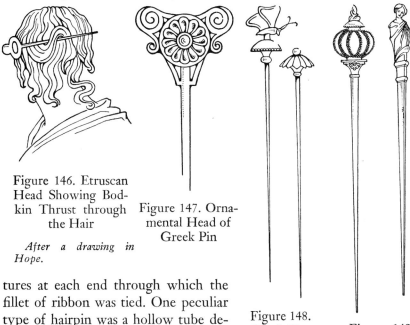

Figure 146. Etruscan Head Showing Bodkin Thrust through the Hair

After a drawing in Hope.

Figure 147. Ornamental Head of Greek Pin

Figure 148. Greek Pins

Figures 149, 150. Roman Pin; Roman Hairpin

tures at each end through which the fillet of ribbon was tied. One peculiar type of hairpin was a hollow tube designed to hold poison. This was similar to the pin that Cleopatra is reputed to have used in poisoning herself. In general, Roman bodkins were ornamented with figures, such as Venus and Cupid, Cupid and Psyche, Isis, and other favored subjects. Ivory hairpins found in London and dating from the Roman occupation are ornamented with the busts of Roman women of the Empire. Figures 149, 150. Others are surmounted with figures of dogs and bears, with spearheads, and various military standards.

In early Britain, bodkins of bone and bronze were in use from a remote period. This is indicated by the many findings of recent times. Among the Saxons such hair ornaments were known as "hair needles." Figure 151 shows three early bodkins in their original sizes. Similar pins have been found in Ireland, where they were probably used as hairpins or possibly to fasten the coarse clothing. Figure 152.

1500-1900

In western Europe during the Middle Ages, bone and wooden skewers as well as jeweled pins were used to hold the hair in place. With the wearer's head veiled and hooded, however, the beauty and richness of these ornaments were entirely concealed. With the coming of the early Renaissance, as heads were gradually uncovered, ribbons, nets, and hairpins filled an important place in milady's coiffure. The first bent-wire hairpins were made in England and imported to France about 1545. Though the use of the simple wire hairpin soon became general, the more elaborate

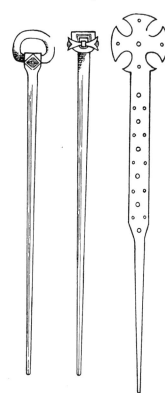

pins were still displayed. These were ornamented not only with all sorts of vegetable and animal forms, but also with handsome jewels. Figure 153. In *Mundus Muliebris*, 1690, occur lines referring to the elaborate pins used in the headdress of English women during the reign of William and Mary:

> Pins tipt with diamond, point and head,
> By which the curls are fastened.

The late eighteenth century headdress with its pads, plumes, and elaborate decoration continued to need the hairpin. Now, however, this demure little accessory slipped far into second place; for tinsel, ribbon, gauze, feathers, and flowers were the supplementary ornaments upon which hairdressers depended for all their novelties.

By the nineteenth century, however, the coiffure had become more simple. Bent hairpins of iron and brass wire were in use, and the orna-

Figure 151. Two Saxon Bodkins and a Bronze Bodkin

mental pin was not without its place. Gradually to the iron and brass pins was added a stronger type. For a long time the growing demand for a more slender and at the same time stiffer pin had been so insistent that the steel-wire hairpin was soon placed upon the market. It has now superseded both iron and brass. The ordinary black-

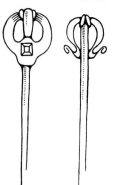

Figure 152. Parts of Hairpins Found in Ireland

lacquered, bronzed hairpin of modern times is made of tempered steel wire. There are two kinds of steel hairpins, the tiny "invisible," made of fine wire usually from 1½ to 2½ inches in length, and that of average size, made of heavier wire, and measuring from 2 to 4 inches in length. Though these simple wire hairpins have a well-established and permanent field, other types have gradually been added. Hairpins of bone, shell, horn, celluloid, and rubber, made in various sizes, shapes, and colors are equally popular. Modern hairpins, whether of wire or of one of the other popular materials, are usually designed either with two straight prongs or prongs crimped in zigzag fashion. This irregularity helps to keep them in place. Aside from the simple hairpins there are those with ornamental tops. These are largely of shell, especially favored for evening wear. Figure 154. Their popularity, however, as well as that of hairpins in general, has gradually dimmed and vanished altogether during the period of bobbed hair.

Twentieth Century

Fashions in coiffure naturally have much to do with the demand for hairpins. With the acceptance of bobbed hair by the feminine world of the twentieth century, hairpins became useless except for tiny invisibles and the later "bobby" pins. Bobby pins which secured stray wisps in

place proved a real boon to the growing bob. These popular pins were about two inches in length; the metal, however, was flattened, crimped on one side, and sufficient "spring" brought the two ends tightly together. This made the pin secure, eliminated the possibility of its falling out of place, and at the same time maintained a tidy coiffure. The bobby pin is the latest form of the ancient pin for the hair. Modern invention, however, still continues to play upon the old motif—the primitive pin, and will create new types for new needs as they arise.

Figure 154. Modern Hair Ornament, 1915–18

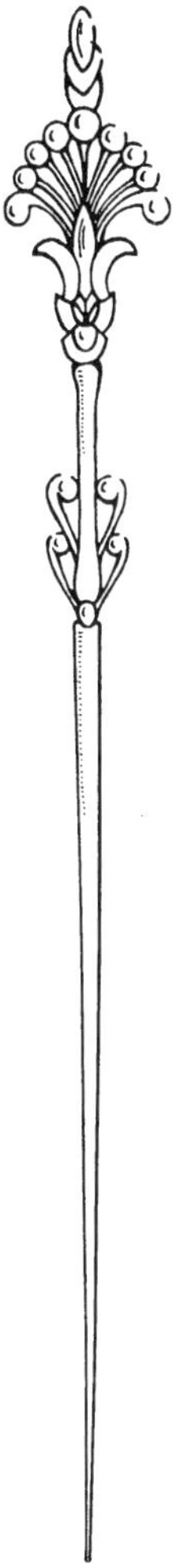

Figure 153. Hairpin, 17th Century

REFERENCES

Child, Theodore, *Wimples and Crisping Pins*, pp. 62, 68.
Cole, George S., *A Dictionary of Dry Goods*, p. 175.
Dooley, William H., *Clothing and Style*, p. 236.
Johnson, Harold, *Private Life of the Romans*, p. 263.
Lester, Katherine Morris, *Historic Costume*, pp. 36, 64.
Sage, Elizabeth, *A Study of Costume*, pp. 34, 93.
Souder, M. Attie, *The Notions Department*, pp. 137-138.
Wilkinson, Sir John Gardiner, *A Popular Account of the Ancient Egyptians*, Vol. I.

CHAPTER 9

The Hair Net

Her head with ringlets of her hair is crown'd,
And in a golden *caul* her curls are bound.

Aeneid VII

FROM earliest recorded time woman has looked upon the choice of
ornaments for the hair as her own peculiar privilege. From the myriad
of bands, crowns, tiaras, veils, pins, and nets which tell the story of hair

Figure 155. Greek Cauls
Drawing after Hope.

ornament, one device alone emerges which, for sheer interest and charm
coupled with its unique development in the late nineteenth and twentieth
centuries, is outstanding. The fashion of the hair net has waxed or waned
through the centuries. In the early periods simple weaves of gold and
silver wire, and gold and silver cord strung with pearls, made up the rich
and showy cauls worn by fashionable women. Later, weavings of ribbon,
chenille, and thread took the place of gold and silver. Finally, the invisible
net of human hair brought the conception of a hair net to the point of
perfection. As the hair net played its fashionable role from ancient times
down to the present, the invisible net of the twentieth century became
the final achievement in the development of this accessory.

It is said that the net for the hair was first used by the Chinese. Made of
silk and worn only by married women, the Chinese net served as a kind
of badge, distinguishing the married from the unmarried woman, who
wore her hair in a long queue hanging at the back.

In ancient Greece the "golden caul" in which the leaders of that day confined their hair was a net usually made of gold wire. Others, made of gold cord, were likewise fashionable. According to Winckelmann, many Grecian coins and vases show the heads of women wearing a net similar to that worn in later times in the home by Italian women. The literature of the period frequently refers to the caul and the mountings of gold used in ancient headdresses. In the following lines from Homer's *Iliad* picturing Andromache's despair at the death of Hector, various ornaments of the headdress are named, among them the net:

> The ornaments
> Dropped from her brow . . . the wreath,
>   the woven band,
> The *net*, the veil, which Venus gave.

From the many examples seen in ancient works of art one realizes that the caul was indeed an ornament of beauty. Figure 155.

Figure 156. Netted Headdress, 14th Century

As with all accessories fashionable in Greece, so with the caul—it passed to Rome. Roman women wore nets of various materials, including gold and silver cord ornamented with jewels and

Figure 157.

Handsome Cylindrical Cauls with Elaborate Coronet

From the Effigy of Queen Philippa, 1350.

Figure 158.
Margaret of Anjou

Wearing the Large Wheel-like Arrangements over the Ears.

From a window in the Bodlein Library.

Figure 159. Joan of Navarre, 1420

pearls. Nets are said to have been worn there for centuries. It was, however, long after the decline of the Roman Empire and toward the fourteenth century that nets again became a conspicuous part of the headdress.

Middle Ages

During the early part of the Middle Ages the hair had been entirely concealed by the various types of hoods and veils generally worn. It is

therefore not surprising that toward the close of the period a new era in hair fashions began to emerge. Women had been experimenting more and more with arranging the hair in various ways, and by the fourteenth century the intricacies of hairdressing had reached a new stage. Soon the fashion was

Figure 160. Beatrice, Countess of
Arundel, 1439

An example of the most extravagant fashion in the reticulated headdress.

set. In the earliest developments of the new mode a netted cap enclosed the hair in a simple way, a headband or other device holding the net in place. Figure 156. Soon the hair was parted and plaited in two long braids. These were coiled in large wheel-like disks over each ear, or, without plaiting, were rolled or twisted into shape at the sides of the head. In due time the cauls of the fourteenth and fifteenth centuries appeared. This particular fashion in hairdressing has passed into history as the "reticulated headdress." Cauls were very handsome and costly accessories. The basic network was of gold and silver wire richly ornamented at the

Figure 161. Miter Headdress
from Effigy of Lady Vernon,
1450

intersections with jewels. Sometimes a single gem, or again a costly cluster of gems, furnished the added enrichment. Small pearls strung on gold wire added a striking note of decoration and also strengthened the framework. The cauls were cylindrical, spherical, or some other appropriate form. They were large or small according to milady's fancy. Indeed, each reticulated headdress came to be a particular masterpiece of the goldsmith's art!

Though the entire headdress is frequently referred to as the *crespine*, *crispine*, and *crispinette*, the word *crespine* probably indicates the rigid gold band fitted across the brow. At the sides of this band were extensions which fitted over the top edges of the cauls, holding them firmly in place. The back hair was usually covered with a net fastened to the crespine at the top and carried tightly to each side where it was attached to the side cauls. The effigy of Queen Philippa (1350), in Westminster Abbey, though very much damaged, shows evidence of the handsome side cylinders, Figure 157, while that of Margaret of Anjou, of a later date, shows the large wheel-like sidepieces. Figure 158. Naturally there were many styles in this fashionable headdress. The effigy of Joan of Navarre (1420) shows little baglike protuberances above each ear, with the gems at the intersections much in evidence. Figure 159. As shown in this monument, the veil gradually came to be draped over the headdress. Some authorities state that the word *crispenette* referred to the veil alone. When the veil was wired, as frequently it was, it could be held out away from and over the cauls, presenting a very elaborate form of headdress. The effigy of Beatrice, Countess of Arundel, who died in 1439,

Figure 162. Margaret of Scotland, 1487

Netted headdress beautifully embellished with pearls and worn with the jeweled coronet.

furnishes a most extravagant example of the reticulated headdress and veil. Figure 160. Here the side ornaments are very large, whereas the veil that covers them is stretched its full length and probably supported by wires. The coronet is of equally extravagant size.

The reticulated headdress continued fashionable well past the middle of the fifteenth century. When worn covering the ears and extending outward and upward, it foreshadowed the double-peaked headdress and towering hennins of the late fifteenth century. The handsome cauls seen in the effigy of Lady Vernon (1450) easily suggest the horned headdress which followed. Figure 161. In the admirable example of the fashion seen on the figure of Margaret of Scotland (1487), the beautifully embellished caul is profusely adorned with pearls and the whole is surmounted by a handsome coronet richly ornamented with jewels. Figure 162.

From time to time there were other forms of the netted headdress. Sometimes the hair was worn loose, filling the pouchlike bag. Figure 163. Sometimes the net was elongated, to form a queue, and tied at selected intervals with ribbon. The netted cap of Beatrice d'Este, as seen in her

portrait by Leonardo da Vinci, is still another version of the popular fashion. PLATE XXIII. The popularity of nets at this period (1492) is vouched for by a lady of the court who describes the dress of the happy Beatrice, Duchess of Bari, saying:

> The Duchess of Bari had a lovely vest of gold brocade worked in red and blue silk, and a blue silk mantle trimmed with long-haired fur, and her hair coiled as usual in a silken *net*.

1500-1800

With slight variations in weave and ornament the netted headdress continued to be worn well into the sixteenth century. Figure 164. Sometimes little kerchiefs and pointed caps were worn over the net-covered hair.

Figure 163. Net Embellished with Pearls, 15th Century

Other portraits show an elaborate head covering set off with plumes suggesting the modern hat. Naturally the thread nets of silk and gold were the luxury of the wealthy. Figure 165. Those of lesser means who must, nevertheless, be in fashion wore nets of crepe.

In the early seventeenth century Fashion decreed a change. Women now began to let their hair fall free to the shoulders, unconfined by a net. It was sometimes gathered at the back and frequently adorned with a string of pearls and an ostrich feather. For evening

Figure 164. Netted Headdress, 16th Century

wear, the long, white plume falling over the back hair was the very height of the mode. It was at this time that the fashion of nets became distinctly passé not to be revived until almost two centuries later.

1800-1900

The nineteenth century is an important period in the further development of the net. Ever whimsical but determined, Fashion wrought many changes in the popular type of net. These changes, fortunately, led to that unrivaled development of the late nineteenth and twentieth centuries— the invisible net of human hair.

PLATE XXIII. Beatrice d'Este.................................*Da Vinci*

The netted cap edged with jewels was a favorite headdress of the late 16th century. Note the jeweled ornaments which decorate the ribbon headband, the shoulder ornament, and the pearl necklace with pendant.

In the early days of the century (1800-40), the net of the past, decorated with pearls, struggled for recognition and soon attained a measure of popularity. It was, however, in the middle of the century (1859-65), that a definite change came. Then nets had a tremendous vogue. The popularity of the fashion led to many new and ingenious types of nets. Of course France set the mode and the world followed. In the late fifties and

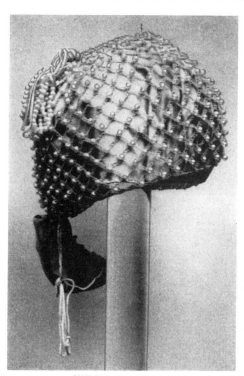

Figure 165. Caul Ornamented with Pearls, French, 18th Century

sixties the hair was fastened up in a shapeless mass and held in nets made of heavy silk thread spangled with jet. Figure 166. By 1863 nets were not only fashionable for indoor wear but were considered a necessity for outdoor wear. The new nets of this date were made of silk or velvet ribbon of varying widths. These were woven "over and under," forming an open network. The overlapping strips were caught with needle and thread and sewed securely to keep them in place. A tiny white braid manufactured for the purpose was frequently sewed along the open edge both inside and outside the net. Then, as a finishing touch, a black velvet bow, a pleated frill of velvet, or a thick ruching was placed

atop the whole. A net for evening wear appears to have been somewhat more venturesome. This was made of scarlet chenille, netted in a half-inch mesh and trimmed at the front with a ruche of black lace and at the top with a scarlet bow. These nets were, indeed, a popular novelty. Women now began making their own nets. Happy was she who could turn out an original net, distinguished in some way by an unusual bit of color or design!

It was at this interesting period that the net made of human hair was first introduced. Peterson's fashion book of the autumn of 1863 states that the new type of net was made of hair "the exact shade of the wearer's." It was customary for the fair client to cut off a generous lock and give it to the hairdresser, who made it into a net. These nets were made in a fine

PLATE XXIV. A Woman Wearing a Caul. . . . *Lucas Cranach, 1472-1553*

Note also the display of chains and rings.

mesh, were exceedingly durable, and when worn correctly upon the head were nearly invisible. Many refinements in the fashioning of the net followed these earlier types until, in the twentieth century, the highest possible attainment was reached. Today's hair net is made of the finest human

hair, in all shades, both single and double mesh, is self-conforming to the contour of the head, and practically invisible when worn. Figure 167.

Figure 166. Net and Coiffure Fashionable in Late 50's and 60's

Twentieth Century

Since 1914, nets of human hair have been used at some time by nearly all women. In America the fashion reached its peak during the World War. At that time it was urged upon all nurses to wear hair nets. This was followed by a ruling that all waitresses in restaurants should adopt the net. Before long all classes had discovered the value of this little device for keeping the coiffure in trim. It was soon adopted everywhere by women for daytime wear, for sports, and for evening wear.

Silk-thread nets, made exclusively in France, differ from the real hair nets not only in material but in the size of mesh, which is much smaller. These, however, are not manufactured for the fashionable trade and in no way compete with the real hair net.

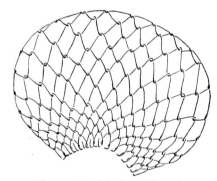

Figure 167. Modern Net of Human Hair

The business of making hair nets began to decline in 1923. This was due to the popular fashion for bobbed hair. When this fashion swept the country it forced forty thousand girls in Shanghai out of employment. This decline in business continued until 1929, when a modified return to long hair increased the demand for nets. By this time, however, a small, cap-shaped net for bobbed hair had entered the field and attained great popularity. Milady of fashion could now call for a "cap" net or, if she preferred, the "fringe," which was made for long hair.

Practically all hair nets used in America are imported from China. The human hair is imported in the raw state, dyed here, and then shipped back to that country to be fashioned into nets. An important fact about the hair net is that it has been found impossible to produce it by machinery. Owing to the fine texture of human hair and the shortness of the strands, no machine has yet been able to knit the delicate sets. Yet when attempts have been made in the United States to manufacture nets *by hand*, all efforts have failed. All the fashioning must be done by hand, and only the Chinese seem to possess the necessary patience and skill for this fine work. An able worker in China requires one day to make one dozen nets of the self-adjusting cap shape of ordinary size. Even if American workers possessed the requisite skill, the manufacture of nets of human hair would still be impracticable because of the prohibitive cost of labor. About ninety-five per cent of the nets imported to this country, therefore, are made in the homes of the Chinese natives. Each of these modern hair nets is wrapped in tissue paper and enclosed in an envelope. Those of a given color are then wrapped and sealed together in dust-proof and germ-proof paraffin parcels, ready for shipment.

The fashion leader of the twentieth century—and, indeed, every woman follows the fashion from at least a safe distance—can for a very nominal sum purchase her net of a required color, for long or short hair, and truly "invisible." The hair net of today has evolved from a comparatively clumsy arrangement of wire, thread, ribbon, velvet, and ornaments of various types into the most delicate, most dainty, and most modest of accessories for the coiffure.

REFERENCES

Calthrop, Dion Clayton, *English Costume*, Vol. II, p. 37.
Child, Theodore, *Wimples and Crisping Pins*, p. 40.
Dooley, William E., *Clothing and Style*, p. 237.
Evans, Mary, *Costume Throughout the Ages*, p. 19.
Lester, Katherine Morris, *Historic Costume*, pp. 57, 75, 92, 193.
Peterson's Fashion Magazine, Volume of 1865.
Planché, J. R., *Cyclopedia of Costume*, Vol. I—*Dictionary;* Vol. II—*General History of Costume in Europe.*
Rhead, C. W., *Chats on Costume.*
Souder, M. Attie, *The Notions Department*, Chapter 17.

CHAPTER 10

The Comb

When you have apparelled yourself handsomely, combe your head softly and easily with an Iuorie *combe;* for nothing recreateth the memorie more.

Babees Book, p. 249

THE use of objects such as thorns, slender bones, and sticks stuck into the hair may have suggested the early comb; or, more likely still, the backbone of a large fish. Though the exact date of the first comb is unknown, many interesting specimens have been found in the region of the Swiss Lake Dwellers. This places the date at a very remote period. It appears that ancient peoples, as do modern, used the comb more for adjusting the hair or holding it in place than as an ornament. Women of tribes in Africa and Central America are said to spend hours in combing the hair. Whatever the distant date of the comb or its varied uses, it has always been considered an essential article of the toilet.

In Egypt combs were made of ebony, boxwood—a very hard wood—and bone. Many examples taken from the tombs show a single row of teeth; others show two rows, both of the same sized teeth. Frequently these varied somewhat, one row being thicker or longer than the other. Figures 168, 169, 170.

COURTESY, MET-
ROPOLITAN MU-
SEUM OF ART

Figure 168. Bone Comb, Egyptian, pre-Dynastic

The early Greek and Roman combs were usually made of ivory and boxwood. Later, however, among the wealthier classes ivory and ebony combs similar to those of the Egyptians came into general use.

These were used only for combing the hair. Metal combs were also used to some extent. The great mass of the people, however, did not use combs. It is recorded of the Britons that up to the time of the Danish invasions (first invasion, 789) the people near the coast wore the hair unkempt. The Danes, however, used combs and, following their own custom, are said to have taught the natives of Britain to comb their hair every day. In Anglo-Saxon graves of both men and women many combs have been found. Figure 171 shows a comb found in an Anglo-Saxon grave antedating the Christian era. It is especially curious on account of the two guards for protecting the teeth.

In early times the comb, as is true of the fan, had a place in religious ceremony. Careful ritualistic directions have been found for combing the abbot's hair in the sacristy before vespers. The tombs of the martyrs in the catacombs have yielded combs of ivory and boxwood. This, likewise, inclines to strengthen the belief that the comb was used in church ceremonies.

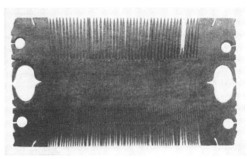

COURTESY, METROPOLITAN MUSEUM OF ART

Figure 169. Egyptian Comb, Ebony

Middle Ages

During the Middle Ages combs for combing the hair were made of a variety of materials; wood, bone, and ivory were in general use. The comb as an ornament was probably used to some extent, though not much evidence of its general popularity exists.

COURTESY, METROPOLITAN MUSEUM OF ART

Figure 170. Egyptian Comb, Boxwood, Empire Period or Later

In the miniatures of the twelfth century and a few of the church windows, however, an ornament appears called the *freiseau*, which is undoubtedly a comb. This ornament seen from the front spreads in radiating form terminating in balls of gold and silver and gives a kind of nimbus effect about the head. Figure 172. At this period women separated their long flowing hair into two queues, bound them about with ribbon, and found the ornamental "freiseau," lending further charm to the coiffure.

During the late Middle Ages and on through the Renaissance period all small articles for personal use, including combs, were fashioned by craftsmen. Instead of being turned out by the thousand from a machine, each bore the stamp of personal care and the love and labor of the maker. Combs of this period were often beautifully carved and sometimes set with jewels. Indeed, it is well said, "No woman of the modern world ever knew the luxury of such combs." Many of these handsome combs are today preserved in museum collections. The various materials then in use were soon supplemented by metal, which continued popular until the next century, when tortoise shell appeared.

1600-1900

A strange superstition prevailed in the seventeenth century with reference to lead combs. It was

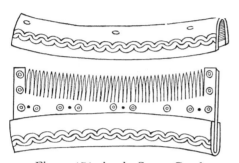

Figure 171. Anglo-Saxon Comb

Curious on account of two guards for protection of teeth.

Found in an Anglo-Saxon grave.

believed that the use of these preserved the color of the hair. If, perchance, milady's hair had faded, the magic of the lead comb was called upon to restore its color. During the same century women's hair was set out at the sides by means of little combs, and the distended ringlets fell to the shoulders. The fashion of the wide effect given the hair continued for many years. With the coming of the peruke and periwig, combs came to be an important accessory in fashions for men. No bewigged gentleman was without his pocket comb of silver or tortoise shell. With these, wigs were kept in perfect order. Previous to this, beard combs and beard brushes had been used by both English and French gentlemen.

Figure 172. A Rare Example of Ornamental Comb, about 1150

After Viollet-le-Duc.

In the history of the comb the eighteenth century is particulary interesting because in 1759 the first factory in America for the manufacture of combs was located, at Newbury, Massachusetts. Horn combs were a speciality. It was not long, however, before automatic machinery was making combs from tortoise shell, ivory, horn, wood, bone, metal, and celluloid. These were largely combs for combing the hair. About 1773, however, the demand for the comb as an ornament for the coiffure caused the industry to produce beautiful ornamental combs in tortoise shell and ivory.

Then, in the early years of the nineteenth century, the high coiffure made by upstanding loops of hair called for a comb as a finishing note to the headdress. The comb increased the apparent height, and height was a very desirable quality. By 1810-20 combs were many and varied. Large tortoise-shell combs were worn with the high coiffure, and women vied with one another in the beauty of these ornaments. Figure 173. In 1840, the hair was parted and brought back into a roll held in place by a large comb. At this time handsome and elaborate ornamental combs were used.

Later, the fashions of 1863 also called for combs, and now and then from this period on Fashion has called for the ornamental comb.

Figure 173. Modern Comb, Tortoise Shell, American, 19th Century

Figure 174. Modern Ornamental Comb, 1915–18

Twentieth Century

In the later years of the nineteenth century and the early years of the twentieth, both back combs and side combs were much in evidence. Then, after a season of popularity,

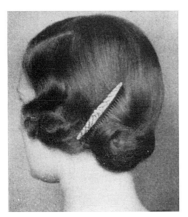
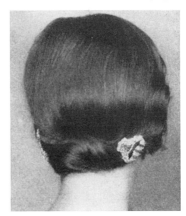

Figure 175. Modern Coiffures, Early 20th Century

combs were accepted only for evening wear, when the hair was dressed high and no hat was worn. Many of the popular combs of this day were designed in a spreading fan shape, in pastel colors, and set with brilliants. During the last decade the fashion of shorter hair has practically eliminated combs as an ornament for the coiffure.

Combs for combing the hair are a necessity which insures them a constant market, while the fashion supporting ornamental combs is controlled by the prevailing mode. In this matter of combs, as well as in other accessories of dress, Fashion constantly repeats herself. In the spring of 1930, with the somewhat reluctant return to long hair, beautiful tuck combs set with rhinestones came into use for formal wear. Figure 175. Rapidly changing custom is the outstanding feature of the twentieth century, and by the fall of 1930, the comb as an ornament had practically disappeared. These transient modes, however, only serve to verify the fickleness of Fashion. Running true to form, she may at any moment again pronounce combs the *sine qua non* of the mode!

REFERENCES

Child, Theodore, *Wimples and Crisping Pins.*
Dooley, William H., *Clothing and Style.*
Earle, Alice Morse, *Two Centuries of Costume in America.*
Guhl and Kohmer, *Life of the Greeks and Romans.*
Kennard, Beulah, *Jewelry and Silverware*, Chapter 19.
New International Encyclopedia, Vol. 5.
Peterson's Fashion Magazine, January, 1863.

CHAPTER 11

Toilet Accessories: Paints and Powders

Barber no more . . . the gay perfumer comes,
On whose soft cheek his own *cosmetic* blooms.

CRABBE

THE use of paint as a decoration for the body has always won the attention of primitive peoples in widely separated sections of the globe. The rudest of ancient barbarians made every effort to bring their personal charms, real or imaginary, up to the prevailing standard of beauty maintained by their tribe. Today even the lowest order of savages living on the islands of the Indian Ocean paint their faces with various colored clays mixed with fats; the savages of Australia paint their bodies with red and yellow ocher and the white earth found in their locality; the early Gauls stained the entire body with a blue dye called *woad*; and the American Indian, when preparing to go on the warpath, daubed his face with patches of color.

The desire to attract attention, to be different from one's fellows, doubtless stimulated this interest in body painting. Primitive man, returning from the hunt or chase, found that the bloodstains which he carried were esteemed as marks of courage and brought notice and admiration. Perhaps these were left on to remain as long as possible. When, however, they finally wore off, a substitute was found in the many-colored clays so near at hand. Face, head, and body were daubed with patches of color.

Modern rouge remains the surviving remnant among civilized peoples of this ancient custom of body painting. Dating far back to antiquity is the use of other cosmetics, including ointments, balms, and powders which from time to time have held a magic lure for both the feminine and masculine worlds. Archaeologists say that women six thousands years ago painted their faces and penciled their eyes in much the same manner as they do today.

Though the use of cosmetics undoubtedly originated in the Orient, Egypt furnishes the first record of the various ingredients and their uses. The ancient tombs have yielded many interesting and useful objects which had to do with the cosmetics of remote periods. Figure 176. In

137

1923, when the tomb of King Tutankhamen, who ruled about 1350 B.C., was opened, many small jars were found containing cosmetics which still possessed an elusive fragrance. Many other tombs have also yielded cosmetic jars, cosmetic spoons, and even the stibium pencil. The little cosmetic jars so evidently popular with Egyptian women were commonly known as kohl pots. Figures 177, 178. In these were carried a supply of the coveted mixture *kohl,* used in darkening the eyes. These small kohl pots were of various sizes, made of glass, ivory, onyx, and alabaster with gold mountings. Egyptian women are believed to have made up their faces by using a crude paint. This reached its greatest extravagance in the time of Cleopatra; but, though the women of Egypt used oils, ungents, and white paint in abundance, it was in the art of embellishing the eye that they particularly excelled. The eye was made to appear larger, its beauty greatly enhanced by painting below with a dark green, and adding kohl to the eyelids, eyelashes, and eyebrows. This was applied with an ivory or wooden stick, or spoon, known as the "cosmetic spoon." Figures 179, 180. The custom of staining the fingers with henna was also an Egyptian custom, probably derived from farther east. The Greek metaphor "rosy-fingered Aurora" may suggest this ancient practice.

Figure 176. Lady Rouging Herself

From the Papyrus of Turin.

The ancient Medes painted eyelashes and eyebrows to give an expression of power to the countenance. The Assyrians followed the same custom. Among the Hebrews distinct notice was taken of skin cosmetics. The custom was probably introduced into the hinterland of Israel by Queen Jezebel, who was a Sidonian princess familiar with the customs of Phoenicia, the center of culture and fashion for the Syria of that day. We read in II Kings 9:30, "And when King Jehu was come to Jezreel, Jezebel heard of it; and she *painted her eyes* and attired her head."* From Asia these tastes and customs were carried into Europe, to come down to modern times somewhat modified, to be sure, but still with the same old interest.

---

* In the original translation, *put her eyes in painting.*

In Greece both young and old painted their faces and used every other artificial means within their knowledge to add to their personal beauty. In fact, the word *cosmetic* comes from the Greek word meaning *I adorn*. The Russian archaeologist Zusser, while opening Greek tombs, came upon the tomb of a woman which contained a small linen bag in which was a mirror, a rouge stick for the lips, and a charcoal pencil for the eyes. In 1930, an archaeological expedition from Princeton University found in a Corinthian tomb dating back to possibly 600 B.C. a vanity box, which upon being opened disclosed cubes of lead carbonate. This dangerous preparation is believed to have been used as a facepowder by ancient Greek women. From many sources it is evident that white lead was commonly used for the face and that *alkanet* was the Athenian substitute for rouge. Literary sources supply many references to the custom among young and old of coating the face with paint:

COURTESY, METROPOLITAN MUSEUM OF ART

Figure 177. Kohl Pot, Egyptian

You dye your hair, but you will not dye your old age, nor will you stretch out the wrinkles of your cheeks. Do not then plaster the whole of your face with paint, so that you have a mask, not a face, for it is of no use. Why, are you mad? A paint and wash will never make a Hecuba a Helen.   LUCIAN

COURTESY, METROPOLITAN MUSEUM OF ART

Figure 178. Kohl Pot and Vases of an Egyptian Princess, Obsidian with Gold Mountings

Ischomacus, in the *Good Husbandry* of Xenophon, speaking of his girl wife of fifteen says:

One day I saw her with a lot of *rouge* to make her redder, and high heels to make her taller. I pointed out to her that in the first place she was doing as dishonorable a thing in trying to deceive me about her looks as I should if I tried to deceive her about my property. As I remarked that though her arts might impose upon others, they could not upon him who saw her at all times. I was sure to catch her in the morning before they had been applied, or tears would betray them, or perspiration, or the bath.

COURTESY, METROPOLITAN
MUSEUM OF ART

Figure 179. Toilet Spoon, Alabaster and Slate, Egyptian, XVIII Dynasty

COURTESY, METROPOLITAN MUSEUM OF ART

Figure 180. Bronze Cosmetic Spoon, Egyptian, Ptolemaic Period

Among the earlier Romans little attention had been given to improving the beauty of the person. At this time it was doubtless considered too effeminate an interest for so sturdy a race. Later, after contacts with Greece and the East, a sense of personal beauty was wakened and more attention was given to the improvement of appearance. By the time of the establishment of the Empire the "horrors" of the mode held full sway. Roman women painted their faces with white lead and chalk; gave a glow to cheeks and lips with *fucus*, a kind of rouge; supplementary eyebrows were bought in shops; and Egyptian kohl was applied to eyelids and lashes. Wigs and artificial hair were commonplace extravagances. Leading beauties of the day, as was said in the chapter on wigs, wore blond wigs imported from Germany at great cost, while those less fortunate bleached their hair with soap imported from Gaul. Barley flour and butter made a kind of paste for correcting skin eruptions, and pumice stone

COURTESY, METROPOLITAN MUSEUM OF ART

Figure 181. Lady's Toilet Box with Cover, Greek, 5th Century, B.C.

was used for whitening the teeth. Poppaea, the wife of Nero, made no effort to conceal the many artificial aids employed in her toilet. It is said that she herself compounded a special pomatum which she used to preserve her beauty. Doubtless Juvenal knew whereof he spoke when he said,

You have your hair curled, Galla, at a hairdresser's in Subura Street, and your eyebrows are brought to you every morning. At night you remove your teeth as you do your dress. Your charms are enclosed in a hundred different pots, and your face does not go to bed with you.

Middle Ages

During the Middle Ages cosmetics and drugs of all sorts were used in large quantities. The eyelids and eyebrows continued to be stained, for brilliancy of eye was still a coveted charm. It is said that the early Britons employed a crude type of face paint, continuing its use until after the Crusades. Many of the returning knights brought back with them the rare perfumes, oils, and other cosmetics prized by the East. During this same early period, however, the young women of Gaul were not permitted to drink wine because it was believed to be injurious to their fair complexions!

1500-1700

Throughout the early Renaissance in both France and Italy, cosmetics were extravagantly indulged in by both men and women. In Italy, women were spending "hours at their mirrors when they should have been attending to domestic duties." Others gave the entire day to beautifying themselves in preparation for the evening amusements. Paint had been introduced into France by Catherine de'Medici, and now the faces of all fashionable women were actually coated with white lead and vermilion. Queer concoctions made up of strange mixtures were believed to produce magic results. The wings and claws of pigeons, pulverized and mixed with fresh eggs, lilies, ground mother-of-pearl, and camphor, the whole distilled with musk, was one of the favorite beautifiers of the day. Bean water, vine water, rosemary, and oil of talc were used on the face, neck, and arms—anything to simulate beauty!

In England about the same time, during Elizabeth's reign (1558-1603), the use of cosmetics became increasingly popular. The ladies of the court kept all these important conveniences in strongly perfumed boxes called "sweet coffers." These were considered a necessary feature of milady's boudoir. About this time, too, the first books on the toilet were published, and professionals appeared who undertook the pleasant task of "make-up" for those ladies who felt themselves unqualified, or preferred to give the "risk" over to others well practiced in the art. Among the popular receipts for beauty of complexion was this: "Take a hot bath, sufficiently hot to induce excessive perspiration, then wash the face with wine to make it fair and ruddy." Because wine was very expensive, its use finally was permitted to older women only. Mary, Queen of Scots, is said to have used wine not only for the face, but for the bath as well. It is not surprising that after frequent ablutions of this sort she applied for an increased allowance! During the reign of Charles II (1660-85), milk baths came to be regarded as an indispensable aid to beauty. In Italy during the same period, face painting ran riot. So great was the extravagance in this direction that pamphlets were issued against the practice. This, naturally, availed nothing. One Italian woman is said to have made a collection of five hundred receipts for toilet preparations. Of this number one third were said to be "magically charmed lotions, prepared with incantations." In Venice, beauty was preserved or wooed by the use of the most commonplace supplies of the household. Raw veal, after being left in hot milk for several hours, was applied to the cheeks at night; alum water, extract of peach seeds, lemon seeds, bread crumbs, and vinegar were used to keep the skin soft and white. Women of this period also gave much care and attention to the hands and nails. Rosy-hued nails were considered most desirable.

1700-1800

By 1760 the craze for powders and rouge surpassed all reason. The French women of the day, with "their wooly white hair and fiery red faces," are said to have resembled "skinned sheep." In England the same fashion was carried to such ridiculous extreme that in 1770, with the hope of checking the custom, a bill was introduced in the British Parliament providing that,

All women of whatsoever rank or degree . . . that shall seduce or betray into matrimony any of His Majesty's subjects, by the scents, paints, cosmetic washes, artificial teeth, false hair, Spanish wool, iron stays, hoop, high-heeled shoes, bolstered hip, shall incur the penalty of the law in force against witch-craft and like demeanors, and that the marriage upon conviction shall stand null and void.

The *Gentlemen's Magazine* for 1792 carried an interesting paper on this irritating subject of face painting. "Great and little, old and young," says the writer, "paint their faces, nay, 'avow the fact, and glory in the deed'." The writer then proceeds to voice his further reflections on the mode:

For the single ladies who follow this fashion there is some excuse. Husbands must be had; and if the young men of this age are so silly as to be allured by a little red paint, why red paint must be used; but for married women, mistresses of families, mothers, for these to be greedy of the gaze and admiration of the other sex is disgusting, and betrays a frivolity of character unbecoming the dignity of a matron's situation. . . . The ladies sometime assert that they put on paint to please their husbands. Is it possible that a British husband can desire his wife to make herself a gazing stock for every coxcomb! But if it is for the good man's personal satisfaction that all these pains are taken, let the fair one remember that to be consistent the rouge box must be had recourse to in the morning before breakfast, as well as before dinner, when she sits alone with her husband, as well as when she issues forth to a rout.

1800-1900

Following this period of wild extravagance came the more sober years of the French Revolution and its aftermath. By 1806 powder and rouge had almost disappeared. During this lull a fashion magazine carried the following:

> Just now the tinting of face and lips is considered admissible only for those upon the stage. Now and then a misguided woman tints her cheeks to replace the glow of health and youth. The artificiality of the effect is apparent to everyone and calls attention to that which the person most desires to conceal. It hardly seems likely that a time will ever come again in which rouge will be well-nigh universally employed, but until that time does come a person could not make a greater mistake than to use it upon the face.

The abatement in the use of "make-up" continued for many years. A modest dusting of powder was generally admissible, but rouge, pencil, and lipstick were taboo. Toward the closing years of the century a general revival in the use of cosmetics brought with it a definite effort on the part of France to place the manufacture of all beauty aids upon a scientific basis. Since that time the status of cosmetics has been distinctly raised. With the production based upon scientific experiments and findings the supply of cosmetics to the trade has become one of the most remunerative branches of modern business.

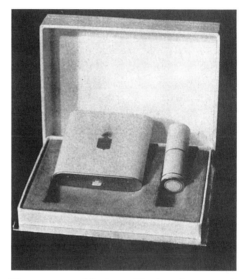

Figure 182. Modern Vanity Set, Small Case Containing Mirror, Rouge, and Powder; Lipstick—1936

Twentieth Century

In the first quarter of the twentieth century the fashion world seemed to have been captured anew by the ancient lure of cosmetics. Powder, rouge, and pencil, with other and more modern beautifiers of every description, became the rage. Figure 182. Though the "balance of power" for the cosmetic trade now lies in face powder, of which more than a thousand brands are registered, hundreds of other articles are now manufactured and used in the business of the cosmetician. There are beauty masks; tissue creams; cleansing creams; foundation creams; skin lotions; rouges; lipsticks of every tint and shade; pencils; astringents; bath, dental, and manicure preparations; and perfumes of every description. In the early days face powder was prepared with a base of bismuth, lead, or arsenic salts. Bismuth was expensive, increasing the cost of the product.

The other bases were not altogether satisfactory. In 1866 a harmless yet satisfactory base was found in oxide of zinc. This was, moreover, inexpensive. Its use helped to give a new impetus to the cosmetic industry. No other developments in powder were made until the closing years of the nineteenth century, when talcum powder appeared. This new toiletry, a powdered silicate, perfumed and put up in attractive tin containers, met with immediate success. Talcum is now used largely for dusting and drying the body as well as a base for face powder. Enormous quantities are consumed every year in North and South America. Strange to say it has never met with great popularity in Europe.

The important step taken by France in the late nineteenth century in the effort to secure scientific standards for the trade led to an increasing attention being given to the compounding of cosmetics. In the early years of the twentieth century legislation in various countries was secured requiring that this study be conducted by authorized physicians, with a view to determining the effects of various mixtures. The chemist has by now eliminated most harmful and questionable substances from cosmetics. Moreover, compounds are prepared under the most scrupulously clean and sanitary conditions. Thus the new-old quest for beauty goes on. Having enlisted not only the feminine world in this wide crusade, but physicians, chemists, and legislators as well, it is not surprising that the modern slogan, "Every woman may be beautiful," has spurred into line an enthusiastic following.

CHAPTER 12

Toilet Accessories:
Cosmetics for the Hair

With odorous oil thy head and hair are sleek. . . .
PERSIUS, *Satires* IV, 89

THROUGHOUT the ages the choice of cosmetics for the hair has been a subject of surprising interest. Besides the various pomades, oils, and tonics which have always been applied to the hair and scalp, there are also the dyes and powders which have descended to the modern world from the venerable past.

The custom of applying dye to the hair dates back to remote antiquity; it has been as popular with savage tribes as with the more civilized nations. Egyptian manuscripts dated approximately 1200 B.C. give two strange receipts for hair dye. One suggests, "dried tadpoles from the canal" crushed in oil; the other, "tortoise shell and the gabgu bird" boiled in oil. It is said that the mother of the first king of Egypt distinguished herself by inventing a dye for the hair. Not only were dyes prescribed for restoring color, but pomades to prevent falling hair, and oils for strengthening the hair, were numerous. For falling hair a special mixture of six kinds of fat—the fats of the hippopotamus, of the lion, the cat, the crocodile, the snake, and the ibex worked into a thick pomade—was recommended as a sure cure. For strengthening the hair, the "tooth of a donkey crushed in oil" worked the miracle. Though the early Egyptians shaved the head and wore wigs as well as false beards, the colors of these were no doubt determined by their knowledge of dyes.

The Assyrians rivaled and even surpassed the Egyptians in their attention to the cosmetic arts, particularly those pertaining to the hair. The long hair, which fell to the shoulders, was carefully and elaborately arranged in a series of curls and ringlets. The beard was allowed to grow its full length and, descending low on the breast, was divided into two or three rows of curls. The mustache was carefully trimmed and curled at the ends. The hair as well as the beard appears to have been dyed. The eyebrows and eyelashes were dyed black, and a dark pigment was used to blacken the edge of the lids and the lashes and thereby increase the brilliance of the eyes.

145

The Persians were remarkable for the length and beauty of their hair. The women of the Orient—especially of China—used the juice from the petals of the hibiscus plant as a dye for their hair.

In Greece during the Homeric period, the greatest possible attention was paid to the beauty of the hair. Long and abundant hair among both men and women was greatly to be desired. So general was the custom of wearing the hair long that in this way the Greeks were distinguished from barbarians, who wore their hair short. Even the gods were praised for their rich and abundant locks. Zeus was described as "magnificent" in long and curling hair. Hera braided her "fragrant and divine curls." Athene and others were described as "long haired" and "beautiful haired."

> . . . When thus her shapely form
> Had been anointed, and her hands had combed
> Her tresses, she arranged the *lustrous* curls,
> *Ambrosial, beautiful,* that clustering hung
> Round her immortal brow.
>
> *Iliad*

Fair hair was especially esteemed, and is attributed to most of the heroes. Achilles, Menelaus, Paris, and others are distinctly described as "fair haired." Baldness was looked upon as an unsightly defect. Somewhat later, judging from frequent references in Greek literature, the use of hair dye as well as other artifices of the toilet became general. The inclination of Greek women for the dye method of rejuvenating their faded locks is plainly evident in the following lines:

> Themistonoe, thrice as old as a crow, after *dyeing* her white hair, has become on a sudden not youth-like but Rhea-like.
>
> LUCIAN

Again:

> You *dye* your hair; but you will not dye your old age.
>
> LUCIAN

Hair dye as well as perfumes and cosmetics in general soon made their way to Rome. The trade of the barber came first to be established as a distinct occupation in Sicily and soon grew to be one of importance. About 303 B.C. the first barbers set up their shops in Rome. The taste of the Romans, even those in modest circumstances, demanded well-kept hair. In fact, if a man's hair showed neglect or careless attention he was likely to be treated with contemptuous scorn or open insult. This popular demand for the barber caused little shops to spring up on many of the leading streets, and the Roman barber of the early centuries soon rivaled the later-day *friseurs, coiffeurs,* and *perruquiers.* Hair dye and other cosmetics were soon fashionably established. Pliny paints a vivid picture of the use of hair dye among Romans. He tells of the black dye produced by boiled walnut shells and leek parings; of a mixture of oil, ashes, and earthworms used to prevent the hair from turning white; of crushed myrtle berries as a popular antidote for baldness; of the generous supply of bear's grease believed to stimulate the growth of hair. As has been said before, when the blonde type came to be admired the hair was bleached, and when wigs came into fashion, large supplies of flaxen wigs were imported into Italy to be worn by the dark-eyed, dark-skinned Romans.

Hair powder is commonly said to date from the luxurious days of ancient Rome. We know, however, that before that period the Assyrians and other peoples of the East practiced dusting their black hair with a yellow powder which resembled gold dust. These powders were made from pulverized starch scented with perfume. The women of Rome used many ointments and tonics which kept the hair soft and lustrous, and added to these the use of hair powder. It is said that the emperors of Rome in her most glorious days also indulged in a hair powder of gold dust.

The Saxons are believed to have practiced either the dyeing or powdering of the hair. Both hair and beard in Saxon drawings are frequently colored blue. In other instances it is sometimes bright red, green, or orange. But whether this coloring indicates dyeing or powdering of the hair has not been definitely decided. The Gauls practiced the dyeing of the hair to give it a reddish hue.

1500-1800

From time to time through the centuries certain fads in hair color have prevailed. In the sixteenth century Italy was the distinct leader in all the artifices of the toilet. Blonde again was the favorite hue. Women spent whole days sitting in the sunshine, for they believed that the sun imparted a golden glint. Those who bleached their hair dried it from the terrace tops of their houses, wearing hats without crowns and with broad brims over which the hair was spread, the brim meantime protecting the wearer from the sun. At this time quantities of false hair were worn. The popular "false heads" when not made of peasant's hair were formed of white and yellow silk. All this extravagance was hotly condemned and women were generally denounced for such "ungodly exploitation" of themselves.

In England, when Queen Elizabeth was arbiter of fashion, the leaders of the day dyed their hair a reddish hue in compliment to the queen.

In France during the reign of Charles IX (1560-74), powdering the hair came to be the ruling fashion. When later the periwig came in, all the European countries, and America as well, made haste to adopt it. Both men and women powdered not only the wig but their shoulders. Indeed, the proper finish to the complete toilet was a liberal dash of perfumed powder. The powder of this day was pulverized starch or, frequently, wheat flour to which a scent had been added.

Throughout the seventeenth and eighteenth centuries the popularity of hair powder continued. In the *History of Potters and Porcelain*, by Marryatt (1715), a highly interesting light is thrown on this subject of hair powder.

John Schnoor, one of the richest iron-mongers of the Erzebirge, when riding on horseback near the Ane, observed that his horse's feet stuck constantly in the soft, white earth, from which the animal could hardly extricate himself. The general use of hair powder at this time was a considerable article of commerce, and the idea immediately suggested itself to Schnoor that this white earth might be a substitute for wheat flour which was then used in its fabrication. He carried a specimen to Carlsfeld and caused hair powder to be prepared, which he sold in great quantities in Dresden, Leipsic, and other places.

The article further relates that some of this powder was purchased by the superintendent of the famous royal porcelain factory at Meissen. One day while using the powder for his hair he noticed that it seemed somewhat heavy. He examined it carefully and decided that it could not have been made from wheat flour, but must be earthy. A happy thought dawned—he would experiment at the factory, using this earthy substance for his ceramics. To his great joy he found that it produced that for which he had been seeking. So it might well be that hair powder led to the development of porcelain at the royal manufactory at Meissen!

Of course, about 1795, at the court of Marie Antoinette, hairdressing among women reached its peak. The professional hairdresser, as we know, combed, curled, and waved the locks, added false hair if necessary to the effect, gathered it all up into high, fantastic towers, then powdered the whole. A writer of the period declares it would require a volume to describe the amazing extravagance in the headdresses of this day and emphasizes the fact that an ever-widening wave of complaint was arising on account of the enormous cost of curls, ribbons, jewels, and flowers. He then adds, "and no wonder, for it had emptied the purse of the unfortunate husband to build it."

1800-1900

In England, 1795, when the use of hair powder was at its height, William Pitt, in order to replenish the public treasury, proposed a tax on this luxury. He estimated that the returns would add approximately £210,000 per year to the public funds. Strange to say the measure passed, but unfortunately for the expected increase in revenue the use of hair powder gradually declined, and finally was largely given up. The few who were loath to part with their powder were compelled to pay a guinea a year for the privilege of using it. Before long those who persisted in its use notwithstanding the tax came to be known as "guinea pigs." Meanwhile, the fashion for various-colored powders had also flourished. In early 1800, dull pink powder was the fashionable hue, at other times gray, violet, blue—each had its day. The *Monthly Magazine* (1800), describing the dress of Charles Fox, English statesman, says he was one of the most fashionable figures about town wearing his "red-heeled shoes and *blue hair powder*. Despite this great vogue for hair powder, soon after the opening years of the century, it rapidly vanished from the fashion scene. The charm of the powdered wig, however, has never been lost, for it frequently adds the note of elegance and distinction to the many costume balls and festivals of our own day.

Twentieth Century

With the coming of the twentieth century changes undreamed by the court of Marie Antoinette and the queens of former centuries were rapidly becoming established. The luxuries which were then the privilege of the few were now conceded to the many. In fact, the new social and economic conditions of the modern world made the luxuries of the past the necessities of the present. An outstanding illustration of this fact is the phenomenal growth of the beauty shop and all it has to offer. The beauty shop of the twentieth century originated about 1918. More and more at this time woman was rapidly finding her place in the industrial and professional world. It was necessary for her to not only do her work well but to be as well dressed and well groomed as time and money would permit. This economic change and its demands, perhaps, were largely responsible for the services and products of the beauty shop.

As women enjoyed their new-found freedom gained through financial independence, they naturally indulged their taste for the luxuries of the toilet. At no time in the history of the world have these luxuries been so easily available to women in all walks of life. Powders, pomades, creams, rouges, perfumes, and countless other beauty aids are to be found in the present-day beauty shop. Here is made available the very latest in shampoos, tonics, waving fluids, brilliantines, and rinses. The array of modern rinses is remarkable; there are lemon, vinegar, and vegetable in many shades. All are for improving the texture of the hair. The recent fashion for auburn hair brought the henna rinse to popularity. Then there are the various waves which have reached their height in the "permanent wave" fixed through the use of electric irons.

So great and so successful has been the business of the beauty shop that large department stores have opened attractive sections devoted to these accessories of the toilet. Here complete lines of cosmetics and many other varieties of toilet articles may be purchased. Beauty specialists are frequently employed by these merchandizing stores to give free information and demonstration of their various beauty aids. It is indeed not surprising to read that the nation's yearly expenditure for toilet accessories runs into the millions.

From the days of ancient Egypt down through the luxury-loving periods of Greece and Rome and in the later Renaissance, woman has always gratified her taste for the accessories of the toilet. Never before, however, in the history of the world has there been so diversified and alluring array of toilet aids as is today at the command of modern woman!

CHAPTER 13

Toilet Accessories: Perfume

She took for *perfume* the ryndes of old rosemary and burned them.

Sir T. Elyot, *Castle of Health*

THE use of sweet-smelling scents is by no means a luxury of only the twentieth century. Long before man knew how to utilize the fragrance of flowers, he delighted in the odor of dry, resinous gums—frankincense, myrrh, cassia, spikenard—and the many aromatic spices. From time immemorial the Arab woman of the desert has perfumed her body by sitting near or actually in the smoke rising from a slow-burning fire of spices. In ancient Scythia, the women bruised the woods of the cedar and cypress tree which, mixed with water, was used to anoint the face and body. The following day it was removed, leaving the skin fresh and fragrant. The entire Far East, particularly Arabia, is the home of aromatic spices and resinous gums. Sesame, olive, and almond oils seem to be the basic ingredients most used for these sweet-smelling gums.

The word *perfume* is compounded from *per,* meaning "by" or "through," and *fumus,* meaning "smoke." In the ancient religious rites of China, Egypt, Greece, and Palestine, the burning of incense caused a filmy, blue haze to float over the altar. The odor of incense reached the people through this thin, blue haze, *through the smoke;* hence the fragrance of incense came to be known as "perfume." The offering of delicate odors was considered a mark of the deepest respect and homage. The burning of incense was also a feature of the Hebrew ritual. Numerous instances of its use are found in the Old Testament. Here, also, is a record of probably the earliest of perfumes:

The Lord said unto Moses, Take unto thee sweet spices, stacte, and onycha, and galbanum; sweet spices with pure frankincense; of each shall there be a like weight; and thou shalt make it a *perfume*, a confection after the art of the apothecary, tempered together, pure and holy.*

It is related that when the Queen of Sheba visited King Solomon, she brought with her a very great train, "with camels that bore spices." The luxury and magnificence of Solomon's court was unrivaled. "Ointment and perfume rejoice the heart," he sings. Perfumes and spices, always highly prized, came into general use during this period.

* Exodus 30:34-35.

By-and-by these aromatics of the East were carried into Egypt. Here again they were offered morning, noon, and night on the altar of the temples. In religious processions, myrrh, cinnamon, iris, and other strongly scented substances were burned. The fumigation of temples by the burning of scented gums was considered an act of purification. The ancient art of embalming pressed into service these aromatics, the costliest gums and spices. In Egypt, perfume for personal use is always associated with the fame of Cleopatra, whose beauty and charm were greatly enhanced by the variety and abundance of her perfumes and lotions. The favorite perfume of this famous beauty was *kyaphi,* said to have been one of the charms used by the enchantress to accomplish the downfall of Mark Antony. When the dark-skinned Cleopatra sailed down the river Cydnus at Tarsus to meet the Roman warrior,

> The barge she sat in like a burnished throne,
> Burned in the water; the poop was beaten gold;
> Purple the sails, and so *perfumed* that
> The winds were love-sick with them.

Antony and Cleopatra, Act II, sc. 2

The mystic-sounding *kyaphi* was kept by special slaves in containers of alabaster, gold, or turquoise. It is said that each time Cleopatra anointed her hands she used an extravagant amount of sweel-smelling ungents of great value. For her feet she employed a lotion called *aegyptium,* a combination of almond oil, honey, and cinnamon treated with orange blossoms and henna.

Figure 183. Alabastron,
Greek, 550–500 B.C.

As the world grew older, the fragrance of flowers began to enter into the compounding of perfumes. The odor of the rose, iris, crocus, and above all the violet, was widely sought. To women of Greece these sweet-smelling odors were indispensable. They kept their clothes in scented chests and made use of innumerable scent bags for sweetening the air as they sat at table. Even the wine was scented with rose, violet, and other aromatics. By-and-by these fragrant powders were mixed with oils making a perfume of liquid form.

In Greek mythology perfume was a gift from the gods. Whenever the Olympian gods honored mortals with a visit they left behind them an ambrosial odor, a token of their divine nature. The Greek nation gradually grew more and more addicted to the use of perfume, and the art of the perfumer rapidly advanced. Solon is said to have tried to restrain the extravagant use of scents by law, but in spite of the law the indulgence increased. It is said that in this day a Greek dandy used one scent for his hair, another for his clothes, and another for his wine! Certain oils and essences were especially recommended as appropriate for each part of the body. The eyebrows and hair were anointed with an oil extracted from marjoram; mint was recommended for the arms; palm-oil for the jaws and breasts; and ground ivory was applied to the neck and knees.

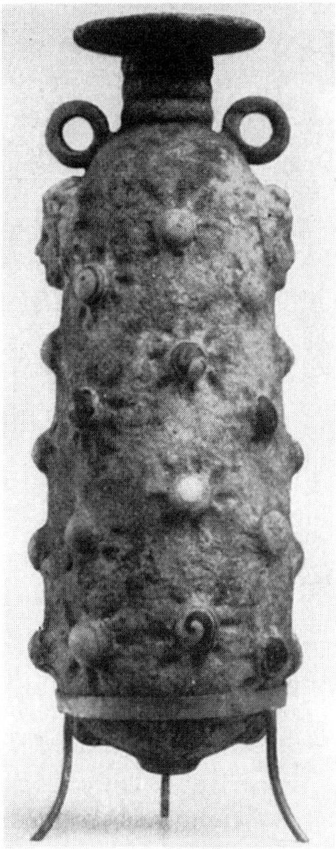

A vase peculiarly Greek—the *albastron* —was used to contain these various perfumes and ungents. This was a long, narrow bottle with wide-spreading neck and small opening. The base was rounded so that a stand of some kind was necessary to hold it upright. These vases were usually made of alabaster or onyx. Figures 183, 184. In a quotation from a Greek poet* who flourished about 350 B.C., one is led to believe that far more fantastic methods were employed in scattering sweet odors than that of dipping the perfume from the alabaster jar:

COURTESY, METROPOLITAN
MUSEUM OF ART

Figure 184.
Alabastron, White Glass with
Glass Inlay, Greek, 5th
Century, B.C.

> . . . . For he t' anoint himself
> Dipped not his finger in Alabaster,
> The vulgar practice of a former age;
> But he let fly four doves, with unguents drenched,
> Not of one sort, but every bird a *perfume* bore
> Peculiar, and differing from the rest;
> And they hovering above us, from their heavy wings
> Showered their scents upon our robes and furniture,
> And I—be not too envious, gentlemen—
> I was myself bedewed with violet odors!

A perfume container of unusual beauty, possibly developed from Egyptian alabaster vases, is now in the Cesnola Collection of the Metropolitan Museum of Art, New York City. This rare ornament goes back probably to the sixth or late fifth century. It was found with other treasure during the excavations made on the island of Cyprus in 1872. Cyprus,

* From *Settler* of Alexis.

of all the Mediterranean islands, lies nearest to the Phoenician coast and was settled early in the general movement westward. This section of the world carried on extensive commerce with neighboring countries, with Egypt, and with the East. Naturally the recovered treasure shows the in-

fluence of all these various peoples and is an eloquent testimony to the richness and beauty of early ornament. This little container is about seven inches in height and made of rock crystal, a material anciently valued as much as, if not more than, gold. It retains the gold-mounted neck, and a gold cover in granular work is attached by a chain to one of the ears of the bottle. It is called a *vinaigrette* because it resembles the perfume container turned out by the modern jeweler, and since women have been very much alike in all ages, it is believed to have served the same purposes. Figure 185.

Figure 185. Rock-Crystal Vinaigrette, 3d Century

Found in the island of Cyprus.

From Greece, perfumes quickly traveled to Rome. At first their sale was prohibited, but by-and-by the appeal of scents and sweet-smelling ointments made such a conquest that Roman battle standards were considered not fit to wave in the face of the enemy unless duly anointed! Soon perfume was in so great demand among the luxury-loving Romans that a guild of perfumers was kept busy supplying the trade. They were called *unguentarii*, and their shops occupied an entire street in one of the seaport towns of Italy. Three types of perfumes were made: solid unguents—that is, scents from only one source, as almond, rose, or quince; or liquids—compounds containing flowers, spices, and gums in oil; and powdered perfumes. These various types of perfume were kept in beautiful containers. Like the Greeks, the Romans lavished perfume upon the apartments and their furniture, besides prescribing special scents for different parts of the body. The Emperor Caligula reveled in perfume; Nero is said to have set the fashion for rose water and to have spent four million sesterces* on roses for one fete. So fond was he of scents that he ordered the ceiling of his dining salon to be made to represent the firmament and apparatus supplied for showering down perfumes and fragrant waters both night and day. At the funeral of his wife, Poppaea, more perfume was used than Arabia could produce in a year. In fact, perfume is said to have been applied to everything with which men and women had to do. Even the mules that took part in the festivals were treated with ointments and scents. It is said that some thoroughly saturated objects have retained their odor for centuries. Gibbon, writing on the festivals and amphitheater of Rome, observed, "The air of the amphitheater was continually

* An Ancient Roman coin; value, something over $.04 in American money.

refreshed by the playing of fountains, and profusely impregnated by the grateful scent of aromatics."*

After the fall of the Roman Empire the manufacture of perfume passed again to the East. In the tenth century an Arab physician discovered a method of distilling fragrant water from leaves. The Arabs were also skilled in the preparation of fragrant ointments, and it was from them, through the Crusaders, that the art of perfume making was reintroduced into medieval Europe.

Middle Ages

One of the oldest and costliest perfumes the Crusaders found was *rose attar*. It is attributed to Nicander (140 B.C.) and the Mohammedan pharmacists. *Attar of rose* is described in pharmacopoeias as the oil distilled from the petals of the damask rose (Rosa Damascene). It is employed chiefly in pharmacy for perfuming lotions and medicinal washes. It requires about two hundred pounds of almost featherweight rose petals to produce one ounce of attar of rose. Considering this, it is not surprising that the perfume in its quaint eastern phials covered with quotations from the Koran is expensive, amounting in some instances to five pounds sterling a fluid ounce. Persia and Turkey now produce most of the attar for commerce.

Coming from the Orient where they had contacted a land of sweet-smelling odors, the returning Crusaders brought with them some knowledge of perfume and many new ideas. This tended to re-establish in Europe the art of perfume making. With the gradual advance in the compounding of perfumes, animal substances came to be of great importance in preparing the finished product. It was found that a small portion of these substances added to the "life" and diffusiveness of these sweet-smelling odors. These important animal substances were musk, ambergris, civet, and castor.

COURTESY, METROPOLITAN MUSEUM OF ART

Figure 186. Perfume Bottle, Roman, 5th Century, A.D.

Musk is a secretion of the musk ox which inhabits the mountainous districts of the Atlas and Himalaya ranges. The most important variety comes from Tibet. Ambergris is a highly perfumed waxy substance cast off from the stomach of the sperm whale. It is the basis of the most expensive extracts and, like musk, is worth its weight in gold. Civet is a soft, waxy substance secreted by the civet cat and derived from the Orient. It is packed in horns and imported principally from Abyssinia. Castor is a scent of animal origin derived from the castor beaver.

---

* Vol. II, Chapter 12, page 104.

1500-1600

About 1500 an Italian perfumer named René established a shop in Paris. René was the pioneer of the new era. Soon the trade grew and developed into a tremendous business. Italy and France were leaders in this extensive trade. During the early Renaissance, Francis I (1515-47) invited the celebrated perfumers of Italy to France. Every opportunity was offered for developing their business, and their scents were in great demand. People believed that "strong odors refreshed the brain" and had a beneficial effect upon the health. Later in the same century, Catherine de' Medici, wife of Henry II, continually fostered the movement for paint, powder, and perfume in France. Like Francis I, she conspired to bring into France the celebrated perfumers of Italy. They came, setting up their shops in the French capital to supply the extravagant demands for perfume. During the whole of the Renaissance period, perfume came more and more into use, and France attained a supremacy in the field which she holds to this day.

It was now discovered that the animal substances—musk, ambergris, civet, and castor—improved with age; consequently, the great Parisian perfumers placed these in vats where they were left for years to ripen. Then a small portion of this substance, with the essence of flowers and distilled waters blended with balsam and other extracts and oils, were found to produce a more delicate odor. Working along these lines the chemist soon brought his perfume nearer and nearer to that exquisite delicacy of odor which is the supreme achievement of the perfumer's art.

As the sixteenth century wore on, the prodigal use of perfume continued. All apparel was scented. Hair, shoes, fans, gloves gave out sweet odors. Even the jewelry of the day contained hidden cavities in which perfume was concealed, to be released at will. Henry III is famous for his love of paint, powder, and sweet scents of every sort. He in France and Henry VIII in England initiated the fashions, and the world followed. The desire of these monarchs was that everything be bathed in amber and musk. Never had such a thing been known before! It is related that Henry VIII used such quantities of perfume that he nearly fainted.

Throughout this entire period musk continued to be most highly prized, while ambergris and other substances mixed with various spices were next in choice. These various scents were rolled into little balls called *pommes de senteur*, enclosed in cases of gold and silver filigree often set with gems, and worn as an ornament suspended from the girdle or pendant to the rosary. Since musk was first choice, the names "musk balls" and "musk apples" were also given to these little ornaments. The fashion had prevailed during the late Middle Ages for mention is made as early as 1300 of such "artificial apples" being worn or carried as a protection against infectious disease. Charles V of France owned several costly specimens set with emeralds, rubies, and pearls. Others were made of amber and gold, agate, gold and enamel, enamel and pearls. In England the same ornament was known as *pomander*. Figure 187.

> The bob of gold
> Which a *pomander* ball does hold
> This to her side she does attach
> By gold crochet or French penache.

The pomander was also originally worn as a preventive against infection, something as the camphor bag was worn in the nineteenth century. It was not long, however, until the craftsmen of England made them into exquisite bits of jewelry so beautiful that they were frequently offered as complimentary tokens of affection. Many are said to have been given Elizabeth as New Year gifts. On the list is this puzzling item which probably refers to a girdle with pomander attached: "a farye girdle of *pomander*.

In well-known portraits of the period the fashionable pomander is much in evidence. In PLATE LV, page 547, the Spanish lady holds a jeweled pomander pendant to her girdle. The girdle, pomander, rings, pendant, tiara, and jeweled fur piece are excellent examples of the various kinds of ornament which prevailed during this century.

Soon after the introduction of the orange into England it, too, was used as a pomander. The substance within was removed and the hollow filled with a sponge saturated with vinegar, cloves, and other spices. This was worn or carried as a preventive against infection. Cavendash describes Cardinal Woolsey entering a crowded room and "holding in his hand a very fair orange . . . against pestilent airs." In portraits of the period the orange is frequently seen either carried in the hand or suspended from the girdle.

The *pouncet-* (perfume) *box* mentioned by Shakespeare is another name for the pomander or dry-scent box:

> HOTSPUR. And twixt his fingers and his thumb he held
> A *pouncet-box*, which ever and anon he gave
> His nose and took't away again.
> *Henry IV*, Act I, sc. 3

Though the pace set for perfumes by Henry III of France and Henry VIII of England is notorious, the example of Elizabeth (1558-1603) was scarcely less prodigal. Handkerchiefs, gloves, ruffs, cuffs, and bags—all were scented. Women soon learned how to distill sweet waters and delicate odors, to make powders and essences. In every great man's house a room known as the "still room" was given over to the ladies, who busied themselves in the art of preparing perfumes and washes. In some of these establishments plants such as the rose, elder flower, balm, primrose, sage, marigold, tansy, and many others were cultivated solely for the use of the still room. In Nichol's *Progress of Queen Elizabeth* he mentions that among the rooms on the ground floor at Hawkstead was one known as the still room, where ladies of the court amused themselves by distilling fragrant scents.

During the reign of Good Queen Bess laws failed to restrain the luxury-loving leaders. Toilet tables groaned with all kinds of cosmetics. Into the bath were thrown myrrh, mint, lavender, and other fragrant herbs and spices. These same perfumes were constantly poured about in public places. This extravagant use of odors and essences gave rise to many remarks by writers of the day. The following verse appeared in the *New Bath Guide* (Bath was then becoming a center for everything fashionable):

> Bring, oh bring the essense pot!
> Amber, musk, and bergamott,
> Eau de Chipre, eau de Luce,
> Sanspareil and citron juice.

1600-1700

In France, following the prodigal habits of Henry III, powders and perfumes suffered a relapse. Henry IV (1589-1610) spent most of his time in camps and had little use for these vanities of the toilet. However, upon the accession of Louis XIII (1610-43), and his queen, the beautiful Ann of Austria, perfumes again added their fragrance to the social life of the period. It was during this reign that the famous *Frangipani* perfume was introduced. The name Frangipani, that of a noble Roman family, has been preserved to posterity because one of its members, a marquis who held an important military office under Louis XIII, discovered that perfume could be obtained in fluid form by treating sweet powders with alcohol. This produced a perfume much like our modern handkerchief perfumes. The new Frangipani perfume is said to have been applied to gloves, which were known as Frangipanni gloves. Every so often the word Frangipani, so well known to the trade, has been revived as a popular name for new scents, pomades, and essences.

Louis XIV (1643-1715) is said to have detested perfumes and, consequently, under his leadership the use of sweet-smelling scents somewhat abated. In 1715, when Louis XV came to the throne, the fashion for perfume was revived with all its old-time popularity. Louis demanded a new odor each day in all his apartments. Consequently, the royal quarters received a bath of a different perfume each twenty-four hours. One day it would be that of musk, another of ambergris, another of rose. Ladies of the court made lavish use of every perfume known, while the King's favorites, Madame de Pompadour and Madame du Barry, set the fashion. Pompadour is said to have spent a half million francs each year for perfumes and cosmetics. Rumor has it that her favorite astringent was composed entirely of crushed wild strawberries and that after a strawberry bath she was massaged with sponges of fine silk saturated with violet-scented milk. It is easily understood why her court became famous as the "Perfumed Court." Madame du Barry, in turn, is said to have preserved her beauty through a receipt given her by an Italian perfumer. At this time the use of perfume was, indeed, lavish. Gloves were scented, rings were supplied with small hollow cavities which held delicate perfume, and all articles of clothing were heavily scented, even those worn in mourning.

Figure 187. Pomander Perfume Container, 1600

And the perfume cases of the day! The contents of these tiny accessories tell the story of perfume in no mistakable language. One item is invariably found in each case, a diminutive funnel. Each case also held at least two bottles which contained the essence of two different flowers. And so milady, with the help of the little funnel, could blend her own perfumes! Thus she secured the exact *odeur* that pleased her discriminating taste. It is said that this custom of blending perfumes goes back to the early seventeenth century. A tiny, trunk-shaped, leather-covered perfume case which once belonged to Louis XIII (1610-43), shows two tiny bottles and the little funnel. In many instances the bottles which held the perfumes were gems of beauty. One set was found cut from rock crystal, another from solid agate, each set capped with tiny porcelain figures.

Figure 188. Renaissance Perfume Flask

1700-1900

The coronation of Louis XVI (1774-89) as King of France brought a new queen to the fashion world. Though Marie Antoinette is famous for her extravagance in all lines of dress, her taste in perfume was modest. She preferred the delicate and subtle odors of the rose and the violet. But during this same period in Italy, Venetian women were saturating their clothes, from underlinens to gloves, in perfumes that filled the air for "three miles distant." Many of the perfumes at this time, especially balsam and musk diluted with water, were considered effective medicinal remedies. Figure 189.

The extravagant use of perfume did not perish with the kings. Though Napoleon and Josephine discouraged cosmetics, they were lavish with perfume. It is understood that after each bath Napoleon poured an entire flask of *eau de cologne* over his head, shoulders, and hands. He was, moreover, a constant user of highly scented soaps and toilet waters. Over a period of three months he used three flagons of essence of jasmine and 163 flasks of eau de cologne. This perfume, obviously his favorite, came to be very popular during the Napoleonic regime. But the favorite perfume of the Empress Josephine was musk. This odor is very penetrating

and persistent. The story is told that a later occupant of the Empress' room at Malmaison found it impossible to rid the atmosphere of the odor of musk, notwithstanding the fact that the walls had been repeatedly washed and painted through several successive years.

Sometime later in the nineteenth century, about 1850, the ladies of the period carried little perfume cases known as scent boxes. Figure 191. These stood from one to two inches high and were made of both gold and silver. The cover of each was hinged, and within, a small sponge saturated with choice perfume was secreted. It was no uncommon sight to see the fair belle of that day passing the tiny box among her friends, permitting each the favor of a stimulating whiff.

Figure 189. Scent Bottle,
Meissen Porcelain, 1750

Twentieth Century

In the twentieth century, the art of the perfumer has reached near-perfection. With this attainment has come a finer discrimination in its use. No longer is wearing apparel drenched in perfume. No longer is the air scented for miles around. In the present day the extravagance of Henry VIII, of the Louis', and of Napoleon would be viewed with alarm, and the taste of Elizabeth, Pompadour, du Barry, and Josephine would be sadly out of place. Whatever love milady may still cherish for perfume and scented waters, this she artfully veils. Their use she gently tempers with restraint, selecting with critical discrimination the precise fragrance that, sparingly indulged, best harmonizes with and most charmingly expresses her own individuality.

Along the banks of the French and Italian Riviera, in the vicinity of Monoco, Nice, Grasse, Cannes, and almost as far as Genoa, one sees choice flower farms cultivated for the perfumer's art. The sunny slopes are covered with rose, jasmine, violet, jonquil, orange-blossom, mignonette, tuberose, and cassia buds. For many decades this had been the flower garden of the world. As long ago as 1550, Catherine de' Medici sent her agents to establish perfume factories in this enchanted spot. To-day during the season which lasts from February to November this picturesque locality becomes a scene of thriving activity. The narrow, winding streets are filled with flower-laden, moving carts; merry, bright-eyed women and girls with baskets of gay-colored flowers troop back and forth; and the air is filled with an elusive fragrance. Here the flowers are distilled the same day as gathered,

COURTESY, METROPOLITAN MUSEUM OF ART

Figure 190. Pair of Perfume Bottles

White porcelain decorated in dark blue, gilt, and various colors; French, late 18th century.

and the essence is placed in large containers and then sent to distant laboratories where modern alchemists theorize, blend, and experiment, until they produce the thousand exquisite fragrances that grace the toilet tables of the world.

Figure 191. Silver Scent Boxes, about 1850

Many countries contribute some individual essence to the perfume industry. England gives lavender and peppermint; Algeria, unsurpassed geranium oils; Italy, citrus oils; Turkey and Bulgaria, attar of rose; the East, fragrance typically Oriental. In America the hundreds of flora in Yellowstone Park make various contributions to the perfume industry.

From the days of Cleopatra to the present, the use of sweet-smelling scents has ever been one of the alluring devices of Fashion. True, their use has sometimes risen as in the sixteenth and seventeenth centuries, and then later fallen, but the fascination has remained. Fads may come and fads may go, but the lure of perfume continues its magic hold upon the world.

REFERENCES

Askinson, George William, *Perfumes and Their Preparation* (translated from the German).

Burckhardt, Jacob, *Civilization of the Renaissance.*

Carter, Howard, *The Tomb of Tut-ankh-Amen.*

Child, Theodore, *Wimples and Crisping Pins.*

Erman, J. P. Adolph, *Life in Ancient Egypt.*

New International Encyclopedia, Vol. 10.

Parsons, Frank Alvah, *The Art of Dress*, pp. 93, 229, 346.

Piesse, G. W. Septimus, *The Art of Perfumery.*

Timayenis, T. T., *Greece in the Time of Homer*, p. 203.

Wilkinson, Sir John Gardiner, *A Popular Account of the Ancient Egyptians.*

Part II

ACCESSORIES WORN AT THE NECK,
SHOULDERS, AND WAIST

CHAPTER 14

Pins and Brooches

His garment, naught but many ragged clouts,
With thorns together *pinn'd* and patched was.

SPENSER, *Faerie Queen*

Figure 192.
Silver Pin,
2000 B.C.

May have
been used as
a hairpin.

*Found in
the Island of
Cyprus.*

STRICT necessity, the proverbial mother of invention, brought the pin, with its many interesting developments, into the field of dress. In its most primitive form the pin goes back to the thorn and fishbone used to fasten together skins and bits of clothing. As soon as clothes appeared, these clothes ornaments came into use. During the Bronze Age the crude pins fashioned by hand were an imitation of the earlier thorn or bone pins. They were, however, a marked improvement upon primitive types, for some displayed artistic merit and served an ornamental as well as a practical purpose.

In Egypt, Sparta, and Cyprus, stiletto pins six to eight inches in length have been found. These were used both for fastening the clothes and holding the curls or plaits of hair in place. In Greece the pin gradually developed into a distinct ornament, Figures 195, 196; later, Roman pins had large heads, usually decorated with a miniature of some divinity, a bust, or an animal. The ruins of Pompeii have yielded many ancient Roman pins of bronze with unusually beautiful heads. In central Europe in the region of the Lake Dwellers, rudely constructed pins of bronze have been recovered. Figure 193. So many of these have been found that it is but reasonable to assume that they were generally worn. Though the thickness of the shaft of these primitive pins would seem to have torn the fabric, it must be remembered that these early robes were coarse and loosely woven, resembling a modern blanket, and the pin, though ever so thick, in no way damaged the cloth. Sometimes the shaft of the early pin was pierced with an eye in which a chain was fastened. Two of these linked together made a distinctly ornamental pin. In others a wire ring was hung through the head of the pin. Figure 194. This "ring and pin" device later developed into an elaborate fastening which reached the highest artistry and came to be the outstanding ornament of the eleventh, twelfth, and thirteenth centuries.

Down through the years the single-shaft pin has held a place more-or-less fashionable in the costumes of all peoples. But, with the introduction of the common pin which answered the same purpose and the development of other attractive forms of fastenings—brooches, buckles, clasps—the single-shaft pin was relegated to second place.

The exact date of the introduction of the common pin into Europe is uncertain. Figure 198. Pins in their present form, however, were used in England and France in the fourteenth century. A record

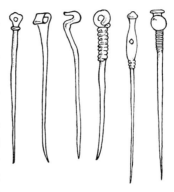

Figure 193. Primitive Pins of the Bronze Age

Figure 194. Primitive Ring and Pin

of 1347 tells of the delivery of twelve thousand pins for the wardrobe of a French princess. As evident from this, the fashions of the period required large quantities of pins, and at times it is said that a great scarcity of this simple item prevailed. With the scarcity of pins, prices mounted so much that the people were taxed to provide the Queen with money to buy pins. In order to prevent too much indulgence in their use an act was passed by the British Parliament allowing pinmakers to sell pins in "open shop" only on the first and second day of January of each year. On these days ladies of high and low degree alike, taking their pin money with them, flocked to the shops to make a purchase of pins. The term "pin money" is said to have originated with this practice of saving money for this particular purpose. In that day the cost of pins made them a popular gift for New Year's day. It was indeed a happy thought to consider presenting a friend with a gift of three or four pins!

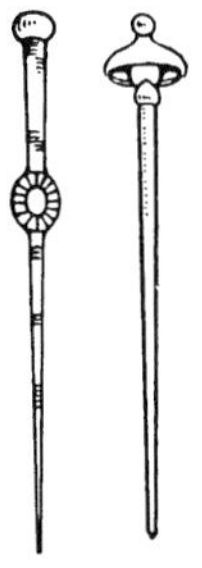

Figures 195, 196. Greek Pins

The Bronze Age was the key which unlocked the door to all future development in personal ornament. Working in metal made it possible to shape objects, to make finger rings, arm rings, and neck rings, and primitive man took keen delight in imitating earlier forms in yielding metal. After the simple, single-shaft pins, came those fastenings which represent the attempt to prevent the pin from working out of the material which it was intended to hold together. These pins were shaped from one unbroken length of wire and bent over until the point could be caught within a looped head. The modern safety pin is a direct descendant of this early type. The ancient forms are among the oldest of ornaments and are known as *fibulae*. Figure 199. Though the term is especially applied to these forms of fastening, all buckles, brooches, and clasps which eventually resulted are also termed fibulae. It is said that the Romans were the first to apply this name to the brooch.

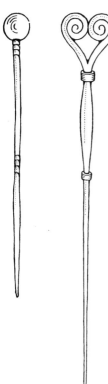

The ancient examples of looped pins show many ingenious ways of coiling the spring, arching the bow, and shaping the catch. Sometimes only single coils are used; sometimes a double coil; and then again the wire is coiled bilaterally, one, two, or three turns on each side of the central pin. By-and-by this primitive pin began to be ornamented. Sometimes the metal was flattened on one side, or sometimes a flat disk was attached to the side, which served as a shield to the pin. Figure 200. These ancient fibulae are important because they undoubtedly represent the first application of the spring. About the fourth century B.C. fibulae were designed in a T-shape form, which came to be the basis for many subsequent designs. In fact, the safety-pin type seemed almost lost in the many new patterns that developed.

The word "brooch" is derived from the French *brocher*, a term applied to several different pointed instruments. From this word also comes the verb "to broach," i.e. "to pierce." These early fibulae were used in the place of buttons and other fastenings common in the world of today. They were worn by men and women of Greece, Rome, and western and central Europe, and continued to be important accessories of dress as late as the early Middle Ages.

Figures 197, 198.
Early Anglo-Saxon
Pin and Irish Bronze
Pin

Greek women of the early archaic period wore long pointed fibulae to fasten the chiton on the shoulder and upper arm. In the classic period a disk or shield was often attached to the pin, and the plate was engraved with quaint designs. Figure 200. Beautiful cameos were also used for the plate. The chalmys, a cloak worn by men, was usually held in position on the right shoulder by a golden brooch. Figure 201 shows a beautiful fibula of the seventh century B.C. The bow is exquisite in granular work and the catch is enriched by a rhythmic border of what would appear to be a procession of lions. In Greek fibulae the bow is small, while the catch is usually large.

Roman fibulae were constructed on the same general principle as those of the Greeks. In the early empire, however, they appear with the hinge instead of the spiral spring. Figure 202. Many of these recovered bronze

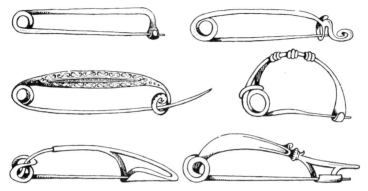

Figure 199. Various Forms of the Early Fibulae

Roman fibulae show that they have been tinned over to give them the appearance of silver. During the first and second centuries the round disk, with pin fixed behind and resembling the modern brooch, was much in use. The circular top was often ornamented with enameled designs and en-

Figure 200. Coiled Fibula with Covering Disk, Greek

riched with settings of jewels. Other fastenings used in Rome were the cameo brooches, generally worn by military leaders to secure the mantle

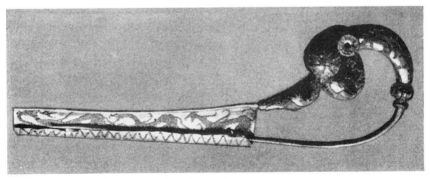

Figure 201. Greek Fibula, 7th Century, B.C.

on the shoulder. Between the fourth and six centuries, under the Eastern or Byzantine influence, the design and workmanship on brooches developed rapidly. They were made of gilt bronze, inlaid with enamel and set with jewels. They were large, elaborate, and heavy.

Middle Ages

In western Europe during the Middle Ages when Romans, Gauls, and

Franks were merging into the French of feudal times, ornament continued to be highly prized. Many important discoveries indicate that in the earlier years the safety-pin type of fibula was worn by the various peoples inhabiting this section of Europe. The T-shaped forms, both large and small, are found in great numbers. Figure 204. In fact, some of the larger ones are most extravagant in size, measuring a foot in length. Those worn by the Franks are peculiarly different than those worn by other peoples, in that the design of the upper section invariably shows a semicircular form with radiating pattern. Figure 205. Later, however, this form of fastening passed into oblivion, and its place was taken by the large brooches which by the eleventh century had gradually evolved from the ancient custom of hanging a wire ring through the head of the primitive pin.

Figure 202. Bronze Fibula, Roman

Often tinned to give appearance of silver.

Figure 203. Roman Fibula

Of particular interest because from it is suspended a large bauble.

Though the Saxons secured their mantles on the shoulder by drawing one corner of the material through a ring and knotting it, Figure 206, they, too, soon followed other peoples of western Europe and were using the "ring-and-pin" fastening. These handsome and highly ornamental ring-and-pin brooches are the distinctive ornaments of the eleventh, twelfth, and thirteenth centuries. They have passed into history as the *annular* and *penannular* brooches. In all annular brooches the ring is a complete circle, while in penannular ornament the circle is open. Figure 207. The pin, set loose upon the ring, was passed through the material and the ring given a twist. The pin, caught over the edge

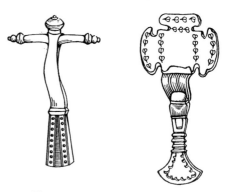

Figure 204. T-shaped Fibulae

of the open ring, held the material in place. One of the finest examples of the annular brooch in existence is the famous Tara brooch in the Royal Irish Academy at Dublin. Figure 208. This remarkable ornament was found in 1850 near Drogheda after a landslide had uncovered the spot where it had lain for centuries. The handsome fastening is made of white bronze, copper, tin, and silver, and the lower half of the ring is broadened out into a much-ornamented lunette. The groundwork is patterned in sections which are filled in with scrollwork in fine wire. The raised edges are set with translucent enamels. Small gold pins with filigree heads and others set with colored glass hold pieces of amber in place. Curious little human masks in red glass or-

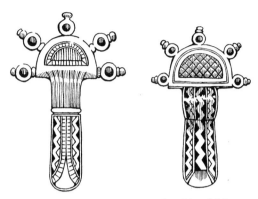

Figure 205. Ancient Fibulae, Frankish

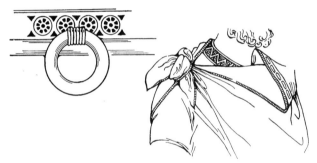

Figure 206. The Saxon Shoulder Ring and the Way
It Was Used in Securing the Mantle

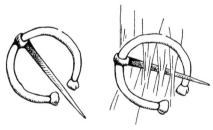

Figure 207. Penannular Brooches

The first shows the pin loose on the ring, the second, the pin pushed through the material and caught over the edge of the ring.

nament the large bosses. The head of the large pin is broadened out, decorated with tracery, and ornamented in keeping with the ring. It is said that nearly every branch of the jeweler's art is represented in this treasure. In all early annular and penannular brooches the pin was much longer than the diameter of the ring. Later, however, the pin was shortened. Those brooches in which the divided ends are fashioned to represent the arbutus berry are known as "arbutus brooches" and are among the best known examples of the penannular brooch. Figure 210.

After the ring of the open, circular brooch had become broad enough to support jewels, enamels, and molded forms, the circle itself was next filled in with gold and other metals and the pin hinged behind. Figure 209. At this point the flattened disk of the ancient fibulae and the filled-up center of the "ring and pin" becomes one with the modern brooch. Many

of these old brooches are remarkable for the beauty of enamel and inlay work. Garnets were perhaps the first stones to be used. These were cut in small, flat pieces, then formed into a pattern laid out in twisted wire on a bronze foundation. Nearly all designs were geometric in form. Rubies, amethysts, opals, emeralds, and sapphires were also in use, usually combined with a blue composition in inlay. Stones used in these settings prior to the thirteenth century were polished but uncut,

COURTESY, ROYAL IRISH ACADEMY, DUBLIN

Figure 208. The Tara Brooch

for it was not until this period that the cut stone appears.

By-and-by the large single brooch inspired the fashion for two circular, square, or diamond-shaped ornaments either sewed firmly or riveted to the opposite edges of the mantle at the neck

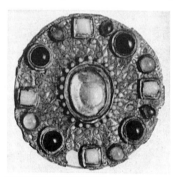

COURTESY, METROPOLITAN MUSEUM OF ART

Figure 209. Brooch, Gold with Wire Scrollwork and Stones Set *en Cabochon*, Anglo-Saxon, 4th to 10th Centuries

opening. These were very handsome, being made of bronze, gold, and silver embossed in elaborate pattern and set with jewels. Under these disk coverings were openings or rings through which the cords of the mantle were passed. By adjustment of the cords the mantle could be either brought up closely around the neck or made to fall loosely about the shoulders. These ornamental brooches were known as *agrafs* or *fermails;* and the word *tasseau,* from the Latin *tassa* meaning "clasp," was also applied to them. Figures 212, 213. At this period our present understanding of the word "tassel" did not exist. That which we today call "tassel" was at that period known as *houppe*. See page 538.

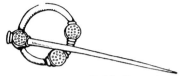

Figure 210. Celtic Brooch

The ends of the ring and the head of the pin are patterned after the arbutus berry.

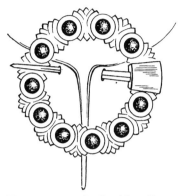

In England in the fourteenth century, circular brooches, those formed in the shape of letters, and others bearing well-chosen words or mottoes were worn by both men and women for fastening the tunic at the neck. Figure 214. Chaucer, in his *Canterbury Tales*, does not over-look the handsome brooches worn by

Figure 211. A Richly Ornamented Brooch Which Secured the Neck of the Tunic

From the effigy of Queen Berengaria, 1235.

two of his company. He describes the carpenter's wife as wearing a brooch "as broad as a buckler," and the prioress wears:

A *broche* of gold full shene,
On which was first ywritten a crowned *A*
And after, AMOR VINCIT OMNIA.

Figures 212, 213. Tasseaus

From Effigy of Lady Marmion and from Effigy of William of Hatfield, York Cathedral.

Figure 214. Brooches, 14th Century

Designed in the shape of letters; worn by both men and women.

In the fifteenth century the brooch came to be a fashionable ornament for the headgear, especially for the tall hat or low bonnet. In fact, no gentleman was considered fully attired unless a handsome brooch set off his hat. These brooches often had a pendant ornament, usually a rare pearl, which hung over the front edge of the hat resting on the forehead. During the late Middle Ages, when the great trade guilds sprang up, the work of the goldsmith brought the brooch to its highest point of perfection.

1500-1700

With the beginning of the Renaissance the love of ornament and the use of jewelry grew apace. Men and women alike 'decked themselves with gold and jewels. In fact, the human figure is said to have been literally smothered in ornament. In England, from the time of Edward III (1327-77) to Henry VIII (1509-47), sumptuary laws forbade the wearing of brooches of gold, silver, or gilt, by all persons under the degree of knight or knight's wife, and to all clergymen under that of bishop. Laws, however, were little respected and handsome ornament continued. The slashed sleeves and doublet of 1600 gave ample opportunity for the use of jeweled pins, and, consequently, little brooches were sewed upon the sleeves or pinned here and there upon the costumes of both men and women. Many portraits of the period show handsome jeweled brooches worn with the necklace popular during the century. Figure 215. Queen Elizabeth is said to have worn many brooches merely as a decoration.

COURTESY, THE PRADO, MADRID

Figure 215. Isabel, Empress of Portugal. . . . *Titian*

The Empress wears the large breast ornament or brooch, a distinctive feature in 16th-century costume.

One of the impressive ornaments in feminine dress during the first decade of the seventeenth century was the large brooch which held the handsome lace collar in place on the breast. Men, too, found the brooch indispensable. Following the fashion of the flat collar came the stock and lace jabot with which a handsome brooch was often worn. The fashion for hat brooches which had started in the fifteenth century continued unabated. In a letter written by James I to his son, the King sent word of a new brooch, a gift, and suggested how it should be worn:

> I send for your wearing the Three brethren [undoubtedly three stones] but newly set . . . which I wolde wish you to weare alone in your hat, with a Littel black feather.

It was also this particular fashion of wearing a brooch in the hat that called forth the much-quoted words of Ben Jonson:

Honor's a good *brooch* to wear in a man's hat at all times.

Saffron-gilt and leather brooches for hats are also mentioned. These, it seems, were worn about 1605 as ornaments on children's caps.

Toward the close of the seventeenth century the fashion for large quantities of jewelry in feminine dress gradually weakened, while it almost disappeared from men's dress. When compared with those of the previous century, portraits of famous beauties are remarkable for the lack of jewelry displayed. However, occasionally brooches were worn; though their design varied from time to time they continued to be built on the safety-pin and circular plan and were both useful and ornamental.

1700-1900

All through the eighteenth century fashionable attention was diverted from brooches and directed toward jeweled buttons, watches, and ornate snuff boxes. This is probably responsible for the decrease in the demand for jewelry. At any rate the period is notably modest in the use it made of the former gorgeous brooches, chains, and pendants.

Following the Revolution and the flair for the classical came a revival of the ancient cameo. So fashionable were these that Napoleon authorized eighty-two handsome antique cameos to be taken from the national collection and combined with 275 pearls to make a diadem, a necklace, a comb, earrings, and a bracelet for Josephine. Though magnificent, the weight of these ornaments made it impossible to wear them. The general demand for the antique stone cameo was so great at this time that it was impossible to supply the market. This circumstance brought forward the shell cameo, which was easier to cut, more speedily supplied, and less expensive. The beauty of the shell cameo made an immediate appeal, and, later during the course of the nineteenth century, it completely supplanted the stone cameo. For a time the taste was for large cameo brooches, and they had a tremendous vogue. After the middle of the century, coral took the fashionable lead, being used for brooches, earrings, and necklaces. Enamel was also in popular demand. Brooches were designed in the form of large bows, later to be enameled in various colors. During the "shawl period" large brooches were used to hold milady's handsome Cashmere or Paisley in place, while smaller ones appropriately served for securing the lace collar or fichu and for other light and dainty purposes. These brooches were made of gold and silver and when not set with precious stones were ornamented with glass of inferior color and cutting. At this time the demand for jewels was in the ascendancy, but the cost of genuine stones made the luxury prohibitive to the great mass of the people.

Toward the close of the nineteenth century the machine manufacture of jewelry came in. Then it was that the long bar pins of pressed gold, so familiar to many of this generation, became fashionable. Figure 217. Though designs were feeble and the brooches bore every mark of the machine made, they were widely worn for many years, chiefly because their cost was modest, within the reach of many. During this interesting nineteenth century, women apparently usurped the whole field of ornament. By this time men had been deprived of their earrings, their bracelets, jeweled collars, and brooches. They were modestly content with a ring, a tiepin, a watch fob, or chain. From this period forth, ornament lies distinctly in the field of feminine dress.

COURTESY, METROPOLITAN MUSEUM OF ART

Figure 216. Brooch, Goldsmith's Work

Italian, 18th century.

Twentieth Century

The twentieth century makes three outstanding contributions to the field of ornament: the revival of hand-wrought jewelry, the manufacture of "costume" jewelry, and the introduction of platinum jewelry.

Toward the close of the nineteenth century and well on into the opening years of the twentieth, the beauty and craftsmanship of hand-wrought ornament gained wide recognition. Rings, bracelets, necklaces, and brooches especially designed and made by the artist-craftsman were in great demand. In the rebirth of this artistic craft no effort was made to compete in mechanical perfection with factory-made pieces. The marks of craftsmanship were instead very apparent and tended to bring out the beauty of the metal, giving a character which machine-made objects do not even suggest. Silver and bronze have been the favored metals, and the stones for the most part have been semiprecious. Enamels have been effectively combined with silver and bronze, thereby adding a distinct color enrichment. The beauty and charm of this hand-wrought jewelry brought immediate response everywhere, and for something over a quarter of a century it has maintained its distinctive place.

The greatest novelty in the field of ornament of the twentieth century is the modern "costume" jewelry. The speed with which style follows style and the constant demand for ornament to meet these changes have, no doubt, hastened the manufacture and acceptance of this new departure in jewelry. About this time a new ornament, the "clip," made its appearance. This served the decorative purpose of the brooch but, in place of the pin, a small piece of metal was hinged behind the ornament, which, as the name suggests, *clipped* with a tight grip over the edge of material. The clip to some extent has succeeded the brooch in popularity and is one of the favored ornaments in the field of modern jewelry.

Today all gems have imitations! The defense of the sponsors of costume jewelry is that the contribution of ornament to dress lies in its beauty and effectiveness, not in its cost. With the choice ranging from daintily set synthetic stones to the heavier models in vegetable "ivory," simulating lapis lazuli and other opaque stones, with chains of every conceivable form of link and pattern, with rings, bracelets, buckles, brooches, and clips of every description—the merry market dances on!

Extremes in the use of ornament sometimes appear side by side with a more restrained use. Especially is this true in the wearing of rare or beautiful jewels and distinctly handsome ornament. In this particular field the modern world has made an unrivaled contribution to the ornament of all time and leaves as a heritage to the future jewelry which is among the most beautiful of the goldsmith's art. This is the platinum ornament of the twentieth cen-

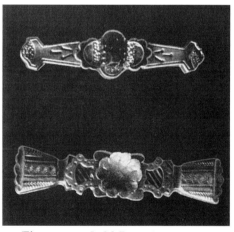

Figure 217. Gold Brooches, 1890

The machine-made brooch of the 90's.

tury. Though platinum had been known to scientists for over a century, its use in jewelry is a recent development. The world's supply of platinum comes largely from Russia, where less than fifty years ago the peasants were wearing this rare metal on the buttons of their clothes. Platinum is light gray in color, shading into a silvery white, and is of sufficient strength to permit the execution of delicate design. Strange to note, the name "white gold" was chosen for platinum in the earliest volume treating exclusively of this subject and published in Paris in 1758. This is of interest today because "white gold," a seventy-five percent alloy of gold with nickel and zinc, is in general use for present-day jewelry,

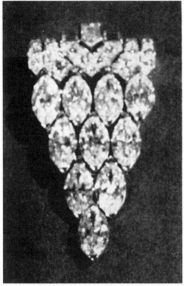

its reduced cost having made it a popular choice. In platinum's silvery white sheen, diamonds and other precious stones have a setting which greatly enhances their beauty. Platinum brooches, clips, bracelets, necklaces, watches, and rings are among the most beautiful creations of the modern designer and craftsman. Figure 218. (Also see pages 190, 319, 347, 383).

Tracing the story of pins and brooches from their beginnings down through succeeding periods—Greek, Roman, the transforming Middle Ages, the extravagant Renaissance, and on through succeeding centuries to our own day—one fact is apparent: however varied the design or excellent the workmanship, the ancient pins and fibulae never

COURTESY, TIFFANY & CO., NEW YORK

Figure 218a. Modern Platinum "Clip" Brooch Set with Marquise Diamonds

COURTESY, TIFFANY & CO., NEW YORK

Figure 218b. Pair of Modern Platinum-and-Diamond Clips

leave the fashion world but simply change their form, adapting themselves to the needs and tastes of each new period. In the sober, useful design of the common safety pin or in the ornamental brilliance of the diamond brooch, the ancient form still persists.

REFERENCES

Boehn, Max von, *Modes and Manners; Ornaments.*

Brereton, Lt. Col. F. S., *Clothing.* The Essentials of Life Series.

Burgess, F. W., *Antique Jewelry and Trinkets,* Chapter 6.

Child, Theodore, *Wimples and Crisping Pins.*

Cole, George S., *Dictionary of Dry Goods,* p. 289.

Davenport, Cyril, *Jewelry.*

Earle, Alice Morse, *Two Centuries of Costume in America.*

Ellsworth, Evelyn Peters, *Textile and Costume Design.*

Hiler, Hilaire, *From Nudity to Raiment, An Introduction to the Study of Costume.*

Kennard, Beulah, *Jewelry and Silverware.*

Lester, Katherine Morris, *Historic Costume,* pp. 48, 56, 79.

Norris, Herbert, *Costume and Fashion,* Vols. I, II.

New International Encyclopedia, Vol. 18.

Quennell, Marjorie and C. H. B., *Everyday Life in the New Stone, Bronze, and Early Iron Ages.*

Smith, J. Moyr, *Ancient Greek Female Costume.*

Wilkinson, Sir John Gardiner, *A Popular Account of the Ancient Egyptians.*

These references include reading on Beads and Necklaces, discussed in Chapter 15.

CHAPTER 15

Beads and Necklace

Ay, with these crystal *beads* heaven shall be bribed.

King John, Act II, sc. 1

BEADS are among the most ancient of ornaments. To primitive man almost anything with a hole through it served as a bead. Nuts, oak balls, shells, teeth, claws of beasts, and seeds of various kinds strung upon a grass blade or a thong suggest the earliest forms of either beads or necklace. Stones were frequently chipped into a suitable size for beads, and clay is known to have been molded by hand into bead shapes. Long before clothing appeared, the string of beads in an infinite variety of form and color was the cherished ornament for the neck and shoulders.

Figure 219. Torques from the Bronze Age

Then followed the working in metal; soon after that came the art of engraving and embossing, and then the making of delicate ornamental work known as filigree. Among the early examples of neck ornaments in metal is that ancient collar worn by the barbaric peoples of northern Europe. This collar, known as the *torque*, a word from the Latin *torquere*, meaning "to twist," fitted close to the neck. Figure 219. A wealth of such personal ornament has been recovered, all of which goes to show that these early peoples had discovered the simple elements of pattern and the added value which this gave to the material. Some were fashioned by lengths of bronze or gold rods laid together like cords and twisted; others were formed like rings and hooks linked together; of those preserved, many are plain or engraved in simple design and have bulbous terminations. These torques were frequently of great weight and represented the wealth of the wearer. Later, when taken as spoils from the

Celtic army by the conquering Romans, as they often were, they were given as rewards to the Roman soldiers.

Countless beautiful examples both of the art of the early worker in metal and the lapidary have been recovered. Excavations on the ancient sites of temple and tomb have furnished an amazing wealth of ornament. In all of these "finds" beads of every description are numerous. Figure 221.

Though the real age of beads began with the later discovery of glass, the Phoenicians of three thousand years ago are known to have manufactured glass beads in much the same way as they are made today. In this early period they were often used as barter in trading with various African peoples. The unusual interest and beauty of Egyptian necklaces are mute witnesses to the taste and lapidary skill of the ancient jeweler.

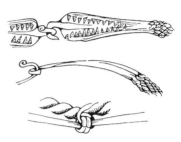

Figure 220. The Clasped Ends of Saxon Torques

Beads were used in abundance—drop beads, diamond-shaped beads, cylindrical beads, and flat disks of lapis lazuli, carnelian, amethyst, felspar,

COURTESY, METROPOLITAN MUSEUM OF ART

Figure 221. Glass Beads, Ptolemaic and Roman

and agate. Figures 222, 223, 224. These same stones used as pendant ornaments were cut and worn as amulets. Egyptian jewelry is largely allegoric and emblematic. The scarab, the sacred beetle; the *utchat*, or the sacred eye; the *uraeus*, the hood-headed snake; and representations of the human-headed hawk appear over and over again. Lotus flowers in enamel, pearls, and amethyst, and figures of birds, reptiles, and insects are used in great variety. These are of various sizes and shapes—spherical, drop, vase, and ring shapes—and are combined in effective design with colored stones. Among the conspicuous favorites of the Egyptian woman is the deep collar of strung beads. This is evidenced not only by the recovery of large numbers of these ornaments but also by the constant repetition of similar de-

signs on mummy cases and painted sculpture. Figure 225.

Colored beads and stones were not generally worn by the Greeks; conse-quently, their jewelry lacks the colorful note so

Figure 223. Black Beads with Blue, Granular Incrustation, Egyptian, Period Unknown

Figure 222. String of Beads and Amulets, Egyptian, VI-XIII Dynasty

charmingly characteristic of Egyptian jewelry. But the goldsmith of Greece excelled in the art of en-graving and embossing and in the making of filigree jewelry. The Greeks of the classical period (600-145 B.C.) wore beau-tiful examples of the goldsmith's art. Figure 226. In fact, it has been said that much of the dis-covered ancient jewelry displays more good taste and judgment than the usual manufactured jewelry of the twentieth century. Many of the Greek necklaces were made of plaited wire ter-minating in pendants of enamel or chased gold. Others are formed by linking various ornaments, such as disks and balls. The characteristic neck-lace of Greek design, however, is that showing a deep fringe made of fine chains and little vaselike drops. Interspersed among the chains are rosette forms in white, green, and blue enamel. Stones set in gold before the fourth century are rare. En-

Figure 224. Necklace, Drop Beads, Egyptian

For detail, see Figure 235, page 186.

gravers of gems came to be most efficient about that time and shortly thereafter the cameo appeared. No other cameos in the world equal in beauty the stone cameos of ancient Greece. For this reason those re-covered are preserved in museums and private collections.

The famous treasure found in the Island of Cyprus* and dating about

* Cesnola Collection, Cyriote Antiquities, Metropolitan Museum of Art, New York.

the fifth century or earlier again testifies to the widespread use of beads and the superior craftsmanship of the early centuries. Earrings, necklaces, bracelets, and rings were found in abundance. In many of these ornaments large quantities of beads, gold beads, agate beads, and beads of enameled gold were combined with drops of gold. The illustration, Figure 228, is that of a necklace made of gold beads of exquisite workmanship. The gold bottle as the center pendant can be opened and probably contained some delicate scent for the use of the Cyprian woman who wore it.

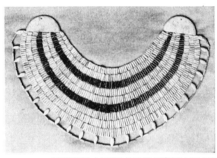

COURTESY, METROPOLITAN MUSEUM OF ART

Figure 225. Bead Collar, Egyptian

All jewelry worn by the Romans was more heavy, more magnificent, and of less grace than that of the Greeks. Diamonds, sapphires, garnets, and opals were the stones generally favored for the necklace. Although the Romans were

COURTESY, ART INSTITUTE OF CHICAGO

Figure 226. Greek Jewelry, 4th to 3d Century, B.C.

the first to use a setting similar to that of modern times, their work differed in that the upper edge of the bezel, or enclosing band, instead of being thinned was kept broad and heavy. Beads were popular, those of cylindrical form in amethyst, chrysoprase, and gold joined by carefully designed links of gold wire being among the choice ornaments for the neck. From early times pearls were a favorite gem. Strung as beads they fashioned the famous "ropes" of pearls with which Roman beauties enhanced their charms.

In 324 A.D., when the Emperor Constantine established his court at Constantinople, that city came to be the fashion center of the empire. The jewelry of this period was composite, a style showing both Greek and Roman characteristics and influenced by Eastern feeling. The goldsmiths of the East furnished the richest of ornaments for the head,

Figure 227. Greek Necklace Showing Beautiful Jeweled Ornament,
4th to 3d Century, B.C.

neck, and arms of the luxury-loving Romans. Necklaces and other ornaments were heavy plates of gold, inlaid with colored pastes, enameled in color, and encrusted with pearls. Stones were polished, set *en cabochon*, and the metal was elaborate with filigree tracery and granulations.

Figure 228. Section of a Necklace,
Gold Beads with Stone Drops, Cyprus,
about 5th Century

Middle Ages

The influence of massive chains and ornament of the Byzantine goldsmith is constantly reflected in the jewelry of the early Middle Ages. Glass beads and metal disks beautifully patterned with colored pastes in geometric design are constant reminders of Roman influence. By-and-by the enveloping couvrechef which covered the head and shoulders of women completely concealed any ornament that may have been worn. Necklaces or collars of some sort, however, must have been the prized possession of these women, for an old Anglian law empowered the mother to bequeath to her son land, slaves, and money; to her daughter necklaces, earrings, and bracelets. The ornaments most in evidence in these early days were the large brooches which fastened the tunic and mantle, and the massive belts and girdles. Earrings are seen in only one illustration, that of a servant. All medieval ornament is large, showing heavy carvings and a liberal use of stones and crystal, together with filigree and enamels. The Gallo-Roman women, the Frankish women, and the daughters of Charlemagne all wore these massive ornaments.

Among the early Anglo-Saxons, beads were used in great quantities. Figure 229. Many of these show designs painted in color, and others were shaped in variegated clay, made with great skill and often exhibiting pleasing patterns. Large beads of clay or stone were habitually worn as a pendant ornament, Figure 230, and stones set in gold and used as pendants are commonly found among Anglo-Saxon ornaments. Figure 231. Large beads of crystal, glass, garnet, amethyst, and amber were strung in graduated form and worn about the neck. At this time amber was especially prized. Its popularity is explained by the prevailing superstition that this substance was a protection from evil spirits. There have been found small lumps of amber merely perforated in order to be hung upon the person. The open tumuli of Britain reveal that both men and women invariably wore the string of beads about the neck. As one archaeologist remarks, "There were Saxon 'exquisites' who were vain enough of their personal appearance."

Figure 229. Anglo-Saxon Beads

Many show designs painted in color.

Over a long period the pendant ornaments and beads of clay,

Figure 230. Amethyst, Amber, and Clay Beads, Anglo-Saxon

stone, shell, and semiprecious stones, hand wrought, or imported from the East, sufficed to furnish the fashion needs of both men and women. Then came the manufactured glass bead. From the fourteenth century down to the present day the manufacture of glass beads has been carried on by the Venetians. It is believed that the industry was introduced into Italy from the East by the Italians themselves. From early times these manufactured beads have been a source of steady revenue to the city. As a fashion, however, the vogue for beads declined with the gradual rise of the artist craftsman, although occasionally through the centuries beads have been revived and worn for a limited period. In the late nineteenth and twentieth century, beads of coral, amber, and crystal were among the smart accessories in fashionable dress.

It was during the late Middle Ages that the work of the artist-craftsmen attained distinction. These were the people who combined with a high order of intelligence an unusual skill in craftsmanship. They developed into the great artisan groups and were the beginning of the famous trade guilds and fraternities of the Middle Ages. With this gradual advance in craftsmanship, beads became passé. They were no longer considered exquisite enough for milady of fashion, who now gave her attention to ornaments of gold. About 1300-99 chains began to appear about the necks of noblemen, and among the sepulchral effigies of women an occasional necklace is seen. Toward the close of the fifteenth century, heads and necks were gradually uncovered; hence a glimpse of the ornament of that day is now posterity's privilege. The

earliest form of necklace to be found in these early brasses and monumental effigies is the simple double chain. About 1390 sections made of enameled or jeweled plaques began to appear and were inserted at regular intervals in the chain. Such necklaces were called "carcanets." Of a somewhat later date are the handsome necklaces seen in the portrait of Marie, wife of Potinari, Margaret of Scotland (1487), and Joan of Navarre (1492). See pages 17, 123, 126. Perhaps the most remarkable specimen of an early necklace is that of Isabel Cheyne* (1482) who was the great-aunt of Queen Ann Boleyn. This necklace is formed of pendant jewels, making an exceedingly massive and handsome ornament.

Figure 231.
Simple Pendant
Ornament

Chains are also seen in the portraits of men of this period. Not only one but several were worn at the same time. Late in the century the elaborate jeweled collar which lay wide across the shoulders was a conspicuous feature in masculine dress and remained an important accessory throughout the sixteenth century. Figure 233. At the close of this interesting period the work of the artist-craftsman flourished. Remarkable originality developed in all branches of creative design and its application in every field.

Figure 232.
Later Anglo-Saxon Pendants
Goldwork and stones set in gold.

1500-1600

With the opening years of the Renaissance the love of ornament, and of the necklace in particular, grew apace. In fact, the Renaissance was outstanding in splendor. The display of metals, precious stones, and enamels, together with the extraordinary care given to design and craftsmanship, made this period one of superior attainment. Among the illustrious craftsmen working in metal and precious stones, the names of Albrecht Dürer, Hans Holbein, and Benvenuto Cellini are preëminent. Elaborate chains and collars of massive link continued to adorn the shoulders of gentle-

* Page 18, Monument in Blickling Church, Norfolk.

men. These were regarded as badges of rank. Scarcely a portrait of the period exists in which a gentleman is without his handsome collar. Figure 233. In the feminine world chains with jeweled settings and an elaborate display of pearls were the order of the day. The well-known portrait of Eleanor of Austria (after Mabuse) expresses well the popular taste for jeweled ornament and pearls. Figure 234. Other portraits* show the massive necklace with the heavy, jeweled pendant. The string of pearls with the large pendant brooch, as seen in the portrait of Isabella, Queen of Portugal (1503-36), was yet another form of neck ornament (see Figure 215, page 172).

During this great revival of the arts the pendant, a favored ornament of

COURTESY, DETROIT INSTITUTE OF ARTS

Figure 233. Sir Henry **Guilford**
....*Holbein*

The handsome collar, together with the low beret, is a distinct characteristic of early 16th-century dress.

antiquity, rose to new heights. One line from the Homeric poems indicates that the pendant was well known in ancient Greece:

Chains, bracelets, *pendants*,
all their toys I wrought.

COURTESY, METROPOLITAN MUSEUM OF ART

Figure 234. Eleanor of Austria....
Van Cleve, the Elder

The extravagant use of pearls and jeweled ornament in the costume of the early 15th century is well exemplified in this portrait of a royal lady.

Now both time and money were spent upon the pendant. In Italy and France, antique cameos were set in frames of gold and worn as pendants. Baroque pearls were a favorite gem and were usually hung from the pendant. The artists' creative abilities were taxed to the utmost in producing designs for this ever-popular ornament. Figure 239 shows a handsome French pendant of this period. It is made of wrought gold and gems; the figure is believed to represent Prudence. The carved sardonyx, set in a gold framework with jewels and pearls, dates from 1520. Figure 238. In the early years these were

* See Plates XXVIII, XXXII; Figures 245, 251, 254.

suspended from the jeweled collars so fashionable at this time. They were also a conspicuous and elegant detail of the chains which were

Figure 235. Pectoral from Necklace of Princess Sat-hathor-iunut

Gold, inlaid and engraved (3½ inches at base)
1849-1801 B.C.

passed twice about the neck, the first loop being brought close while the second, supporting the pendant, hung lower. During the last quarter of the century, when Henry of Valois (1574-89) adopted rings, earrings, and the necklace, gentlemen of fashion everywhere followed the King's lead and were wearing jewels and ornament of every description. Women, not to be outdone, loaded themselves with gold, pearls, and colored stones. Excess in decoration was the keynote of sixteenth century costume. These excesses were carried to such an extravagant degree that later fashion periods have looked back in amazement at the "barbarous taste" displayed. PLATE XXV.

1600-1800

During the following century the necklace of diamonds, pearls, and colored glass mounted as jewels was in great demand. History records that under Louis XIV (1643-1715) the abuse of the precious stone began. The goldsmith and enameler were overtaken and outstripped by the lapidary and mounter. Jewelry became a mass of diamonds or colored stones set in

Figure 236.
Renaissance
Pendant

After a design by Holbein.

Figure 237.
Initial-Letter
Pendant

After a design by Holbein.

gold. So crowded was the surface with stones that the setting was scarcely visible. In fact, the element of design as practiced in the previous century had just about disappeared. Gradually, however, the great display ended. Necklaces and other ornament were never again seen in such extravagance as they had been during this period. About 1680, Jaquin of Paris had completed a process for making imitation pearls. This created an enthusiasm for the gem, and imitation pearls were ac-

PHOTOGRAPH, KUNSTVERLAG WOLFRUM, VIENNA

PLATE XXV. Young Woman................*Lucas Cranach, the Younger*

In this early period, 1564, women in some localities are said to have worn at one time all the ornament they possessed. Note chains, rings, cuff bands, and the elaborate caul set with pearls.

cepted everywhere as the crowning achievement in ornament. In making the new pearl the beads were first blown from glass tubes; then they were lined with powdered fish scales and filled with wax. It is said that sixteen thousand fish were needed to furnish one pound of essence of pearl. Though pearls were first worn as a long necklace, later in the same cen-

Figure 238. Pendant with Sardonyx Carved with Portrait of Boni Sforza

Reverse shows arms of Sforza family, Italian, 1526.

Figure 239. Wrought Gold Pendant with Jewels

Figure symbolizes Truth or possibly Prudence; French, 16th century.

tury a single string closely encircling the neck and without a pendant was the fashion accepted by beauties of the day, whose rare personal charms made unnecessary the excessive use of ornament. PLATE XXVI.

Feminine costume of the early eighteenth century was incomplete without some simple ornament at the neck. For a while pearls continued to be highly favored, for then as now women believed that pearls enhanced their coloring and beauty. Everywhere these lustrous gems were in evidence. But as the century wore on the vogue for jeweled buttons, watches, and snuff boxes challenged the popularity of the necklace, and it gradually retreated to second place. At the end of the century, while the fires of the French Revolution were smoldering, all conspicuous ornament was laid aside and a simple ribbon was substituted for the necklace. Following this came the vogue for miniatures and pendants

PLATE XXVI. Marie de Rabutin, Marquise de Sevigne (1626-96)....*Chantel*

This portrait is a witness to the great change that had taken place in the choice of jewels. The former heavy and grandiose ornament was in the late 17th century supplanted by pearls.

suspended from ribbon. When, later, the Bastille was taken, fragments of its stones were polished, set in gold, and worn as pendants and brooches.

1800-1900

The grave, unsettled condition of affairs of state in both France and England during the final years of the eighteenth century and the opening years of the nineteenth had much to do with the waning popularity of ornament. By 1830 the necklace was seldom seen. Pearls and garnets occasionally were worn but only for formal occasions. The many

delightful portraits of English and American women of the early nineteenth century testify to the simplicity and charm in the dress of this this period. In many of these the necklace is conspicuously absent, the neckline being softened by lace, lawn, and tulle. However, toward the middle of the century jewelry gradually regained its lost favor. Many revivals of old fashions, and new designs as well, were pressed into service. At this time cameos were reborn. Every fashionable woman prided herself on possessing a beautiful shell-cameo pendant or brooch. Black velvet ribbon with a cameo, a gold locket or cross suspended was characteristic of these mid-century days. During the last quarter of the century gold chains, from a yard to a yard and a quarter in length and supporting a watch were the fav-

Figure 240. Renaissance Pendant

From a portrait.

ored ornament in dress. The "watch and chain" had completely displaced the chain and locket and was indeed a coveted possession. The chain supplied with a slide, usually cameo set, could easily be adjusted to the proper V-shape neckline. The suspended watch was then tucked in at the girdle or hidden in a diminutive pocket at the waistline.

During the nineteenth century the making of jewelry was carried on in factories, largely by machines, which were indeed marvels of construction. Beads, gems, semiprecious stones, and chains with a great variety of link have each contributed to the make-up of the modern manufactured necklace. Perhaps it was the reaction against the monotonous repetition in the designs of manufactured jewelry that brought forth a striking change in the last quarter of the century. This was the revival of hand-wrought jewelry. Again the work of the artist-craftsman was in demand. Silver and bronze with settings of semiprecious stones and enamels furnished a wealth of inspiration for creative design. Rings, brooches, bracelets, and necklaces bearing the mark of superior craftsmanship were the coveted ornaments of the new period. With the rise of hand-wrought jewelry came also the popular form of pendant named after the French beauty Louise de la Vallière. Lavalieres, the latest note in the pendant family, were made in choice designs set with both precious and semi-precious stones. They represent the successful achievement of the artist goldsmith, who aims to enhance the beauty of the stone by the setting instead of making it a mere background for the gem.

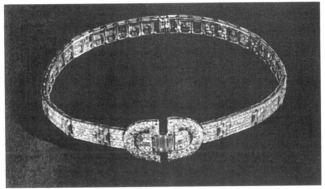

Figure 241. Platinum and Diamond Collar, Modern

Twentieth Century

Somewhat removed from the charm which "personally designed" and "hand-fashioned" jewelry holds for the discriminating woman is the recent innovation in the field of ornament—the popular costume jewelry. The fleeting fashions in dress and the rapidity with which change follows change, demanding an ever-ready supply of available ornament, has had much to do with the introduction of this new industry. In this field imitation stones and metals of every variety are employed. Though the imitation of stones has been practiced for centuries it is today a thriving industry. Synthetic stones made in the modern laboratory are in great demand. In fact, both semiprecious and imitation stones are used in the manufacture of costume jewelry. Milady of the twentieth century purchases for a modest sum a necklace, brooch, or pendant, which she wears as a finishing note to each of her many costumes. Moreover, women who are fortunate enough to possess rare jewels wear them only on formal occasions, preferring at other times the costume jewelry which so easily keeps pace with the fleeting changes in fashion. With the use of costume jewelry women, generally, have come to appreciate the fact that it is not the cost of a necklace or of other bits of jewelry that is of first importance but that its value lies in the contribution it makes to the color, line, and texture of the entire costume.

In a field quite apart from the popular costume jewelry are the handsome modern ornaments in platinum, which are among the most beautiful of the jeweler's art. Platinum, a metal of modern times, is both rare and costly, yet the most exclusive styles in ornament are confined largely to this medium. A rich, light gray in color and shading to a silvery white, it affords an admirable setting for diamonds and other gems, greatly enhancing their beauty. Necklaces, bracelets, brooches, clips, and other personal ornament in platinum represent the contribution of the modern world to the field of ornament conceded to be among the most beautiful of all time. Figure 241.

In some countries in our modern world the women, disregarding fashion, still cling to the traditional types of national ornament. The Hindu woman wears a great variety of beads and chains. Some fit snugly about the neck; others hang to the waist. Polish women wear many strands of coral and amber. The women of Rumania favor heavy strings of coin and glass. The Serbian women prefer many strands of beads.

Though the wearing of elaborate jewelry has become a thing of the past, the love of beautiful ornament is instinctive. In time to come this instinct may lead the designer still further into new, untried fields where creative skill may achieve still finer forms of personal ornament, undreamed of by our world.

CHAPTER 16

Collars and Cuffs

Two thirds of the greatest beauties about town will have cambric *collars* on their necks.

RICHARD STEELE, Tatler, No. 118

T HE collar and cuff of linen, lawn, lace, or similar material is of comparatively modern development. It is true that the ancient Egyptians and probably other Eastern peoples wore neckbands and collarlike ornaments of embroidered stuffs. These, however, show no particular development as did collars in the sixteenth century. The Romans wore chin cloths or mufflers known as *focalia* for protecting the neck and throat. These were adopted particularly by public speakers, who were solicitous for their own comfort and well-being, and were looked upon as rather effeminate additions to dress. Horace, in his *Satires* asks:

Will you lay aside those ensigns of your disease, your rollers,* your mantles, your *mufflers?†*

1500-1600

The collar and cuff began to appear about 1530, when little ruffles are seen at the edge of the neck or shirtband and about the wristband of sleeves. They were unpretentious little ruffles, often daintily embroidered, and were worn by both men and women of fashion. The exact type of ruffle is seen in several famous portraits by the German master, Hans Holbein. One of these, the portrait of Christina, Duchess of Milan, now hanging in the National Gallery, London, shows these same little ruffles embroidered in black at both the neck and wrists. PLATE XXVII. This fair lady was a widow at eighteen, and Holbein, court painter to Henry VIII, who was contemplating another alliance, was sent to paint her portrait. It is said that when informed of Henry's proposal she promptly declined, and, in the next breath, observed with a show of spirit that had she possessed *two heads* she might have looked with favor upon the suit!

An interesting contemporary reference to these early ruffles occurs in an inventory which appeared in the time of Henry VIII:

4 shirts with bands of silver and *ruffles* of the same, whereof one is perled with gold.

---

* Wrappings for the legs.

† Chin cloths, *focalia*.

193

Another records the ruffles on the sleeves:

One payer of sleeves, passed over the arms with gold and silver, quilted with black silk and *ruffled* at the hand with strawberry leaves and flowers of gold embroidered with black silk.

No doubt cuffs were originally formed by turning back the sleeves at the wrist. Figure 242. Early in this century, however, the word "cuff" was in use, for an inventory taken in the eighth year of the reign of Henry VIII (1509-47) states that three yards of "cloth of gold of damask" was allowed for "the edging, facing, and *cuffs* of a gown for the queen." An old play of the time of James I mentions cuffs as among the accessories of a fashionable woman's attire.

Figure 242.
Extended Cuff
From Cotton ms.

These unpretentious little ruffles which distinguished the neckline of costume in the early sixteenth century gradually grew in length and breadth until about 1540, when a new type of collar was evolved—the ruff. This distinguished accessory is said to have come into being first in Spain. Here a certain Spanish woman of position worried and wept because an ugly wen disfigured her throat. Intolerant of such a ban to her beauty she set about to hide it. She gathered a full ruffle of lace, fitted it close about the neck under the chin, and dried her tears. She had made the first ruff! Forthwith ruffs blossomed on every neck. They next appeared in Italy, from where they were carried by Catherine de' Medici into France. They reached England about the time of Queen Mary's marriage with Philip of Spain. The portraits of these two monarchs with their ruffs appeared upon the Great Seal of England. The whole world, in fact, was now wearing ruffs!

Ruffs had a comparatively long and interesting career. They were born, reached their zenith, and passed away in the course of a century. From the little ruffs which in the sixteenth century adorned the neckband of the shirt to the elaborate, starched, wired, and lace-trimmed ruff of Elizabeth's day, they present a fashion which was altogether charming. Here at their zenith they present a fashion that was indeed charming but, nevertheless, exasperating to the moralists of that day, who heaped tirades of abuse and scathing denunciation upon this modest offender. In his critical but characteristic vein, Phillip Stubbes, that energetic observer of the mode, has this to say:

They have great and monstrous *ruffs*, made either of cambrike, holland, lawne, or els of some other the finest cloth that can be got for money, yea, some more, very few lesse, so that they stande a full quarter of a yearde (and more) from their necks hanging over their shoulder points insteade of a vaile.

PLATE XXVII. Christina, Princess of Denmark

The Princess wears the little white ruffles which started the fashion of the elaborate ruffs and cuffs. Note ring, glove, fur-trimmed cloak, hood.

PLATE XXVIII. An Unknown Lady of the Spanish Court (1621)....
Pantzo de la Cruz

The rich details of the costume are remarkable. Note the rings on the thumb and index finger of the right hand, and on the fourth and little finger of the left hand.

196

PLATE XXIX. Isabella Clara Eugenia, Archduchess of Austria......*Pourbus II*

The magnificent ruff with its geometric-patterned lace and deep-pointed scallop represents the very height of the mode and is one of the most elaborate in the history of ruffs. Note lace handkerchief and use of jewelry.

197

John King, bishop of London, as late as 1611 was particularly hostile to ruffs. Said he in a vigorous attack:

Fashion has brought in deep *ruffs* and shallow *ruffs*, thick *ruffs* and thin *ruffs*, double *ruffs* and no *ruffs*. When the judge of the quick and dead shall appear he will not know those who hath so defaced the fashion he hath created.

The early ruffs were made of starched linen or Holland cambric. The material was plaited and arranged in flutes of one layer or more. Gradually the layers grew in number until there were as many as the neck would allow, and they usually extended to the shoulders. Ruffs grew all the way from the small ruff, as seen in the portrait of

COURTESY, METROPOLITAN MUSEUM OF ART

Figure 243. Elizabeth of Austria
....*Clouet*

The moderate ruff, lace edged, represents the earlier fashion. Note the elaborate ornamentation of the dress; pearls and jewels are used in profusion.

Elizabeth of Austria by Clouet, to the great "cartwheel" of the Infanta Isabella Clara Eugenia. Figure 243. PLATE XXIX. They were elaborate in drawn and cut work, and proved a stimulating influence to lacemaking, which from this period on developed as one of the great industrial arts. Cuffs were equally extravagant. They were frequently turned back but many times appeared with elaborate flutes matching the ruff. Figure 244.

THE PRADO, MADRID

Figure 244. Marie de Medici....*Frans Pourbus, the Younger*

The Queen wears an unusual ruff of very fine material edged with deep scallops instead of the usual lace. Note fine lace handkerchief and pearls.

These early ruffs of starched Holland linen were expensive, for the art of starching was not widely known, and ruffs were unsightly after having been once laundered. Urged by necessity, however, before long starch was generally introduced. Forthwith its influence spread throughout the fashion world. The magic material, in yellow, blue, purple, and white,

PLATE XXX. Volkera van Bereseijn..........................*Rembrandt*

This handsomely goffered ruff is an example of just what the "perfect ruff" should be. Note the precision of the flutes, and the care given the stiffly starched lace of the edge.

was introduced into England from Holland by a Madame van der Plasse. This incited the wrath of Stubbes, who dubbed it the "divell's liquid."

> The one arch or pillar whereby his [the devil's] Kingdom is underpropped, is a certaine kind of liquid matter, which they call *starch*, wherein the divèll hath willed them to washe and dive their ruffs well, whiche, beeying drie, will stande stiff and inflexible about their necks.

At the same time that starch appeared, setting sticks, strutts, and poking sticks for ironing were introduced. The setting sticks of bone or wood were used in arranging the starched material into pleats; strutts were wooden sticks placed between the pleats to hold them apart; the poking stick, a steel or iron rod heated, added the finishing touch by ironing or drying the starched lawn. When the process was completed, the collar came forth a perfectly fluted ruff, a thing of beauty.

Many are the famous portraits, of both men and women, picturing the reign of the ruff. These great pictures reveal the delicate whims in ruff fashion, ranging all the way from the modest close ruff, through the medium standing ruff, to the great ruff, known as the "divell's cart-wheel," which ruled about 1580. Catherine de' Medici, queen of Henry II, induced an Italian maker of ruffs and garooned (pleated) collars to come to France, where she gave him the sole right of selling such articles. This encouraged him to collect patterns especially suitable for trimming these ruffs, and he finally published the most complete set of designs known for all sorts of stitches, cut- and drawn work, and lace. The fastidious Henry, the most carefully groomed of all his court, is said to have worn a ruff made of fifteen widths of cambric, half a yard in depth. To insure the perfect fluting of his lace-edged, stiffly starched ruff he used, with his own royal hands, the poking sticks of steel—a deed which scandalized the court. The ruffs of Queen Elizabeth, which were among the finest in the world, were made of lawn and cambric enriched with gold and silver needlework, very fashionable at that time, and adorned with the richest of lace. The same extravagant ruffs were worn all over the fashionable world. In France, they were known as the "English monster," in England as the "French fashion." Men and women, alike, vied with one another in the depth and beauty of their ruffs.

The days of the ruff were gala days! It was brought to the height of its extravagance in France and England in the late sixteenth century, under the Medici and Elizabeth. In Holland the ruff took on the sturdy character of the people, and, though fine lace is frequently worn, many portraits of the period picture the untrimmed ruff of characteristic Holland linen. Invariably, with the ruff, cuffs of a similar material are pictured.

The first change in the elaborately pleated ruff came when women hesitated to continue to cover the line of the throat with encumbering

PLATE XXXI. Marie Louisa de Tassis . . . . *Van Dyck*

The handsome whisk edged with lace sets off with unmistakable charm the attractive head with its mass of dark hair and delightful expression of the eyes and mouth. The costume is superb in richness of materials and ornament.

material. Consequently, the ruff was opened in front, revealing the throat. There were many interesting changes in this style of ruff. The high, flaring, open style is a note of distinguishing elegance in many famous portraits. Anne of Denmark, queen of James I, is usually seen wearing this elaborate standing ruff. Figure 245. In the portrait of the charming Marie Louisa de Tassis the ruff begins to fall, and before long has changed into the flat collar of lawn, linen, or handsome lace. PLATES XXXI, XXXII.

COURTESY, H. CLIFFORD SMITH, VICTORIA AND ALBERT MUSEUM

Figure 245. Anne of Denmark....
Marc Gheeraerts

The Queen wears the handsome, standing ruff of the favorite reticello. Note the unusual use of pearls and other jewels.

These standing, open collars were both plain and lace trimmed, and, like ruffs, in order to maintain a correct position, were sometimes supported by an understructure known as "underpropper" or "supertasse." The testy Stubbes, writing of the devices used to make the ruff support itself, and having had his fling at starch, describes the "other piller":

The other piller is a certaine device made of wires, crested for the purpose; whipped over either with gold thread, silver, or silke, and this he calleth a *supportasse* or *underpropper;* this is to be applied round their neckes under the ruffe, upon the one side of the hande, to beare up the whole frame and bodie of the ruffe, from falling and hangying doune.

Later the wired collar was superseded for a time in France and Spain by small collars of crisp, white lawn, set in the high neckband of the doublet. This is the collar seen in the famous portrait of Philip IV of Spain by Velasquez. In England a somewhat similar collar, starched and either plain or lace trimmed, was known as the *picardil.* It was no doubt the succession of stiff lace points around the spreading collar that started the new name on its way, for the word evidently is derived from *picca,* meaning "spearhead" or "spike." Piccadilly, the famous London street, is said to have derived its name from the sale by one Higgins, a tailor, of these same small collars. Though "piccadill" usually refers

PLATE XXXII. Helena du Bois......................*Van Dyck*

The elaborate ruff, having passed through various forms, finally falls into the wide flat collar of handsome lace seen in the portraits of the late 17th century.

PLATE XXXIII. Paul Christian van Bereseijn..................*Rembrandt*

The "falling band" succeeded the ruff; it was often equally handsome in cutwork, drawn work, and lace, but always unstarched.

to the stiff diminutive collars, it must also have been applied to large collars as well, for Drayton says of one fair lady:

> In everything she must be monstrous;
> Her *pickadil* above her crown appears.

Gradually collars began to fall, and were referred to as "bands" and and "falling bands," "whisks" and "falling whisks."

A woman's neck-*whisk* is used both plain and laced, and is called of most a gorget or *falling whisk*, because it falleth about the shoulders.

Randle Holme

1600-1700

The final steps in the transition of the standing ruff to the falling band took place about 1635. It appears that many of the early falling bands were similar to the unstarched ruff, which though very full, lay in a soft mass about the neck. Plate XXXIII. Evelyn, describing a medal of Charles I struck in the year 1633, made the following observation: "The King wears a *falling band*, a new mode which has succeeded the cumbersome ruff." By this period lacemaking had made great strides and the beautiful Venetian point was being used for many falling bands. With the broad, falling

DRESDEN GALLERY

Figure 246. Charles I. . . .
Van Dyck

The King wears the falling collar of handsome lace. Note the fashionable earring.

collars of lace, turned-back cuffs of the same pattern completed the costume. Likewise, when collars were plain, cuffs were untrimmed. By-and-by the falling band flattened, and was transformed into the modern collar. Figure 246. Many of these were plain; others were of handsome lace. The plain band is that associated with the Cromwellian period in England and seen likewise in the famous portraits of Hollanders. The handsome lace collars of the Cavaliers are forever linked with the name of Charles. No more worthy record of the fashion of the falling band and the exquisite richness of the period exists than that left to the world in the magnificent portraits by Sir Anthony Van Dyck. Lords and ladies alike, in falling bands, standing whisks, and their ultimate development, the handsome lace collar, are delightful witnesses to this luxurious fashion.

1700-1800

Then came the monstrous periwig! Periwigs abolished collars. The great mass of false hair resting on the shoulders made the handsome collar unnecessary, and it finally gave way to the cravat and neck-cloth.

The bands of the Roundheads were now confined to the learned professions. They eventually became two shortened strips of lawn or cambric attached to a tape or band which passed around the neck, fastening at the back. These bands are especially familiar to Americans for they appear in the portraits of many of the New England clergy. Figure 247. Among these distinguished figures some wear the full short wig, while others still cling to the fashionable periwig. These bands when not in use were kept in boxes designated as "band boxes." Figure 248. It is from this period that the band box has descended to modern times.

During the debonair days of wigs and lace jabots, the cuffs were transformed into frills of beautiful lace, which finished the sleeves falling over the hand. Indeed, the hands

COURTESY, AMERICAN ANTIQUARIAN SOCIETY,
WORCESTER, MASSACHUSETTS

Figure 247. Cotton Mather. . . .
Pelham

This distinguished New England clergyman, author, and scholar, though possessing a Puritan conscience, is here pictured in an elegant, richly curled periwig. The "band" with its two tabs distinguished the clergy of that day.

were hidden to the tips of the fingers. "His hands must be covered with fine Brussels lace," is the direction given in *Monsieur a la Mode,* 1753. In the *Beau,* under date of 1755, appears these lines:

> Let the *ruffle* grace the hand,
> *Ruffle,* pride of Gallic land.

COURTESY, METROPOLITAN MUSEUM OF ART

Figure 248. The Indispensable
Band Box, Early 19th Century

These lovely frills were also attached to the short sleeves of women's gowns under the name of *ruffles.* In 1685 double ruffles had been the rage and in this subsequent century they grew into sweeping billows of lace and lawn. Collars had given away to the low bodice, and by the end of the century the dainty "Marie Antoinette" fichu draped the neck and shoulders of all fashionable women (see PLATE XIV, page 44).

1800-1900

Many years passed before men were willing to part with their wigs, their cravats, and lace jabots; consequently, collars remained out until the great period had run its course. As the wig changed into the bob wig, the Ramilie, and less ponderous affairs, the plain folded stocks appeared. Figure 250. These were followed in the opening quarter of the new century by the very high collar, usually attached to the shirt. The collar, standing high at each side of the face, was supported by a fashionable cravat which swathed the neck. Collars with or

Figure 249. Captain George Curwen, 1610–85

Captain Curwen wears the handsome lace cravat of the period; the fine lawn of the sleeves is edged with lace. Note the gold-mounted walking stick, also ring on right forefinger.

Defects are in the original.

Figure 250. The Reverend James Everett. . . . *Jarvis*

Note the high, folded stock.

without points showing continued to be worn under the stocks. Figure 251. The points sometimes turned down, were a forecast of the winged collars of the late sixties and seventies. Figure 252. By 1852 the fashion of the high collar began to wane and in its place came a narrow, stiff standing collar. The detachable collar and tie were now considered correct. Throughout the late Victorian period collars changed many times. There were the turned-down collars of the sixties, straight-standing and winged collars of the seventies, and the stiff-standing and turnovers of the eighties and nineties. Figures 254, 255, 256. Though the detachable collar varied from the narrow turnover to the deep turnover, from the straight-standing to the standing with turned corners, and from the soft to the starched, it soon established itself as an indispensable accessory in men's dress. Cuffs also were ordered detached to be adjusted only as milord saw fit.

Figure 251. Van Brugh Livingston
.... *Raeburn*

The high collar and the white cravat of the early 19th century are here pictured with the very high, rolling coat collar.

Figure 253.
Detached Collar
Worn in 1830

From an old print.

Figure 252. William Coleman....
Attributed to William Dunlap

The high, white collar with outward-turned points, the loosely tied, white cravat, and the goffered shirt, early 19th century.

With crinoline days (1852-70), collars were revived in woman's dress, and worn large, particularly where the line rounded in a deep curve at the back. At this period, according to August Challamel, "an immense crinoline and enormous collar constituted the principal part of a costume." With the early eighties the jersey and polonaise descended upon society and milady was buttoned up to the neck in a snug upper garment. This was invariably tipped with a standing collar of linen set inside the neckband and extending above it for the space of one-half inch or less. The cuffs were set up under the sleeve, permitting only the accredited edge to be displayed. Frequently narrow, turned-down collars and matching,

COURTESY, PENNSYLVANIA MUSEUM, MEMORIAL HALL, PHILADELPHIA

Figure 254. Stephen Foster, Composer of "My Old Kentucky Home" and "Old Black Joe," 1826–64

The turned-down collar and black cravat are characteristic of the 60's.

COURTESY, METROPOLITAN MUSEUM OF ART

Figure 255. Arthur Hoppock Hern
....Alphonse Jougers

The popular, "winged" collars with the fashionable cravat and jeweled scarf pin are seen in many portraits of the late 19th century.

turned-back cuffs gave the finishing accent to the costume.

By-and-by, at the very end of the century, the stiffened collar and cuffs rose to new heights in the pronounced fashion of the "shirtwaist period." Both standing and turn-over collars were now worn with the fashionable shirtwaist, and cuffs attached to the waist were heavily starched. For several years following the vogue of the shirtwaist stiffened collars continued to be worn by women. After a period, however, toward the end of the century their place gradually was taken by collars and jabots of lace, lawn, organdie, and other light, dainty materials. Many times these were an integral part of the blouse and were not looked upon as accessories. No doubt the twentieth-century demand for easy and comfortable clothes had much to do with the disappearance of the stiffened collar and cuff.

In men's dress, the collar and cuff of the nineties were carried over

PLATE XXXIV. The Art Jury . . . . *Wayman Adams*

An interested group depicted in the prevailing styles of collar and tie worn during the early years of the 20th century.

with slight modification to the twentieth century. As the years passed the collar gradually assumed a more comfortable form. The height was reduced, particularly in front, and the points of the turnover varied in length, in some instances becoming much longer than ever before. This tended to suggest height and at the same time allay discomfort. Collars and cuffs, both fully or only slightly starched, continued to be either attached or detachable. Though white was always in vogue, solid colors and stripes in delicate hue, matching the shirt, were equally popular choices. While the collar and cuff in men's dress has met with little change, in woman's world the constant

COURTESY, FOGG ART MUSEUM, HARVARD UNIVERSITY

Figure 256. Theodore Roosevelt. . . .
Joseph Rodefer de Camp

This portrait, ordered by the Harvard class of 1880 for Memorial Hall, pictures this great American in the typical dress of his day. The collar and tie are those worn during the late years of the 19th and early years of the 20th centuries.

Figure 257. Fashionable Collar
1910

variety is bewildering. The detachable collar and cuffs of beautiful materials—lace, silks, crepes, and lawn— offer an alluring array, and are worn by those who find them particularly becoming in color and line.

It is a long way from the unpretentious little ruffles which appeared at the neck and wrists in the late sixteenth century to the practical collar of modern times. However, the intervening centuries with their handsome ruffs, standing whisks, lace collars, jabots, and cravats are gentle reminders both of the richness and charm which once prevailed in fashions in neckware. It is impossible to separate fashion from life, and therefore it is not surprising that the great ruff made its first appearance during the early Renaissance when dress had become a matter of ornamental display and the sole object seemed the desire to attract by showiness. In the modern world, so practical by contrast, fashions again reflect the times. Men's collars and cuffs have taken a comfortable and practical form, while in women's dress these dainty accessories add

Figures 258-260. Collars of the Fashionable
Shirtwaist Period

much of the old-time charm without the accompanying extravagance. These will undoubtedly hold their place for a while, changing only in line and material as the new times and new fabrics make their demands.

REFERENCES

Blanc, Charles, *Art in Ornament and Dress.*
Calthrop, Dion Clayton, *English Costume*, Vols. III, IV.
Earle, Alice Morse, *Two Centuries of Costume in America*, Vols. I, II.
Hughes, Talbot, *Dress Design*, pp. 16, 278.
Kelly and Schwabe, *Historic Costume*, pp. 79.
Peterson's Magazine, May, June, September, November, 1863.
Rhead, G. W., *Chats on Costume.*
Sage, Elizabeth, *A Study of Costume*, pp. 25, 155.
Vogue, July 5, 1930.

CHAPTER 17

The Cravat and Tie

Virtue may flourish in an old *cravat*
But men and nature scorn the stocking hat.

OLIVER WENDELL HOLMES, *The Rhymed Lesson*

WHEN compared with the older accessories of dress—the earring, necklace, fans, and fur—the cravat or tie is a modern invention. The tie, as it is today, goes back in its line of ancestry approximately three hundred years. Previous to that time

Figure 261. Governor John Leverett, 1616–79

The "playne bands," which succeeded the falling ruff were in the late 17th century tied with cord and tassel. Following this collar came the cravat.

Figure 262. Chief Justice Samuel Sewall, 1652–1738

The first cravats were lengths of material placed about the neck, lapped, and drawn up under the chin, leaving the ends falling free.

our menfolk were well satisfied with themselves in their beautiful ruffs, handsome lace collars, wired-out whisks, and "playne bands"—all so conspicuous in the evolving fashions in men's dress. As stated in Chapter 16, it was only after the wig had been adopted that ruffs and collars quit the scene. The huge wig completely

213

covered the shoulders and concealed the handsome collar. Why conceal so handsome an accessory? Apparently both wigs and collars were impossible. Wigs were indispensable, consequently, collars had to go!

Figure 263.
Early Cravat

Figure 264.
The Steinkirk

Twisted ends drawn through ring. In other examples one end of the cravat is pulled through a buttonhole of the waistcoat.

1600-1700

With the passing of the handsome lace collar there came first the turned-down linen "bands" with strings or cords to tie under the chin. These were known as "bandstrings" and were ornamented with tassels of silk or tufts of ribbon which proved a rather flattering note at the throat. Figure 261. Then about 1660 came the cravat.

Originally the cravat was a wrap or scarf worn about the neck. The name "cravat" was derived from the French *cravates*, the term used with reference to the Croats who were in the French military service. A regiment of Croats visiting Paris in 1636 wore wraps of cloth about their necks as amulets or charms against sword cuts. This novelty in men's apparel captured the French fancy, and gave impetus to a new fashion in neckwear which was destined to capture the world. Soon Parisians were wearing this same scarf which they called *cravat*. Paris had no sooner set the style than it spread abroad. England first accepted the fashion and America followed.

These fashionable neck scarfs were strips of fine material carried about the neck, lapped, and then drawn up under the chin, leaving the ends hanging free. Figure 262. By-and-by the strip of cloth came to be caught and tied with a brisk bow of ribbon, suggesting the somewhat earlier bandstrings. The most fashionable cravats of this day were made of soft, white linen, lawn, mull, and lace; many were lace trimmed or embroidered. The love of fine laces which began with the fashion of the falling

Figure 265.
Madame la Duchesse de
Lude *en Steinkerke*

From an old engraving after Planché.

band had by no means relinquished its hold, and during the early years of the picturesque wig period the handsome lace cravats were notes of accepted elegance in dress. Figure 263. Toward the end of the century the cravat was lengthened, frequently reaching the extreme of two yards. The many famous portraits of this elegant period testify to the great popularity of the lace, and lace-trimmed, cravat (see Figure 111, page 96).

About 1684 a new type of cravat appeared. The victory at the battle of Steinkirk was responsible for this novelty. The French officers, so the story runs, were so taken by surprise that they had no time to prepare their elaborate toilets; so they hurriedly threw their cravats about their necks, gave them a twist or two to secure them, pulled the ends through a buttonhole and rushed forth to meet the English. Their victory immediately set the new style of tie, the *steinkirk*. Figure 264.

1700-1800

Many prints of the period show the new scarf with the long ends twisted several times and caught through a buttonhole at the waistline. Though black silk is said to have been favored for a few of the early steinkirks, fine white linen, lawn, mull, and lace soon took the lead. These fashionable neck scarfs were worn not only by men but also by women. The old French print of

COURTESY, ESSEX INSTITUTE

Figure 266. Governor Simon Bradstreet, 1603–97

The simple cravat of white lawn, mull, or cambric, loosely tied with long ends hanging free, had succeeded the handsome lace collars of the early part of the century and were now generally worn.

Madame la Duchesse de Lude, Figure 265, pictures the graceful drapery of the steinkirk in the costume of women. Not only lace but other materials and various colors were fashionable. An entry in the account book of Isabella, Duchess of Grafton, under date of 1708 reads, "To a green steinkirk, 1s, 6d."*

Side-by-side with the fashionable steinkirk, the early form of cravat continued to be worn. Figure 266. At times this cravat was so adjusted that the two falling ends were of uneven length. Some "fashionables"

---

* Mrs. Bury Palliser, *History of Lace.*

affecting the steinkirk caught the long end of the scarf through the buttonhole of the waistcoat. Though the steinkirk lasted only through the first quarter of the eighteenth century, the simple and effective cravat persisted for many years.

About 1720 this style of neckscarf gradually gave way to the soft, folded stock of cambric which buttoned or buckled behind. Figure 250, page 207.

Figure 267.
The Solitaire

This shows the black ribbon from the bag brought to the front and tied.

The *stock* with buckle made of plate
Has put the cravat out of date.

WHYTE'S *Poems*, 1742.

The open space above the waistcoat was now filled in with jabots and frills of lace and lawn. Wigs were in their heyday. The bag wig worn with the high cambric stock gave rise to an unusual fashion, which is said to have originated at the court of Louis XVI. A broad black ribbon called the *solitaire* was attached to the underside of the top of the bag. This was brought snugly around the white stock and then either pinned or tied in front. Figure 267. The black solitaire, the white stock, the frill of handsome lace with cuffs to match, together with the well-arranged wig, proclaimed the gentleman of that day.

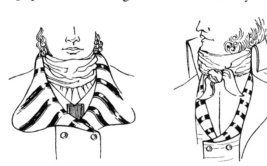

Figure 268. High Cravats of the Directoire, 1795–99

1800-1940

By the end of the century the French Revolution and the *Directoire* which followed brought in many exaggerated styles in general dress and the cravat did not escape. The fashionable "bloods" of the period adopted huge cravats which swathed the neck and muffled the chin. "The white muslin cravat is a big thing," writes a contemporary; "it is higher than ever, covering not only the chin but the mouth as well." Figure 268. This

French fashion was reflected in both English and American dress. Soon the fashion was set for two cravats, both to be worn at the same time! The first, invariably white, was wrapped twice about the neck, in imitation of the stock, and tied. Over this a black cravat of the same size was

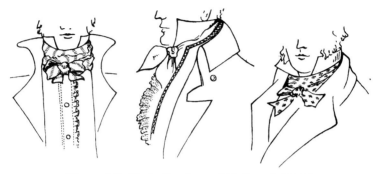

Figure 269. Early Stocks and Collars, 1800–12

placed, making the thickness of the neck equal to the width of the head and the chin seem buried in the cloth. These were the exaggerated cravats that Southey in his *Commonplace Book* describes as "pudding cravats," suggesting that they were invented by someone with a poulticed throat to conceal. In the combination of the black and white cravats the white edge of the under stock extended above the black folds of the second. Later, about 1809, the white cravat was removed and its place taken by a high collar which supplied the white edge above the black silk cravat. These collars were of linen, starched or unstarched, and their points stood high at each side of the face. The enveloping cravat often hid all but the upstanding points of the collar. This is the particular cravat which Charles Dickens, in *Dombey and Son*, so aptly describes:

Figure 270. Stocks l'Oriental and Sentimental, Worn in 1829

From an old print.

"Perhaps, Louise," said Mr. Dombey, slightly turning his head in his *cravat* as if it were a socket, "you would have preferred a fire."

The stocks or cravats of this period were either white or black tied with a front bow and usually seen with a frilled or goffered shirt. Figure 269. Dandies affected high collars with upstanding points and large cravats tied so loosely that their chins disappeared within them. To be in fashion, a man was supposed to change his cravat three times each day. A cravat was at this time any kind of a scarf not made up.

'Twould be as convenient to buy satires against women ready made, as it is to buy *cravats* ready tied.

WYCHERLEY, *Love in Wood*, III, 1

Figure 271. Samuel Jaudon
.... *Sully*

The high collar and the dark cravat filling the open front of the coat was one of the favored fashions during the early 19th century.

The part of the cravat that fitted the neck was usually wide and narrowed toward the ends. Many were the fashions in tying this important accessory! Indeed, the proper tying of a cravat came to be regarded as the enviable accomplishment of a gentleman!

The cravat in the early years of the century is always associated with the fashionable Beau Brummel, for it was he who grew famous for his many innovations in the tying of this important accessory. One characteristic account of the famous beau says that his collars were "always fixed to his shirts and so large that before being folded down they completely hid the face and head; the neckcloth was almost a foot in height, the collar was fastened down to its proper size and Brummel standing before the glass, by the gradual declension of his lower jaw, creased the cravat to reasonable dimensions."

All is unprofitable, flat,
And stale, without a
   smart *cravat*
Muslined enough to hold
   its starch—
That last keynote of
   Fashion's arch!

In 1828 a pamphlet was published in London which gave exact directions for tying the cravat in no less than thirty-two different ways. The importance of tying the cravat properly was given no end of attention. The starched muslin was difficult to manage, and naturally the correct tying was of considerable moment, for a second experiment with the same tie was impossible!

Figure 272. Fashionable Cravats, 1820, 1830, 1847

Two stocks which were the extreme of fashion about 1829 are pictured in Figure 270; one was known as the "stock sentimental" and the other as the "stock *l'oriental*," the latter receiving its name from the crescentlike ends of the tie.

About 1837 the points of the collar began to turn out and down. Black satin and serge cravats were favored, while white was *de rigueur* for evening and formal occasions. By 1840 various styles were being worn. While the flaring high collar with a black cravat tied in front was gen-

eral, some favored a simple neckcloth, often of heavy silk, filled in like a muffler over the shirt front. Figure 271. Others wore a gay-colored handkerchief, tied at the back and covering the whole expanse of shirt front. Another cravat of muffler form was the simple neckcloth

Figure 273. Cravats, 1850–60

Cravat with stiffened lining; narrow, stiff, standing collar, tied cravat; and stiff open collar, tied cravat.

of two pieces—one to swathe the neck; the other, after being placed about the neck, to fill in the open space above the waistcoat, completely hiding the shirt. Between 1846 and 1849 dapper young men wore a long neckcloth with the high collar. This was simply knotted in front, the long ends being left to fall free. About 1850 the soft scarf was superseded by a cravat with a stiffened inner lining. This was fastened at the back usually by a buckle and strap, and a flat bow of generous size was sewed on at the center front. Figure 273. A similar cravat in white satin was worn for dress occasions.

Gradually collars began to fall and the same type of cravat was now worn with the turned-down collar. Pictures of Lincoln and other Civil War heroes have made this mid-century collar and tie familiar. Figure 275. At the same time both a narrow, standing collar and a new type of tie appeared. The tie, of considerable width, was laid in length-

COURTESY, METROPOLITAN MUSEUM OF ART

Figure 274. Captain Henry Rice
....*Gilbert Stuart*

The flaring collar and white stock are made even more effective by the high, rolling collar of the dark coat.

wise folds, passed around the neck and, while still folded, tied in a bow in front. The new tie was also worn with the turned-down collar, the open space in front being filled with the generous black bow. By 1868 "winged" collars were on the horizon, and with the changing trends in collars, cravats were taking on new forms. In fact, the last quarter of the nineteenth century witnessed more new fancies than had been seen in any previous century. Bow ties, string ties, and the four-in-hand flourished. Figures 276-282. The four-in-hand of the early days was a shaped scarf and depended entirely upon the proper tying for its effect.

Figure 275. Abraham Lincoln....
Tyng

During the 60's, the lined cravat with generous bow was worn with the turned-down collar.

Figure 281. Though the general shape of the scarf varied from season to season, the various styles were all based upon the same principle in tying. During the seventies a popular scarf was one having two broad ends which were crossed in front and held together by a tie pin. This is an important scarf because it ushered in the Ascot puff which was an outstanding cravat of the late century. This popular scarf was tied so that the ends, typically square, were brought out horizontally at each side of the knot and then dropped diagonally across each other. The two ends were usually held in place by a jeweled scarf-

Figure 276. Ready-Made Bows

One adjusted by ring, hook, and elastic. The others simply hook behind collar wings.

pin. This scarf caught the popular fancy and immediately led to the outstanding innovation of the late century—the ready-made cravat. Instant popularity attended this new departure in neckware! Large and varied was the array of ready-made cravats. Though these were inspired by the earlier scarf, they were now given new names. There was the "puff" scarf, the "knot" scarf, the "flat" scarf, the "Ascot," the "Teck," the "de Joinville," and an innumerable variety of band-bow ties. Figures 276, 277, 278. Cravats and ties were now made of various materials and colors. Silks, satins, moires, and various novelty textures were in constant use. While the ready-made tie remained popular, long, bias scarfs, rolled and—while still rolled—passed around the collar and tied in a sailor knot, were also widely worn.

These were shown in repped silk, moire, and grenadine. Very light tints—pale blues, lavendars, and grays—were especially favored. To-

Figure 277. Ready-made Cravats of the 1890's

Enlarged views of the ready-made ties discussed on page 220. Reading from the left, the flat scarf, the Ascot puff, Teck scarf, de Joinville, a Teck scarf inspired by the four-in-hand, the knot very tightly drawn.

ward the end of the century the vogue for the ready-made cravats began to decline, and the four-in-hand forged ahead to first place. Figure 280. This scarf has held the field for years, and though other types are worn, it still continues in this mid-twentieth century to be the general fa-

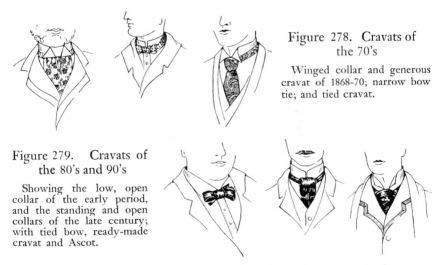

Figure 278. Cravats of the 70's

Winged collar and generous cravat of 1868-70; narrow bow tie; and tied cravat.

Figure 279. Cravats of the 80's and 90's

Showing the low, open collar of the early period, and the standing and open collars of the late century; with tied bow, ready-made cravat and Ascot.

vorite. Figures 282, 283. Its present-day form, however, is far more simple than when it was first introduced. This modern four-in-hand comes in all sorts of materials—silks, satins, crepes, brocades, crocheted silk—and in an unlimited number of colors and color combinations. In today's mode, it is particularly the tie that adds a distinctive note of color to the ofttimes somber dress of gentlemen.

The tie has never been a popular accessory in women's dress for any long period of time. It was an important note, however, during the late nineteenth century, when the shirtwaist flourished. Both the little bow

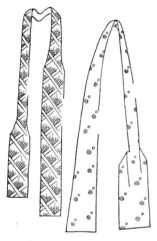

Figure 280. The Early Four-in-Hand Types

Note pleats in second tie.

Figure 281. Cravats of 1900

Low, open collar and winged collars with four-in-hand and bow.

tie and the four-in-hand were worn with the fashionable stiff collar. Later the collar and tie were gradually metamorphosed into various styles of more dainty neck accessories.

In the modern dress of children and young people the tie often is worn as a finish to the neckline. These ties are frequently of the same material as the dress or blouse, and are either cut as part of the pattern or sewed in place. This detail, though quite

Figure 282. Ties, 1930–36

This shows the informal bow tie, the white tie for formal occasions, and the four-in-hand.

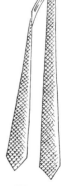

Figure 283. Modern Four-in-Hand

removed, is a late descendant of the old-time neckcloth or cravat.

The evolving of fashions may not always mean the evolving of comfort. Looking back over the history of the modern tie, one finds both rare comfort and charm in its early form—the simple looped cravat with flowing ends. Through the years ties have changed from one form to another—stock, jabot, "pudding cravats," bow ties, the ready-made cravat, and four-in-hand. Among them all, however, one only, both for its charm and its comfort, has been revived again and again—the simple and effective neckcloth, the first of ties! So artistic to modern eyes is this early form of cravat that repeatedly it appears as the distinctive note in the swagger sport clothes of the twentieth century.

Figure 284. Women's Ties of the
Shirtwaist Period

REFERENCES

Cole, George S., *Dictionary of Dry Goods*, p. 102.
Earle, Alice Morse, *Two Centuries of Costume in America*, Vol. I, p. 192.
Hughes, Talbot, *Dress design*, p. 346.
Lester, Katherine Morris, *Historic Costume*, pp. 127, 188.
Norris, Herbert, and Curtis, Oswald, *Costume and Fashion. The Nineteenth Century*, Vol. 6.
Peterson's Fashion Magazine, March and July, 1863.
Rhead, G. W., *Chats on Costume*, pp. 194, 201.
The Delineator, January, 1860, 1870, 1880.

CHAPTER 18

The Shawl

Matrons flung gloves,
Ladies and maids their *scarfs* and handkerchiefs,
Upon him as he passed . . .

Coriolanus. Act II, sc. 1

IN the language of Fashion the shawl belongs entirely to the nineteenth
century. It is true, however, that mantles resembling shawls have been
worn from earliest times. The nineteenth century shawl is merely an
adaptation of this ancient mantle. In earliest times the mantle was worn
chiefly as a protection, with perhaps little thought of its decorative possibilities. In the nineteenth century, however, when the fashion for shawls
was at its height, the decorative effect in color, design, and draping was
an important consideration; every woman took a personal pride in the
selection of her shawl. An English writer of the "shawl period" expounds
upon the unprecedented vogue for the shawl at this time and gives some
interesting sidelights on its use in other countries:

The passion for *shawls* among all women everywhere is remarkable. In
one country the *shawl* may flow from the head like a veil; in another it is
knotted around the loins like a sash; in yet another it is swathed around the
body like a petticoat. Wherever worn at all it is the pet article of dress.*

The same author then touches upon the distinguished ancestry of the
shawl, its design, its brilliant dyes, and its matchless weave:

From a time remote beyond computation the sheep of Cashmere have
been cherished on their hills, and the goats of Tibet on their plains, and the
camels of Tartary on their Steppes, to furnish material for the finest *shawls*.
From time immemorial the patterns which we know so well have been handed
down as a half-sacred tradition from a Hindu ancestry which puts even
Welsh pedigrees to shame. For thousands of years have the bright dyes which
are the despair of our science and art, been glittering in Indian looms. For
thousands of years have Eastern potentates made presents of *shawls* to distinguished strangers together with diamonds and pearls.

In Egypt during the Nineteenth and Twentieth Dynasties (1350-1090
B.C.), the long mantle was draped over both shoulders and fastened in
front; or, as was sometimes the custom, it was thrown over one shoulder,

* *Living Age,* October, 1852.

PLATE XXXV .... Diana of Gabii
   The mantle is here folded and about to be fastened on the
shoulder.

passed under the opposite arm, and then fastened. In Assyria both men and women wore the enveloping mantle edged with fringe. It was so draped that it crossed the chest and the back in a diagonal line, passing from the left shoulder where it was fastened under the right arm. Both men and women of Greece wore an outer garment as a protection against the cold. This was usually woolen, frequently referred to as *thick* and *great, purple, woolly,* or *red*. This same outer garment was spoken of as "double," which no doubt means "folded," resembling, in a sense, the modern fashion of the folded shawl. The well-known sculpture Diana of Gabii shows the goddess in the act of fastening the folded mantle. PLATE XXXV. During the long period of the Middle Ages the enveloping mantle was an important article in the wardrobe of both men and women. From time to time little changes appeared—a variation in the length, the width, or the manner of adjusting—but it still remained the mantle.

Just when the ancient mantle was transformed into the modern shawl of our western world cannot be definitely stated. The year 1770, near the close of the reign of Louis XV, is generally accepted as the date when the fashion for shawls "set in." The word "shawl" is of oriental origin, having been derived from the Persian and Hindu word *shāl*. Records of the shawl-weaving industry point to Bokhara as the most ancient seat of this exquisite craft. Here the fine, downy hair of the camel was spun into yarn. The yarn was dyed with vegetable dyes and then woven into strips of shawl pattern each about eight inches wide. The strips were then joined so artfully that the joinings were invisible. The shawls were carried out of the country by caravan. Russia, fifteen hundred miles away, was the usual destination. Here they were sold at princely prices to the Russian nobility. In the Russian market they brought sums equivalent to twelve thousand dollars each. Very few of the finest Bokhara shawls, however, ever reached Europe, and today they are extremely rare.

1800-1900

It was during the period when French and English armies were contending in Egypt (1798) that handsome oriental shawls began to appear in Europe. The cultivated tastes of the French and English stationed in Egypt were captivated by the rare beauty of the Egyptian, Persian, and Turkish shawls. As a gift to wife or sweetheart at home, nothing could compare with the shawl! There they were sent in large numbers; whereupon the vogue for the shawl made its initial bow to the fashion leaders of Europe. Soon the new trade interests brought these luxuries to the interested attention of importers, and within a short time Persian, Egyptian, and Turkish shawls, along with the rare Cashmeres from India, which were but little inferior to the Bokharas, were being carried into France.

It is suggested that the wives and daughters of ambassadors to India were responsible in large measure for introducing this product of the Kashmir looms to the beauty-loving French.

The earliest Cashmere shawls were made in the valley of Kashmir, in northwestern India. Kashmir lies in a cup of the Himalayas, a portion of whose snow-covered peaks enclose the little valley. Legend says that before the dawn of history, this fertile valley was a lake which a mighty king, wishing to give his people greater fields, caused to be drained and so made one of the "dream spots of the earth"—the "Vale of Kashmir." An altitude of from five thousand to eight thousand feet made warm clothing essential; hence the use of wool was developed. The excellence of the fine soft wools woven here was due to the unusual quality of the underfleece of the shawl goat which roamed the neighboring plateau of Tibet. The Tibetan goat produced a long, fine fleece called *pashm*, which seemed neither wool, silk, nor hair, but finer and softer than any similar product known. Each strand was approximately eighteen inches long, and in color white, yellow, or black. So much for the quality of material. Next one must understand that the beauty of design and color worked into these woolens were developed by the most expert weavers that Kashmir afforded. Generations of weavers—for the trade passed from father to son—furnished a tradition of deft fingers and sensitive feeling for design and color. Moreover, the weaving was under the direct patronage of the maharaja himself. For over two hundred years these leaders had jealously guarded the production of its wool and never allowed one ounce to leave India. For centuries these shawls had been produced for the courts of India alone. It is said that as far back as 1586, when the Sultan Akbar conquered Kashmir, there were approximately one thousand establishments employing forty thousand looms. Since one loom averaged five shawls a year, this would make an annual output of two hundred thousand shawls. And this, long before Dame Fashion demanded Cashmere for her market!

There were two main types of Cashmere shawls—those that were woven and those embroidered in imitation of weaving. The woven shawl was of far greater value. Rarely were these woven in one piece. As a rule they were woven in sections, sometimes the various pieces on different looms, and later sewn together with such expert exactness that the joinings could not be detected. In shape they were both square and oblong, one type being known as the "square shawl" and the other as the "long shawl." Figure 285. The finest shawls were about three and one-half yards long by one and one-half yards wide, sometimes woven the same on both sides, making them reversible. Many times these shawls were woven in pairs to be caught together and thus made reversible, which explains the term "twin" or "double shawl."

The embroidered Cashmere shawl was a supreme work of craftsman-ship. The shawl proper was first woven in a plain or one-color scheme—white, red, or green—and then the embroidered design was added. The surface of the shawl was first prepared for the design by being carefully smoothed with a polished agate. Next, the design was transferred to the surface by the rubbing of colored powder or charcoal through a pricked pattern. The pattern was then carried out by hand in silk, gold, and silver thread. The familiar stitches in embroidering used were the chain, darn, and stem stitches. The embroidered shawl was indeed beautiful but, compared to the woven shawl, it lacked in depth and play of color. This was due to the fact that the jewel-like design, though worked with finest wools and an expert needle, was an overlay and not an underweave. In some in-stances, however, irregular patches of the woven pieces, sometimes only a half inch in diameter, were set together in such a way as to suggest a pattern, and then a darning stitch was used to bring the pattern together. So expertly was this carried out that the effect was that of a woven fabric.

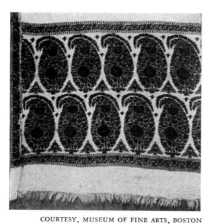

COURTESY, MUSEUM OF FINE ARTS, BOSTON

Figure 285. Cashmere, Border of a Long Shawl

The characteristic design of the Cashmere shawls as well as all Persian and Indian art is the "cone" pattern. Figure 286. This pattern was un-doubtedly inspired by the jeweled ornament worn in the turban of the Mogul emperors. This resembled a cone, usually set off with feathers. At one time this design was woven into a scarf for the great Emperor Baber. He was immensely pleased with it; forthwith the cone pattern was set for all time! Over and over again it appears. Of course, this constant repetition of the design—always, however, with some slight change in its form—naturally resulted in a wide variation of pattern.

The price of Cashmere shawls varied; their size, whether they were single or double, and the fineness of design were all considered. A pair of the finest type, which usually kept a dozen men employed for a year, was frequently valued at fifteen thousand dollars.

Though the changing years of the Consulate (1799-1804) and the First Empire (1804-14) brought shawls, scarfs, and kerchiefs into fashion, the rare Cashmere bided its time and came into recognition a few years later. During these early years scarfs and large handkerchiefs served as diminu-tive shawls. PLATE XXXVI. This was not, however, the first appearance

PLATE XXXVI. Lady Willoughby d'Eresby...............*Hoppner*

The filmy scarf in rhythmic swing with the washing waves adds a delicate, poetic charm to this early 19th-century figure. Note the shoes, the gloves, and the lack of jewels.

of the scarf. As far back as the age of Elizabeth scarfs were mentioned. They were at this time an important item in the wardrobe of every fashionable woman. The famous commentator of this period, Philip Stubbes, says of the fashion:

They must have their *scarfs* cast about their faces and fluttering in the wind, with tassels at every end, either of gold, silver, or silk, which they say they wear to keep them from sun-burning.

Evidently scarfs in one form or another continued popular well into the following century for *Post Boy*, published November 15, 1709, carried an advertisement to the effect that a "black silk furbelowed *scarf*" had disappeared. In another advertisement quoted by Malcolm, dated March, 1731, mention is made of a "long velvet *scarf* lined with shot silk of pink and blue." From 1795 to 1804 scarfs were in their heyday. Scarfs, in fact, have never been out of fashion unless it was when handsome shawls held center stage of the fashion world.

Figure 286. Silk-and-Wool Shawl, English, 19th Century

In America, the Quakers, who strictly adhered to simple lines in dress, found in the diminutive shawl an article of clothing that conformed to their strict demand for "plainness of apparel." It was quickly adopted and so generally worn that the little square of gray cashmere has come to be regarded as a distinguishing characteristic of Quaker dress. During the same period, women of fashion wore diminutive squares and scarfs draped gracefully about the shoulders or carried on the arm. The artistic draping of shawls and scarfs received so much consideration that women were instructed in the art of both draping and posing.

It was about the year 1820 that Cashmere shawls became not only the fashion but "the rage." These beautiful creations had come in with the first Napoleon; they gradually reached their zenith during his time, and then with the third Napoleon (1870) slowly passed from the fashion scene. This was the day when the finest gift to a bride-to-be was a piece of real lace or a Cashmere shawl. If the family purse would not permit of the shawl from India, a worthy substitute was found in the "French Cashmere" or the Paisley, both new adaptations of the shawl from India. As can easily be judged, during this entire period the Cashmere shawl was considered one of "the most splendid adornments of feminine dress."

Augustin Challamel, a French chronicler, pays his respects to the shawl in these words, "When an occasion arises in which very grand and imposing attire is required, a woman of fashion buys one of those splendid products of India." And again: "At solemn family gatherings a Cashmere is indispensable, it proclaims the wealth of the wearer."*

In the fashion centers of Europe, so insistent and continuous was the demand for the Cashmere shawl that soon France and Austria set up manufacturing plants to supply the market. In 1882 a pure strain of Cashmere goat was brought into France from Tibet by Guillaume Louis Ternaux, who first conceived the idea of naturalizing the Tibetan goat in France. Two hundred and fifty-six of these goats were scattered throughout southern France. It proved impossible, however, to acclimatize them, and the quality of their wool gradually deteriorated. In the end, dyed yarn had to be imported for the production of French Cashmeres. The French manufacturers did succeed, however, in making a shawl very similar in external appearance to the Cashmere. At Barèges, France, a light fabric of silk and wool was manufactured for shawls; these were known as *barège* shawls. These were very beautiful and highly prized by women of fashion.

At the same time that the manufactured shawl was being placed on the market in France, the manufacture of shawls resembling the Cashmere was begun in Paisley, Scotland. Paisley had been famous for centuries for its fine muslins, linens, silk, gauzes, threads, and dyes. Silk Street, Lawn Street, Gauze Street, Thread, and Needle Street all testify to the industries which made Paisley a thriving center of trade. Then, too, her weavers were experienced, able to cope with all the difficulties of the new industry. The manufacture of the Paisley was an attempt to produce in large quantity on a power loom the effects in color and pattern which in the Indian shawls were made by needle and hand weaving. To consider the Paisley as an imitation of the Cashmere is unfair to the beautiful shawl produced in Scotland. Throwing all comparisons aside, the Paisley shawls are in themselves works of art and are best considered not as imitations but as adaptations of the Cashmere to the demands and fashions of that day.

There were, naturally, some interesting differences between the handwoven Cashmere and the manufactured Paisley. Figure 287. The Cashmere was usually woven in strips later to be put together, while the Paisley was woven as a unit, field and border in one continuous piece. Cashmere shawls show many different colors, usually ranging from fourteen to sixteen in number, while the Paisley is made up of four or five in various interesting combinations. In the Cashmere hand-woven shawl there are always certain irregularities which lend an artistic charm to the

---

*Augustin Challamel, *History of Fashion in France*.

cloth; these are never seen in the manufactured shawl. As can be seen, the two shawls are distinctly different, yet one was the sole inspiration of the other.

Paisley shawls immediately attained an unrivaled popularity. The patterns so closely followed the intricate oriental designs that it required four months to draw the pattern and one week to weave the shawl on an English loom. An interested observer of that day tells how Queen Victoria and other women of fashion aided the manufacturer in his effort to match the beauty of the oriental patterns:

COURTESY, MUSEUM OF FINE ARTS, BOSTON

Figure 287. Detail of Paisley Shawl

> Some of our greatest ladies of all, even the Queen, and certain Duchesses and Countesses offer to our manufacturers a sight of their treasures from India — their Cashmeres and other *shawls* — from a patriotic desire for the improvement of our English pattern.[*]

The Paisley long shawl measured approximately eleven feet by five-and-a-half, the square shawl about five or six feet each way. Many of these showed the same pattern on each side, but with the color reversed, suggesting the Cashmere double shawl. The *broché*, a very popular type Paisley, was woven in strips of different colors, the alternate strips being patterned. The manufactured shawls sold in England for from one pound to ten pounds each, and in America they brought a still higher return. So great indeed was the demand for this shawl that the industry outdistanced all others that had been set up in France and Austria. It is said that in 1834 the yearly output was five million dollars worth of shawls. By 1850 the Cashmere or Paisley shawls were generally worn. "Imagine," says a recent writer, "a mid-Victorian garden party with one hundred or so of those gorgeous shawls, white, scarlet, turquoise, green, and orange, gracefully draped over crinoline skirts!"

Though the woven shawls made Paisley famous, the little town manufactured two other types of shawl which were both beautiful and fashionable. These were the printed shawl and the "tartan" or plaid. The printed shawls were light and thin when compared with the woven. They graded all the way from a medium weight barège to the lightest gossamer. The important note, however, lay not in the shawl proper but in the printed borders. These were carried out with the same painstaking care as the

[*] *Living Age*, October, 1852.

woven shawl. Many of these printed shawls showed a red or white ground on which was printed the Cashmere border, leaving the plain red or white center. Though these shawls were very showy and enjoyed a great popularity, they were less valuable than the woven Paisley.

The "tartan" or plaid is a third type of shawl made at Paisley. Though the Scottish Highlanders wore a kind of plaid shawl whose pattern has given the name "plaid" to all checkered designs, the "tartan" refers not only to checkered patterns but to all mixed or mottled colors woven in squares or lengths and used to cover the shoulders. The comparative value of these three Paisleys may be easily understood when one realizes that in the one week necessary to weave a Paisley, ten or twelve tartans could be produced, and twenty or thirty printed shawls.

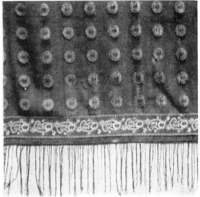

All through this period of shawl popularity Queen Victoria set the fashion by wearing delicate Persian and Cashmere designs, and embroidered antique squares. The finest collection of shawls in existence is said to be the gorgeous examples presented to the Queen by maharajahs of India.

COURTESY, METROPOLITAN MUSEUM OF ART

Figure 288. Shawl, Black Gauze with Colored Figures, French, Early 19th Century

As noted before, while the colorful Cashmeres and Paisleys were at the height of their popularity other shawls began to appear. The shoulders of the feminine figure of that day were draped with scarfs, boas, and shawls of silk, wool, and crepe. As usual milady of fashion indulged her taste for many, frequently choosing a particular type for each costume. Worn folded half or in triangular fashion they always imparted that air which was considered correct for that particular period.

So exclusively has the shawl been considered a part of feminine costume, that the imagination receives a decided jolt when it contemplates this comfortable garment as a part of masculine dress. However, in the early sixties, and probably as early as 1840, the shawl was worn as a fashionable accessory by prominent men of the day. Though the custom never reached the extreme it did in women's dress, it was no uncommon sight to see, especially in the fall of the year, a gentleman of influence with a folded shawl thrown across his shoulders. The choice of shawl naturally turned to dark, somber woolens. In the famous production *Abraham Lincoln*, by the English dramatist, John Drinkwater, Lincoln is pictured as visiting the army headquarters wearing the typical dress of his day— the silk hat and the folded woolen shawl thrown across his shoulders.

About 1870 the demand for large domestic shawls and those of oriental pattern began to wane. Now the demand was for newer types, and they forthwith appeared. Entire shawls of lace, some of Maltese bobbin lace, others of net with Brussels applique, and still others of black Chantilly lace, were the vogue. Black silk and crepe shawls, embroidered and carrying a deep fringe, were looked upon as very elegant accessories, as indeed they were. Never, since the period of the Cashmere and Paisley, has there been a decided vogue for the large shawl. The fashion belongs dictinctly to the nineteenth century.

Twentieth Century

Within recent years the Spanish shawl, embroidered and edged with a deep fringe met with great popularity. Curiously enough, however, these Spanish shawls are not Spanish at all. They are Chinese. The large, embroidered squares were completed in China and then sent to Spain where the deep fringe was added. This shawl was introduced a little more than 150 years ago. It is true that in centuries past the great galleons of Spain returning from Eastern ports brought back to their dark-skinned beauties at home many handsome Indian shawls. These, however, belong to another day. The modern shawl is known as the *manton de manilla*. In an earlier period Spain had taken steps to protect her silk industry by prohibiting importations of silk from China. To circumvent this law merchants succeeded in sending their embroidered squares to Manilla, a Spanish port, and then to Spain where the deep fringe was added; hence *manton de manilla*.

Though Spanish shawls are borrowed from the Orient, the graceful ways of wearing them is an expression of old Spain. In the characteristic Spanish fashion the shawl is carefully folded on the diagonal and placed over the bust, the double point falling exactly at the center of the lower edge of the skirt. The ends are crossed at the back and brought forward rather tightly—outlining the figure—carried over the shoulders, and pinned at each side. This, the usual arrangement, gives a very picturesque effect in dancing. When used as a wrap the shawl is folded in triangular fashion, the deep point falling at the back and one long end thrown carelessly over the left shoulder.

The vogue for the shawl as it flourished in Victorian days, has never returned. Instead, scarfs, boas, and mufflers, diminutive forms of the shawl, continue to come and go with the seasons. Though the scarf is usually associated with feminine dress, it has, under the guise of "muffler," also been a fashionable note in men's attire. The present-day muffler is a protecting scarf worn about the neck and inside the coat. Very different is it from the muffler of old which goes back to the days of ancient Rome. There, the chin cloth or muffler was worn by public speakers as a pro-

PLATE XXXVII. The Lady with the White Shawl....*Chase*
The handsome, white, wool shawl with decorative border and deep
fringe, popular in the 90's, is here worn by the artist's wife.

tection to the neck and throat. It was considered a very effeminate fashion. Of a much later period are the old drawings from the time of Henry VIII and James I showing both men and women with their mouths covered with mufflers. In Scotland, under James II, a sumptuary law ordered that no woman come to church with her face "muffled" under forfeiture of the muffler.

In the modern world wool, silk, and knitted mufflers have become the choice for winter months, while for formal occasions, gentlemen find the white silk muffler indispensable. As for the modern sport scarfs, the great array in shape, color, and material is unlimited. One season silk, crepe, and velvet hold sway; the next, gay knitted scarfs with bold stripes sound the sport note, to be followed, after a brief space, by dainty chiffons and georgettes. In fact, scarfs of every hue and material have added their note of color and accent to all costumes of the twentieth century.

Among various peoples the world over the shawl or the shawl-like mantle is still a favorite article of dress. From the blanket of the American Indian to the *sari* of the Hindu woman it continues to hold an important place in tribal and national dress. In the field of fashion, however, changes in size, material, and pattern have been swift and varied. It is a long way from the shawl-like mantles of the ancients to the diminutive scarfs of the present day. The interim, however, is happily filled with those brightest and most charming patches of color—the Cashmeres and Paisleys of yesterday!

REFERENCES

Cole, George S., *Dictionary of Dry Goods*, p. 313.
Dooley, William H., *Clothing and Style*.
Earle, Alice Morse, *Two Centuries of Costume in America*, Vol. I.
Fales, Jane, *Dressmaking*.
Hughes, Talbot, *Dress Design*, p. 272.
International Studio, February, March, 1924.
New International Encyclopedia, Vol. 20.
Peterson's Fashion Magazine, Volume of 1863.
Sage, Elizabeth, *A Study of Costume*, pp. 11, 201.

CHAPTER 19

The Girdle and Belt

And by hire *girdel* heng a purs of lether
Tasseled with grene and perled with latoun.
Chaucer, *Miller's Tale*, I, 64

THE modern waist belt or girdle comes straight down from antiquity. It is not surprising that man everywhere early discovered the great convenience of the girdle and immediately appropriated it to his use. Early peoples in all parts of the world have used the leathern thong to gird the waist. Egypt and the near Asiatics, as well as the Franks, Saxons, and Gauls of western Europe, commonly wore this useful and convenient accessory. Naturally it was merely the service of the girdle that led to its early adoption. Later, however, this utilitarian value was augmented by some element of beauty, which greatly enhanced its attractiveness. With the development of civilization the girdle came more and more to be an ornamental as well as useful detail of dress. Indeed, so highly did the beauty of

Figure 289. Egyptian Figures Showing Adjustment of Girdle

After Wilkinson.

the girdle come to be regarded that it soon challenged the genius of both artist and goldsmith. During the Middle Ages designers and workers in metal were lavishing the best of their talent and skill upon it, producing belts and girdles of rare pattern and superior craftsmanship.

In ancient Egypt both men and women wore straight-hanging tunics, usually without a girdle. During the later dynasties, however, the girdle came more and more into use. The long, loose robe of the woman of the higher orders was confined by a girdle or sash of colored ribbon. Figure 289. Though in Egyptian paintings the figures are represented in side view, their sashes are understood to have been tied in front. In the king's dress one of the badges of royalty was the handsome apron which hung from the front of the girdle. This was richly ornamented with gold, opaque polychrome glass, and colored leathers arranged in pattern. Figure 290. One of the rare treasures found upon the mummy of King Tutankhamen, when the royal tomb was opened in 1923, was the handsome ceremonial apron. This was composed of several gold plates graduated in size, each inlaid with opaque polychrome glass. The plates were held together by a border of threaded beads. This apron was, no doubt,

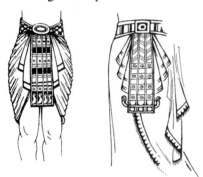

Figure 290. The Girdle and Apron of an Egyptian King

suspended from a handsome golden girdle which encircled the waist. Three very beautiful girdles were found within the tomb. One, from which the apron was probably suspended, was of fine chased gold; a second was also of chased gold and under this was tucked a dagger; and a third was formed of cylindrical and disk-shaped beads in gold and faience. This again testifies to the enormous number of beads used by the Egyptian jeweler. Girded garments were usually worn at religious celebrations by the priests and those women who took part in the processionals. The mourning habits of the ancient Egyptians were quite the opposite of the later Greeks and Romans. Instead of discarding the girdle and allowing their tunics to trail in the dust, the Egyptians girded their garments.

Though the Greek chiton, when pictured as worn by men not in action and of great dignity, is usually ungirded, numerous references indicate that the tunic was always girded for action. Nestor, as he lay in camp outside Troy, kept at his side his "belt" with which to gird himself for battle. On the third day of battle, Agamemnon shouts to his men to "gird" themselves for the fray. Among the women of Greece the girdle was an indispensable accessory. It was known as the "zone" and corresponds to the belt worn by men. These girdles were frequently of leather, and since they are often described as "gleaming" it is very probable that they were ornamented with thin plates of metal. The girdles of Calypso and Circe were adorned with gold; that of Hera had a fringe or tassels of gold wire. These were probably exceptional, the ordinary girdles being made of leather, cord, and common metal.

The various ways of adjusting the girdle had much to do with the beauty of the Greek dress. Often the chiton was confined by a girdle just below the bosom. Figure 292. A person so girded was said to be "tucked up high." Homer and other Greek poets frequently speak of

Greek women so girded; also the phrases "deep girded," "gracefully girded," and the term "beautiful girdles" are often used. In many instances the girdle was of unusual length serving both as a shoulder strap and girdle. This is apparently the type of girdle seen in the Themis of Rhamnous. PLATE XXXVIII. When so used the long loop of the girdle was let down at the back to the waistline. The ends falling to the front of the shoulders were passed under the arms and through this back loop. They were then slightly tightened, brought to the front or side, and tied. Another arrangement shows the long girdle crossed over the bosom before being passed through the loop at the back. This gives a very pleasing effect. Perhaps the most familiar type of girded chiton is that seen in the Caryatids of

Figure 291. Girdle of Courie Shells

Beads of carnelian, gold, and green felspar. Belonged to Princess Sat-Hathor-Iunut, XII Dynasty, 2000-1788 B.C.

the Erectheum at Athens. In these figures the material of the chiton is pulled up, falls over, and completely hides the girdle. Figure 293. When the chiton was unusually long it was not uncommon for Greek women to wear two girdles—one high and the other low about the hips. The material of the chiton between the two girdles was given a nicely puckered arrangement, or it was drawn up, shortening the length of the tunic. In this fashion it fell over the lower girdle, completely hiding it from view. The double-girded chiton was worn by women active in the games and the chase. Diana,

COURTESY, MUSEUM OF FINE ARTS, BOSTON

Figure 292. Draped Torso with Girded Drapery, Hellenistic Marble

the huntress, is frequently represented in the double-girded chiton. Figure 294. Girdles varied in width. Those found on some figures, according to Winckelmann, are as "broad as a horse girth," and some of these seem to be embroidered.

Strange to relate, the girdle also played an important role in the mourning customs of the Greeks. When suffering from great affliction both men and women are represented in trailing garments and without girdles. The

PLATE XXXVIII. Themis of Rhamnous

This unusual adjustment of the girdle gives the effect of a strap or cord over the shoulders.

Trojan women, with loosened garments, mourned the death of Hector. The sad Andromache, with other women, their garments ungirded and trailing, received the body of her husband. This custom was also observed among the Romans. When the body of the great Augustus was consigned to the tomb, it was accompanied by Roman knights with ungirded garments.

The women of Rome regarded the belt and girdle as very necessary articles of dress. The Roman girdles were made of various materials and usually signified the wealth and position of the wearer. The imperial girdle of the Roman Empire was woven of silk and gold, having an inscription on the narrow border, and fastened by a heavy gilt buckle. In the fourth century when the capital of the Roman Empire was moved to Constantinople, Byzantium became the dictator of the world's fashions. Byzantine richness was expressed in every phase of costume. The artisans of Greece and Rome flocked to Constantinople, and in this rich and fashionable capital found a ready market for their handsome, elaborate chains, brooches, rings, belts, and girdles. The belts worn by men were usually either of leather, ornamented with disks or bosses of gold and jewels, or they were made of plaques of gold, each elaborately chased and set with stones. These plaques were then hinged together, forming a girdle of unusual flexibility. After the fashions of the Byzantine world had spread to Rome, they invaded western Europe, particularly that section which we now know as France—the same France which inspires the stylists of the modern world! Here the Merovingians, Carlovingians, and Captains were gradually developing into the French of feudal times. Both men and women of this section of Europe naturally looked to the influential Roman families

PHOTOGRAPH, W. F. MANSELL, LONDON

Figure 293. Caryatid from the Southwest Porch of the Erectheum, Athens

This famous sculpture pictures the typical Greek dress. The chiton is here girded and the upper part, drawn up, falls over and completely hides the girdle.

for their fashions in dress. The many brasses and sepulchral effigies of this period, which are a rich legacy to the modern world, furnish an authentic record of the beauty and costliness of the girdle. The French women of this time wore girdles of gold and other precious materials which held the tunic in place at the waistline just above the hips. Charlemagne assisted in making the girdle more popular among men by wearing a jeweled belt at the waistline from which hung the state sword.

Late Middle Ages

By the eleventh and twelfth centuries the influence of the Crusades began to be seen in dress. The outstanding figure of the late Middle Ages is the knight in armor. What a contrast to the draped and mantled figure of Roman times! In marked change from the loose flowing tunics and

Figure 294. The Double-girded Chiton

After Hope.

mantles of the Romans was the highly-polished armor of the knight, which clearly defined the figure. This gave a new inspiration to costume. Though the flowing garment, belted and girded, lingered, by the twelfth century the "fitted garment" was on its way. The twelfth century is remarkable for the many new and surprising changes in dress. At this time the chin strap, the wimple, and the gorget appeared; in men's dress the beard was introduced; and gloves appeared as a part of fashionable dress. The fitted bodice, defining the figure and molding the hips, was now the accepted order. The skirt was full, falling from the fitted upper section in numerous folds about the feet. A handsome girdle added the distinctive note to the costume. Many of these girdles were long, twisted strands of silk, woolen, or golden cord, held together at frequent intervals by jeweled ornaments, and usually ending in a handsome silk or golden tassel falling to the hemline. Figure 296. Others were strips of material elaborately embroidered and invariably terminating in tasseled ends. Soon these ladies of the twelfth century were encircling both the waist and the hips with this important detail of dress. The girdle was now placed high about the waist, crossed at the back, brought forward low about the hips, and tied or clasped in front.

In men's fashions the belt was an equally important accessory. The effigy of King John of England, in Worcester Cathedral, is the earliest monumental effigy of an English sovereign. In this he wears a crimson tunic embroidered in gold, and a golden girdle, richly jeweled, one end of which falls below the knee. Later, men of fashion adopted belts of leather, the main purpose of which seemed to be to carry a pouch or purse, and a dagger. Figure 300. This was another influence which had come in with the Crusaders. The pouch, bag, or purse fastened to the belt was supposed to carry coins and alms for the poor. It was the custom for wealthy men and women to distribute money and other gifts to the

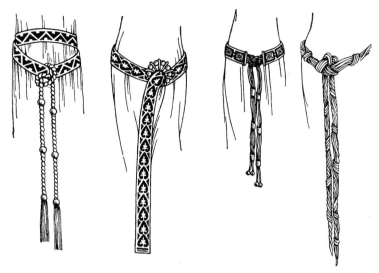

Figure 295. Girdles Showing Byzantine Influence,
12th and 13th Centuries

needy, and the purse came to be a popular companion to the belt and girdle. These little purses were originally called "*amônières sarrasinoises*, meaning "Saracen almsbags," but they now carried other things than coins for the poor. So popular were these little bags that they were worn by both men and women

Figure 296.
Girdle, 1100

From a tapestry.

Figure 297. Belt, 1321

Belonged to Humphrey de Bohun, Earl of Hereford.

Figure 298. Belt,
1400

throughout the period of the late Middle Ages. In addition, the dagger was looked upon as a very important detail in the dress of men, and later gave way to the custom of wearing the sword at the hip. Each of these accessories, the belt, the dagger, and the sword guard was a chef-d'æuvre of the goldsmith's art. Later, in the fourteenth century, one's favorite book was often attached to the girdle, and many early drawings show also the pen and inkhorn carried at the belt. Still later a bunch of keys at the girdle was no uncommon sight. So general was this custom during

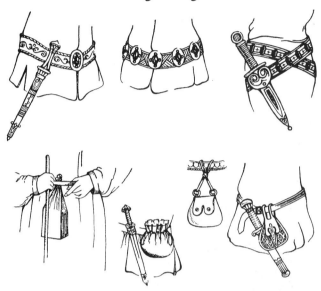

Figure 299. Belts, 1300
With pouches, dagger, and book.

**Figure 300. Fig-
ure with Fitted
Cotehardie and
Elaborate Hip
Belt**

After Viollet-le-Duc.

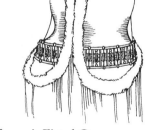

Figure 301. Woman's Fitted Garment
With open armscye displaying massive, jeweled hip belt.

After Viollet-le-Duc.

the Middle Ages that every portrayal of Shylock upon the modern stage pictures him wearing a bunch of keys at the girdle.

. . . wear nothing but high shoes, and bunches of keys at their *girdles*.
Henry IV. Act I, sc. 2

By the fourteenth century men had adopted long hose and the fitted tunic—the *cotehardie*, which extended below the waist. Now both men and women were wearing the fitted garment. With this new fashion the dominant note is the massive girdle set low about the hips. Figures 300, 301. The hip belt was a most important accessory, composed entirely of goldsmith's work. It was made up of a series of large gold or bronze squares, oblongs, or circular disks hinged together. The disks were ornamented by engraving, repoussé, or filigree used with stones or enamel. Often the relief work upon them was so high that it extended two inches

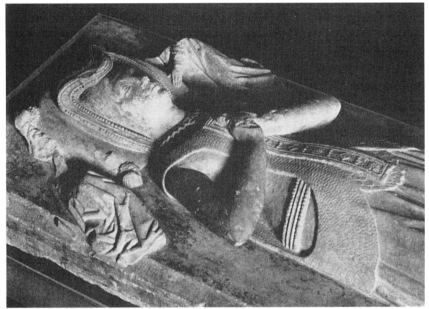

Figure 302. Detail from Tomb of Countess de Vipart de Lunay, 15th Century

The monumental effigies of the Middle Ages are authentic records of costume. The fashionable surcoat with open armscye displaying the girdle is here delineated with accuracy.

above the surface. When not hinged the handsome disks were frequently sewn to a band of ribbon or velvet which gave the girdle the necessary flexibility. The extravagant richness displayed in the girdle again set the moralist to work. Prophecies rang out on every side: "Those who wear these *girdles* shall the lions and dragons of hell one day destroy." While the nobles and other modish young men continued to wear these luxurious belts, those who followed the fashion at a little distance adopted belts of leather with the inevitable purse or dagger attached. Women continued to wear the fitted gown with the elegant girdle about the hips. Soon the sleeveless supertunic, the *surcoat*, was introduced to be adjusted over the gown proper. The armscye of this modish new garment was so large that the front and back were reduced to a few inches. With the large openings at the sides the handsome girdle was much in evidence and, as was intended, imparted a note of great elegance to the dress of the period. Figures 301, 302.

1500-1600

The distinguishing feature in women's costume of the new century was the deep-pointed bodice, to which the open skirt was attached. This was worn over a handsome underskirt which harmonized in color and

texture with the overdress. At this time the elaborate girdle worn about the waist grew narrower though none the less handsome. Figure 304. It was caught at the center front, and from this point a long chain, known as the *troussoire*, from which a silk purse, jeweled ornament, or rosary was suspended, fell to the hem. Other pretty trifles such as scent boxes, a fan, keys, or a seal, were also hung from the chain. It is recorded that toying with these gewgaws "during a delicate conversation gave confidence to the wearer." Eleanor of Castile added to these a small mirror, and

Figure 303. Fashionable Girdles, 1300, 1400

immediately a new fashion was set! Mirrors were framed in ivory with carved handles or set in frames of wrought gold. Later, they were occasionally inserted at the back of the feathered fan. Thus milady might by happy chance catch a vision of her loveliness while toying with her fan.

1600-1800

Men's clothes had also changed with the century. The doublet took the place of the tight cotehardie, and the belt crept from the hip up to

Figure 304. Fashionable Girdles, 1500

the waistline. Belts and girdles continued to be worn, but the padded hips of men and the looped dresses of women tended to lessen their popularity. From 1660 to 1670 men wore colorful sashes loosely knotted about the waist. Women, too, attempted narrow sashes. From this period on, for something over a hundred years, the girdle had no conspicuous place in the costume of either men or women. The fitted bodice and paniers of the ladies were quite sufficient unto themselves; the long coats and waistcoats of the gentlemen had no need of a girdle. In 1792 when rumblings of the Revolution were heard in France, little ornament was worn, though ribbon sashes often added a note of color to the waistline of women.

1800-1900

During the nineteenth century the belt and girdle scarcely functioned. This was the period of the hooped skirt and trussed-up overdress, and other excrescences that so cluttered up the feminine silhouette that belt

Figure 305. Women's Belts of the 90's

and girdle had no place. In the nineties, however, with the coming of the shirtwaist period, belts and girdles were revived. Figure 305. The belt of the skirt was now cut with a downward swing in front, known as the *dip;* and the girdle followed the same line. Belts were of various colored leathers, with buckles in enamel and colored stones. As if to revive the old styles, metal belts and girdles made of filigree disks hinged together were popular. Figure 306. Belts, girdles, and sashes made of velvet, silk, and various widths of assorted ribbons were a fashionable addition to the smart toilet. The shirtwaist period is synonymous with the athletic period of the late nineteenth century. The sport world at this time had opened new fields of activity to men and women, and the belt came to be a definite feature in both masculine and feminine dress.

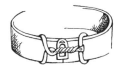

Figure 306. Metal Belts, Early 90's

Figure 307. Man's Modern Belt

Men adopted leather belts with nickle buckles in lieu of suspenders, and from that day to this, the leather belt has held a place in men's dress. It is particularly favored during the warm summer months, when modern man disdains the added warmth of a coat. Figure 307. With many men, however, the leather belt has, in this twentieth century, gradually become a year-round favorite, worn in all seasons.

The old adage "There's nothing new under the sun," may well apply to belts and girdles. Though in this twentieth century these accessories are again in full usage it appears that revolutionary ideas in the fashioning of belts and girdles have been exhausted, and that nothing remains but to adopt materials appropriate for belts to the various types of costume as they appear.

REFERENCES

Blanc, Charles, *Art in Ornament and Dress.*
Carter, Howard, *The Tomb of Tut-ankh-Amen.*
Lester, Katherine Morris, *Historic Costume.*
Norris, Herbert, *Costume and Fashion*, Vol. I.
Planché, J. R., *Cyclopedia of Costume*—Vol. I—*Dictionary;* Vol. II—*General History of Costume in Europe.*
Rhead, C. W., *Chats on Costume.*
Sage, Elizabeth, *A Study of Costume.*
Smith, J. Moyr, *Ancient Greek Female Dress.*
The Delineator, June, 1921.
Wilkinson, Sir John Gardiner, *A Popular Account of the Ancient Egyptians.*

Part III

ACCESSORIES WORN ON THE FEET AND LEGS

CHAPTER 20

Shoes

How beautiful are thy feet with *shoes*, O prince's daughter!
Song of Solomon, VII:1

THROUGHOUT the history of dress, shoes have played an important role. Even in fairyland, it was the glass slipper that brought

Figure 308. Shoes of the Early Britons

Cinderella her prince, and who knows, it may still be the shoe, its style and beauty, that brings miracles to pass in the modern world! At any rate shoes have had a long, varied, and romantic career.

The prehistoric foot covering was undoubtedly a bit of woven rush, bark, hide, or skin tied about the foot as a protection to the sole. In all parts of the world earliest peoples have worn a similar covering for the feet. In northern climates,

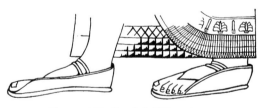

Figure 309. Sandals Worn by an Assyrian King

where more protection was needed, pieces of skins or hides were brought up around the foot in folds and bound with a thong. In that this made an undesirable mass of material at both heel and toe, it is not surprising that the ancient inhabitants of both Britain and Gaul cut out the numerous folds at both heel and toe, laced the heel together at the back, and brought together the strips over the instep by means of a thong. Figure 308. The warmth and mildness of the East, however, where history really begins, made a close-fitting shoe unnecessary, and the earliest form of protection was only a sole of skin or woven fiber, bound to the foot. A relief from the palace at Nimrod shows a king wearing open sandals bound across the instep. Figure 309. Many of the later Egyptian sandals were made by interlacing palms and papyrus leaves. Figure 310.

Frequently they were lined with cloth, and occasionally fitted with buckles. Among the higher classes, both men and women gave much attention to the beauty of their sandals, which were usually pointed and turned up at the toe. Others had a sharp, flat point, and still others were simply rounded. In one of the early pictures of the First Dynasty a king in full costume is shown walking barefoot while a servant carries his sandals. From this record it would appear that sandals were probably worn out-of-doors only when needed and the occasion demanded the services of the sandal bearer.

COURTESY, METROPOLITAN MUSEUM OF ART

Figure 310. Woven Egyptian Sandals

Probably palm leaves and papyrus, XII Dynasty.

Though the earliest form of foot covering developed solely as a protection, it is evident also that the element of beauty was not overlooked. One cannot say just when beauty came to be considered a desirable quality in foot coverings; it must be conceded, however, that the evidence leads back to the beginnings of history, to the beautiful sandals worn by the kings and queens of Egypt. In the tomb of King Tutankhamen were several pairs of sandals. Some were evidently worn at court or indoors, for they were very elaborately decorated with gold and semiprecious stones. The mummy of this youthful king wore sandals of sheet gold embossed. With the sharp point of the sandal turned up and back over the toes, a thong from be-

COURTESY, METROPOLITAN MUSEUM OF ART

Figure 311. Fragment of Egyptian Sandal, XII Dynasty

tween the first and second toe extended to the ankle, where it met the ankle band. In another pair of these historic sandals the part that covered the instep was exquisitely embellished with gold. In the center of the instep band was a remarkable golden ornament in the form of a lotus flower, with little rosettes on each side. Here and there the design was inlaid with semiprecious stones. Other tombs of the royal families of Egypt have furnished ample evidence of the beauty this ancient people bestowed upon their sandals.

Though the pharaohs and their queens of Egypt's Middle Kingdom are usually represented as wearing sandals, they were probably seldom worn indoors, and only occasionally out-of-doors. It is at the beginning of the New Empire (1495 B.C.) that representations of various types of

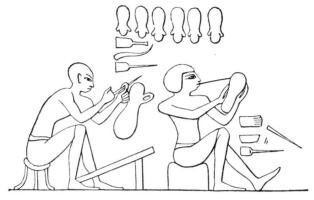

Figure 312. Egyptian Shoemakers
From a wall painting at Thebes. After Wilkinson.

sandals are frequently seen. In an ancient record found on the wall of a temple at Thebes, one may read in picture the story of primitive shoe-making. Figure 312. Two shoemakers are seated upon low stools, busily engaged in shaping the sandals then worn in Egypt. The first work-man is piercing with his awl the leather thong at the side of the sole, through which the straps were passed. His fellow workman is equally busy sewing the sandal and tightening the thong with his teeth.

The people of the Near East, including the Phrygians, Persians, Medes, Syrians, Parthians, and other peoples bordering the Mediterranean, particularly those of an-cient Crete, have all contributed interesting variations to the shoe. In contrast with those of Egypt, the ancient records of these people picture leather shoes covering the entire foot and extending to the ankles. They are frequently fastened with leather thongs sufficiently long to be bound several times about the ankle. Figure 313. A second type of shoe worn by these people of

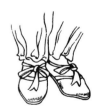

Figure 313.
Shoes of the
Dacians

the East was the laced half boot, made of skins and ornamented with long flaps suggesting the legs of the animal. Figure 314. In previous times the sandal had been tied. The lacing of boots is a departure from the earlier custom and was not uncommon among peoples living along the Mediter-ranean. In ancient Crete men and women wore sandals, shoes, and even boots. The surprising fact is that some of these show a heel—perhaps the only ancient example of the heel.

Among Eastern peoples it is a general custom to remove the shoes as a mark of reverence. Even today, in Mohammedan countries, shoes are always removed before entering the mosque, and the "call to prayer" meets the same response as of old. The native spreads his rug, removes his shoes, and kneels with face to the East. Inasmuch as the Mohammedan religion is based on the Old Testament of the Jews, this observance so generally practiced is in obedience to the command given to Moses from the burning bush at Horeb: "Put off thy shoes from off thy feet, for the place whereon thou standest is holy ground."* In the Apocrypha, Judith sings in triumph: "Her *sandals* ravished his eyes, and her beauty took his soul prisoner."

Among the Greeks during Homeric times, it was the custom to re-

Figure 314. The Phrygian Boot
After Hope.

move the shoes upon entering one's own or a stranger's house and, consequently, no shoes were worn in the home. The early forms of Greek sandal were extremely primitive. A simple felt, wooden, or leather sole with thongs for binding sufficed to meet the simple needs. Later, straps of leather were added to the sole, and a leather piece with straps was fixed at the back to cover the heel. The various straps were then brought up over the foot and given

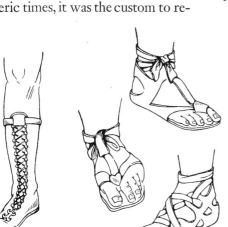

Figure 315. Greek High Boot and Sandals

a variety of arrangement over the instep and about the ankle. Indeed, in time the lacing and fastening of the Greek sandal came to be its distinguishing characteristic. ". . . round his shapely foot laced the becoming sandal." Somewhat later, not only sandals but both shoes and boots were commonly worn by all classes. Shoes were fitted to the foot and were tied about the ankle or bound over the instep and ankle. The boots were high, with wooden soles and leather tops, laced up the front almost

* Exodus III:5.

to the knee. Figure 315. When Greek national life had attained its highest development, about 480 B.C., the various types of boot and shoe gave way largely to the sandal, which is regarded as the characteristic foot covering of the age. In classic times sandals were usually made of leather in its natural color. Among the nobles, however, gilting was often employed as a means of adding further distinction to their dress. Grecian women also gave great attention to footwear. Embroidery and other decorative features were often used to enrich the sandals, which came to be one of the costliest accessories of Greek dress. Greek literature gives many interesting glimpses into the fastidious grooming of these beauty-loving women. Lines from the *Iliad* reveal all the intricacies of bath, perfume, jewels, robes, veils, and then adds:

> Last, her fair feet celestial
> *sandals* graced.
>   *Iliad XIV*

Figure 316. Ivory Foot with Sandal Roman imperial period.

As far back as 600 B.C., Sappho, the Greek poetess, sang of the "broidered *shoes* of varied and delightful colors wrought with Lydian art." To Sappho is attributed the charming Graeco-Egyptian tale of Rhodopis, which is similar to the Cinderella legend. Rhodopis was a beautiful Greek slave owned by the rich Xanthes, who carried her off to Egypt to be sold to the highest bidder. One day, so the story runs, while bathing in the Nile, Rhodopis laid her sandals on the sand near by. An eagle soaring aloft espied them. Down he swooped, seized one, and carried it off. In Memphis, not far distant, the mighty Pharaoh Psammetichus sat administering justice. The eagle circled above, and dropped the tiny sandal. It fell into the King's lap. So awed was he by the strange incident, and so enthralled by the tiny shoe, that he immediately sent forth his emissaries to find the owner. With little delay—continues the story—the demure Rhodopis was brought before the King. So smitten was he with her beauty—and considering the incident an act of the gods—he straightway made her his queen, and even in that distant day is said to have "lived happy ever after."

The simplicity of the Greek sandal, as well as of other details of Greek dress, naturally appealed to the beauty-loving Romans. Patriotic sentiment, however, is said to have prevented them from adopting the sandal, which was essentially Greek. They found, instead, in Etruscan models, a foot covering more to their liking. These sandals and half shoes were somewhat higher than Greek models and were therefore in general use in early Republican Rome. Though "rights" and "lefts" in shoes are generally supposed to have appeared many centuries later, it is an undeniable fact that soles at this early date were cut to fit the left and right foot. Unlike the Greeks, the Romans seldom walked barefoot either in- or out-of-doors. Within the home, sandals or other light coverings were worn, and, without, the sandal, shoe, or buckskin graced the foot. In Rome some types of shoe were distinct badges of position. The *baxea*, a woven sandal, similar to the palm and papyrus of the Egyptians, was worn by the peasant classes. The priests and philosophers adopted this sandal because to them it was an expression of humility. The *soccus* was a light sock, usually worn as an intermediate covering for the foot. It was roomy and comfortable and could be easily pulled on or cast off. The *crepida* was a light

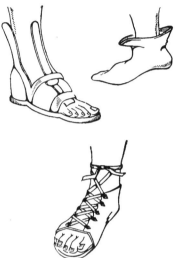

Figure 317. The Roman Sandal, Soccus, and Crepida

type of sandal or half shoe worn both in- and out-of-doors. This sandal, unlike that of the Greeks, covered the sides and heel of the foot. The low-cut leather was attached to the back and sides of the sole, leaving the toes free. It was held in place by leather laces passing through eyelets set in the sidepieces. Figure 317. Another type, the *calceus*, was a kind of shoe which encased the foot and extended somewhat above

Figure 318. Roman Calcei

the ankle. Figure 318. The leather was cut at the side, permitting easy access of the foot. These leather uppers were then fastened to a shaped sole and leather straps were set at the back of the uppers. The straps were brought forward about the ankle and tied, holding the upper front in place. Frequently these straps were quite long, to be wrapped high about the leg just short of the calf and tied. A second pair of straps were then attached at the sides of the widest part of the sole. These were brought up over the instep, crossed, carried around the ankle, and brought to the front and tied. The *calcei* were very important foot coverings usually indicative of rank. The buckskin or *corthurnus* was worn by men of position. Figure 319. Roman senators are often pictured wearing this half boot which reached above the calf, sometimes to the knee, and was laced down the front. It was frequently ornamented with the head and claws of wild animals. If height of figure was desired the thickness of the sole was increased by added layers of cork. This boot, im-

parting as it did a sense of stature to the wearer, no doubt struck awe to the hearts of lesser folk.

The sandals, boots, and shoes of the wealthy were of the finest leathers, often ornamented with gold, silver, and precious stones. The Emperor Heliogabalus indulged in settings of diamonds and other valuable stones, but prohibited this luxury to the women of his empire. Later however, Poppaea, the wife of Nero, is reputed to have worn sandals encrusted with jewels. Seneca records that Julius Caesar wore shoes with soles of gold. Color, as well as jewels, played an important role in the shoes of these luxurious Romans. The high buskin was often of leather, dyed purple. Red shoes were worn by senators. Magistrates wore red shoes with crescent-shaped ornaments at the inside of the ankle. The fashionable Roman matrons, when

Figure 319. The
Corthurnus

not wearing dyed leathers, chose to have their shoes and sandals otherwise decorated in color. Consequently, at various periods painted shoes were much in vogue. Narrow bands of colored silk, used instead of straps, added a further note of gaiety. The Emperor Aurelius reserved

Figure 320. Roman Sandals

the use of white, green, and red shoes for women, prohibiting these colors to men.

For an example of sturdy shoe one may look to the Roman soldier, for he needed to be well shod. Examples of these early boots, which may be seen in the British Museum, show that they resembled the modern idea of just what a boot should be. They were strong and heavy soled, giving protection to the foot by entirely covering it.

Many references in early writings suggest the great care and attention given to their sandals by both men and women of Rome. In advising his soldiers to give less attention to civil dress, Philopoemon suggests they be "less nice" about their sandals and more particular about keeping their greaves (leg armor) bright and well fitted to the leg.

The custom of removing the sandals when dining suggests one of the familiar pictures of Roman life. At such a time guests reclined upon couches. Before partaking of the feast, slaves were summoned to quietly remove all sandals. It was no uncommon occurrence for slaves to bathe the feet of the guests. It is recorded that on one occasion a wealthy Roman, Trimalchio, wishing to display his riches, ordered his slaves to bathe the feet of his guests in wine.

With the fall of the Roman Empire (476 A.D.) civilization moved westward. In that fair section of Europe which we now call France, Romans, Gauls, Franks, and Saxons mingled. Here during the Middle Ages the beginnings were laid for that new type of costume which was to eventually emerge as the dress of moderns. Shoes at this period were not the least of dress accessories which hold a peculiar interest, for they, too, began to change and take on new forms which, centuries later, merged into the modern shoe.

Middle Ages

The study of costume during the Middle Ages is always of absorbing interest, and throughout the period the story of shoes is especially fascinating. During these centuries the much-loved story of Cinderella and her slipper was born. Likewise, at this time many of the old superstitions relating to the shoe had their beginnings. The custom of throwing an old shoe after the departing bride dates back to the Anglo-Saxon wedding, when the father of the bride presented one of her shoes to the bridegroom, symbolizing by this act the transfer of his authority to the new husband. The throwing of a shoe as a symbol of good luck has lingered through the centuries. In deference to the superstition, Ben Jonson penned the following lines:

> Hurl after me a *shoe*,
> I'll be merry whatever I do.

Under the inspiration of the same superstition, John Hayward wrote:

> And home again hitherward quick as a bee,
> Now for good luck, cast an old *shoe* at me.

The characteristic shoe of the early Middle Ages was the soft, pliable, clinging, moccasin type, extending to the ankles. Figure 321. It was easily adjusted to the foot and was fastened with straps, laces, or ribbons. Some of these early shoes show V-shaped places cut out at the sides to afford greater ease in slipping them off and on. Bands of embroidery were frequently sewed around the top and down the front of the shoes of both men and women. Sometimes the top edge of the shoe was cut or snipped, for, says Francois Rabelais, encyclopaedic writer: "The slippers or *shoes* of crimson, red, or violet velvet were snipped like the edges of a crab's claw."

The shoes of the nobles of this day were among the most beautiful

Figure 321. Half Boots, 11th to 15th Centuries

accessories of dress. The ankle shoe and half boot were frequently of colored leather ornamented with gold. Figure 322. The effigy of Henry II of England shows half boots of a green color ornamented with gold; that of Henry III, in Westminster Abbey, shows boots the entire surface of which is crossed at right angles with gold bands, and in each intervening space is the figure of a lion. In opening the tomb of Henry VI of Sicily, who died in 1197, his shoes were seen to have been made of cloth-of-gold embroidered with pearls.

Those of his queen, who died a year later, were also of cloth-of-gold and fashioned with leather tie straps. These were embroidered, and contained small openings which suggested that jewels had been added as ornament. It has been said that the beauty of the

Figure 322. Notes of Elegance in Soft, Pliable Foot Coverings, Middle Ages

shoes of this particular period, designed and executed with rare pattern and workmanship, are "above all Greek, above all Roman fame."

It was during the Middle Ages that men engaged in the various skills, such as saddle making, shoemaking, and other crafts which were gradually increasing, banded themselves together into unions or guilds. We judge from this that shoes and boots of various kinds were coming more and more into general use. In that day the shoemaker was known as the *cobeler* and *cordwainer*, and so we read of the "Cordwainer's and Cobeler's Guild"; also of the "Worshipful Company of Cordwainers." The name cordwainer is said to have been given the shoemaker probably because he used a special kind of leather then imported from Cordova, Spain. The guilds chose as their protecting saint the good St. Crispin, himself a royal cobbler. According to the legend, Crispin was the son of King Logrid of Britain. Toward the close of the third century he traveled about the country, by day preaching the new tenets of the Christian faith, and by night making shoes for the poor. The leather for these was said to

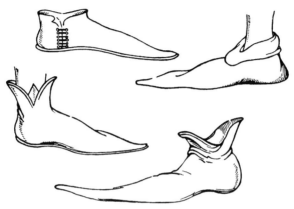

Figure 323. Fashionable Long-toed Shoes,
1460-83

have been miraculously supplied by an angel. In 287 A.D. St. Crispin suffered martyrdom for his religious teaching.

In the isolated villages and towns of the late Middle Ages, the shoemaker was a very important person, for the people of his community depended upon him alone to provide them with shoes. Each village in this early day was sufficient unto itself. The neighboring farmer supplied the hides to the local tanner; the tanner in turn furnished the shoemaker with leather; and the people came to the shoemaker, who took their measure and made their shoes to order.

As the years passed leather came to be used more and more in the making of shoes for both men and women. The popularity of soft, pliable materials, however, such as cloth-of-gold, velvet, and others of a similar quality, still lingered. In the late thirteenth century a striking change took place in the shape of the shoe. The toe was carried out to an exaggerated length. Figure 323. This fashion had come from Cracow, Poland; hence in England such shoes were known as *crackows*. Even in this early day it is plain that political influence played a part in the rise and fall of fashions, for the grandfather of England's Queen, Ann of Bohemia, had only recently incorporated Poland with Bohemia. The new name for shoes suggested to all the world his political affluence. In France, Italy, and, in fact, all over the fashionable world the modish crackows were the last word in style achievement. These long points gradually grew in length, until shortly a man's wealth came to be gauged by the length of his shoe!

Figure 324. Various Types of Pattens

By-and-by the long point was so difficult to manage that a showy device was hit upon. One end of a chain was caught in the point; this was gradually pulled up to the proper angle, and the opposite end was adjusted about the knee. Then a little bell was attached to the point and a tinkling sound accompanied milord as he walked about. The extreme toes remained in style for a long time, although after the death of Richard II (1399) their popularity waned for a while, to emerge with greater show a little later. From 1422-61, under Henry VI of England and Charles VII of France, the toes grew into exaggerated needlelike points that had to be pinned back in order for the wearer to get about. Now the term *poulaine* was often applied to the long-toed shoe. Toes were constantly stuffed with hay, tow, or moss to keep them in shape, and frequently they took on the appearance of a ram's horn. Many times the tops of the shoes were turned back to show the gay-colored lining. Philip Stubbes, that acrid observer of fashion, says of the long-toed shoes:

Their shoes and pattens were snouted and picked [piked] more than a finger long, crooking upwards, which they call "*crackows*," resembling Devil's claws, and fastened to the knees with chains of gold and silver.

The exaggerated "claws" and chains of gold and silver which so irritated Stubbes apply only to gentlemen's shoes; for women, toes were far more modest.

By-and-by the Law had to be called upon to regulate the length of shoes. Princes were permitted two feet while the great mass of the people were limited to six inches. Toward the last years of the century, about 1483, the long, pointed toe began to go and soon passed out of the picture.

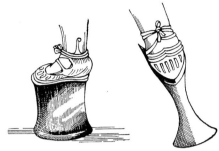

Figure 325. Chopines

Meanwhile, with the long, tapering shoe there had come an innovation in footwear, one which presaged the heel of the modern shoe. This was a wooden clog with the same drawn-out toe and also called "poulaine." Later this wooden clog, with a shortened toe, came to be familiarly known as the *patten*. Figure 324. This protecting shoe made its first appearance about 1377 and continued in varying forms until the eighteenth century. It is not surprising that some device was hit upon to preserve the rich and beautiful footwear, for shoes of the period were wholly unsuited to the deep mud and hard stones of medieval cities. Both poulaines and pattens were supplied with heels about one inch in height and very thick soles of cork or wood. This set the ladies and gentlemen of that distant day high above the cold, damp ground!

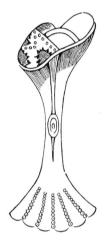

Figure 326. Very High Chopine

A similar development of the heel was the *chopine*, which had been introduced into Italy from Turkey, and thence into France. Figures 325, 326. This was an ornamental stilt, either purchased singly, one for each foot, or in pairs, one for the heel and one for the ball of each foot. It is described as a "thing made of wood and covered with leather of sundry colors, some white, some red, some blue." When not covered it was painted or gilded. In Venice the chopine had met with great favor. Some women are said to have worn them a foot and a half in height. So difficult were they to walk upon that the fair wearer had to be supported by her husband or the women of her household.

1500-1600

By the dawn of the Renaissance (1500) ankle shoes of various styles were still worn. They continued to be made of soft leathers, velvet, silk, satin, and brocade, and were always without a heel. The outstanding change, however, was in the shape of the shoe. When the long, pointed toe had run its course and was gradually going out of fashion, all toes began to round. The former exaggeration in length now veered to an exaggeration in width. Figure 327. No one was considered fashionable unless his shoe measured a foot across the toe! Moreover, many times these broad toes were stuffed with moss which turned them into veritable rolls. Again the law had to be called upon—this time to regulate the width of the shoe!

With the broad toe came the new manner of decoration, the slashing of the instep and the toe. In this way the prevailing style in doublet and sleeve was carried out in the shoe. The immortal painter, Hans Holbein, and others of the period have preserved for all time the unusual fashions of this day.

During the second half of the century the chopine and the patten con-

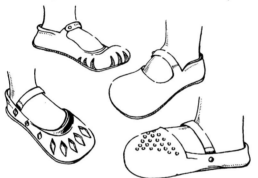

Figure 327. Soft, Heelless Shoe with Wide Toe, 1500

spired to bring in the heel. One of the earliest shoes showing the heel is said to have been worn by Catherine de' Medici (1519-89) wife of Henry II of France. This heel was very modest in height, but the curious connection of the heel with the ball of the shoe by a kind of second sole suggested the development of the heel from the patten. Figure 328. Next to the shoe of Queen Catherine is that of Mary, Queen of Scots, and of Queen Elizabeth, both preserved in museum collections. These are believed to be the earliest known shoes which show the high heel disconnected from the sole. Queen Mary's shoe is black satin with a slightly curved heel; that of Queen Elizabeth is white satin with a low, curved heel and square-cut toe.

1600-1800

In this period of innovations in footwear, the soles of shoes were frequently corked. Figure 328. These shoes show, between the upper leather and the sole, a pad of cork rising considerably toward the heel. When the cork-soled shoes were without uppers at the heel, resembling the modern "mule," they were known as *pantofles*. These were in great favor at court during the later years of the sixteenth century. Corked soles continued to be worn well on toward 1650. In a comedy of 1615 a lady inquires why the citizens are wearing corks in their shoes, and is told:

Tis, madam, to keep up the customs of the citie, only to be light-heeled.

Again, in a play of 1623, a country girl is made to say:

I come trip, trip, trip over the Market Hill, holding up my petticoats to the calves of my legs, to show my fine colored stockings and how trimly I could foot it in a new pair of *corked* shoes I had bought.

Figure 328. Women's Shoes Popular during Reigns of Elizabeth and James I, 1590-1620

The soft, heelless shoes, the corked sole, and shoe with second sole, which probably inspired the patten.

And, of course, the inimitable Stubbes vigorously raises his voice:

They have *corked* shoes, puismets, pantoffles, and slippers, some of black velvet, some of white, some of green, and some of yellow; some of Spanish leather and some of English; stitched with silk and embroidered with gold and silver over the foot, with gewgaws innumerable.

Gentlemen were also wearing corked shoes and Stubbes, not content with his summary of women's styles, continues:

The men have *corked* shoes, puismets, and fine pantoffles which bear them up two inches or more above the ground, whereof some be made of white leather, some of black, and some of red, some of black velvet, some of white, some of green—razed, carved, cut, and stitched all over with silk, and laid with gold, silver, and such like.

It is interesting to observe in passing that no example of slippers, as we understand the term, antedates Elizabeth's time. Though the word *slipor*, from which the word "slipper" is derived, was in the vocabulary of the Anglo-Saxons and would indicate that such foot coverings were familiar, no illustration of slippers as such is seen in the old manuscripts. Up to the sixteenth century foot coverings were always at least ankle high. It is during and after this period that slippers are constantly mentioned.

With Elizabeth came the heel, and once set upon the fashion stage it continued to rise. Soon it grew disgracefully high and inordinately gay. Red, blue, violet, and yellow heels, and shoes embroidered in silk, gold, and silver were the order of the day. At this time "shoe roses," bunches of ribbon shaped like a rose, and fluffs of silver lace came into fashion. It is said that James I, noticing the elaborate shoe roses brought to him by his gentlemen of the wardrobe, asked if they intended to make of him a "ruff-footed dove." Peacham, in 1638, spoke of the exorbitant cost of these new accessories:

Some types that go under the name of *roses*, from thirty shillings to two, three, and four pounds the pair. Yes, a gallant of the time not long since paid thirty pounds for a pair.

Dramatic writers, also, frequently referred to these fashionable shoe roses:

With over-blown *roses* to hide his gouty ankles.

The Devil's Law Case, 1623

Rich Pantoffles in ostentation shown, and *roses* worth a family.

Massenger's *City Madam*

By the latter part of the century shoes were fastened by two short straps held together by ribbon ties. Ribbons were of many colors, and the same color which so lavishly trimmed the costume were repeated in the shoe ties. It is interesting to note that during Elizabeth's reign, "pumps" are first mentioned. Judging from an old record of 1728 pumps were low shoes fitted to the foot without ties, usually worn by footmen. This record happens to be an account of the wages paid to the servants of an Englishman, and the following are mentioned as part of the dress of his running footman, "Drawers, stockings, *pumps*, caps, sash, and petticoat breeches." In *Midsummer Night's Dream* this line occurs:

Get your apparel together, good strings for your beards, new ribbon for your *pumps*.

Act IV, sc. 2

In France, during the reign of Henry III (1574-89), high boots with a slight heel had been introduced. Soon the high top of the boot was increased in width and fell out in a flare from the leg or was turned down, displaying the silk hose so fashionable at this time. This was the day when it was said, "a lady admires the good wrinkle of a gallant's boot." Figure 329. The falling top was the result of a Spanish influence that had come into the field of fashion when Louis XIII married Anne of Austria, the daughter of Philip III of Spain. The heels of these boots grew still higher, and to add to the gaiety of the mode, were frequently painted red. The boot and falling top is a detail of the charming cavalier dress made familiar through the paintings of Sir Anthony Van Dyck and the Dutch masters.

Boots were out of fashion by 1660, but about 1665 the rigid jack boot had made its appearance and was generally worn. This was the popular footwear of the early American planter who spent much of his time on horseback. Figure 330. At this period spatterdashes or leather leggings buttoned or buckled to fit the leg were also worn. Toward the close of the century, low shoes with square toes, high tongue-like projections,

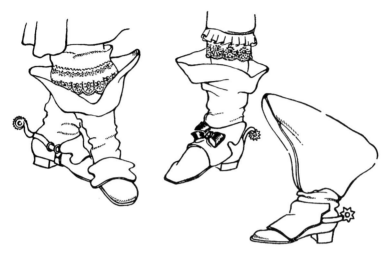

Figure 329. Cavalier Boot of 1600

red heels, and stiffened "butterfly" bows captured the fashion world. Figure 331. So exaggerated were the long bows and ends projecting at each side of the shoe, that they are said to have literally cast a shadow.

> Madame, I do as is my duty,
> Honor the shadow of your shoe-tie.
> HUDIBRAS

Butterfly bows and red heels proclaimed the dandyism of this day. The red heel continued well into the following century. Fashionable folk seemed loath to part with it. One of the necessary qualifications of a beau of 1727 was "red heels to his shoes."

Figure 330. Jack Boot

Even as late as 1765, Horace Walpole wrote to Lady Suffolk, "I am twenty years on the right side of red heels."

During the early years of the new century the shoes with exaggerated square toes and high fronts continued, although they began to take on a more normal and inconspicuous shape. Figure 332. Large square buckles succeeded the fanciful butterfly bows, but the red heels endured to the very threshold of the Revolution. Ever since cavalier days boots had occasionally been worn, and now about the middle of the century they were again returning. It was not, however, until the early years of the nineteenth century that they attained their greatest popularity.

Meanwhile, throughout the eventful eighteenth century the world of women's fashions was swayed first this way, then that, by the changing whims of the favorites of the Louis's. These beauties, Madame Montes-

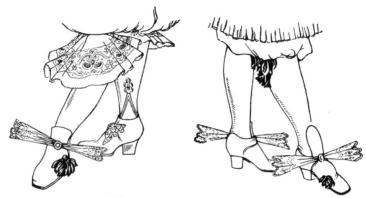

Figure 331. Butterfly Bows

Figure 332. Shoes of Late 1600-1700

The fashionable square toe, red heel, and high tongue were set off with stiff bow or buckle. Silk hose with embroidered clocks completed the picture.

pan, Madame Pompadour, Madame du Barry, and Marie Antoinette, each in her succeeding day set the mode for all the world. And behold, the high heel did not vanish, but grew still higher! In the earliest years of the century under Madame Montespan's influence, shoes were covered with handsome embroidery, and in addition were graced by costly buckles, which soon usurped the place of the exaggerated shoe roses and butterfly bows. The artist craftsman of the day designed and wrought the buckles. Many of these were among the costliest accessories of dress so popular at this period. So high were women's heels at this time that the fair wearer was thrown forward on her toes and walked with the greatest difficulty. Figure 337. Madame Pompadour, however, possessed inherent good taste, and under her regime (1721-64) shoes became an elegant detail of costume. In her day, dress and shoes were expected to make a harmonious unit. Various colors of leather were employed, as well as satin,

Figure 333. Women's Shoes, Early 1700

silk, and brocade. Heels were high and narrow, and buckles were veritable jewels. In the rare collection of shoes in the Hotel de Cluny, Paris, is a dainty pair of high-heeled, yellow-dotted silk slippers, said to be the same seen in the celebrated pastel portrait of this famous beauty, Figure 338. When Marie Antoinette set her pretty foot upon the stage of fashion, every detail of dress was given a further spurt. So elaborate was her wardrobe and her collection of matching shoes that they had to be indexed by color, date, and style! About 1780, when the rumblings of the Revolution were heard, the high heel grew lower and was thrust far under the foot; the following year the low flat heel made by a thickening of the sole elevated the foot slightly, but this was really not a heel at all. Figure 339. As the statesmen of the day were harking back to Greek democracy as a model for world government, the Greek idea took hold of the popular mind and a craze for the classic set in. The bouffante dress

Figure 334. Women's Fabric Shoes, Early 1700

of former years changed to the long, scant, diaphanous tunic; the hair was dressed *à la Minerva*, *à la Diana*, or *à la Sappho*, and the shoe, in keeping with the classic ideals, changed to the heelless sandal held in place by a ribbon tie. Indeed, some even disdained to cover the foot and, like the Greeks of old, went about unshod. In men's dress the unconventional shoestring, though an offence to many, gradually supplanted the handsome buckle. At the very end of the century boots again were rapidly finding a popular place in the fashion world.

These fashions made popular in France ruled the world. In America, low heels and silver buckles are always associated with the colonial dress of the period. Naturally the moccasin of the American Indian was the first foot covering used in this country. It followed in its main lines the easy comfortable form used by all primitive peoples. But during Pilgrim days (1620) boots and shoes followed the same general lines as those set in the fashion center of the world, Paris. These had passed to England and thence to America. Here, however, they lacked the extravagance seen in the French shoe. They

COURTESY, METROPOLITAN MUSEUM OF ART

Figure 335. Shoes, White Kid Embroidered in Silk, French, 17th Century

were strong and durable, with wooden heels. A bronze statue, *The Pilgrim*, by John Quincy Adams Ward, which stands in Central Park, New York City, shows every detail of the seventeenth-century costume minus the extravagance seen in the European centers.

COURTESY, METROPOLITAN MUSEUM OF ART

Figure 336. Fabric Shoes, Late 1700

Figure 341. The tall beaver without its plume, the doublet without its lace and embroidery, and the great top boots without sign of silk hose or furbelows express the rugged character of the pioneer.

As times grew prosperous with the colonists, the tendency toward extravagant dress was held somewhat in check by the Quakers and "women friends," who advised that all "Friends are careful to avoid wearing Striped *Shoes* or red and white heels or clogs or *Shoes* trimmed with gaudy colors."

COURTESY, METROPOLITAN MUSEUM OF ART

Figure 337. English Shoes with Extreme Heel

Nevertheless, in spite of the Quaker stand, even in William Penn's day Philadelphia took the lead in fashionable dress, and later we find the wealthy planters, together with their wives and daughters and others of influence, displaying the rich materials and fashionable modes prevailing in Paris and London.

The real beginning of the shoe trade in America was made in Salem,

Massachusetts, about 1680. Little shops were started in the farmhouses of the outlying districts north and south of Boston. Here, through the long winter evenings, the shoemaker, with his family, worked at his craft. After the Revolution the trade expanded. Enterprising shoemakers set up shops in the villages and hired others to work for them. Parts of shoes were sent to the country cobbler to be stitched, and then returned to the shop to be soled and finished. Both the shoe and the tanning industry centered in New England. Boston early became a great shoe center, and today it is the greatest leather and shoe market in the world.

1800-1900

The French Empire was proclaimed in 1804, and at this date Napoleon and Josephine held the fashion lead. Military boots became the vogue for men. Napoleon's favorite boot was cut away at the upper edge at the back, leaving the front as a kind of mask for the knee. This set the mode for the popular Hessian boot. Short breeches with white stockings and Hessian boots were the "top of the mode" in 1804. Later the height of the boot came to be regulated by the length of the trouser. Breeches soon extended over the knee and were fast creeping

COURTESY, MUSEE DU LOUVRE

Figure 338.
Madame de Pompadour . . . . . . *LaTour*

The dainty, high-heeled shoe of yellow silk is only one fashionable item in this exquisite costume. Note the handsome, flowered silk of the gown, the lace ruffles of the sleeves, and the ribbon bows of the corsage—all dominant notes in the modes of the period.

down the leg. In 1818 boots were only about fifteen inches high. Top boots, the tops turned down and of different colored leather or beige and gray cloth, were a close second to the popular Hessians. The dandies of the day with their tight trousers extending well down the leg to meet the light-topped boot, took a worthy pride in the appearance of the "lowers." They were always kept in a highly polished condition. Various kinds of oils and wax mixtures were sold for this purpose, and great was the sale thereof, for not one dull spot must appear upon the black leather dress boot! It is said that the light top or cap of the boot was the outcome of an effort to keep the black polish off the light trouser leg.

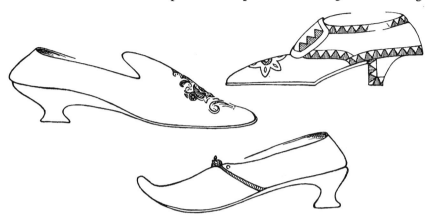

Figure 339. Types of Heel Worn in Late 1700's

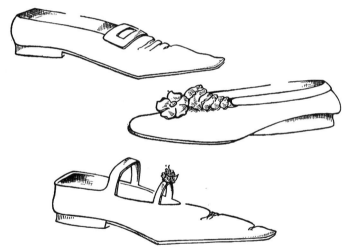

Figure 340. Shoes at the End of the Century. Just before
the Heel Vanished

From 1820 to 1830, short Hessian and Wellington boots with curved tops and sometimes a swinging tassel were in great favor. Of course, though the boot was the popular favorite one must not forget that the shoe still had a following. Heels were broad and low, toes were rounded, and small lachets were fastened over a short tongue.

About 1829 gaiters or spatterdashes were a fashionable item in men's dress. Though the novelty was rather short-lived its influence was seen in the changing modes. By 1830 smart gentlemen were wearing a kind of drill trouser with the lower part shaped like a gaiter. The Wellington boot, which fitted the leg closely as far as the knee, was still popular. The long trouser was now pulled down over the boot and fastened like the gaiter with a strap under the boot arch. Trousers gradually grew wider and were shaped more loosely at the ankle and the understrap omitted. But even after long trousers had come to stay the boot was still worn, though covered by the very loose trouser.

During this period women were wearing the low, soft, pliable slipper without a heel. Figure 344. Though no decided innovation in shoes was made by Josephine, it is said that she loved beautiful clothes, slippers in particular, and that her wardrobe consisted of hundreds of gowns with slippers to match. These were probably not worn for service so much as to complete the effect of the full costume. It is said that the Empress once showed to her shoemaker a dainty slipper which revealed a hole after one day's wear. "Ah! I see what it is," he sighed. "Madame, you have walked in them!"

Figure 341. The Pilgrim
.... *John Quincy Adams Ward*

The "cavalier" boots of 1600, the fashionable tall hat, and the slashed doublet are here well exemplified in early American or pioneer costume.

Slippers at this time were so simple in form and made of materials so easy to fit that both English and American women began to make their own shoes. We hear of "half shoes of lavender kid," others of "pale amber velvet," "grass green velvet," and "pale buff brocade." This suggests something of the daintiness with which some of our forebears were shod. In 1810, the fashionable brocade or embroidered walking shoe appeared. In South Kensington Museum, London, is a pair of black satin walking shoes laced up the front and embroidered with gay colored flowers. Other such shoes were made of nankeen. For evening, slippers in light, delicate colors were always fashionable. Figure 345. Until 1830 the rounded toe was worn; it then gave way to the square toe. These same shoes were often fastened by narrow ribbons crossed and tied about the ankle. The instep was frequently decorated with a pretty bow or rosette.

Though this soft, sandal-like shoe continued popular, by 1840 most shoes for outdoor wear had a heel. At first these were low and comfortable, but gradually began to grow higher. The first boots side-laced to the

Figure 342. Boots, 1785-1800

ankle came into fashion about 1828. Figure 346. They had a seam down the center-front and often a leather toe cap. Frequently they were finished with fringe and a swinging tassel hung from the center-front.

The nineteenth century was a period of remarkable industrial achievement. Outstanding was the shoe industry. The coming of machinery into

Figure 343. Boots, 1800

the realm of shoemaking brought changes undreamed of by the cordwainer of old. In 1833, a machine was invented for attaching the outer sole to the inner sole by means of wooden pegs. A little later, about 1841, the invention of the sewing machine by Elias Howe Jr., furnished new inspiration for the maker of shoes. In 1861, a machine was invented by Lyman K. Blake of Massachusetts which sewed the outer sole through to the inner sole. This machine revolutionized shoemaking, and modern manufacture began. Then followed a machine with a curved needle, developed by Charles Goodyear, which sewed a narrow strip of leather or welt to the inner sole and sewed the outer sole to the welt. Thus the welt sole was born. This sole has since been used universally in the manufacture of shoes. All through this period French, English, and American genius worked toward the improvement of methods and the perfection

Figure 344. Soft, Pliable, Heelless Shoe with Square Toe, Early 1800's

of boot-making machines. However, although the making of shoes by machine displaced the former methods, it still continued to be the privilege and pleasure of fashionable belles of the nineteenth century to be measured and fitted for shoes.

During the mid-Victorian period the extremely high heel was looked upon askance. The crinoline and trailing skirts of the fifties, sixties, and seventies completely hid the shoe. Indeed, a lady was not even supposed to allow her feet to be seen! But the queen of fashion at the French court, Eugénie, possessed trim ankles. She resolved that they should be seen, and, consequently, looped her overdress to ankle length. Gay Parisian life accepted the innovation, but the mid-Victorians looked with

COURTESY, METROPOLITAN MUSEUM OF ART

Figure 345. Slippers, Early 1800's, American

consternation. It is reported that one day Frans Joseph of Austria, in assisting his empress and the lively Eugénie into his carriage, remarked quietly but pointedly to his consort, "Be very careful, Madame, you are showing your feet."

Shoes of this period of dignified restraint were, indeed, an echo of the times. The soles were practically archless, the heels small and low. Materials were kid, cloth, and silk. However, toward the seventies skirts began to clear the ground, and with this change high heels, which had been esteemed a "wicked invention," began to appear. High boots with rounded toes also became popular. They were made of the softest kid with soles as thin and dainty as paper. Figure 347. Carriage shoes for the amazingly small feet of that day were made of brocade, laced or buttoned high and ornamented with a swinging tassel. Soon patent leather, which is leather with a varnished surface, made its appearance and was accepted as one of the popular materials for the low shoe and half shoe. Attempts were made, during the late seventies and early eighties, to hold the shoe in place by means of elastic inserts at the sides or over the instep. These shoes were known as the *congress*. They proved popular for a short period, but as the elastic failed to retain its elasticity for any considerable time, at least during the lifetime of the shoe, it gradually disappeared from the market.

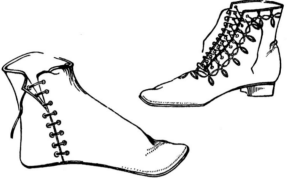

Figure 346. Early Laced, Heelless Boot, Ankle
High, 1820-30, and the Front-laced Boot
with Heel, 1860-65

While woman's footwear was taking on these new and many forms, men's shoes were likewise changing. Though the boot worn beneath the trouser was favored for many years, by the fifties the laced-up shoe had made great inroads, Figure 348, and in the sixties was followed by the side-buttoned shoe slightly above ankle height.

The many dress-reform movements that came in toward the late seventies and early eighties also affected milady's shoes. New avenues of interest, the sport world, business, and professional life, all so foreign to women of other days, likewise brought a transformation in the conception of shoes. "Shoes for comfort," was the slogan of this transition period. Not only women's shoes, but men's as well, were affected by the new times. The manufacture of shoes had, by this time, become an industry in which thousands found employment. The manufacturers seized upon these new demands from both men and women, and the market was supplied with afternoon, evening, and sport shoes. These were made of various leathers, with soles of different thickness, and medium heels, neither too high nor too low for everyday comfort. Men's shoes ranged from the low to those just above the ankle. They were either laced or buttoned, with soles of different weight. Sometimes the shoe tapered to a long narrow point; again it was short with a broad toe tipped with a leather cap. Toward the end of the century men's shoes were taking on a very modern appearance. The fashionable walking shoe for women was known as the *commonsense shoe*, and a very comfortable shoe it was with its broad heel and medium sole. Figure 349. Leather was now fast usurping the shoe field, and by 1900 was used for all shoes for practical wear. Fabrics of silk, satin, and brocade, however, continued in the manufacture of the dress shoe, and heels remained high.

Twentieth Century

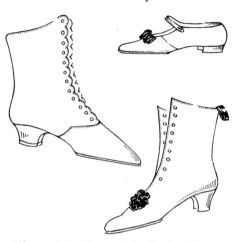

Figure 347. Shoes of the Early 70's

With the beginning of the twentieth century the demand for comfortable shoes continued. In the industrial field new inventions followed one another so rapidly that not less than eighty different types of machines were used for the making of a single shoe. These machines operated so quickly and accurately that the various operations of stitching, eyelet making, and decoration were accomplished in a few minutes. This made possible the mass production of the twentieth century. All the different types of machines used today in shoe manufacture have been brought together under one management known as the "United Shoe Machinery Company." The company leases its system of machines to all manufacturers on the same terms, and this has produced a highly competitive market.

Another of the great modern industries which has to do with foot coverings came into the world during this epoch-making century. This was the rubber industry. The process of vulcanization, by which rubber is made into an enduring, elastic, heat-and-cold-defying material, was discovered in 1839, by Charles Goodyear. It was not until 1844 that he obtained his patents, and upon these the great rubber industries of the world have since been based. Among multitudinous products of these factories is the rubber overshoe, commonly designated as "rubbers," and various other types of overshoe made of rubber combined with rubberized cloth, all of which are waterproof. The high rubber or rubberized cloth overshoes are today known as *galoshes*.* Figures 350, 351. This, however, is

---

*According to M. Quicherat, *History of Costume in France*, the word is derived from the name given the leathern shoes with thick or wooden soles worn by the Gauls and adopted by the Romans with other Gallic fashions. Fr. *galloche*, It. *galoza*.

not a new word, for *galoches de bois* were worn in France in stormy weather as early as the fourteenth century. It is believed that the word was first applied to the high leathern shoes worn by the Gauls. An amusing reference to galoshes appears in a record of Pepys under date of November 15, 1665:

Lady Bettin walking in the dirt, dropped one of her *goloshes*, which she wore over spic and span white shoes.

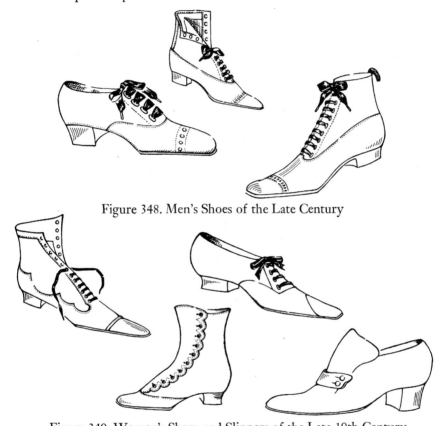

Figure 348. Men's Shoes of the Late Century

Figure 349. Women's Shoes and Slippers of the Late 19th Century

The long vamp of 1898 and the short vamp of 1893. Extreme right, "commonsense shoe."

Twentieth-century galoshes serve the same purpose, they protect the shoes of moderns when they walk abroad and are, indeed, a worthy successor to the clog and patten of old.

In the early days of the twentieth century high shoes were worn during the fall and winter months. They were either buttoned or laced. During the spring and summer months of this period the fashionable favorites in women's footwear were the low shoes known as the *oxford* and *pump*. Figure 352. Simple ties or laces supported the oxford, while the pump was without ties or buttons of any kind. Following the World War (1914-18), when skirts grew shorter, high kid boots in pearl gray, tan, blue, and bronze were the fashionable note in footwear. These colored shoes so completely took over the fashion field that the all-black shoe was crowded off the market. But Fashion is fickle, and by 1920 the high shoe of every type began to go. Low shoes, for all seasons and all climates, took the fashionable lead. So unexpected was this sudden change that well-stocked boot and shoe establishments were almost forced to give away their supply of high shoes. From this period, the low shoe seems to have come

Figure 350. Popular Style, Women's Galoshes, Early 1900's

Figure 351. Type of Men's Galoshes, Early 1900's

to stay, and today remains the favorite form of footwear. Figure 353.

Comparing the shoes of men and women of modern times, one finds the balance of novelty falling on the side of women's footwear. Men's shoes, like men's clothes in general, follow well-established lines which change slightly. The low broad heel and comfortable sole has become what seems to be a permanent feature in shoe fashions for men. Figure 354. Even in color there is a note of constancy, for, while women flit from black to beige, to rust, to gray, to blue, to green, to white, men follow the conservative blacks and browns, relieved by white canvas, calf, or buck for summer.

In this century the automobile, the world of sport, and the general complexity of modern life have all contributed in styling shoes for both men and women. Designers are constantly looking forward to the necessity of creating new patterns and novel modes of decoration. Looking back, they gather new inspiration from historic footgear. Occasionally a worldwide interest gives a popular flare for some particular style. For instance, in 1924 after the rare treasures of the tomb of King Tutankhamen had been revealed, shoe designers, as well as designers in general, seized upon the Egyptian motif. Sandals with and without heels, of leather and woven fiber, strapped in a multiplicity of styles, were the novelties of the period. Their popularity, especially during the summer months, extended down to 1932.

But how useless to discuss the variety in styles of the twentieth century! It is impossible to say that *one* style is the mode, for each occasion has its distinct style. There is the shoe for walking, the shoe for golf, for

Figure 352. Women's Fashionable Shoes,
Early 1900's

The pump, sandal, and ties.

Figure 353. Shoe Modes, 1930-36

The strap pump; oxford, perforated kid with high heel;
and oxford with medium heel.

tennis, for camp; the shoe for morning, for afternoon, for evening; the shoe for the promenade, the opera, the dance. Industry is searching the ends of the earth for material for milady's shoes. Snakes from India, lizards from Java, boa-constrictors from the tropics, alligators from southern swamps, fish from the deep sea, and the skins of the kangaroo, the kid, the calf, the buck, the antelope, the horse, the cow—all are conspiring to bring to pass the most comfortable and beautiful types of footwear that the world has known.

It is a far cry back to the primitive sole bound by a thong or reed to the foot. Man has come a long way in his journey through the centuries. Looking back history records that as his needs arose, his genius first stirred, then asserted itself, and finally produced a foot-covering not only practical and comfortable, but more and more satisfying to his growing sense of beauty. After ages of modest effort and worthy achievement, he reached the nineteenth century. Then he swept aside all handicaps. He produced the machinery which turned the foot swathing of old into the modern shoe. With the manufacture of shoes left to the machine, the vital elements—the line, the form, the color of all footgear—have become the highly specialized field of the designer. His is a work of importance, far removed from that of the cordwainer of old. Not only does he furnish designs for the shoes of kings and queens, but the whole work-a-day world looks to him for that essential note—the element of beauty in modern footwear.

Figure 354. Men's Sport Shoes, 1930-36

White and black leather, rubber heel; white canvas, rubber heel; and black-and-tan elkskin, perforated, rubber heel.

REFERENCES

Erman, J. P. Adolph, *Life in Ancient Egypt*.
Fairholt, F. W., *Costume in England*.
Guhl and Kohner, *Life of the Greeks and Romans*.
Johnson, Harold, *Private Life of the Romans*, pp. 252, 262.
Lester, Katherine Morris, *Historic Costume*.
McClellan, Elizabeth, *Historic Dress in America*, 1607-1800; 1800-70.
Norris and Curtis, *Costume and Fashion*, Vol. VI, *The Nineteenth Century*.
Peterson's Fashion Magazine, April, September, 1863.
Planché, J. R., *Cyclopedia of Costume*, Vols. I, II.
Rhead, C. W., *Chats on Costume*.
Sage, Elizabeth, *A Study of Costume*.
Story, Margaret, *Individuality and Clothes*, p. 32.

CHAPTER 21

Buckles

Why, Petruchio is coming in a new hat, and an old jerkin; a pair of old breeches, thrice turned; a pair of boots that have been candle-cases, one *buckled*, another laced. . . .

Taming of the Shrew. Act III, sc. 2

UPON the mere mention of buckles as an accessory of dress, the mind instantly conjures up the debonair charm, stateliness, and extravagance that distinguishes the eighteenth century. This was the day when red heels and costly buckles were the supreme dictate of Fashion. Buckles were not a new accessory at this time, but they were a most important one; for they supplied the distinctively elegant note in the gay galaxy of dress.

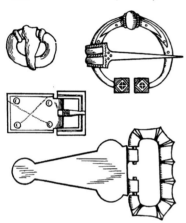

Figure 355. Buckles of the Bronze Age

Upper right and left represent the "ring and pin" device—the forerunner of the modern buckle.

Buckles have existed for so long a period in such a variety of form that it is "obviously impossible to enumerate or engrave their many varieties," according to the eminent English authority F. W. Fairholt.*

The earliest form of buckle is seen on those primitive belts of the Bronze Age, which show one end fashioned as a hook that catches into an opening in the opposite end. This is similar to the modern clasp which consists of two parts generally symmetrical. Others show the fastening complete in itself consisting of a ring or hoop and pin. Sometimes the ring was open and the pin, after being passed through the material, was turned slightly, caught over the edge of the ring, and thus secured. When the ring was closed the end of the girdle was drawn and held by the pin. This brought in another form of fastening, the "tong and slot." The "ring and pin" device is the forerunner of the modern buckle. Figure 355.

---

* Fairholt, F. W. *Costume in England.*

As a fastening for belts, girdles, and mantles, buckles have long been in use. In Figure 356 there are four of the "tong" ends of bronze buckles dating from the ancient Roman world. Figure 357 shows one side of an old Roman clasp, the twelve sections of which are laid in yellow, red, and gray enamel.

Middle Ages

Throughout the long period of the Middle Ages buckles (also called brooches) were in common use as dress and mantle fastenings. They varied in size from the tiny buckle to one of eight or ten inches in

Figure 356. Buckle Ends of Belt, Bronze, 53 B.C.-500 A.D.

length. Many of these were massive in form, studded either with colored glass and semiprecious stones or with ornamental bosses of bronze. Figure 358. Those worn by the Franks and Saxons were especially conspicuous for size and decoration, sometimes being further enriched by adjoining plates beautifully chased or set with stones. Figures 359, 360. By the late fourteenth century many of the soft moccasinlike shoes were buckled at the instep; garters, a fashionable accessory of the time, were frequently fastened with ornamental buckles. In *Piers Ploughman's Crede*, a fourteenth-century poem, the Franciscan brothers, who had been accustomed to go barefoot, are hotly denounced. "Now," says the indignant critic, "they have *buckled* shoes!"

However, the use of buckles increased. They were found useful for fastening the various parts of armor, as the following lines from *Richard III* indicate:

Your friends are up, and *buckle* on their armor.

Richard III, Act. V, sc. 3

And in *Henry II* occur these lines:

You live in great infamy . . . he that *buckles* him in my belt cannot live in less.

Henry II, Act I, sc. 2

1600-1700

Though these varied uses of the buckle are interesting, it is a much later day that brings this useful accessory to "its place in the sun." The fashionable era of buckles began about 1660, when the shoe buckle supplanted the elaborate shoe roses and ribbon ties. Though first accepted in Italy and France, buckles came into fashion about the same time in England, that is, during the reign of Charles II. Soon they passed to America. Under date of January 22, 1659, Pepys makes this note in his diary, "This day I began to put *buckles* on my shoes." Evelyn, writing

Figure 357. Part of a Clasp or Fibula Found in the British Isles

Ornamented with twelve sections in yellow, red, and gray enamel.

in 1666, refers to the dress of ladies of the period, and mentions their diamond buckles "for garters and as rich for shoes." When first introduced, buckles were small, set high on the instep, and used with the extravagant butterfly bows so fashionable from 1660 to 1685. By 1685 the buckle had usurped the place of every other fastening for shoes, and gradually grew larger and more imposing. Many buckles were elaborate in gold and silver work and studded with jewels. It is said that Louis XIV wore no other jewels than those on his shoe buckles and garters. The fashion continued to grow, and reached its full flower in the next century.

In London, during the popular reign of the buckle, a watchmaker, Christopher Pinchbeck by name, developed a new alloy for the manufacture of this much priced accessory. It came to be known as *pinchbeck*. This was a composition of five parts copper to one part zinc. It was soon in general use for the casting of buckles. All buckles cast in pinchbeck carried a surface design which was covered with a thin plating of silver. They were frequently set with colored glass and paste brilliants, which added the final note of color and glitter. A more valuable buckle was produced from a compound metal known as *tutaunia*, and called the "close-plate" buckle. This was cast in molds, and in some countries the trade was carried on in the public streets. Anyone in need of new shoe buckles stopped, selected his pattern, watched the

Figure 358. Heavy, Bronze Buckles, Merovingian Period

process of casting, and within ten or fifteen minutes marched off with his finished buckles.

1700-1800

The following year brought in the fashionable knee buckles. Gentlemen's knee breeches were fastened at the side with one, two, or three buckles. Figure 362. These were usually small and oval in form while the shoe buckles were large, square, or oblong. In France, the brother of the King, the Comte d'Artois, a fashion leader of the day, adopted buckles of enormous size. Naturally this set the fashion, and soon no buckles would please the fastidious taste of the hour but the largest that could be had. Out of compliment to the Count, these enormous buckles were known as the buckles *d'Artois*.

Throughout the reign of the shoe buckle America played her part to the full. The wealthy colonists followed the dictates of fashion quite as closely as did their English cousins. Large buckles were worn on the shoes and smaller ones on the knee breeches.

During the entire period, one of great prosperity, an extensive business in buckle manufacture was carried on, particularly in England. It is said that not less than 2,500,000 pairs of buckles were turned out annually from the manufacturing city of Birmingham alone. In 1771, while the vogue was at its height, the fashion suddenly changed, for the shoestring was destined to take the place of the buckle. This change in fashion wrought great distress among the buckle makers, and they petitioned the Prince of Wales to re-

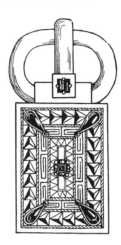
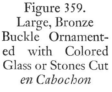

Figure 359. Large, Bronze Buckle Ornamented with Colored Glass or Stones Cut *en Cabochon*

Figure 360. Anglo-Saxon Bronze Buckle in Which the Design Follows Roman Types

instate the buckle and thus bolster up the dwindling business. The Prince responded immediately. He adopted the buckle and demanded that all his household do likewise. This, however, proved only temporary aid and was very short-lived. Later, despite the Prince's efforts and the buckle-makers' pleas, the buckle gradually gave way to the shoestring. Now, even in Paris shoes were tied with the unconventional string!

This was, indeed, an offense to many, for there were still strong champions of the elegant buckle. It is said that in France during the stirring times of the Revolution (1793), Minister Roland, who had been appointed by Louis XVI, appeared before him with strings in his shoes. The King regarded this as a personal affront and remained silent. Finally by a sign to one of his courtiers, he indicated the offending strings. The courtier, in turn, with a fretful and hopeless gesture, murmured, "Alas, Sir, indeed all is lost." In America the same apathy was shown toward this unworthy successor of the buckle. It is said that admittance to exclusive places of entertainment was denied to all but the silver-buckled. Tickets distinctly read: "Gentlemen with shoe-strings not admitted." So passed the shoe buckle, that patrician of ornaments!

COURTESY, METROPOLITAN MUSEUM OF ART

Figure 361. Gold Buckle and End for Belt, Frankish, 4th to 8th Centuries

1800-1900

Approximately a hundred years later buckles were revived. About 1870 they appeared on the low-cut shoe with the high heel and rounded toe. These buckles were large, usually square, and set with rhinestones. This revival, however, was not to play a role of any importance in the fashion world, for it soon disappeared. It was not until the late nineteenth and early twentieth centuries that this fashionable accessory returned with redoubled popularity. At this time, however, an unexpected transition had taken place. Instead of gracing the exquisitely shod foot of gentlemen it had passed, apparently forever, into the world of women. In the twentieth century the shoe buckle

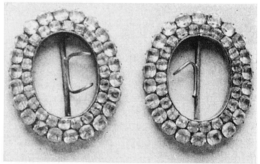

COURTESY, METROPOLITAN MUSEUM OF ART

Figure 362. Knee Buckles, Silver and Paste, English, 18th Century

is an item of feminine luxury alone. Men's shoes like men's clothes are adapted to the life they lead. Silk stockings, red heels, and costly buckles would be sadly out of place in a business day of the twentieth century. At the same time women's shoes have become as varied as women's interests. With the passing of the years the manufacture of women's footwear has grown into one of the great industries of the world.

Twentieth Century

In this century it has been truly said, "'There is a shoe for each occasion.'" During these years the buckle, as if in an effort to find its most fitting place in the modern world, has been worn on all types of shoes. Low street shoes, afternoon shoes, evening shoes, and sport shoes have, each in turn, had their fling with the buckle. On the low strap slipper, and pumps as well, buckles of bone, metal, and composition are seen. For afternoon and evening shoes of silk, satin, and moire, the cut steel buckle and the silver buckle set with rhinestones have struck a popular note. The cut steel buckle of the twentieth century is of unusual design, fine workmanship, and has a jewel-like quality that rivals the eighteenth century buckle. The sport shoes of buck, calf, and popular russet leathers are frequently fastened with buckles and strap. Though the fashion for shoe buckles waxes and wanes through the years, the world of femininity concedes that the cut steel buckle still adds a note of elegance and distinction to the formal afternoon or evening costume.

While the buckle as an ornament for the shoe continues to hold a fashionable place, it also serves in a less conspicuous field. In ancient times the buckle was an ornamental fastening for belt and girdle. Modern men and women find a similar use for this convenient accessory. During the late nineteenth and early twentieth century the sport world exerted a marked influence upon costume. In men's dress the leather belt with the plain metal buckle was a permanent feature, not only for sport but for occasional everyday wear as well. In the world of women the use of the belt varies with the fashion silhouette. When belts are "in," buckles are worn. When belts are out, buckles do not appear. During the late nineties, when the modish shirtwaist occupied the center of the fashion stage, belts and buckles flourished. After a lapse of several years forth they came again. In 1930, the belt and buckle loomed large on the horizon of fashion. Wardrobes of the twentieth century are indeed varied, but when they call for belts and buckles, belts and buckles appear. An infinite variety in silver, gilt, enameled, jeweled, and composition buckles are set before woman's enchanted gaze and the only task is one of choosing.

Though buckles from time to time have been both popular and useful ornaments for various parts of the costume, the reign of the buckle belongs distinctly to the eighteenth century, and culminated in that period, when handsome men and beautiful women, in silver buckled shoes stepped lightly to the strains of the minuet. One cannot be surprised that the leaders of that day were loath to part with this handsome accessory of dress, especially when its place was usurped by that niggardly rival, the shoestring. Champions of the buckle, however, may view with pride its survival in England, where tradition furnishes a mellowed background. Here the silver buckle still retains a place of prominence, not in everyday life to be sure; but upon distinguished occasions it continues to grace the shoe of judge and bishop, and is always a detail of the courtly costume worn for presentation to the king.

CHAPTER 22

Hose

Play not the peacock, looking everywhere about you to see if you are well decked,
if your shoes fit well, if your *stockings* sit neatly, and your clothes handsomely.
GEORGE WASHINGTON, *Rules of Courtesy and Decency of Behaviour*

IT has been truly said that women of the twentieth century wear the
clothes that only yesterday were designed for queens. This is especially true of hosiery, for it is a matter of history that in the third year
of her reign (1561) Queen Elizabeth was presented with her first pair
of knitted silk stockings. So rare and beautiful was this new accessory of
dress that Elizabeth, in her delight, forever after refused to wear any
other than silk stockings. Today every woman may wear silk stockings;
and milady's hose of modern times must appear as gossamer of fairyland
when compared with those of England's queen in 1561.

The story of the modern stocking is an involved one. The word "stocking" does not appear in the vocabulary of dress until the sixteenth century and, according to Tooke, is derived from the Anglo-Saxon *prican*
meaning "to stick." He implies that the word was probably first written
stoken or *stocken*—that is, *stock* with addition of the participial ter-
mination *en* because it was "stuck" or made with sticking pins, now
called knitting needles. Modern sources say the word is derived from
the Anglo-Saxon *stocc,* meaning "post," "stocking" being the "post
wrapping."

Middle Ages

It is undoubtedly true that throughout the Middle Ages women were
familiar with the stocking. Though in these early days the long, enveloping mantle was worn and there was no display of hosiery, it is not
too much to conjecture that women had developed a leg covering similar
to that worn by men. As early as Chaucer's time, women had adopted
the word *hose*. Of the wife of Bath we read:

> Hir *hosen* weren of fine skarlet redde,
> Ful straite y-tyed.

Of approximately the same time is a naïve and interesting drawing which
appears in a manuscript of the fourteenth century (1307-27), repre-

286

senting a woman in the act of dressing her feet. She holds in her hand the hose, which resembles the modern long stocking, and is about to draw it over her foot. Figure 363. The drawings in these old manuscripts are invaluable as authentic records of costume. Though both men and women in these early times had adopted leg coverings, it was not until the late eighteenth century that woman shortened her skirt and exhibited her hose, hence the past history of hosiery is confined largely to the types displayed by our gentlemen of yesterday. It is the hose of men that passed through successive and interesting changes before emerging in the form of the handsome stockings of the seventeenth and eighteenth centuries.

During the Middle Ages western Europe held the key to modern costume. It was here, in this early period when Romans, Franks, Gauls, and Saxons mingled, that various details of dress evolved; and not the least among these was the stocking. The binding of

Figure 363. Medieval Hose

From Royal ms. 2B, VII.

the legs with hides was, no doubt, the most primitive method of protection. Even in modern times, the peasants of backward countries commonly wrap the legs to the knee and bind them with thongs or strips of cloth. In western Europe the early Britons, Gauls, Franks, and neighboring peoples bound coarse cloth or skins about the legs, cross gartering them to the knees. Figure 364. These same peoples, frequently mentioned by the haughty Romans as "trousered barbarians," wore a loose trouser which extended to the ankle and was there secured by a thong. This long, loose pantaloon was known to the Anglo-Saxons as *brōc* and to the Romans as *bracco*. Figure 365. French trousers, which were practically the same, though somewhat closer in fit, were known as *braies*. These were usually of linen, woolen cloth, or hide. It appears that these loose leg coverings were also frequently bandaged or cross gartered to the knee. Figure 366. This custom gradually grew into a common practice. It kept the pantaloon close to the leg and made for greater freedom of movement. This was essential as man came to be more active and laid aside the encumbering mantles brought over by the Romans. Toward the sixth century the cross-gartered braccae and braies, so long associated with barbarians, had been generally adopted. Over this garment was worn a simple tunic reaching

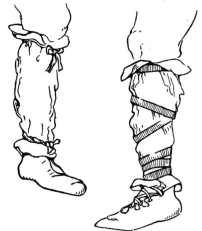

to the knee. Following the general acceptance of the cross-gartered pantaloon came the use of closer fitting bracco—the *brēc* (Anglo-Saxon plural of *brōc*) or *brech*,—and, finally, *breeches*. By-and-by the lower part of this same trouser, from the knee down, was fitted well to the form of the leg. About the eleventh century the

Figure 364. Types of Early Leg Coverings

breeches were shortened to the knee, and the lower leg, instead of going about undressed, was covered to the knee with a fitted cloth form. These fitted cloth forms were known to the French as *chausses*, to the Saxons as *hose* (akin to the Danish *hoos*). Very soon, however, the term "hose" was accepted, and, consequently, these cloth forms have passed through history under that name. The word "stocking," however, had not yet been coined. Cloth hose, though fitted, were inclined to wrinkle or ruck. Therefore they no doubt were kept in place by some sort of band or garter. As early as the twelfth century hose appeared

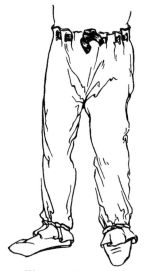

Figure 365. Anglo-Saxon Brōc

The *braie* of the French was the *brōc* of the Anglo-Saxons.

with feet to which something resembling a thin leather sole was supplied. When without feet, other foot coverings were worn. When not covered with hose the leg was bandaged or cross gartered. Occasionally the bandages were wrapped continuously, overlapping so closely as to form a bandaged covering, the necessary protection. The illustration of a bandaged leg, Figure 367, after Fairholt, is from an illuminated manuscript of the tenth century. These bandages were of gold cloth, lapped tightly and tied just under the knee with cord and tassel. They undoubtedly represent those worn by a prince or other noble. The English puttee is a distinctly modern adaptation of this ancient bandage.

Following the twelfth century, breeches continued to become still shorter and tighter, and hose longer. As hose lengthened they widened at the top and the breeches were tucked into them. Gradually the breeches began to take the place of underwear, continuing to shrink more and more until toward 1400 they bore a marked resemblance to the abbreviated "trunks" of modern times. The tunic was soon displaced by the fitted cotehardie; every dandy took pride not only in the smooth fit of his cotehardie but of his long hose as well. Indeed, every beau desired to display to the best advantage his claim to a shapely leg. Hosiers of that period, after much practice, became expert in cutting and fitting the fashionable hose, which were fitted and seamed by hand. The fitting took the form of gussets laid in about the ankle, and these no doubt were the origin of the modern "clock." The embroidery stitches were probably added to hide the seam. This distinct note of artistry in the modern stocking is only a vestige of the embroidered seam of the ancient hose.

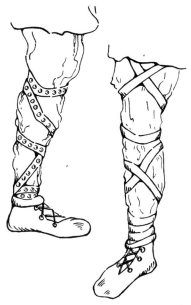

Figure 366. The Cross-gartered Brōc

The front of the hose now formed a high point and was fastened by means of a cord to the breeches girdle or band. By the middle of the century the hose had reached the hip and was fastened by means of points to the doublet. Figure 368. *Points* were ties or laces, often of silk or braid and equipped with metal tags. These were generally used for fastening various parts of civilian attire. A book of interesting instructions to a valet, dated about this time, sets forth explicit directions for dressing his master:

> Pull up his *hosen* and tie them up,
> Lace his doublet hole by hole,
> Comb his hair with an ivory comb,
> Set his garments goodly—scarlet, or green,
>   satin, cendal, or velvet.

During the early centuries hose had crept gradually up the leg; now toward the end of the fifteenth century (about 1489-90) the inevitable happened: the two hose met, were sewed together, and formed one garment which resembled the "tights" of modern days. The word *hose* was now applied to the united garment. Figure 369. This new hose, as *one* garment, extended from the waist to the ankles and sometimes covered the feet. Though the wearing of this type of hose was a new fashion and the last word in gentlemen's styles, the old form, a hose for each leg, continued for a time along with the new.

These days of the fitted hose were far removed from the earlier period of the "trousered barbarian." Fresh contacts with other peoples, the growth of the crafts, and the introduction of silk all found expression in the field of dress. Hose were made of the finest materials. Though loosely woven woolen cloth was, no doubt, in general use, the medieval inventories record that silk

Figure 367. A
Cross-gartered
Leg

After Fairholt.

and velvet, added to the fabrics of earlier periods, had also found their way into the making of hose.

This was a great day in the history of leg coverings! The close-fitting hose had become gay-colored tights, which in the extreme of their fashion quite

Figure 368. Long Hose Fastened
by Points

shocked, even in that day, the more conservative. People had been accustomed to the long doublet and mantles, but when the "exquisites" of the late fifteenth century appeared in short jacket—only hip length—and "tights," it is not surprising that such clothes were stigmatized for "their horrible inordinate scantiness." Figure 370. And added to this was color! Colors were in stripes, embroidered or emblazoned. The dandies were not abashed to clad one leg in white, yellow, or green, and the other in black, blue, or red. Legs, in fact, were not only different in color, but in pattern as well. By-and-by the upper part of the hose came to be patterned in such a way as to appear as a separate garment, resembling the decorated trunks of the acrobat. This appearance was first accomplished by adding to the upper part of the long hose bands and strips sewed on in the form of appliqué. Then followed a decidedly novel form of decoration—that of slashes and puffs.

1500-1600

In the early years of the new century when Fashion had decreed slashes in shoes, sleeves, and doublets, this mode also affected the hose, and slashes appeared at knees and hips. No doubt the former decorative

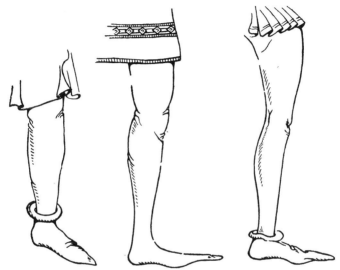

Figure 369. Hose of 1300, 1400, and 1500

work on the upper part of the hose, and now the slashing about the knees, suggested to some fashionable member of society the complete separation of upper and lower hose. Forthwith he applied the shears, and the long hose divided! Thus did the "stocking" of modern dress appear upon the field of fashion. The upper part of the hose was now called *upper stocks* and the lower *nether stocks*. The term *trunk hose* was later applied to the upper part, and the lower was termed *stocking of hose*. In time the lower part was known simply as *stocking*. Today in common parlance, the terms *stocking*, or *stockings*, and *hose* are synonymous.

While the transition in men's attire was taking place, women continued to wear the early form of stocking, taking personal delight in its colors and the added touches of embroidery. Says François Rabelais:

The ladies wore scarlet or crimson stocking, the said stockings reaching three inches above the knee, and the edge thereof finely embroidered or cut out. The garters were of the same color as their bracelets and fitted tight above and below the knee.

He also states that men's hose were made of milled serge of scarlet color, a hue somewhat darker, and black and white. Between 1485 and 1509, we also read of "caliber web hose" being in use by both men and women. This is understood to mean a cotton stocking.

Following the division of hose into trunk and stocking, each part of the garment pursued its own divergent path. Trunks changed into the bombasted breeches of 1600, filled as they were with bran, moss, and hair; then into full knickers; then into petticoat breeches, knee breeches, and finally long trousers. Nether stocks or stockings were, for a period, fastened to the upper stocks by laces or points. Knitted hose, however, appeared about this time, and, with this, the stocking was generally recognized as an entirely independent accessory of dress.

As to the antiquity of knitting, it has always been believed that the ancient nations versed in weaving, dyeing, and kindred arts must have been familiar with the practice of knitting. It has been proved by specimens of Egyptian knitted stockings of fine wool, now in the Louvre collection, that the art was known and practiced by this ancient people. Knitted wool stockings of the modern sort are said to have been first produced in Scotland toward the close of the fifteenth century (1499). A record of 1499 lists two pairs of knitted stockings as part of the wardrobe of the Princess Mary, sister of Henry VIII. Bluff King Hal, himself, is said to have had in his wardrobe six pairs of black-silk, knitted hose. This record, however, may refer, as some writers believe, to the full hose rather than to stockings. In France, hand-knitted silk stockings were worn first by Henry II, in June, 1559, when he was attending a royal wedding. At this early date, however, the great mass of the people continued to wear stockings made of various materials shaped and sewed together.

Figure 370. Fashionable Long Hose, Short Doublet, Tall Hat, and Crackows, 1400

In the early years of the knitted stocking it probably required one week to knit two pairs of ordinary hose. If the stockings were to be unusually fine, six months were consumed in the making of a single pair. By the end of the sixteenth century, however, stockings were of every fabric. Some were knitted; others were of woolen cloth, silk, and velvet, cut and seamed to fit the leg and foot. Clocks in gold and silver thread and gay embroidery began to appear. Women soon began wearing the most expensive silk hose, costing as much as seventy-five francs per pair. Red hose, called *bas flamette*, were especially popular, and with these, blue and red slippers were worn. As proof that women must have continued to indulge their extravagant taste, we have the assertions of Philip Stubbes. He says mildly of the ladies:

Their *stockings* are either of silk, Jarnsey, worsted, crewell; or at least of fine yarn, thread, or cloth as is possible to be had. They are not ashamed to wear those of all kinds of changeable colors, as green, red, white, russet, tawny, and else what, cunningly cut and curiously indented at every point with quirks, clocks, open seams, and everything else accordingly.

On the heads of gentlemen, however, he vents his contempt:

Then have they *neather stocks* to those gay hosen, not of cloth (though never so fine), for that is thought too base, but of Jarnsey, worsted, crewell, silke, thread, and such like, or else, at the least the finest yarn that can be got; and so curiously knit with open seam down the leg, with quirks and clocks about the ancles, and sometime, (haplie) interlaced about the ancles with gold or silver threads, as is wonderful to behold. And to such impudent insolency and shameful outrage it has now growne, that everyone almost, though otherwise very poor, having scarce forty shillings wages by the year, will not stick to have two or three pairs of these silk *neather stocks*, or else of the finest yarn that can be got, though the price of them be a royal, or twenty shillings, or more, as commonly is; for how can they be lesse, when as the very knitting of them is worth a noble, or a royal, and some much more? The time hath been when one might have clothed all his body well, from top to toe, for lesse than a pair of these *neather stocks* will cost.

Anatomie of Abuses, 1596

It is not surprising that these luxurious accessories, handknit as they were, were expensive, for knitting was comparatively a new art, having been practiced for only approximately a century. Few, indeed, were those sufficiently skilled in transforming yarn into hose. It had been only a short time before the outburst of Mr. Stubbes that the first knitting machine appeared (1589). This machine was developed by an Englishman, William Lee of Nottinghamshire. The story is told that this gentleman sat day after day watching his wife ply the needles, stitch by stitch, row upon row, until the "stock" was completed. By-and-by he conceived the idea of making a complete row in one operation of the needles. He soon produced a knitting frame which made a continuous flat area of fabric which could be seamed in tubular shape. He was thrilled with the idea of revolutionizing the whole world of dress, and of hose in particular, by introducing machine-knitted hose instead of those made by patient hand knitters. He laid his invention before the Queen. Even in this early day

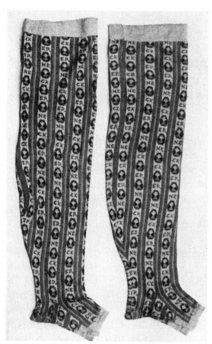

Queen Elizabeth must have recognized the machine as something of a Frankenstein, for she refused to aid him, saying, "Would you take the bread out of the mouths of hand-knitters?" Then she added by way of compromise, "If your machine could knit silk stockings, I might perchance assist you." Taking renewed courage the inventor knit a pair of silk stockings and returned to the palace to assure the Queen that he had further demonstrated the possibilities of his machine. Her Majesty, however, was in no mood to assist, and completely ignored him. Lee, downcast but not discouraged, crossed the channel, and at last, at the French court, found that which he sought in the person of Henry

Figure 371. Silk Stockings, French, 1783-93

IV. The King immediately offered his patronage. As a result Lee set up his frames at Rouen and began a work which in time revolutionized the hosiery trade. The industry rapidly spread and Lee continually prospered. After the assassination of Henry and the death of Lee, his workmen carried the valuable invention back to England.

Having been started on their career, stockings continued their way through the centuries. Refreshingly interesting are the Shakespearian references to the hose—*stockings, hose, cross gartered*, each is mentioned by name:

He will come to her in yellow *stockings*, and 'tis a color she abhors; and *cross-gartered*, a fashion she detests.   *Twelfth Night*. Act II, sc. 5

What a pretty thing man is when he goes in his doublet and *hose* and leaves off his wit!   *Much Ado about Nothing*. Act V, sc. 1

Doublet and *hose* ought to show itself courageous to petticoat.
                    As You Like It. Act II, sc. 4

1600-1700

During the seventeenth century the silk stocking was the fashionable choice. Many were the colors of this modish accessory—green, russet, silver, gray, carnation, black, and white. White silk stockings were preferred by gentlemen who had not adopted the fashionable high boot. Even in winter, silk stockings must be worn. To secure a little warmth several pairs had to be worn at once, one over the other. Three was the popular number, but it is recorded that one gentleman (whether it was unusually cold or unusually stylish is not stated) ventured forth wearing twelve pairs of silk stockings. This century marks the vogue for the high boot introduced by Henry IV of France. About 1620 the top of this boot was greatly increased in width and turned down, displaying the silk hose to advantage. Between the silk stocking and the cavalier boot a linen hose, edged with lace, was worn as a protection to the stocking. This was known as "boot hose." In time it grew very elaborate. It became wide at the top and trimmed with ruffles of billowy lace which formed a kind of lining to the turned-down cavalier boot. So fashionable was this conceit that many "exquisites" of the day, who did not care to encumber the foot with a second hose,

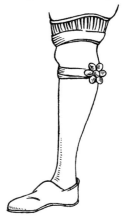

Figure 372. Hose of 1590

Figure 373. Lace Ruffs, 1700

wore only the fluffy tops fastened about the leg. Many of these are said to have reached the extravagant width of two yards. They were set with eyelets, were caught over or under the breeches by points, and then each was further confined by a garter below the knee. Being wide above the knee and loosely held by points, a much-admired bagging effect over the garter was produced. These elaborate effects led to the later fashion of wearing drooping valances of lace and lawn about the knee. Figure 373. Though silk hose were the *sine qua non* of fashion, after 1680 the cotton stocking came into favor. This was made in England and chiefly supplied by the stocking trade. By the end of the century long and short stockings of kersey, wool, and worsted, as well as silk and cotton, were in use. Figure 373.

1700-1800

With the beginning of the extravagant eighteenth century there came the blithe days of the Louis's and their favorites, Madame du Barry, Madame de Pompadour, and Marie Antoinette, who ruled the fashion world. In men's fashions this was the day of the knee trouser and silk stocking. Blue and scarlet hose beautifully clocked in gold and silver thread were a mark of great elegance in dress. These gay, silken hose were usually accompanied by the famous shoes with red heels. During the earlier years of the century stockings were pulled up over the short breeches and gartered below the knee, a fashion which lasted well toward the middle of the period. Then fashion changed a little and a short, close trouser, fitted well down over the knee, was buttoned or buckled to confine the stocking. Figure 374. The gay silk hose of this century continued to be beautifully clocked, and stripes were exceedingly popular.

In colonial America, woolen stockings were worn from approximately 1620 to 1725. Many of these were heavy homespun, in russet, blue, browns, and gray greens. Styles in hosiery in America followed, in the main, the fashion set in France and England. The wives and daughters of our provincial governors, wealthy Virginia planters, and the few others who could afford it, adopted the silk stockings so fashionable in that modish center of the world, Paris. Various colors rose in favor as the years went by, swaying for a while the popular trend in hosiery, only to make way a little later for other colors and color combinations. During the early years of American independence, fashions were tempered with wisdom. Though Dame Fashion recommended silk stockings, they were doubtless worn with discretion. Toward the very close of the century, however, a man's silk stockings were the most important detail of his dress and might easily be more costly than any other article of his attire. They were, indeed, the object of great pride and solicitous care. Though silk stockings held first place, there were, of course, other materials in common use. Cloth, knitted homespun, and knitted worsted stockings were serviceable hose fitted to the life and need of a vast number of Americans.

The Lee knitting frames had worked a miracle in the hosiery industry. With the passing of the years, however, new types of machines and various improvements were destined to replace the earlier frames. In 1790 a circular machine was invented in France. This knitted in tubular form, but, strange to say, it did not come into general use. It was followed by various improved machines and other inventions until 1864, when the original machine upon which all modern hosiery is knit was patented by

William Cotton, an Englishman. Since that date this machine has been ever improved, and in 1889 the automatic machine was introduced.

The knitting industry in America probably began when the German immigrants, in 1869, set up their knitting factories in Germantown, Pennsylvania. The honor of establishing the first knitting mill in this country also falls to Germantown. This took place in 1825. As early as 1790 the stocking industry had been organized in several towns in Connecticut,

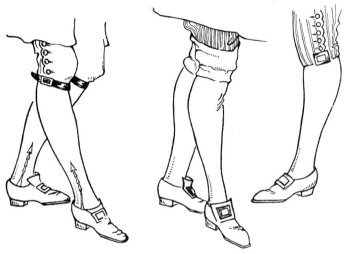

Figure 374. Fashion Trends through 1700

and in 1822 stocking machinery was secretly brought to this country and the industry started at Ipswich, Massachusetts. In this twentieth century New England and Pennsylvania support the largest cotton mills.

1800-1900

With the coming of the nineteenth century the trouser was gradually coaxed to the shoe top. When in the early years of the century it was finally accepted, the long hose so fashionable in the eighteenth was shortened. By-and-by it extended up and over the calf of the leg and was familiarly called the *sock*. This was not a new word in the vocabulary of hosiery, for it too, had come down from ancient times. Among the Romans a light covering for the foot resembling the modern sock and known as the *soccus* had been worn. In the ninth century A.D. the Franks and Anglo-Saxons wore a leg covering, a kind of short stocking made of cloth or thin leather. This was fitted loosely and could easily be drawn over the foot and heel. Figure 375. The illustration, Figure 376, after Fairholt makes clear this custom of the early Saxons. The sock is worn over the hose and within the shoe. These ancient *soccus* and *socque* suggest the half hose or sock of modern times.

With the establishment of cotton mills and the cotton industry in America, cotton stockings soon came to be generally fashionable. In 1863 milady selected the hose that exactly corresponded in color with her petticoat. Violet was a favorite hue for both petticoat and stockings, especially since this color had been recently manufactured "fast" and guar-

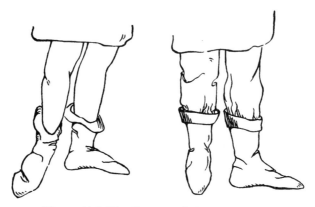

Figure 375. The Socque of the Franks and
Anglo-Saxons

anteed "to stand any amount of washing."* The economic stress occasioned by the Civil War naturally had its effect upon clothes, and hosiery kept to the inexpensive fabrics of cotton and wool. The long skirts of women, preventing even a glimpse of an ankle, and the long trousers of men, had much to do with the prevalence of the more simple types of hosiery. Even as late as 1890 the woman who possessed silk stockings was the envy of her associates. During these years of the hidden stocking, the improvement in dyestuffs, and the infinite number of new and possible hues were preparing every day for the beauty of modern hose. These years were destined to bring forth the most beautiful and varied styles in hosiery that the world had witnessed.

Twentieth Century

The full flower of the hosiery industry blossomed in the early twentieth century. Now cotton, lisle, wool, silk of various weights, combinations of silk and cotton, silk and wool, and the gossamer silk chiffon—all beckoned to milady of fashion. Figure 377. These were machine made. In the cotton stocking of this period the grade of cotton used was an important factor in the character and value of the product. The lisle stocking was made of combed Egyptian cotton. This cotton was twisted slightly and run through a flame of gas to singe the lint which is always seen in yarns made from cotton. The singeing process gives a very fine

* *Peterson's Fashion Magazine,* March, 1863.

"feel" to the stocking. Added to this is a silky luster which is imparted by treating it scientifically with caustic soda. This process is known as *mercerizing*. In treating the fiber in this process the yarn loses its flat, twisted shape and becomes more round. Cotton treated to the mercerizing process takes dye more readily. Mercerized hosiery is distinctly a modern product. In the realm of silk hosiery the modern manufacturer turns out two types of stockings, the seamless and the full-fashioned hose. The seamless hose was formerly knitted in one piece on a circular machine, leaving an opening for the toe to be looped together. The leg, heel, and toe were usually shaped by steaming and then dried on boards cut in the proper shape. Today, however, a later invention knits and shapes the stocking in one process. "Full-fashioned" is the most recent adjective to be applied to distinctive hosiery. This hose is also made on a modern machine, and the art of shaping it is given great consideration. As this machine knits, it automatically drops the required number of stitches to make it conform to the leg, ankle, and foot. The leg is knitted in a flat piece on one machine and then seamed on another. The demand in these days for silk stockings has led to the use of artificial or vegetable silk made from wood fiber. Hosiery made of this material is attractive in appearance but has not succeeded in taking the place of the all-silk stocking. Another miracle thread spun from the same chemical elements as are found in coal, air, and water is called "nylon," and this new material is considered a most important textile discovery. Indications are that nylon hose may assume first place; indeed, may even outmode the fashionable silk hosiery of the present day.

Figure 376. The Sock Worn with a Shoe

After Fairholt.

In these days of the twentieth century the many whims and fancies in hosiery would all but confuse the feminine mind. One season says "no stockings"; another, "silk stockings"; for sport, "silk and wool mixtures"; and so it goes. The 1930 fashion for sun-tanned legs, without stockings, seemed a novel departure in those days, but it was only a repetition of a custom sanctioned long ago by the belles of the Nile, by the Greeks, and by the Romans. During the Middle Ages and the Renaissance, the long, trailing skirts concealed the hose, and milady was content with cloth. When skirts grew shorter cotton all but vanished and only silk was accepted. And now milady is so wedded to silk hose that a longer skirt has no influence whatever on fashions in hosiery. Fashion authorities believe that women, whatever their economic position, have become so accustomed to the luxury of silk hose that there is no possible return to cotton and lisle for general wear. Cotton manufacturers, however, have appealed to the economic sense of women in presenting their arguments for a return to cotton for the garter tops and feet of silk hosiery. These have been generally accepted. Time only, however, will prove whether cotton man-

ufacturers by their modern methods and appeal to service can persuade women to return to the all-cotton hose. The trend toward new discoveries in textile threads —indeed, it may be said that these are present-day accomplishments — leaves much in the field of modern hosiery to the very near future.

The popular materials favored for women's hose also lead in fashions for men. Silk, cotton, wool, rayon, and mixtures make up the modern list of fabrics for men's shortened hose. These are usually woven with a deep-ribbed top which is very elastic and assists in keeping the hose in place. Figure 378. Colors are beautiful and varied. Em-

Figure 377. Women's
Modern Silk Hose

broidery clocks and dropped stitches add to the artistry of the modern sock. The sport hose so fashionable for both men and women strikes a gay note of color in modern dress. These hose are knitted in wool, mixtures of silk and wool, and wool and cotton, and are usually strikingly pronounced in both color and pattern. The sport hose is a distinctive type of leg covering that has gradually developed with the widening interests in modern athletic life.

In looking back over the field of

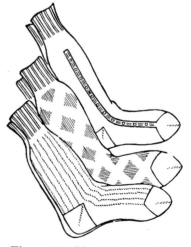

Figure 378. Men's Modern Hose

hosiery, it is almost startling to observe the fascinating role played by men in the history of hose. For centuries only gentlemen's hose were considered. Shapely legs encased in finest silk and displayed with gartered top left women quite out of the picture. Today, however, with women's shortened skirts and gentlemen's lengthened trousers the scene has shifted. Attention is now lavished upon milady's silk hose, while gentlemen are content to stand on the sidelines. The aim of the stocking industry is centered upon the achievement of the most beautiful in hosiery that the world has known, a hose which fulfills in color, texture, and service the every wish of modern women; a hose which not only improves the art of dress, but increases its charm as well. One is reminded of the significant words of the distinguished French author, August Challamel, in his *History of Fashion in France:*

We must not limit the causes of fashion to three only—the love of change, the influence of those with whom we live and the desire of pleasing them, the interest of traders in a transient reign of luxury. . . . There remains to be pointed out a fourth and much nobler cause. There is frequently the desire, though not always successful, to *improve the art of dress, to increase its charm, and to intelligently and sanely advance its progress.*

A review of the history of hose places the modern stocking within the province of the "nobler cause"—*to improve the art of dress, to increase its charm, and to intelligently and sanely advance its progress.*

REFERENCES

Calthrop, Dion Clayton, *English Costume*, Vol. III, p. 53.
Hartley, Dorothy, *Medieval Costume and Life.*
Kelly and Schwabe, *Historic Costume.*
Lester, Katherine Morris, *Historic Costume*, pp. 106, 230.
Norris, Herbert, *Costume and Fashion*, Vols. I, II.
Peterson's Fashion Magazine, March, 1863.
Planché, J. R., *Cyclopedia of Costume*, Vols. I, II.
Rhead, C. W., *Chats on Costume*, pp. 114, 118.

CHAPTER 23

Garters

A pair of silver *garters* buckled below the knee.
ADDISON, *Spectator,* No. 16

THE primitive ancestor of the modern garter filled its ancient role in much the same way as does its present-day successor. As a leather

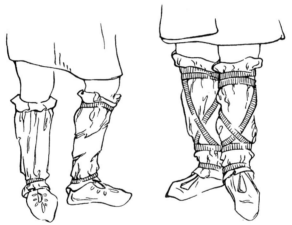

Figure 379. Primitive Ancestor of the Garter

thong tied below the knee or about the ankle it confined a sort of loose legging. True, with the passing of the centuries, ribbon, silk, lace, and silver buckles were substituted for the thong, and today elastic cloth has superseded these, yet the modern garter, as of old, is still worn to confine the "loose legging."

Middle Ages

The early legging was no more than a piece of hide or cloth wrapped about the leg as a protection. Following the use of the simple thong came the bandages cross gartered to the knee and serving the same purpose. Figure 379. In a detail of the Bayeux Tapestry several examples of the garter worn by Norman nobles of the eleventh century are pictured. One is tied below the knee and confines what appears to be a knitted hose. The fringed ends hang at the side while the top of the hose seems to be rolled over the garter. Figure 380. The earliest mention of the garter in literature is probably in the *Decameron* of Boccaccio, written sometime before 1353. In the second story of the second day Rinaldo, who had been robbed of all his apparel, even to his shoes, gets back everything but his garters, "*un paro di cintolini.*"

The various types of dress worn by men and women through the ages have had much to do with our historical knowledge of this sometimes visible, sometimes invisible acces- sory. When the long robes of men and the trailing garments of women prevailed, they disappeared from view. In 1300, when men adopted the long, close- fitting hose and the cotehardie, a fitted tunic reach- ing to the thigh, the garter was brought more and more into prominence. At this early date it was not an article of use but purely ornamental, worn largely by fashionable gentlemen. The custom is said to have first developed in Italy, and soon after was carried into France. In view of this an engraving from a portrait of Cimabue painted in 1300 is interesting. Figure 381. As an artist, Cimabue, appreciating the touch of variety which the golden garter imparts to the otherwise plain surface of the long, tight hose, wears this fashionable accessory fixed just below the knee.

Figure 380. A Type of Knitted Hose and Orna- mental Garter Seen in the Bay- eux Tapestry

During this century records show that gentle- men of fashion wore elaborate garters ornamented with jewels and beautiful buckles. Women of this day also confined the long cloth stocking, cut and sewed by hand, with a silk or velvet garter embroidered with gold and silver thread and ornamented with jewels and tassels. François Rabelais, the encyclopediac writer, speaking of the scarlet or crimson stockings worn by women, says that their garters "were the same color as their bracelets and fitted close above and below the knee." Throughout the early history of the garter, however, it was men, not women, who were conspicuous in their extrava- gant taste and showy display of this accessory.

It was in this period that the famous order of knighthood, the *Most Noble Order of the Garter*, was instituted by Richard III of England. Earlier orders of knighthood had made service the great objective. The purpose of the new order was solely to enable the sovereign to confer added dignity upon distinguished persons whom he wished to honor. Eminent, authoritative writers of the period say that the institution of the order grew out of an accident which occurred at a state ball given by the King. Among the guests at this royal function were the Earl of Salis- bury and his charming wife, the Lady Catherine. Gossip had already noted the attachment of the King for this beautiful lady. During the course of the ball, while in the midst of the dance, Lady Catherine met with the embarrassing misfortune of dropping her garter. The gay company was greatly amused, and did not hesitate to pass jesting and indelicate remarks. The tactful King quickly stopped, picked up the blue garter, and returned it to the fair lady, who immediately withdrew. Thereupon the King turned upon the company and rebuked them hotly,

exclaiming, *"Honi soit qui mal y pense,"** and added that he would make this blue garter so glorious that all nobles would desire it. At the foundation of the order in 1348 the various insignia were named— the belt, and sword, the surcoat, the hood, the garter. The garter, the principal badge of the order, was a band of sky-blue velvet edged with gold, and bore upon it in letters of gold the famous words: *Honi soit qui mal y pense.* A golden buckle also adorned this historic garter, which was worn on the left leg by knights and upon the left forearm or wrist by the few women who were so honored. The color of the garter remained the same through the centuries until George I (1707-27), changed the sky-blue color to dark blue.

Figure 381. Cimabue
From an old engraving.

The following lines, from Shakespeare's *Henry VI*, state in unmistakable terms that only the worthy were sufficiently distinguished for this honor:

> I vowed, base knight, when I did meet thee next,
> To tear the *garter* from thy craven's leg,
> Which I have done, because unworthily
> Thou wast installed in that high degree.
>
> *Henry VI.* Act IV, sc. 1

Though centuries have rolled by, the blue garter still remains the insignia of this most famous, premier order of knighthood in England.

---

* Translated, "Evil to him who thinks evil."

1500-1600

It is an illuminating fact that throughout the manuscripts of the four-teenth and fifteenth centuries nothing appears which resembles the garter as a useful rather than an ornamental detail in men's attire. In the sixteenth

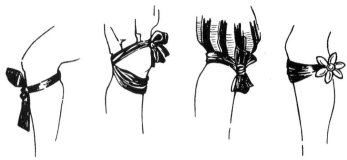

Figure 382. Fashionable Garters of 1500

and seventeenth centuries, however, its usefulness came more and more into prominence. We naturally infer from this that the separation of the long, tight hose into "upper stocks" and "nether stocks" undoubtedly brought the garter more and more into use. Though the early "nether hose" or "stocking of hose" were fastened to the trunk hose by points,

Figure 383. Garters of 1600 Transformed into Sashes
and Elaborate Knee Ornaments

the garter was frequently added as an additional aid. During the reign of Francis I (1515-47), when long stockings and slashed breeches were the fashionable order of the day, garters became visible for a short time. Figure 382. Under Henry II (1547-59), the great trunk hose and their tubular extensions called *canons* frequently covered the garters. During the same century, however, when Charles IX (1560-74), and Henry IV (1589-1610), led the fashion world, they again came into prominence. In the early years of the century garters were merely ties of ribbon knotted below the knee. With the passing of the years and the growing extravagance in every field of dress, it is not surprising that the possibilities of the garter as a decoration were rapidly developed. Garters of these later days were among the most important accessories of dress. They were very showy, with deep-fringed and lace-trimmed ends. As early as 1525 a type of cross garter was used which gave a very handsome effect. This was placed below the knee, the long ends crossed at the back and brought forward above the knee where they were tied. Figure 382. In the later years of the century, writers of the period frequently call attention to "garters fringed with gold" and "garters rich with silver roses." No doubt the women of this day wore a similar type of garter.

Figure 384. Garter Bows, Gold Galloon, French, Early 1800's

Contrast with earlier, ribbon bows.

Though the voluminous skirts of the period hid them from view, it is not to be supposed that woman's fastidious taste was to be outstripped by men of her day.

1600-1700

The dress of the early seventeenth century is distinguished by the Spanish mode of wasplike waist and short, bombasted breeches, which had been carried over from the preceding years. A little later breeches narrowed from the waistband to the knee, where they met the garters, which were tied in fanciful bows or finished with large rosettes of lace, lawn, and ribbon. Figure 383. Many of these garters took the form of a sash swathing the leg below the knee and were tied in a huge bow with long ends of richest lace. Another type of the popular garter was a band set on the outer side with bows and bunches of ribbon. Figure 383. Frequently these bunches of ribbon appear both on the inner and outer side of the garter. Then followed cavalier days when the great-top boots led to all sorts of extravagance in breeches, hose, points, and knee decorations. Frills of rich lace falling to the middle of the leg hung from the garter. Figure 385. This fashion, no doubt, grew out of the earlier custom of wearing the boot hose between the boot and silk stocking. The latter was fastened to the short trouser by points; a garter below the knee kept the boot hose in place, while the loose top fell over the garter forming a kind of valance. These elaborate knee decorations may or may not have been a part of the garter. At any rate they were worn at the place where the hose is gartered. So general were all these fopperies of fashion that stern reprimands were constantly sounded forth. One poet hints his opinion of the mode when he chides those who,

Wear a farm in shoe-strings edged with gold,
And spangled *garters* worth a copyhold.

JOHN TAYLOR, the Water Poet

Others ridicule the "spangled *garters* pendant to the shoe . . . with a thousand such fooleries unknown to our manly forefathers."*

Toward the end of the century the fanciful knee trimmings began to go. The stockings were now rolled up over the breeches, and the garter was reduced to a buckled band fixed below the knee or hidden in the roll of the stocking. Figure 386. In the eighteenth century the knee trouser fitted well down over the knee, concealing the garter.

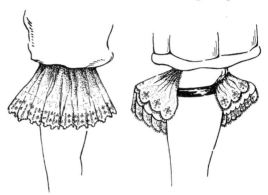

Figure 385. Fanciful Knee Ornaments, 1600

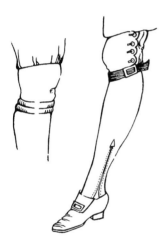

Figure 386. Fashions of Late 1700's

The trouser was finished at the side just below the knee with a buckle or several buttons. Figure 387. Following the short trousers of 1700 came the lengthened trouser which gradually approached the boot top. The garter continued to remain invisible.

1800-1900

During the first quarter of the nineteenth century, the beginning of the great rubber industry was destined to revolutionize not only the nation's business but its dress as well. Among the accessories of dress first affected by the great discoveries in the rubber world was the shoe. Following this came rubberized cloth for use in overshoes, raincoats, and caps. Soon followed a method of weaving an elastic cloth. In this process threads of rubber are stretched upon a frame, and the linen, silk, or cotton thread is woven over the stretched rubber. This elastic cloth or *webbing*, as it was known, was first manufactured in England and used for the wrists of gloves. Later it was woven into bands of different size to be used for various purposes.

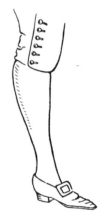

Figure 387. Trouser, 1800 Concealing garter.

* Henry Peachum, *Truth of Our Times.*

With the coming of elastic bands, the ribbon garter was forced off the market. The woven elastic band supplanted all other methods for garter-

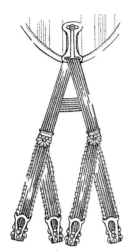

ing the hose. From that day to this, in the field of gartering, nothing has taken the place of elastic webbing. About 1875 the various dress-reform movements which sprang up simultaneously in France, England, and America did much to set people thinking about hygienic and comfortable clothes, particularly for women. At this time many changes in fashion were advocated, and not the least among these was the new method of gartering the hose. The elastic band either above or below the knee was denounced as an impedi-ment to circulation and, consequently, a menace to health. Doctors and nurses, alike, advocated the elastic supporter suspended from the front or side of a stay, girdle, or belt. Manufacturers imme-diately put this improved accessory on the market and it was readily adopted. Figure 388 illustrates the fashionable front supporter of the nineties.

Figure 388. Early
Elastic Front
Supporter

This was attached to the lowest stud of the stay or girdle. Aside from its useful-ness as a supporter of hose, it was claimed that this particular model would impart to the wearer "that straight-front military effect" which was the key phrase in wom-en's fashions. Side supporters followed front supporters, and these were in popular demand. Figure 389. They were made in a number of attractive colors—yellow, red, pink, lavender; and also black and white. The introduction in the nineties of a rub-ber-covered metal button added a new feature which has persisted to the present day.

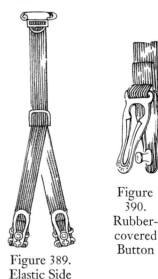

Figure
390.
Rubber-
covered
Button

Twentieth Century

Though from year to year there have

Figure 389.
Elastic Side
Supporter

been some changes in style, the side supporter continues, in this twen-tieth century, to be the choice form for gartering the hose. Along with the elastic supporter, however, are dainty elastic bands, trimmed with rosettes, bows, flowers, and rhinestone ornaments, which still hold a place in Fashion's field.

The garter worn by men of the modern world is far removed from the silken, lace-trimmed sash which swathed the leg of the "exquisites" of 1600. Today they are without ornamentation, serving only as a support for the hose. Figure 391. Verily, the garter of gentlemen has passed from the gayest and most fantastic to the drabbest of accessories.

In reviewing from ancient times the fascinating role of the garter, it would seem that it reached the height of its capricious development in the seventeenth century. Following this, it quietly subsided into the place of a less conspicuous accessory. The modern elastic band, so generally worn is only the thong of old improved by the efforts of man in the field of invention. The side supporter, the most recent phase of the ancient thong, is the result of the same inventive effort. The great interests of the present-day world, discovery, invention, and science, continue happily to contribute to the smallest of accessories which go to make up the story of dress.

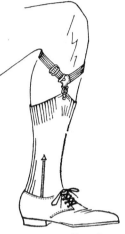

Figure 391. Gentleman's Modern Garter

REFERENCES

Calthrop, Dion Clayton, *English Costume.*
Cole, George, *Dictionary of Dry Goods*, pp. 159, 160.
Fairholt, F. W., *Costume in England.*
Kelly and Schwabe, *Historic Costume.*
New International Encyclopedia, Vol. I.
Planché, J. R., *Cyclopedia of Costume*, Vols. I, II.
Rhead, C. W., *Chats on Costume.*
Sage, Elizabeth, *A Study of Costume.*

CHAPTER 24

Gaiters

The eloquent Pickwick . . . his elevated position revealing those tights and *gaiters*
which, had they clothed an ordinary man, might have passed unnoticed.

CHARLES DICKENS, *Pickwick Papers*

GAITERS, like hose, may be traced back to the earliest form of leg
covering. This was a piece of cloth or hide wrapped about the leg
to the knee and bound with a thong, or cross gartered. Aside from this
most primitive type, the more modern progenitor of the gaiter is the jack boot, which was adopted about 1660. Figure 392. It was worn only for riding. It was made of leather and, being a stiff form unshaped to the leg, was both clumsy and uncomfortable. From this boot, however, there was developed some years later a lighter form which fitted more neatly over the instep and about the ankle and leg.

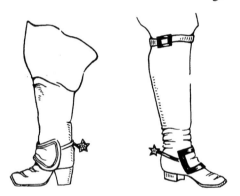

Figures 392, 393. Jack Boot with Spur Leather, and Fitted Boot

Figure 393. Over the instep the spur leather, which supported the spur, continued to be worn. This light boot in time developed into a legging of leather which was buttoned or buckled down the side.

1700-1800

Though this type of legging had been introduced about 1710 by the infantry and was soon adopted by civilians, it was not until 1770 that it became a fashionable form of leg covering. A writer of 1736 says of the leggings of that date that they were "a sort of light boot without soles." F. W. Fairholt, eminent English authority, says that leggings were "coverings for the legs used by soldiers, which fasten at the side like gaiters but were secured more tightly to the leg by straps and bands about the knee."

The cavalry must be saddled, the artillery horses harnessed and the infantry *gaitered.*

Trial of Lord G. Sackville (1760)

In medieval drawings there appear many instances in which a protection for the leg is worn. These have much the character of boots without soles but are fastened at the sides. The word *gaiter* is from the French *guêtre* and does not appear in the English language until about 1750.

About 1770 leggings came to be very fashionable and were especially adopted for wear in stormy weather. They were made of leather and were buttoned or buckled down the side. They were known as *spatterdashes*, probably because they protected the hose from the spatters of rain and dashes of mud.

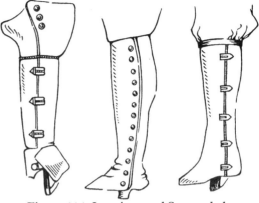

Figure 394. Leggings and Spatterdashes

Here's a fellow made for a soldier; there's a leg for a *spatterdash*, with an eye like the king of Prussia.

SHERIDAN, *The Camp.* Act I, sc. 2

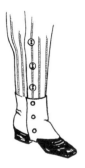

Figure 395. The Fashionable Short Gaiter, Early 1800

Figure 396. Trousers Held by a Strap beneath the Boot Arch

Figure 397. Modern Gaiters or Spats

1800-1900

It is surprising to know that even in that day in some parts of England, these leggings were called "spats." Today Fashion has definitely abbreviated the name as well as the leggings and the modern world knows them as spats.

It was during the nineteenth century that long leggings began to grow shorter. Then they were still generally known as gaiters. In the first years of the century gaiters were a fashionable feature in men's dress. As the trouser descended the leg, approaching first the shoe top, then the ankle, gaiters gradually took the place of the high boot. Figure 395. Even the black boot with light gray or biege top, though a fashionable note in gentlemen's attire, was soon rivaled by the black shoe with the gray cloth gaiter. It is said that all young men who hesitated to give up their boots but still wanted to appear fashionable, adopted boots with a black foot and gray top which resembled the gaitered shoe. In 1820 dark pantaloons and gaiters were very fashionable. So marked was the influence of the gaiter that as trousers grew longer, they were fitted at the ankle, sometimes provided with buttons, and a strap passing under the shoe arch held each leg in place. Figure 396.

From the early days of the nineteenth century to the present, gaiters have held a modest place among accessories of dress. At times they have been short, again they have lengthened into fashionable leggings so generally worn with knickerbockers. This was another influence of the popular sport world, an influence which so quickly registered in the general dress of both men and women.

In the twentieth century the fashion for spats waxes and wanes. Figure 397. At rare intervals they are worn by women. Far more frequently, however, they are both a fashionable and distinctive note in the modern dress of gentlemen.

REFERENCES

Fairholt, F. W., *Costume in England*.
Giafferri, Paul-Louis de, *History of French Masculine Costume*.
Planché, J. R., *Cyclopedia of Costume*, Vol. I.

Part IV

ACCESSORIES WORN ON THE ARM AND HAND

CHAPTER 25

The Bracelet

Will he return unto his father's house
And revel it as bravely as the best,
With silken coats, and caps, and golden rings,
With ruffs, and cuffs, farthingales and things;
With scarfs, and fans, and double change of bravery,
With amber *bracelets*, beads, and all this knavery?

Taming of the Shrew. Act IV, sc. 3

THE bracelet as an ornament for the wrist and arm belongs to all peoples, both savage and civilized, and its use extends from most ancient times to the present. The word "bracelet" is derived from the

Figure 398. Bracelets of the Bronze Age

Latin *bracum*, which means "arm." This ornament has usually been worn about the wrist. The "armlet," named from *armilla*, is a circular ornament worn above and below the elbow.

The earliest collections of savage ornament show bracelets of plaited grass, shell, wood, and ivory. Later, among more advanced peoples, metal was used, and this ultimately developed to a point where it was enriched by engravings, enamels, inlays of glass, and settings of stones. Many bracelets of the Bronze Age have been recovered. Figure 398. These were made of both bronze and gold. The bronze bracelets are usually deco-

314

rated, while those of gold are plain bands. Coming down to later times we read in Exodus XXXV:22,

And they came, both men and women, as many as were willing-hearted and brought *bracelets*, and earrings, and rings and tablets, all jewels of gold; and every man that offered an offering of gold unto the Lord.

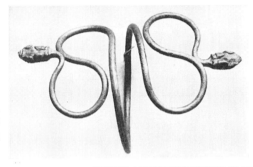

Again in Ezekial XVI:2, God's love for Jerusalem is expressed thus:

I decked thee also with ornaments, and I put *bracelets* upon thine hands and a chain on thine neck.

The Egyptians wore gold anklets as well as bracelets, frequently ornamented with

COURTESY, METROPOLITAN MUSEUM OF ART

Figure 399. Bracelet, Egyptian, Ptolemaic Period, 332-30 B.C.

stones and enriched with enamels. Many were in the form of serpents; others were simple, gold, band rings. In the Leyden Museum is a gold anklet one-and-a-half inches high by three inches in diameter

COURTESY, METROPOLITAN MUSEUM OF ART

Figure 400. Jewelry of Princess Sat-Hathor-Iunit, Egyptian, XII Dynasty

Bracelets—beads of gold, carnelian, and turquoise. Sliding gold clasps inlaid with name and titles of A-men-em-het.

Anklets—beads of gold, carnelian, and turquoise. Sliding gold clasps.

bearing the name of Thotmes III. This inscription would indicate that it had been worn by that monarch. In an early period the glass industry of Egypt had attained a high degree of perfection. Armlets, bracelets, and rings of glass of many widths were worn. Glass beads and beads of gold, turquoise, carnelian, and other semiprecious stones, both light and dark in color, were in general use. Not a few of these ornaments were made of beads, the light and dark repeated at certain intervals, showing a fine sense of design. A pair of anklets and bracelets belonging to a princess of the

Twelfth Dynasty shows rows upon rows of gold, carnelian, and turquoise beads. The elaborate sliding clasps are inlaid with the name and titles of Amenemhet. Figure 400. Among the interesting treasures found in the tomb of the youthful King Tutankhamen are the bracelets which

decorated the arms of the mummy. Seven were found upon the right forearm and six upon the left. These were made of gold and silver, many of them inlaid with precious stones and pieces of colored glass. The scarab was also much in evidence.

From antiquity the people of all oriental countries, both men and women, have displayed great admiration for bracelets on both the upper and lower arm. The ancient Persians and As-syrians, as well as the Egyp-

COURTESY, METROPOLITAN MUSEUM OF ART

Figure 401. Silver Armlet, Egyptian, 332-30 B.C.

tians, commonly wore the bracelet. Among these peoples it was always an evidence of wealth and a symbol of power. In the British Museum are bas-reliefs from Nineveh showing a king wearing heavy chain bracelets similar to those shown in Figure 402. This unusual bracelet is

one from the famous Cesnola Collection of the Metropolitan Museum, New York City. It was found with other valuable ornaments during the excavations carried on in the island of Cyprus in 1872 and therefore dates from a very early period. The band of the bracelet is formed by a number of ribbed gold beads soldered together

Figure 402. Section of Handsome Gold Bracelet with Onyx and Gold Medallion

Cesnola Collection, Metropolitan Museum of Art.

three by three. In the center is a large gold medallion, within which is an onyx setting. The onyx was originally held in a silver mounting but the silver was so oxidized that it fell to dust when the clinging earth was being removed. From the medallion hang four chains, and at the end of each one is a gold amulet. This, like other ornaments found at the same time, indicates that the people of Cyprus carried on extensive commercial relations with the neighboring world.

The Greeks gradually came to use jewelry. Chains, necklaces, bracelets, and other articles of personal ornament did not become popular in Greece until the workers in metal had achieved a high degree of skill, about the fourth century, B.C.; and from this period on magnificent ornaments of gold, silver, and bronze appeared. Patterns were embossed on thin, metal plates, or designs were outlined by thin, gold wire arranged in various curves. Jewels or gems were rarely used before the third century. Many examples of the classic period (600-146 B.C.) show Grecian women wearing bracelets of various types. The broad, flat, gold surfaces of many of the ancient bracelets are covered with cloissons into which stones or composition had formerly been laid. The most familiar design among Greek bracelets is that of heavy gold, silver, or bronze wire twisted around the arm in imitation of a serpent. Others are penannular with the

COURTESY, METROPOLITAN MUSEUM OF ART

Figure 403. Bracelets, Gold Cloissoné Work

The enamel from cloissons missing, Cypriote, 6th century, B.C.

ends finished in elaborately worked ornamental forms usually representing animals' heads. Figures 404, 405. Many of these bracelets were worn on the upper arm as well as below the elbow. A statue of Aphrodite which stands in the Glyptotek, Munich, shows a broad band or ring about the upper arm. Greek men do not seem to have worn bracelets.

Roman luxury and the taste for ornament date from 68 B.C., when Pompey brought to Rome the captured treasures of Greece and with great ceremony set them before the eyes of an amazed populace. The beauty of Greek jewelry greatly stimulated the desire for ornament among the Romans. Greek artists were brought to Rome and were soon producing Greek designs for the Roman citizenry. Designs from ancient Etruscan ornament were also copied for this luxury-loving people. As always, however, the tendency among Romans ran to display. Consequently, bracelets were very showy. Massive were they in form and elaborate in their settings of vari-colored stones and precious gems. The most popular style of Roman bracelet was that twisted about the arm in imitation of a serpent. Figure 407. The ends were often flattened, suggesting the head and tail. Frequently two or three bands of gold or carved stone were worn on the upper arm as well as about the wrist. Some were made to open and close with hinges and fasteners. Bracelets are frequently seen upon the many existing statutes in Roman sculpture. History points out that Nero was greatly given to the fashion of wearing bracelets and that as a reward of merit or mark of distinction bracelets of silver were awarded to Roman soldiers.

Middle Ages

Nearing the Middle Ages, the fashion scene gradually

COURTESY, METROPOLITAN MUSEUM OF ART

Figure 404. Gold-plated Bracelet with Lions' Heads, Greek, 5th Century, B.C.

shifted from Rome to western Europe. Now the styles of the old world were carried to this corner of the new, where from now on modern dress evolved. Naturally the Gallo-Roman women affected the styles followed by the wives of their Roman conquerors, and for a time the fashion of the bracelet continued. Wide ornamental bands, many of them sent from Byzantium, the capital of the Roman Empire, were a popular fashion. They were frequently made to open with a hinge and were sometimes set with cameos or enriched with enamels. In the ninth and tenth centuries when

COURTESY, METROPOLITAN MUSEUM OF ART

Figure 405. Silver Bracelet, Greek, 4th Century, B.C.

the Danes were invading England, they came wearing gold and bronze bands about the arm. For a time this popularized the bracelet in England. The Vikings, like their kinsmen the Jutes and Angles, considered gold and bronze bracelets a sign of honor, and in England the bracelet gradually came to be regarded as an emblem of rank. In the early and even later days of British sovereignty bracelets, like gloves and rings, were used in the coronation ceremony. In the ceremonies at the coronation of Richard II, Henry VIII, Edward VI, Mary, Elizabeth, and Charles II, the royal, official bracelets were used. Those of Charles II were flat bands of gold, one-and-one-fourth inches wide. The outer surface was beautifully ornamented with colored enamels, the inner was lined with rich red velvet. Other royal and official bracelets are now kept on exhibition in the Tower of London.

1500-1800

The long, flowing sleeve and enveloping mantle of the Middle Ages gradually did much to offset the popularity of bracelets. Invariably when sleeves are long and close fitting, as they were during this period and well

Figure 406. Characteristic Roman Bracelets

on into the sixteenth and seventeenth centuries, bracelets are seldom seen. They were now of minor consequence in the fashion world.

In France toward the close of the eighteenth century, while the Revolution threatened, very little jewelry was worn; bracelets, however, were considered an elegant accessory, especially if set with miniatures and locks of hair. About 1793 short sleeves attained popularity and with this innovation in dress the bracelet again rose in favor, so that during the Revolution and Empire periods bracelets were fashionable accessories in the costume of both men and women.

1800-1900

As the nineteenth century wore on changes appeared. From approximately 1830-60, fewer bracelets were seen, chiefly because the type of sleeve was changing. The sleeveless evening gown, however, was never complete unless bracelets of gold were worn. By-and-by the simpler, lighter forms of jewelry gradually took the place of the massive, showy patterns of earlier years. With the lighter designs which were essentially feminine, it was no longer considered good taste for men to wear the bracelet.

Fashion says there is nothing new under the sun, only new combinations and variations of the old. So again in the late nineteenth century (1882) there came a modified return of the ancient forms of bracelet—serpents twining about the wrist, heavy circlets of gold ending in some favored animal's head, and others of similar style. During the late eighties and nineties, when "sets" of jewelery—that is, bracelets and brooch, or bracelets and chain having the same type of ornament—were the vogue, the cameo was revived, appearing in heavy mountings in these jewelry sets. On the chain it took the form of a slide which pulled the long chain down in a V shape about the neck. On the bracelet, as a slide, it regulated the fit about the wrist. These bracelets were approximately an inch in width, very flexible, the link being in a close mesh resembling woven gold, the loose end finished with gold fringe. They were looked upon as very handsome ornaments and were a part of the elegance of the "watch and chain" period.

Twentieth Century

With the constant change in sleeves, bracelets continued to come and go. Styles played about the old order—a circlet of gold or silver for the arm. With the early years of the new century, however, a new type of ornament was introduced—the beautiful as well as useful wrist watch. This practical adornment was adopted for men's wear shortly before the

COURTESY, METROPOLITAN MUSEUM OF ART
Figure 407. Bracelet, Roman, Probably 300 B.C.

World War and has remained with varying popularity to the present day. The wrist watches worn by men are usually adjusted to silver bracelets or leather straps which fit about the wrist. Women's watches are gold, silver, or platinum, affixed to a bracelet of the same metal. Sometimes a narrow black cord or a ribbon is preferred for securing the dainty watch about the wrist. Though the wrist watch has continued a fashionable note in costume it has by no means usurped the place of the bracelet. Milady of the twentieth century, wearing her watch fixed about the wrist, at the same time finds a use for the many and popular types of bracelets.

Bracelets were of many styles during the early years of the century. Gold, silver, and platinum were the favorite metals, while various forms of composition were also the vogue. Some were set with precious stones and others with stones not so precious. In 1930 bracelets were narrow or wide, linked, hinged, clasped, or slipover.

As with all forms of jewelry in the twentieth century, so it is with the bracelet: the machine has largely taken the place of the craftsman. To be sure, the designer and maker of beautiful jewelry has today a following, but it is indeed limited. The abundant supply of manufactured jewelry placed on the market is beautiful, much less expensive, and offers a tempting variety in size, shape, and decoration.

Bracelets have never gone entirely out of fashion, but their vogue is largely determined by the type of sleeve. The function of the modern bracelet is to "dress" the arm. The short sleeve leaves an unbroken expanse of arm which is far more attractive broken with a note of gold, silver, or color. For this reason bracelets will always have a place in fash-

COURTESY, TIFFANY & CO., NEW YORK

Figure 408. Platinum-and-Diamond, Flexible Bracelet, Early 20th Century

ion. There is a lasting love and indefinable desire in human nature for beautiful ornament and the bracelet as an ornament of beauty may often add the necessary and finishing note to a costume. Though all modern forms of the bracelet may be found among Greek and Etruscan designs, the present gold, silver, and platinum combined with the wealth of precious and semiprecious stones available provide unlimited opportunity for the creative talent of the modern designer and craftsman. Figure 408.

REFERENCES

Carter, Howard, *The Tomb of Tut-ankh-Amen*.
Earle, Alice Morse, *Two Centuries of Costume in America*, pp. 70, 740.
Guhl and Kohner, *Life of the Greeks and Romans*.
Hiler, Hilaire, *From Nudity to Raiment; An Introduction to the Study of Costume*.
Kennard, Beulah, *Jewelry and Silverware*, Chapter 16.
Lester, Katherine Morris, *Historic Costume*, pp. 34, 157.
Norris, Herbert, *Costume and Fashion*, 3 Volumes.
Sage, Elizabeth, *A Study of Costume*, pp. 5, 203.
Wilkinson, Sir John Gardiner, *A Popular Account of the Ancient Egyptians*.

The Ring

THE finger ring, though not the most ancient accessory used in personal adornment, is a very old one. Long before the glitter of rings, as ornament, captured the eye of man, they were used as barter, and later as money. The ancient Egyptians were probably the first to use the ring as money. These money rings were made of common metal linked together. In that day a man's ring money was easily cared for: he simply increased his chain as rings came in and decreased it as he paid money out. This system of ring money has descended from the pharaohs and is said to be still in use in some parts of Africa. Similar systems are known to have existed in other parts of the world. In some of these the smaller rings were strung upon a large metal ring left slightly open. With rings coming in or going out in exchange it was an easy matter to slip the ring money on and off the large ring. Figure 409.

Figure 409. Bronze Money Ring

Found in a pile village in Switzerland.

Bound up with the ring in its history as an object of personal adornment is the Promethean myth. According to the legend, Prometheus had dared to steal the sacred fire from heaven. This so angered the gods that he was condemned to a living death, to be chained forever to a rock on Mount Caucasus while a vulture continually fed upon his vitals. In the course of time, however, Zeus repented of the severity of his sentence and, while keeping the letter of the law, adroitly changed its spirit. He now ordained that Prometheus should wear a ring made from one of the links of the chain set in a piece of the huge rock. In this way he still continued to be linked with the ancient rock. In the account of the wedding feast of Peleus and Thetis given by Catulus, reference is made to this ring, the first one with a stone setting, which was worn by Prometheus when he came to the feast:

Sage Prometheus, on his hand he wore
The slender symbol of his doom of yore,
When fettered fast in adamantine chains,
Hung from the craggy steep, he groaned in endless pain.

From earliest times the ring has been a pledge and seal of faith. Its use as a stamp indicating power and authority dates back to ancient times.

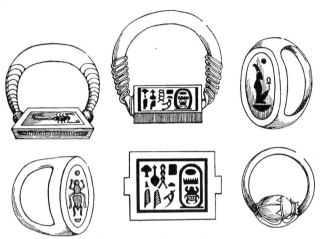

Figure 410. Signet Rings

Reading from upper left: massive ring with revolving bezel, royal gold signet ring said to resemble the ring put by the Pharaoh upon the hand of Joseph, bronze rings probably worn by Egyptian soldiers, a lighter form, showing gold loop passing through scarab setting.

Such rings, known as "signet rings," have been revived, with interesting variations again and again through the centuries. Among the ancient Egyptians, Assyrians, Hebrews, Greeks, and Romans they were used officially as a seal by which all important orders were given the mark of authority. Later, during the Renaissance, the importance of the science of heraldry led to the custom of engraving the family coat of arms upon the signet ring. In modern times a motto, a crest, or a monogram takes the place of the ancient seal.

The ring as a seal grew out of the earlier custom of wearing a cylindrical seal suspended about the neck or arm. In time it gradually grew smaller, finally being so much reduced that it could be worn upon the finger. In the authorizing of all important transactions the necessary papers were always stamped with the owner's signet ring. Such an impression gave the force of a royal decree to any paper to which it was attached. Figure 410. In the third chapter of Esther we read that King Ahasuerus gave Haman authority to avenge himself upon Mordecai by killing all the Jews, and that he gave him his ring that Haman's writing or command might be "sealed with the King's seal." In the early days this was the simplest way of delegating power, and so the custom of entrusting one's signet ring to another came to be a symbol of confidence. A woman receiving a man's ring might issue her commands in his name; with the possession of his ring she was in every respect his representative and he thereby endowed her with all the power he himself possessed. Jezebel wrote letters in her husband's name, "sealed them with his seal," and gained for him the coveted vineyard which had belonged to his neighbor.* When Daniel was placed in the lion's den, a stone was brought and laid upon the mouth of the den, and King Darius "sealed it with his own signet and with the signet of his lords."† At the time the Pharaoh set

Joseph over all the land, he "took off his ring from his hand and put it upon Joseph's hand."‡

The red carnelian cut in the form of a scarab was the stone most often used in the signet ring of the pharaohs. Other popular stones were the agate, granite, lapis lazuli, serpentine, and amethyst. For the ancient Egyptians the scarab, or sacred beetle, was an emblem of immortality and for that reason was held in great veneration. Many designs were inspired by this sacred symbol; its form cut in stone served for necklaces, pendants, rings, and official seals. The device carved on the underside of the scarab varied according to the taste of the individual. Some markings indicated the name of the owner, others of the monarch in whose reign he lived, and still others were emblems of certain deities. Sometimes the settings in the rings were fixed, but usually they turned upon pins or were mounted on gold wire which passed through them. In this way the stone could be revolved at will and easily used as a seal. In the tomb of King Tutankhamen several signet rings, and others as well, all of massive gold and richly decorated with inlay, were found. Figure 411. Egyptian rings were generally of gold. Silver was seldom used, and bronze rarely. Rings made entirely of precious stone have been recovered—dating, however, not earlier than the time of Rameses III (1202-1100 b.c.). Ivory and porcelain were the materials used by the less fortunate classes in Egypt, the scarab also being their favorite symbol.

COURTESY, METROPOLITAN MUSEUM OF ART

Figure 411. Signet Ring,
XVIII Dynasty

Engraved with name of King Tutankhamen.

---

* I Kings XXI:8.
† Daniel VI:17.
‡ Genesis XLI:42.

Besides the scarab and various engraved stones, frequently worn by Egyptian women, other patterns, such as the snake, the snail, and a knot, have been found. It was, moreover, the fashion for these women of ancient days to wear many rings, sometimes two and three on a finger. The thumb was not forgotten, as many of the old mummy cases testify.

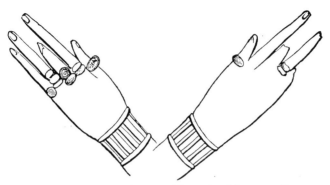

Figure 412. Hands from an Egyptian Mummy Case
After Wilkinson.

Though the fashion of thumb rings is outstanding in Roman times and in the sixteenth century, the fact must not be overlooked that the fashion dates back to ancient Egypt. A portrait painted upon a mummy case shows a great lady of that distant day wearing rings on both her thumbs. Figure 412. The one on the left hand appears to be the signet ring. On the index finger of the same hand are two rings, two on the middle finger, three on the ring finger, and one on the little finger. The right hand is not so highly favored. Besides the thumb ring, two, only, are worn, both on the third finger. It is an interesting fact, by the way, that the third finger was usually privileged to wear more rings than any other; it must, even in that remote period, have been looked upon as the ring finger. Wedding rings were not unknown. In fact, the use of the ring in the marriage service began in Egypt. The custom was also favored by the Greeks and Romans, but was not adopted for the Christian ritual until about 860 A.D. Previous to that time it was looked upon as a pagan idea.

Ancient Egyptian writings reveal that the wedding ring was worn on the third finger of the left hand because this finger was believed to be connected by an artery with the heart. The more generally accepted theory, however, is that inasmuch as the right hand signified power and authority and the left hand subjection and dependence, the ring was placed on the left hand to denote the wife's place as subordinate to her spouse. Another interesting reason for the third finger being the choice for the wedding ring is found in the ancient ritual of marriage in England. At the ceremony the ring was first placed upon the thumb of the bride with the words, "In the name of the Father"; it was then removed and placed upon the first finger with the words, "and of the Son"; then removed again and placed upon the second finger with the words, "and of the Holy Ghost"; it was then removed once again and placed upon the third finger with the pronouncement of "Amen."

According to an old Norse tradition the taking of an oath or pledge was anciently performed by passing the hand through a silver ring. Among other peoples the betrothal custom consisted in clasping hands through a large ring or a perforated stone.

The wedding ring was used by the Hebrews before the coming of Christ. Wheatley says that the

Figure 413.
Gold Rings,
about 500 A.D.
Found at
Cyprus

. . . reason a ring was pitched upon rather than anything else was because the ring was anciently a seal by which orders were signed, and others of value secured, and therefore the delivery of it was a sign that the person to whom it was given was admitted into the highest friendship and trust. For that reason it was adopted as a ceremony in marriage, to denote that the wife in consideration of being espoused to the man was admitted as a sharer in her husband's council and a joint partner in his honor and estate, and therefore we find not only the ring, but the keys, were in former times delivered to her in marriage.

Among ancient rings showing an Egyptian influence are those in the remarkable Cesnola Collection of the Metropolitan Museum of New York City. Many of these are of the swivel type, the engraved scarab appearing frequently. The illustration, Figure 413, shows two rings of this collection which are of unusual interest. Both are of gold. One is set with three stones; the other shows a small container, which probably held perfume or a portrait, covered with a rosette top of very delicate goldwork.

Among the Greeks, rings had, no doubt, been introduced from Asia. In the earlier period they were worn sparingly, especially when compared with ring fashions of the first century, A.D. The third finger of the left hand is said to have been the favored ring finger. The left hand was used less than the right, and the stone on the third finger seemed to be less exposed to injury. Later, however, popular taste shifted to the index and little finger. The earlier rings were usually plain bands of gold; later they were cut from various semiprecious material. Some Greek rings have been found which are formed entirely of jasper, rock crystal, and chalcedony. The art of engraving on stone reached its highest development in Greece about 480 to 400 B.C. These engraved stones were in settings similar to signet rings and used as seals. The *intaglio* and *cameo* are two methods of engraving which are always associated with Greek life. The intaglio, which is the older method, is that of cutting the design below the surface of the gem. Carnelian, quartz, and jasper were among the favored stones for this type of engraving. The cameo, which was the reverse of the intaglio, was a method of cutting in relief, the design being raised above the main body of the stone. Sardonyx and chalcedony were used for the most part in cameo cutting. Portraits were the popular subjects, and in this the Greek artist achieved distinction. Cameos were used not only for rings but for pendants, bracelets, and other ornaments. Figures 238, 239, page 188. During the Hellenistic period, hard, brilliant stones from India were engraved, set in metal rings and used as seals. Jacinth, famous for its rich, ruddy hue, was one of the favorite stones of this period.

It is interesting to read that in these far-off days counterfeit stones were frequently used in rings. Many transparent stones, when removed from the original setting, are found to be backed with a leaf of red gold as a foil. The use of this material gave to a transparent stone of no value the finest color, intended to deceive the unwary. This same practice in a later century was punished both by fines and at the whipping post.

The custom of wearing "charm" or "talismanic" rings was one which also prevailed in ancient Greece; and later, during the Middle Ages, it was revived. In ancient mythology it was the god Mercury who was the giver of these wonder-working rings. Rings that preserved the health, rings that gave the strength of ten, rings that made the wearer invisible, rings that brought love, wealth, and happiness—all these were among the many charm rings. Charm rings, pendants, necklaces, bracelets, and earrings were the prized possessions of these women of Greece. So highly were these feminine trinkets regarded that a jewel treasury was the choice and fitting receptacle for this wealth of ornament. The famous *Stela of Hegaso*, one of the most delicate and beautifully modeled masterpieces of that great age, pictures the departed matron, as she had been in life, interested in the wealth and beauty of her jewels. PLATE XXXIX. In this way the Greek artist worked to perpetuate in marble the interests and enjoyments which filled the life of the Greek woman of old.

In the early days of republican Rome (527-09 B.C.), most rings were of iron. Even after gold rings had been introduced, these iron rings were worn late into the Empire period. Many were made in the form of a plain hoop or a coiled serpent. Figure 414. Others were given their particular value by the artistic cutting of the stone and its setting. Figure 415. Many of these rings were not mere ornaments but were used as seals worn by men only. In these early days even the Roman wedding ring was iron, presumably indicating the enduring nature of the union. A lodestone, which suggests the highly attractive power of love, was frequently used as a setting. In the later, more luxurious days of the empire, the engagement ring was the first article of gold ever worn by the Roman maiden.

Records show that in the third century, B.C., no one but a Roman senator upon a diplomatic mission was permitted to wear the ring of gold. In private life he still wore his iron ring. All others, as well, wore iron rings. Later during the third century under the reign of Tiberius, rings of gold

Figure 414. Ancient Roman Rings Showing Form of
Coiled Serpent, a Type Far Spread in the Old World

were bestowed upon young men attaining knighthood, and the honor of wearing a gold ring was granted to all knights. The ring of gold then gradually became a badge of civil and military rank. These rings were regarded with great pride and passed as heirlooms through succeeding generations. In his eleventh Satire, Juvenal pictures the spendthrift who after consuming all he possesses has nothing left but his ring:

At length when naught remains a meal to bring,
The last poor shift, off comes the knightly *ring*,
And sad Sir Pollio begs his daily fare,
With undistinguished hands and fingers bare.

Figure 415.
Roman Rings

One with large bosses and signet ring with projecting shoulders.

At the time of the Second Punic War (218 B.C.), when the momentous question to be settled was whether Rome or Carthage should rule the world, the gold ring was distinctly a badge of position. Only patricians and knights of the highest standing were permitted to wear it. With the crushing defeat of the Romans by the Carthaginian general Hannibal, his order went forth to take the gold rings from the hands of the fallen Romans as a proof of the slaughter of patricians. So humiliated was Rome by this disaster that a day of mourning was proclaimed, when all Romans laid aside their rings of gold and substituted rings of iron. This custom came to be a national practice: for centuries afterward all mourning days were observed by the wearing of iron rings. Gradually, however, other laws were enacted granting greater liberty in the use of the ring of gold. At a later date only freeborn men and women were permitted the use of the gold ring; freedmen, only the silver ring; and slaves, the iron ring. A special decree of the senate was necessary

Plate XXXIX..........................Grave Relief of Hegeso

This monument in low relief represents the deceased as she had been in life, interested in her jewels. It thus recalled to friends and relatives a very pleasing memory of one who had gone.

to allow a freedman the privilege of the ring of gold. In later Roman times, under the luxurious days of the Empire (27 B.C.-400 A.D.), the fingers of both men and women, without restriction, were laden with rings. Among stones the sardonyx was highly prized. In describing a celebrated player of the lyre, Juvenal remarks upon the popularity of this stone, saying that the strings of the instrument were "lighted by the sheen of his many sardonyx rings."

Figure 416. Thumb Ring of Roman Imperial Family

Bears bust of Plotina, consort of Trajan. Coiffure shows three rows of faceted gems.

After Montfaucon.

The Romans were particularly given to the fashion of thumb rings. Figure 416. Since their thumb rings were very heavy and massive the patricians inaugurated the fashion of changing their rings with the season. Lighter rings, worn during the warm season, were known as "summer rings"; during the cold portion of the year the large, heavy rings, known as "winter rings," were the fashion. In the following lines, Juvenal refers to these "season" rings:

> Charged with light *summer rings*, his fingers sweat,
> Unable to support a gem of weight.

The Emperor Trajan is said to have worn a "winter" thumb ring measuring three-and-one-half inches in width.

Figure 417. Roman Amber and Glass Rings

A beautiful thumb ring, probably belonging to the elder Faustina, wife of Antoninus Pius (86-161 A.D.), is entirely of sapphire; to protect the band from wearing, it is lined with a circlet of gold. Many of the other beautiful rings of this period were made entirely of amber, and other semiprecious materials. Figure 417. Diamonds, pearls, and amber from the Baltic were being transported in great quantities to Rome, and gold and silver were annually imported. The Roman goldsmiths, following their Greek masters, reached a high standard of excellence and turned out all kinds of personal ornament enriched with precious stones. This was an age of ornamentation, and the Romans were masters in display.

Many of the rings worn were used as seals. Distinguished families had their personal seals passed on to them from one generation to another. The sapphire and ruby engraved with the owner's seal and set in gold were the favorite stones for this type of ring. Also, various interesting symbols were engraved upon these Roman rings. Sometimes subjects referring to religion or mythology were suggested; at other times portraits of the family, friends, or ancestors. Figure 418. Julius Caesar wore a ring on which an armed Venus was represented, for he claimed to be a descendant of that goddess. The ring of Augustus showed first a sphinx, later the portrait of Alexander the Great, and finally, his own portrait. On the ring worn by Pompey were emblems of his three wars in Europe, Asia, and Africa. Caligula's iron ring bore the portraits of Drusilla and himself. Figure 419. The stone in this ring was made to turn from one side to the other. An unusual fashion of Roman society was that of wearing rings above the second joint of the finger and thumb as well as below it. Figure 420. Apparently this was designed to make a greater display of wealth. Seneca speaks of this extravagant custom when he says, "We adorn our fingers with rings and a jewel is displayed on every joint." This fashion was again revived in the luxurious days of the sixteenth century.

Figure 418. Ancient Roman Ring

Engraved with portrait of Galba.

Figure 419. Caligula's Iron Ring with Portrait of Himself and Drusilla

Roman women spent incalculable sums upon adornment. Rings of gold, and others cut from lapis lazuli, crystal, amber, and various precious stones were fashionable. Cameos and intaglios, especially those in portrait form, were highly favored. Though a great variety of gems were in use, the pearl was always a favorite. It is said that Julius Caesar spent for a single pearl which he presented to Servilia, the mother of Marcus Brutus, six million sesterces,* and that the wife of Caligula possessed a set of pearls valued at forty million sesterces. Two other valuable rings of Roman days were that of Faustina, valued at approximately fifty thousand sesterces, and that of Domitia, said to be worth fifteen thousand sesterces.

---

* An ancient Roman coin, value something over \$.04 in American money.

When the fashion for rings set with precious stones had grown so general that leaders of the fashionable world, both men and women, owned large quantities of them, the ring treasury again became popular. Among the first of these on record was that owned by the son-in-law of Sylla, Emelius Scaurius (138-78 B.C.). These probably resembled the treasure boxes of the ancient Greeks, and, like them, may have held other ornaments than rings.

Figure 420. Forefinger Showing Ring on Second Joint

From a bronze statue.

An unusual type of ring which was peculiarly Roman was the "key ring." Figure 421. Roman wives first wore signet rings to designate that they were mistresses of the household and had the right of sealing up the cupboards and wine bottles. By-and-by, instead of the seal, real keys were used; many of these have been found in which the key is part of a ring. It is difficult for the modern world to understand just how these key rings were worn. They were at first undoubtedly carried upon the thumb or finger. Many of them, however, are so large and inconvenient to wear that it is very probable they were suspended from the girdle. The key ring which the Roman matron so proudly wore symbolized, as had the seal, her authority to carry the keys of the house.

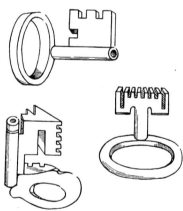

Figure 421. Roman Key Rings

To pass from the fascinating subject of seal rings, jeweled rings, and Roman key rings to the historic poison rings is, indeed, an abrupt transition! Though poison rings date from ancient Roman times, as late as the sixteenth and seventeenth centuries they were not uncommon. Figure 422. It is presumed that these rings were first designed as an easy means of escape from imposed torture, humiliating slavery, or death. Hannibal is known to have turned to the poison in his ring when about to be delivered to the Romans. The Emperor Heliogabalus also wore a poison ring in order to be prepared for any emergency. His murder, however, took place so suddenly that his ring was of no avail. Pliny the historian tells how an erring custodian of the capitol was arrested and sentenced to torture. He escaped the sentence by biting his ring, the setting of which was a thin shell containing a strong poison. Back of the bezel of the signet ring of Cesare Borgia, dated 1503 and still in existence, is a small sliding panel which, opened, reveals a shallow cavity formerly containing poison. Another poison ring, of Venetian workmanship, is set with a high-pointed diamond with a ruby on each side. A secret spring at the side of the middle stone lifts the diamond setting, and below there is a small recess large enough to contain several drops of poison. Figure 422. Though the earlier poison rings were worn as a means of quick and easy escape from life, later the same ring was designed as an instrument of murder. One of these later rings shows a recumbent lion with sharp claws. The claws connected with a small receptacle filled with poison. With the bezel of the ring turned inward, a hearty handclasp punctured the skin of the enemy. Such a ring is said to have been found in an antique shop in Paris. The collector, not acquainted with the device, received an accidental scratch which almost proved disastrous.

Figure 422.
Poison Ring

Richly engraved and set with two rubies and a pyramidal diamond. The bezel securing the diamond opens with a spring, revealing receptacle for poison.

Middle Ages

With the removal of the Roman government to Constantinople, Byzantium took the lead as arbiter of fashion. Models in jewelry as well as other details of personal attire were soon carried to western Europe, where, during the period of the Middle Ages, Byzantine jewelry was in demand. Rings were massive in design and engraved with inscriptions or the sign of the cross with the initials of the owner distributed between the arms. Figure 423. Somewhat later Byzantine rings took on a more ornate design very different from the classical simplicity of former times. A famous old ring found at Lyons in 1841, in the jewel casket of a Roman lady, who evidently had carried it there during this early period, has three cup-shaped settings supported by double leaves at each side. Two of the settings have disappeared but the third, an Arabian emerald, is intact. Figure 424.

During this period the rings worn by the dignitaries of the Church came to be an important item in ring history. Closely akin to the king's ring in its indication of power and authority was the ring worn by ecclesiastical leaders. This ring had a twofold significance—it was a mark of priestly dignity and authority and also symbolic of the mystical union of the priesthood and the Church. Chief among the ecclesiastical rings are the pope's ring and the rings of cardinals, bishops, and sometimes abbots. The pope's ring of investiture, called the *Fisherman's Ring*, is of gold; on the stone is engraved the figure of St. Peter seated in a fisherman's boat and holding a net, while the name of the reigning pope appears above. Figure 425. According to early records, the custom of breaking the ring at the time of the pope's death has obtained for a long time. This prevented the signing of any pontifical documents while the papal see was unoccupied.

Each pope, however, had a replica made for himself with the addition of his name and initials. Among other famous rings of the Church was the official ring of Thomas à Becket. This was set with a large ruby, a gift from Louis XII. Pope Paul upon his entry into Rome in 1536, was presented by Charles V with a handsome ring set with a magnificent diamond. Benvenuto Cellini, in his *Memoirs*, tells about this unusual ring and relates that he succeeded in giving the diamond a singular tint which surpassed anything that had previously been accomplished. Following the example of the Church, Christian kings and queens at the imposing coronation ceremony came to be presented by the officiating bishop with coronation rings.

Figure 423. Early
Byzantine Rings

Figure 424.

A ring found at Lyons in 1841, in the jewel case of a Roman lady. One cup-shaped setting still retained its jewel. Ring of Byzantine design, illustrates a type more ornate and distinctly different from classical simplicity of early times.

Figure 425. The "Fisherman's Ring"

Among the rings found in France and belonging to this very early period are three of unusual interest. Figure 427. The gold ring with the initials "S.R.," believed to mean *Sigbert Rex*, probably belonged to one of three kings, each of whom bore the name Sigbert and ruled over the eastern possessions of the Merovingians. Each of the other two rings, a gold signet inscribed *Helva*, and one which bears an imposing seal, probably belongs to the same period. In the north, particularly in the British Isles, large numbers of spiral rings and rings of gold wire with various kinds of twists have been recovered. These date, no doubt, from the same early age. Figure 429. It was in the late Middle Ages that the perfection of the goldsmith's work, especially in the designing of rings, began to display itself. It is said that at no other period have a greater number of ring forms been produced. Though most of these were for sealing official documents and for ceremonial purposes, the fashion world also made heavy demands upon the goldsmith. Intaglios and cameos showing the portrait of the owner were among the favorite styles. These were most frequently used as betrothal, wedding, and gift rings. In medieval romance the gift ring was especially in vogue. In *Sir Degrevant* one reads:

> Lo! here is a red gold
>   *ring*
> With a rich stone.
> The lady looked at the
>   *ring*,
> It was a gift for a king.

About 1363, the fad for rings reached such extravagance that a law was passed to restrain "the evil." No one below the rank of knighthood, except those

COURTESY, METROPOLITAN MUSEUM OF ART

Figure 426. Silver Ring with Pontifical Seal Probably effigy of a pope, 18th century.

whose property reached a value of £200, was permitted to wear rings. In *The Vision of Piers Plowman* (1363) the poet tells of a richly adorned lady whose fingers were laden with rings set with diamonds, rubies, and sapphires. In the *Lais* of Marie de France we read of rings of "fine gold, weighing full an ounce, set with garnets most precious with letters graven thereon." In a parchment roll of prayers to the Virgin, now preserved at Oxford, is a portrait of Margaret of Anjou (1429-82). The lady wears two rings on each finger except the fourth; these are placed on the second as well as the third joint, a fashion which was revived later, in the sixteenth century.

The sepulchral effigy* of the wife of Sir Humphrey Stafford (1450) is remarkable for its courtly costume and profusion of rings. Figure 430. Each finger except the little one of the right hand is adorned with rings, which show a remarkable variety in design. During this interesting period, the charm rings which had once flourished in ancient Greece

---

* In Bloomsgrove Church, Staffordshire.

were revived. Figure 431. These rings, believed to possess magical powers, were worn by commoner and noble alike. In the *Squire's Tale* Chaucer mentions a magical thumb ring worn by the daughter of "Cambustan bold" which gave the fair lady full knowledge of all medicinal herbs and enabled her to converse with birds in their own language. Other charm rings possessed still other magical powers, many of them rendering the wearer invisible. The ring of Gyges, king of Lydia, possessed this peculiar power; when the stone was turned in-

Figure 427. Western European Rings

Ring probably belonging to Merovingian period; gold signet ring inscribed *heva*; a gold ring with initials *S.R.* believed to mean *Sigbertus Rex*. Three kings of Austrasia (name given to eastern possessions of Franks) bore the name Sigbert, and the ring doubtless belonged to one of these.

Figure 428. Gallo-Roman Ring

Of huge proportions, showing seated cow with bell about neck.

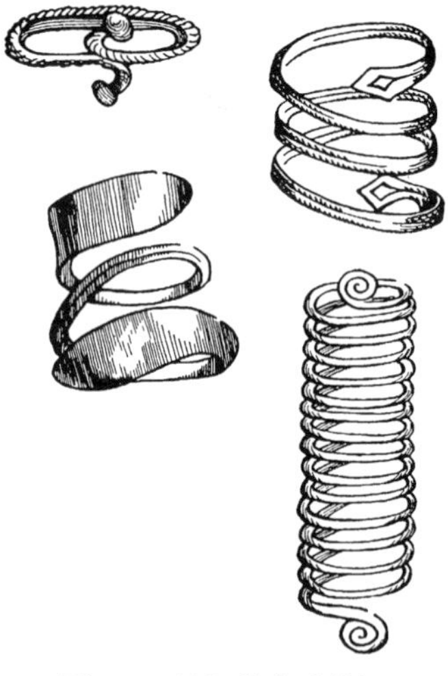

ward, Gyges became invisible; when reversed he reappeared! All kinds of talismanic pieces were set in rings in the belief that they possessed certain powers. For instance, a wolf's tooth was believed to act as a charm against assault; a badger's tooth brought wealth and general good luck; and the toadstone was supposed to have various mystical qualities. Among these was the power to change color, thus warning the wearer of the presence of poison in his food or drink. Words and legends lettered upon rings also gave mystical protection. The word *anamyaptus* was engraved upon the band as a charm against epilepsy or cramp. This was in accord with the old superstition which gave this word as a cure. Such cramp rings were first blessed by the sovereign at high mass and then given to the persons so afflicted. According to an old tradition, the "pilgrim" ring of Edward the Con-

Figure 429. Spiral Rings

Found in graves of old Northmen in British Isles. Bronze, upper left; rest gold.

fessor contained a sapphire which later adorned the British crown and gave English sovereigns the power to pronounce a blessing over these cramp rings. In *Introduction to Knowledge*, the author, Andrew Boorde, who lived in the time of Henry VIII, says:

Kynges of England doth halow every year crampe *rynges* whych *rynges* worn on one's finger doth help them whych have the crampe.

Another favorite charm against disease was a ring bearing the names of the three wise men from the East — Jasper, Melchoir, and Balthazar. Others were engraved with the mystical swastika.

During the late Middle Ages the peculiar be-trothal ring favored in

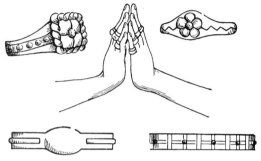

Figure 430. Rings Shown upon the Effigy of Lady Stafford, 1450

Figure 431. Charm Rings

Left, a thumb ring of mixed metals. Center face shows a conventional representation of a monkey with hand mirror, while at each side is a large stone setting. Inside is the mystic word, *anamzapta*, with the cross and sacred monogram. This indicates a charm ring. Right, a massive thumb ring with tooth of some animal as its principal setting. This was believed to have mystic power for its possessor; precious stones set around the ring made this power enduring.

ancient times and known to history as the *geminel*, *gemmel*, *gimmel*, or "twin ring," rose to new heights of popularity. Figure 432. "Geminel" is derived from *gemelli*, meaning "twins." Though this type of ring later came to be made triple and quadruple, the name remained the same. Such rings, formed of two, three, or four circlets, fitted together as one when upon the finger. Sometimes the two circlet rings ended in miniature hands which, given the proper twist, clasped firmly when upon the finger. Figure 433. Others show several circlets held together by one pivot. This type of ring was popular from the fourteenth to the sixteenth century in France, Italy, and England. The contemporary English poet Robert Herrick (1591-1674) wrote:

> Thou sent'st to me a true love knot; but I
> Return a ring of *jimmals*, to imply
> Thy love had one knot, mine a triple tye.

Figure 432. Triple Gimmel Ring

Another type of ring curious to modern eyes flourished during this period. This was the "devotional ring." Figure 434. It was made of various materials, chiefly gold, bronze, or ivory marked with small spherical projections for the saying of *Aves* and a cross for the *Paternoster*. Others were constructed with a hinged bezel under which was concealed a gem stone, engraved with a sacred symbol, inscription, or portrait.

In medieval times rings were frequently classified by being strung upon a wand or small rod known as the *bacula*. Each bacula held its own peculiar assortment of rings, especially if the owner possessed a large ring collection. An inventory of King John's jewels (1205), shows an interesting statement of such ring rods. One bacula carries twenty-six diamonds, another forty emeralds, another forty-seven

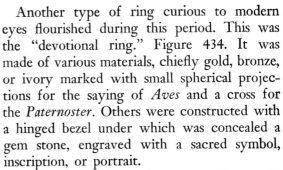

Figure 433. Gimmel Rings

Left, a gimmel ring not later than 1650. Clasped hands originated among ancient Romans. Right, a remarkably fine gimmel ring, set with sapphire and amethyst and enriched with colored enamels.

emeralds, another several topazes, and still another nine turquoises. Jewelers were supposed to keep their store of rings strung upon a bacula. The famous painting "The Goldsmith," by Jacque Louis David, shows a jeweler with the ring rod, which had been in use for centuries.

1500-1600

Throughout the sixteenth, seventeenth, and eighteenth centuries the ring continued. During the sixteenth century men and women alike vied with one another in the elegance of their dress and the display of their jewels. Figure 435. When one possessed more than sufficient for the fingers, rings were worn on a chain or band about the neck, or placed on the hat or cap. In a portrait by Lucas Cranach (1472-1553), a Dutch woman of his time wears eight rings suspended upon a chain and five upon her hands. So general was the use of rings in the sixteenth century in England that, among the various articles carried by the

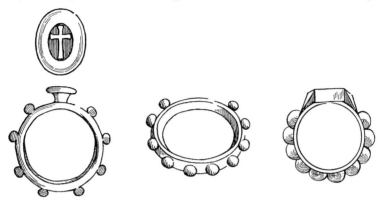

Figure 434. Devotional Rings

Reading from left: Silver ring with bosses for the Creed and large bezel showing cross for Paternoster; ring with ten bosses for prayers; ring with ten bosses for Ave Maria and large boss for Paternoster.

peddler, rings were an item of importance. In the old ballad of *Redisdale and Wise William* the peddler entices the fair lady with these words:

> Come down, come down, my lady fair,
> A sight of you I'll see,
> And bonny jewels, brooches, *rings*
> I will give unto thee.

To which the lady replies:

> If you have bonny brooches, *rings*,
> Oh, mine are bonny tee,
> Go from my yettes, now, Redisdale,
> For me ye shall not see.

Posy rings, which had been fashionable during the late Middle Ages, reached their full flower in the sixteenth century. Figure 436. These rings were inscribed with such lines as, "Let Love endure," "Faithful and true," or "Be of good heart;" others carried two lines:

Let us love
Like turtle dove.

God saw thee
Most fit for me.

A most refreshing reference to such a ring is that in the *Merchant of Venice*. Portia and Narissa had each presented Bassanio and Gratiano with rings and each had sworn he would never part with it. Later, Gratiano, being chided for parting with his ring, tries to treat it lightly:

Figure 435. Benedict von Hertenstein
....*Holbein*

A signet ring appears upon the Index finger, two on the third, and three on the little finger of the left hand.

A paltry *ring*
That she did give me, whose posy was
For all the world like cutler's poetry
Upon a knife—LOVE ME AND LEAVE ME NOT.

Act V, sc. 1

Related to posy rings were the so-called "regard rings." These were set with stones the initials of which spelled a favorite sentiment or enshrined the name of the beloved:

L apus lazuli
O pal
V erd antique
E merald

M alachia
E merald

S apphire
A methyst
R uby
A methyst

D iamond
O pal
R uby
A methyst

Frequently betrothal rings were broken in two, one to be kept by the lover and the other by the maiden fair. Four lines from the *Exeter Garland* plainly express the sentiment attached to this custom:

A ring of pure gold she from her finger took,
And just in the middle the same she broke;
Quoth she, *As a token of love you take this,*
And this, as a pledge, I will keep for your sake.

Again, thumb rings, a revival of the ancient fashion, became the vogue.

Thumb rings had passed out of fashion about the thirteenth century, but were revived immediately after the devastation of the shrine of Thomas à Becket. While the spoils of this and neighboring shrines were being carted off, Henry VIII seized the famous gem the "Regale of France," then the finest diamond in the world, and appropriated it for his personal use. The stone was set in a ring worn upon the thumb. When last seen this gem was in the necklace of Henry's daughter, Queen Mary.

With the King setting the fashion, thumb rings were immediately adopted by all men and women of fashion. Many are the portraits of famous folk of that day pictured with massive rings upon the thumb. Figure 437, PLATE XXVIII, page 196. The popular charm rings of this century were often worn upon the thumb, and English ladies are said to have worn their wedding rings permanently upon the thumb. The plain gold, band wedding ring is said to date from this century. In 1553, when Princess Mary and Philip of Spain were married, much discussion took place as to the proper ring for the royal marriage. The Princess finally decided the matter for herself, declaring that she preferred to be married with "a plain hoop of gold like other maidens." This incident, no doubt, did much to establish the prestige of the plain-band wedding ring. An interesting feature of the wedding ceremony of this day was the giving way of gold rings as favors. One gentleman, generous to an extravagant degree, at the marriage of one of his servants gave away gold rings to the value of £4000. From time to time during the following centuries the custom was revived, and at the marriage of Queen Victoria, in 1840, rings having the royal profile in gold and the legend *Victoria Regina* were distributed. The Queen was so pleased with the beauty and superior craftsmanship of this delicate work that she ordered many more, planning to distribute them from time to time as gifts to distinguished visitors.

Among the famous portraits of the sixteenth century, those of Anne of Cleves, Jane Seymour, the Duchess of Savoy, and many others testify to the love of rings among the fashionables of the period. Painters of this day, chief among them the German master, Hans Holbein, showed a great fondness for drawing the finely wrought gold and adding the touches of color found in the precious gems. The hands of kings, queens, and lesser folk of the period are painted with a realism so perfect that no doubt remains of the exquisite craftsmanship of that day. Figures 437, 438. The gold used in the rings of the Renaissance, like that in which the ancients delighted, was yellow gold, 22 carats fine. This yellow gold of the past, with only two parts alloy to give it the necessary resistance, not only retained its fine yellow color but even improved with age. Never did these rings of the past need polishing. In contrast, the 18-carat gold used by modern jewelers changes color under the action of fire and must be polished, and sometimes dipped into a bath of salts and acids to restore its yellow tint. Even at its best, it is not comparable with the rich yellow of the 22-carat gold. Also, the gold loses much in wear and has to be refinished or polished at intervals. Among the famous jewelers of this great period were the illustrious artists of the Renaissance. Bervenuto Cellini,

Figure 436.
Posy Rings

Ghirlandjo, Mantegna, Del Verrocchio, Leonardo da Vinci, Michelangelo, Albrecht Dürer, and others, who used their genius in the designing and execution of jewelry as effectively as in the creation of the world's great masterpieces. The famous ring collections of the Louvre, the British Museum, and those in private collections boast many handsome rings once the treasured possession of illustrious persons of the Renaissance. The signet ring of Mary, Queen of Scots, the ring of Darnley, of the Jane Seymour family, of Martin Luther, Shakespeare, and others equally historic may be seen in these valued collections. Figure 442.

Elizabeth's love of jewels, and of rings in particular, is well known. It

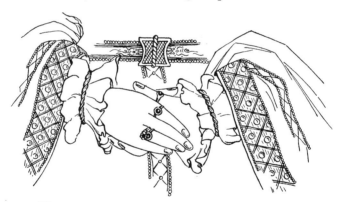

Figure 437. Detail from Portrait of Ann of Cleves
Shows fashionable thumb ring and others.

is said that frequently as a mark of particular favor she pulled off her glove and extended her hand, sparkling with rings, to be kissed. One of the most interesting stories about the rings of Elizabeth is that of the famed "Essex ring." As a mark of esteem, the Queen once presented a ring to the Earl of Essex, promising him that if the ring should ever come back with any request, the request would be granted. Sometime later Essex was imprisoned for high treason and sentenced to death. In this unfortunate situation he remembered Elizabeth's promise. Not trusting the keeper, he sent a boy, directing that the ring be given to a favorite lady in waiting. Unluckily, however, the ring fell into the hands of Lady Nottingham, whose husband was the Earl's enemy. Receiving no word from Essex, and believing that obstinacy possessed him, Elizabeth left him to his fate. Sometime later Lady Nottingham fell ill; knowing that her

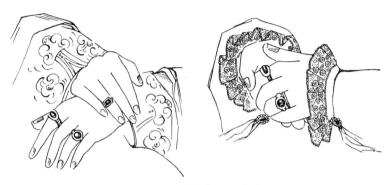

Figure 438. Ring Styles, 16th Century

Left, hands from portrait of Magdalena Dona, showing ring on second joint of third finger, and others; right, hands from portrait of Jane Seymour, showing large ring on index finger and two on third finger.

illness was fatal, she sent for Elizabeth and revealed the story of the Essex ring. Elizabeth, indignant and incensed beyond control, gave the dying woman a severe shaking, slapped her face, and left the room exclaiming, "God may forgive you, I never can!" The incident so affected the Queen that she fell ill, and some weeks later passed forever from her world of jealousy and intrigue.

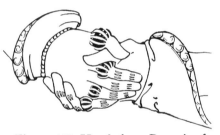

Figure 439. Hands from Portrait of Judith by Cranach

Gloves show slits to relieve pressure of rings.

During the late Renaissance period the development of the science of heraldry and the great importance attached to armorial bearings led to the engraving of the family crest upon the signet ring. Every gentleman of consequence owned such a signet ring and wore it. This constant revival of the old seal ring—always, however, with a new meaning suited to its time—is one of the interesting recurrences in ring fashions.

1600-1700

In contrast with the extravagant vogue for rings in the sixteenth century was the fashion of the seventeenth. Portraits of famous folk of this century wearing rings are far less frequent than in the preceding period.

The portrait artists of the seventeenth century did not favor the adorning of the hands with many rings. They regarded these costly accessories as not in any way indicative of a worthy portrait. Few, if any, are found upon the hands of court beauties or other famous or influential men or women. Sir Peter Lely's portraits of beautiful women are invariably without rings, all the artistry of the painter being lavished upon the beautifully

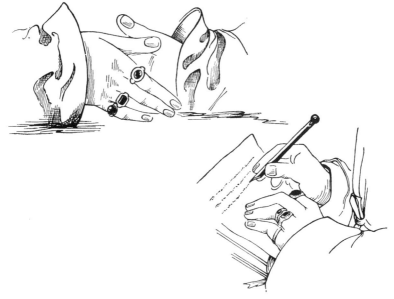

Figure 440. Rings from Old Paintings

Left, hands from portrait of Cardinal of Brandenburg, showing ring on index, third, and fourth fingers. Right, hands from portraits of Erasmus, showing large ring on index finger, two on third finger, and one on fourth finger of left hand.

modeled hands. Where rings do appear, they are few in number and very inconspicuous.

In England, during the Commonwealth (1649-60), even the use of the wedding ring was given up for a time. It was condemned for its "heathenish origin."

> They will not hear of *wedding-rings*
> For to be us'd in their marriage;
> They say they're superstitious things,
> And do religion much disparage.
>
> Loyal Songs, *A Curtain Lecture*, Vol. I, No. 15

In the *British Apollo* one speaker asks the question,

Why is it that the person to be married is enjoined to put a ring upon the fourth finger of his spouse's left hand?

The answer is:

There is nothing more in this than that the custom was handed down to the present age from our ancestors, who found the left hand more convenient for such ornaments than the right, in that 'tis ever less employed; for the same reason they choose the fourth finger, which is not less used than either of the rest, but is more capable of preserving a ring from bruises, having this one quality peculiar to itself, that it cannot be extended but in company with some other finger whenever the rest may be singly stretched to their full length and straightened. Some of the ancients' opinions of this matter, viz., that the ring was so worn because to that finger, and to that only, comes an artery to the heart; but, the politer knowledge of our modern anatomists having clearly demonstrated the absurdity of that notion, we are rather inclined the continuance of the custom owing to the reason above mentioned.*

Figure 441. Hand from Portrait of Mary, Queen of Scots

Note ring on second joint of third finger.

During the period of two centuries, from the sixteenth through the eighteenth, Italian goldsmiths popularized the pleasing *giardinetti* rings. Figure 443. The settings of these rings represented flower baskets, nosegays, and jardinieres. The flowers were suggested by bits of precious and semi-precious stones, or colored glass and pearls, while the stems and leaves were gold. Many unusual examples of this fashion may be seen in the ring collections of the museums.

Figure 442. Shakespeare's Ring

Among the famous rings of the seventeenth century are two *memorial* rings of Charles I. Figure 444. One is gold with a large diamond set in an oval face which opens. Within is revealed the portrait of Charles made in enamel. The other has a diamond with two smaller diamonds on each side. The shank is designed in the form of a skeleton, within which is engraved, "C.R. January 30, 1649, Martyr." Other rings of the unfortunate Charles bear miniatures of the King. One is engraved, "January 30, 1649, Martyr Populi"; on another the miniature is set in small brilliants, with the words: "*Sic transit gloria mundi.*" The lasting impression made on his loyal supporters by the execution of Charles in 1649 led them to carry out his final injunction, "Remember." Great numbers of these memorial rings were made and worn by the Royalists. This event more than any other did

* *British Apollo,* Vol. I, p. 123. Edition MDCCXXVI.

much to establish the general custom of memorial rings. A signet ring believed to have been the seal of Charles' queen, Henrietta Maria, is also in existence. It has a circular bezel with a sapphire and bears the arms of England and the letters *M.R.*

Closely akin to the memorial rings were the *mourning* rings which came into fashion during this century. These were, indeed, ghastly ornaments, massive in design, and frequently black in color. Black rings were later displaced by others in blue enamel. Many bore portraits of the deceased, emblems, or inscriptions. Among these were such melancholy legends as:

Prepared be   Death parts
To follow me.   United hearts.

Figure 443.
Giardinetti Rings

Others had the hair of the departed daintily plaited or formed into a design and placed under a crystal or a white sapphire. These were worn as both rings and lockets. George Washington is said to have left several such rings to friends and relatives as "Mementos of esteem." It is further related that as late as 1783, on the occasion of a funeral in Boston, rings valued approximately at seven dollars each were given away. Other types of rings were undoubtedly popular during the century, for Samuel Pepys in his diary mentions a "Turkeystone, set with little sparks of diamonds." This refers to the setting fashionable in England—a turquoise surrounded by small diamonds.

1700-1900

In the early years of the eighteenth century restraint in the use of rings

Figure 444. Memorial Rings
of Charles I

continued, but toward the later half of the period they were again worn in great profusion. Of course France set the mode and the world followed. In 1783, when the jewels of Mlle. de Beauvoisi were placed on sale, two hundred magnificent rings found a new owner. Mercier, in his *Tableau de France* says that at the end of the eighteenth century enormous rings were worn. He says that when one takes the "hand of a pretty woman, one only has the sensation of holding a quantity of rings and angular stones, and it would be necessary to strip these off the hands before we could perceive of its formed delicacy." He adds that the "nuptial ring is now unnoticed on the fingers of women; wide and profane rings altogether conceal this warrant of their faith." During the period of the Revolution fragments of stone from the Bastille were set in rings and brooches, and wedding rings were enameled in the republican colors, red, white, and blue. During the Reign of Terror portrait rings engraved with the leading spirits of the times were popular. Rings at this period were not limited to finger decoration, but milady walked forth, sandal shod, with rings upon her toes!

Among the rings of the early nineteenth century are those linked with the name of Napoleon. In the collection of the British Museum is a ring, one of six, said to have been made by the conspirators who planned his escape from Elba in 1815. The bezel of this famous ring has a hinged lid. Figure 446. On the inner side of this is engraved in relief the head of Napoleon. The outer side is simply engraved with an enamel decoration. Such rings had been worn in France ever since the Emperor's abdication and indicated a following among

COURTESY, METROPOLITAN MUSEUM OF ART
Figure 445. Mourning Ring

Gold and cloissoné enamel with portrait of Washington, 1800.

the people. This, however, necessarily had to be kept secret. These rings closed could be worn with impunity, and yet testified without undue publicity to the loyalty of the wearer. Another famous ring of the early nineteenth century is the historical geminel ring made for the Prince Regent of England, George IV. Geminal rings as betrothal rings had been worn in ancient times, were revived during the Middle Ages when they were in great demand, and now again the style was renewed in this historic ring made for the Prince. In the traditional manner, this ring was in two pieces which, when properly adjusted, fitted accurately together. Each was provided with a secret spring which on being pressed revealed on the one the portrait of the beautiful Mrs. Fitzherbert, and on the other that of the Prince. Before his death, the King had entrusted one part of this ring to the Duke of Wellington with the solemn promise that he would place it upon his breast as he lay in his casket. Some years later, the Duke, meeting a fashionable lady at dinner noticed that she wore a ring of unusual pattern. It appeared to him as a duplicate of the ring that George IV had given him. He was naturally both interested and curious. He showed the lady how to touch the spring, and lo! there was the King's portrait. The ring had been bequeathed to the lady by Mrs. Fitzherbert, but she was entirely unaware of its significance. The Duke then told the story of the twin ring and how he had fulfilled to the letter his promise to the King.

Though various fashions in rings have come and gone, the signet or seal has persisted. From 1865 to 1885 it was worn extensively. At the end of the century it was again revived and worn by both men and women. Sometimes a crest or monogram was engraved upon the gold

Figure 446. Napoleon Memorial Ring

disks; other times an engraved stone—onyx, bloodstone, or carnelian—was preferred. This flair for seal rings was followed by the great popularity of cameo rings, the choice being either white on brown, or brown on white, black on white, or the reverse. In fact, cameos in brooches or bracelets, as well as rings, were the last word in ornament. With the popularity of the cameo it is not surprising that a taste for the intaglio developed. These were usually cut in black onyx, carnelian, or a stone of a dark brown color known as "sard." Then in the early years of the new century there followed a whole procession of "dinner rings," large and decorative, reaching from knuckle to knuckle and sparkling with brilliants and gems in color.

Twentieth Century

Though the ring from earliest times has had certain *style* periods, the fact remains that irrespective of style the ring remains. Time was when the ancient alchemists called gold the metal of the sun and silver that of the moon, and these two metals fashioned the rings of the world. Today, an alloy known as "white gold" has become as popular as yellow gold. Ancient inventories indicate that a pale alloy of gold known as *electrum* was used at a very early period for ring making in Greece. Several rings found in Cyprus dating from the fifth century, B.C. are of this composition which resembles modern white gold. The metal, however, which leads all others of the twentieth century is platinum. Figures 447, 448.

Diamonds, emeralds, sapphires, and many other stones favored of old appear and reappear in these new and beautiful settings. Men's rings, like much else in men's dress, have taken on a conservative air. Thumb rings and "rings on every joint" are a thing of the past. Only one of the ancient forms finds favor with men of the modern world. This is the seal ring of gold or platinum. Many of these show designs incised in the gold disk; others are set with engraved stones. The popular stones used in men's rings are suggestive of masculine character—the carnelian, black onyx, tiger eye, bloodstone, and diamond. Akin to the seal rings are the vast number of rings representing the various secret societies at universities, colleges, and certain fraternal orders. These are in many styles, and the use of symbols is an important feature of the design. Such rings are made in the several metals, combined with enamels, precious, and semiprecious stones.

Though hand-wrought jewelry still retains its place for an exclusive clientele, by far the greater demand is for the machine-made product. The modern methods of ring making, like those of gloves, shoes, and hose, have been gradually linked with the machine. Instead of the ring being completed by a single craftsman as of old, it now passes through the hands of many workers. There is the blanket maker, who rolls the metal to the proper thickness, the jeweler, the stone setter, the engraver, and the polisher. This quantity production has greatly reduced the price of rings. Yet, although manufacturers vary in the quality of their product, many are as discriminating and exacting as were the crafts-

COURTESY, TIFFANY & CO., NEW YORK

Figure 447. Platinum Rings, Early 20th Century

Upper, large emerald-cut diamond set in platinum; lower, fancy platinum ring with diamonds and emeralds.

COURTESY, TIFFANY & CO., NEW YORK

Figure 448. Platinum Band Ring

Showing one row of sapphires and four rows of diamonds. Early 20th century.

men of old. Certainly our lady of the twentieth century makes her choice from fully as bewildering an array as did ever her kinsmen of yore. Gone are the old complex forms of the ring with their poison chambers and mystic meanings; in their place, however, the modern designer presents both a charm and variety in setting, unequalled in the history of ring fashions.

REFERENCES

Child, Theodore, *Wimples and Crisping Pins.*
Encyclopedia Britannica, Vol. 6.
Fairholt, F. W., *Rambles of an Artist.*
Jones, William F. S. A., *Finger-Ring Lore.*
Johnston, Harold, *Private Life of the Romans.*
Kennard, Beulah, *Jewelry and Silverware*, Chapter 16.
Kunz, George Frederick, *Rings for the Finger.*
Lester, Katherine Morris, *Historic Costume*, pp. 34, 119.
New International Encyclopedia, Vol. 20.
Norris, Herbert, *Costume and Fashion.*
Sage, Elizabeth, *A Study of Costume*, pp. 36, 203.

CHAPTER 27

Gloves

These *gloves* the Count sent me; they are an excellent perfume.

Much Ado About Nothing, Act III, sc. 4

THE time-honored traditions of the glove make it one of the most aristocratic of dress accessories. Even in the modern world an air of old-time distinction accompanies every well-gloved individual. Though the various usages and interesting traditions of the glove were developed during the Middle Ages, the history of the glove begins with the cave man. The period when men lived in caves is uncertain but is supposed to date sometime before the Glacial period. This would place that remote age something over 240,000 years ago. At that date the idea of gloves developed naturally out of a need for protection for the hands, probably from the cold. Among the numerous remains found in various parts of Europe are gloves or "bags" of roughly dressed skins, without separate fingers, reaching to the elbow.

Looking back to ancient Egypt, that land which cradled the very beginnings of dress, we find that gloves were by no means unknown. Though they do not seem to have been worn by women, several instances testify to their use by men. Among the discoveries made in the Valley of the Kings were gloves once worn by the now famous King Tutankhamen. Lying in the ancient tomb, bundled with many pieces of clothing, were a pair of linen gloves and a tapestry glove woven in colored thread. Tape attached to the wrist indicates that the gloves were fastened by being tied about the wrist, and the separate fingers and thumb prove beyond a doubt that the modern form of glove was known to this ancient people.

The early Greeks are known to have been familiar with the glove, and had, no doubt, adopted it from Eastern peoples, for it is an established fact that not only the Egyptians but also the Israelites, Chaldeans, and Persians had worn this particular form of hand covering. In Genesis, the record states that Rebecca put skins on the hands of her younger son to secure for him the birthright of his elder brother.* In the language of the Chaldeans the word *mugubh*† is said to mean a covering for the hands.

---

* Genesis XXVII:16.

† Talmud Dictionary.

Complaining of the luxury of the Persians, Xenophon says,

> It is not sufficient for them to clothe their heads and bodies, but they have coverings made of hair for their hands and fingers.

Cyclopedia, Book VIII

Among the Greeks these earliest gloves were worn solely as a protection to the hands and not in any way as a decorative detail of Greek dress. In the *Odessey* Homer tells that Ulysses, returning to his home, found his father, Laertes, working in the garden wearing gloves—"while *gloves* secured his hand to shield them from the thorns."* The belief that gloves were generally worn, when shoes were rarely used, is, of course, absurd. In later days both Greeks and Romans are said to have worn gloves when feasting, dipping their food from a common bowl. Two reasons are assigned for this custom: first, to keep the hands from the food; secondly, to protect them from burns. Athenaeus speaks of a celebrated glutton who always came to table habited in gloves, so that he might be able to devour more than the rest of the company. Pliny, the younger, in giving an account of his uncle's visit to Vesuvius, states that his amanuensis wore gloves upon his hands in winter lest the cold should prevent him from making use of his writing implements.† Under the emperors it is known that the glove was made both with fingers and also in the shape of the "bag" or mitten, the original form of glove. Though this shows that the ancients were by no means strangers to the glove, its use as a fashionable note in costume did not become general until the days of Roman supremacy. Then the glove was accepted as a note of refinement in dress and a means of displaying both wealth and taste.

Middle Ages

During the Middle Ages it is quite probable that the Romans introduced the glove to western Europe. The Romans came as conquerors, and the subject peoples naturally adopted the manners and clothes of their masters. Like many other fashions in dress, the rise of the glove belongs to this interesting period. Although there is mere speculation as to the derivation of the word "glove," the general opinion favors the Anglo-Saxon *glōf*, meaning "palm of the hand."‡ The early etymologists, how-

---

* *Odessey*, 229.
† Pliny, Ep. III, 5.
‡ Anglo-Saxon: *glof*
  Celtic: *golof*
  French: *gant*
  Scandinavian: *glof* or *glofar*
  English: *glove* or *gauntlet*
  Spanish: *guandi*

ever, claim to have found the root of the word in the Belgic *gheloove*, meaning "faithfulness." One of these early students wrote, "Gloves signify fidelity, since they are in a certain sense the witness of constancy and love." This significance of the glove and its use as a pledge of honor are inextricably woven into the fabric of glove tradition.*

During the early centuries of the Middle Ages, the enveloping mantles and long-sleeved gowns of both men and women, extending as they did over the hand, served to fulfill the purpose of the glove as a protection. As early as 486, however, Frankish men and women were wearing coverings for the hands. These were not in the form of the modern glove, but resembled the familiar mitten, that is, a bag with a separate compartment for the thumb. They were made of finely dressed skins with the fur on the inside. Sometimes the fur was worn outside and the glove lined with warm material. Skins of the stag, kid, or goat were especially favored. The back of this glove was frequently ornamented with gold and set with gems. These gloves were worn only during the cold season of the year. In a manuscript of the tenth century a drawing depicts a woman wearing a glove in the form of a mitten

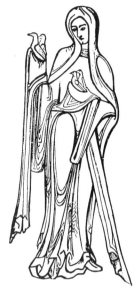

Figure 449. Early Gloves in the Form of Mittens

From the Cotton ms., Nero, CIV.

with only the thumb separated, and another shows long streamers attached to the glove. Figure 449. Though the discoveries made in recent years point undeniably to the fact that gloves with separated sections for the fingers were known to the ancient Egyptians and, if to them, no doubt to other Eastern peoples, their use was probably not general. At any rate, for several centuries during the Middle Ages the separated fingers do not appear. It is not until the eleventh century that the records begin to picture the sections designed for fingers and thumb. It is safe, then, to conjecture that the modern glove began to take form at this period.

As with many of the luxurious details of dress, so it was with gloves—they were first worn exclusively by those of wealth and high position. As early as the seventh, eighth, and ninth centuries kings, princes, and prelates were adopting the glove. There is mention of gloves in a seventh-century poem of Beowulf, and a record in old archives of the tenth cen-

---

* The existence of a word signifying such an object indicates that *glove* in a primitive form, a bag, was familiar to the various peoples.

tury shows that five pairs of gloves formed a part of the duty paid by German merchants to the English sovereign Ethelred II (976-1016). An illumination from the time of Edward I (1272-1307), shows the assassination of the youthful Richard I, in which the unfortunate young prince carries a white glove.

Royal gloves of this early period were invariably set with gems. The monumental effigies of Henry II (1154-89) and Richard I (1189-19) at Fontevraud display gloves with jewels on the back. Such effigies appear to have been a literal representation of a deceased king's appearance. A writer of the period, describing the ceremony conducted for Henry II, says:

On the morrow when he should be carried to be buried, he was arrayed in regal vestments, having a golden crown on his head, and *gloves* on his hands; boots wrought with gold on his feet, and spurs; a great ring on the finger and a scepter in the hand, and girt with a sword; he lay with his face uncovered.

King John's effigy at the same place, and also the one at Worcester where he is buried, display jeweled gloves. In 1797 when his casket was opened such gloves were found upon his hands. No effigy of King Edward is in existence, but it is stated that when his tomb was opened in 1774, the body was found arrayed in royal vestments without the gloves, which had undoubtedly perished, for the ornaments which had been a part of them were found lying upon the backs of the hands.

Like the gloves worn by kings and princes, those of Church officials were also badges of distinction. As early as 790, Charlemagne gave unlimited rights of hunting to certain monks. In turn, with the skins of the deer they killed they were pledged to make gloves and girdles, and covers for their books. Gloves were given a distinctive place in the rites and ceremonies of the church. The early priests wore white gloves, probably linen, at mass so that they might offer the Holy Sacrament with clean and pure hands. The symbolism of the Church invested these gloves with a certain significance, "It was specified that by these gloves the hands would be preserved white, chaste, clean during work, and free from every stain."* At the time of the interment of Pope Boniface VIII, his hands were clothed in gloves of white silk, beautifully embroidered and ornamented with pearls. White as a symbol of purity had much to do in determining this choice in prelates' gloves. In later years, however, they were made in color following the colors of the vestments. Among the most famous gloves in church history are those of William of Wykeman, bishop of Winchester. They are still preserved in New College, Oxford. They are red silk with the sacred monogram surrounded by a glory embroidered in gold on the back. Many monumental effigies of the

---

* Durandus, bishop of Mende, 1287.

period picture interesting examples of the gloves worn by the dignitaries of the church. The lower clergy were not permitted to wear gloves.

Adopted first by the Throne and then by the Church, gloves were from then on imbued with dignity and meaning. As a symbol of kingly power and a badge of priestly office they came to be the most significant articles of official dress. Gradually other usages, both grave and gay, developed and passed into a tradition. The twentieth century looks back in wonder and fascination, charmed with the solemn uses and mystic meanings once attached to this seemingly unromantic detail of modern dress.

Figure 450. Pontifical Glove, Knitted and Embroidered, 1500

From earliest feudal times the king's glove represented regal power. By sending his glove with an envoy the sovereign delegated power to others. His glove served as his ambassador. One of the most important occasions to which the king's glove gave royal sanction was that of holding public fairs or markets. It was customary to display at the entrance to the fair or market a large glove, dyed or gilded.

No one is allowed to set up a market or a mint without the consent of the ordinary or judge of the place; the king, also, ought to send a *glove* as a sign of his consent to the same.

Speculum Saxonicum, Lib. II

Another interesting custom of these early days was the use of the glove as a pledge of security. It frequently entered into many transactions connected with the transfer and tenure of property:

a. To ratify a grant of land, gloves were often deposited with the deed.

b. As part payment for rent, gloves frequently figured as one of the items. It is related that a manor house in Nottinghamshire was held by the annual payment of "one pound of cumin seed, a steel needle, and a pair of *gloves.*"

c. A register of the Parliament of Paris, dated 1294, reads: "The Earl of Flanders by the delivery of a *glove* into the hands of the King, Philip the Fair, gave him permission of the good town of Flanders."

The glove as the instrument in a challenge to duel brings to mind the familiar phrase, "Throw down the gauntlet." Throwing down the glove was a symbol of challenge and, when picked up by the adversary, signified acceptance. A duel to the death was often the result of such an encounter.

As gifts at weddings and funerals, gloves were distributed among guests. This extravagance gradually diminished, however, till gifts of gloves were made only to relatives and friends. In 1639, one Francis Pynner, an Englishman, left by his will, "to everyone that shall be my household servant at the time of my death, twenty shillings apiece and everyone of them a pair of *gloves.*" Another funeral statement shows an account of £45 5s "to Mr. John Sleigh, his Bill for *Gloves*, Scarves, and Hatband." A modern survival of this old custom occurred in 1736 in Boston, when, at the funeral of the wife of Governor Belcher, over one thousand pairs of gloves were given away.

In contrast with these gifts presented at weddings and funerals were the gloves given to friends and distinguished persons as an expression of courtesy or compliment. New Year's Day was a great day for the exchanging of gifts. These gifts usually took the form of small articles of wearing apparel in which the glove was the favorite. Such are frequently mentioned as "gift gloves." By-and-by the custom prevailed of giving, instead, the price of a pair of gloves, bringing into use the term "glove money" or "glove silver."

In the field of romance, as tokens of love, gloves have played a charming role. In this early day gloves were looked upon as binding gifts in courtship—"seals of the truth of hearts."* In Durfrey's *Wit and Mirth,* one hears the song of the *Jolly Pedlar:*

> I have fine perfumed *gloves*
> Made of the best doeskin,
> Such as young men do give their loves
> When they their favor win.

Many a gallant knight appearing at the jousting tourney wore the glove of his lady fixed in his hat. In Drayton's *Battle of Agincourt,* we read:

---

* *Countryman,* 1618.

> The noble youth, the common rank above,
>   On their courvetting coursers mounted fair.
> One wore his mistress' garter, one her *glove*,
>   And he a lock of his deir lady's hair:
> And he her colours whom he most did love—
>   There was not one but did some favor wear.

Before gloves were exchanged as a symbol of fidelity, the sleeve of the lady was worn as a favor by the knight upon his helmet. Sir Lancelot consented to wear in the lists at Camelot the fair favor brought him by the Lily Maid of Astolat:

> "A scarlet *sleeve* broidered with great pearls."

Describing a tournament of 1500, Hull, the chronicler, says of one of the knights:

> One wore on his headpiece his lady's sleeve,
> Another the *glove* of his dearlyng.

So it is that the glove comes down to modern times with a history old and princely, imbued at once with gravest meanings and happiest fancies.

In the history of dress, the twelfth century is especially interesting because at this period many new departures in costume first appeared. Gloves at this time gradually came to be a part of fashionable dress. Though mittens, leaving the fingers free, had been adopted somewhat earlier, they continued to be occasionally worn as late as the twelfth century. Sometimes the mitten or glove was made a part of the sleeve, and so appears upon several monumental effigies of 1300. Up to this time gloves, as previously said, had been worn almost exclusively by men, but now ladies of the most exalted rank began to adopt them. The gloves worn by women of this early day were usually of leather. They were frequently ornamented with precious stones, or a single gem was set on the back after the fashion of prince and prelate. It is believed, and indeed fair to conjecture, that the pursuit of hawking had much to do with the rising popularity of gloves. The hawk was always borne upon the wrist, and thus protection was needed to shield the flesh from the sharp talons of the powerful bird. Figure 451. In the thirteenth century ladies adopted this sport and are said to have outdistanced their lords in skill. We find reference to one medieval lady who "hunted, hawked, snared birds with nets, and ferreted rabbits." A manuscript of the early fourteenth century, preserved among the Royal Collection in England, shows a group of women, one of whom carries a hawking glove and another who bears a hawk on her gloved hand.

About the thirteenth century the metal gauntlet as a part of defensive armor came into use. It is well to note this in passing, because it gradually developed, in 1600, into an historically interesting type of gauntlet glove. The early gauntlets were made of overlapping plates of metal on a leather foundation. With many variations in style, they continued to be worn until 1660. At this period they were often wholly of steel with cuffs shaped to the arm and reaching to the elbow. Others were made of plates of overlapping leather. Later, at the time of Cromwell, the "buff glove" was adopted by his troopers and the steel gauntlet fell into disuse. The hands of the famous "buff gloves" were made of heavy sheepskin and the deep cuffs, extending almost to the elbow, of stout buffalo hide. Often the deep cuff or gauntlet was covered with leather or horn scalework. Figure 452.

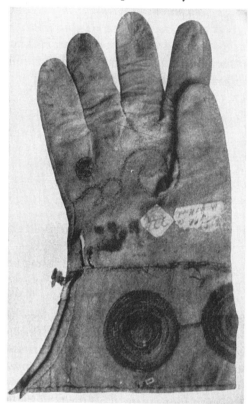

ASHMOLEAN MUSEUM, OXFORD

Figure 451. Hawking Glove of Henry VIII

With the acceptance of the glove as a fashionable detail of dress by the leaders of the twelfth and thirteenth centuries it soon came to be a coveted accessory of lesser folk. With the new demand for gloves which arose at this time several small towns in France did such a thriving business that it was not long before they were meeting all the demands of the trade. Gloves were made of sheepskin, doeskin, and hareskin; to make them even more attractive they were soon being heavily scented. During the next century, approximately between 1380 and 1461, under Charles VI and VII, "violet-scented gloves" were introduced. The craze for scented gloves had set in, and for the next two centuries the perfumed gloves were an indispensable detail in the fashions of the hour. The scented glove as well as other luxuries in dress is said to have been introduced into Italy (Venice) about the year 1071, when Domenico Sievo, the Doge, married a lady of the East who brought with her many Eastern customs, among them the scented glove. The fashion was a long time in spreading but it finally permeated every section of the fashion world.

Many were the methods of imparting a permanent fragrance to gloves! In one instance animal essences—civet, musk, or ambergris—were mixed with oil and all kinds of fragrant drugs and spices. One simple recipe directed thus:

Put into angelica water and rose water the powder of cloves, ambergris, musk, and ligum aloes; benzamin and carduus aromatic. Boil them until half consumed, then strain and put your gloves therein. Hang them in the sun to dry and turn them often. Do this three times wetting and drying them again. Or wet your gloves in rose water, and hang them up until almost dry then grind half an ounce of benzamin with oil of almonds, and rub them on the gloves. Then hang them up to dry, or let them dry in your bosom, and so, after use them at your pleasure.*

Figure 452. Buff Glove Showing Cuff of Horn Scale Work, 1600

1500-1600

Many were the recipes for this coveted fragrance. No doubt milady of fashion, as well as milord, tried them all—for, at any price, gloves must be perfumed! Although perfumed gloves held their own for the next two hundred years, their popularity in France, Italy, Spain, and Germany preceded by two centuries their acceptance by Fashion in England. Though worn by Henry VIII and his court, it was not until the days of Good Queen Bess that the fashion of the perfumed glove was the rule in Britain. Then followed the golden age in gloves—the sixteenth and seventeenth centuries. It is at this interesting period that portraits of famous men and women begin to appear, and reference is constantly made to this fashionable accessory. *The Book of Quarterly Payments* for the household of Henry VIII shows that His Majesty on New Year's Day was presented with a pair of perfumed gloves. In 1532, the King's *Privy Purse Expenses* shows that 7s 6d was paid "for a dousen and a half of Spanyshe gloves." Spanish gloves at this time were famous for the perfume skillfully applied to them. Their fragrance was of a permanent character, very different from the French perfume made from distilled oils of natural flowers, which failed to be of enduring quality. As the result of her reputation for scented gloves, Spain's trade in embroidered and perfumed gloves, as well as in skins, scented but not cut up, is said to have flourished for several centuries.

A familiar story in the annals of gloves is that of the Earl of Oxford, who, returning to England after a period of several years in Italy,

---

* After Mark. See *Gloves, Their Annals and Associations* by S. William Beck, F.R.H.S.

brought back a pair of perfumed gloves, which in that day were known as "sweete bagges." He presented the gloves to Queen Elizabeth, then in the fifteenth year of her reign. According to John Stour, a chronicler of that period, Elizabeth was delighted; "she took such pleasure in these gloves that she was pictured with these gloves upon her hands"; and he adds that the particular scent was called, "the Earl of Oxford scent." In 1556, among the gifts to the Queen on New Year's Day were: from "Mr. Frankewell, a peire of perfumed *gloves*," from "Pascal, a peire of *gloves* perfumed and cuffed with gold and silver"; and from "Hannyball, a peire of perfumed *gloves*." The Queen's love for these beautiful accessories brought more and more similar gifts to her wardrobe. Further, at this period and even earlier it was the custom of universities and corporations to present a gift of gloves to those whom they wished to honor. In 1566, Queen Elizabeth upon her visit to Oxford was presented with a handsome pair of embroidered gloves which to this day are preserved in Ashmolean Museum, Oxford. These unusual gloves show very long fingers and a deep cuff edged with fringe and covered with a rich embroidery carried up and around the base of the thumb. PLATE XL. Many are the distinguished persons listed in the ancient archives as recipients of this distinctive gift. In 1451, Oriel College presented the bishop of Lincoln with a pair of handsome gloves. In 1571 Magdalen College presented Wolsey with a pair of gloves costing 6s 4d. In 1561 Corpus Christi College presented Lord and Lady Bedford with a handsome pair of gloves costing 4s. This interesting custom probably grew out of an earlier tradition, to wit, the habit of the courteous in the presence of superiors to "do off his hood, his *gloves* also." A gift of gloves now indicated that one so distinguished was worthy to stand with hands covered, even in the presence of the highest collegiate dignitaries of the land. Such a gift was, consequently, considered the highest of honors. In Nichol's *Progresses of Queen Elizabeth* there is still further mention of the gift of perfumed gloves:

By the Lady Mary Grey, 1 peir of swete *gloves* with fower dozen buttons of gold, in every one a seed perle.

By Lady Mary Sidney, one peir of perfumed *gloves* with XXIII small buttons of golde, in every one of them a small diamond.

By Petro Lupo, a peire of swete *gloves*.

By Joseph Lupo, a peire of swete *gloves*.

By Caesar Caliardo, a peire of swete *gloves*.

Elizabeth was very proud of her beautiful hands, and gloves served as a captivating foil to attract attention. De Maurier, in his *Memoires*, relates his experience when sent to interview the Queen, speaking of the "coquettish restlessness" with which she played with her gloves . . . "at every audience . . . she pulled off her *gloves* more than a hundred times

PLATE XL. Gloves Presented to Queen Elizabeth on Her Visit to Oxford in 1566

to display her hands, which, indeed, were very beautiful and white." Elizabeth was very much given to bestowing her glove as a favor upon those whom she admired and those whose admiration she sought. At one time Her Majesty is credited with pulling from her hands gloves of rich Spanish leather, embossed on the back with marvellous embroidery and heavily fringed, and, passing them to a favorite, Glisson, she remarked,

"Here Glisson, wear them for my sake." At another time she presented to Clifford, Earl of Cumberland, a glove which she had dropped and which he had gallantly restored to her. The Earl was so flattered by the Queen's attention and so pleased with this mark of her esteem that he wore the glove constantly where all could see it, in the front of his helmet. At another time when Shakespeare and his company were giving

Figure 453. Gloves of Mary, Queen of Scots

a court performance, the Queen was present. No doubt the presence of their Queen stimulated the actors, the great dramatist in particular. Elizabeth is said to have greatly admired handsome men, and Shakespeare, cast well in his part, appeared so highly to her satisfaction that she threw her glove to him on the stage. This has sometimes been regarded as a bit of coquettish flirtation on the part of the Queen. The poet, however, with wise discretion, choosing to consider it an accident, picked up the glove, returned it to the Queen, and bowing deeply said:

> Altho now bent on this high embassy,
> Yet stoop we to pick up our cousin's *glove*.

In the plays of the great poet reference is constantly made to the glove. Autolycus sings of

> "*Gloves* as sweet as damask roses."
>
> *Winter's Tale*. Act IV, sc. 3

and in *Much Ado About Nothing*, Hero says to Beatrice:

> These *gloves* the Count sent me, they are an excellent perfume!
>
> Act III, sc. 4

Still again, under the spell of a passionate devotion Romeo says:

> Oh, that I were a *glove* upon that hand
> That I might touch that cheek!
>
> *Romeo and Juliet.* Act II, sc. 2

These days of the sixteenth century were, indeed, happy days for the glove. With Elizabeth setting the mode, they were soon adopted by people in general. Closely associated with Elizabeth in life and lying near her in death is that other queen of melancholy fate, Mary, Queen of Scots. A very handsome glove presented by the unfortunate queen on the morning of her execution to a gentleman of the Dayrel family who was in attendance upon her, is preserved in the Saffron Walden Museum, Oxford. Figure 453. A copy of a letter found in the Tower Records, presumably written by the gentleman himself and dated, "ffrom ffatheringaie Castle, VIIjth of ffebruarye 1587," gives an account of what he had seen on that tragic morning, describing in full the manner of procedure and the bearing of the Scottish queen. It is believed that the writer, in whatever capacity he may have served was recognized by the Queen as a gentleman of quality and given her glove as a token of regard. The glove is fully described in an antiquarian magazine, the *Relinquary*, from which S. William Beck, in his valuable book, *Gloves, Their Annals and Associations*, quotes:

The *glove* is made of light cool, buff-colored leather, the elaborate embroidery on the gauntlet being worked with silver wire and silk of various colours. The roses are of pale and dark blue, and two shades of very pale crimson; the foliage represents trees, and is composed of two shades of aesthetic green. A bird in flight, with a long tail, figures conspicuously among the work. It should be here mentioned that the embroidery shown in the drawing is repeated *fac simile* on the other side of the *glove*, and this having been lying against the glass case, has retained the color better than the side which has been so many years exposed to the light. The part of the *glove* which formed the gauntlet is lined with crimson satin (which is as bright and fresh as the day it was made) a narrow band being turned outward as a binding to the gauntlet, unto which is sewn the gold fringe or lace, on the points of which are fastened groups of small pendent steel or silver spangles. The opening at the side of the gauntlet is connected by two broad bands of crimson silk, faded now almost to a pink colour, and each band is decorated with pieces of tarnished silver lace on each side.

A melancholy interest attaches to the glove of Lady Jane Gray, a queen of nine days. It is said that after being led to the scaffold and kneeling before the block, she "stode up and gave her maiden, Mistress Tilney, her *glove* and handkerchief." Charles I, on the scaffold, is said to have passed his gloves to William Juxon, bishop of London, in whose family they are believed to be preserved to this day. It is said that the glove played no small part in the effort of Catherine, the first queen of Henry VIII, to win him from his growing attachment for the Lady Ann Boleyn. By arranging a game of cards for the King, the Queen hoped the Lady Ann might pull off her glove and reveal a deformed finger.

Among the more noted historic gloves of this period are those believed to have once belonged to Shakespeare. Figure 454. These are of substantial leather ornamented with a scroll stitching in gold and red. A yellow silk ribbon marks the cuff, the lower edge of which is edged with a crimson-and-yellow fringe. The cuff is double, with an openwork pattern cut in the upper skin.

During this important century a new leather glove made its appearance. This was the *cheverell* glove. "Cheverell" is from the French *chevre*, meaning "goat," and was a kind of kid leather, finer and more pliable than had hitherto been worn. "Knitted gloves" are also frequently mentioned in records of this century; likewise "silk knitted gloves." This does not mean, however, that the history of knitting begins here. It is known that as far back as the ancient Egyptians stockings of fine wool were knit, and bonnets were knitted before they were felted. Knitted gloves of silk were worn in France during the reigns of Henry II (1137-80) and Henry III (1223-26). In a list of articles imported to England from Holland in 1536 appears, *gloves knitte of silk*. Each item in this list is checked either as "superfluous" or "necessarye," and interesting to note, gloves come under the former head.

Figure 454. Drawing from a Glove, 1500

Said to have belonged to Shakespeare.

Surveying the gloves of the century, they are, without doubt, remarkable. Magnificent embroidery in color usually covered the cuff. The needlework was so skillfully done that it was often referred to as "needle-painting." The deep cuff was frequently lined with gay-colored silk, usually crimson, and edged with gold fringe. The gloves of this century, in fact, were gorgeous with colored embroidery and gold fringe.

1600-1700

During the seventeenth century the perfumed glove, with new scents, still continued. The Marquis Frangipani, *Marechal des Armees* of Louis XIII, invented a new perfume for gloves, and instantly the gloves *à la Frangipani* became a sensation (see Perfume, page 158). Again, gloves *à la Nervoli* perpetuated the name of a princess who had invented a new and wonderful scent. Perfumed gloves were everywhere!

Under Louis XIV the glove merchants were privileged to make and sell gloves, mittens, skins, and perfumes. During this century and probably earlier than 1600, gloves made of "chicken skin" were manufactured.* There seemed to be some particular value in this skin which made the hands soft and white.

> Some of *chicken skin* for night
> To keep their hands plump, soft and white.
> *Mundus Muliebris*

Both the gentlemen and ladies of the perfumed court of France made a practice of wearing these gloves at night, heavily lined with scented pomades, hoping to acquire thereby a peculiar delicacy of hand. This practice continued in England as late as the reign of George III. There is little definite information about the manufacture of

Figure 455. Glove
From Portrait of the Earl of Exeter, 1621.

Figure 456. Glove

From Portrait of the Earl of Southampton, 1624.

chicken-skin gloves, but their use developed a taste for fine materials, and, before long, gloves were being made of the skin of unborn calves. The main seat of this manufacture was in Limerick, Ireland, and such gloves came to be known as *limericks*. They are said to have been so fine that they could be folded up and packed in a walnut shell; history says that the shop windows of the day exhibited gilded walnut shells with dainty "limericks" hidden therein.

Sleeves and gloves have always had much in common. In the earlier days, it has been noted, the wide cuffs of gloves took care of the full sleeves, and now in the seventeenth century this relation of sleeve and glove is again very fashionably manifest. During this period the sleeves of women's gowns grew short and ever shorter and the glove followed the sleeve up the arm. When the sleeves came to be mere puffs on the

---

* A kind of vellum prepared from the skins of very young animals. Extremely thin, very delicate and supple. It has no grain but held up to the light has a slightly mottled appearance which shows at once what it is and distinguishes it from paper.

shoulder the gloves leaped the elbow. In 1675 mits of white kid thirty-two inches long were Fashion's favorite. They were very wide at the top and had three draw strings with gilt tassels which were used to draw up this width to form two puffs above the elbow. Moreover, every fashionable woman had gloves for each occasion. It is said that when Marie of

Figure 457. Embroidered Gauntlets, English, 1700

Austria died in 1666, she left three hundred pairs of gloves. The fascinating prints of Menceslaus Holler (1607-77) picture the ladies of his day wearing the long, close-fitting gloves. The gay cavaliers of the period wore gloves of white leather with wide cuffs. They were often embroidered and frequently loaded with other ornament. Figure 457. Though embroidered gauntlets continued fashionable for many years, the love for embroidery gradually gave way to the heavily fringed glove which was the favorite in later cavalier days. Figure 458. It was considered a very smart thing at this time to carry the gloves in the hand or tuck them in at the girdle.

Toward the last quarter of the century, ribbon was worn in profusion. In fact, men and women of the day were swathed in ribbon. Gloves were not spared. They, too, were:

. . . top't with narrow Ribbands of various colors and textures with gold or silver interwoven . . . white *gloves* with broad black lace ruffles and heavy fringe; *gloves* pearl coleur and gold . . . large rolls of ribband round the tops and down to the hand.*

---

* See S. William Beck, F.R.H.S., *Gloves, Their Annals and Associations*, p. 128.

Evelyn, who is best known for his playful satire on the subject of dress, records his impression of a dandy he had seen in Westminster Hall: "It was a fine silken thing I espied the other day . . . that had so much ribbon about him as would have plundered six shops and set up twenty country pedlars." Soon France started the fashion of wearing foreign laces upon the glove. So extravagant did this fashion become that the King took the lead in reinforcing an act of Charles I, his father, forbidding foreign lace coming into the country. We are amused, however, to read that the King gave his license to one merchant to import:

Such laces as may be for the weare of . . . our dear mother, the Queen; our dear brother James, the Duke of York, and the rest of the royal family, to the end the same may be patterned for the manufacture of those commodities here, notwithstanding the late statue forbidding their importation.

Figure 458. Fashionable Fringed Gauntlets, English, 1600

This exclusiveness of the decree, however, defeated its purpose and soon laces of all description were being smuggled into the country. Presently the deep lace ruffles, which were soon added to the cuffs of men's dress and completely covered the hand, made gloves less essential. Women continued to wear white kid beautifully embroidered and of varying length. Gradually, however, ornamentation diminished and gloves, having passed their golden age, entered upon a period of simplicity.

1700-1900

During the late eighteenth and early nineteenth centuries gloves settled into a kind of unadorned beauty, compared with the fringed, embroidered, and perfumed gloves of bygone days. The chief merit of gloves in the new era had passed from that of elegance through ornamentation to that of perfection in fit. This is in marked contrast to the days of Good Queen Bess, for her gloves were of such liberal dimensions that they would to modern eyes appear ridiculously clumsy. New ideas and new methods, however, had now entered the field, and gloves like shoes were made to measure. During the later days of the century, long gloves of glacé kid and mitts of knitted silk were the fashionable choice in women's gloves. Long gloves were expensive, and since a soiled glove was not permissible, tan became a favorite color. The vogue for this color continued of its own momentum well into the nineteenth century; then, by cleverly giving the color a new name, "York tan," its life was still further prolonged. Though men generally had neglected the use of gloves, Napoleon, who had small, well-shaped hands of which he was very proud, wore gloves on many occasions. It is said that in 1806 he possessed 235 pairs of cream-colored gloves, and had purchased in December of that year 42 pairs of fur-lined gloves. During the century there were whimsical changes in the length of women's gloves. As usual this depended upon the sleeve. Wrist-length gloves were worn with the long-sleeved street dress; gloves to the elbow with the medium-short sleeve; and shoulder-length gloves with the evening gown. Lace mitts in black or white, and gloves trimmed with lace or ruching were also very fashionable. Figure 459; PLATE XLII. During the sixties one-button gloves captured the fashion world and were worn with both long and short sleeves. This was quite an innovation; eyes unaccustomed to seeing the arms uncovered received a jolt. But by-and-by everybody succumbed to the mode. From 1875 to 1878, long gloves of openwork China silk of extraordinary fineness and elasticity were fashionable. These were of many colors, and are said to have been "perfection in fit." One of the outstanding fashions of this century was that introduced by Sarah Bernhardt. This world-famous actress possessed very slender arms, and in 1870 at the height of her career, appeared in long gloves that lay in horizontal folds all the way up the arm. This was the glove *à la mousquetaire*. This new fashion instantly became the vogue. Everybody was now wearing the glove *mousquetaire!* From that time to the present, glacé kid and a softer suede have appeared and re-appeared in this attractive form.

During the early seventies, as Augustin Challamel in his delightful *History of Fashion in France* records, a strange rumor was current in

PLATE XLI. A Cavalier, Time of Louis XIII.................*Meissonier*

Every detail of dress is indicative of the extreme of the mode—the high boots with spur leather, the full-skirted jerkin, the lace collar, the elaborate sash, the rolling-brimmed beaver, the sword, and, last but by no means least, the gloves.

fashionable circles. This was nothing less than the abolition of gloves! Economy was not the aim, for "women of fashion proposed to wear clusters of rings between each finger joint; each hand to wear a fortune." Then the vivacious Frenchman adds: "This was a fantastic dream of some blasé lady longing for novelty at any price. It was not realized, as may be imagined; and gloves kept their place—an important one—among articles of feminine attire." Toward the end of the century the laced glove was the final word in glove styles. Tiny metal "holds," four to six in number, were riveted down each side of the glove opening, and a short cord securely fastened to the first "hold" was carried back and forth down the opening until the glove was entirely laced; the tas-

COURTESY, METROPOLITAN MUSEUM OF ART

Figure 459. Mitts, Black Silk Netted
American, early 19th century.

seled end was then left to fall free. By the twentieth century, however, the laced glove had passed out of the picture, and its place was taken by the "slip-on" and one-button glove, each of which easily adjusts itself to the hand. As for men's gloves of the nineteenth century, one finds them usually black and wrist length. Doeskin and kid stitched in black were generally worn. In Paris, the center of world fashions, color was established as a feature in men's gloves for evening wear and garnet red, blue, and straw yellow were the fashionable hues.

Twentieth Century

With the passing of the years the great variety in gloves, like that in shoes, hose, handkerchiefs, buttons, and other accessories has passed far beyond all limits. It is quite impossible, without going into a statistical report, to enumerate the various styles and materials popular for gloves in the twentieth century. Hand coverings of this day are adapted to the life of the present. The sport world, including that of the automobile and airplane, demands a certain type of glove; that of the street, another; and formal wear still another. Milady chooses from a wide range of colors, textures, and types the glove for each occasion. It may be a sport glove of pigskin, doeskin, or hand-sewn calf; driving gloves of dogskin; street gloves of kid, doeskin, or suede; or evening gloves of the finest kid or velvet, delicate hued and faultless of fit.

PLATE XLII. Mrs. Robert Hooper.............................*Copley*

The very elegant costume is enriched by both fur and lace. The lace mitts with the turned-back point are especially worthy of note.

In the making of leather gloves, various skins which come from all over the world are used. These leathers are treated by a different process from that used in shoes and other leatherwork. The finest dress gloves are made from the skins of kids, though the name "kid" is applied to other skins as well. The larger number of gloves is made from the skin of calves, lambs, sheep, and goats, cured in different ways. Those gloves known to the trade as doeskin, buckskin, and dogskin are the hides of deer, dogs, sheep, and calves. Chamois gloves are made from sheepskin which has been tanned by an oil dressing. The development of aeronautics has created a demand for fur gloves. These are made from pelts with the hair left on and properly treated.

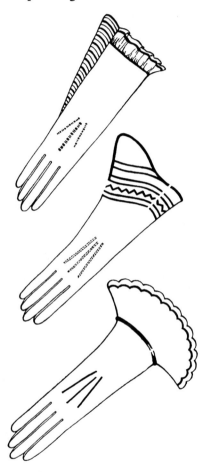

Figure 460. Modern Fabric Gloves, 1930-36

The cotton glove industry sprang up in the United States during the World War, but the quality of the American cotton glove was much inferior to that made in Saxony and other parts of Germany; consequently, notwithstanding the high rate of duty on them, Europe supplies our entire consumption of women's cotton chamois and suede gloves. Woolen and knitted gloves are largely made by the hosiery trade.

Following through the centuries the development of manufactured gloves, one naturally wonders about the beginnings of the trade. When did the craft of the glover become a recognized trade, and how did it come about? Probably as soon as gloves began to be worn and made with profit these ancient glovers formed themselves into groups for mutual protection and gain. Perth, in Scotland, is the recognized home of the first glovemakers. Here, in 1165, the Incorporation of Glovers of Perth received their first charter, "admitting them to the free right and privilege of being in corporate craftsmen." The ancient glovers chose for their patron saint Bartholomew, who according to legendary accounts was flayed before his crucifixion. A little later, in 1190, the glovers united under a settled code of statutes. The patron saint of the French glovemakers was Saint Anne, the mother of Mary, for according to tradition, she was a knitter of gloves. All good glovers of France hold her memory in tender veneration. In England, glovemaking was first carried on by those who worked with skins, the tanners and cobblers. In the fourteenth century the city of London fixed the price for various articles made of leather. On this list appears, "One pair of gloves of sheep leather for one penny half penny, and the best for two pence." In the United States, the manufacture of gloves dates back to 1760, when William Jonson induced several families of glovemakers from Perth, Scotland, to settle on his grants of land in New York State. They brought with them their glove patterns and the necessary needles and thread for glovemaking and settled in what is now Fulton County, New York. This proved to be the beginning of the present town of Gloversville. During the long winter evenings these Scotchmen made gloves and mittens for the farmers living in the vicinity. So readily did the gloves sell that shortly a little industry grew up. It was not, however, until after 1800 that the gloves sold outside the village and its immediate vicinity. In 1825, a lumber

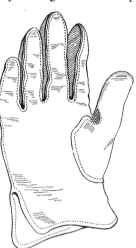

Figure 461. A Gentleman's Modern Stitched Glove

wagon filled with gloves was taken from there to Boston. Today Gloversville and its neighboring town, Johnstown, supply over half the gloves made in the United States.

The first gloves made by these early settlers were crude and clumsy. They were cut by men from pasteboard patterns with shears, and the sewing was done by women. Later steel dies, or patterns, were introduced for cutting. A number of sizes of dies were provided, for hands vary as do feet. In 1852, the invention of the sewing machine marked a new era. Later, in 1875, steam power was introduced to run the machines. This has now been superseded by electrically driven machines.

In this twentieth century one glove passes through the hands of many workmen before it is ready for the market. It is the business of one set of glovers to do the cutting; others sew in the fingers and insert the thumbs; still others do the hemming and ornamental lines on the back. These three ornamental lines, which follow the V-shaped line seen on the back of the hand, are a vestige of the old form of glove. In the early glove the pieces which formed the inside of the fingers, known as *fourchettes*, met in a long V-shaped point, and the stitching had to be carried down some distance on the back of the glove. Sometimes bits of embroidery terminated each of the three elongated stitchings. Gradually, with the improvement in glovemaking, the fourchettes became much shorter, but the embroidery still remained, and as the glove grew simple in form, the stitched line survived the more elaborate embroidered line. In today's glove this stitched line is often of the same color as the glove; or it may be accented by a different color and embroidery.

After the modern glove has passed through the hands of various workers and is completed, it is ready for the "finish." It is now stretched over a hollow metal hand of the same size as the glove—for hand forms now come in as many sizes as there are sizes of hands—and into this steam is passed. The action of the heat causes the soft leather to be smoothed out and easily shaped. When this is completed, the glove is taken from the form, inspected carefully, folded, and packed.

Thus endeth the story of the glove! The regal beginnings, the strange usages, and the delightful spirit of romance that hallowed the old-time glove *must* give a little more color, a little more meaning, create a little more fondness for this very personal accessory of modern dress. Happy is she of the twentieth century who, as she draws on her gloves, catches the vision of their old-time charm.

REFERENCES

Beck, S. William, *Gloves, Their Annals and Associations.*
Blanc, Charles, *Art in Ornament and Dress.*
Boehn, Max von, *Modes and Manners; Ornament*, Chapter 3.
Carter, Howard, *The Tomb of Tut-ankh-Amen.*
Ellsworth, Evelyn Peters, *Textiles and Costume Design.*
Guhl and Kohmer, *Life of the Greeks and Romans.*
Lehman, Helen, *The Leather Goods and Gloves Department*, Chapter 26.
Lester, Katherine Morris, *Historic Costume*, pp. 93, 228.
McClellan, Elizabeth, *Historic Dress in America*, Vols. I, II.
Norris, Herbert, *Costume and Fashion*, Vols. I, II.
Picken, Mary Brooks, *The Secrets of Distinctive Dress.*

CHAPTER 28

The Watch

And I lent my *watch* last night to one that dines today at the sheriff's.
BEN JONSON, *The Alchemist*, Act I, sc. 1.

THE modern watch carried in the pocket or worn upon the wrist is so indispensable, so matter-of-fact as an accessory of dress, that it is difficult to understand how the world ever moved on without it. Today, one scarcely pauses to consider those primitive periods when the progress of time was marked only by the journey of the sun across the heavens. In considering the fashion in watches it is interesting to recall that the very earliest form of timepiece was the sundial. According to some authorities sundials date back to 700 B.C. The earliest mention of a sundial is found in Isaiah XXXVIII: 8, "Behold I will bring again the shadow of degrees, which is gone down in the *sundial* of Ahaz, ten degrees backward." Babylonians, Egyptians, Greeks, Romans, and Chinese all used the sundial. Today, although sundials are used largely in garden decoration, pocket or portable sundials, in use in the first century, have been employed for hundreds of years and are still manufactured. Figures 462, 463. In *As You Like It*, it is the pocket sundial that Shakespeare placed in the hand of Touchstone. Says Jacques:

> "Good morrow, fool," quoth I. "No Sir," quoth he,
> "Call me not fool, till heaven hath sent me fortune."
> And then he drew a *dial* from his poke,
> And looking on it with lack-lustre eye,
> Says very wisely, "It is ten o'clock."
>
> Act II, sc. 7

Admiral Byrd is said to have carried a sundial in his flight to the South Pole. During the World War, pocket sundials were carried by the United States Army Engineers.

Middle Ages

Sundials, the later water clocks, and hourglasses, all devices for measuring time, belong technically to ancient civilizations. In the Middle Ages, new methods evolved. Gradually the world found itself in the land of clocks. The word "clock" originally meant "bell" and arose from the custom of striking a bell to tell the hour. The mechanism was known as "horologe," not as "clock." These early clocks were without dials. In many towns in France and Germany automatic figures were set up, men in armor and others often in grotesque make-up, who, at the proper moment, were timed to tone the hour by striking a large bell. The Clock Tower at Venice, the Strassburg clock—set up in 1352—and the clock of the Neues Rathaus in Munich are vivid reminders of that period. In the fourteenth century clocks really worthy of the name began to appear. They were set up in towers and other high places where their dials could be easily seen by the populace. One of the most celebrated of these clocks is

COURTESY, METROPOLITAN MUSEUM OF ART

Figure 462. Folding Pocket Dial with Compass and Plumb

Brass, late 17th century.

the De Vick clock, the first of which the world has a full description. It was set up by the inventor himself in Paris, in the palace of Charles V. This building is now the *Palais de Justice.*

This famous tower clock was constructed on the same general principles which are the basis of all modern timepieces. Soon artists and craftsmen of this great age were vying with one another in devising new and unusual forms for the time-measuring clock. Gradually there emerged the table clock, the immediate forerunner of the watch. Figures 464, 465. Tower clocks

COURTESY, METROPOLITAN MUSEUM OF ART

Figure 463. Ivory Pocket Dial with Compass

German, 17th century.

were driven by hanging weights. This was impossible with the dial in horizontal position on a table or desk. The new timepiece, of necessity, involved a new motive power. This proved to be the coiled spring. This epoch-making invention is attributed to Peter Henlein, of Nuremburg. Writing in 1511, Johannes Cockläus says that Henlein, "out of a little iron constructs clocks with numerous wheels which can be wound up at will, have no pendalum, go for forty-eight hours, and strike, and can be carried in the purse as well as the pocket." This achievement was considered so remarkable that, to commemorate the event, a monument was erected in his native city to this ingenious locksmith.

1500-1600

These early, portable, table timepieces or clocks, and those which followed, bore little resemblance to the modern watch. They were made entirely by hand—with expert workmanship, to be sure—and the works were iron. The cases were thick and round, resembling the sector of a cylinder; they had no crystal and only one hand, the hour hand. Later they were made oval in shape and, coming from Nurem-

COURTESY, METROPOLITAN MUSEUM OF ART
Figure 464. Table Clock

English, 1565.

COURTESY, METROPOLITAN MUSEUM OF ART
Figure 465. Table Clock

Bronze gilt with engraved decoration, German, 16th century.

burg, have passed into history as "Nuremburg eggs." When compared with the modern demand for precision of performance these early timepieces were crude and inaccurate. Large and clumsy they were, awkward to carry in the hand and uncomfortable in the pocket; consequently, they were invariably hung from the girdle. With all their shortcomings however, they were better than anything previously devised and so answered in a measure the need of the period.

During approximately two hundred years following the invention of the watch it was altogether too expensive for general use and was worn only by the wealthy. By day the great mass of the people depended upon the dials and clock towers. By night the town watch patrolled the streets and called the hours. Watches in this early period were not the necessity they are to modern life and were regarded as "ornaments" or "possessions"; a man's watch simply indicated his wealth and position. Several portraits of this interesting period in watch development picture the watch suspended upon a chain and worn as an ornament about the neck.

Presently the locksmiths of this day began to devise more ornate and

beautiful cases for these little ma-chines. Several outside covers were supplied and made to fit on over the case which held the mechanism. The dial was now not visible until the outer case was opened. These cases were made of gold, silver, tortoise shell, and intricate, pierced goldwork. Figure 466. Many times the covers were decorated with beautiful miniature paintings or set with rare and costly gems. The un-usual shapes which prevailed at this time are so characteristic of the

COURTESY, METROPOLITAN MUSEUM OF ART

Figure 466. English Watch

Gilt metal and silver with pierced case, 1660.

period, the late sixteenth century, that they do not occur at any later time. Some of these were in the shape of a seashell, a tulip or other flowers, butterflies, and other in-sects, a cross, or a skull bearing appropriate phrases with reference to time and death. Figures 467, 468. Mary, Queen of Scots, possessed a silver gilt watch in the shape of a skull. Edward VI is said to have been the

COURTESY, METROPOLITAN MUSEUM
OF ART

Figure 467. Silver Watch, French, 17th Century

Intended to remind the wearer that each second brought death nearer.

first Englishman to own a watch. Queen Elizabeth is reported to have se-lected her watches as the modern woman chooses her hats, one for each costume. Her Majesty's inventory, however, appears quite modest for it mentions only twenty-four watches and "smale clocks." Of course, most of these were jeweled with "faier rubies, diamonds, emerodes and opolls."

Like gloves and rings, watches had long been looked upon as tokens of love and esteem, and Good Queen Bess is said to have received many gifts of rare and beautiful watches.

By 1580 watchmaking had begun as a home industry in both England and Switzerland. Soon the craft spread throughout Germany and France. Switzerland, however, rapidly forged ahead and soon the Swiss people were recognized as the great watchmakers of the world. Toward the close of the sixteenth century (1590) tiny spherical watches were fashionable. Many of these were fitted with chimes. Young men who were "the glass of fashion" carried these fanciful little watches about with them. Charles V of France possessed a tiny watch with chimes which he had set in an earring that he wore. At this period these midget watches were also set in finger rings. Watches with rock-crystal cases and enamel watches are said to date from the middle of this century. Figures 469, 470. Throughout the period this expensive accessory was always worn where it could be seen and admired.

1600-1700

The seventeenth century was indeed a century of achievement in watchmaking. Many of the marvelous mechanisms of the modern timepiece were then devised. The perfection of the various parts of the watch was greatly stimulated by

COURTESY, METROPOLITAN MUSEUM OF ART

Figure 468. Rock Crystal Watch, French, 16th Century

English enterprise. There was a general demand for accurate timepieces for finding longitudes at sea and a watch that would keep correct time notwithstanding the heavy rolling of a ship at sea. England offered many rewards for the best inventions, and, finally, there was invented in 1676 the spiral spring with a balance wheel, which made the minute hand possible eleven years later, in 1687.

Previous to this, watches continued to be set with chimes, and tiny watches to be set in rings. Handsome watches continued to be given as presents among the royal families of Europe. Some of these are the most beautiful known in the history of watches. In 1647, the great Elector of Brandenburg gave his bride, Louisa Henrietta of Orange, a wedding gift of a little watch set with forty-seven diamonds and valued at four hundred florins.* By 1650, the enameling of watches with opaque color was almost perfected. Figure 472. Pictorial representations of biblical history, Roman history, and mythological subjects were exquisitely carried out in enamel in various colors. This art had been developed by a Frenchman, Jean Toutin, who discovered the process by which thick colors applied

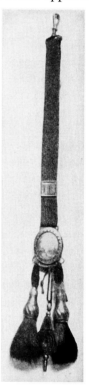

COURTESY, METROPOLTAN MUSEUM OF ART

COURTESY, METROPOLTAN MUSEUM OF ART

METROPOLITAN

Figure 469. Gold, Yellow Crystal, and Enamel Watch

French, 17th century.

Figure 470. Rock-Crystal-and-Enamel Watch

French, 17th century.

Figure 471. Watch Fob, English

Late 18th century.

to thin plates of gold could be melted and still retain their luster.

1700-1800

During the eighteenth century, the technique of watchmaking was brought to so high a degree of perfection that it has not been surpassed to this day. Switzerland, Germany, France, and England did much to promote this attainment. Watch jewels and the first keyless watches were introduced about 1700; the balance spring and seconds hand were first used about 1780. Before this, in 1721, a new material for the making

* Florin, about $.41½.

of watch cases was introduced by Christopher Pinchbeck, who had discovered an alloy of metals which closely resembled gold in both color
and ductility. This new alloy, one part zinc to five parts copper, was
called after its inventor, "Pinchbeck gold," and during his entire life the

formula of its composition was
jealously guarded. At this time
"Pinchbeck" was being used for
clocks, stock buckles, shoe buckles,
sword hilts, cane heads, whip
handles, spurs, snuffboxes, and in
particular, "watches plain and
chased in so curious a Manner as
not to be distinguished by the nicest
eye from real Gold, and which are
highly necessary for Gentlemen and
Ladies when they travel." Watches
were now beginning to be recognized as a necessity and were being
carried by all leaders of fashion.
History records that the exquisite
Comte d'Artois, who later became
Charles X, wore buttons on his coat
each set with a tiny watch. During
the reign of Louis XVI women
wore watches with small fobs at-

Figure 472. Watch, Geneva
Enamel on Gold

18th century.

tached. As the waistcoat of gentlemen grew shorter, watches and fobs
increased in popularity and came to be considered an essential part
of masculine dress. It was then the fashion for men to wear two watches
with fobs, one in each pocket of his waistcoat. Figure 473. In Germany
the possession of a watch among the middle class was a mark of distinction. The story is told that in 1745, when the Austrians captured Vils-
hofen, a noncommissioned officer took a watch from a lieutenant of the
captured town, and was forced to ask the lieutenant to wind it, for he
was unacquainted with its mechanism. By the close of the eighteenth century, watches had become fairly accurate. The Swiss and French took
the lead in producing both beautiful and dependable timepieces. Watches
were now almost exclusively carried in the pocket and, consequently,
grew thinner, lighter, and more simple in decoration. In 1776, Lepin the
French watchmaker made the first thin watches.

With watches coming more and more into use and carried by both
men and women, a curious fad developed. This was the fashion of carrying within the case little papers on which appeared a treasured likeness
or a bit of sentimental verse. These little papers, fitted very carefully to

the watchcase, were known as "watch-papers." They continued fashionable as late as 1837. In the following century the gathering of watch-papers came to be a hobby of collectors both in England and America. With what zeal these happy hunters must have seized upon a treasured portrait or a bit of tender rhyme! One gentle sentiment under date of 1730 reads like this:

> With me while present may thy lovely eyes
>   Be never turned upon this golden toy,
> Think every pleasing hour too swiftly flies,
>   And measures time by joy succeeding joy.
> And when the cares that interrupt our bliss
>   To me not always will thy sight allow,
> Then oft with kind impatience look on this,
>   And every minute count as I do now.

Another admonishes thus:

> Little monitor, impart
> Some instruction to the heart.
>   Show the busy and the gay
>   Life is hasting swift away.
> Follies cannot long endure,
> Life is short and death is sure.
>   Happy those who wisely learn
>   Truth from error to discern.

And still another:

> *Time is*—the present moment well employ;
>
> *Time was*—is past—thou canst not it enjoy;
>
> *Time future*—is not and may never be;
>
> *Time present*—is the only time for thee.

1800-1900

By the nineteenth century watches were rapidly becoming a commercial product. They were losing much of their former elegance and taking on an air of practical utility. More and more they were recognized as a necessity. With this turn in the fashion, watches grew very plain, the case no longer being studded with gems; instead of the former elaborate decoration, patterns in interlacing lines were now engraved on the case. The nineteenth century is remarkable in many ways for the progress made in watchmaking. It was during this century in America, in 1838, that the first machine-made watch was produced. This was known as the "Pitkin watch," for it had been made by two brothers by that name living in Hartford, Connecticut. The watch was crude in manufacture and too costly to compete with the Swiss watches then on the market.

About 1850, a system of making timepieces by machinery was begun in England. In 1853 an American watch company began producing watches in quantity. This establishment was the forerunner of thirty more American watch factories. Today one company alone, in New England, occupies a building equivalent in area to a four-story structure half a mile in length. It employs from three to four thousand workers, and turns out approximately sixteen thousand watches per week. Though the important first inventions which led to the perfection of the watch were not of American origin, America has made her contribution to the watchmaking industry in improvements upon earlier inventions and in producing a watch so efficient and reasonable in price that people the world over demand and use it.

Figure 473. Gentleman with Two Watch Fobs, about 1785

Toward the close of the nineteenth century, women were wearing the watch suspended upon a long chain worn about the neck. The watch was then tucked into a small watch pocket near the waistline. In 1890, the open-face watch was very popular for both men and women's wear. In the twentieth century, this type of watch vied with that of the closed case for men's wear, while women everywhere adopted the open-face watch. Figure 474.

Watches were not now regarded as a "possession" or an "ornament," but as a necessity. People needed them. The business of the world demanded them. It was now the ambition of American manufacturers to produce a watch so low in cost that every man could have a watch in his pocket. Then emerged, "The watch that made the dollar famous." The early dollar watches were thick, clumsy, and noisy, but were, nevertheless, reliable timekeepers. By-and-by time and experiment improved the watch so materially that the public responded generously to the idea of a dollar watch. Before long millions were in use. Though not a fashionable watch, as fashions go, the inexpensiveness and accuracy of these timekeepers brought the watch idea home to workers everywhere. Today every man has a watch in his pocket.

During the same history-making century the world was startled by the announcement of the discovery of radium (1896). For years experiments with paint made from phosphorous which would give off a glow in darkness had been progressing. Phosphorus paint, however, had its limitations. With radium the problem was solved. A luminous coat was now developed and applied to the numerals and hands of the watch. A miracle was wrought! With its luminous glow the little watch in the inky blackness of night revealed the hour.

Twentieth Century

From 1900 to 1908 Fashion decreed that women's watches be displayed upon the blouse. They were consequently secured by an ornamental brooch just below the left shoulder. This fashion naturally

Figure 474. Open-Face Watch with Reverse View, 1880-1900

brought out many beautiful specimens of jeweled and enameled watches. The handsome Swiss enameled watches of the early twentieth century were works of art. They were tiny, usually open faced, and in various tones of blue, green, yellow, and lavender enamels. Enamel brooches and chains of the same color were the order of the day. Thus the watch could be pinned upon the blouse or suspended about the neck as milady chose.

It was just previous to the first World War that the latest fashion in watches was introduced. The wrist watch is said to have originated with the French, away back when watches were looked upon as mechanical toys and their makers as *toymen*. Be that as it may, since the early days of the century the convenience of the wrist watch has been demonstrated so completely that it has continued to hold first place in popularity. These very practical watches have been worn by both men and women and are of various shapes—round, square, oblong, and oval. Those adopted by men are sometimes encased in leather, with a leather strap adjusting them to the wrist. Others are of silver or gold, often beautiful, held by a wide silver or gold bracelet, usually a chain mesh. Men of more conservative tastes, however, continue to favor the thin gold watch, with either the closed or open face, which is so easily carried in the pocket.

Women's wrist watches are diminutive in size, more delicate in design, and offer rather a generous choice in form. Some are round, others are square, and still others are narrow oblongs or elongated ovals. These vary all the way from the simple timepiece of gold or silver adjusted by a black ribbon about the wrist to the most exquisite specimens of the watchmaker's art. Many of the handsome modern watches are of unusual design, wrought in platinum, and set with jewels. These are invariably adjusted about the wrist by a jeweled bracelet. Figure 475.

In reaching its present jewel-like perfection, the watch idea has traveled forward something over four hundred years. The "Nuremburg eggs" and the heavy dials suspended from the girdle, hopelessly inaccurate, were only mute auguries of a later day when the perfection of the timepiece should be accomplished. The watch of modern times, so indispensable, so vital, so timed to the pace of the twentieth century, is the watch idea perfected. Not only does the delicate mechanism of the modern watch mark the hour for the twentieth century, it also marks progress—progress from those primitive periods when the journey of time was indicated only by the passing of the sun across the heavens.

Figure 475. 20th Century Watch

Platinum-and-diamond wrist-watch.

REFERENCES

Boehn, Max von, *Modes and Manners; Ornaments*, pp. 230, 240.
Brearley, Harry, *Time Telling Through the Ages*.
Encyclopedia Britannica, Vol. 23.
Evans, Mary, *Costume Throughout the Ages*, pp. 74, 99, 143, 164.
Kelly and Schwabe, *Historic Costume*.
Kennard, Beulah, *Jewelry and Silverware*, Chapter 27.
Moore, Mrs. N. Hudson, *The Old Clock Book*.
Story, Margaret, *Individuality and Clothes*, p. 342.

Part V

ACCESSORIES CARRIED IN THE HAND

CHAPTER 29

The Walking Stick

By his cockle hat and *staff*,
And his sandal shoon.
Hamlet, Act IV, sc. 5

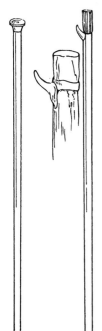

Figure 476.
Walking Sticks
Found at
Thebes

THE walking stick or modern "cane" dates from a very ancient period of history. One eminent Spanish physician claims that man inherited the cane from the apes. Be that as it may, it is no difficult task for the modern mind to picture primitive man reinforcing his power for either assault or defense with the "big stick." The big stick lay so close at hand that it was a ready weapon. This same stick later, by easy transitions, gradually came to be a symbol of strength, then of power, and eventually of authority. The scepter of kingly power and the staff of ecclesiastical authority, as well as the modern cane, are present-day descendants of this same "big stick." With this regal, authoritative development on the one side, there continued through the centuries the more homely use of the stick as a staff to aid in walking. The pilgrim's *bourdon*, that sturdy staff so generally carried by doughty travelers on pilgrimage, has indeed changed much. It has lost its ancient crudities and, as has been truly said, "since admitted to the world of fashion, has grown a bit more frivolous!"

The ancient Egyptians, Assyrians, and Persians each represented their rulers and powerful gods carrying the symbolic staff. Many discoveries in Egypt would indicate that sticks from three to six feet long were frequently carried by Egyptians of exalted rank. These were often surmounted by an ornamental knob resembling the lotus. Others, and these are very characteristic of Egyptian sticks, show a peg projecting from one side near the top from which a bag or bottle could be suspended. Figure 476. Some sticks found at Thebes are made of cherry wood painted and gilded. Acacia, which is a very hard wood, is believed to

388

have been generally used. Upon entering a house it was customary to leave the stick with a servant who generally cared for all the sticks of the guests. The name of the owner was frequently inscribed upon each man's stick. On one found at Thebes the markings, deciphered,

read, "O my stick! The support of my legs." Among the finds made in the tomb of King Tutankhamen was an ebony box which contained a number of sticks, some of which were remarkable in workmanship. The handles of two terminated in a curve, and on each was fashioned in relief the figure of a captive. One, an African, was cut in ebony; the second,

Figure 477. Egyptians Walking with Sticks

From a wall painting.

Figure 478. Pedagogue with Staff
From a Greek vase.

an Asiatic, in ivory. Another with a curved handle was decorated with gilt and colored barks. Several were gold, or wood embossed with gold.

Among the Greeks the staff was likewise a symbol of distinction. Several of the Greek gods are represented with staff in hand symbolizing their superhuman power. Homer sings of the scepter staff of Achilles: "I will swear," says the hero, "by this *staff,* which will never again bear shoots, since the axe has stripped it of leaves and bark." This early association with gods and heroes probably prevailed over a long period, before the staff gradually descended to the lesser folk. Figures frequently appear upon Greek vases showing the long walking stick fitted to the hand. Upon one a seated pedagogue is pictured with his staff in hand. Figure 478.

Middle Ages

During the Middle Ages kingly power came to be symbolized by the scepter carried in the right hand, while a second staff or scepter known as the "Hand of Justice" was carried in the left. This scepter was surmounted by a hand in the act of blessing. In France, this custom of investing authority with two scepters dates from about 987 A.D. In England, during the latter part of the twelfth century, two scepters were bestowed upon Richard Coeur de Lion. Not to be outdone, the Church, always a keen rival of civil power, bestowed the staff as a symbol of authority upon its highest officers. Early in this period, the pastoral staff was a symbol of the bishop's prestige,

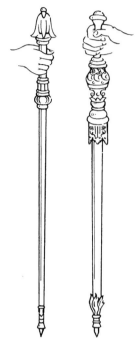

Figure 479. Official
Staffs

Decorated with metal-work and gilt. Spiked ferules gave much secur-ity in walking.

From a brass in Canter-bury Cathedral, 1578, and from a portrait of Sir G. Hart, 1587.

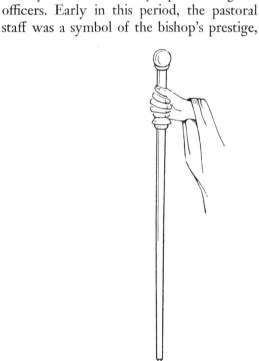

Figure 480.
Pilgrim's
Staff

From 14th-century ms.

and by the sixth century it directly represented his supremacy as shep-herd of his people. Figure 479. The oldest examples of pastoral staffs were long, with crooked handles. The crook signified the bishop draw-ing the believers to him, while with the point he urged on the indifferent. The judges and officers of this period also carried the staff as a symbol of office. As late as the seventeenth century, all who exercised authority —kings, priests, judges, and military commanders—were represented with some type of staff indicative of the power each possessed.

Travelers or pilgrims, shepherds, and tillers of the soil usually carried the long stick or staff as a part of their daily equipment. The pilgrim's *bourdon* of this period was a heavy stick five feet in length tipped with an iron spike which was intended to assist in walking and climbing. Figure 480. Ten inches from the top was a projection upon which the hand rested, or, when carried over the shoulder, upon which the pilgrim's belongings tied up in a bag were hung. The head was pierced and through this the palm branch, a proof of authentic pilgrimage, was fixed. The upper part of the staff unscrewed, and, within the hollow, relics were often concealed. Many are the tales told about this hollow staff and the part it played in various historic episodes. One of these relates the story of two monks who, traveling in the Orient, came to be greatly interested in the silkworms of China. Knowing that silk had always been imported into Rome from the East, they hit upon the idea of carrying back to their emperor a gift of these curiosities. Accordingly, they packed their long walking sticks with the eggs of the silkworm and carried them to Rome. It is, therefore, to the ingenuity of two monks and the hollow walking stick that the European silk industry owes its inception. Other instances similar to this are recorded: it was a hollow staff that bore from Greece the first head of saffron when the penalty for taking the living plant out of the country was death. It was a similar staff which carried into Holland the first tulip bulb, the cultivation of which in later years was a

Figure 481. A Carlovingian Woman, with Staff, 1000 A.D.
From an old print.

source of increased national income. The asparagus traces its introduction in England to a Templar's hollow cane, and the seeds of the melon, apricot, tomato, onion, cauliflower, and quince, all indigenous to oriental countries, were transported in the hollow of the pilgrim's staff.

It was during the eleventh century in that part of the world whence the modern French woman eventually emerged, that the walking stick was first carried as a caprice in feminine fashion. The Carlovingian women (1000) carried walking sticks cut from apple wood, and usually ornamented at the top with a carved bird or other device. A few surviving prints picture the belles of the day in flowing robes, carrying the fashionable stick. Figure 481. It was not, however, until the close of the fifteenth century that the walking stick was generally adopted as an accessory of dress. Late in this century, about 1495, Agnes Sorrel the famous "Lady of Beauty" of the French court and the acknowledged queen of fashion, among other innovations, introduced the walking stick. This was made of valuable wood ornamented with a handsome top. For reasons unrecorded, however, women soon gave up the fashion, and not until the late eighteenth century was it revived.

1500-1600

The word "cane" had not been applied to the fashionable walking stick up to the sixteenth century. During this period, however, the thick, jointed stems of tropical grasses known as bamboo and cane, and the reed-like stem of several species of palm and rattan were introduced for the stick. These were called "canes." From that day forth the walking stick of the past merged into the cane of the future. Today the terms are used interchangeably, though the saying, "One strolls with a walking stick, and swaggers with a *cane*," tends to give greater dignity to the former. Among interesting references of ancient date to the cane are those contained in an old manuscript of the time of Henry VIII. One item reads, "A *cane* garnished with silver and gilte with astronomie upon it." This stick no doubt belonged to Henry himself. Another described a stick as, "garnished with golde, having a perfume in the toppe under that a diall, with a pair of tweezers, and a paire of compasses of golde, and a foot rule of golde, a knife, a file, the hilt of golde, and a whetstone tipped with golde." Human ingenuity at this time had introduced many novel ideas for filling the space in a hollow walking stick. During the period when it was no uncommon occurrence to dispose of men in authority by poison, those subject to danger carried harmless-looking walking sticks for protection. These were by no means harmless, however, for cunningly concealed within them were deadly rapiers. These canes were known as "sword sticks," and they are still found in countries where the government is unstable.

1600-1700

It was in France during the reign of the Louis's that the cane came to be an indispensable accessory in the dress of gentlemen of fashion. These were very valuable and handsome, made of ivory, whalebone, ebony, and various other woods ornamented with handles and knobs of amber, jasper, and gold set with rubies, turquoises, amethysts, and diamonds. Henry IV, who preceded Louis XIII, is said to have been the first person to possess a walking stick which might be classed as a luxury. Louis XIII carried a long, ebony staff with ivory top frequently decorated with streamers of ribbon. Louis XIV was so ardent an advocate of the walking stick that he never appeared in public without it. Moreover, the fashion he set was quickly adopted by all French officials of the day. This same king is said, when in a temper, to have broken a handsome rosewood stick over the back of a lackey— thus the cane occasionally suffers a reversion to type, becoming the "big stick" again.

It was about the middle of this century that canes grew more slender and of a con-

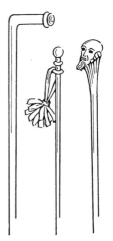

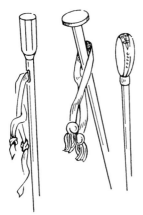

Figure 483. Fashionable Canes of 1600

Figure 482. Sticks, 1500-1730

Hooked stick used by older men of the 14th and 15th centuries; French walking stick, 1600; grotesque heads appeared in England about 1730.

venient length to use in walking. They were made the length now common, from about two feet ten inches to three feet. At this time a silken cord, or ribbon and tassel, decorated the handle. This was slipped over the wrist. Though it served as an aid in carrying the cane, it was largely ornamental. Figure 482.

In England during the reign of Charles I (1600-49) gold- and ivory-headed canes were fashionable. Charles himself possessed many handsome walking sticks. The extensive use of the oaken stick began when the Stuarts were driven out in 1688. During the early years of the following century, oak sticks were ornamented with grotesque heads. The *Universal Spectator*, under date of 1734, comments on the fashion thus: "The large oaken sticks, with great heads and ugly faces carved thereon are carried at the court end of town by polite young gentlemen instead of swords." Ever and anon heads for handles have appeared. Old cynics of Greek days used them. In Rome they were the badge of tribunes. Jesters of the Middle Ages, and even later, carried them as baubles distinctive of their class. As late as 1852, when Kossuth made his memorable visit to America, members of his train carried sticks with carved ivory heads which attracted considerable attention. The sturdy, oaken stick remained popular for years. A writer in the *London Evening Post*, 1738, expressed her surprise and disgust over the taste of certain

men at the theater who "appear in scanty frocks, little shabby hats put on one side, and *clubs* in their hand." It is this same oaken stick which carried over into the dress of our Puritan forebears and is always regarded as an expressive detail in early American costume. Figure 484.

1700-1800

During this century canes again lengthened to approximately four feet and were decorated with bows and streamers of ribbon. The importance of the cane in the life of the period, particularly in England, is set down in the *Tatler* under date of 1702. Here one is amazed to read that it was necessary to procure a license for the privilege of carrying a cane. Other fashionable accessories such as snuffboxes, perfumed handkerchiefs, and similar trifles also required a permit. An interesting example of such a license issued for the carrying of a cane reads:

COURTESY, ART INSTITUTE OF CHICAGO

Figure 484. The Puritan......*Saint-Gaudens*

The heavy oaken stick, coming into fashion in England about 1686, carried over into the dress of the Puritans of America. Note hat of the same period, shoes, and heavy, knitted hose.

> You are hereby required to permit the bearer of this *cane* to pass and repass through the streets and suburbs of London, or any place within ten miles of it without lett or molestation; provided that he does not walk with it under his arm, brandish it in the air, or hang it on a button; in which case it shall be forfeited; and I hereby declare it forfeited to anyone who shall think it safe to take it from him.

Signed.................................

One petition, very interesting today, seeking the privilege of carrying a cane may serve as an illuminating example of the times and is therefore given in full:

The humble petition of Simon Trippet,
Sheweth

That the petitioner having been bred up to a cane from his youth, it is now become necessary to him as any other of his limbs.

That a great part of his behaviour is depending upon it, he should be reduced to the utmost necessities if he should lose the use of it.

That the knocking of it upon his shoe, leaning one leg upon it, or whistling with it on his mouth, are such great reliefs to him in conversation, that he does not know how to be good company without it.

That he is at present engaged in an amour, and must dispair of success if it be taken from him.

Your petitioner, therefore, hopes that (the premises tenderly considered) your worship will not deprive him of so useful and necessary a support.

And your petitioner shall ever, etc.

The above petition, though carefully prepared, did not receive the tender consideration implored, for the Censor upon investigation found the petitioner to be a prig. He was consequently ordered to produce his cane in court. Thereupon it was found to be a very costly cane, curiously clouded, with a transparent amber head and a ribbon to hang upon the wrist. The stern Censor looked with disapproval upon such luxury and ordered the clerk of the court to "lay it up" and "deliver out to him a plain jointed head of walnut," and then in order to wean this from him by degrees permitted him to use it "three days in the week, and to abate proportionally till he found himself able to go alone."

By the middle of the century canes were well established as an indication of rank. They were slender in form, made of agate, marble, ebony, horn, and bone, richly ornamented with gems. Usually they were bent at the top and tipped at the lower end with ivory. When not in use they were carefully protected in shagreen cases. Today many of these may be seen in the collection of the Tower of London, where they are looked upon as curious relics. These canes of the eighteenth century, curious looking to modern eyes, far surpassed in richness of finish anything of the kind produced in later periods. It was during this interesting age that members of the leading professions, especially clergymen, physicians, and surgeons, adopted the cane. Beadles stationed themselves at church doors to relieve the parishioners of their sticks. With physicians and surgeons the stick came to be a kind of insignia of office; they continued to carry it for more than a hundred years.

During the last quarter of the century, after Marie Antoinette had established her dairy at the Petite Trianon and adopted the shepherdess crook as a novelty, the long staff again entered upon the fashion scene. The grand ladies of this regime carried their tall sticks mounted in gold or silver and knotted with bows of ribbon. The handsome mounts of some of these opened to disclose little receptacles for powder or perfume. Somewhat later, shorter sticks displaced the shepherdess staff. The bouffant skirts with pretty ankles displayed, the towering headdress, quantities of rouge, powder, and perfume, and the walking stick were the very essence of style in that picturesque day. Figure 485. Soon, however, milady tired of the stick and laid it aside for the fan. Gentlemen, not so capricious, continued in their loyal support of the cane. The eighteenth century is distinctly the period of the fan for women and the walking stick for men.

Figure 485. A Fashion Figure of 1780

While there were various woods used in the making of canes, Bengal wood was the choice. The tops of these were fitted with many ingenious devices. Some contained perfume bottles and vinaigrettes, others were fitted with eyeglasses which could be opened and closed, and still others with miniature telescopes. Many of these ornamental heads were made of porcelain, enameled metals, and other rich materials. Charles III of Spain sponsored a porcelain factory at Naples which furnished eighteen different kind of walking-stick handles, costing from one to sixty ducats each.* By the nineteenth century the fashion of the heavier bamboo staff had succumbed to the taste of the dandies, who carried a very fine, lightweight bamboo cane, topped with a tiny gold knob or cube.

In Germany during this century, the fashion for very elaborate walking sticks flourished. Frederick the Great of Prussia (1712-86), though known for his conservative spending of money for luxuries, made a hobby of collecting handsome sticks. Figures 486, 487. In 1719, the favorite sticks carried by Frederick William I were ornamented with

---

* *Ducat*, coin ranging in value from about $.83 to $2.25.

jasper handles set with rubies and rose-cut stones. In 1731 his hobby was
for walking sticks set with diamonds. In Bavaria, the Elector Maxmillian
Joseph III (1745-77), a man of wealth and fashion, owned a stick made
of amethyst and set with thirty diamonds. Toward the middle of the
century, when canes were again useful as well as ornamental, Austria

SCHLOSS MONBIJOU   HOHENZOLLERN MUSEUM, BERLIN

Figure 486. Canes of Frederick the Great

and Hungary added to the fashionable telescope and pedometer canes a
cane which carried a flute. An even more curious example of a useful
walking stick was one made up of three adjustable sections. In the lowest
was a quill pen, with ink and paper; in the second a measuring rod; and
in the third a telescope. In France, toward the end of the eighteenth
century, gentlemen spent money recklessly for walking sticks. It is said
that as many as 40,000 francs or about 7,600 dollars was expended for
sticks by one leader of fashion. Rousseau, who was considered a poor
man, is said to have purchased forty sticks; and Voltaire, who was not a
follower of fashion, owned eighty. Indeed, the demand for sticks was
so great in France that the originality of their makers was taxed to the
utmost.

This virtually universal vogue for the walking stick gradually developed certain manners which were no more to be ignored by the fashionable than the etiquette of the fan, glove, and handkerchief. For instance,
the cane was never carried when calling upon persons of consequences;
it was a flagrant violation of cane convention to carry it under the arm;
to lean upon the cane when standing was unpardonable, and shocking
beyond measure was the sight of one trailing his cane in walking. Further, taboo was the use of the cane for writing idly in the dust!

1800-1900

In the nineteenth century both men and women of the Empire Period carried the stick. Figure 489. The twisted walking stick was the favorite with fashionable "bloods" of this day, but Napoleon is said to have carried a tortoise-shell stick with a musical box attached. In Germany, the students used their walking sticks as a record of friendship. Friends wrote their names upon them until they were completely encircled from top

SCHLOSS MONBIJOU   HOHENZOLLERN MUSEUM, BERLIN

Figure 487. Canes of Frederick the Great

to bottom with inscriptions. When Prussia organized her standing army in the early nineteenth century, commissioned and noncommissioned officers, who carried canes, were often guilty of beating their men with them. This was the period when both military and civil authority ruled by the rod, the same time that the students at a famous bonfire burned a Prussian military corset, a Hessian soldier's pigtail, and an Austrian corporal's cane, all three symbolizing the abuses they hoped to see abolished. Throughout the entire nineteenth century, the walking stick was an indispensable article with both French and English gentlemen. In America men were addicted to the same fashion. Men of affairs and of the professions, particularly those in the medical field, carried handsome, gold-headed canes. In 1894, a French newspaper desirous of exploiting the usefulness of the walking stick reproduced twenty-two different designs showing it in its possible adaptations to various conveniences—as a tripod for a camera, a toilet table, a footstool, a shotgun, and a lantern. Since that time medicine chests and ear trumpets have been added to the list. With the discovery of electricity some walking sticks were adapted to this added novelty and emitted an electric shock!

Twentieth Century

As men acquired the habit of carrying a newspaper, together with an occasional package, the popularity of the walking stick gradually began to wane. Modern life finds the cane a rather formal accessory of men's dress, worn when on parade or attending functions of special importance. Canes with elaborate tops are seldom seen in this century. In fact, modern canes scarcely resemble in any way the canes of a hundred years ago. The various materials formerly used—whalebone, ivory, shell, bone, horn, and hide—have given place to rare woods. Whalebone was monopolized by the umbrella industry. Ivory, shell, and bone have proved too valuable in making other things. Horn, which was once heated and drawn out into rods, has become too costly. Rhinoceros hide, tough and elastic and so affected by chemical treatment that it becomes translucent, has also been given up on account of cost. Some twenty-five years ago when Charles Goodyear introduced vulcanized rubber, it was thought that this new material would take the place of all others in the manufacture of walking sticks. Rubber under special treatment takes on the appearance and hardness of ebony, may be highly polished, is of light weight, and is impervious to extremes of heat and cold. It seemed an ideal material for canes.

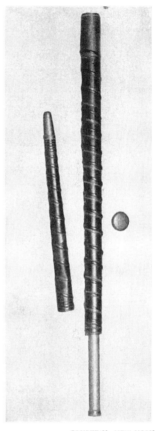

COURTESY, NEW YORK
HISTORICAL SOCIETY

Figure 488. Telescope Cane

For several years rubber walking sticks were the height of fashion in London, Paris, and Berlin. By-and-by, however, they were found to lack the quality most essential in a cane, elasticity. Thus, one by one the materials so popular in former centuries passed, and the modern choice fell to the rare woods of the tropical forests, rosewood, dogwood, and Malacca. Today, it is the quality of the wood that gives distinction to the walking stick.

The coveted Malacca canes are obtained from a peculiar species of the rattan plant. This is a natural stem with possible slight irregularities in

PLATE XLIII. James McNeil Whistler
.... *William Merritt Chase*

This famous portrait interprets the striking personality of the artist as given by his friend, William Merritt Chase: "He wore yellow gloves and carried a long slender cane two thirds his own height. This he invariably held at a graceful angle."

marking. These unusual spottings are caused by the action of the sun during the process of drying. In that the great stems of the Malacca plant are dried in sheaves, naturally those nearest the outer edge are most readily affected by the sun. These are the most highly prized stems used in making Malaccas.

Among the unique collections of canes is that once owned by King Edward VII as Prince of Wales. In this large collection is a stick said to have been used by Queen Victoria, cut from the limb of an oak tree in which Charles II sought refuge from his pursuers in 1651. Other canes in this collection are fine examples of artistry from India, showing specimens of rare woods and fine ivory carvings. Many valuable cane collections exist in other parts of the world. These not only testify to the rare and beautiful woods used at different periods, but, to the strange, ingenious devices as well, which, in the effort to make the cane useful as well as ornamental, came into vogue through the centuries.

Up through the lane of history the walking stick has always been a symbol of dignity and power. Originally a man became a peer or a king by sheer force of the "big stick." Today, as late as the twentieth century, there is still a haunting suggestion of the old prestige. Somehow, canes seem to have a natural affinity for the distinguished, or vice versa, the distinguished for canes.

Figure 489. A Beau, 1830

REFERENCES

Boehn, Max von, *Modes and Manners; Ornaments*, Chapter IV.
Fales, Jane, *Dressmaking*.
Guhl and Kohner, *Life of the Greeks and Romans*.
Kelly and Schwabe, *Historic Costume*.
Lester, Katherine Morris, *Historic Costume*, pp. 25, 159.
Sage, Elizabeth, *A Study of Costume*, pp. 57, 190.
Wilkinson, Sir John Gardiner, *A Popular Account of the Ancient Egyptians*, Vol. II.

CHAPTER 30

The Umbrella and Parasol

The tucked-up semptress walks with hasty strides,
While streams ran down her oil'd *umbrella's* side.
JONATHAN SWIFT's description of a *City Shower*

THE umbrella is of great antiquity. It is at least two thousand years older than its modern descendant, the parasol. Yet the original purpose of the umbrella was distinctly that of a sunshade. It was "an instrument for casting a shadow," and was in ancient times regarded as the privilege only of monarchs, priests, and others of high rank. It was not used as a protection against the rain until the late sixteenth century, when it was introduced into the western world. In France, the umbrella then became the *parapluie* (against the rain). Although the modern world frequently uses the word "umbrella" with the old-time meaning of sunshade, at the same time "umbrella" is the only word in the English language which refers to the covering carried to ward off rain.

Figure 490. Egyptian Chariot with Umbrella

From a wall painting at Thebes.

In ancient Egypt and Nineveh, remains in both sculpture and painting testify to the use of the umbrella as a sunshade. It is invariably carried by the attendants of some great dignitary. Ancient Egyptian art depicts a pharaoh enthroned beneath an umbrella, and a wall painting at Thebes shows the umbrella attached to the chariot of a king. Figure 490. A relief from the palace at Kuyunjik, now in the British Museum, shows the Assyrian king Ashurbanipal standing beneath the official umbrella receiving prisoners from the Babylonian king. Figure 491. The Persians also, according to Xenophon, used umbrellas to protect themselves from the heat of the sun. Figure 492.

From the Far East—China, Japan, and India—come many interesting accounts of the pomp and splendor associated with the ancient umbrella. Many of these customs, unspoiled by the centuries, have survived to modern times. An ancient Chinese legend attributes the invention of the umbrella to a Chinese woman who lived some three thousand years ago. It was named the *san kai,* and was used as a protection against the hot, oriental sun. Its use was permitted only to those of royal blood and other

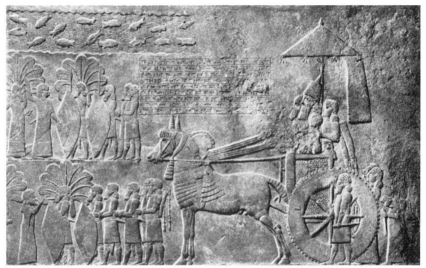

Figure 491. Relief from the Palace of Ashurbanipal, King of Assyria, 668-626 B.C.

Shows the official umbrella attached to the King's chariot. He is here receiving prisoners and spoils after the defeat of his brother, the King of Babylon.

high authority. A man's rank was indicated not only by the umbrella itself, but by the number carried in his train. One of the powerful emperors of China is said to have had twenty-four great state umbrellas carried before him. During one important celebration in China, three hundred umbrellas are said to have been carried in procession. Many of these were very handsome, made of cloth of gold and enriched with gems. In 1898, when Prince Henry of Prussia visited the Emperor of China, he was received under a red umbrella, a sign of executive authority.

In Japan, the umbrella has been popular in all outdoor ceremonies. In the old days of the Empire the mikado never appeared in public without his umbrella bearer. Today both Chinese and Japanese men and women carry sunshades. The frames of bamboo are covered with a tough, oiled paper which is frequently decorated with pictures and designs in bright colors.

In India also, as in other Asiatic countries, the umbrella has an ancient record. The Indian poet Kalidasa, who wrote in the sixteenth century, mentions the sunshade in his play *Sakuntala*. In India, as was general in the East, the sunshade was an emblem of rank. An umbrella with seven

coverings was the badge of a monarch. In 1877, when Edward VII, then Prince of Wales, made a tour of India, he was required, in order to command the respect of the natives, to ride upon an elephant beneath a sunshade with frame of gold, covered with an embroidered cloth set with precious stones. While being entertained in India the Prince was the recipient of many handsome umbrellas, gifts from Indian princes. One outstanding umbrella of this collection was made of blue silk stitched in gold thread and heavily strung with pearls.

In Burma, white umbrellas were reserved for the use of the king and the sacred white elephant. Others, in tints graduated to correspond to the various degrees of rank, were carried by those

Figure 492. Darius with His Attendants, the Fan and Umbrella Bearers

of lesser authority. The king of Burma, among other titles, claimed for himself that of, "Lord of the Great Parasol."

The Greeks have been credited with introducing the sunshade into Europe. Grecian women carried shades similar in shape to the flat type of Japanese umbrella. The paintings on Greek vases suggest the umbrella was an article in common use. The women sit in the shade or walk accompanied by a slave or attendant as umbrella bearer. Records show that the handles of some Greek sunshades were set at the edge instead of the center. With this arrangement the full benefit of the shade fell to the one over whom it was carried. Figure 493. In the classic period umbrellas were used to protect the sacred offerings as they were carried in processions to the temple.

The sunshades of Roman women were similar to those used by the Greeks. Figure 494. Pliny describes them as having frames of bamboo covered with palm leaves. Sunshades appear later with frame and handle made of ivory set with jewels, and a covering of silk embroidered in gold. Purple was a favorite color used in the Roman umbrella. Observing the advantages of the umbrella to womankind, men too soon acquired the habit of carrying them. Though it is said that the Emperor Claudius condemned them as effeminate some continued to indulge in their use. One Roman youth is said to have suffered sunstroke because he neglected to carry an umbrella. From the Latin classics one is led to believe that the umbrella's use as a protection from the rain originated with the Romans.

Martial, in his fourteenth book, says: "Do not forget when you go out in fair weather, to take an umbrella in case of bad weather."

1500-1600

The umbrella became almost extinct during the Middle Ages. It served neither an ornamental nor practical purpose for the people of these times. Though a curious drawing in an early manuscript* shows an Anglo-Saxon umbrella, and Joseph Strutt, a commentator of the nineteenth century, states that

Figure 493. A Sunshade Pictured on a Greek Vase

the umbrella was known as far back as the reign of Stephen, it is not until the sixteenth century that it begins to take an important place in modern life. Italy seems to have been the first to recognize its usefulness, and then not till the latter half of the century. The clergy adopted it as a symbol of dignity and honor rather than for more practical purposes. The pope claimed not only the right to use the umbrella as a mark of authority but also the privilege to bestow it upon others as a symbol of distinction and power. Whenever the pope appeared in public an umbrella was carried over him. The papal court is the only one to this day that retains an umbrella as a symbol of power and authority. In 1578 the Italian umbrella was very large, easily covering three or four persons; when closed and folded it occupied comparatively little space, but these earliest umbrellas were so awkward to carry that they proved as much a burden to the arm as a protection from the sun. During the latter days of the century, travelers from France and England observed Italian women carrying the umbrella, and the fact that their diaries make mention of the "strange structures" shows that

---

* Harleian Ms., 603.

it was an unusual sight. Henry Estienne, who wrote his *Dialogues* in 1578, refers to the sunshades of both Spain and Italy:

Have you ever seen a device which certain persons of rank in Spain and Italy carry, or have carried less to protect themselves against flies than against

Figure 494. Greek Lady with an Umbrella
After Hope.

the sun? It is supported upon a stick, and is so constructed that it takes up little room when it is folded; but when it is needed it can be opened forthwith and spread out in a round that can well cover three or four persons.

1600-1700

Another of the earliest references to the umbrella made by an English traveler is that by Thomas Coryate, whose *Crudities*, published in 1611, tells of the many unusual sights met with in his travels. His minute description of this novel accessory is indeed amusing to modern ears:

And many of them do carry other fine things of a far greater price, that will cost at the least a ducket, which they commonly call in the Italian tongue *umbrellas*, that is, things which minister shadow unto them for a shelter against the scorching heate of the sunne. These are made of leather, something answerable to the form of a little canopy, and hooked on the inside with divers little wooden hoopes that extend the umbrella in a pretty large compass. They are used especially by horsemen who carry them in their hands when they ride, fastening the end of the handle upon their thighs, and they impart so large a shadow upon them that it keepeth the heat of the sunne from the upper part of their bodies.

It was not until 1680 that the umbrella appeared in France, and later, about the beginning of the eighteenth century, in England. The first umbrellas used in France were so clumsy and ill made that history says they did not "take." Montaigne is credited with saying:

There is no season more inimical than the burning heat of the hot sun, for the *umbrellas* that have been used in Italy from the time of the ancient Romans fatigue the arm more than they relieve the head.

Though the ancient Romans have been credited with first using the umbrella for protection against the rain, the real origin of this use is lost in obscurity. Sometime during the sixteenth century a Frenchman, Marius of Paris, developed an umbrella for rain with a jointed stock that could be folded and, when not needed, carried in the pocket. This contrivance, however, never came into general use.

1700-1800

By the eighteenth century the use of the umbrella was known generally in Italy, France, England, Germany, and Holland. In these days it is said that venders sold them on the streets of Paris for from fifteen to twenty-two francs each. Carrying an umbrella at this time, however, was regarded with some question. Ladies seldom walked. They rode in carriages. Carrying an umbrella, therefore was a silent confession of the lack of a carriage. Caraccioli, writing in this century (1750), tells of the fashion in Italy which was doubtless prevalent elsewhere:

It has long been the custom not to go out save with one's *umbrella*. . . . But those who wish not to be confounded with the vulgar, prefer the risk of getting wet or being regarded as people who walk on foot, for the *umbrella* is the sign of having no carriage.

Someone has said that northern Europe owes the umbrella to Robinson Crusoe, whose famous story was told by Defoe in 1719. Robinson Crusoe's umbrella was covered with skins, as a protection from both rain and sun. "I covered it with skins," wrote Crusoe, "the hair upward so that it cast off the rain like a penthouse, and kept off the sun so effectively that I could walk out in the hottest weather, with greater advantage than I could before in the coolest." Whether northern Europe owes the umbrella to Crusoe or not, the fact remains that both French and English were following Thomas Coryate's example and traveling considerably at this time. Many of the ideas gained abroad were carried home. In 1757, an Englishman traveling in France wrote home:

The people here use *umbrellas* in hot weather to defend them from the sun, and something of the same kind to save them from the snow and rain. I wonder a practice so useful is not introduced into England.

Later the custom was adopted by English women, who continued to use this practical article for some time before it was accepted by men.

There are many popular accounts of the first courageous citizens of Great Britain who ventured forth with the umbrella. The honor of being the first Englishman to carry an umbrella falls to Jonas Hanway, a famous traveler and philanthropist. In 1780 he stepped upon London streets with a large umbrella which he had purchased in China. The appearance of a gentleman carrying an object so unusual created a great deal of merriment. Cab drivers tried to hoot him off the street, but he persisted in what he believed to be a good custom, and lived to see it generally adopted. There is today a street in London called after Hanway. As early as 1772, John McDonald, a footman, appeared in the streets of London carrying a fine silk umbrella which he had purchased in Spain. He was immediately jeered, and cabmen called in derision, "Frenchman, why don't you get a cab?" This cry explained in a measure the early opposition to the umbrella, for it appeared as the inevitable enemy of the cabmen.

It is an interesting fact that in England the umbrella seems to have been continually rediscovered. It appeared at intervals, then disappeared as if utterly forgotten, only to be brought forth at a latter day. Today, however, one could as easily imagine an English gentleman in the streets of London without his coat as without his "rainstick."

The first appearance of the umbrella in Scotland is given in Dr. Cleland's *Statistical Account of Glasgow*. Here it is stated that the first umbrella carried by a man to protect himself from the rain was seen in 1781. The Scotchman who dared venture forth was James Jackson, who had just returned from France, bringing his umbrella with him. It was a ponderous affair with rattan ribs covered with heavy waxed cloth.

It is said that the first umbrella that appeared in the American colonies created consternation. This was in 1772, eight years before Jonas Hanway had astonished Londoners with his revolutionary deed. A little shop in Baltimore had in that year purchased an umbrella from a ship just returned from India. When the hesitating proprietor ventured forth with his prize, pedestrians stood transfixed, women were frightened, horses ran away, and naughty children threw stones. Finally the town watch was called out to quiet the disturbance. When Philadelphia, the early fashion center of America, heard of the innovation, no time was lost; unsuccessful efforts were immediately made to introduce it, particularly in summer, as a protection against the sun. Notwithstanding the fact that doctors recommended it to "keep off fever and sore eyes," it was scouted in the public *Gazette* as a ridiculous effeminacy. Shortly, however, fashion sentiment won the day—the umbrella was accepted, New York soon followed the example of Philadelphia.

In 1787, umbrellas, which had hitherto been imported, were being manufactured in England. One manufacturer offered "umbrellas superior to the imported"; another advertisement ran thus:

All kinds of common umbrellas repaired in a particular way that will never stick together.

When umbrellas were first produced in England, an old superstition led the manufacturers to attach acorns to the handles. In England, many years previous, acorns were worn about the neck as a protection against lightning, for, according to tradition the oak tree was sacred to the god of thunder; therefore, any one who wore an acorn was mercifully spared the unpleasant experience of being struck by lightning. The acorns which the manufacturers attached to the handle of the early umbrella reassured hesitating customers of the merit of their purchase. The silken and bone ornaments, sometimes resembling acorns, seen dangling from a cord fastened to the handle of the modern umbrella are an interesting vestige of this old superstition linked with the early rainstick.

Figure 495. A Fashion Figure, about 1785

1800-1900

The general construction of umbrellas has changed little through the centuries, the ancient Chinese pattern having been generally adopted by European nations. The earliest umbrella had twenty-eight curved branches or ribs, covered with a strong material. The chief improvements have been in the mechanism of folding and in the material used for the supporting ribs and covering. During the latter part of the eighteenth century, industry undertook the manufacture of this important accessory with such enthusiasm that it ceased to be looked upon as a novelty, and came to be regarded as a necessity. The earliest ribs were bamboo, rattan, or oak. The wooden frame continued from 1806 to 1826. The coverings of these early examples were oiled and waxed silk and linen. The stickiness of this cloth as well as the inconvenience and weight of the clumsy frame led to much experimenting. In their effort to secure lighter and less bulky umbrellas for rain, manufacturers soon produced the whalebone frame. This was much lighter than the

former wooden frame, which in 1806 had weighed approximately ten pounds. By 1826 the weight was reduced to two pounds. Then, in 1850, followed the triumph of the steel ribs and the alpaca, gloria, silk, and other types of cover, which produced a strong umbrella of little weight. In China, Japan, and the Philippines, umbrellas are now formed with thirty-six ribs covered with waterproof, oiled paper.

With this rapid development in the ribs and covering of the umbrella, studious attention came to be given the handle. The earliest orien-

Figure 496. Hinged Parasol, 1840

tal sunshades had been supported by long, highly polished handles fashioned from rare woods. The later Eastern sunshades show handles of etched gold, carved ivory, or damascene. With the use of the umbrella in Europe came the bent wood handle, which, when not in use, was so easily carried caught over the arm. In 1890 the bent-wood handle gave place to wooden knobs and carved sticks. By-and-by a piece of carved wood was inserted, passing through the handle and forming a cross. Gradually umbrella manufacturers of the fashion centers of Europe began to call in trained artisans for this work. Various beautiful woods, leathers, vegetable ivory, precious metals, and synthetic gems soon found a place in their designs. In England, woodworkers turned out carved handles, many with realistic heads of

Figure 497. Parasol, 1850

dogs. These were regarded as very fashionable. From Siberia came animal bone and walrus tusks which were polished and etched for men's umbrella handles. In Vienna, wooden handles were mounted with brilliant feathers of birds; other wooden handles were covered with reptile skins and leathers; vegetable ivory nuts were polished by the thousand to be used for round-knobbed umbrella handles. From Hungary, northern Italy, Germany, and Japan, came many of the bent-wood handles for men's umbrellas. Since the first World War, discovery of a modified pyralin composition which is inexpensive, indestructible (except by fire), and easily modeled, has led to the manufacture of synthetic handles. The modern imitations of jade, amber, glass, and pearl are fashioned from this composition. This accounts for the market being supplied with an unlimited variety of most attractive umbrella handles.

While the umbrella was changing in form and special attention was given to ribs, covering, and handle, its use as a sunshade came to be more general. Gradually with the lighter frame, materials took on fineness of texture and by-and-by added color. Then, as a definite accessory of dress, emerged the parasol. Figure 497. In the course of half a century, the new sunshade by its appropriation of silk, lace, ribbon, and fringe, had become so dainty and smart as to be scarcely

Figure 498. Fringed Parasol of the Late 19th Century

recognizable beside its ancient and practical forebear, the umbrella. In France, during the close of the Second Republic (1852), parasols were the same size as umbrellas. They were usually light on the outside and lined with a darker color, preferably dark blue. Soon parasols grew somewhat smaller in size, and coverings of moire and batiste were introduced. By the middle of the century taffeta was the fashionable covering, and gold lace as a trimming was elaborately used. Parasols were now of various shapes. Some were flat, others rounded, and still others were given a pagoda shape. We now begin to hear of parasols of shaded silk lined with white satin; white silk parasols with borders of painted flowers, and parasols lined and edged with a deep fringe. In 1865, braid-trimmed parasols were the vogue. Sometimes the pattern braided the edge; sometimes the design fitted each division between the ribs. This was the period of both braid and fringe, and one is not surprised to read that heavily fringed parasols, at first the novelty in France, rapidly spread over the entire fashion world. Figure 498.

In America, as on the continent, the parasol was so popular a favorite that it almost outrivaled the fan. The latest styles from Paris and London were promptly displayed in all the principal shops. A woman

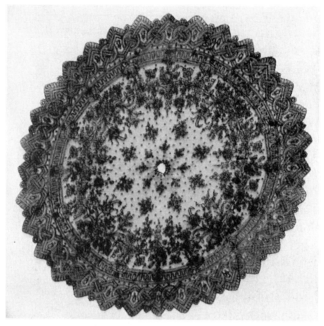

Figure 499. Chantilly Lace Cover for Parasol, French,
Late 19th Century

of fashion was seldom seen, either on the promenade or drive, without her lace or fringed parasol. It was the fashion during the late century for ladies to drive out in small carts without tops or in phaetons with the top "let back." Then it was that the parasol flourished. It was, indeed, a charming picture, these smart "turnouts" with the belles of the period atop carrying their gay-colored parasols. Older ladies with tastes more restrained carried very diminutive sunshades of black silk or lace, twelve to fourteen inches in diameter. These were almost flat and hinged at the top of the handle so that they could be easily turned upon the stem. When not in use they were closed just as were other parasols. These were known as "carriage parasols." They suggest the modern folding umbrella, which comes in various sizes and is designed for traveling, because so easily packed in a trunk, suitcase or handbag. This practical development originated in Paris but has been copied by modern American manufacturers.

Twentieth Century

As the years rolled by, fashions in umbrellas continued to keep pace with the changing modes in dress. In the early years of the twentieth century there came a general swing to Directoire modes. Milady must be tall and slim. High hats and tall feathers added to this effect. Parasols and umbrellas followed the same lines and sticks grew immoderately long. These continued for several years; then Fashion did as Fashion always has done—swung to the opposite extreme. Handles grew short, astonishingly short. Indeed, the stick which in 1910 measured approximately forty-two inches had, by 1930, shrunk to little more than half that length. These short, sturdy sticks averaged about twenty-four inches from tip to tip. Figure 500.

In the modern world the motor car is largely responsible for the many rapid fashion changes. Today milady seldom walks for any considerable distance, and the charming parasols of the past century have become a lingering memory. The umbrella for rain, however, still holds a place among the convenient accessories of dress. Moreover, modern umbrellas have lost entirely their aspect of drabness and gloom, for they are now seldom black. Indeed, bright greens, reds, blues, and violets make gay spots of color in the grayness of a rainy

Figure 500. Modern Umbrellas, 1910, 1936

day. Handles, too, are highly attractive for their varieties of color and shape. But while milady of the twentieth century adds these touches of color to dreary days, men insist on the established order and carry modest rainsticks of durable black cotton or silk.

Though the umbrella goes back to ancient days its general form has changed little. Though the crudities of antiquity have completely vanished and in their place have come all the refinements of the twentieth century, it still functions as the *parapluie* (against the rain) and the *parasol* (against the sun).

REFERENCES

Boehn, Max von, *Modes and Manners: Ornaments*, Chapter V.
Evans, Mary, *Costume Throughout the Ages*, pp. 82, 283.
Hughes, Talbot, *Dress Design*, p. 116.
New International Encyclopedia, Vol. 18.
New York Times, March 23, 1930.
Parsons, Frank Alvah, *The Art in Dress*, pp. 254, 255.
Peterson's Fashion Magazine, July, 1863.
Sage, Elizabeth, *A Study of Costume*, pp. 8, 32, 197.

CHAPTER 31

The Handbag

Or tie my treasure up in silken *bags*,
To please the fool and death.

Pericles, Act III, sc. 2

THE convenience and decorative qualities of the modern handbag or purse were undoubtedly known to women of long ago. Zusser, the Russian archaeologist who in his excavations in Greece uncovered many ancient burial places, found in the tomb of a woman a small linen bag showing signs of having been decorated with stitches of embroidery. Since such an article was known to the women of Greece, other women of that ancient day may have found it equally useful. Authentic record, however, is nearly barren, due to the great frailty of materials used. Unquestionably the simplest form of bag was such as is represented in Figure 501. This bag was without doubt carried by lesser folk, both men and women, for centuries.

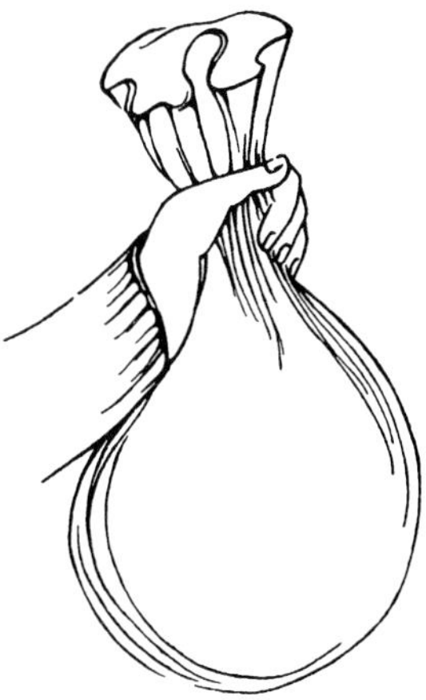

Figure 501. Early Handbag

From Cotton ms., Nero, D 4.

Middle Ages

Beginning with the interesting period of the Middle Ages, we find unmistakable evidence of the ancestor of the modern handbag. In the excavations of Saxon barrows (Saxon period, 460-1066 A.D.) recoveries indicate that Saxon women were interred in full costume. The dress in many instances shows a girdle from which, suspended by chains, are numerous trinkets—scissors, tweezers, knives, combs, keys, and also the little purse hanging from the same belt. During the later years of this eventful age the returning Crusaders came wearing little bags appended to their girdles. These were originally called *amônières sarrasimoises*, meaning "Saracen almsbags," and were supposed to carry coins for the poor. They were soon adopted, coming to be an indispensable accessory in the costume of both men and women. Figures 502, 503.

415

It was the custom for ladies of wealth to distribute either food or money to the needy, and the little amônière, though it often carried other things than coin for the poor, was a very practical as well as attractive accessory to the dress of that day—it is worthy of notice here

Figure 502. Bag, from a Statue at St. Denis, 1200

that the word *lady* is believed by some to have been derived from the early Anglo-Saxon meaning *giver of bread*. Many interesting examples of the amônière, also *aulmônière*, are preserved in old manuscript drawings and in the effigies of distinguished persons. One of the most pleasing of these early bags is that seen in the effigy of Queen Berengaria, widow of Richard I, who died in 1235. Her tomb in the Abbey l'Espau, near Mans, pictures several details in the costume of that period. Among these the little amônière, suspended from the gem-set girdle by strings of unusual length, is of important historical interest. Judging from an early thirteenth century poem, these fashionable bags were usually made of silk and leather. Says a merchant of that day, "I have good *amônières* of silk and leather."

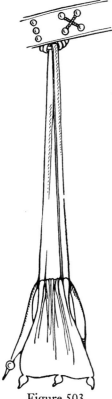

Figure 503. Amônière, from the Effigy of Berengaria of Navarre, 1235

During the period of the later Middle Ages, when customs and fashions of the old world were slowly merging into those of the new, women employed much of their leisure time in embroidering their shoes, gloves, girdles, and bags. In fact, many of the great families had their professional embroidresses who carried out in elaborate pattern the decoration upon various articles of apparel, upon the bag in particular. As early as the thirteenth century records exist which show that embroiderers were included in the craft guilds, a fact which testifies to the demand for such needlework. A few famous bags now treasured in collections bear mute evidence of the handsome work lavished upon these very personal accessories. One of the finest known is that said to have belonged to the Count of Campagne, Thibaut IV (1201-33). It is made of crimson velvet with figures and arabesque pattern which had first been embroidered with silk and Cyprus gold thread; the reverse side is green, flowered damask. Many of these handsome bags were finished at the lower edge with knots and tassels of thread and metal, and others are mentioned as having been hung with bells. Some of these bags, especially those of square shape, were undoubtedly designed to hold the prayer book. An example of such a bag is seen in a fourteenth-century brass which was erected in Bruges to a nun of the Séquin Sisterhood. She is robed in the habiliments of the order and carries on her left arm a pendant bag described as "holding her book of devotion." Figure 504 is representative of a bag designed for this

COURTESY, METROPOLITAN MUSEUM OF ART

Figure 504. Bag of Canvas, Embroidered with Silk and Metal Threads, French, 14th Century

COURTESY, METROPOLITAN MUSEUM OF ART

Figure 505. Bag, Showing "Stump Work," English, 17th Century

purpose. It is executed in tent stitch. The face is divided into quadrangular fields, two of these showing animal forms, the stag and unicorn; and two, bird forms with human heads, one that of a jester, recognized by his cap and bells, and the other of a woman. The reverse side, which is sadly frayed, shows a tall, central tree form with figures arranged at each side. All of these motifs are usual in the thirteenth and fourteenth century embroidery. Though most of the subjects chosen for bag design were selected from contemporary literature, the *Romance of the Rose*, a poem rich in romantic episodes, has supplied by far the larger number of motifs. Marie de France, in her lovely *Lais*, says:

"This doleful lady took a fair piece of white samite, broidered with gold, and wrought thereon the story of this adventure." Another bag, which, however, is fitted with a drawstring and embroidered with a conventional surface pattern, is shown in the drawing after Viollet-le-Duc. Figure 581, page 494. This was carried by a woman of the fourteenth century to hold her book of prayers.

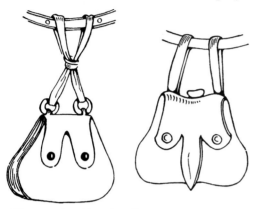

Figure 506. Popular Forms of the Pouch, 12th and 16th Centuries

1500-1600

Another type of embroidery which was applied to the indispensable bag was that known as "stump work." Figure 505. This form of stitchery made its appearance in England about 1600, but as early as 1500 and perhaps even earlier it had been practiced by the nuns living in various sections of the continent. The unusual feature of stump work was the raised patterns. These raised portions were liberally padded with bits of wool, tow, or horsehair called "stumps." Many times the raised work was completed separately and then applied to the foundation material. This popular form of embroidery was used not only for bags but for wall hangings, picture frames, mirror frames, jewel boxes, and other objects about the home. Though the work with its high relief and elaborate detail often appears grotesque, it is interesting by reason of the marvelous skill with which it was executed. It continued a popular form of embroidery design to about 1688, when it completely disappeared.

Figure 507.
A Pouch of the
14th Century

During the period of the Middle Ages, when bags were in their heyday, there gradually came a change in form. From the late twelfth to the sixteenth centuries many of the popular bags took on a flat shape, grew smaller, and were worn at the belt. These were called pouches. Figures 506, 507, 508, 509.

> One of these wore a jerkin made of buff,
> A mighty *pouch* of canvas at his belt.
>
> THYNNE, *Pride and Loneliness*

These flat pouches in time came to be very handsome, and were worn with a knife or dagger thrust through the strap. The illustration, Figure 509, is an example of a striking fourteenth-century pouch ornamented with a beautiful foliated pattern. From the fourteenth to the sixteenth century the city of Caen was especially noted for the beauty of its embroidered bags and pouches. These were sold all over Europe. In a book published in 1588, "Margaret the emblazoner" is mentioned as a "maker of pouches" whose delicate handwork brought renown to the city.

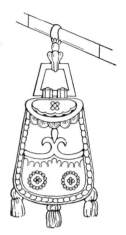

As for Caen *pouches* none made in other towns can compare with them for choiceness, character, and excellent materials, such as velvets of all colors, gold, silver, and other threads, or in suitability for the use of nobles, justices, ladies and maidens, so that it is a common proverb to speak of "caen *pouches* above all others."
CHARLES DE BOURGUEVILLE,
Recherches et Antiquities sur le Ville de Caen

Figure 508. A Bag
of 1400

From a very splendid tapestry preserved in the Cathedral of Sens.

Various names have been applied to this handy little accessory—amônière, bag, pouch, purse. The last, from the French *bourse*, is now in general use. As far back as Chaucer's time, however, the little bag was called a purse. In the *Miller's Tale*, the young wife is thus described:

Figure 509. A Handsome
Pouch in Foliated
Pattern, 1300

And by hire girdel heng a *purs* of lether
Tasseled with grene and perled with latoun.

"Perled with latoun" suggests a kind of beadwork in pearls, similar to the modern decorative work in steel beads. In the inventory of the palace at Greenwich, made during the reign of Henry VIII, there appears:

A *purse* of crimson salm, embroidered in gold.
Harleian Ms., 1412

As time went on these little girdle pouches continued to carry a greater and greater variety of trinkets: keys, combs, pincushions, cosmetics, mirrors, strings of beads, scent apples, little remedies for illness, and whatnot were hidden away in their depths. Some of the interesting bags of the sixteenth century show several compartments, each furnished with a drawstring which concealed the precious pack. Figure 510.

Handsome bags with frames of bronze and gold came into fashion at this period and continued to reappear at intervals throughout the centuries, taking their place as a permanent and indispensable accessory of dress. A very fine example of a fifteenth-century purse is preserved in the Louvre. Figure 512. It is of velvet, bound with gold thread and finished with gold lace tassels. On the upper section is a coat of arms in colored silk. The handsome clasp is of steel, richly chased. At the top of the elaborate frame is a ring by which it was attached to the girdle. The metal frames of many of the bags of this period were frequently

Figure 510. Bags of the Renaissance
After Racinet.

inscribed with moral and religious sentiments. On one the following line appears: "*Soli Deo honor et gloria, Laus tibi soli, O Domine Christi.*" On another: "*Ave maria gratiae plene, Dominus tecum.*" These probably belonged to ecclesiastics of the period.

1600-1800

With the beginning of the seventeenth century and the wide use of pockets in the costume of men, the appended pouch gradually withdrew from sight. Real pockets appeared with the puffed breeches, about 1630, when vertical openings were cut on each side the front near the waistline. These openings were usually bound with braid and sometimes treated in a decorative manner. In women's dress, pockets were hidden under the enveloping skirt. These pockets were bags of linen, lawn, dimity, chintz, calico, or other unpretentious materials worn suspended from the waist. Figure 513. An amusing print of Cromwell's time (1599-1658) pictures an interested group listening with close attention to a stirring speaker, while a pickpocket lifts the skirt of a rapt woman listener and is about to rifle her hanging pocket. These pockets, though very useful accessories of this century, did not take the place of the handbag or purse but were more likely the forerunner of the pocket. They were highly prized as recep-

Figure 511. A Purse Hanging from an Elaborate Girdle Seen in a Portrait by Holbein, 1500

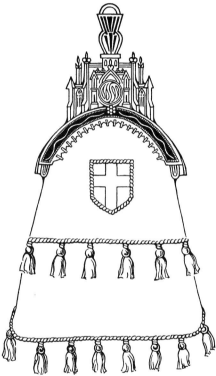

Figure 512. A 16th Century Purse Showing an Elaborate Mount

tacles for the little purse, handkerchief, mirror, and keys, and were often left by will to deserving friends. Women of fashion, however, continued to carry in the hand or at the girdle the handsome purse or bag, suspended by cord or ribbon. The richest and costliest materials were used, embellished with colored silks and metal threads. Figure 514 shows a beautiful bag of the eighteenth century. The foundation material is white satin, and the elaborate embroidery is carried out in colored silks combined with metal thread. Throughout the eighteenth century purses continued to be works of art and the beaded bag came to be the chef d'oeuvre in purses. Figure 515. This highly prized bag was usually worked on canvas or made with knitting needles, or crochet hook with purse silk and beads. Other purses fashionable during the late century were those long and narrow in shape, carried by rings adjusted about the center. Small, large, circular, and bag-shaped purses made of linen, silk, or velvet and embroidered in colored silks or enriched with steel, gilt, or colored beads were the choice of many modish women. These bags were either drawn with long cords or set in chased metal mounts.

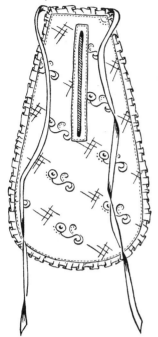

1800-1900

It was during the Empire period when scant, diaphanous garments were the mode, that the little bag or purse was reborn under the name *reticule*. The dress of this day was too scant for underpockets, so the little reticule was not only useful but a very necessary accessory. Reticules seem to be a revival of the bags carried by Greek women of long ago. Generally formed, in part, of cardboard or lacquered tin, many resemble in shape the old Etruscan vase

Figure 513. The Practical Hanging Pocket, 1600

forms. They were invariably supported by long strings. Figures 516, 517. It is said that in 1806, during the famous trial of Lord Melvell, women carried within these little reticules of silk dainty sandwiches to eat in court. When not in use these handy bags were hung on the back of the chair milady occupied. Reticules had a long and popular vogue; every lady who made any pretence to fashion carried one, and often possessed several, matching her various gowns. In a periodical of 1808 we read that:

COURTESY, METROPOLITAN MUSEUM OF ART

Figure 514. Purse, English, 18th Century

Satin embroidered in silk and metal.

No lady of fashion appears in public without her *reticule* which contains her handkerchief, fan, card-money, and essence-bottle. They are at this season made up of rich figured sarcenet, plaid satin or silver tissue with strings and tassels, their color appropriate to the robes with which they are worn.

Indeed, reticules were so generally carried that during the first quarter of the nineteenth century they were popularly called "indispensables" and, ironically, a few years later "ridicules."

By the middle of the nineteenth century women had discovered the pocket, and pocket openings were left in the seam of the skirt. For many years the little leather purse was carried within the shelter of the new pocket. Fashion, however, is a creature of whims, and no custom is permitted to stay overtime. Consequently, ere long, little purses came out of seclusion, and bags were again the mode. Handsome

COURTESY, METROPOLITAN MUSEUM OF ART

Figure 515. French Beaded Bag, Early 18th Century

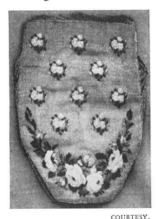

COURTESY,
METROPOLITAN MUSEUM OF ART

Figure 516. Reticule,
English, 1800

COURTESY, METROPOLITAN MUSEUM OF ART

Figure 517. Reticule, English, 1800

bags made of tortoise and pearl were carried during the latter half of the century. They were frequently inlaid with silver and gold. Some of the more elaborate were jeweled and mounted with handsome frames, supported by a chain. Sometimes they were carried in the hand or, more frequently, attached to the girdle. They were followed by flat, pouchlike purses of leather or beads, invariably attached to the belt or girdle and commonly called *chatelaines*.

Twentieth Century

In the opening years of the twentieth century, bags of silk, beads, and leather in a great variety of shapes and sizes were fashionable. The flat envelope purse and the pouchlike bag, each had its day. The popular leathers—calf, deer, kangaroo, seal, walrus, pigeon, alligator, lizard and snakeskin—each found a place in bag making. Fabrics were also much in vogue—silk, satin, crepe de chine, and other attractive materials. The

interior of these modern bags was fully as important as the exterior. Linings, pockets, mirrors, and other tempting details were all considered. The fair purchaser of this day inspected with concern the silk and suede lining, the number of inner pockets, and the vanity accessories which must accompany every up-to-date bag. Distinction in the modern bag, aside from material, is gained by the use of handsome clasps and handles. Bags for winter, bags for summer, bags for day, bags for evening—each had its particular fabric, form, and color.

Among the novelty bags of the early twentieth century were the beautiful mesh bags of sterling silver, gilt, and gold. Figure 518. These did not take the place of the leather bag but were largely used for only coin and handkerchief. Choice speci-

Figure 518. Silver Mesh Bag with Vinaigrette, Florentine, 1910

mens of these bags were of Florentine design. They were formed of fine links of silver, gilt, and gold wire woven into a close mesh. The frame of these attractive bags were sometimes further enriched by the use of colored enamels.

Among the distinctive bags of 1924 were the flat envelope shapes of leather to be carried under the arm, and also the practical bag with a handle. Figures 519, 520. Beaded bags, exquisite revivals of an earlier period, were also in demand. These were very handsome and, being woven with a silvered background, were well adapted to different costumes. The inspiration of the modern beaded bag has undoubtedly come from those of 1800.

Thus it is that Fashion ever repeats herself, building upon the old, and adding new touches in size, form, color, or material reflecting the spirit of the new times. The line of ancestry of the modern handbag runs far back into the past, even beyond the simple little bag of leather or silk designed to carry coins for the poor. Through the centuries it has taken

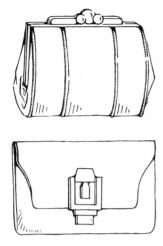

Figure 519. Modern Handbags

Figure 520. A Practical Bag of the 20th Century

on enrichment and distinction in shape, yet it still serves its ancient purpose—to carry the coin, and if need be, the kerchief and mirror of our modern lady of fashion.

REFERENCES

Burgess, F. W., *Antique Jewelry and Trinkets.*
Calthrop, Dion Clayton, *English Costume*, Vol. II.
Fairholt, F. W., *Costume in England.*
Lehman, Helen, *The Leather Goods and Gloves Department*, Chapter 14.
Peterson's Fashion Magazine, July, 1863.
Planché, J. R., *Cyclopedia of Costume*, Vols. I, II.
Style Sources, November, 1929.
Vogue, July, 1930.

CHAPTER 32

The Handkerchief

It was a *handkerchief*, an antique token
My father gave my mother.

Othello, Act V, sc. 2

THE handkerchief, which in earlier times was carried in the hand, today seeks the seclusion of purse or pocket. Time was when the belles of fashion exhibited their large, handsome handkerchiefs with the same pride as milady of today displays her scarf. The famous portrait of the Infanta Marie Theresa by Velasquez pictures that distinguished lady with the very large handkerchief carried where all may see. PLATE XLIV. At this period handkerchiefs were new. They had only recently come into general use and one cannot be overcritical of the conspicuous place they were given in the dress of the period. Sometime later, though still carried in the hand, they grew smaller and were very elaborate in drawn-work embroidery and the handsome needlepoint and bobbin laces. Figure 243, page 192.

Going back down the lane of history, records show that savage races wove small mats of grasses and wore these both as a covering for the head and also for wiping the perspiration from the brow. The first handkerchiefs for the face alone are believed to have been used in the service of religion. These were small pieces of silk tissue used only by the priests at the altar. In that ancient day these handkerchiefs were called *facials*, and were left at the altar with other vestments when the service was finished.

In literature of the classic age there is frequent mention of "perspiration" and "mouth cloths." The general populace, however, not following the fashions, mopped their brows and wept their tears upon their mantles. In Greece, handkerchiefs were made of fine cotton, often perfumed. In Rome the handkerchief, known as the *sudarium*, was carried chiefly by men and used largely for wiping the perspiration from the face and hands. Patrician women are said to have carried handkerchiefs at games and festivals and used them to wave as a sign of approval, a custom which is, no doubt, the origin of the Chautauqua salute of modern times. According to an account given in Foosbroke's *Encyclopedia of Antiquities*, 1843, these early handkerchiefs were always oblong in shape. The writer

PLATE XLIV. Infanta Marie Theresa........................*Velasquez*

At this period (1600) the handkerchief of generous size was carried where it could be seen and admired.

states that they were always "more long than broad" and continues that they were "used by spectators at the publick shows to wave in token of appreciation. They were used in the church of the first Christians in applause of the sermon, and afterward they were used as handkerchiefs." He adds: "It was a piece of linen cloth which the deacons wore upon the left arm. It was not square but oblong and in use by all citizens."

In later days Roman handkerchiefs, particularly those carried by women, were simple squares of cotton or silk. It is further known that in lieu of the handkerchief these Roman beauties carried crystal and amber balls for cooling the hands. This was an ancient Egyptian custom which had been adopted by Roman society. It was a fashionable caprice to carry these little balls in gold and silver nets and allay the perspiration of the hands by rolling and pressing the balls, which gave off a delightful odor when warmed. The handkerchief as a refinement of Roman civilization, being exclusively the property of the nobles, was regarded as a badge of distinction or a symbol of power.

Middle Ages

All through the Middle Ages the handkerchief was looked upon as a

showy dress accessory— the privilege only of the wealthy. Many leaders of fashion possessed *one* of such rare fineness, however, that it frequently found a place in the pages of history. As early as 1328 a "handkerchief of silk" is mentioned as an important item in the wardrobe effects of the lady Clemence of Austria.

COURTESY, METROPOLITAN MUSEUM OF ART

Figure 521. Handkerchief, Drawn Work, 1500

1500-1600

During the early Renaissance handkerchiefs came to be more general. Observations and writings on the use of the handkerchief began to appear. Erasmus, writing in the early years of the century, particularly urged upon children the correct use of the handkerchief. "To wipe your nose on your sleeve is boorish," he says scornfully. During this century the handkerchief was commonly known as a *napkyn*.

Your *napkyn* is too little.
Othello, Act III, sc. 3

With the gradual spread in the popularity of the handkerchief it soon came to be a very general and fashionable item in dress. In Italy, handsome drawn-thread work was applied to the handkerchief and many of those now in museum collections are a witness to the beauty of this work. Figure 521. Others were made of cambric embroidered in red silk in the popular tent stitch. Somewhat later, as the lace era neared, the finer lawn was used; this sometimes was striped with gold thread and frequently edged with the new, popular bobbin and needle laces. Figure 522.

COURTESY, METROPOLITAN MUSEUM OF ART

Figure 522. Handkerchief, Bobbin Lace, French, 18th Century

In France, silk and linen were the popular materials. As the use of lace grew more and more widespread gentlemen as well as ladies carried the lace-trimmed handkerchief. Very elaborate and expensive were those carried by people of wealth. They were so important a "possession" that inventories of the period frequently mention a handsome handkerchief as a valuable part of the estate. It is said that in 1594 Gabrielle d'Estrées displayed a handkerchief costing one thousand francs.

In England silk and cambric were the fashionable materials. During the reign of Elizabeth, the handkerchief made rapid progress. It was at this period that the lace handkerchief first appeared in England. These handsome handkerchiefs were "wrought with names and true love knots" and were given as favors to admirers, who wore them in their hats. Howe writes of this custom in his *Addition to Stowe's Chronicle*. He says:

Maydes and gentlewomen give to their favorites, as tokens of their love, little *handkerchiefs* of about three or four inches square, wrought round about, and with a button or a tassel at each corner, and a little one in the middle, with silke and threed; the best edged with a small gold lace, or twist, which being doubled up in foure crosse foldes, so as the middle might be seen, gentlemen and others did usually weare them in their hatts as favors of their loves and mistresses. Some cost six pence apiece, some twelve pence, and the richest sixteene pence.

Indeed, it was at this period that milady's lace handkerchief gradually developed into both an ingenious and dainty lure in flirtation.

A favorite occupation of women then was that of embroidering the handkerchief. Some were stitched in blue thread, and others were carried out in the fashionable cutwork embroidery.

> A cut-work *handkerchief* she gave me.
> BEN JONSON, *Bartholomew Fair*, 1614

Queen Elizabeth was a lover of all these dainty accessories of dress and set the fashion in handkerchiefs as well as gloves, ruffs, and jewels for the ladies of her court and the other fashion leaders of her day.

1600-1800

As mentioned before, with the development of needlepoint and bobbin laces handkerchiefs came to be even more elegant and costly affairs. Under date of August 12, 1666, Pepys made this entry in his diary:

> I and my wife up to the closet to examine her kitchen accounts and then I took occasion to fall out with her for buying a *laced* handkerchief . . . without my leave.

The quarrel over the expensive lace handkerchief was not easily overlooked for the following day, the 13th, he adds:

> Up, without being friends with my wife, nor great enemies, both being quiet and silent.

The lace handkerchief continued to be the important detail in milady's dress. And exquisite bits they were! Squares of dainty linen edged with the finest of bobbin or handsome needlepoint. Figure 523 shows a dainty insertion of Mechlin with an edge of the same. In Figure 524 the handsome edge in Brussels needlepoint.

Individual fancy was rampant during the late seventeenth and eighteenth centuries in dictating the shapes of handkerchiefs. They were now oval, round, or oblong. The story is told that when Marie Antoinette happened to mention to Louis XVI that she was tired of these various shapes, instantly the King declared that "the length of the handkerchief shall equal its width throughout the kingdom." The little square has ever since remained the accepted form for the handkerchief. At the end of the century the French Revolution brought forward many novel types of accessories, and handkerchiefs did not escape. Men wore high stocks and these in turn were swathed with a figured-silk handkerchief which muffled the chin.

In the American colonies fashions in handkerchiefs kept pace with

Figure 523. Handkerchief, Mechlin Insertion and Edge, 19th Century

those in Europe. Colonial dames displayed their dainty, lace-trimmed squares with the same pride as did their cousins across the Atlantic. Linen, silk, and handsome lace handkerchiefs were the mode. The Quakers of Pennsylvania considered the plain, white handkerchief as an absolute necessity in completing the dress of the well-groomed Quakeress!

1800-1900

When Napoleon and Josephine came to their "place in the sun," Josephine set the mode in handkerchiefs. Gossip said that during conversation the Empress with unwonted frequency raised a dainty lace handkerchief to her lips to offset the ill effect of her "not pretty" teeth. It was not long before the fashion set by Josephine was adopted, and ladies the world over were carrying in their hands dainty handkerchiefs of fashionable lace. It was during the later days of the Napoleonic régime, however, that the public display of the handkerchief became "anathema" to social leaders of the period. Its public use was so opposed that gradually it crept under cover. Later in the same century, however,

COURTESY, METROPOLITAN MUSEUM OF ART

Figure 524. Handkerchief, Brussels Needlepoint, 19th Century

it emerged and was accepted as an indispensable accessory of dress, suitable alike for the private or public covering of coughs and sneezes.

A handsome handkerchief of this period is that shown in Figure 526. This was the wedding handkerchief made for Marie Henriette, Archduchess of Austria, on the occasion of her marriage to Leopold II of Belgium in 1853. The handsome Brussels needlepoint is given a royal significance by the arms of Belgium and Austria worked in medallions and the initials LM surmounted by the crown.

In 1863 England popularized the cambric handkerchief with colored border and hemstitched edge. The scalloped and embroidered edge with the initial in Gothic letters also had a decided vogue. Young ladies carried "pocket handkerchiefs" which were finished with a narrow frill or slightly scalloped edge and worked with colored embroidery. The French considered the hand-embroidered or lace-trimmed handkerchief an important accessory to the costume of every well-dressed woman. By 1893, the Dress Reform Movement, which began in Germany, advocated that every article of clothing be made of wool, even the handkerchiefs. This is the only instance on record where handkerchiefs have been made of wool.

During these later centuries men's handkerchiefs like men's dress had become more simple and inconspicuous. While woman's handkerchiefs were dainty in size and embroidered or lace-trimmed, men's settled down into an established order. They were large, approximately eighteen inches square, with a simple hemstitched edge, and

COURTESY, METROPOLITAN MUSEUM OF ART

Figure 525. Handkerchief, Embroidered, Monogrammed and Edged with Lace, French, about 1822

sometimes a corner monogram. White linen was always accepted as "good form," though Fashion permitted a small amount of color and colored borders. From time to time the very fastidious wore silk handkerchiefs of various colors, and occasionally with decorative borders which harmonized with some other detail of dress, preferably the tie, the hatband, or a subtle tone in the wearing apparel.

Twentieth Century

The twentieth century sees the fashion of the handkerchief still continued. It is not the accessory, however, to be displayed as ostentatiously as in the earlier centuries. The handkerchief is now invariably carried in the purse or pocket, sometimes completely hidden, and sometimes only half concealed. Occasionally, however, in her effort to initiate a novelty, Fashion decrees that a large or small handkerchief, crepe, chiffon, or silk, gaily decorated or severely plain, be added as a conspicuous note to costume. In 1928, large chiffon handkerchiefs with allover designs or borders were invariably worn for fashionable evening dances and assemblies. Sometimes this same decorative handkerchief was tucked into the jacket pocket of a daytime costume, leaving one long end to fall over the skirt to relieve the severe line of a tailor-made garment. In 1929, the linen handkerchief with very narrow hem and a corner monogram was popular for general use. Occasionally monograms were embroidered in color which added another interesting note. Further, small designs cut

Figure 526. Wedding Handkerchief of Marie Henrietta, Archduchess of Austria, Who Married Leopold II of Belgium in 1853

Brussels needlepoint showing royal arms of Austria and Belgium.

from gay-colored linen and dexterously set on or applied to the white background was still another style which added to the attractiveness of the white linen square. Though the modern handkerchief may vary from season to season in details of style and materials, linen holds a foremost place. As a material, linen is soft, absorbs moisture quickly, and launders so easily that the handkerchief of linen will evidently go on forever.

Linen handkerchiefs are made in Ireland, Scotland, Belgium, Germany, France, and Switzerland. France and Italy also produce many fine lawn handkerchiefs. China and Japan are famous for their silk handkerchiefs. These are often printed in interesting patterns or embroidered in fine stitching by hand.

So important are handkerchiefs to us that statistics report that in the year 1929 350,000,000 were sold in the United States.

It is a far cry back to the days when the handkerchief emerged as a fashionable accessory of dress. Then it was worn on "occasions." Milady possessed *one*. It was a rare and much-prized belonging. She gowned herself with the display of the handsome handkerchief in mind. Today our lady purchases her squares by the dozen. They are choice but simple accessories of dress, worn not for display but as a useful and practical addition to the toilet of this most practical of centuries.

Figure 527. Silk Embroidered Handkerchiefs, Modern Chinese

REFERENCES

Cole, George S., *Dictionary of Dry Goods*, p. 175.
Evans, Mary, *Costume Throughout the Ages*, pp. 57, 99.
Fales, Jane, *Dressmaking*, pp. 36, 40.
Lester, Katherine Morris, *Historic Costume*.
Parsons, Frank Alvah, *The Art in Dress*, pp. 88, 230.
Peterson's Fashion Magazine, Volume of 1863.
Rhead, G. W., *Chats on Costume*, p. 201.
Sage, Elizabeth, *A Study of Costume*, pp. 57, 170.
Thompson, Eliza, *The Cotton and Linen Departments*, pp. 88, 230.
Vogue, July 5, 1930.

CHAPTER 33

The Fan

What daring Bard shall e'er attempt to tell
The powers that in this little engine dwell?
What verse can e'er explain its various parts,
Its numerous uses, motions, charms and arts?
Its shake triumphant, its virtuous clap,
Its angry flutter, and its wanton tap.

SOAME JENYN, *Art of Dancing*

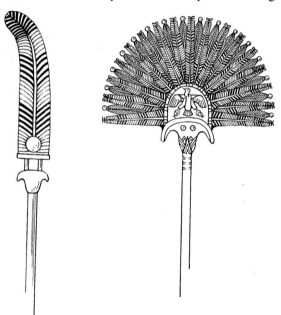

Figure 528. Egyptian Fans

THE fan, like the sunshade, originated in tropical countries. Here it was in daily service as a protection against the sun, as a means of cooling the air, driving away bothersome insects and, when necessary, fanning the fire into a flame. In the Far East the fan was extensively employed in the service of religion, but its use as a costume accessory also dates back to remote antiquity. Some authorities state that the fan was known in China three thousand years ago. The Egyptians, Assyrians, Persians, Hebrews, Chinese, Japanese, and the people of India used fans as far back as their records of history go.

Among Eastern potentates, the fan was a badge of rank. The dignity of these rulers required that their fans be carried by slaves or attendants. The ancient form of the fan is therefore pictured with a long handle, and resembles a standard. Figure 528. A wall painting at Thebes pictures

436

twenty-three sons of Rameses the Great in a procession, each carrying a ceremonial fan of semicircular shape attached to a long staff. The office of fan bearer to an Egyptian king was one of high honor, one to which only princes and other sons of the highest nobility could aspire. Figure 529. These attendants served standing at the right and left of the monarch as he sat in state; they attended him when he rode forth and during ceremonies in the temple. When not serving in the capacity of fan bearer, they waited upon the king as members of his staff or in some other service of distinction.

Another ancient record of the fan is seen in an Assyrian bas-relief, now in the British Museum. This pictures a king of 880-860 B.C. being fanned by attendants. Figure 530. A Persian relief likewise represents the king of that country seated on his throne with attendants behind him bearing fans. In China, at the palace of Peking, a number of fans sawed from ivory are exhibited which date from about 1000 B.C. They have handles of gold and silver filigree combined with mother-

Figure 529. Rameses III and His Fan Bearers

From a temple at Thebes.

of-pearl. It is the Chinese, in fact, who claim to have invented the fan, and they trace its origin to legendary sources. According to the tale, Langsen, the daughter of an all-powerful mandarin, was present at the Feast of the Lanterns. About to succumb from the heat, she broke all traditions by removing the mask which she wore. She held it near enough, however, to hide her features, waving it rapidly to and fro. Immediately, says legend, this caprice set the fashion of fans.

Europe acquired the fan from the East. Ancient Greek writers often refer to fans, and illustrations of fans may be seen on Greek vases. Figure 531. Here, as in oriental countries, the large fans with long handles were usually carried by slaves in the service of their masters. In Orestes, the words of the Phrygian slave affirm:

I fanned Helen's cheeks and airy curls with a winged *fan* of round and graceful shape.

Euripides, Orestes

However, small fans carried by Greek women occasionally appear in vase paintings. About 500 B.C. the fan made of peacock feathers was in use. Some of these were probably only a tuft of feathers set in a handle; others no doubt were arranged so that their color and markings formed a pattern. The peacock was known as the bird of Hera (Juno, to the Romans) and was held as a symbol of refinement and luxury; hence it is not difficult to understand the Grecian woman's preference for the fan of peacock feathers. During the late centuries, fans were made by stretching linen or silk over a frame shaped like a leaf. According to Winckelmann, the first fans in imitation of leaves were triangular in shape. They were inspired, without doubt, by the palm leaf and other fronds which had been used in earliest times and had furnished the original idea.

Figure 530. An Assyrian King Being Fanned by His Attendants

Roman authorities refer to the fan as being of service in keeping away the flies. Their fans continued the curved leaf shape but were made of thin, delicately carved wood, elaborately gilded and painted. The patrician woman of Rome was provided with slaves who attended her as fan bearers, for no high-born lady was even to be suspected of fanning herself. We hear, however, that later Roman beauties carried their own fans. For general cooling of the air within the lofty apartments of the Roman villas, great bunches of ostrich plumes tinted in various colors were suspended from gilded ceilings.

Middle Ages

In western Europe during the Middle Ages nothing is heard of the fan in the everyday life of the people, and the inference is that it had disappeared. The old ceremonial use, however, coming down from the ancients, was kept alive in the churches. The long-handled, disk-shaped fan was held by the deacons and used by them to drive away insects from the sacramental vessels. In the early inventories, the *flabellum*, this large fan carried by church attendants, is frequently mentioned as used in this service. These ceremonial fans were radial in form, with long handles. The fan proper was made of various materials, feathers, parchment, silk, and wood; many of them could be folded, *à la cocarde*, and resembled the wheel-shaped fan of later days. One of the most famous of these early fans is that from the Abbey of Tournus, dating from the ninth century and now preserved in the National Museum of Florence. Figure 532. This remarkable example is formed of a strip of vellum folded *à la cocarde*. It is painted on both sides. The outer border consists of a continuous scroll of Romanesque ornament. Inscriptions in Latin fill in the three concentric circles. Figures of the saints separated by little conventional trees fill the second large space. The handle is formed by four cylinders of white bone. The two larger pieces are ornamented by semi-

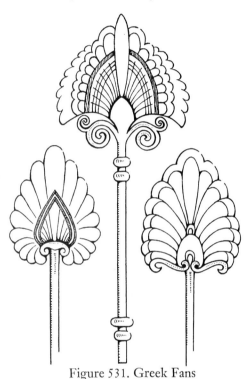

Figure 531. Greek Fans

After paintings on Greek vases.

naturalistic foliage and running spirals; the two lower are fluted. The cylinders are joined by pommels painted green. The upper one supports a capital with four figures of saints. On the capital rests the long guard or box which receives the fan when closed. The four sides are white bone elaborately carved. This famous specimen, one of the few which has been preserved, may be regarded as a characteristic type of the ancient flabellum.

The gradual reappearance of the fan in Europe during the early thirteenth and fourteenth centuries was due to the many unique examples of Eastern fans brought into the country by returning Crusaders. Japan is credited with having invented the folding fan about 670 A.D. In the tenth century it was introduced into China, and from there it undoubtedly reached Europe. Authorities disagree as to which of the

European countries first introduced it, though a general feeling exists that Italy was probably the leader.

Among the earliest records of fans are the *esmouchoirs** or "fly whisks." This particular type of fan seems to have been employed for

the same purpose as the modern fly brush—so generally used in Egypt—to keep away insects. Figure 533. Following the fly whisk there probably came the fly fan, that is, a fixed fan with the blade set firmly in a handle. Proof of these fly fans in the fourteenth century is contained in a record of 1316 in which it is stated that the Countess Mahant d'Artois had a "fly-fan with the handle all silver." A "fly-fan of cloth of gold fleur-de-lis ornamented with the arms of France and Navarre, with a bastion of ivory and jet valued at five francs of gold," is mentioned in the will of Jeanne d'Evereau. An inventory of Charles V of France (1364-80) records a "fan of round form which folds." These two types, the fixed fan and the folding, wheel-shaped or cockade fan were the earliest forms in use on the continent. These were in the possession only of the wealthy and may not have been considered a part of personal costume, for they were always carried by servants or used as part of the furnishings of private chapels. Fans did not become a distinct part of costume until milady carried her own fan in her own hand. This came to be general in the early sixteenth century. Miniatures of this period begin to show women with long-handled, disk-shaped fans, tuft fans, and a little flag fan.

PHOTOGRAPH, ALINARI NATIONAL MUSEUM, FLORENCE

Figure 532. Flabellum, from Tournus Abbey, France

1500-1600

The flag fan, the long-handled, disk-shaped fan, and the tuft fan were

* Latin name, *muscarium,* from *musca,* meaning "fly."

in use in the fourteenth century and even earlier. Figures 534, 535, 536. The tuft fan had been in use as early as the twelfth century. In the sixteenth century these were made of the plumage of the ostrich and peacock dyed various colors, with feathers varying in number from one to twenty. Sometimes feathers were arranged in overlapping series suggesting their natural growth. They were set in beautiful handles of carved ivory, gold, or silver, frequently richly jeweled. Figure 537. These costly handles were a very important item of a permanent value. The feathers, vellum, or parchment were less durable and could be replaced from time to time. For the folding fans, which appeared later, the precious metals were not so suitable and consequently ivory, bone, tortoise shell, and mother-of-pearl came to be the popular materials for sticks.

The flag fan, sometimes called the "key" or "weather vane" fan, Figure 534, seems to have been in use during the earlier centuries. Its form had undoubtedly come from the East, where a similar type was in use. It was during the early sixteenth century that it came to be very fashionable in Italy, particularly in Venice. This was a fixed fan of oblong shape with the handle attached to one long edge. The blade was made of plaited straw of various

Figure 533. Early Fly Whisk

colors, of linen painted or embroidered, of parchment, vellum, or silk. Figure 538. The more ornate of these were carried by matrons, while newly married women or those betrothed carried flag fans of a dainty whiteness. Since the popularity of these fans were largely limited to Italy, they are always associated with the fashions of this country. Lavinia, the daughter of Titian, in her portrait as a young girl (1550) carries a flag fan; some years later she is pictured with a feathered fan, significant of Venetian nobility. Figure 540. In several famous portraits both Titian and Veronese have each preserved the exact type of flag fan.

Figure 534. Weathercock or Flag Fan

From a painting, 1500.

In 1550 screen fans, which resembled the disk fan, reached France. These were called "screen fans" because they served admirably as a screen, shielding the eyes of the fair bearer from the hot rays of Parisian

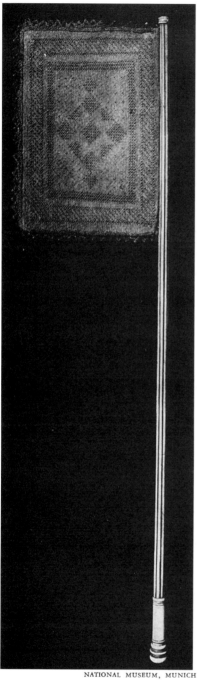

Figure 535. Flag Fan

Plaited straw with ivory handle, Italian, 16th century.

sunshine. Many of these resembled a folding fan but did not fold. They were spread in deep, permanent pleats. During the same period Catherine de' Medici brought the new folding fan from Italy into France. These fans of heavily scented leather coming from the Orient had been in use for some time in Spain and reached the continent through that country.

The earliest form of folding fan used in Italy was probably the so-called "duck's foot" fan, so popular with the ladies of Ferrara. Figure 538. This opened only a quarter of a circle, and instead of being made of leather it was formed of alternate strips of mica and vellum, sometimes daintily painted. Others were formed of paper, the surface cut in geometric patterns of circles and lozenges with bits of mica inserted at intervals, giving unusual richness to the fan. The sticks were usually of ivory. The popularity of mica, introduced about the middle of the sixteenth century, grew to such an extent that all the leaves of fans frequently came to be made of this material. These various styles of the early folded fan represent the type which reached its ultimate perfection in the seventeenth and eighteenth centuries.

Commenting on the new folding fans, Henri Estienne, who wrote in the late sixteenth century, describes it in the hands of King Henry III, "In his right hand was placed an instrument which extended and folded again with the touch of a finger. We call it here a *fan*." According to

Pierre de l'Etoile, Henry's fan could be unfurled with a swift motion of the hand and was large enough to shield his delicate complexion from the sun. And now handsome folding fans vied with beautiful feathered fans. The fan was, indeed, the indispensable accessory of every toilet. "So much are they used now," says Henri Estienne, "that once used, they cannot abandon them; but they use them in summer to make air and keep away the heat of the sun, and in winter to keep away the heat of the fire."

Under Henry IV (1589-1610), the fashion for fans was sufficiently general to give rise to a manufacture of considerable extent. The right to manufacture was first authorized in December 1564 by an act which established a company made up of tradesmen

Figure 536. Disk Fan of Rice Straw, 1400

From a ms. of the 15th century.

who made the fans, and master gilders, who decorated them. The gilders were authorized "to garnish fans made of sheepskin, silk, goatskin, enriched and ornamented, as may please the merchant and the lord who may order them." A later decree, passed about 1660, deprived them of this right and gave the tradesmen "the right of having painted and gilded fans done by *any* painters and gilders and of having them mounted as might please them."

Figure 537. Tuft Fan
From a portrait, 1500.

Though the earliest record of a fan in England is said to date about 1307, the general acceptance of this fashionable accessory was almost contemporary with its use in France. The fan was brought into England from Italy during the Renaissance period. Throughout the reigns of Henry VIII, Mary, Elizabeth, and James, the fan maintained its place in fashion. As in France, the most popular fans were the large screen fans of ostrich feathers with carved ivory, gold, and silver handles. Queen Elizabeth found particular delight in fans, as she did in gloves, ruffs, and kerchiefs. She is said to have remarked at one time that a fan was the only gift a sovereign should receive from her subjects. She is, consequently, said to have been presented with innumerable fans. Leicester's New Year's gift in 1574 is recorded thus:

A fan of white feathers set in a handle of gold garnished on one side with two very fair emeralds, and fully garnished with diamonds and rubies; the other side garnished with rubies and diamonds. . . .

The famous portrait of the Queen by Zuccario pictures the royal lady carrying a handsome fan of the period. PLATE XLV. Other historic paintings show that the beautiful fan of feathers continued to hold first place for years to come. The portrait of the delightful Marie Louise de Tassis, painted in the early seventeenth century, shows a handsome example of the plumed fan, while a century later the Hon. Mrs. Graham carries a whisk of one, curling plume. PLATES XXXI, XIII, Chapters 16 and 1.

Figure 538. The "Duck's Foot" Fan, 1500

From a portrait.

1600-1700

As in France, the folly of the fan had also invaded the masculine realm, and in the early years of the century several English notables are said to have appropriated it for their own use. In 1617, Greene wrote:

We strive to be accounted womanish by keeping of beauty, by curling the hair, by *plumes* of feathers in our hands, which in war our ancestors wore on their heads.

In Hall's *Satires* one reads of the English dandies, "Tir'd with pinn'd ruffs and *fans*." The plays of the immortal Shakespeare constantly refer to fashionable accessories of dress popular in his day, and the fan is not overlooked. In *The Taming of the Shrew* one scans a generous list of accessories, and among them the indispensable fan:

> With silken coats, and caps, and golden rings,
> With ruffs, and cuffs, and farthingales, and things;
> With scarfs, and *fans*, and double change of bravery.
>
> Act IV, sc. 3

Again, in *Anthony and Cleopatra:*

> . . . . on each side her
> Stood pretty dimpled boys, like smiling cupids,
> With divers-colour'd *fans*. . . .
>
> Act II, sc. 2

At this time the fashion of the fan was well-nigh general throughout Europe. An English traveler, Coryat, writing in 1609, says:

Men and women carry *fans* to refresh themselves in the heat, and often fan their faces. Almost all these are pretty and elegant. The mounting is composed of a piece of painted paper which is pasted on it on both sides, very curiously ornamented with excellent paintings, either of love scenes with Italian verses written below, or of some famous Italian city with a short description. These fans are cheap for one can be bought for what is called a *groat* in England.

In France under Louis XIII (1610-43) and Louis XIV (1643-1715) the same fashions were coming rapidly into vogue. The popularity of the folding fan, introduced much earlier but for a time supplanted by the feather fan, was now going forward by leaps and bounds. By the first half of the seventeenth century it held undisputed sway. Tight stays and high heels were the order of the day. The fan was looked upon as a necessary means of allaying the great discomfort caused by torturous Fashion. During the reign of Louis XIV the sticks of many of the folding fans were so broad that they overlapped to form a solid background. Gradually, however, they began to narrow and were set wider and wider apart, making the fan lighter and giving a more satisfactory background for decoration.

Figure 539. Fan Handle

From a portrait by del Piombo in Stadel Museum at Frankford-on-the Main.

After Viollet-le-Duc.

During this century the fan industry leaped forward. Guilds were soon formed for their manufacture. In Paris alone, in the late seventeenth century, there were more than five hundred manufacturers of this dainty accessory. Fans of French manufacture were in demand everywhere. Even in Spain, where a native artist, Cano de Arevalo, gave himself to the painting of French fans, the fans were sold as soon as decorated. An old record states:

The season for sale having come, our painter supposed that he had received

PLATE XLV. Queen Elizabeth.....................*Frederigo Zuccario*

The Queen carries a handsome fan of six plumes set in an elaborate jeweled mount. Note the ruff with cuffs to match, the embroidery (dark on light), and the array of jeweled ornament.

from Paris an ample supply to be painted, and in a few days he had not a single remaining, having finished and sold the whole.

It was during the latter half of this century that the first all-lace fan appeared. Figure 541. This was produced in Flanders for the Duke of Brabant. Previously, lace had been sewed or gummed upon parchment. Now with the great strides in lacemaking this new phase of the fan appears. Handsome needlepoints gave priceless value to the fashionable toy.

1700-1800

In the eighteenth century fans reached their zenith. Figures 542, 543. Folding fans, used almost exclusively, were among the most daintily beautiful accessories that have ever formed a part of costume. They were indeed costly and elegant ornaments. Many were mounted in gold, silver, ivory, or mother-of-pearl. Handles, too, were looked upon as a field for design. They were beautifully carved, pierced, decorated with *piqué* work, or set with precious stones, and some

PHOTOGRAPH, KUNSTVERLAG WOLFRUM, VIENNA

Figure 540. Lavinia................*Titian*

The daughter of the artist carries the fashionable fan of short ostrich plumes. Note other details of her dress—the earrings, beads, chain, bracelets, rings, buttons, and tussoire.

were fitted with small watches. The piqué work of this century is unique. Minute holes were drilled into the sticks of ivory and shell. Tiny silver or gold pins were pressed into these in such a way as to form elaborate patterns. Silver was usually combined with ivory and tortoise; gold with light tortoise, and gold and silver with dark shell. The mother-of-pearl sticks were marvels of delicate workmanship, for these were built up from small pieces to those sufficiently large to make the sticks. The chief glory of the more elaborate sticks lay in the intricacy of the design, the blending together of the different materials, and methods of decoration. The craftsmen of that day were masters in devising the most suitable technique to display the qualities of the different materials used.

Over the gold or ivory stays were stretched satin, kid, and vellum leaf, and upon this as a dainty background the famous artists of the day reproduced in miniature, each in his own peculiar style, charming pastoral scenes, dancing nymphs, cupids, wreaths, and lovely ladies of the

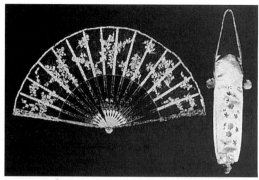

Figure 541. Lace Fan Mounted on Painted Ivory Sticks

Also note the satin bag in which the fan was carried. Late 18th century.

COURTESY, METROPOLITAN MUSEUM OF ART

Figure 542. French Fan, 18th Century

The popular painted vellum with sticks and guards of carved and gilded ivory.

COURTESY, METROPOLITAN MUSEUM OF ART

period. Fan painting came to be a profession of distinction. The names of Boucher, Lancret, Watteau, Greuze, and Fragonard are always associated with the fans carried by du Barry and Pompadour, the favorites of Louis XV.

During this century the gift of wedding fans came to be an established convention. French brides always included a large number as part of the wedding outfit. These were presented to lady guests as a gift from the bride. Such fans were often a costly item, and when royal weddings were celebrated the returns to fanmakers must have been enormous. The fans for the wedding of Marie Leckzinski, bride of Louis XV, were furnished by Tiequet, fanmaker to the King, at a cost of 3,627 livres.* Since it was *de rigueur* for the bride to present her lady guests with fans there were many thousands of them distributed. It is quite possible that many of the beautiful fans which are shown and admired today in museum exhibits were originally wedding fans.

* Livre, an old French money of account; value, 19½ cents.

Since fans of this great period were very expensive they could be carried only by persons of wealth. To meet the demand for "picture" fans a less expensive style was produced. These were made of white paper tinted, and outstanding events of the day were pictured upon them. "Fan prints" were designed and engraved. One of these commemorative fans pictured the famous balloon ascension of L'Homme and Roger, which took place in March, 1785. Figure 544. In England, many pleasing "fan prints" were suggested by scenes from the *Beggar's Opera*. Hogarth's drawings, likewise, furnished many popular themes.

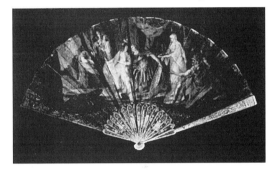

The great triumph of the fan in the eighteenth century led to the establishment of certain conventions and gestures in handling the fan which were considered of first importance. In gesture, in repose, the lady was invariably revealed by the way she managed her fan! Though she possessed all the charms of beauty and distinction and failed in this, she passed quietly into social oblivion.

COURTESY, ART INSTITUTE OF CHICAGO

Figure 543. French Fans, 18th Century

Other examples of painted mounts with carved and gilded ivory sticks and guards.

The grave importance attached to the management of the fan is set forth by Addison in the *Spectator:*

Women are armed with *fans* as men with swords and sometimes do more execution with them. To the end, therefore, that ladies may be entire mistress of the weapon they bear, I have erected an Academy for the training of young women in the exercise of the *fan*, according to the most fashionable airs and notions that are practiced at court. The ladies who carry *fans* under me are exercised by the following words of command: Handle your *fan*, Unfurl your *fan*, Discharge your *fan*, Ground your *fan*, Recover your *fan*, Flutter your *fan*. By the right observation of the few plain words of command, a woman of tolerable genius who will apply herself for the space of one year shall be able to give her *fan* all the graces that can possibly enter into the modish little machine.

There is an infinite variety of motions to be made use of in the flutter of

Figure 544. Fan Print Commemorating the Balloon Ascension of L'Homme and Roger, March 3, 1785

COURTESY, METROPOLITAN MUSEUM OF ART

Figure 545. English Fan, Late 18th Century

This shows very fine filigree sticks and guards.

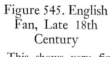

COURTESY, METROPOLITAN MUSEUM OF ART

a *fan*. There is the angry flutter, the modern flutter, the modest flutter, the timorous flutter, the merry flutter and the amorous flutter. There is scarcely an emotion of the mind which does not produce a suitable agitation in the *fan* of a disciplined lady. I know well whether she laughs, frowns, or blushes. I have seen a *fan* so very angry that it would have been dangerous for the absent lover who provoked it; and at other times so languishing that I have been glad for the lady's sake, that the lover was at a certain distance from it.

A letter written by Madame de Staël to a friend sets forth with emphasis unmistakable the great importance of the fan and its management:

Let us picture to ourselves a most charming woman, splendidly dressed, graceful and gracious to the highest degree; yet with all these advantages if she manages her *fan* in a bourgeoise way, she may at any moment become a laughing stock. There are many ways of playing with that precious appendage that by mere movement of the *fan* one can tell a princess from a countess, a marchioness from a plebian. And then it imparts such gracefulness to those who know how to manage it; twisting, closing, spreading, rising, or falling according to circumstances.

We are told that Madame de Staël never acquired the art of using her fan and therefore never carried one; she chose in its place a spray of leaves with which to occupy her fingers! Charles Blanc, in his *Art in Ornament and Dress*, says:

> In all the paraphernalia of the lovliest and best-dressed woman in the world, there is no ornament with which she can produce so great an effect.

As early as 1732 fanmakers were setting up their shops in America. Boston was the center of the trade, and women within a wide radius were earning their livelihood by fanmaking, and mending and painting them as well. Fan mounters came to town and established their little shops near the Common. One advertisement tells of the arrival of such a dealer in fans, and adds:

> He likewise hath a large Sortment of curious mounts which he will dispose of very reasonably, not proposing to stay long in these Parts.

Colonial women at this time were carrying their fans with all the grace and charm of their cousins across the Atlantic.

The French Revolution changed the tide of many fashions. With these somber days the fan was deprived of a measure of its elegance but not of its popularity. It grew smaller, and gauze and tulle, scented and spangled, took the place of the more expensive decoration. Referring to the contrast in the size of fans at this time, Madame de Genlis, in her *Dictionaire des Etiquettes*, places the cause for the change to the fact that, "in the time when women blushed, when they wished to hide their timidity they sheltered themselves behind large *fans;* now that they blush no longer, that nothing intimidates them, they do not wish to screen their faces, and consequently they carry imperceptable *fans.*" Instead of the charming scenes and fêtes of earlier days, there appeared various emblems and decorations suggesting republican ideas then prevalent— figures of Liberty, the letters "R.F.," *Republique Française*, and portraits of popular leaders. In fact, it is said that the fans of this day recorded every phase of the dark period. After the execution of Louis XVI, mourning fans with the leaves decorated in black were carried. Pen and ink drawings, uncolored etchings, and sketches of a sad nature, sometimes taken from the Bible, were depicted. In some of these the portrait of the King and Queen were ingeniously hidden among the leaves of weeping willow trees and could be detected only when the fan was opened to a certain degree. In England also, after the death of George III (1820) mourning fans were carried.

1800-1900

With the coming of Josephine and her "faultless taste," the fan resumed its former reign. The victories of Napoleon now suggested many of the subjects for decoration. Josephine was a lover of all these little

Figure 546. Elaborate Fan of 19th Century

Painted vellum mount and sticks and guards of carved and gilded mother-of-pearl.

accessories of dress—jewels, slippers, turbans, handkerchiefs, fans. The handkerchief and fan were particularly kind to the Empress for they furnished a screen for the one blemish to her beauty—her faulty teeth. It is said that Josephine never appeared in public without her fan.

Among the famous fans of this period are two which Napoleon presented to the Empress Marie Louise as a wedding gift. One of these was set with diamonds, the other with diamonds and rubies. The pair is reported to have cost nine thousand francs. After the restoration of the Bourbon king, Louis XVIII, the court took on great elegance, and fans again were the luxurious note in dress. At this time new artists appeared, who painted fans that rivaled all others. The art of Ingres, Vernet, and Isabey made the French fans of the early nineteenth century the most beautiful of a generation. Figure 546.

About 1828, an effort was made to interest men in fans. The attempt failed, however, possibly because the masculine mind had become convinced that the art of the fan was limited alone to the coquetry of the feminine mind.

From 1830 to 1860 the fan remained of medium size and still continued to play an important role in social life. Painted fans were much in vogue, but the novelty of the period was the autograph fan. These elaborate, folding fans made of paper were carried from 1863 to 1890. It was a popular custom at gala balls for gentlemen to write their names for the various dances upon the leaves of these fans. Sometimes a witty verse was treasured as a souvenir of the ball. During the latter part of the century the most fashionable fans were made of black-and-white lace, lined with silk or satin the exact shade of the dress. They were usually set in handsome ivory sticks. Until the present day each period has produced its fan appropriate for the time. Never, however, has the fan occupied so enviable a place in costume as in the debonair eighteenth and nineteenth centuries.

Twentieth Century

The twentieth century finds the fashion of the fan on the wane. This is in marked contrast to the use of the fan in the East.

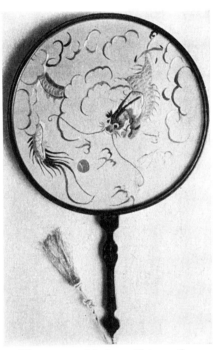

Figure 547. Modern Chinese Fan, Embroidery on Silk

In Japan the fan is as generally used as a garment, and in all seasons and under all conditions it is an inseparable part of costume. Almost every city and province in Japan has its characteristic fan distinguished by its color and ornament and made to please each class from mandarin to peasant.

In the modern western world the fan has lost much of its old-time charm. The lure and romance of the fan, fan play, and fan coquetry are a part of the fascinating charms of other days, long past. The fans of the twentieth century are wholly utilitarian, convenient objects for service on a hot day. They are useful rather than luxurious, and no longer considered an indispensable part of costume. Strange to say, however, the practical fans of this great age follow, in general, the centuries-old pattern used by the ancient Greeks and Romans—the simple leaf patterns. The serviceable palm-leaf and other Chinese and Japanese makes are the popular fans of this very practical century.

REFERENCES

Blanc, Charles, *Art in Ornament and Dress*, p. 187.
Blondel, M. S., *History of Fans*.
Boehn, Max von, *Modes and Manners; Ornaments*, Chapter 2.
Earle, Alice Morse, *Two Centuries of Costume in America*.
Evans, Mary, *Costume Throughout the Ages*, pp. 9, 286.
Encyclopedia Britannica, Vol. VIII.
Flory, M. A., *A Book about Fans; the History of Fans and Fan-Painting*.
Johnson, Harold, *Private Life of the Romans*, p. 266.
New International Encyclopedia, Vol. VIII.
Peterson's Fashion Magazine, Volume of 1863.
Rhead, G. W., *History of the Fan*.
Uzanne, Louis O., *The Fan*.

CHAPTER 34

The Muff

A coxcomb, a fop, a dainty milk-sop;
Who, essence'd and dizen'd from bottom to top,
Looks just like a doll for a milliner's shop.
A thing full of prate, and pride and conceit;
　　All fashion, no weight;
Who shrugs and takes snuff; and carries a *muff*,
A minnikin, finicking, French powder-puff!

　　　　"Isaac Bickerstaff," character in the comic opera,
　　　　　　　　　　Lionel and Clarissa, 1760

IN the long list of accessories of costume there are two especially marked with the charm of femininity—the fan and the muff. Throughout its many changes in size, material, and shape, the muff has long been a favored detail of woman's dress. But during the seventeenth and eighteenth centuries its usefulness and charm so appealed to the masculine world that it was immediately adopted and worn by swanky gentlemen of that day.

1500-1600

The history of the muff follows the usual rule in fashionable costume accessories—it was first the exclusive property of kings, queens, and others of highest rank. Muffs appeared in Italy as early as 1499. These first Venetian muffs were small, made of a single piece of velvet, brocade, or silk and lined with fur. Though the fifteenth century marks the appearance of the first muffs, their general popularity was reserved for the sixteenth, seventeenth, and eighteenth centuries. Muffs first appeared in France about 1550 and were called *countenances*. These early muffs were carried only by women of rank and were especially fashionable during the reign of Charles IX (1560-74). Many of the bourgeois at this time, in imitation of their more fortunate sisters, made themselves muffs of various inexpensive materials. The religious wars then overshadowing France brought edict after edict from the King in his effort to control extravagance in dress. Among the royal commands there went forth the order permitting the bourgeois to carry only black muffs, while ladies of rank were privileged to continue the use of various colors. The records of the period bear witness, however, that women gave little heed to the King's decree and continued to wear muffs as they chose.

1600-1700

The first authentic record of an English muff is that in an engraving by Caspar Rutz, 1588. This pictures an English woman of rank wearing a small muff suspended on a long chain attached to her girdle. Figure 548.

Then, during the next century (1600), fashionable gentlemen of the court of Charles I and Charles II developed a new fashion, a pair of muffs! These were in the form of long, loose cuffs attached to the coat sleeves, providing a separate covering for each hand. This led to the fashion of *muffetees*, a small muff for each wrist. These were made of either fur or worsted materials of various colors and were especially fashionable dur-

Figure 548. English Lady Wearing the Early Muff Suspended from the Girdle, 1588

From an old engraving.

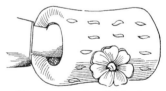

ing the reign of Queen Anne. By 1663, small, single muffs were again the mode and were being carried by both men and women in England and France. They were attached by a cord to a button of the coat or suspended by a ribbon about the neck. The fur was turned inside at

Figure 549. Small Muffs, 1689-94

First, yellow silk muff, thickly wadded and edged with black fur; second, white fur muff, decorated with black tails and blue bow.

this time because of the belief that it kept the hands beautifully soft and white.

In France, while the vogue for the small muff was at its height, a surprise entered upon the fashion stage. During the reign of Louis XIV (1643-1715), every lady who prided herself upon her correct appearance carried a lively little muff dog. These diminutive creatures were concealed within the cosy depths of milady's muff. Modish women, as well

PLATE XLVI. Mrs. Siddons ....*Gainsborough*

This portrait of the famous lady of the stage pictures the fashionable fur muff of the period.

as men, are said to have passed the time when on the promenade in feeding dainty bits of sweets to these little creatures and in lavishing endearing phrases upon them. Special muffs for the purpose are said to have

been made at the shop of Demoiselle Guerin in the Rue de Bac, Paris. Women of the great middle class who could not avail themselves of fine fur muffs, carried those made of cat and dog skins costing the modest price of fifteen or twenty francs. Muffs remained small, with little change in form until about 1692 when they began to grow larger. Figure 549.

1700-1800

With the coming of Louis XV to the throne of France (1715) there was no abatement in the extravagance of the previous reign. Fashions continued to be set by the court leaders. At this time the muff developed into an object of great beauty. It was made of handsome fur whose richness and color furnished a very becoming note to the wearer. The many charming women who were carried about in sedan chairs or filled the walk at Versailles during the visiting hour took this occasion to parade their beautiful muffs of fur.

Figure 550. The Man's Muff, 1787

After Jacquemin.

During the following reign, that of Louis XVI, women decreed that fur should be discarded and muffs should be made of cloth. This caused great excitement among the furriers, who at once petitioned the Pope asking that anyone wearing a cloth muff be excommunicated. The petition, however, was denied. All manner of schemes were played upon the public to coax, cajole, or force women to give up the cloth muff. Nothing availed. Happily someone suggested bribing the headsman of the guillotine to carry a cloth muff on the day of execution. This alone stayed the march of the new mode! Women immediately shrank from such an association, and, to the great joy of the furriers, fur returned to "its place in the sun." At this time muffs were carried at all seasons, in warm as well as cold weather, when walking or driving, and particularly

PLATE XLVII. Miss Farren ....*Raeburn*

In the early 19th century large muffs of fine fur decorated with a knot of ribbon or a nosegay were especially favored during the summer months.

when attending the fashionable balls of the day. During this century the muff attained a place of real dignity and distinction in the dress of gentlemen. Figure 550. Frenchmen wore muffs of great beauty, many of them elaborate with frills of lace and ribbon. Englishmen, in general, preferred those more plain, though a few followed the French fashion. All Englishmen of high office carried their muffs. Dr. Joseph Tucker, dean of Gloucester, wore his muff in the cathedral; Francis, second Earl of Guilford, Charles James Fox, Dr. Samuel Parr, and others famous in the annals of English life carried their muffs. Horace Walpole, who also carried a muff, is said to have found great pleasure in presenting muffs as gifts to his friends. On Christmas Eve, 1764, he wrote to George Montague, "I send you a decent smallish muff, that you may put in your pocket, and it cost but fourteen shillings." The inimitable Pepys records that he took his "wife's last year's muff for my own wearing."

Although the American colonies were naturally in direct line for the fashions from England, it is a severe strain upon the imagination to picture our sturdy forebears carrying the fashionable muff. The muff was, nevertheless, believed to lend an air of great dignity to the wearer; consequently, churchmen, judges, and doctors—all carried the muff! The *Boston News Letter* of March 5, 1715, announces:

> Any man that took up a man's *muff* dropt on the Lord's Day between old meeting house and the South are desired to bring it to the Printer's office and shall be rewarded.

These early muffs were made of rich materials trimmed with gold and silver lace and bows of ribbon. Later, the all-fur muff came to be the popular choice and continued to about 1780. At this time the fashion for muffs in gentlemen's dress gradually declined, though it lingered for a time with men of eccentric taste. Women's muffs up to 1780 were small and often made of silk and satin beautifully embroidered and trimmed with bows of ribbon. Fur or feather muffs were also worn.

1800-1900

From 1790 on, women's muffs gradually grew larger, reaching their largest size about 1810. They were now barrel shaped, of huge proportions, being large enough to conceal the arms to the elbows. Fox, sable, and squirrel were the favorite furs, while flat cloth and velvet, fur-trimmed, were the modish, less expensive materials. The fashionable Roxburgh muff of this period was white satin trimmed with swans'-down. Many of the muffs of this and later days were decorated with tiny rosettes of ribbon, sprigs of artificial flowers, ribbon with paste buckles, and hung with a multitude of tails. Among the famous portraits in which the muff plays an important role is "Miss Farren" by Lawrence. PLATE

PLATE XLVIII. Madame Molé Raymond.........................*Lebrun*

The large, barrel-shaped muff, in its heyday about 1810, added an enviable charm to feminine costume.

461

XLVII. It was the good fortune of Lawrence to have as his model one of the most beautiful women in England and a popular actress. The huge muff with its bow of ribbon is a striking example of the style in vogue at this period. The portrait of the charming actress of the *Comédie Français*, Madame Molé Raymond, likewise pictures the muff in this heyday of its popularity. PLATE XLVIII.

Twentieth Century

Feminine whims from this time forth have dictated the styles in muffs. In 1830, muffs of chinchilla and fox, moderate in size, were popular; these were frequently worn with straw hats and slippers. About 1870, muffs came to be very small—tiny, enveloping shapes only big enough to protect the two hands. Those of Russian sable were especially prized. These were very expensive, being made entirely of the tails of these little animals. In the early years of the twentieth century muffs grew very large and flat, resembling pillowlike envelopes. Fine furs, such as fox, sable, lynx, squirrel, mink, and ermine, were fashionable. Materials of velvet, silk, and flat cloth, combined with satin, ribbon, and fur, though not so costly were equally popular. Until the year 1924 muffs had always, since their introduction in 1500, been in style. By that year the general use of the motorcar had overtaken the world and muffs disappeared. Though fashion experts have from time to time attempted to lead the fashion parade with handsome muffs, their following up to the fall of 1939 had been negligible.

The coming of the motorcar has brought about many changes in dress. The fashion for muffs developed out of a real need for warmth, which, with our well-heated cars, scarcely exists today. But the wheel of fashion turns, forever turns, and the little muff, always a fascinating subject for designers, may in time to come regain its former high command in the world of dress.

REFERENCES

Cole, George S., *Dictionary of Dry Goods*, p. 263.
Cosmopolitan Magazine, Vol. 26, 1898-99.
Dooley, William H., *Clothing and Style*, p. 155.
Earle, Alice Morse, *Two Centuries of Costume in America*.
Elite Styles, October, November, 1921.
Ellsworth, Evelyn Peters, *Textiles and Costume Design*, p. 25.
Harper's Weekly, February 6, 1909.
Rhead, G. W., *Chats on Costume*, p. 104.

CHAPTER 35

The Mirror

Behavior is a *mirror* in which everyone shows his image.
GOETHE, *Die Wahlverwandtschaften*

THE first glimpse of her mirrored reflection caught by primitive woman in the still waters of pools and lakes is responsible for all the later magic of the looking glass. This primitive urge for seeing ourselves soon led to the discovery of a polished metal surface, and this paved the way for that

Figure 551. Egyptian Necklace, and Mirror

With favored lotus pattern in handle, 2000-1788 B.C.

Figure 552. Bronze Mirror

Handle blue marble with tip of black, Egyptian, XII Dynasty.

indispensable modern accessory, the mirror. After centuries of metal reflectors the genius of man finally discovered the mirror of glass, which, with its later refinements, has been passed on to the modern world.

The use of man-made mirrors is of great antiquity. Among the later Egyptians the mirror was one of the principal articles of the toilet. It was made of copper or mixed metals, and these mirror plates were capable of being polished to an amazingly high luster. Today, after centuries of burial, many of those found in the ancient tombs of Thebes have been partially repolished. Egyptian mirrors were usually round, oval, or pear shaped, inserted in handles of ivory, wood, faience, or metal. These

handles were often of beautiful design. Some represented the conventional form of the lotus, others, a column ornamented with a bird or other form. Figure 551. Judging from the number recovered, a favorite type of handle was that of a figure upholding the mirror. The same type of metal mirror was used by the Israelites, who doubtless carried them from Egypt. We read of the early Hebrews using mirrors of brass. When Moses made brazen vessels for the tabernacle, he commanded the women of Israel to surrender their hand mirrors for this purpose:

And he made the laver of brass, and the foot of it of brass, of the *looking-glasses* of the women assembled at the door of the congregation.

Figure 553. Greek Figure with Mirror
After Hope.

Mirrors of bronze were commonly used by the ancient Greeks. It is said that Praxiteles, the great sculptor of 328 B.C., had discovered the beauty of polished metals and maintained a school where he taught the art of polishing silver for mirrors. Greek mirrors may be divided into two classes—disk mirrors and box mirrors. Disk mirrors were highly polished on one side only; the reverse was usually engraved or decorated with designs in relief work. Disk mirrors with handles were very general. In many of these the handle was so constructed that it served as a support or foot so that the mirror could be set upon a table. Figure 554. The box mirrors were formed of two disks which could be easily fitted together. The lower disk was highly polished, serving as the mirror proper, while the upper disk was used as a cover to protect the polished surface. Instances have been found in which the cover was hinged to the lower disk. These two disks when fitted together formed a kind of round box; hence the name "box mirror." Figure 555.

Among the Etruscans and Romans, the manufacture of mirrors was a flourishing business. These people used every kind of metal that would polish. The Etruscans employed a higher grade of bronze than that used in antiquity, one which was nineteen or twenty times richer in tin. A marked characteristic of the Etruscan mirror is the engraved work which decorates the back. Figure 556. The

Figure 554. Greek Mirror
Figure supporting disk, 480-460 B.C.

Romans overlaid the bronze surface of their mirrors with silver. In the days of Pompey, gold came to be more popular than silver, and these mirrors were often enriched with chased work, set with precious stones. So great was the "craze" for golden mirrors that even the maidservants made their demands and would have nothing but mirrors of gold.

Figure 555. Greek Box Mirror with Cover, Bronze, 5th Century B.C.

Middle Ages

All through the period of the Middle Ages woman was generally content with her little hand mirror of polished metal. Not until 1284 was there a change in this favored article of the toilet. By-and-by experiments in pouring molten metal upon hot plates of glass were made. The resulting mirrors were very small but at that time there was no way of making large pieces of glass for this purpose. In Venice, in 1300, glass mirrors made their bow to the world! These first glass mirrors were very crude, especially when compared with those of later date. Naturally these useful little ornaments were the coveted possession of the wealthy. Women wore them as ornaments suspended about the neck or attached to the girdle. Men carried swords with little mirrors set in the hilt. Pres-

Figure 556. Mirror Back

Bronze, engraved with toilet scene, Greek or Etruscan, 5th century.

ently little mirrors were set in cases of ivory and silver and could be carried in the pocket. These were no sooner inaugurated than they captured the fashion world. Now everyone carried the pocket mirror! Charles V of France possessed a number of great value. All French women during the sixteenth century carried these mirrors concealed in their bags or purses. So general was their use that not only ladies of the court, but peasant girls as well indulged in this attractive luxury. In early 1400, according to the Duc de Berry, men carried these little pocket mirrors concealed in silken cases. These were later made to open like a book. They were often very beautiful, made of silk, ivory, and other costly materials.

1500-1900

At her death in 1547, a little mirror concealed in "a book with an embroidered cover" was among the possessions of Anne of Brittany. Queen Margaret of Spain, in 1547 owned a pocket mirror worth sixty ducats.* The dandies of the court of Henry III of France carried their mirrors in book form in the right breeches pocket, where they were easily accessible for any occasion.

The pocket mirror was in general use as a costume accessory up to the middle of the seventeenth century. About this time hanging mirrors for the wall, giving a larger reflection, began to be made. It was not, however, until 1673 that the manufacture of mirrors was introduced into England. In 1688, a French craftsman named Louis Lucas discovered a method of casting glass for mirrors. Up to this time blown glass had been used. This discovery was the beginning of a new era, and the manufacture of mirrors spread from Europe to America. The mirror was now not only a personal ornament but a useful and highly decorative unit in the home and in public buildings. When so used it was not generally treated as a movable object but as an integral part of the room. The great Hall of Mirrors at Versailles is an illustrious example of the mirror being incorporated into the paneling of an interior. After the rise of the mirror to such distinction, the little pocket mirror subsided into a purely utilitarian costume accessory.

Figure 557.
Mirror from the Ms. *Romance of Renaud*

Printed in the 15th century and now preserved in the Library of the Arsenal of Paris (No. 224).

In this twentieth century, every vanity case, purse, or bag turned out by a manufacturer is fitted with this indispensable accessory. By the use of this little mirror milady of the modern world removes the ravages of heat, cold, rain, hurry, worry, even as did her sister of two thousand years ago.

REFERENCES

Boehn, Max von, *Modes and Manners; Ornaments*, Chapter VI.
Child, Theodore, *Wimples and Crisping Pins*, pp. 62, 203.
Earle, Alice Morse, *Two Centuries of Costume in America*, Vol. I.
Guhl and Kuhner, *Life of the Greeks and Romans*.
Kelly and Schwabe, *Historic Costume*.
Lester, Katherine Morris, *Historic Costume*, pp. 36, 75, 80, 130.
New International Encyclopedia, Vol. 15.

---

* European coin ranging in value from about $.83 to $2.25.

Part VI

ACCESSORIES USED ON THE COSTUME

CHAPTER 36

Buttons

Now old Tredgortha's dead and gone,
We ne'er shall see him more;
He used to wear an old grey coat,
All *buttoned* down before.

RUPERT, Lines leading the list of John
Tredgortha's works in Bibloi-
theca Staffordiensis, 1894.

BUTTONS began to appear during the late centuries of that long period known as the Dark Ages. At this time the greatest transition in costume, the change from the loose-flowing dress of the ancients to the fitted garment of modern times, was gradually taking place. The twelfth century marks definitely the beginning of the fitted garment, and closely thereafter followed that almost indispensable accessory of modern dress—the button.

Because the garments of the ancients, loose robes and enveloping mantles, were not fitted, strings,

Figure 558. Bone Buttons

Egyptian, XX Dynasty.

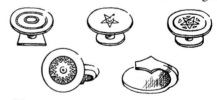

Figure 559. Studs of the Bronze Age

After Racinet.

girdles, and, if need be, thorns and pegs of wood or bone were sufficient to hold them in place. It is undoubtedly true, however, that a kind of button was not only known to these ancient people but to prehistoric man as well. Prehistoric bone buttons have been found. Figure 558. Buttons, and studs of bronze with the upper button marked in simple design, are definitely linked with the Bronze Age. Figure 559. These bronze studs are the same which the modern world uses as a fastening for starched linens. Excavations made in Egypt reveal that a form of button was used as a fastening in that day. Figure 560. It appears, however, that the

470

marking upon these buttons are not Egyptian, and, consequently, they are believed to have been carried into Egypt by immigrants. They date between the VI and XIX Dynasties (2500-1300 B.C.).

Figure 560. Primitive Dress Ornaments

The early fibulae used by the Greeks for fastening the sleeve of the chiton were simple pins resembling the modern safety pin. These were followed by disks of gold and bronze with pins beneath. At a later day, buttons were used instead of these fibulae. Among the numerous treasures unearthed by Dr. Schliemann at Mycenae in 1876 were many ornamental disks of gold, which in earliest times were fastened to the Greek dress, thereby adding a note of splendor to the costume. A Greek button made of wood covered with embossed gold was also found. If not used to fasten garments it probably belonged to the large class of ornamental disks. Figure 561.

Figure 561. Greek Button

Like the Greeks, the luxury-loving Romans are known to have worn handsome jeweled buttons to some extent as fastenings. These, however, must have been rare, as indicated in the following lines:

> Rare as the *button* of a Roman breeches,
> In antiquarian eyes surpasses riches.

> JOHN WALCOTT, M.P., *Peter's Prophesy*

Middle Ages

The word "button" is derived from the French *bouton*, meaning "any round thing, a bud, a knob, or a projection." The first buttons in fashion-

Figure 562. Earliest Types of Buttons Seen on Monumental Effigies

Large button with depressed center, embossed button, and large button with small metal bosses.

Figure 563. Pyramidal and Half-Sphere Buttons, 1300

From upper left: Bronze button, each face decorated with a trefoil; bronze button. Lower: Wooden form covered with sheet brass; silk-covered wooden form.

Figure 564. A Lady at Sawtrey, Hampshire, 1404

able use during the interesting period of the Middle Ages were merely ornamental. These were disks or projections fastened to the garment. They are seen closely set down the sleeve from shoulder to elbow or from elbow to wrist. For the fastening of garments at this time, "points" or lacings with metal tips continued to be used. Then, about 1300, the coming of the fitted garment brought buttons into more practical prominence. No doubt some genius passing the lace through a small slit saw that a button could likewise be passed through an opening, and lo! the buttonhole was born. The button and buttonhole were new, but the popularity of this fastening grew apace. They were now set down the front of the long, fitted tunic and the cottehardie. In the *Romance of Sir Degrevant*, the writer says of the dress of the Earl's daughter—"to tell her *botennes* was toore." Planché, commenting on this, says that "toore" means *dure*, hard; he then adds: "In other words to count her buttons was too much trouble."

The earliest types of button seen upon monumental effigies were circular in shape, sometimes with depressed centers and frequently showing ornamental bosses. Figure 562. Other designs, especially the half sphere and pyramidal shapes, are often seen upon effigies of 1300. In Figure 563 are, first, two drawings after bronze buttons of the fourteenth century which had been dredged up from the bottom of the Thames; secondly, a wooden form, the face of which was covered with a thin sheet of brass, the shank made of catgut; and thirdly, a wooden button, probably worked over with silk.* These effigies of the late twelfth, thirteenth, and fourteenth centuries are a fascinating source of authentic information with reference to the fashion in buttons. In the church of St. Mary at King's Lynn is the brass of John Brandon and his two wives (1364). Here one may see a vest of the period supporting forty buttons from the elbow to the hand. Numerous examples of the close-fitting sleeve with buttons set in this fashion are seen in the

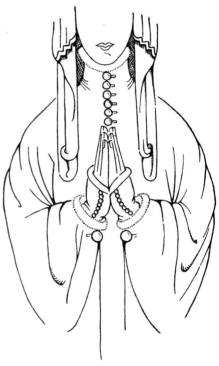

Figure 565. From a Brass of 1400, Tilbrook Church, Bedfordshire

illuminations and effigies of this early date. In a brass at Sawtrey, Hampshire, dated 1414, the sleeves, which extend over the hand, show a closely set row of buttons from elbow to the sleeve opening. Figure 564. A poem dated not later than 1300 suggests this same fashion:

> *Botones* azur'd [azure blue] wor ilke ane
> From his elboth to his hand.

Another brass dating 1400 shows large buttons extending well up under the chin. Figure 565. The undersleeves reach to the knuckles and are ornamented with buttons set touching one another. Other figures of the period show the tunic with buttons extending down the entire length of the front.

---

* Fairholt, F. W., *Costume in England*.

Though the earliest buttons were probably bronze or bone the popularity of the new fashion set the artisans to work, and before long gold

buttons, silk-covered buttons, and others of ornamental design were being made. By 1500, buttons were the height of the mode, as seen in the costumes of both men and women. At this period buttons of diamonds and other precious stones combined with gold are frequently mentioned.

As with all novelties in costume the

Figure 566. Gold Renaissance Buttons, Enameled and Set with Pearls

Figure 567. Renaissance Button
From a portrait.

most handsome buttons were at first the privilege of kings, queens, and other members of the various courts. Francis I (1515-47) ordered from his jeweler 13,400 gold buttons which were to be set upon a black, velvet suit. Henry VIII of England (1509-47) exhibited the same pride in his buttons. His famous portrait by Holbein shows the doublet set with jeweled buttons which are the same in pattern as the rings he wears. Hans Meinhard von Schonberg, a wealthy citizen, owned forty-two gold doublet buttons, each set with seven diamonds. An interesting reference to these jeweled buttons is given in a record of the fifteenth century:

> For one set of twenty-five golden *buttons*, each *button* with four pearls surrounding a diamond, purchased from Symon de Damputart . . . each *button* at the price of eight gold crowns; total, 200 gold pieces.

Indeed, jeweled buttons were the buttons par excellence during the sixteenth and seventeenth centuries! Four-dozen gold buttons each set with a seed pearl ornamented a pair of gloves presented by a lady of the court to Queen Elizabeth. The portrait of Sir Walter Raleigh well illus-

PLATE XLIX. Sir Walter Raleigh

The handsome busked doublet is ornamented with a closely set row of costly buttons.
Note the pearl earrings.

trates the vogue for handsome buttons. Here a row of costly buttons, closely set, extends down the front of the handsome busked doublet. PLATE XLIX.

All through the sixteenth century buttons were in their heyday. Gold and jeweled buttons were reserved for the few, but paste buttons almost excelling the finest jewels in luster were also worn. The usual buttons turned out by artisans were large, wooden molds worked over with silk. Gradually according to the *Annals* of Stow, "The very best sort" began wearing buttons "of the same stuffe, their doublets, coats, or jerkins were made of." These, no doubt, were all covered buttons. Stow continues to give reliable information on the use of buttons in the sixteenth century:

Many very honorable personages, and others, as well women and men, did weare borders of great Christall *buttons* about their cappes, and hatbands, as a worthy garment, to distinguish betweene the Gentry and others. But about the ten yeere of Queen Elizabeth [1567-8] many young citizens and others began to weare Christall *buttons* upon their doublets, coats, and Jerkins, and then the former wearing of borders and hatbands, set with Christall *buttons* ceased. And within a few yeeres after, began the general wearing of *buttons*, of thread, silke, haire, and of gold and silver thread.

STOW, *Annals of England*

Toward the end of the century a kind of metal button called *fers* was used profusely as ornamental disks on the handsome slashed and puffed costumes of both men and women. The increase in accessories of dress led to the employment of men, women, and children in the making of these various ornaments, among which the elaborate buttons were conspicuous.

1600-1700

Under Louis XIII (1610-43) many ornamental buttons adorned the fashionable doublet, and later, under Louis XIV (1643-1715) buttons were the only jewelry worn by men. Louis XIV wore buttons which indeed were veritable jewels. "He sank beneath the weight of them," wrote Saint Simon. In 1683 the studs of his waistcoat, which ran up in value to 360,000 francs, were set with diamonds and other precious gems. In 1687 he purchased a set of twenty-one coat buttons, each a single diamond, costing the exorbitant sum of 377,500 francs. When he was six years old he owned a waistcoat with thirty-one ruby buttons. In England during the same century buttons were equally popular. Not only were they worn upon the handsome doublets and coats but they also ornamented the handkerchiefs of the day. "Handkerchief buttons," says

Planché, "was one of the crys of London in the time of Charles I." Among the ornate buttons of this period is one pictured by Fairholt having a face of silver with the body of blue glaze. Figure 568. Writing in his diary under date of July 1, 1660, the incomparable Pepys has a word to say about fashionable buttons:

> This morning came home my fine camlet cloak with gold *buttons* and a suit which cost me much money, and I pray God to make me able to pay for it.

Figure 568. Silver-faced Button with Body of Blue Glaze

In America the fashions in buttons kept pace with the rest of the world. On the finest Holland shirts as well as those of canvas, buttons of pewter and silver were used. The colonial Puritans, however, wore no buttons at all, for they considered this a "sign of vanity." In place of buttons, hooks and eyes were used. It is interesting to note further that buttons were used as a medium of trade in bartering with the Indians. In 1653, John Eliot ordered three gross of pewter buttons for traffic with the Indians. Robert Keayne, of Boston, writing in the same year, said repeatedly that a "haynous offense" of his had been selling buttons at too large a profit—that they were "gold" buttons and he had sold them in Boston for a shilling and nine pence each, when they had cost him two shillings a dozen in London. During the eighteenth century a large variety of magnificent buttons were worn on the dress of colonial gentlemen. Fashionable button-makers of the day covered button molds with the cloth of the coat, and then embroidered the surface with silk, gilt, steel beads, and spangles.

Figure 569. Buttons of the 18th Century

1700-1800

In 1700 the demand for buttons was enormous. They were used largely as ornament with trimmings of braid. The gentlemen's full-skirted coats of the period were set with buttons down the front, cuffs were ornamented with braid and buttons, and the pocket slits, either vertical or horizontal, were finished with buttons and loops of braid. At one period the full-skirted coats were gathered at each side into fan-shaped pleats radiating from the hip, and this point was finished with a button. Figure 570. Later in the century the divided skirt of the coat was edged with buttons. In order that each side of the opening be nicely balanced, the buttons on one side and the braid on the other were set upon bands of em-

broidery exactly alike. The costume of men was very handsome and buttons continued to be important items. By 1777, the buttons of the coat were very large, sometimes measuring one and three-fourths inches across. They were at one time adorned with miniature heads in profile of persons of distinction. These profiles were usually mounted on black silk or satin and edged with a rim of tin. Figure 571. Ever and again new designs entered the fashion field. "Picture buttons" were among the most popular. These were designs with trees, figures, and flowers cut from ivory or bone in various degrees of relief and mounted against

Figure 570. Time of Charles I. Fan-pleated Coat Skirt with Hip Button

COURTESY, METROPOLITAN MUSEUM OF ART

Figure 571. French Portrait Buttons, 1790

Upper row, left to right: C. de Lameth, Mirabeau, Necker; lower row: La Fayette, Louis XVI, d'Aiguillon.

a dark background. Others were designed in white metal against a gilt ground. Toward the end of the century metal buttons assumed the shape of the ancient pyramids, and were engraved with meaningless markings suggesting hieroglyphics. During the Revolutionary period, buttons were made of cloth, surrounded by a plain, copper-gilt ring.

1800-1900

By 1805, metal buttons, which had not been seen for a long time, were more fashionable than ever. Figure 572. A smart young man was supposed to wear them on his coat, his breeches, his waistcoat, and his gaiters. The lapels of his coat usually carried six or eight; the breeches, as a rule, had three at the side of each knee; and the remaining number were dispersed throughout other parts of the costume. The most exclusive style demanded that five- or six-dozen buttons should be worn. By

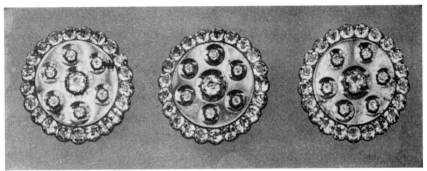

Figure 572. Buttons, Cut Steel Set with Paste, French, 18th Century

1821 gold buttons were again in style. An item appeared at this time reading, "Some dandies have gold buttons made for them." The close-fitting kerseymere trousers of this century had mother-of-pearl buttons set just above the ankle. Figure 573. About the middle of this period metal buttons with colored stones were the modish fastening for the front of milady's bodice, and these were followed by others of steel and oxidized silver.

The nineteenth century is important in the history of the button, for during this period many ingenious inventions appeared, and the button began to be manufactured on a large scale. The shell button with a metal shank was invented in 1807 by a Dane, B. Sander, who moved from Copenhagen to Birmingham, England, which city was then taking the lead as a button manufacturing center. The metal shank was soon replaced by a layer of cotton cloth secured to the back of the button by a metal plate, and by this it was sewed to the garment. By the end of the century, however, Fashion looked with less favor upon both these types and returned to the earlier two- and four-hole buttons. About 1812, "horn" buttons made from the hooves of animals were introduced. These were also made at Birmingham. Materials quickly followed one another until the variety in buttons offered the public was almost without limit. Vegetable ivory was a material greatly favored because it could be readily turned upon the lathe and easily dyed. This is the fruit of the South American coroza nut; it resembles true ivory, though somewhat softer. The manufacture of buttons from this material was introduced into the United States in 1859. The buttons used in modern suits, overcoats, and cloaks are generally made of vegetable ivory. Glass and porcelain buttons are still other types that have gained popularity. Metal buttons have also had a wide field and range all the way from trouser buttons stamped out of iron to the various types of brass buttons seen on uniforms and to the more handsome silver or gold buttons.

The year 1826 is conspicuous in button history, for it definitely marks the period when the manufacture of buttons began in America. According to the story, the good wife of Samuel Williston, a storekeeper in East Hampshire, Massachusetts, is responsible for the industry. Like a dutiful wife she helped to augment the family income by covering wooden button molds by hand. In this way she earned many extra pennies. From this humble beginning she gradually worked out a machine for covering buttons which was the first used in this country. By degrees an industry developed, and soon the Williston factories were credited with making half the buttons of the world.

The manufacture of pearl buttons was introduced into the United States about 1885. At first the raw material was imported from China, but during the last years of the century the manufacture was greatly stimulated by the discovery of fresh-water mollusks in the Mississippi River. These are admirably adapted to button manufacture. The plastic button is probably the most recent to be added to the button list. The smallest buttons made are shoe buttons, glove buttons, and small waist buttons. The cheapest in modern manufacture are those known as composition buttons. These are made of such materials as clay, ground slate, and similar substances molded into form with shellac as a binder.

Twentieth Century

Though the button in modern dress is usually employed as a fastening, it persists in some instances only as an ornament, a vestige of its former usefulness. The buttons often seen upon the sleeves of men's coats are among these interesting survivals. In the days of lace cuffs and cravats, the large coat cuff, supplied with braid and buttons, was turned back to display the handsome lace frills. In case milord wished to protect his lace, the coat cuffs could be turned down over the frill and buttoned. These buttons on the modern coat sleeve serve as reminders of this former custom. The buttons used as mere ornaments on the knee trousers of young lads formerly served a useful purpose. The very tight-fitting knee trousers of the eighteenth century were frequently finished with button and buttonhole. By unbuttoning the knee buttons they could more readily be put off and on. Again, the buttons at the back of a man's cutaway coat at the waistline remain as a survivor of the time when men looped up their coattails when traveling by horseback. A small loop of braid sewed to the edge of each coattail made it a very simple matter to keep them from being sat upon or creased.

One of the peculiarities in the use of the button as a fastening is the difference in its position in masculine and feminine dress. Milady's habit always buttons from right to left, while milord fastens his in the reverse order—from left to right. And now the reason for this extraordinary custom! It is believed that originally all garments fastened from right to left. In the early days, however, when man was engaged in the hunt and chase, and later, when wielding the sword as a knight, he invariably drew his weapon with his right hand from the left side. With the garment fastened, the right edge over the left, his quick action was greatly hindered. This awkward situation changed the order of fastening the garment, and it was reversed. For this reason men's coats continue to button from left to right, while women's keep to the original form of right to left.

Figure 573. Buttons in Fashionable Masculine Dress, 1816-26

Among the Chinese, buttons have had a peculiar symbolic interest. Five buttons were usually worn on the coat fronts, each a reminder of the five great virtues emphasized by Confucius—Humility, Justice, Order, Prudence, Rectitude. When worn upon the peak of the Chinese hat, the rank was indicated by the material of which the button was made. A ruby button indicated the highest rank; a coral, the second; the third, a sapphire; the fourth, lapis lazuli; fifth, crystal; sixth, white stone; seventh, plain gold; eighth and ninth, differently marked gold.

Since the twelfth century, when costume began to be fitted, buttons, at first ornamental, then useful, have continued to shift from one to the other through the centuries. Woman's dress of the twentieth century has been so designed as to be almost independent of buttons as practical fastenings. Dresses are slipped on over the head, snapped, or fastened by zippers; coats are wrapped round or caught with few buttons, a belt, or a girdle. Although today the button is used generally as an inconspicuous fastening for clothes, sometimes it is made the most conspicuous note in the costume. In this case, as in the days of its earliest popularity, it is often ornamental rather than useful. Again and again through the centuries it has added a pleasing note to sleeves or cuffs, or even formed a continuous line of ornament down the front of garments. Thus does history repeat itself.

In the modern world milady holds a monopoly on all those luxuries in dress which formerly bolstered up the vanity of gentlemen of fashion. Lace, ribbon, embroidery, braid, tassel, fringe, and, indeed, all but buttons have disappeared from the dress of men. The more elegant details now belong distinctly to the feminine world, while buttons remain one of the few ornaments permitted the sober garb of gentlemen.

REFERENCES

Boutell, Charles, *The Monumental Brasses of England.*
Brereton, Lt. Col. F. S., *Clothing.* The Essentials of Life Series.
Blanc, Charles, *Art in Ornament and Dress*, pp. 87, 154.
Cole, George S., *Dictionary of Dry Goods*, p. 43.
Dress Decoration and Ornamentation, p. 30, Woman's Institute.
Druitt, Herbert, *A Manual of Costume as Illustrated by Ornamental Brasses.*
Earle, Alice Morse, *Two Centuries of Costume in America*, Vol. I.
New International Encyclopedia, Vol. IV.
Rhead, G. W., *Chats on Costume*, pp. 3, 116.
Sage, Elizabeth, *A Story of Costume*, pp. 3, 116.
Souder, M. Attie, *The Notions Department*, Chapter 9.

CHAPTER 37

Embroidery

Ferne-stitch, finny-stitch, new-stitch, and chain-stitch,
Brave bred-stitch, Fisher-stitch, Irish-stitch and Queen-stitch,
The Spanish-stitch, Rosemary-stitch and mowse-stitch,
The smarting whip-stitch, back-stitch and the cross-stitch
All these are good and these we must allow,
And these are everywhere in practice now.

> From "Praise of the Needle," prefixed to a 1640
> edition of a pattern book called *The Needle's*
> *Excellency* by John Taylor, the "Water Poet."

EMBROIDERY in its most primitive form is one of the oldest of the decorative arts. Use of the bone and wooden needle was probably first discovered in sewing together skins and other stuffs, and it was only a step from this to further decoration of the material with stitches. From this beginning the art of embroidery developed. The first threads were wool, cotton, and flax, then gold and silver. These were later followed by silk. Like the brilliant daubs of color which served to distinguish primitive man from his fellows, so embroidery stitches gratified the desire of later man for marks of social distinction.

The art of embroidery was widely practiced among the ancient Egyptians. Tomb paintings and paintings on temple and palace walls and on the ancient mummy cases would indicate that embroidered fabrics were well known. Moreover fragments of mummy cloth found in upper Egypt in burial places along the Nile, dating from the first to the sixth century, show plain stitches on linen. Other garments show linen worked with wool in tufted loops. Those tunics showing allover patterns, usually pictured as worn by women of rank, resemble modern chintz effects; many appear to have been worked with the needle, while others were probably woven. In the figure of Takushet, Figure 574, the lady wears a sheathlike tunic which molds the figure. The neck is high, the sleeves long and close fitting. The entire surface of the dress is covered as with an embroidery of religious inscriptions and scenes of religious significance. These are incised and then filled in with a silver line. An interesting reference which touches upon the dress of a pharaoh's daughter is found in Psalms XLV: 13, 14, "She shall be brought before the king in a raiment of *needlework*," and "her clothing is of wrought gold."

It is evident that the Egyptians had arrived at perfection in the art of working with gold thread. This gold is supposed to have been beaten out with a hammer, cut into fine ribbons, and rounded. Silver thread was doubtless used in a similar manner, though no mention of silver stuffs appears in the writings of ancient authors. Pliny attributes the idea of using gold thread to Attalus, King of Asia. He states, "To weave cloth with gold thread was the invention of the Asiatic King, Attalus, from whom the name 'Attalic' was derived." After attributing the use of gold thread in weaving to the Asiatic king, he then speaks of the beautiful needlework practiced by the Phrygians, who, he says, "were the first to divine the method of giving the same effect with the needle." Phrygia was a land of gold; so it is not surprising that this precious metal found its way into the needlework of the period. We read of the "purple and fine linen" and note the beautiful designs which edge the tunics and mantles. Figure 575. The Phrygians are believed to have taught the art of gold embroidery to the Egyptians. The Hebrews in captivity learned much of the art, and on leaving Egypt carried this knowledge with them. Allusions are frequently made to "bordered work" and "needle work." In Ezekiel XXVII:7, reference is made to the "fine linen with bordered work from Egypt." Like other arts, embroidery also served as the handmaid of religion. In the making of the tabernacle we read:

Figure 574. Sheathlike Tunic of Tahushet

Covered with an incised pattern which has been filled in with silver, suggesting embroidery.

And thou shall make a hanging for the door of the tent, of blue and purple, and scarlet and fine twisted linen, wrought with *needlework*.

Exodus XXVI: 36

In this early day reference is also made to the gold thread used in needle-work and the manner in which it was prepared:

And they beat the gold into thin plates, and cut it into wires to work it in the blue, and the purple, and in the scarlet, and in the fine linen.

Exodus XXXIX: 3

The ancient Assyrians, Persians, Baby-lonians, and Phoenicians were all familiar with the art of embroidery. Among the oldest records of embroidered design are the Nimroud reliefs in the British museum, dated 884 B.C., picturing the embroidered vestments of King Ashurbanipal and his attendants. The royal robes are heavy with rich embroidery which almost hides the material. Borders of flowers and palm leaves enrich the pattern to such extent that one is held in utter amazement at this evidence of skill on the part of Assyrian women who virtually painted their fragile designs with the needle. Another stone in the same collection pictures the Baby-lonian king Merodack-Idin-Akhy wearing embroidered robes which indicate that the art was practiced eleven hundred years before Christ. In his account of the cam-paign of Alexander against the Persians, Strabo tells of the amazement of the Greeks upon seeing the rich costumes of the Persians, embroidered as they were

Figure 575. Phrygian Needlework Design

After Hope.

with gold and jewels, with the more filmy stuffs embroidered in flowers. Alexander later took possession of the richly embroidered tent of Darius. Aristobulus, in describing the tomb of Cyrus, refers to the sumptuous embroideries of Babylon. He says the King's body was covered "with a magnificent Babylonian fabric, gorgeously *embroidered.*" Though not a vestige of these ancient embroideries remain, the fineness of the work is questioned because of the coarseness of the needles, either bone, boxwood, or metal, and the fiber of the threads in use.

In Greek civilization the art of embroidery was practiced by women of the highest rank. They were famous alike for their skill with the needle and their work at the loom. The greatest attainment in needle-work was attributed to Athene. According to Ovid, Arachne, who dared compete with this beloved goddess, was changed into a spider. The

Greeks, no doubt, borrowed both stitches and designs from oriental examples. Tyre and Sidon in the early period were at the peak of their reputation for rich oriental embroideries, and Homer states that Paris

Figure 576. Greek Border Arrangements

From Greek vases.

had brought talented Sidonian embroideresses to Troy. During the early years embroidery had been executed in woolen, cotton, and flaxen threads, often intermixed with strands of gold which gave a very sumptuous effect to the patterns. Silk was the last thread to be introduced into Europe and that not until the first century of our era.

The phrases "richly decorated" and "flowered garments" frequently appear describing the embroidered

Figure 577. The Embroidered Band

This, as well as single units, is frequently seen in Greek vase painting.

robes made by Greek women. Numerous references in Greek literature suggest the beauty and richness of their embroidered garments. The third canto of the *Iliad* pictures Helen "in her palace embroidering a large cloth, white as alabaster, with the story of the combats in which Trojan heroes skilled in taming steeds and Greeks in brazen cuirrasses contended for love of her." In the *Odyssey* Penelope describes the vest of Ulysses which she herself had embroidered:

The vest much envied on your native coast,
The regal robe with figured gold embossed,
   In happier hours my artful hand employ'd
   When my loved lord this blissful bower enjoy'd.

In the *Orestes* of Aeschylus, Agamemnon on his return to Troy recoils
from placing his foot upon the rich stuffs laid in his way by Clytem-
nestra. Avoiding them, he exclaims:

A mortal to walk upon purple
richly *embroidered* and tissues purchased at great cost! No; I dare not
do so!

The famous peplos of Athene,
renewed every four years and dedi-
cated to the Panathenic festival,
was white, embroidered in gold.
Greek dresses, as seen in both
sculpture and vase painting, show
a general use of borders. Figures
576, 577, 578. The borders enrich
the lower edge of the chiton and
are seen running along the over-
fold of the peplos. Strips or bands
of embroidery finish the neckline,
edge the armholes, and frequently
extend vertically down the center-
front of the tunic. Some Greek
dresses show a pattern of stars and
floral designs scattered all over the
material. Naturally the question
arises whether these were woven
or embroidered. No doubt some

Figure 578. Greek Borders

After Hope.

of the designs appearing as borders were woven into the material; it is,
however, far more likely that the patterns appearing in bands were embroidered and set on the material. As for designs distributed over the
surface of materials, it is quite probable that many of them were embroidered. A woven pattern carrying elaborate design would have a
tapestrylike appearance unsuitable for such costumes.

The patterns seen in the borders generally take the form of broad
bands in parallel lines, the zigzag, the meander, the key pattern—varying
from a simple running border to a complicated fret—the guilloche, simple spirals, and flower forms. The "honeysuckle" or "palmette" was a
very popular subject, its delicate stems and spirals lending themselves

well to needlework. In the earlier centuries the enrichment of costume was very elaborate, while in later periods it expressed more delicacy and refinement. A vase painting of the sixth century B.C. shows a figure wearing a heavily patterned garment, while in the fifth and fourth centuries the lighter floral patterns appear and the decoration is confined to the lower edge or border of the garment.

Among Roman women as well as Grecian the ability to embroider was looked upon as an accomplishment. It was with great pride that the Roman matron wrought her length of embroidery for tunic or girdle. This was usually worked in wool, in one color, and appeared very rich and beautiful against the light linen, cotton, or woolen background. Figure 579. Wool was used for all early embroidery, for silk did not

Figure 579. Patterns Seen on Roman Tunics

Wool embroidered work in one color on white linen.

come into general use until about the sixth century. Both Greeks and Romans adopted the various processes of embroidery work from the Oriental. Phrygian, Babylonian, and other Asiatic embroideries were constantly coming into both these countries. The embroideries in which gold thread was extensively used came from Phrygia; therefore the Romans called these embroideries *Phrygonae* and the embroiderer *Phrygio*. Since the use of gold thread appealed to the Romans they made extensive use of it. Pliny mentions cloth made of such thread without the usual background of linen or woolen material, creating a veritable cloth of gold. Such was a robe worn by Agrippina and a tunic of Heliogabalus. In the early centuries senators wore a white toga with a border of two purple bands, either woven or embroidered; later, under the empire, as many as seven bands were worn. When a Roman conqueror returned with the honors of victory upon him he was given a *toga palmata*, a robe embroidered in palm design similar to those seen in the Cashmere shawls. Indeed, so highly was this needlework esteemed that whenever a distinguished mark of any kind was needed, embroidery was chosen as the most fitting decoration. The elaborate display of embroidery used in Rome during imperial times was outshone only by that used at Byzantium where, in the fourth century, Constantine had established his court.

Middle Ages

Wealth and luxury centered first in Rome under the imperial rule of the Caesars, and then in Byzantium. These centers entered into active commerce with the East, whence beautiful embroideries were constantly pouring into the western world. The Emperor imported for his festivals and triumphs in Rome quantities of embroidered stuffs from Persia and China. Marvelous couch covers of Babylonian embroidery, which were valued at enormous sums; table napkins, heavy with needlework depicting the viands and dainties of the table, and other elaborate pieces were among the rich embroideries entering these important European centers. In Byzantium, religious subjects drawn from the New Testament were worked into altar cloths, great hangings, and curtains to swing between colonnades both within and without churches and palace. On the occasion of funerals, richly embroidered palls were thrown over the dead while lying in state.

Aside from these elaborate specimens of needlework was the use of embroidery in costume. Borders and bands rich in color and combined with gold threads gave the traditional sumptuousness to the dress of the fourth century. Robes loaded with rich embroideries hung in stiff folds. At this period the wife of the Emperor Honorious died. When her tomb was opened in 1544 the gold tissue which formed the shroud had melted and its weight amounted to thirty-six pounds. Though most of the elaborate needlework has utterly perished, a few pieces, especially those used to enrich ecclesiastical dress—the robes, shoes, gloves, cope, chasuble, and dalmatic—are today preserved in various churches and museums. With the passing of this heavily decorative period, however, it must be understood that the art of embroidery by no means became extinct. Of all textile processes this was the one generally known and most widely employed throughout Europe.

In western Europe, during the period of the early Middle Ages, the monasteries were gradually becoming the workshops in which the arts were fostered. Here special workrooms for weavers and embroiderers were fitted up. Much of the material turned out by the workers was used in the service of the Church and in ceremonies of state. We are told that Charlemagne on solemn occasions wore a close-fitting vest or jacket of gold embroidery and sandals embroidered and set with gems. The wife and daughter of Charlemagne are said to have been greatly skilled in needlework. St. Gisella, the sister of the Emperor's mother and founder of several convents took particular pride in her belief that girls should be taught the art of embroidery. Judith, mother of Charles the Bold, embroidered and bejeweled with her own hands the mantle for King Harold of Denmark, to wear at his baptismal ceremony in 826.

The striking characteristic of eleventh- and twelfth-century costume is the embroidered bands which appear at the hem of dresses, about the neck, around the wrists, upon the upper arm of the sleeve, and on the edge of the mantle. As a rule materials were somewhat coarse in texture, threads were large, stitches of little variety, and color flat in tone. Embroidery was usually worked upon linen with either worsteds or

Figure 580. A Band of Embroidery

Made in little geometric patterns in goldwork with stones and pearls, 12th and 13th centuries.

After Viollet-le-Duc.

Figure 581. Embroidered Band in Which Pearls Are Set in Little Metal Plaques

These are held in place by threads of the material, 12th and 13th centuries.

After Viollet-le-Duc.

silk. Occasionally gold thread was used and the ground showed between the various parts of the pattern. Figure 580 is an example of the borders worn about the middle of the twelfth century. The design shows little geometric figures of goldwork combined with stones and pearls. In Figure 581 the embroidery pattern is carried out in heavy stitches as indicated. The unusual note about this piece, however, is the setting of little metal plaques at each corner of the squares. These are held firm by embroidery threads, and each supports a pearl.

The year 1202 marks the beginning of the fourth Crusade, and from this time on the demand for colorful embroidery in costume increased. It is an important point in the record of embroidery that the Crusades exerted a marked influence. Returning Crusaders came wearing beautifully embroidered pouches, girdles, and other specimens of the colorful art of the East. Figure 582. This naturally created a demand for these luxuries. The art of embroidery came to be looked upon as an accomplishment much to be desired and milady's leisure time was spent in adding fine stitches to gloves, shoes, girdles, bags (see The Handbag, Chapter 31), and other personal accessories. Further, the thirteenth century is conspicuous for the wide popularity of a new method of embroidering which had been introduced to the western world during the previous century. This was known as *appliqué*, a form of decoration probably invented by the ancient Persians as an inexpensive imitation of their rich embroideries. Figure 583. Later it was borrowed by the Egyptians and Greeks, who made general use of it. In this form of decoration various shapes were cut from one material, placed upon a foundation of another, and embroidery stitches used to unify the pattern. Coming in during the Crusades it was invariably employed in the decoration of banners, horse trappings, tents, and the surcoats worn by knights. At this time the nobles were granted the right to appropriate to themselves certain emblems signifying prestige or rank. These marks of distinction took the form of a family crest or coat of arms. New stitches were introduced and this gave greater variety to the patterns. So strong was the significance attached to the personal escutcheon that all women of position applied them-

Figure 582.
Embroidered Bag

Probably used to carry the book of prayers, 14th century.

After Viollet-le-Duc.

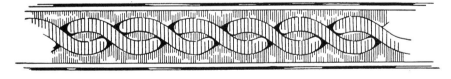

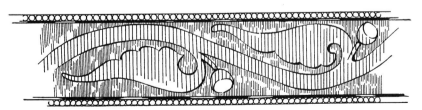

Figure 583. Appliqué Bands Seen on Garments of the 12th Century
After Viollet-le-Duc.

selves diligently to the embroidering not only of gloves, shoes, girdles, bags, but of banners and hanging canopies, all of which displayed the family rank. Further, these same leaders presided over the colorful tournaments where the family banners were displayed. In the costume of the period appliqué bands and borders are dominant. By 1389, the use of pearls and spangles set among the embroidery stitches was the "last word." A single instance of the use of pearls is worthy of note: In 1414, Charles of Orleans wore a fashionable tunic with wide, flowing sleeves. Forming a deep border around the lower half of the sleeves were the words and music of a song beginning, *Madame, I Am All Joyous*. The lines were fashioned of gold thread and each note (of square shape in those days) was formed of four pearls. Approximately nine hundred pearls, costing an enormous sum, were used in this elaborate border of gold and gems.

At the close of the fourteenth century (1395) these women of the nobility found still another way to distinguish themselves from lesser folk. They began to embroider the family coat of arms upon the dress; the crest of the husband's family was emblazoned upon the right side and that of the lady upon the left. So popular did this fashion become that a large part of the costume was soon covered with rampant lions and leopards, fishes, birds, and fleur-de-lis. Out of this fashion for heraldic display grew the particolored gown. This was the costume one half of which was of one color and the opposite side of another. A noble lady of Provence is said to have worn a dress with the left side and sleeve white and the opposite side blue.

Great attention was now directed to the preparation of colors for dyeing threads and fabrics. One Parisian, Jean le Beque, journeyed to Italy to study the process of color dyeing. At Bologne he met an embroiderer of great experience who gave him new ideas about color and the methods of dyeing. Le Begue set this down and later gave a full account in writing. The manuscript is preserved to this day. Another famous dyer of this period was Jean Gobelin (1450) whose name is forever linked with the manufacture of Gobelin tapestries developed in his workshop.

By-and-by, toward the end of this interesting period, the increasing demand for all sorts of dress accessories—gloves, belts, buttons, bags, and pouches—brought large numbers of men and women into these various fields of employment. This led to the formation of the great trade guilds and fraternities of the Middle Ages. Among the spinners, weavers, makers of silk, velvet, and fringe, there were also listed the "embroiderers and embroideresses."

1500-1600

In the opening years of the early Renaissance, Italy held a foremost place in the field of embroidery. Spain followed, and soon France, England, Germany, and Holland were adopting many of the handsome embroideries popular in Italy and Spain. Fabrics for the Church, the home, and the costume each developed certain types which belong distinctly to the sixteenth century. In Italy the Medici, the Venetian Doges, and the Court of the Popes were the great patrons of art, and under their inspiring leadership the field of embroidery widened. About 1545, the introduction of the steel needle, probably from India, did much in refining the art. The steel needle was so far superior to the bone bodkin and coarse metal tools previously employed that it is not surprising to hear of the great forward movement in the art of embroidery, as related especially to costume.

In the field of clothes the Renaissance is outstanding because at this time embroidery began to play a conspicuous part in dress. True, embroidery had previously been applied to costume and had been a beautiful detail of girdles, shoes, and bags, but now the real period of embroidery in dress began. As usual, it was first the luxury set aside for kings and queens and other men and women of rank. It was rich in color and in the use of gold and silver thread, pearls, and other gems. Deep-piled velvets, rich brocades, and heavy silks were increasingly used for the ground of garments, and, on this, embroidery was worked in colored silks and gold thread. In fact, costume came to be little more than a mass of embroidery. In men's dress, black velvet, with its threads of gold traceries, touched here and there with gay bits of color, was very handsome. Plate L. In women's dress embroidery massed the sleeves and bodice (see Plate LI, Chapter 38). The long stomachers were encrusted with jewels and embroidery, and invariably a handsome, embroidered panel extended down the front of the skirt, often passing around the lower edge to form a border. A little later in the century the skirt of the dress was made open in front to show the handsome petticoat, often embroidered.

Not only costume but gloves, bags, girdles, and shoes each received its share of embroidery. Gloves in this century, clumsy and ill fitting though they were, were still among the most distinctive of costume accessories. Scarcely a portrait of Henry VIII exists in which he is not carrying a glove. White kid, buff, and brown leather, and gloves with gauntlet tops of silk or leather were all elaborately embroidered and in many instances edged with heavy gold fringe (see Gloves, Chapter 27). The little French hood, so popular in this period, was likewise stiffened at the outer edge with embroidery in gold and pearls. In France, effeminate men adopted the art in which ladies had excelled and embroidered their gloves, shoes, and knitted stockings.

One of the famous types of embroidery developed in England during this century was the *Spanish blackwork*, which is said to have been introduced from Spain by Katherine of Aragon, the first unhappy queen of Henry VIII. Though called "Spanish," it is of great antiquity, probably having been adopted from the Moors, who, in turn, had borrowed it from the ancient Persians. Blackwork was carried out in black silk embroidery on white linen, often combined with gold thread (see Plate LII, Chapter 38). The designs usually showed continuous curved stems from which grew graceful flower shapes of honeysuckle, carnation, or rose. The admirable results achieved in this black-and-white work were quite remarkable. So great was its popularity that it continued for nearly a century. Henry VIII wore shirts elaborate in blackwork; Queen Katherine's bodices were blackwork; and when the reign of Elizabeth was reached, blackwork was still the height of fashion. Not only costume but household furnishings as well were adorned with this attractive embroidery. Queen Katherine trimmed her sheets of "fyne Holland clothe" with blackwork, and Elizabeth received as a gift pillowcases of blackwork.

About the middle of this extravagant century a new type of needlework was introduced which soon found its way into the elaborate ruffs and cuffs for which the century is famous. This was the popular *drawn* and *cutwork*. Figures 584, 585. Before this period much embroidery upon canvas and coarse linen had been done in colored threads. It was an easy matter for the worker to draw the coarse linen threads from this foundation material and join together those that were left with various stitches in geometric pattern. As the manufacture of linen improved in quality, becoming finer, its use in costume grew more popular. Drawn work in fine linen with white embroidery stitches came to be the vogue. Sometimes the threads of the foundation material were not withdrawn but only separated, and groups of varying size were caught together, forming a ground work of small square meshes. Presently much of the fine drawn work in linen came to be less and less dependent upon the foundation material. This foundation was gradually reduced to a narrow strip into which a row of buttonhole stitches was made; the embroidery stitches were then supported upon this. Soon the supporting row of material vanished altogether, and from this moment dates the beginning of lacemaking—but that is another story.

During the vogue for drawn-work embroidery, cutwork was equally fashionable. In this work certain parts of the embroidered pattern were cut away and the open space filled in with various designs in needlework patterns. Figures 584-86. Both forms of embroidery were exceedingly popular, especially in relation to the fashionable ruffs and cuffs, the conspicuous accessories of dress during the latter half of the century. Of these elaborate fashions set with drawn- and cutwork, Philip Stubbes, the period's sharpest critic, says that some of these were wrought with

PLATE L. Charles IX......................*Clouet*

The King wears the elaborate costume of the early Elizabethan period. The velvet jerkin with cape is rich with embroidery. The little toque is set off with feathers and jeweled
brooches. Note the cutwork of sleeves and bombasted
breeches.

"*open-work* down to the middle of the ruff and further, some with close-work, some with purled lace, so closed and other gewgaws so pestered, as the ruff is the least part of itself."

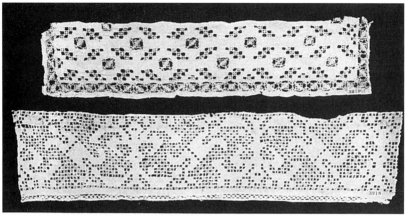

Figure 584. Cut- and Drawn Work, Italian, 16th Century

Throughout the period the application of embroidery to costume grew more and more lavish, reaching its greatest extravagance in the reign of Elizabeth. At Elizabeth's death her wardrobe boasted not fewer than three thousand gowns, most of them embroidered. These embroidered gowns were heavy with gold thread and spangles; others were

Figure 585. Cutwork, Italian, 16th Century; Drawn Work with
Punto in Aria Edging, Italian, 17th Century

lighter, being silk of delicate color exquisitely wrought in realistic flowers and vines. Still others were covered with embroidered emblems; among these the famous dress embroidered all over with eyes and ears. So handsome were these costumes that James I, who succeeded Elizabeth, advised his queen, Anne of Denmark, to make use of the elaborate wardrobe. A glance at the famous portraits of this day—Elizabeth, the Archduchess

Clara Eugenia, Marie de Medici, the Countess of Pembroke, Anne of
Denmark, and hosts of others, robed in their "embroidered stuffs" and
"sumptuous ruffs," convince one that this was the day of outstanding
grandeur in costume (see PLATE XXIX and Figure 245, Chapter 16;
Figure 541, Chapter 33). The art of embroidery was so fascinating to
the ladies of this period that they applied themselves diligently, and
many attained more than ordinary skill. Catherine de' Medici was famous

COURTESY, METROPOLITAN MUSEUM OF ART

Figure 586. Cutwork, with Embroidery Stitches, Italian, 16th Century

for her needlework. Katherine of Aragon is said to have consoled herself
with the needle,

> Although a Queen, yet she her days did pass,
> In working with the needle curiously.

Elizabeth, and Mary, Queen of Scots, were likewise famed as skilled
needlewomen. During Elizabeth's reign, *petit point*, the single square
stitch on canvas, was popularized. Further, it was in the reign of Good
Queen Bess that there was incorporated in London "The London Company of Broderers," which flourished until the time of Charles I.

Contemporary with this age of embroidery was the darned net called
lacis. This form of embroidery was worked in squares which were later
joined. However, it was more favored for household linens, bed hangings, coverlets, and curtains than for costume. It was also extensively
used for ecclesiastical purposes. Patterns ranged from the simple, geometric to the more fanciful creations. A little later, the darning of lengths
of net to be used as insertion was a popular form of needlework. Running
the stitches through the netted background and keeping the regularity
of the design by counting the open meshes was both an easy and pleasant
pastime for these ladies of 1500. It is said that Catherine de' Medici kept
her court busy darning these squares of network which were later to
be used in the decoration of her boudoir. An inventory of the Queen's
household goods records that one chest contained 380 unmounted
darned squares, and another 538. It was in this period that the popular

forms of needlework lacis, drawn and cutwork, laid the foundation for the handsome lacemaking of the following century.

The use of embroidery in furniture coverings, hangings, and needlework pictures continued to occupy the time and wits of the famed embroiderers of the day. As early as 1520, particularly on the occasion of the historic meeting of Henry VIII and Francis I on the Field of the Cloth of Gold, we read of the lavish use of embroidery. According to contemporary writers, the tents, the banners, the horse trappings, and the costumes of the long retinue of knights were splendid with embroidery beyond the power of mortals to describe. Silks, velvets, and cloth of gold and silver were embroidered with quaint mottoes and other legends in colored silks and gold and silver thread.

The embroidering of large portable pictures was another field in which the art of needlework flourished. Many of the pictures, which resembled real paintings in their fine gradations, blendings, and smooth shadings of color, are today preserved in the museums of Europe. So important was this field that great artists gave of their skill in making designs for the embroiderers. Among these Raphael is said to have given generously of his time and talent. In the Cluny Museum in Paris is a specimen of picture embroidery said to have been worked over a design of Raphael's which was the result of an order from Francis I.

1600-1700

During the early years of the following century, embroidery continued to hold its place in the fashion world. Men were particularly gorgeous. The bombasted breeches of James I (1603-08), and other leaders of these years show excellent examples of embroidery in men's fashions. Slashed trousers, slashed doublets, slashed sleeves were the order of the day! A contrasting lining was pulled up through the slashes to form a series of puffs, while each opening was elaborately outlined with embroidery combined with silk gimp and gold and silver thread. In France, display of embroidery was carried to such extravagance that Louis XIII, in 1629, published an edict forbidding its use:

> We forbid men and women to wear in any way whatsoever *embroidery* on cloth or flax, imitation of *embroidery*, or bordering made up with cloth and thread, and of cut-work for "rebatos" capes, sleeves, done upon quintain, and other linens, laces, "passamaynes," and other thread-work made with bobbins.

Though, despite this, embroidery continued to hold its place in the fashion world the use of gold threads gradually grew less and less. Thread laces soon entered the costume field, and white embroidery together with these new thread laces began, slowly but surely, to usurp the place of the former sumptuous embroideries. Stomachers, which continued to be fashionable, were usually enriched with embroidery, but "gold and glitter" was not so evident. In fact, women of the late century are said to have ridiculed the "outrageous taste" of the previous period when gold bullion weighed heavily upon all wearing apparel.

Gloves continued to be embroidered and, though very handsome, were less ornate than formerly. By 1680 the highly decorated "sweete bagges" of former days were on the wane, but dainty shoes were still decorated with choice bits of stitchery combined with seed pearls and metal threads. With the coming of lace the elaborate ruffs and cuffs of drawn- and cutwork gradually gave way to those edged with lace. These were succeeded by the "falling bands" edged with a narrow, pointed, and wiry lace, and, finally, by the handsome lace collars of exquisite needlepoint. In fact, lace had, to a very great extent, succeeded embroidery in costume.

In England little embroidery was worn in dress after the time of James I, but, toward the end of the century, about 1688, it was again introduced. Then, however, instead of covering the entire costume, it was reserved for certain details such as sleeves, stomachers, and bags. In France, Louis XIV, unlike his predecessor, gave the greatest encouragement to those working in the field of embroidery. Embroidered furniture hangings, as well as accessories of costume, received his enthusiastic support. Attached to his court were a number of skilled embroiderers who carried out his instructions. Madame Maintenon—who had secretly married Louis XIV in 1685—after his death, 1715, established a school for girls at St. Cyr and devoted much of her time to instructing the young ladies in needlework. Elaborate wallpieces executed by these girls still hang in the palace at Versailles. Madame Maintenon worked at her embroideries at all times, whether sitting in the royal apartments, walking, or driving. According to a statement of the time she was "hardly ensconced in her carriage, and before the coachman had flicked his horses, this good lady put on her spectacles and pulled the needlework out of the bag she carried with her." Workboxes and little cases containing scissors, thimble, and needles were the dainty companions of every lady of leisure. Such a case was known as a *nécessaire*. Figure 587.

Toward the end of the century the fashion of quilting in backstitch embroidery was used in hangings, bed coverlets, furniture coverings, and also in costume. Petticoats, capes, and waistcoats were often made of two thicknesses of material held together with backstitch embroidery, usually in diaper pattern. This was further embellished with realistic flowers, vines, and sprays of green. The popularity of this style in embroidery reached its zenith in the following century.

The embroideries of 1600, especially those used in wall hangings, furniture coverings, and other forms of interior decoration were in grandiose style. The luxuriance of floral designs and bold, ornamental emblems contributed to the impressiveness of the effect. In costume, taste gradually grew more and more discriminating: embroideries came to be delicate rather than sumptuous, exquisite rather than rich. These tendencies blossomed in the following century, a period conspicuous for the simple beauty of its embroidered handwork.

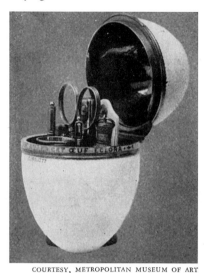

COURTESY, METROPOLITAN MUSEUM OF ART

Figure 587. *Necessaire*, Gold and Enamel, French, 17th Century

1700-1800

Early in the eighteenth century the embroideries which enriched the coats of the Louis XV and XVI periods were outstanding. Colored silks and metal threads were used in working elaborate patterns on both heavy silks and satins. Figure 590. By-and-by more dainty designs gradually came into fashion. New threads, chenilles and gimp, were now being made of spun silk and silk floss, and these combined with gold and silver thread, spangles, and narrow, flat braids are responsible for the dainty designs of this delightful period. St. Albans, writing "Embroideries

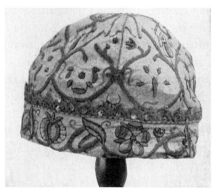

COURTESY, METROPOLITAN MUSEUM OF ART

Figure 588. Embroidered Cap, Late 17th Century

This type of work became most popular in the early 18th century.

done with fine whipcord or *guimps* came into fashion," declares that China was responsible for this new fashion demand. Fastidious gentlemen and ladies, their tastes growing more and more refined, were no longer satisfied with the embroideries of the past and were now sending their materials, cut to pattern, to China for the enrichment of stitches. No doubt, the work sent back from China greatly influenced the designs of the century. From 1720 on, the French embroideries attained a high degree of charm in pattern and finish in execution. In fact, so widely recognized was the superiority of French work that a constant market for French goods was established in all European centers. Delicate patterns were now seen bordering the pockets, rambling about buttonholes, and adding their delightful color to the admirable waistcoats of the period. The coat of embroidered brocade, the waistcoat of blue, cream, or white silk embroidered in dainty sprays

COURTESY, METROPOLITAN MUSEUM OF ART

Figure 589. Detail of Lady's Jacket

White, embroidered in gold and colored threads, English, 17th century.

of many-colored flowers, the lace cravat, knee breeches, silken hose, silver buckles, and powdered hair made this one of the most elegant and charming periods in gentlemen's dress.

Gowns and petticoats worn by women were also executed in the new embroidery threads. During the century the fashion of the quilted petticoat, which had begun in 1688, was revived. While women adopted the petticoat, men indulged in quilted coattails. The type of quilting varied all the way from a simple running stitch to elaborate diaper patterns in colored silks, over which were dispersed flowers in color and in gold and silver thread. Quilting had been used occasionally for garments in earlier times, but as a phase of embroidery the art falls between the years 1688 and 1714.

Figure 590. Coat, White Grosgrain Silk

Embroidered in silk and metal threads, English, about 1720.

An interesting revival of this period was that of the apron. The *barm cloth** or *napron†* had been worn as a protection to the dress as early as 1300, was again adopted in 1500, and now in the eighteenth century it was taken up by fashionable ladies and, embroidered in elaborate stitchery, came to be looked upon as a favorite article of dress. Figure 591.

---

* *Barm cloth,* from the Anglo-Saxon, meaning "lap." The leathern aprons worn by the smiths were known as *barm skin.*

† *Napron,* from the French *nappe,* meaning "cloth."

Even in the earlier days the barm cloth was not without its decoration, for witness the figure from an old manuscript drawing which shows the upper part set with reticulations. Figure 592.

These aprons white of
 finest thred,
So choicely tide, so
 dearly bought,
So finely fringed, so nicely spred,
So quaintlie cut, so
 richlie wrought;
Were they in work to
 save their cotes,
They need not cost so
 many grotes.

STEPHEN GOSSON's *Pleasant Quippes for Upstart New-fangled Gentlewomen*, 1596

COURTESY, METROPOLITAN MUSEUM OF ART

Figure 591. Embroidered Apron, English, 1700

Figure 592. An Early Apron

The upper part is ornamented with reticulations.

From the Sloane ms., 346.

Later, during the lace era, aprons were made of the finest needlepoint and bobbin laces and these were considered the ultra-smart detail in feminine dress.

It was toward the later years of the century that the daintiest of muslins, cambrics, and finest of linens came to be embroidered in white cotton and used for collars, cuffs, scarfs, and other accessories. Saxony was outstanding in this work. The beauty of design was so delicate and the execution of the work so perfect that Queen Marie Antoinette chose this dainty embroidery for her own wardrobe. This, much to the joy of the Saxon workers, set the fashion for the world. These white cotton embroideries on the sheerest of muslins, together with the handsome laces now in use, had completely eclipsed the popularity of embroidery as used in previous periods. By 1780, the fashion in needlework had traveled a long road. The dainty white cambrics and embroideries of Marie Antoinette and her world were far removed from their gorgeous beginnings in the days of the Good Queen Bess.

Soon the horrors of the Revolution upset the social order, and this wrought havoc among the gentle embroiderers. It is said that after the tumult embroiderers were set to work to pick and pull out the gold and silver threads which had been used in the priceless embroideries of former times. They were made to unstitch braid used in the ornamentation of hangings, curtains, and costumes, and from these extricate all gold and silver thread. This was then sent to the melting pot and the returns are said to have been used "for the good of the nation." It is one of the regrettable facts of history that many of the treasured embroideries of church and palace alike were at this time utterly destroyed.

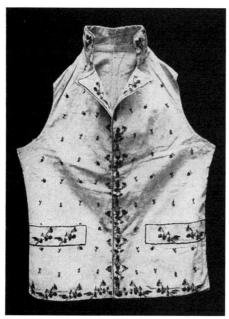

COURTESY, METROPOLITAN MUSEUM OF ART

Figure 593. Vest, White Cotton, Embroidered in Colored Silks and Gold Thread

French, 18th and 19th centuries.

1800-1900

In the early years of the new century the popularity of muslins and other dainty and sheer materials embroidered in white cotton in flowing de-

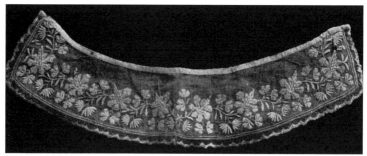

COURTESY, METROPOLITAN MUSEUM OF ART

Figure 594. Collar, Embroidered on Net with Bobbin-Lace Edge, American, 19th century

signs with scattered flowers continued to be the quiet demand of milady of taste. In men's clothes embroidery had all but vanished. It lingered, however, in the fashionable ties embroidered at each end and in the short, embroidered vests which added a note of color to the otherwise somber tone of men's dress. Figure 593.

During the Victorian period (1837-1901), the most popular use of embroidery was in the underlinens. As in other fields of industry the machine had entered, and now the needs of the great mass of the people

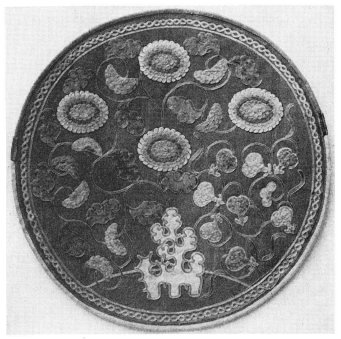

COURTESY, METROPOLITAN MUSEUM OF ART

Figure 595. Chinese Mirror Case

The floral pattern is in silk appliqué, of the Ch'ien Lung period.

were easily and rapidly met. By the twentieth century mechanical processes had been so perfected that any and all types of embroidery, whether copies of ancient patterns or modern designs, were produced at little expense. The bonnaz* and other machines, so generally used in Switzerland, Saxony, and other parts of central Europe and in the Philippine Islands as well, furnish in this day of fast living the great quantities of embroidery and embroidery materials demanded by the fashion world. Not so, however, in sections of the world not so fast moving. It is said that today women of primitive tribes in Central America continue to embroider skins with designs of flowers and animals. The people of the Orient as in ancient times, still excel in the art of embroidery. The Persians, Turks, and natives of Hindustan use not only silk but gold and silver threads, beads, spangles, pearls, and precious

* A machine used to embroider patterns on net and other materials in chain stitch.

stones. Feathers also frequently appear in design. Coins, which unmarried women wear in their hair, are also worked into embroidery for their dresses. The women of India often work into their embroideries their own hair together with that of animals. The Chinese are perhaps the most industrious and elaborate hand-embroiderers, their best work being on silk. Their designs are either embroidered in colored silks or combined with gold and silver thread. Figures 595, 596, 597.

Twentieth Century

The source of inspiration for much modern embroidery has been the

Figure 596. Imperial Chinese Court Robe

This is the *k'o ssu* (silk tapestry) of the K'ang Hsi or Ch'ien Lung period. Although no two Chinese embroidery designs were alike, they were all governed by formal distinctions and rules.

peasant embroidery of central Europe. The earlier peoples of this district, working under the supervision of their lords, copied many designs brought in by invading tribes from the East. The beautiful patterns, with slight changes, were handed down from one generation to another. In this way there developed the various types of embroidery — the Russian, Hungarian, French, and Rumanian.

The story of embroidery is long and varied. Though introduced into costume at a very early period, its chief glory, like that of sculpture

Figure 597. Chinese Lady's Robe

The imperial theatrical costume of a court lady of the 13th century.

and painting, was in the service of religion. It is in the early Church that one finds the most elaborate and exquisite examples of this highly decorative art. From the Renaissance on, the world of fashion appropriated to her own use this oldest of the arts. To add color and pattern to the dress of men and women, first in sumptuous richness and later in delicate refinement, was Fashion's decree. From the gorgeous elegance in the sixteenth century, through the handsome but less conspicuous embroidery of the seventeenth and the flowerlike daintiness of the eighteenth, to the modest refinements of the Victorian era, Fashion has led the way. Sometimes elaborate, sometimes dainty, at all times it has added a note of charm to the world's apparel.

REFERENCES

Abrahams, Ethel B., *Greek Dress; A Study of the Costume Worn in Ancient Greece from pre-Hellenic Times to the Hellenic Age.*

Calthrop, Dion Clayton, *English Costume*, Vol. I, p. 3.

Druitt, Herbert, *A Manual of Costumes as Illustrated by Monumental Brasses.*

Ellsworth, Evelyn Peters, *Textiles and Costume.*

Fales, Jane, *Dressmaking*, pp. 481-485.

Goddard, Eunice R., *Women's Costume in French Texts of the Eleventh and Twelfth Centuries.*

Houston, Mary G., *Ancient Greek, Roman, and Byzantine Costume.*

New International Encyclopedia, Vol. 7.

Lefébure, Ernest, *Embroidery and Lace.*

Rhead, G. W., *Chats on Costume.*

Sage, Elizabeth, *A Story of Costume*, pp. 3, 104.

Shaw, Henry, *Dress and Decoration of the Middle Ages*, Vols. I, II.

CHAPTER 38

Lace

Of many arts, one surpasses all;
　The threads woven by the strange power of the hand—
Threads which the dropping of the spider would in vain attempt to imitate,
　And which Pallas herself would confess she had never known.

An early Flemish poet. From his rhapsodies
over his countrywomen's handiwork.

THE most ancient specimens of any textiles resembling lace are the knotted nets found in the tombs of ancient Thebes, dating back to 2500 B.C. These nets were often adorned with beads and tiny porcelain

COURTESY, METROPOLITAN MUSEUM OF ART

Figure 598. Cutwork, Combined with Embroidery
Stitches, Italian, 16th and 17th Centuries

figures strung among the meshes. Constant reference is made by Homer, Herodotus, and other Greek writers to the *networks* and gold embroidered garments of the patricians of Egypt. Isaiah speaks of the Egyptians as "they that work in flax and weave *networks*."* According to Pliny, "so delicate were some of these that they could pass through a man's ring and a single person could carry a sufficient number to surround a whole wood."

These nets, however, fine as they were, were not lace in our modern sense of the term, for lace involves much more than this. Lace implies a highly developed, refined sense of pattern, combined with artistic methods of execution which have reached near-perfection.

* Isaiah XIX:9

1500-1600

The earliest authentic lace began to appear in the sixteenth century. It had grown out of the fine needlework known as *drawn work, cutwork*, and *lacis*. These types of needlework, however, fall entirely within

Figure 599. Reticello

Needle lace, with bobbin-lace edge, 1500, and needle lace, 1600.

the field of embroidery, not that of lace. In drawn work, threads were drawn from the linen, and portions of the remaining threads, caught together by thread stitches, formed lacelike designs. In cutwork, part of the design was cut away and the intervening space filled with thread stitches in simple pattern (Figures 584, 585, 586, Chapter 37). Figure 598. "Lacis" was at first a name given to the net upon which patterns were darned. In time the finished pattern came to be known as lacis. These darned patterns cover a wide range of design varying from the simple geometric to the more fanciful creations of the imagination. The work was carried out on squares of net, and these were later sewed together. These three types of embroidery, drawn work, cutwork, and lacis, are outstanding as the contributing factors in the development of lace.

It is in the field of drawn thread work, in particular, that the transition of embroidery into lace is so easily apparent. As more and more threads were drawn from the material the pattern gradually grew less and less dependent upon the number of threads in the remaining ground. By-and-by only a row or two of original ground was left and into this the first row of looped stitches was worked and the remainder of the pattern was then supported upon this. Next, the ground vanished altogether. The design or pattern to be made was then drawn upon parchment; the principal line of the pattern was first laid in with a couching or button-hole stitch which served as a support for the complete pattern. Such stitches were called *punto in aria*, meaning "stitches in the air," for they were seemingly made out of nothing. The earliest lace developed from this method was made in Venice and known as *reticello*, meaning "geo-metric." Figure 599. The feeling for geometric form had naturally car-ried over from the lacis, drawn work, and cutwork into the new *punto in aria*. The first punto in aria was a narrow, dentated edging which was seized upon for trimming the hitherto plain ruffs and cuffs of the six-teenth century. Figure 602. Gradually as this lace grew wider and de-veloped into geometric pattern or reticello it was used as insertion and

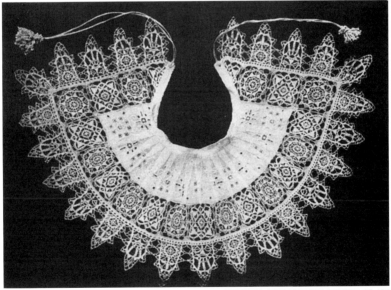

COURTESY, METROPOLITAN MUSEUM OF ART

Figure 600. Collar, 17th Century

Embroidered linen with border of reticello and *punto in aria* edge.

bands, often edged with the narrow, pointed punto in aria. So popular was reticello that it was soon employed for garments of every description and was imitated in every country in Europe.

From this beginning made with "stitches in the air" there gradually developed through the centuries the exquisite needlepoints, *point de Venice, point de France,* and *point d'Angleterre* with all their charming variations which ultimately reached the highest standards of excellence.

Bobbin lace, called "pillow lace" because made on a cushion or pillow and also called "bone lace" because made with bone bobbins, appeared only a little later than punto in aria. Figure 601. Bobbin laces are tissues made by interweaving and plaiting threads rolled at one end around bobbins and at the other end fastened by means of pins upon cushions. The making of this lace points back to the plaiting and tying of fringes. This age-old craft of plaiting, knotting, and tying the projecting warp threads in oblique or transverse lines was practiced by the Assyrians and Babylonians and passed on from them to western civilization. Bobbin lace gradually forged ahead, and very soon came to interpret lace design in a highly artistic manner. The earliest mention of bobbin lace occurs in

LOUVRE, PARIS

Figure 601. The Lace Maker. . . .
Van der Meer

This Flemish woman is busy with her pillow and bobbins making the fashionable pillow lace.

a deed which was drawn up in Milan in 1495. Milan, Venice, and Genoa were the early centers for bobbin lace; then the art passed to the cities of Flanders, where it reached its zenith in the eighteenth century. These two distinct principles upon which all lace evolved, that is, punto in aria or needlepoint and the pillow or bobbin-made, cover the whole range of exquisite laces developed during the seventeenth and eighteenth centuries. Needlepoint emerged in the seventeenth century as the handsome lace which distinguishes the Louis XIV period; bobbin lace came to its own in the eighteenth century under Louis XV.

The vogue for lace on the dress started about 1540, when the fluted ruff absorbed the attention of both men and women. No sooner had the narrow punto in aria appeared than it captivated the fashion world, and the era of lace began. Early portraits show this narrow dentated edging trimming the ruffs and cuffs. Figure 602. A little later the earliest bobbin lace appeared in the form of twisted or plaited thread edgings. These have the same pointed effect but are more wiry with larger portions of openwork and consequently present a very pleasing contrast to the lawn ruff. This admiration for a pointed edge or "finish" to material is historic. Throughout the Middle Ages both men and women cut the edges of their mantles, doublets, and hoods into jagged points or scallops, these remaining fashionable for a long time. Now in the sixteenth century the same desire for a pointed edge was carried out in lace. Later, insertions in drawn and cutwork were set midway of the ruff and the edge set off with the pointed scallop. Many of the "Medici" collars, the standing, open collars which succeeded the ruff, were enriched with drawn work so fine that the original linen foundation had dwindled to a few threads. So extravagant were these ruffs and their trimmings of lace and embroidery that the irrepressible Stubbes again speaks. He regarded the ruffs themselves as inventions of the "devill in the fulness of his malice." He adds that they were,

COURTESY, THE PRADO, MADRID

Figure 602. Philip II of Spain....
Pantaja de la Cruz

The high hat of this period is a forecast of the tall beavers of 1600. The ruff shows the wiry, pointed edging fashionable in the early period. This modest edging inspired the development of the extravagant ruffs of lace or lace-trimmed cambric of the court of James I in early 1600.

Clogged with gold, silver, or silk *lace* of stately price, wrought all over with needlework; speckled and sparkled here and there with the sunne, moone, and starres and many other antiques rare to behold. Some are wrought with open-work down to the middle of the ruff and further, some with closed-work, some with purled *lace* so closed and other gewgaws so pestered as the ruff is the least part of itself.

During this century pattern books began to appear, and with the spread of these designs through Italy, France, and the Netherlands, the making of lace became more and more a lay industry. Women's dresses and men's doublets were set with lace insertion and garnished with lace points.

Though bobbin lace reached its zenith at a later day, it is known to have been used, probably in a limited way, in the late sixteenth century. Quicherat says that it was the fashion in France at this time to wear waistbands and girdles edged with a pleating of meshes called *bissette*. This was probably a bobbin mesh worked in gold and silver thread. In the account of the entry of Henry II into Lyons in 1548, we read that "the costumes were of velvet and satin, the humblest being taffetas some ornamented with guimp applications and others trimmed with *bissette*, or with edgings of silver thread." This gold and silver mesh, or bobbin-made edging, was admirably keyed to the deep-toned velvets and heavy brocades of this luxurious period. We read that in 1577 Henry III wore four-thousand yards of real gold lace on his person; and the fashion queens of the period wore velvet dresses "trimmed all over with gold and silver lace"—all bobbin-made meshes.

All through this century little of the thread laces were known other than the reticello used with the narrow, pointed edging for collars and cuffs and for bands of insertion. All of these kept more or less to the geometric in design. Not until the following century did the patterns break away from the established form and assume a new character.

1600-1700

In the early years of 1600 the ruff reached outrageous proportions. King James I wore ruffs which consumed twenty-five yards of material. These were usually of lace but if of fine cambric were always lace trimmed. Lace insertions were used not only in the ruff but in men's shirts as well. Women were equally extravagant.

One of the charming portraits which show the great beauty attained in the geometric-patterned lace of this period is that of Lady Powlett preserved in the Ashmolean Museum, Oxford. PLATE LI. The portrait was painted about 1621, just before the monstrous ruff gave way to the falling collar. The handsome apron, without doubt made by the lady herself, falls to the hem of the dress. It shows row upon row of the geometric-patterned lace. The whole is edged with a deep-pointed scallop matching that on the ruff and the lace-trimmed sleeves. This lady was probably famed for her skill with the needle for there is mention in the *English Connoisseur* (Vol. II, page 80) of a "Lady Betty Paulet, an ingenious lady of the Duke of Bolton's family, in the reign of James I, drawn in a dress of her own work full length." It is also stated that a gift of certain admirable needlework "of Lady Elizabeth Paulet," who is undoubtedly the same person, was accepted by the "University of Oxford

PLATE LI. Lady Elizabeth Powlett

The handsome apron shows the alternate rows and the deep-scalloped edge of the fashionable reticello. Note that the same pattern appears in the ruff, the cuffs, and the edging about the open neck. No doubt all the needle lace appearing in the costume was made by the lady herself.

English school, 1625.

515

in convocation, on the 9th of July, 1636." Many verses written in her honor have been preserved in the Bodleian Library.

Other admirable examples of the lace of this early period are to be seen in existing portraits. The portrait of Mary Sidney, Countess of Pembroke, shows cuffs and headdress of geometric-patterned lace with the deep-pointed scallop. The bodice, rich in embroidery, is a beautiful example of the scroll pattern, dark on light, so popular during this century. PLATE LII. Following the fluted ruff came the standing ruffs, magnificent in their patterned lace and scalloped borders. (PLATE XXIX and others, Chapter 16).

Soon the great ruffs began to fall. The large, flat collar succeeded the standing ruff and lace was more and more in demand. Wide collars of Holland cambric edged with deep lace fell over the shoulders of both men and women. Many of these still retained the beautiful insertions formerly popular and their borders grew into deep points and finely-turned scallops. The cavaliers strode about in their plumed hats, falling-topped boots, lace collars, and turned-back cuffs, while ladies of fashion took similar pride in their deep berthas and matching cuffs. Figure 605. Not only collars and cuffs in this era of lace but gloves, doublets, breeches, and even boots were profusely trimmed. Lace laid siege not only to clothes but to furniture and the general decoration of the home. Canopies, hangings, coverings—all were developed with lacework. Windows of carriages and coaches were likewise hung with lace. With this great extravagance in the use of lace one is not surprised to hear the edicts come forth. In 1629, Louis XIII promulgated an order under the title, *Regulation as to Superfluities in Costume*. This aimed particularly at the extravagant use of lace and embroidery. A few surviving cartoons of the day picture the sorry belles and beaus reluctantly dressing themselves in clothes without lace. A lady of fashion, seeing her enviable aids to beauty laid aside, comments thus:

In spite of my personal beauty which, without vanity, cannot be surpassed by that of another woman, it still seems to my eyes that with gold and silver lace I further enhance my charms.

The sympathetic valet of one gallant is made to say:

It is with regret that my master doffs the fine clothes covered with trimmings which gave him such a handsome appearance. . . . I go then and put all of these superfluous garments in the cupboard, and as he will wear them no more, I shall not fear he will give them to me.

One is scarcely surprised at the King's edict when informed that one favored courtier, at his death in 1642, left behind three hundred sets of collars and cuffs lavishly enriched with the finest lace.

PLATE LII. Mary Sidney, Countess of Pembroke

This portrait, painted in 1614, pictures an elaborate costume of cut velvet, embroidery, and lace. The bodice is covered with the fashionable scroll pattern, dark on light; the lace headdress and cuffs are magnificent examples of the early geometric-patterned lace and the deep-scalloped edge.

During this century of extravagance in the use of lace, the handsome gold and silver laces of Spain known as *point d'Espagne* or Spanish point, must not be overlooked. Though Spain was never outstanding in the production of thread laces, she did achieve distinction for her rich, metallic laces, all bobbin made and sometimes rendered more gorgeous

Figure 603. Collar with Tassels
Gros Point, Italian, 17th Century.

by the addition of colored embroidery silks. From the beginning of the seventeenth century these gold and silver laces were used lavishly on the dress. Not only clothes but furnishings—sheets and hangings, and draperies in coaches and coffins were generously trimmed. Indeed, in Spain as in France, the extravagant use of gold lace in dress caused Philip III to follow the same course as had the French king and pronounce a ban against this reckless expenditure for finery. Men were permitted only plain, falling collars without lace or cutwork, and women were likewise doomed to wear plain collars and cuffs without starch. It is interesting to note that the Queen of Spain herself was the first to overstep the ban, for upon hearing that Prince Charles of England, visiting Spain, had lost his baggage and was consequently short of clothes, she graciously sent him "as much richly laced linen as filled ten trunks." Not all gold and silver lace, however, was made in Spain, for both Italy and France achieved a large measure of success in the production of metallic laces. These were known to the trade under the same commercial name, *point d'Espagne.*

In England the period of the falling ruff and the collar of exquisite point lace is always linked with the name of Charles I. The King was a great lover of beautiful clothes. At one time he purchased a thousand yards of choicest lace for his own personal use. His handsome dress, usually set off with collars and cuffs of stately needlepoint, has been made familiar through the many portraits of that great Flemish master, Sir Anton Van Dyck (see PLATE VIII, Chapter 1; Figure 246, Chapter 16). The use of lace in England was unbounded. Both the dress and house furnishings were loaded with lace. One gentleman returning from an English country house declared he could not sleep at night, for the Brussels lace with which the sheets were edged tickled his nose. In fact, the craze for lace at this time sent many an extravagant citizen into bankruptcy. In Puritan days the women of England gave up the use of lace, believing the filmy meshes to be "the temptation of Satan." To wear lace at this time was looked upon as a "step toward pride," and, consequently, many lacemakers were forced into other occupations. Colonial women began to make lace after they reached Massachusetts, but the art did not thrive in the Colonies. The lace was never as satisfactory as that made in Europe. Peddlers were sent about the country to sell or trade it for butter, eggs, or cheese, but laws prohibiting its purchase were enacted to prevent the frivolous minded from indulging in its use. Prohibition of the use of lace continued from year to year until the beginning of the eighteenth century, when fine clothes were again permitted.

Toward the close of the reign of Louis XIII (1643), lacemaking began to grow into an established industry. With the ascendancy of Louis XIV (1643-1715), and his able minister, Colbert, the lacemaking business attained even greater heights. Colbert determined to develop the lace industry of France so that the wealth being lavished upon this luxury should not be sent out of the country. In 1665 he gave a handsome endowment to a Madame Gilbert for the establishment of a lace school in his own chateau at Alençon. This experienced lacemaker employed thirty equally experienced workers from Venice. After a short period all the handsome laces made by her workers were carried to Paris and displayed at Colbert's town house. They were arranged in a most artistic manner on the walls of a room hung with crimson damask, naturally being shown to the best advantage. Inspired by Colbert to see the exhibit, the King announced to his courtiers that he had established a manufactory for lace point at Alençon and set a day for a general inspection of the exhibit. At the appointed time the King with his nobles visited Colbert's house, and upon entering the room hung with handsome laces no one hesitated to express his great surprise and delight. The "Grande Monarque," thrilled with the sight, ordered a large sum of money be presented to Madame Gilbert and, turning to his nobles, emphatically addressed them: "Gentlemen, I hope I will see no other lace worn at court than this new fabric, upon which I bestow the name *point de France!*" Scarcely had the King left the room when the courtiers rushed back and at exorbitant prices purchased all the lace on ex-

COURTESY, ART INSTITUTE OF CHICAGO

Figure 604. Point d' Venice

After French design, 18th century.

hibit. This approval of the King brought fame and fortune to Alençon. Other centers were soon set up and all needlepoint *made in France* came to be known as "point de France." This was the lace now demanded for all important occasions. Ladies appeared with headdresses and trimmings and men with cravats and ruffles of the royal manufactories. The continued production and perfection of the stately needlepoints and the encouragement and development of widely distributed centers for the making of bobbin lace were among the important achievements of the century.

By this time Holland and Belgium were both known for the excellence of their bobbin and pillow laces. Many of these were made of silk or gold or silver thread. Linen thread laces, the finest in the world, were made for trimming the broad collars and cuffs of the Hollanders. The designs of these laces, quite distinct from those of Italy and France, may be seen in the famous portraits of this period (see Figure 39, Chapter 1). Figure 605. Flanders soon attained first place in the making of bobbin lace. Lying close to Flanders, England was among the first to use the beautiful Flemish laces. In such quantities were they consumed that England almost monopolized all Flemish lace produced; consequently, English coin was going out of the country at an alarming rate. This compelled the English Parliament to pass an act prohibiting all importation of foreign laces and led to the Flemish lacemakers being invited to England and encouraged to establish their lace centers there. England, however, did not have the right-quality flax, and the lace did not measure up in quality to that of the homeland. English capital, consequently, bought up all the choicest Flemish lace; then it was smuggled into Britain and sold under the new name *point d'Angleterre*, or English point. This eventually came to be the name by which all Flemish lace was known in England and France.

With the coming of the periwig, which covered the shoulders, lace collars were forced off the scene. Then came the cravat. The history of the early cravat is closely linked with lace, for the earliest of these were of fine linen or cambric with ends of handsome Venetian point. It was truly said at this period, "A man is known by the cravat he wears." Skirts flounced in vertical and horizontal rows, sleeves were set with tiers of ruffles called "engageants," and undergarments were profusely trimmed. The use of lace-trimmed undergarments was, indeed, an innovation. Having caught

Figure 605. Agatha Gelvinck. . . .
Dirck Dirchsz

About 1610-43 pleated and garooned ruffs disappear and are replaced by wide flat collars of Dutch linen trimmed with laces showing finely rounded and wide scallops instead of the earlier points.

the popular fancy, however, the fad continued and reached amazing popularity after the machine appeared. In 1662, Pepys records that while walking in Whitehall Gardens he observed hanging in the Priory Gardens "the finest smocks and linen petticoats of my Lady Castlemine's laced with rich *lace* at the bottom, that ever I saw, and it did me good to look at them." Besides underlinens, many handkerchiefs, caps, lappets, aprons, and the little pelerine were lace trimmed or made entirely of lace. The pelerine made its first appearance in 1672. This was a deep-pointed cape of lace which the Princess Palatine had evolved. This young Princess, upon viewing her French-made trousseau, was so shocked at the low bodices, cut strictly according to the mode, that she contrived this dainty lace cape to make up for lack of bodice. Ever and anon the pelerine, with slight modifications, has reappeared in the fashion world.

During the last thirty years of the century a fad "broke loose" for black lace dresses worn over the finest gold and azure brocade. The shimmer of gold and black was the coveted sign of elegance. The fashionable Madame de Sevigne, writing to a friend, informs her of the new mode:

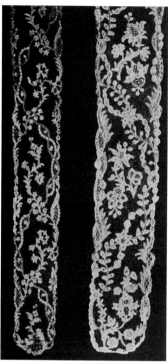

Figure 606. Lappets, 18th Century

Point d' Argentan and Italian needle lace, after French design.

> Have you heard of *transparents?* They are complete dresses of the finest gold and azure brocade and over them is worn a transparent black gown of beautiful English *lace*, or of chenille velvet, like that winter *lace* that you saw. They form a "transparent" which is a black dress with a gold, silver, or colored dress, just as one likes, and this is fashion.

In 1680, the *fontange* headdress had appeared. At first this was a simple band of ribbon but it soon grew into an elaborate headdress of stiffened silk or cambric and fluted lace. To this were often attached the beautiful lappets of expensive needlepoint. Figures 606, 607. Lappets continued to be worn throughout the seventeenth and eighteenth centuries. Sometimes they were looped, as worn in full dress, sometimes left hanging straight, but in whatever style they appeared they added the finishing note of elegance to the modish costume.

It was in Flanders during the early half of this century that the first "all lace" fan was made, probably for the Duke of Brabant. Previous to this period fans had been lace trimmed, the leaf being silk or parchment upon which the lace was either sewed or gummed. Several of these fans with the fan leaf entirely of lace are seen in contemporary portraits (see Figure 541, Chapter 33).

At the end of the century aprons were again the mode. Instead of the earlier bobbin lace fashionable during the previous century, they were now made entirely of fine needlepoint. These continued to be worn well into the eighteenth century, when they were followed by short aprons of silk or satin embroidered in simple pattern or trimmed with gold or silver bobbin lace and fringe. By the end of the eighteenth century these were replaced by the soft, white muslin aprons with dainty drawn work and white satin-stitch embroidery.

1700-1800

The highest development of bobbin lace belongs preëminently to the reign of Louis XV (1715-74). During this period these laces became beautiful, filmy creations, which, instead of imitating the favored needle-point, were designed to meet certain requirements of the bobbin and pillow method. There arose at this time those lighter, gayer, and more flowery patterns known as *Valenciennes, Mechlin, Chantilly*, and *Alen-*

Figure 607. Lappet, Bobbin Lace
Flemish point d'Angleterre, about 1750.

çon. In 1757 *blonde* lace, made of silk in natural color, was produced. The fashionable Madame Vigée le Brun, famous French painter, is said to have designed many of the most beautiful laces produced in the later years of the reign of Louis XV. Her celebrated portrait in the Uffizi Gallery at Florence pictures the artist in her dainty ruffles of Alençon, probably of her own design. PLATE LIII.

With their light, flowing patterns these later bobbin laces decked the underlinens and negligees of all women of fashion. They were lavishly used in the decoration of rooms. The luxury displayed by Louis XV and others of his court is well known. It is said that the toilet table of the Duchess of Bourbon was completely draped with spotted muslin and lengths of beautiful lace. The Princess de Conde had, "two bathing cloaks trimmed with lace, and drapery about the bath edged with d'Angleterre." Lace dresses were again fashionable, and Madame de Pompadour, the favorite of Louis XV, is said to have purchased a dress of point d'Angleterre costing, in American money, approximately fifteen thousand dollars. The lace dresses of this century were especially coveted as wedding dresses. Soon the fad for black lace descended upon the fashion-minded public, and with due haste shawls, scarfs, and mantles were being supplied. In the late eighteenth century, Chantilly in both black and white silk was winning its way to popularity in France. Other black laces soon followed. Normandy black lace and that of Belgium were highly prized. Madame Maintenon, who after the death of Louis XIV in 1775 had established a school for girls at St. Cyr, is said to have constantly worn about her shoulders a shawl of black Chantilly lace.

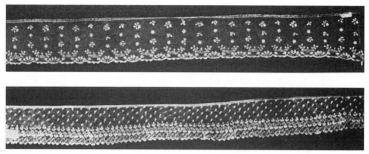

COURTESY, ART INSTITUTE OF CHICAGO

Figure 608. French Lace of the 1700's

The edging above is a copy of French point d' Alençon, late 18th century. The needle lace below is point d'Alençon, French, 18th century.

Toward the close of the century Queen Marie Antoinette wore quantities of blonde lace in natural color. The accounts of her dressmaker show on every page a record of the favorite blonde. This was a period of flounced gowns worn over the enormous hoop. Flounces of Valenciennes, blonde, and other favorite laces were festooned around the

COURTESY, METROPOLITAN MUSEUM OF ART

Figure 609. Collar, Point d'Alençon, French, 19th Century

skirt; and the front of the long narrow bodice was crossed with lace frills and the sleeves finished with "engageants" or ruffles of lace. Figure 610; PLATE LVII, page 565.

The coming of the Revolution did much to ruin the lace industry. Whole districts suffered losses, and many flourishing centers made lace no more. Valenciennes never recovered and Chantilly gradually declined. Lacemaking practically disappeared from France, and this same

PLATE LIII. Madame Vigée-Lebrun

The artist wears ruffs and cuffs of point d' Alençon, probably of her own design.

525

condition was reflected in other countries. These were, indeed, days of gloom. The Queen, formerly gay in her favorite blonde, now wore black net only. When leaving Versailles for the last time, October 6, 1789, she distributed among her ladies all that remained of her beautiful collection of laces.

COURTESY, METROPOLITAN MUSEUM OF ART

Figure 610. Madame Favart.......*Drouais*

Deep ruffles of lace finished the fashionable sleeve of the middle 1700's.

1800-1900

With the coming of the Empire period lace again entered upon the fashion scene. Napoleon interested himself in the lace indus-

COURTESY,
METROPOLITAN MUSEUM OF ART

Figure 611. Cape

Handmade net with embroidered sprays; American, early 19th century.

tries and is said to have shown an unusual appreciation for this beautiful work. Once upon viewing the soaring spire of the Cathedral of Antwerp, he is said to have exclaimed, *"C'est comme la dentelle de Malines!"* Fichus, long aprons trimmed with deep lace, and caps with extravagantly deep lace frills were among the most coveted accessories of dress. Then came a brief change: from 1820 to 1830 lace was strictly "out." When it did return it met with unbounded enthusiasm.

During the early years of the century lacemaking machines began to appear. As far back, however, as 1760, the mechanical manufacture of bobbin net was started by a workman in a stocking factory at Nottingham. He had conceived the idea of making the background mesh on a stocking machine and eventually had succeeded. In 1809 this was improved by a "bobbinet loom" or frame for weaving net. This invention, which falls to the honor of John Heathcoat, broke away entirely from the stocking frame. It was followed, in 1813, by a machine made in Eng-

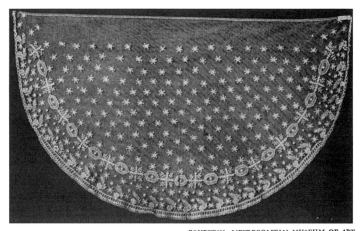

COURTESY, METROPOLITAN MUSEUM OF ART

Figure 612. Veil

Applied bobbin sprays on machine-made net; French, 19th century.

land by John Levers. This made a plain net or tulle eighteen inches wide; moreover, upon this machine figured laces could be turned out. Large shawls, handsome bridal veils, and other pieces of considerable size were now made by machine. In 1832, cotton thread began to take the place of linen. In 1837, Jacquard invented his machine for making flowered nets, which still more closely resembled the handsome laces. This new possibility of manufacture, with the attending low cost, brought unusual prosperity to those in the lacemaking business. The making of machine-made lace had now become an established industry.

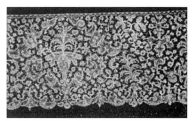

COURTESY, ART INSTITUTE OF CHICAGO

Figure 613. Flounces

Milanese bobbin lace, Italian, 18th century, and Flemish bobbin lace, 18th century.

From 1830 on, lace was in great demand. Chantilly and other patterns were revived and remained in favor for many years. Chantilly was especially popular between the years 1830 and 1840. It trimmed evening dresses in full, gathered flounces, and at times it was used for covering the skirt entirely save for a few inches at the waistline. It was also seen in the large, falling berthas, scarfs, and capes. Many famous portraits of the period are witnesses to the flounced gown in black, white, or natural-colored lace. PLATE LIV; Figures 613, 614. The apron, which had been intermittently fashionable since the seventeenth century, made its final appearance in the dainty, lace-trimmed tea apron of 1874-80.

During the early years of the century England was producing large quantities of pillow lace, most of it coming from Honiton, in Devonshire. This lace was brought into fashionable notice by Queen Victoria who, with the interest of the lacemakers at heart, ordered Honiton for her wedding dress. Though the lace could not compare with other laces in beauty its adoption by the Queen and later by her daughters and the Princess of Wales brought great demand for it; almost immediately Honiton came to be the most fashionable and expensive of English laces.

PHOTOGRAPH, GIRAUDON

Figure 614. Duchess d' Aumale. . . .
Winterhalter

The popularity of black lace is well exemplified in this fashionable gown of the late 19th century. Deep flounces of black lace almost cover the skirt, while the bodice carries its share of the favored material. Note the *boutonnière*. The black-gauze shawl or scarf completes the picture.

The lace shawl had also appeared about 1840 and continued a popular wrap for more than twenty years. Many of these were in black Chantilly, Maltese bobbin lace, or Brussels appliqué. Proud, indeed, was she who could display a handsome Chantilly shawl! Others less expensive were machine made in silk or cotton thread in imitation of the more expensive lace. During the

PLATE LIV. The Empress Eugénie......................*Winterhalter*

Flounces of what appears to be her favorite *blonde* cover the skirt and trim the bodice of this regal costume. Note the pearls and coronet.

century the lace pelerine was metamorphosed into the mantelet of lace and somewhat later into the dolman. The mantelet usually had double capes of lace reaching to the elbow, and long ends in front. The dolman was sometimes lace trimmed but it belongs definitely to a later period, from 1873-83, when trimmings of braid and fringe flourished. From 1870 to the opening years of the new century lace manufacture in France and

COURTESY, METROPOLITAN MUSEUM OF ART

Figure 615. Gown, Irish Crochet Lace
Made by Tardou, Paris, 1905-10.

Germany was sadly interrupted by the Franco-Prussian war and little lace was worn.

Twentieth Century

In the early years of the twentieth century lace was again revived. Though there was some demand for "real" lace, its cost made it largely prohibitive. The great stocks of lace in general use were all machine made. Old patterns were revived, modified, and produced under the name of *cluny* lace. Crochet lace, particularly the Irish crochet, had an unprecedented vogue in the early years of the century. Crochet lace-making had started back in the fifties in Ireland and had been given great attention by the nuns living in the convents. At first, the aim was to copy, as near as possible in crochet, the Venetian Point. In the effort, however, the nuns became interested in designing the crochet and lost interest in the needlepoint copy. Soon they were developing their own designs or patterns which have become celebrated the world over as *Irish crochet*. Figure 615.

By 1924 all kinds of laces were being used. Old laces, new laces, costly laces, cheap laces, all were in demand. Hats made entirely of lace were featured as the outstanding mode in the fashion world. Lace and narrow pleatings of lace were popular trimmings for hat and costume. Dyed laces in hues of blue, orchid, and brown were especially favored either for entire costumes or trimmings. By 1930 the use of lace in costume began to wane and was relegated largely to the popular accessories—the detachable collar and cuffs. Thus has the tide of lace ever risen and fallen with Fashion's demand. Though the extensive use of lace has fluctuated with the centuries, never have the glorious days of Louis XIV and XV returned. The world of today looks back to the seventeenth and eighteenth centuries as the period of handsome laces—a period when gallant gentlemen and lovely ladies, alike, looked with discriminating eye to the fitness of their laces, to the texture, the pattern, and withal to the exquisite effect of this most important detail of their dress.

REFERENCES

Blanc, Charles, *Art in Ornament and Dress*, pp. 193-210.
Boehn, Max von, *Modes and Manners; Ornaments*, Chapter I.
Bray, Helen A., *Textile Fibers, Yarns and Fabrics*, p. 104.
Ellsworth, Evelyn Peters, *Textiles and Costume Design*.
Head, Mrs. R. E., *The Lace and Embroidery Collector*.
Jackson, Mrs. F. Nevil, *History of Handmade Lace*.
Lefébure, Ernest, *Embroidery and Lace*.
Lester, Katherine Morris, *Historic Costume*, pp. 105, 200.
Moore, Mrs. N. Hudson, *The Lace Book*.
Palliser, Mrs. Bury, *History of Lace*.
Peterson's Fashion Magazine, February, 1863.
Pollen, Mrs. Hungerford, *Seven Centuries of Lace*.

CHAPTER 39

Fringe and Tassel

She shaw'd me a mantle o'red scarlet
Wi gouden flowers and *fringes* fine.

CHILD, *Ballads*

THE use of fringe is a very old form of dress decoration. Originally
it was made by the projecting threads of warp left at the edge of
woven stuffs. These were twisted and tied in one or more knots to prevent unraveling and thus formed a natural decoration along the edge
of the material. When the cloth was woven with many colors, the fringe
also showed many colors; when gold thread was used the fringe was,
of course, shot with gold.

During the Nineteenth and Twentieth Dynasties (1350-1090 B.C.) the
Egyptians wore a mantle edged with fringe. This mantle was no doubt
the forerunner of the modern shawl. The fringe of the Egyptian garment was made by the projecting threads of the warp. Speaking of this
fringed mantle, Herodotus says that the Egyptians "had a custom of
leaving *fringe* to their pieces of linen which, when the dresses were made,
formed a deep border around the legs." Deep fringes were also worn
about the neck. It is said by historians that these neck fringes are seen
on women usually pictured performing some menial service. This would
indicate that the custom prevailed among the lower classes. Bas-reliefs
from the Nineteenth and Twentieth Dynasties, found in the royal
tombs, furnish several instances of the use of fringe. In one, a Phoenician
prince brings gifts to a pharaoh of the Eighteenth Dynasty (1900 B.C.).
The garments of the prince are beautifully worked and adorned with
fringe, cord, and tassels. The tassel is of great antiquity. The original,
no doubt, was simply a knotted cord, the knot being intended to keep
the cord from unraveling.

The reliefs found in Khorsabad, Nineveh, and elsewhere show that
the Asiatics, particularly the Assyrians, wore their tunics and mantles
fringed and tasseled in elaborate form. Figure 616. This fringe, however,
was not a part of the woven material as was that of the Egyptians but
was added to the garment as a decoration. The loose, roomy garments
of the early Hebrews were likewise fringed and decorated with tassels
and embroidery. Several references to the fringe worn upon the ancient

Hebrew dress occur in the Old Testament. In Numbers XV:38, Moses is commanded to speak to the children of Israel and "bid them that they make them *fringes* in the borders of their garments throughout their generation, and that they put upon the *fringe* a ribband of blue." The blue "ribband" was a selvage intended to strengthen the fringed edge and keep it from unraveling. Many fragments of linen with these blue selvages are to be seen in the various collections. Further, the religious significance of the fringe is implied in the added words, "that ye may look upon it, and remember all the commandments of the Lord." Again, in Deuteronomy, occur these words, "Thou shall make the *fringes* upon the four quarters of the vesture, wherewith thou coverest thyself." Originally, the outer garment which the Jew wore was trimmed with fringe for religious reasons, but later, because of the persecution of the Jews, the fringe was hidden. It was then, and later as well, worn on an undergarment covered by the outer clothing.

Figure 616. The Elaborately Fringed and Tasseled Robes of an Assyrian King

After Layard.

In contrast with the generous use of fringe and tassel as seen in the East, the Greeks used this form of decoration sparingly. They never added fringe to the material; whenever it is seen it may always be understood as an integral part of the woven fabric. In Rome, the palla worn by women was sometimes edged with fringe, and a veil of transparent material, more or less richly fringed according to the wearer's position, was draped over the head so that it fell to the shoulders—sometimes even to the feet.

Middle Ages

During the Middle Ages, fringes of many colors frequently trimmed the loosely draped gown. Tassels, too, were in use. Figure 617. In the eleventh and twelfth centuries the word "tasseau" was applied by the French to the metal ornaments worn on the front edge of the mantle at the height of the shoulders. These were large, square or diamond-shaped plates, very handsome, resembling the modern clasp (see Figures 212 and 213, Chapter 14). However, instead of being provided with a hook for fastening, ribbons or cords were run through the openings in such a way that the mantle could be easily adjusted. By pulling the cords it could be drawn close about the neck, or by loosening them it was made to fall from the shoulders. The tasseau, which in no way resembled the modern tassel, was probably derived from the Latin tassa, which is described as a "clasp" or "fibula." The cause of the change in meaning which has taken place is not clear, but it is definitely asserted that our present meaning of "tassel" did not exist in the twelfth century. The object which is today everywhere called "tassel" was by the French of the period called *houppe*.

Figure 617. Tassel and Cord from a Girdle of the 12th Century

After Viollet-le-Duc.

Many of the monumental effigies of the Middle Ages show elaborate tassels as a part of the cord which held the enveloping mantle. The tomb of Lady Tiptoft (1446) gives a record of just such a handsome cord fastening; another is from that of the tomb of Christina Philip (1470). Figures 618, 620. Invariably the heavy cord was terminated by silken tassels. This period also marks the beginning of the fitted garment, and with this a girdle completed the fashionable effect. Strips of embroidered cloth, twisted silks, and strands of gold and silver cord were transformed into these modish girdles, usually secured by long cords terminating in various types of tassel. Figure 619. Tassels were at

Figure 618. Mantle Ties, 1446

Shows the ornamental tassels and the long cord which held the mantle in place.

From the brass of Lady Tiptoft.

this time elaborate ornaments. They were frequently made of gold thread set with jewels. Fringe, though recognized, was not generally adopted into civil costume until the fifteenth century. The Church, however, found much use for it as a decoration for the vestments, using it to enrich the ends of the stole, the veils, and the open sides and lower edge of the dalmatics. By the latter half of the fif-

teenth century fringe-making had become a craft. Then it was that Fashion encouraged its use in costume, and from this period records frequently mention various fringes and their cost. In the wardrobe accounts of Edward I of England are listed, "fringes of Venice gold at six shillings and four pence an ounce."

Figure 619.
Girdle, 1558

A girdle of yellow and red silk, the ends drawn through rings, giving the effect of tassels.

1500-1600

The modern world is greatly indebted to the German master Hans Holbein, court painter to Henry VIII, for accurate knowledge of the costume of the sixteenth century. Not only cloaks, hats, ruffs, girdles,

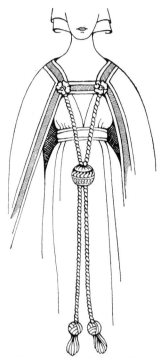

Figure 620. Mantle Ties, 1470

Shows the long cord with tassels which held the mantle in place.

From the brass of Cristina Philip.

bags, chains, and other important accessories are pictured but an equally painstaking care has been bestowed upon lesser details. The illustration, Figure 621, is a drawing of two tassels after designs by Holbein. Not only tassels but fringe as well decorated the costume of the period. Figure 622. In Hall's description of a court masque during the reign of Henry VIII, women are said to have been attired in garments resembling "fringed gold." Later, in Elizabeth's reign, fringed and embroidered petticoats were the vogue. These petticoats were sometimes adorned by a single row of fringe; at other times four or six rows, one above the other, were worn. The rows were called "feet;" consequently, milady with six rows of fringe on her petticoat was said to have a petticoat of six feet. Another coveted accessory of this period was the embroidered and fringed glove. The handsome gauntlets of the sixteenth and early seventeenth centuries, particularly those of cavalier days, were heavily edged with gold fringe (see PLATE XXV, Chapter 15). About 1638, when the ban was placed on the wearing of excessive decoration and accessories very little fringe was used. Later, however, fringe came into still greater favor. Figures 623, 624, 625. In the *Tale of the Tub* by Jonathan Swift, three brothers are found twisting their father's will to get permission to wear

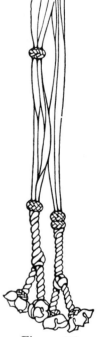

Figure 621. Tassels
After designs by Holbein.

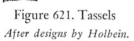

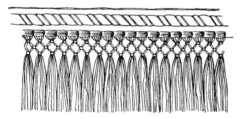

Figure 622. Silver Fringe, Renaissance

Figure 623.
Leather Tassel
from a Lady's
Bag, Renaissance

on their dress braid, tufts of ribbon, and the enviable fringe.

1700-1800

During the early years of the eighteenth century both fringe and tassels were in demand as decoration for costume. An inventory of the wearing apparel of Charles II bears out the fact that fringe was worn on the charming waistcoats of the period, for it mentions: "Fringe of gold for waistcoat." It was during this same century that the fashion of fly fringe laid siege to the hearts of women. Figure 626. This was made of simple tufts of silk, matching the gown, alternating two and four tufts. Usually made by women themselves, it was a popular trimming over a

COURTESY, METROPOLITAN MUSEUM OF ART

Figure 624. Various Types of Tassels Worn from the
16th to the 19th Centuries

COURTESY, METROPOLITAN MUSEUM OF ART

Figure 625. Various Types of Fringes Popular from the
16th to 19th Centuries

considerable period of time. There were also colored fringes, frequently used to trim the popular white dresses of the period. When fringe appeared, tassels, a decorative form of fringe, were always near at hand.

As far back as Chaucer's time reference is made to tied fringe in the form of tassels. The purse of one of the Canterbury company is described thus:

> And by hire girdel heng a purs of lether
> *Tasseled* with grene and perled with latoun.
>
> CHAUCER, *Miller's Tale*, I, 64

1800-1900

Beginning about 1780 and on through the following century, fringe and tassels were conspicuous trimmings. In fact, moderns look back to the nineteenth century as the period of the fringe and tassel. In France,

Figure 626. Fly Fringe

This was the most popular trimming of the 18th century. Made with tufts of silk alternating two and four.

England, and America all women were wearing these handsome trimmings. Chenille fringe, fringe made of sewing silks, and fringe made of ribbon were the novelties of the period. All through the early years these were worn intermittently; then about 1860 fashion books began to display tassels on women's capes, hoods, and sometimes a single swinging tassel was added to the top center-front of the high shoe. From 1873 on, tassels and fringe were in their heyday. Handsome fringes were festooned over the skirt of the fashionable gown, hung in a silken mass from the trussed-up overdress, or worn with the popular dolman. Figure 627. On scarfs, sashes, or wherever else a finishing edge was needed, fringe or tassels were employed. On fringed parasols carried by the belles of the century, tassel and cord invariably decorated the handle. Then, after this unprecedented popularity of the late nineteenth century the pendulum swings in the opposite direction and fringe and tassels are "out."

With the passing of the years both tassels and fringe have been made of many materials and have constantly varied in length and general style. The days of their popularity come and go as the wheel of fashion turns. When tassels and fringe are "in," no detail of dress is more effective in giving an enviable smartness to clothes. Quite the reverse, however, is true when tassels and fringe are "out." How utterly passé is she who persists in tassels and fringe after their knell has been sounded!

Twentieth Century

During the early years of the twentieth century, handsome fringes were revived and used upon various articles of dress. They trimmed the blouse and the sash and were sufficiently deep to form the larger part of the

Figure 627. The Elaborately Fringed Costume of the 70's

skirt of an afternoon or evening frock. In contrast with the earlier centuries when handsome fringes graced the mantle and later the waistcoat and gloves of gentlemen, the twentieth century finds this decoration in the exclusive possession of women. As with lace, embroidery, ribbon, and jewels, fringe and tassels have also been eliminated from masculine fashions, and men's dress reflects the very practical life of this twentieth century.

REFERENCES

Blanc, Charles, *Art in Ornament and Dress*, p. 123.
Boehn, Max von, *Modes and Manners; Ornament*, Chapter VI.
Dress Decoration and Ornamentation, p. 26. Woman's Institute.
Evans, Mary, *Costume Throughout the Ages*, pp. 2, 11, 65, 98.
Harper's Bazaar, 1870-75.
Lester, Katherine Morris, *Historic Costume*.
New International Encyclopedia, Vol. IX.
Peterson's Fashion Magazine, August, 1863.
Sage, Elizabeth, *A Study of Costume*, pp. 8, 201.
Wilkinson, Sir John Gardiner, *A Popular Account of the Ancient Egyptians*.

CHAPTER 40

Fur

Clad them all in clothes of price
And *furred* them with ermine.

From the story of King Robert of Sicily,
printed in HALLIWELL'S *Nagae Poeticae*

IN the early history of clothing, fur was worn only for warmth. Later it came to be a medium of barter between tribes. Then as civilization advanced other materials were substituted for this purpose and fur came more and more to be used as a decoration to dress.

The Egyptians, Greeks, Romans, and Gallo-Romans all wore fur for warmth and not as a trimming or decoration. Herodotus relates that the natives living along the shores of the Caspian Sea wore sealskins. The Greeks received their skins from southern Europe and Russia. The Romans bought furs from the barbarians across the Alps. We read that the early Roman Church fathers deplored the excessive use of fur as a "barbarous luxury." During the Middle Ages and a long time thereafter, the great fur centers were the ports about the Baltic Sea. From this region came many of the fine furs which soon began to play an important role in costume and which from that distant day to the present continued to maintain their challenging hold in the realm of dress.

Middle Ages

As modern dress evolved during the Middle Ages, fur was destined to hold an important place. As early as the fifth century Frankish men and women were wearing a covering for the hands lined with fur and resembling the modern mittens. During the following centuries fur continued to be used in the various types of handcovering. Though fur was undoubtedly worn for warmth by lesser folk, it was those of wealth, power, and influence who set the mode. In the eighth century, when Charlemagne appeared in his great semicircular cloak lined throughout with fine fur, he did much to establish the fashion for centuries to come. His use of a short, sleeveless jacket of otter for extra warmth also brought this into high favor among his followers. The state robes of the early Normans were very elaborate: their mantles or cloaks, which were of great importance, were lined with fine furs. The luxurious, furred mantles of kings and peers of succeeding centuries had their beginnings in these official robes of earlier date.

By the thirteenth century fur was in general use. According to Joseph Strutt, who has given a full account of the habits of the people of England from the time of the early Saxons to the nineteenth century, "the fur of sables, beavers, foxes, cats, and lambs were used

Figure 628. Marguerite de Beaujeau

The fur-lined mantle was an important article of dress in 1300.

From a collection of engravings of French women, "Celebrated for Their Talent, Their Rank, or Their Beauty," published in 1827.

Figure 629. The Surcoat, Rich in Ermine, a Fashionable Feature in The Dress of the 13th and 14th Centuries

After Viollet-le-Duc.

in England before the Conquest; to which afterward were added those of the ermine, squirrel, marten, rabbit, goat, and many other animals." While the poor used fur only for warmth the more costly pelts gradually came to be a prized luxury in the dress of the wealthy. The latter used small, expensive skins such as the ermine, miniver, and sable; the former contented themselves with sheep, goat, and badger skins.

The enveloping mantle was an item of much significance in the dress

of both men and women. Figure 628. From earliest times it had been regarded as a symbol of superiority worn only by persons of distinction.
Many mantles of the twelfth and thirteenth centuries were lined through-

Figure 630. Madame Maintenon, Wife of Louis XIV

The Queen wears a costume rich in ermine. Note the fontange headdress and the hood.

From French collection of 1827 (see Figure 628).

out with fur, ermine and sable being used for this purpose. The first
appearance of sable was in the reign of Henry I of England (1100-35).
It is said that this king was presented with a mantle of "exquisitely fine
cloth lined with black sables with white spots, and of great value." During the thirteenth century ermine was one of the choice furs used to
enrich the modish surcoat so fashionable in the dress of women of the
period. Figure 629. In fact ermine continued to be most highly esteemed,
its use being limited to the dress of kings, queens, and others of high
official distinction. Figure 630.

By the fourteenth century the use of fur had greatly increased. In an
old manuscript of this period, preserved in the British Museum, the
author admonishes that dress be chosen with a view to health and sug-

gests for each successive season various materials at times combined with fur. For spring he advises, "clothing neither hot nor cold, such as cloths of cotton *furred* with lamb skin." For summer, linen and silk is recommended; for autumn, "clothing something similar to that of spring or something thicker and warmer;" for winter, "a good substantial woolen lined with *furs*." He speaks especially of the fur of the fox as the warmest and advises that if this is not obtainable that the rabbit or cat be substituted. At this period, sable; miniver, a white ermine without tails or spots; gris, the fur of the marten; and "vair," a composite fur made of the white of the ermine and the bluish gray of the squirrel, were in use. Another fur, also known as "vair," was that of a species of squirrel, black on the back and white on the throat and breast. During the twelfth century this was imported to western Europe from Hungary and was worn extensively. As early as the reign of Edward III (1327-77), laws were being enacted restricting the use of ermine to the royal family and to those other nobles whose incomes reached one thousand pounds per year. Later the privilege was extended to the entire nobility. The wearing of sable was likewise limited to the nobility and special heads of the official household. As late as the time of Edward IV (1461-83), no one below the estate of lord was permitted to wear sable. Besides ermine and sable, miniver was also highly esteemed at this time.

Figure 631. Queen Claude, First Wife of Francis I, 1500

The Queen wears the great furred cuffs. Note the French hood with hanging veil and the elaborate *troussoire*.

From French collection of 1827.

1500-1600

The early Renaissance finds fur even more desirable as an adornment to dress. The famous portraits and numerous drawings of distinguished persons furnish ample proof of the popularity of fur. Modish women wore great hanging cuffs of fur. Sleeves, very close at the shoulders and extended to the elbow, widened out into great bell-shaped openings lined with fur and then turned back, often as far as the elbow, giving the effect of an enormous fur cuff. Figure 631. Portraits of Queen Mary, daughter of Henry VIII, Ann Boleyn, Catherine Parr, Queen Claude, first wife of Francis I, and other fashionables of the period show these great hanging cuffs of fur. Gowns of this interesting age were made of taffeta trimmed with the fur of the lynx, black genet, marten, sable, and others of value. Ladies wrapped themselves in fur mantles in cold weather and when it was not so cold wore a scarf of sable, fox, or marten with head and claws mounted in gold and enriched with jewels. Figure 632. These of course were of great value. Designs were carried out by the artist craftsmen of the period, who were unlimited in their use of gold and precious stones. Records show that one duchess had a sable fur the head of which was gold set with rubies, diamonds, emeralds, and pearls. Another possessed one having the head ornamented with five rubies and five emeralds; the eyes were garnets and a pearl was held in the mouth; the golden claws were likewise set with emeralds and rubies. In the "Portrait of a Lady" attributed to Antonio Moro, the handsome scarf shows an ornamental head, probably of gold set with jewels. The velvet gown is trimmed with narrow bands of fur which emphasize the form of the sleeve and edge the open front of the skirt. The rich-

NATIONAL MUSEUM, MUNICH

Figure 632. Fashionable Fur Piece, Late 16th Century

Note gold and jeweled ornamentation of the head and claws.

ness of material and wealth of ornament, which are rendered with exacting care, bespeak a lady of wealth and taste. PLATE LV.

While women of the period were indulging their taste for fine furs, gentlemen were not to be outdone. They adopted great coats with wide fur collars which lay out on the shoulders and then continued down each side of the front. Very imposing coats these were. The many portraits of famous personalities of the period leave no doubt as to their popularity. Figure 633. Hans Holbein, court painter to Henry VIII, and Albrecht Dürer of Nuremberg have left a galaxy of portraits picturing the great furred coats of this century. In 1515, fur-trimmed hats for men were also the vogue. At the same time gloves claimed their share of fur. They were lined with various kinds and colors, which were displayed by turning back the cuff. Cat and fox were the popular lining furs for gloves, while the fur of the Polish wolf lined the fashionable mittens. In this century, as in former times, fur was an enrichment for dress possible only to the wealthy. As late as 1558 England passed a law prohibiting the use of sable to anyone below the rank of viscount, and only the royal family were permitted to wear the "fur of the black genet."

COURTESY, METROPOLITAN MUSEUM OF ART

Figure 633. Portrait of a Man....
Francesco Torbido

The great coat with massive collar and revers of fine fur distinguished many portraits of early 1500. The little white ruffles at collar and wrists are a prophecy of the ruffs and cuffs to come.

1600-1700

With fur's continued popularity through the next century, the two outstanding items of importance are: first, the growing fur trade carried on by the colonists in America; secondly, that modish development in costume, the fur muff. Early in the century the American colonists, particularly in the French and Dutch colonies, saw the great possibilities of the fur trade in this new, open country. It is said that the first ship which returned to England from Plymouth carried two hogsheads of beaver. Later, after the middle of the century, quantities ranging from forty to fifty thousand pelts were sent to Amsterdam. Beaver and otter were both sought in the trade, but beaver was considered the more valuable. A rate of exchange was set up by the colonists which today furnishes interesting information as to the value set upon the pelt of our native beaver during the period of colonization in America:

PLATE LV. Portrait of a Lady...............*Attributed to Antonio Moro*

The lady wears the fashionable gold-and-jewel-headed fur piece. Her handsome gown follows the prevailing mode (1500), and the elaborate ornament, necklace and pendant, rings and troussoire, are likewise characteristic of the period. In her hand she carries the jeweled scent box, or pomander.

Guns—12 winter beaver skins for largest; 10 for medium; 8 for smallest.
Powder—a beaver for ½ lb.
Shot—a beaver for 4 lbs.
Hatchets—a beaver for a great and little hatchet.
Knives—a beaver for 8 great knives and 8 jack knives.
Beads—a beaver for ½ lb. of beads.
Laced coats—6 beavers for one.
Plain coats—5 beavers for one plain coat.
Coats for women, laced, 2 yds.—6 beavers.
       "   "   " , plain—5 beavers.
Tobacco—6 beavers for 1 lb.
Powder horn—a beaver for a large powder horn and two small ones.
Kettles—a beaver for 1 wt. of kettle.
Looking glass and comb—2 skins.

So immensely lucrative did the fur business become and so great was the competition that it finally passed from the hands of the French and Dutch settlers into those of a company of English noblemen under the imposing name of the Hudson Bay Fur Company. With the increased supply of beaver skins, this fur rapidly came to be a fashionable feature in the dress of the period. These pelts were not always sent to England, but many of them reached Russia, where they were highly prized for their glossiness. Here they were used to line mantles and also, cut in strips, to enrich the costume with bandings and borders. Another contribution of the little beaver was the beaver hat, for centuries so choice and costly an accessory of dress. True, beaver hats had been worn as far back as the days of Chaucer. In the *Canterbury Tales*, the Merchant is described as wearing:

> On his head a Flaundrish *bever* hat.

It was in the early days of the seventeenth century, however, after Charles I of England had ruled that no fur except that of the beaver be used in the manufacture of hats, that the little beaver made its major contribution to the famous headgear of the world.

1700-1800

And now to the muff! True enough, muffs had been carried in earlier days but these were the very tiny *countenances* made of silk, velvet, and other materials. Later, the muff of material came to be banded with fur. Then followed the all-fur muff. Muffs for men came in about 1668, but by the end of the century both men and women were carrying them. The priceless old prints of this period show not only the belles and beaux with their fanciful muffs but also men of affairs, the dignified leaders of the day (see Figure 550, Chapter 34). Figure 634. They are seen carrying their great fur muffs with an air of imposing grace well-nigh unbelievable in this practical twentieth century. These large muffs, often of luxurious sables, were decorated with bows, artificial flowers, and knots of ribbon and lace. During this flair for muffs, the colonists of America, not one whit behind their cousins across the sea, were also carrying muffs. As late as 1725 Dr. Price, serving the old South Church, Boston, lost his "black bearskin muff" and somebody else lost his "sableskin muff." Men continued to carry muffs until about 1780, when the fashion gradually declined. In women's dress muffs were at their largest about 1810, continuing fashionable to about 1830 (see PLATES XLVII, XLVIII, Chapter 34). After a period of enormous size they gradually grew smaller. Muffs were always, however, considered an important item in the fashionable dress of the period.

Figure 634. Gentleman in Winter Dress, 1688

From an old engraving.

1800-1900

The early nineteenth century brought in the round boa, which later broadened into the stole. Stole and the muff of similar skins brought in the "sets" of furs which every fashion-bent woman was determined to possess—and did. Sable sets, seal sets, mink sets, marten sets, and chinchilla sets were the order of the day. Later in the century after the hoopskirt had run its course came the sealskin coat usually reaching to the knee but in some instances falling to the hem of the skirt. These were both costly and handsome, and when worn with the rustling black grosgrain silk dress milady was indeed formidable! The sealskin coat of this day was unusually lovely in color, the fur being dark brown at the ends and changing into a tawny, golden glint near the skin. The art of achieving this effect was lost with the death of the London crafts-man who discovered it. While the sealskin coat was having its day varia-tions were introduced in the way of bandings, collar, and cuffs. Fre-quently an eight- to ten-inch band of beaver was set about the lower edge of the coat, with matching collar and cuffs added. She who could not afford the coat of seal contented herself with one of silk plush with the beaver trim. During the reign of the sealskin coat an innovation appeared in the form of a sealskin hat. This was shaped like the English walking hat with rounded crown, in derby shape. A long, golden-brown plume was set at the front, passed over the crown, and drooped behind. Such a hat with its companion, the sealskin coat, represented the very height of the mode from 1875-77.

Figure 635. The Circular and Silk Coat

Lined throughout with fur and edged with marten, they were outstanding modes in the late 19th century.

During the same period there came a revival of the long, enveloping mantle or cape. In the early days of the fashion, these were cut in a perfect, semicircular form and, consequently, came to be known as "circulars." Fashioned of silk, satin, or other fine cloth of extra width manufactured for the purpose, they were lined throughout with rabbit or gray squirrel combined with white, which resembled to a marked degree the ancient vair. With this enveloping mantle milady of the modern world wrapped herself in fur and enjoyed its luxury quite as much as had her ancient forbear. Figure 635.

Fur linings for circulars led to fur linings for coats. Old fashion plates of the period show three-quarter cloth and silk coats lined throughout with fur, usually squirrel, edged with marten. Finally, after three decades of fur coats and enveloping wraps, the fashion had run its course, and milady then gave her attention to shorter capes of seal, mink, marten, and the matching "sets" of furs which had again invaded the ranks of fashion. By this time the former stole had merged into various types of the collar and "neckpiece." During the nineties when the fashion emphasis was at the shoulders, the neckpiece took the

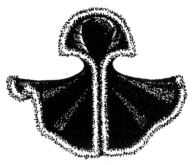

Figure 636. Neckpiece, 1897

Figure 637. Fur Muffs, 1897

form of a wide collar that lay in waves and flutes and stood protectingly high about the throat. Figure 636. Milady chose her matching set of a favorite fur, a fur-trimmed material, or the popular *astrakan*, a black lambskin from southern Russia. Still another version of the fur fashions of the late century were the long boa, probably a yard and a half to two yards in length, and the matching muff worn with it. These were usually of lynx, fox, sable, or other expensive furs. The boa was wrapped about the neck with one long end flung carelessly over the left shoulder. Figure 638. Women of fashion now came to select their furs with discriminating eye, choosing hues harmonious to individual coloring. Many blue-eyed blondes were seen in blue-gray fox; others with brilliant coloring chose glossy lynx or black fox. Not only did fur find a place in street costumes, but distinctive evening gowns courted the same luxury. Narrow bandings and edgings of sable were worn with yellow velvet, astrakan was combined with pink velvet, and combinations of lace and fur were fashionable. Such fashions continued to make heavy demands upon the fur trade, which was constantly enlarging its field to supply the market in this country and in Europe, where fur was equally popular.

PLATE LVI. Booth Tarkington... *Wayman Adams*

Fur, for collars and as a lining for greatcoats, is as highly regarded in the modern world as it has been in periods long past.

Twentieth Century

By the twentieth century great changes had come upon the world. Well-heated homes and heated cars had modified to some extent the use of fur in costume. To be appropriately clothed within as well as out-of-doors was the problem. With homes at summer heat and no draughts to chill one's winter ease, there was no necessity for the flannels and petticoats of our grandmothers. Out-of-doors, however, one was confronted with the same long, cold winter. To bridge the gap between inside, where one was lightly clad, and outside, where protection was necessary, the fur coat again entered upon the fashion scene.

In the modern world the fur coat has become a very popular luxury. With its almost universal adoption the demand for furs has grown enormous; to supply the market the genius of man has been taxed to the utmost! Moreover, the modern use of fur has become a matter of choice, not edicts. It is worn by the wealthy, and with equal grace by those not so wealthy. The great demand has inspired the trappers and dealers in furs to press into service the humbler rodents and the drabber branches of the fox and marten families. Today, by the artful handling of dresser and designer, these lowly pelts have been rescued from obscurity. The demand of the age is for beautiful but less expensive skins so skillfully dyed and dressed that they take on the beauty of the rare, costlier furs.

One of the most favored skins is the "Hudson seal," the trade name for the little muskrat, the tiny rodent that furnishes innumerable coats for milady of fashion. Two other popular skins parading under equally glorified names in the trade are rabbit and lamb. Rabbit pelts prepared in various ways are known in the market under such names as Austrian seal, Baltic seal, Baltic tiger, beaverette, electric seal, sealine, electric mole, squirrelette, and coney; processed lamb has the trade names astrakan, broadtail, and caracul.

Outstanding among the fashionable coats of the twentieth century are those fitted with collars and cuffs of contrasting color. Seal coats with fitch collars and cuffs, seal with kolinsky, tiger with seal, or seal with tiger, are among the popular combinations. For general sport wear the long coat of racoon holds first place. Other pelts used in coats subject to rough usage are tiger, leopard, opossum, Russian pony, and beaver. As in the past, men prefer only the collar with sometimes cuffs of fur. Occasionally, however, coats are lined throughout with fur. PLATE LVI. Among the fur scarfs, collars, and muffs of the early century were many full-sized pelts of silver fox, black fox, red fox, and lynx with ornamental head and tail added. The full skins lying flat about the shoulders were lined with silk, satin, or soft crepe. When a full-sized pelt was rolled into a large muff it was likewise padded and carefully lined. This, in its day, was a much-coveted luxury. For mid-season wear, the long boa so fashionable in an earlier period was a popular choice; this usually was worn without the accompanying muff. Muffs since 1924 have rapidly declined in popularity, forced off the fashion scene by the well-heated motor car.

Figure 638. The Long Boa Worn with the Little Beret of 1929

During the centuries the fur trade has steadily grown in importance. Prior to the World War, London, Leipzig, and Paris were the great fur markets of the world. Since that time, however, many changes have come about, and today the United States markets furs all over the world and imports foreign furs for re-export. New York has become one of the greatest fur markets of the world. Many of the choicest pelts of modern times come from the far north, Alaska, Siberia, and the rest of that land fringing the Arctic Ocean. Here are found the seal, sable, otter, mink, lynx, marten, ermine, bear, and fox. From Persia, Russia, and the highlands of Tibet and Mongolia comes the fur known as "Persian lamb." From high up in the Andes comes the chinchilla, a member of the rat family whose fur is among the most beautiful and most valuable known. From South America comes the coypu, an animal resembling the American beaver whose fur is called "nutria." Various parts of the North-American continent furnish the world with skins constantly used in costume. Among these are the fox, raccoon, skunk, muskrat, opossum, badger, hare, and squirrel. Indeed, both in production and use of fur, North America leads all the other continents in the fur trade.

Through the centuries fur has played a stellar role in the world's dress. Valued first for warmth and then for adornment it soon came to be the luxury of kings and nobles, a badge of distinction, a symbol of office. Indeed, a man's social prominence was gauged by the amount and kind of fur he wore! From that day to this the demand for furs has never ceased. Today, Fashion, that wily old dame of the centuries, still nods her approval of the enviable leadership of fur in the dress of the modern world.

REFERENCES

Brereton, Lt. Col. F. S., *Clothing*. The Essentials of Life Series.
Boehn, Max von, *Modes and Manners; Ornaments*, p. 240.
Carpenter, Frank George, *How the World Is Clothed*.
Davey, Richard, *Fur and Fur Garments*.
Evans, Mary, *Costume Throughout the Ages*, p. 224.
Gottleib, Abraham, *Fur Truths*, Chapter I.
Sage, Elizabeth, *A Study of Costume*.
Vogue, November 24, 1930; January 15, 1931.

CHAPTER 41

Ribbon

She's torn the *ribbon* frae her head
They were baith thick and narrow.

CHILD, *The Braes o' Yarrow*

RIBBON or *ribband* originally signified a stripe in material, usually a narrow band, either applied or woven, forming a border. In Numbers XV:38, Moses is commanded to speak to the children of Israel and direct them in the making of their garments, specifying that they "put upon the fringe of the borders a *ribband* of blue." The blue ribbon was a selvage added to the fringed edge to strengthen it and keep it from unraveling. Many fragments of material with the blue selvage or *ribband* are preserved in the various museum collections. Some of these specimens are bordered with blue stripes alternating with narrow lines of another color. Patterns vary in width from one half to an inch and a quarter. Aside from the use of ribband as a selvage, narrow strips of material, probably a kind of tape, were often employed for the decoration of the hair. The Egyptian tomb paintings picture the women of that day wearing a fillet, such a strip or tape, sometimes ornamented with a lotus bud falling over the forehead. We read that the women of ancient Greece and Rome bound their hair with a fillet or ribbon.

In perfect view their hair with fillets tied.

VIRGIL's *Aeneid*

This, however, was probably a similar tape, very different from our modern ribbons with two selvages, for these did not appear until the Renaissance period (1500). The Gallo-Roman women twisted similar ribbons through the braids of their long, luxuriant hair. The Merovingians, who also wore long plaits of hair, intertwined the braids with ribbon and flowers.

Middle Ages

In Chretien de Troyes' medieval romance, *Eric et Enid*, we find a delightful description of costume in which ribbons were the finishing touches of elegance:

The Queen . . . gave orders to bring quickly the fresh tunic and the greenish-purple mantle, embroidered with little crosses, which was lined with white ermine even to the sleeves. . . . This tunic was very rich, but not a whit less precious, I trow, was the mantle. As yet, there were no *ribbons* on it; for the mantle like the tunic was brand new. The mantle was very rich and fine: laid about the neck were two sable skins, and in the tassels there was more than an ounce of gold; on one a hyacinth, and on the other a ruby flashed more bright than burning candle. . . . The fur lining was white ermine; never was finer seen or found. The cloth was skillfully embroidered with little crosses, all different, indigo, vermilion, dark blue, white, green, blue, and yellow. The Queen called for some *ribbons* four ells long, made of silken thread and gold. The *ribbons* are given to her, handsome and well-matched. Quickly she had them fastened to the mantle by some one who knew how to do it, and who was master of the art. . . . Strung upon a *ribbon* about her neck, a damsel hung two brooches of enamelled gold.

1500-1700

It was not until the sixteenth century that ribbon as it is now known, with two selvages, was either seen or heard of. It was then for the first time introduced into Europe in the form of strips of various widths, separate from the woven border of garments. The first ribbon manufactured was probably cloth interwoven with gold and silver thread. This made it very expensive, and doubtless it was regarded as an article of great luxury. So thought the English Parliament for, in the sixteenth century, it saw fit to reserve to the nobility alone the right to wear ribbon, forbidding its use to the tradesmen of the realm.

It was in the early years of the seventeenth century that ribbon began to invade the ranks of fashion, and by the middle of the century it had risen in popular favor to the important place which it has maintained to the present day. The profusion with which ribbon was used in the costume of both men and women during the seventeenth century is well-nigh incredible. Every portion of the attire was decorated with bows, bands, and loops of ribbon. The walking stick, as well, was graced with bunches of ribbon tied near the head. The dandies are said to have used ribbon, usually red, as a leash to lead their white poodles about. The short trousers of the gay cavaliers, the fashionable *rhingraves*, were profusely trimmed with loops of ribbon about the knee and up the sides; doublets were graced with loops and bows of ribbon; sleeves were puffed and tied with ribbon bows; elaborate shoulder knots of ribbon were a fashionable conceit. Figure 639. Evelyn, upon seeing a fop of his day strutting through Westminster Hall, voiced his feeling in no uncertain language:

It was a fine silken thing I espied th' other day walking through Westminster Hall, that had so much *ribbon* about him as would have plundered six shops and set up twenty country peddlers.

Later, sashes of ribbon, in lieu of garters, were worn at the knee, gay-colored ribbons were sewed to the sleeves and waist of the doublet, and rosettes of ribbon, the fashionable shoe-roses, graced the instep.

Figure 639. An Elegant, Late 1600's

After Jacquemin.

My heart was in my mouth
Till I had viewed his shoes well; for the *roses*
Were big enough to hide a cloven hoof.
                          BEN JONSON

Shortly after this profuse use of ribbon in men's attire, it gradually lessened.

In women's dress the fitted bodice tapering to a long point was the fashionable note. In her efforts to match the taste of the gallant of her day, milady's pointed bodice was decorated with ribbon arranged in graduated loops or "tiers" on each side of the front. These were known as "ladders." The sleeves were finished wide, and a fringe of lace or ribbon was added about the edge. Bunches of ribbon, arranged at the side, adorned the hair. About 1680, the high headdress known as the *fontange* or *commode,* made up of graceful loops of ribbon backed with lace, captured feminine fancy (see Figure 42, Chapter 1). In fact, ribbon was everywhere in evidence as a fashionable decoration. As with all fads and fancies, however, ribbon, too, gradually ran its course and by 1700 had subsided into a very modest part of costume.

1700-1800

During the early years of the eighteenth century men appropriated the use of black ribbon for the Ramilie wig and for the bag of the bag wig (see Figures 104, 105, Chapter 4). At this period watches were worn in pairs, and short ribbon fobs became the vogue. In woman's dress, the deep-pointed bodice which encased the wasplike waist was decorated from bosom to point with a series of graduated ribbon bows. Figure 640. Later, during the reign of Marie Antoinette, when towering headdresses were the rage, ribbon with lace, flowers, and other dainty creations was generously employed to ornament the structure. Though ribbon, when compared with its popularity in the previous century, had somewhat declined, bows and knots were still used as a finishing note to the bodice, sleeve, or elaborately flaired skirt. This was the period when handsome laces held first place in the hearts of women, when flounces and ruffles of lace were the final word in fashion, so naturally ribbon quietly retreated to second place. In colonial America very little ribbon was worn. This was an expression of general feeling against the extravagance of the English court customs.

COURTESY, METROPOLITAN MUSEUM OF ART

Figure 640. Portrait of a Lady....
Sir Joshua Reynolds

Ribbon bows and loops trimmed the costume of all fashionable women from 1768-92.

1800-1900

With the opening of the nineteenth century ribbon was again in demand. As an important phase of the millinery field it rose to new heights. In 1820, pretty ribbon streamers hung from ladies' hats. The pokes of 1840 and thereabout were trimmed with loops of ribbon and secured under the chin by long ribbon ties (see Figure 61, Chapter 1). The quaint dresses of the period were trimmed with ribbon, and a narrow black ribbon took, for a time, the place of the bracelet upon milady's wrist. In 1870, ribbon streamers, together with bits of lace and flowers hanging from the back of the little forward-tilted hat, fell over the big chignon (see Figure 63, Chapter 1). At the same period plaid or tartan ribbons were fashionable touches of color for the black horsehair bonnets. In 1890, a bow of "feather-edge" ribbon, a ribbon with a *picot* selvage, was worn at the left side of the high collar of milady's bodice.

Twentieth Century

As the twentieth century dawned, ribbon continued to maintain its role in the millinery world. In 1909, hats were made entirely of ribbon. Velvet ribbon with a satin back was a popular type for bows, bands, and streamers. Two-toned satins or failles, tinsel-shot metallic effects, and gorgeous brocades in rich, lovely colors were the order of the day. Indeed, feminine apparel of all sorts was being made of ribbon! Matched sets of ribbon accessories consisting of hat, scarf, and bag were the vogue. Coiffure bands made of ribbon matching the gown were attractive novelties for evening wear. Ribbon fancies, ever new and varied, were constantly making a place for themselves in the fashion world.

Two novel ideas which have come to be constantly associated with ribbon must be credited to England. The first of these is the standard for measuring ribbon. The measuring rod used for this purpose was the thickness of an English penny. A "number one" ribbon was the width of one of these pennies set on edge; a "number two" equalled the width of two set edgewise, "number three" the width of

COURTESY, METROPOLITAN MUSEUM OF ART

Figure 641. Dress of Brocaded, Changeable Silk, Showing Use of Ribbon, American, 1845

three, and so on. The second idea has to do with the terms "blue ribbon" and "red ribbon" used as marks of excellence. The blue ribbon was used to designate the Order of the Garter, the highest order of English knighthood; the red ribbon designated the Order of the Bath, which is the next highest in rank. Our present day custom of awarding excellence in any direction with a "blue" or "red" ribbon descends from the honor associated with these two famous English orders.

When compared with the simple narrow stripe or *ribband* of earliest times, modern ribbons appear as miracles of texture and color. Their infinite variety, as well, is cause for wonder. Ribbons of today are fanciful or plain, wide or narrow, of silk, satin, metallic cloth, calico, or paper. Loops, rosettes and bows continue to be a part of the ribbon world. The *ribband* of the ancients has become the *ribbon* of moderns. It has passed from the narrow stripe or woven border to a separate world of its own. In ever new and beautiful textures it continues to add its dainty charm to the changing fashion show.

REFERENCES

Earle, Alice Morse, *Two Centuries of Costume in America.*
Ellsworth, Evelyn Peters, *Textiles and Costume Design.*
Erman, John, *Life in Ancient Egypt.*
Evans, Mary, *Costume Throughout the Ages.*
Hughes, Talbot, *Dress Design.*
Illustrated Milliner, February, March, August, October, 1919; May, 1921; May, 1924.
Kelly and Schwabe, *Historic Costume.*
Lester, Katherine Morris, *Historic Costume,* pp. 123, 225.
Peterson's Fashion Magazine, Volume of 1863.
Sage, Elizabeth, *A Study of Costume,* pp. 18, 208.
Thompson, Eliza, *The Silk Department,* Chapter 16.
Wilkinson, Sir John Gardiner, *A Popular Account of the Ancient Egyptians.*

CHAPTER 42

Braid

A gentleman enveloped in mustachios, whiskers, fur collars, and *braiding*.

B RAIDS," says M. Charles Blanc, "have been invented to relieve the uniformity of plain materials; above all, of those in dull surfaces."* Like the story of many accessories of dress, that of braid, also, goes back to ancient days. In fact, the story of braiding or plaiting antedates historic records. Primitive peoples braided twigs into mats, which they formed into huts. This matting may also have been worn as a bodily protection. The women of Egypt plaited by hand the pretty bits of cloth for girdles, headdresses, and neck and arm ornaments. Many of these braided girdles may be seen in the collections of modern museums. Braids also enriched the official robes and headdresses of the ancient Assyrians.

In modern costume, the sixteenth, seventeenth, eighteenth, and nineteenth centuries stand forth, boldly marked with the use of braid. This fashion is conspicuously linked with the slashed costume distinguishing the sixteenth century. Its popularity continued through the following centuries, enriching the long coats and waistcoats of men, and the dresses, capes, and mantles of women. Previous to the sixteenth century the decoration of costume, aside from the beautiful hand embroidery, was largely confined to bands and borders made with appliqué needlework. This was a method of decoration in which designs were cut from one material, set upon another, and embroidery stitches employed to unify the pattern (see Figure 583, Chapter 37). The fine damasks and brocades of the period inspired many of the designs used in appliqué. Frequent mention is made to the *passaments* of this early day. This word was a general term for all gimps and braids used in forming patterns. The word was also applied to thread braids which by additional thread stitches were formed into geometric designs. Sometimes silk and worsted threads were used in the making of these braids or passaments.

1500-1600

In the sixteenth century, gimp, at present considered a member of

* M. Charles Blanc, *Art in Ornament and Dress.*

562

the braid family of modern times, was gradually coming into general use. Gimp was not a plaited braid, but was used in much the same way as plaited braids of a later day. It was made with a heavy cord or light wire center, closely and completely covered with a fine silk thread, as well as threads of gold and silver. It was frequently used in diaper pattern over coats, capes, and gowns. In men's clothes the fashion of the slashed doublet, sleeves, hose, and other parts of the costume created a demand for gimps, twists, and metallic threads, and, consequently, a great variety of these edgings were introduced. They, with embroidery, outlined the slashes in coats, sleeves, and breeches, thereby furnishing a proper finish to these openings through which the contrasting lining was pulled up in the form of little puffs. The handsome coats of Henry VIII show this use of the fashionable gimp, and it is said that one of Elizabeth's dresses was completely diapered in gold and silver gimp set with gems, to which little embroidery was added. In women's dress, the stomacher bodice also usually received these dainty designs in gimp, embroidery, and gems. The borders of skirts as well as the characteristic panel running down the center-front also supported patterns in which gimp was combined with the rich embroidery of the period. Gimp ornaments were made and stitched upon materials, and these patterns were further enriched with embroidery and jewels. Braided epaulets likewise furnished a distinctive note to sixteenth century costume. Indeed, much of the decorative detail in the dress of the century was achieved by the use of these gimps and fine metal cords which called for just as much skill in handling as did the threads of twisted silks. In later years of the century gold and silver braid on skirt, bodice, and sleeves was the one note that proclaimed fashion.

1600-1700

With the opening years of the following century the popularity of braid continued. In women's dress the long stomacher remained, and braiding and embroidery were the ever popular trimmings (see PLATES XXVIII, XXIX, Chapter 16). In the portrait of Queen Elizabeth, by Heere, rosettes of braid, presumably gold and silver set with jewels, cover the sleeves and ornament the deep-pointed front. The same braid in straight lengths decorates the bodice front. Pearls and jewels complete the lavish display. PLATE LVII. In men's clothes the small slashings began to appear. In passing, however, they lingered in the form of long openings extending from the shoulder down to a distance of six or eight inches over the chest. In the sleeves, also, the long slashings are seen. Frequently the sleeves were open on the front seam from the shoulder to the cuff, showing the handsome undersleeve. The edges of the slashes were still ornamented with braids. Sometimes buttons were set along the open edge, and loops of braid or button holes outlined in braid were set opposite. These, however, were purely ornamental, for the sleeve was never buttoned. About 1685 came the long-skirted coats which made a tempting foundation for braid. Though the coat was never buttoned below the waistline, buttons extended from the collar to the bottom of the coat skirt. All the seams as well as the front were now marked with braid. The cuffs and pockets were likewise enriched with narrow gold and black braid combined with colorful embroidery stitches. Waistcoats were long, embroidered, and often edged with deep gold fringe.

1700-1800

Gold braid had its gala day in the eighteenth century. It was worn on coat fronts, pockets and seams. The back openings of the coats were now decorated with several horizontal bands of braiding, frequently gold, extending to the two side pleats. The fashionable waistcoats of the middle century were heavily braided, or embroidered, or enriched with a combination of braid and embroidery, and the white felt hat so fashionable at this time was banded with gold braid. PLATE LVIII. The ladies, not to be outdone in this matter of braid, wore braid-trimmed skirts and short silk capes elaborately decorated with designs wrought in braided pattern. Many beautiful gimp trimmings were seen at this time.

1800-1900

In the early years of the nineteenth century, these attractive braids continued to be used, particularly in France. An authoritative French publication says of men's styles in 1818:

The wearing of *braid* is somewhat exaggerated. Young men order *braid* sewn on all seams of their redincoats, they go so far as to wear patterns on their backs and sleeves resembling those of a footman or drummer.*

During a large part of the Victorian era (1837-1909) braid combined with tassels and fringe had no rival. Through the thirties a combination of braiding with tassels formed the very elaborate decoration down the front of the popular polonaise, and in 1850 a wide band of flat braid was used to finish the large square-cut sleeve of milady's coat. By 1870-75 braids of every description were in use. Flat braids, especially soutache, which was very popular, were formed into elaborate patterns and used to enrich women's gowns, mantles, jackets, Figure 642, and the fashionable capes with long fronts known as "dolmans." In 1875, when women were wearing long trains, these were chiefly remarkable for their trimmings of gold and silver braid, twists, and fanciful knots, bows, and

---

* Paul-Louis de Giaferri, *French Costume.*

PLATE LVII. Queen Elizabeth . . . . *Heere*

The gown is elaborate with what appear to be little rosettes formed of the same braid which, in lengths, adorns the long front of the bodice. In the center of each rosette is a jewel setting. Note the extravagant use of pearls in the costume and the strings of pearls about the wrists.

fringes. Metal braids were exceedingly popular. Throughout the period, handbags and parasols alike were trimmed with braid and patterned with braided ornaments. Beginning about 1850 and continuing all through the century, narrow, flat, black silk braid was a distinctive note in the dress of men. It was stitched flat down the side seam of the fashionable trouser, and often bound the edges of the coats.

Figure 642. Braided Gown, 1873

Patterns formed of soutache braid are the elaborate trimming used in this fashionable afternoon costume.

As far as is known the first braiding machine was invented by an Englishman and patented in 1748. Receiving no encouragement at home, he crossed the channel and settled in France. About the same time a braiding machine appeared in Germany. This, however, is believed to have been the same machine carried there by French immigrants during the French Revolution. However, Germany soon came to be the center of the braid industry. As late as 1912 there were 100,000 machines for the manufacture of braid in the city of Bremen alone.

From time to time improvements upon the early machine gradually produced the modern braiding machine, which appeared about 1870. The first commercial products from the new machines were shoelaces. Tubular braids as well as flat braids were now woven in these machines. The flat braids are those generally used as a trimming upon costume. The more familiar flat braids of modern times are binding braids, soutache, rickrack, stickerei, lingerie, and the fashionable horsehair braids. The most useful braid ever produced is the serpentine edging known as "rickrack." "Horsehair" braid is today extensively used in the field of modern millinery. The pyroxylin fiber produces this popular braid. This fiber is obtained by treating cotton with an acid which reduces it to a semiliquid form. It is then forced through perforations of the desired

PLATE LVIII. Theodore Atkinson, Jr.....................*Joseph Blackburn*

The handsome waistcoat is elaborate in braiding combined with embroidery. As was the custom, he carries the tricorne under his arm.

size. As it hardens it becomes a stiff fiber resembling horsehair. During the late nineties, when distended skirts were fashionable, horsehair braid was employed as a stiffening. Practically all yarns—cottons, linens, wools, mohairs, silks, and tinsel—can be braided upon the modern machines. A mercerized cotton gives the braid a silk appearance. Silk itself is used for many of the fine dress braids. Artificial silk or rayon, which has a brighter luster than natural silk, is used to a large extent for trimming braids. Metal braids have been used in the military dress of all nations.

The popularity of all the various braids applied to costume may be attributed, no doubt, to the fact that they combine so effectively with other materials used in dress decoration—embroidery, lace, ribbon, fringe, and tassel. Remarking on the extensive use of braids, and of gimp in particular, one commentator cynically asserts, "Guimp is never out of fashion; it is too valuable to the dressmakers as a means of increasing their bills."

Twentieth Century

Though some form of braid is constantly marketed, the popularity of braid as a dress trimming comes and goes with the varying whims of Fashion. Two periods stand distinctly marked as periods of braid—first, the sixteenth century, which definitely marks the beginning of braid in costume, and secondly the Victorian era, during which braid surpassed all other trimming in popularity. The interval of two centuries, the seventeenth and eighteenth, is happily patterned with the rich doublets and the charming coats and waistcoats of men, and the handsome gowns of women, each enriched with the popular braids of silk and gold.

REFERENCES

Blanc, M. Charles, *Art in Ornament and Dress*.
Cole, George S., *Dictionary of Dry Goods*.
Dress Decoration and Ornament, p. 26. Woman's Institute.
Giafferi, Paul-Louis de, Histories of French Costume.
Hughes, Talbot, *Dress Design*, pp. 111-113, 142, 145.
Souder, M. Attie, *The Notions Department*, Chapter IX.

CHAPTER 43

Artificial Flowers

She hath made me four and twenty *nosegays* for the shearers.

Winter's Tale, Act IV, sc. 3

THE use of flowers as a decoration goes back to the same primitive urge that led uncivilized man to deck himself with feathers, beads, and bones. The entrance of artificial flowers into the fashion world followed the custom of wearing natural flowers either as a garland for the hair or shoulders or as a decoration pinned upon the costume or drawn through the buttonhole. The long effort constantly exerted to keep these cut flowers fresh and attractive naturally led to their imitation in material. Though records show that the earliest artificial flowers were worn as early as 1650, it was not until the last quarter of the eighteenth century, about 1775 to 1800, that the fashion came to be widespread, and not until 1800 that the art of imitating the color and texture of natural flowers with any great degree of success was attained. For this reason the general introduction of artificial flowers into the fashion world may be placed at a comparatively recent date, considered between 1800 and 1810.

The Italians, who had long practiced the art of producing artificial flowers, were the first to bring it to success. In 1738, France, having learned the art from Italy, sponsored a similar industry, but, unfortunately, it did not attain any great success. In the early years of the nineteenth century, one Séquin, a French chemist and botanist, succeeded in making artificial flowers equal in color and texture to those of Italy. These were made after the Chinese method—from the pith of the elder tree. He was the first, also, to introduce a kind of silver leaf which later was generally used in feminine costume. Another worker, Wenzel by name, who succeeded in making artificial flowers out of various materials, received recognition for his work at the International Exposition in Paris in 1802. Since that time artificial flowers have been generally used in costume and have had a particularly triumphant career in the field of millinery.

Turning back the pages of history we find that the ancient Egyptians made artificial flowers and leaves of painted linen. Horn shavings stained in various colors were also formed into floral shapes. In Athenian life one finds the garlands or wreaths worn by the women of classic times:

> . . . The ornaments
> Dropped from her brow, the *wreath*, the woven band,
> The net, the veil, which Venus gave.

It was the custom for the women of Greece to adorn their heads on festive occasions with wreaths and garlands of native flowers. The brilliant flower market, then as now, was always supplied with garlands, and these were twined about the head and upper part of the body. Roses in gilt, shaped in imitation of natural flowers, were also worn upon the head. Roman women of later days likewise wore crowns and diadems ornamented with flowers formed from metal. Crassus of Rome is said to have made artificial flowers of gold.

Middle Ages to 1700

During the Middle Ages, natural flowers and ribbons were frequently intertwined among the long plaits of hair, which, falling over the shoulders, often reached to the knee. Later, wreaths of simple garden and wild flowers were worn. The illuminated manuscripts of the fourteenth and fifteenth centuries depict natural flowers tied on hoops which fitted the head. About 1553 flowers were worn at the neck opening of the bodice and frequently used as a finishing note to the coiffure. By and large, flower shapes were constructed of metal and in this form were more lasting as an ornament for the hair.

During the reign of Louis XIV (1643-1715), his able prime minister, Colbert, was the one influence back of the great forward movement in all the industries. It was at this time that lacemaking reached its zenith. Beautiful gardens were built to furnish artists with inspiration for excellence in design. This interest in and appreciation of the garden again brought natural flowers into the fashion world. The dainty *boutonnière* came to be the popular accent in costume. These dainty sprays and bunches of gay-colored flowers were worn not only by the leaders in dress but by every woman who made any pretense of following the mode. In the atmosphere of the court of Versailles, however, these delicate flowers quickly languished. To preserve them a singular device was employed. They were set in little, water-filled bottles or glass tubes about four inches long and deftly hidden in the lace or ribbon of the bodice. These were known as "bosom-bottles." Sometimes these same bottles were securely pinned among the curls of the hair. When this novel gadget reached England in 1754, Horace Walpole wrote: "A new fashion has milady brought from France; it is a tin funnel covered with green ribbon, and it holds water which the ladies wear to keep their bouquets fresh." These were at first an awkward contrivance, but soon more dainty receptacles were devised.

1700-1800

The trend for flowers as costume accessories grew stronger. Gradually the inconvenience of carrying glass and silver containers to keep the natural flowers fresh led to a mild revolt among fashion leaders, and artificial flowers were devised as a substitute (see PLATE XII, Chapter 1.) In 1650 the dainty *boutonnière* of silk was in demand. PLATE LIX, Figure 643. Many of these were charming bits of color, adding a definite note of cheer to the costume. During the reigns of both Louis XV and Louis XVI (1715-89), a great many artificial flowers were worn. In 1770, men of fashion as well as modish women affected the dainty nosegay. Women wore the *boutonnière* on the left shoulder, similar to the manner so highly favored in modern times. The massive, powdered headdress of the late century did not escape. It, too, was enlivened with flowers as accents of color. The fashion in France and England carried over to America, and both men and women of the colonial period added artificial flowers to their already charming dress. French immigrants had probably introduced the making of these novelties into America, for as early as 1760 the newspapers of Boston tell of a new and thriving industry, "the bizness of making flowers." Teachers of flower making set up little shops and advertised for students. A letter dated 1766, written by the sister of Benjamin Franklin, throws an interesting light upon this new diversion:

COURTESY, METROPOLITAN MUSEUM OF ART

Figure 643. *Boutonnière*, Green and Brown Silk, English, about 1650

> And I have a small request to make. It is to procure me some fine old linen or cambric dyed into bright colours, such as red and green, a little blue but chiefly red, for with all my art and good old Benjamin's memorandums, I cannot make good colours. My daughter Jenny with a little of my assistance, has taken to making *flowers* for ladies' heads and bosoms with pretty good acceptance, and if I can procure these colours, I am in hope we shall get something by it worth our pains.

1800-1900

In Napoleon's day, the early nineteenth century, artificial flowers were in great demand. Elegant ladies who were friends of the Little Corporal wore bouquets of violets, his favorite flower. It was at this time that the discoveries of Séquin and Wenzel were greatly advanced, and the making of artificial flowers grew into a thriving industry. When the field of millinery, with its diversified styles, opened, the success of their discoveries was assured. In 1806, high, standing arrangements of artificial

flowers were worn on ladies' hats. From 1815-30, during the years of the Restoration, dainty, artificial flowers were arranged in wreaths or small bunches and worn in the hair as well as on the hat. Figure 644. By 1840 there were ten flower-making establishments in New York City. Nine years later the United States census reported twenty-three establishments making artificial flowers.

From 1873 on, artificial flowers held an honored place as a decoration for feminine headgear. At

COURTESY, METROPOLITAN MUSEUM OF ART

Figure 644. Nosegay, Artificial Flowers, American, 19th Century

times, it is true, the fashion waned, but, on the whole, flowers have held a place in the millinery world since the early nineteenth century. In 1875, flowers combined with ribbon and lace were piled high upon the little forward-tilted hats so popular at that date. Tendrils and dainty vines fell at the back with streamers of lace and ribbon (see Figures 63, 64, Chapter 1).

Twentieth Century

Later, in 1900, when transparent hats became the vogue, flowers in wreath arrangement were pressed flat and placed within the wide brim between the layers of open net. These hats were indeed a charming headdress; the fineness of the black net veiling the brilliancy of the flowers supplied the subtle touch of color necessary to many summer costumes. Then came a time when flowers were "out," and no matter how beautiful or charming the arrangement, milady was indeed passé if she yielded to the flower urge. Fashion, however, has ever been kindly

PLATE LIX. The Marquise de Pompadour.......................*Boucher*

This famous beauty of the court of Louis XV wears the fashionable *boutonnière*, adding one more note of charm to the flowerlike costume of silk, ribbon, and lace.

disposed toward the manufacturer of flowers, for no sooner are they out in millinery than they become the vogue as a dress accessory. Colorful nosegays of every textile, including glass, feathers, and leather, are worn as an added note of smartness to the costume. Sport suits, afternoon dresses, evening gowns, and wraps—each is given a distinctive touch in the dainty and colorful *boutonnière*.

During the winter of 1920, artificial flowers came back again. They were now made of chenille and ribbon, pressed flat, and forming a decorative band around the crown of the popular velvet and plush hat. To the multitude of lovely millinery flowers there were added, in the winter of 1921, many interesting and colorful yarn flowers in hand crochet. These quaint bits of color served innumerable uses. They added to the beauty of the woolen scarf, the tam-o-shanter, and the fur scarf. In 1925, when flowers for hats began to wane, Fashion again provided an opportunity for the use of flowers on coats and dresses. Tinsel chrysanthemums of gold and silver were worn at the shoulder of gowns, coats, and suits. Small bouquets for daytime wear and corsages of artificial orchard flowers for formal wear distinguished the smart ensemble. Indeed, the simplest frock seemed incomplete without its nosegay. Never before had there been such an abundance of artificial flowers when natural flowers were plentiful!

By 1927 the flower-trimmed hat was again revived. Small hats were entirely covered with flowers; large hats had flower-covered crowns. As the twentieth century wears on the flair for artificial flowers comes and goes. Invariably when flowers invade the millinery world, the *boutonnière* and corsage fade. As these rise in popularity, however, versatile Fashion decrees something new, something different in flowers for hats. Each season the manufacturers of artificial flowers have brought new and unusual arrangements, which invariably add color and individuality to costume.

The great skill of the Chinese and Japanese in the field of artificial flowers is noteworthy. The modern Chinese form beautiful flowers of rice paper. The Japanese show wonderful skill in reproducing both the form and color of natural flowers. In Italy the cocoons of the silkworm are dyed and used extensively in the making of artificial flowers. Even among peoples not so highly cultivated has the art been practiced. The natives of the Bahama Islands arrange small, daintily colored shells in flower sprays; feathers of highly colored birds are also shaped into flower forms. Today such materials as paper, fine calico, muslin, gauze, silk, velvet, crepe, leather, and the thin laminae of whalebone, are commonly used in this interesting industry. The twentieth century industry is highly specialized, and the many operations necessary to perfect artificial flowers are performed by many separate hands.

Notwithstanding the amusing satire of an eminent Frenchman who in 1700 proclaimed that artificial flowers were "the offspring of imposture," Fashion pays no heed, and artificial flowers continue to play their pretty part in the world of modes.

REFERENCES

Challamel, Augustin, *History of Fashion in France*.
Illustrated Milliner, March, 1919; September, November, 1921; March, November, 1927.
Planché, J. R., *Cyclopedia of Costume*.
Rhead, G. W., *Chats on Costume*.
Wilkinson, Sir John Gardiner, *A Popular Account of the Ancient Egyptians*.
Vogue, July 5, 1930.

Bibliography[*]

Abrahams, Ethel B., *Greek Dress; A Study of the Costume Worn in Ancient Greece from pre-Hellenic Times to the Hellenic Age.* John Murray, London, 1908.

Ashdown, Mrs. Charles H., *British Costume During Nineteen Centuries.* Frederick A. Stokes Co., New York, 1910.

Askinson, George William, *Perfumes and Their Preparation.* N. W. Henley & Co., New York, 1907.

Beck, S. William, *Gloves, Their Annals and Associations.* Hamilton Adams Co., London, 1883.

Blanc, Charles, *Art in Ornament and Dress.* Frederick Ware & Co., London, 1877.

Blondel, M. S., *Histoire des éventails,* Renouard, Paris, 1875.

Boehn, Max von, *Modes and Manners; Ornaments.* E. P. Dutton & Co., New York, 1929.

Boutell, Charles, *The Monumental Brasses of England;* A Series of Engravings Accompanied with Brief Descriptive Notes, London, 1849.

Bray, Helen A., *Textile Fibers, Yarns, and Fabrics.* Century Company, New York, 1929.

Brearley, Harry, *Time Telling Through the Ages.* Doubleday, Page & Co., New York, 1919.

Brereton, Lt. Col. F. S., *Clothing. Essentials of Life Series.* B. T. Batsford, Ltd., London, 1933.

Brooke, Iris, *English Costume in the Age of Elizabeth.* A. and C. Black, London, 1935.

Burckhardt, Jacob, *The Civilization of the Renaissance in Italy.* Hamilton & Co., New York, 1890.

Burgess, F. W., *Antique Jewelry and Trinkets.* G. P. Putnam's Sons, New York, 1919.

Calthrop, Dion Clayton, *English Costume.* A. and C. Black, London, 1926.

Carpenter, Frank George, *How the World Is Clothed.* American Book Co., New York, 1908.

Carter, Howard, *The Tomb of Tut-ankh-Amen.* George H. Doran Co., New York, 1923.

Challamel, Augustin, *History of Fashion in France.* Scribner and Welford, New York, 1882.

Child, Theodore, *Wimples and Crisping Pins.* Harper & Brothers, New York, 1895.

Cole, George S., *Dictionary of Dry Goods.* W. B. Conkey Co., Chicago, 1892.

Cook, William, *Things Indian.* Charles Scribner's Sons, New York, 1906.

Cooley, Arnold J., *The Toilet in Ancient and Modern Times.* Robert Hardwicke, London, 1868.

Davenport, Cyril, *Jewelry.* A. C. McClurg & Co., Chicago, 1908.

Davey, Richard, *Fur and Fur Garments.* The International Fur Store, London, 1895.

Diez, William H., *Zur Geschichte der Kostüme.* Braun & Schneider, Munich, 1891.

Dooley, William H., *Clothing and Style.* D. C. Heath & Co., Boston, 1930.

Druitt, Herbert, *A Manual of Costume as Illustrated by Monumental Brasses.* A. Moring, London, 1906.

Dutton, W. H., *Boots and Shoes of Our Ancestors.* Chapman & Hall, Ltd., London, 1898.

Earle, Alice Morse, *Two Centuries of Costume in America,* 2 Volumes. The Macmillan Company, New York, 1903.

Ellsworth, Evelyn Peters. *Textile and Costume Design.* Paul Elder & Co., San Francisco, 1917.

[*] Also see Hiler, Hilaire, *Bibliography of Costume,* H. W. Wilson Co., New York, 1939.

Bibliography (continued)

Erman, J. P. Adolph, *Life in Ancient Egypt.* The Macmillan Company, New York, 1894.

Evans, Mary, *Costume Throughout the Ages.* J. P. Lippincott Co., Philadelphia, 1930.

Evans, M. M., *Chapters on Greek Dress.* The Macmillan Company, New York, 1893.

Fairholt, F. W., *Costume in England.* Chapman & Hall, London, 1846.

Fairholt, F. W., *Rambles of an Archaeologist.* Virtue, London, 1871.

Fales, Jane, *Dressmaking.* Charles Scribner's Sons, New York, 1917.

Flory, M. A., *A Book about Fans; The History of Fans and Fan-Painting.* The Macmillan Company, New York, 1895.

Giaferri, Paul-Louis de, *L'historie du Costume Feminin Francais.* Editions Nilsson, 8 Rue Havery, Paris, 1922.

Giaferri, Paul-Louis de, *The History of French Masculine Costume.* Foreign Publications, Inc., 13 West 47th St., New York, 1928.

Giaferri, Paul-Louis de, *Millinery in the Fashion History of the World.* The Illustrated Millinery Co., New York.

Goddard, Eunice R., *Women's Costume in French Texts of the Eleventh and Twelfth Centuries.* Las Presses Universitaires de la France, 1927.

Gottleib, Abraham, *Fur Truths.* Harper & Brothers, New York and London, 1927.

Guhl, E. K., and Kohmer, W. D., *Life of the Greeks and Romans.* D. Appleton Co., New York, 1898.

Hare, Christopher, *Most Illustrious Ladies of the Italian Renaissance.* Charles Scribner's Sons, New York, 1931.

Hartley, Dorothy, *Medieval Costume and Life.* Charles Scribner's Sons, New York, 1931.

Havemeyer, Loomis, *The Drama of Savage Peoples.* Yale University Press, New Haven, 1916.

Head, Mrs. R. E., *The Lace and Embroidery Collector.* Dodd, Mead & Co., New York, 1922.

Hiler, Hilaire, *From Nudity to Raiment, An Introduction to the Study of Costume.* W. and G. Foyle, Ltd., London, 1929.

Hope, Thomas, *Costume of the Ancients.* Bolmer and Co., London, 1841.

Houston, Mary G., *Ancient Greek, Roman, and Byzantine Costume.* The Macmillan Company, New York, 1931.

Hughes, Talbot, *Dress Design.* John Hogg, London, 1913.

Jackson, Mrs. F. Nevil, *The History of Handmade Lace.* Charles Scribner's Sons, New York, 1900.

Jacquemin, Raphael, *Histoire General au Costume.* Paris, 1866.

Johnson, Harold, *Private Life of the Romans.* Scott, Foresman & Co., Chicago, 1903.

Jones, William, *Finger Ring Lore.* Chatto & Windus, London, 1877.

Kelly, Francis M., and Schwabe, Randolph, *Historic Costume.* Charles Scribner's Sons, New York, 1925.

Kennard, Beulah, *The Jewelry and Silverware Departments.* The Ronald Press, New York, 1917.

King, George Frederick, *Rings for the Finger.* J. B. Lippincott Co., Philadelphia, 1917.

Lefébure, Ernest, *Embroidery and Lace.* J. B. Lippincott Co., Philadelphia, 1889.

Lehman, Helen, *The Leather Goods and Gloves Department.* The Ronald Press, New York, 1917.

Lester, Katherine Morris, *Historic Costume.* The Manual Arts Press, Peoria, Ill., 1925.

Lowes, Mrs. Emily Leigh, *Chats on Old Lace and Needlework.* Frederick A. Stokes Co., London, 1908.

Macklin, Herbert, *Brasses of England.* E. P. Dutton & Co., New York, 1907.

McClellan, Elizabeth, *Historic Dress in America,* 2 Volumes. McCrae Smith, Philadelphia, 1910.

Macgowan, Kenneth, and Rosse, Herman, *Masks and Demons*. Harcourt, Brace & Co., New York, 1923.

Moore, Mrs. N. Hudson, *The Lace Book*. Frederick A. Stokes Co., New York, 1925.

Moore, Mrs. N. Hudson, *The Old Clock Book*. Frederick A. Stokes Co., New York, 1911.

Norris, Herbert, *Costume and Fashion*, 2 Volumes. E. P. Dutton & Co., New York, 1925.

Norris, Herbert, and Curtis, Oswald, *Costume and Fashion: The Nineteenth Century*. E. P. Dutton & Co., New York, 1933.

Pallister, Mrs. Bury, *History of Lace*. Sampson, Marston & Low, London, 1865.

Parsons, Frank Alvah, *The Art in Dress*. Doubleday, Doran & Co., New York, 1928.

Pauquet, Freres, *Modes and Costume Historique*, 2 Volumes, Aux Bureaux des modes et costume historiques, Paris, 1865.

Picken, Mary Brooks, *The Secrets of Distinctive Dress*. International Text Book Press, Scranton, Pa., 1925.

Piesse, G. W. Septimus, *The Art of Perfumery*. Blakiston, Philadelphia, 1880.

Planché, J. R., *A Cyclopedia of Costume:* Vol. I–*The Dictionary;* Vol. II–*A General History of Costume in Europe.* Chatto & Windus, London, 1879.

Pollen, Mrs. Hungerford, *Seven Centuries of Lace.* The Macmillan Company, New York, 1908.

Quennell, Marjorie and C. H. B., *Everyday Life in the New Stone, Bronze, and Early Iron Ages.* G. P. Putnam's Sons, New York, 1923.

Quicherat, J., *History of Costume in France.* Paris, 1877.

Racinet, A. C. A., *Le Costume Historique.* Firmin-Didot et Cie, Paris, 1888.

Redfern, W. B., *Royal and Historical Gloves and Shoes.* Methuen and Company, London, 1904.

Rhead, G. W., *Chats on Costume.* T. F. Unwin, London, 1926.

Rhead, G. W., *History of the Fan.* Kegan, Paul, Trench, Truber & Co., Ltd., London, 1910.

Sage, Elizabeth, *A Study of Costume.* Frederick A. Stokes Co., New York, 1926.

Sharpe, A. M., *Point and Pillow Lace.* E. P. Dutton & Co., New York, 1913.

Shaw, Henry, *Dresses and Decorations of the Middle Ages.* Henry G. Bohn, London, 1858.

Smith, J. Moyr, *Ancient Greek Female Costume.* Sampson, Low, Marston, Searle, and Livingston, London, 1882.

Souder, M. Attie, *The Notions Department.* The Ronald Press, New York, 1917.

Story, Margaret, *Individuality and Clothes.* Funk & Wagnall Co., New York, 1930.

Strutt, Joseph, *Complete View of the Dress and Habits of the People of England, from the Establishment of the Saxons to the Present Time.* Henry G. Bohn, London, 1842.

Suffing, E. R., *English Church Brasses from the Thirteenth to Seventeenth Century.* L. Upcott Gill, London, 1910.

Thompson, Eliza, *The Cotton and Linen Departments.* The Ronald Press, New York, 1917.

Thompson, Eliza, *The Silk Department.* The Ronald Press, New York, 1918.

Timayenis, T. T., *Greece in the Time of Homer.* D. Appleton & Co., New York, 1885.

Uzanne, Louis O., *The Fan* (English trans.), Nimmo & Bain, London, 1895.

Viollet-le-Duc., E. E., *Dictionnaire du Mobilier Francais*, Vols. III and IV. Paris, 1858.

Webb, Winifred Mark, *Heritage of Dress.* Revised Edition. The Times Book Club, London, 1912.

Wilkinson, Sir John Gardiner, *A Popular Account of the Ancient Egyptians,* Vol. II. Harper & Brothers, New York, 1854.

Wright, Thomas, *The Celt, the Roman, and the Saxon.* J. B. Lippincott Co., Philadelphia, 1875.

Index to the Illustrations

Index to the Text

A CATALOG OF SELECTED DOVER
BOOKS IN ALL FIELDS OF INTEREST

CONCERNING THE SPIRITUAL IN ART, Wassily Kandinsky. Pioneering work by father of abstract art. Thoughts on color theory, nature of art. Analysis of earlier masters. 12 illustrations. 80pp. of text. 5⅜ x 8½.   0-486-23411-8

CELTIC ART: The Methods of Construction, George Bain. Simple geometric techniques for making Celtic interlacements, spirals, Kells-type initials, animals, humans, etc. Over 500 illustrations. 160pp. 9 x 12. (Available in U.S. only.)   0-486-22923-8

AN ATLAS OF ANATOMY FOR ARTISTS, Fritz Schider. Most thorough reference work on art anatomy in the world. Hundreds of illustrations, including selections from works by Vesalius, Leonardo, Goya, Ingres, Michelangelo, others. 593 illustrations. 192pp. 7⅛ x 10¼.   0-486-20241-0

CELTIC HAND STROKE-BY-STROKE (Irish Half-Uncial from "The Book of Kells"): An Arthur Baker Calligraphy Manual, Arthur Baker. Complete guide to creating each letter of the alphabet in distinctive Celtic manner. Covers hand position, strokes, pens, inks, paper, more. Illustrated. 48pp. 8¼ x 11.   0-486-24336-2

EASY ORIGAMI, John Montroll. Charming collection of 32 projects (hat, cup, pelican, piano, swan, many more) specially designed for the novice origami hobbyist. Clearly illustrated easy-to-follow instructions insure that even beginning papercrafters will achieve successful results. 48pp. 8¼ x 11.   0-486-27298-2

BLOOMINGDALE'S ILLUSTRATED 1886 CATALOG: Fashions, Dry Goods and Housewares, Bloomingdale Brothers. Famed merchants' extremely rare catalog depicting about 1,700 products: clothing, housewares, firearms, dry goods, jewelry, more. Invaluable for dating, identifying vintage items. Also, copyright-free graphics for artists, designers. Co-published with Henry Ford Museum & Greenfield Village. 160pp. 8¼ x 11.   0-486-25780-0

THE ART OF WORLDLY WISDOM, Baltasar Gracian. "Think with the few and speak with the many," "Friends are a second existence," and "Be able to forget" are among this 1637 volume's 300 pithy maxims. A perfect source of mental and spiritual refreshment, it can be opened at random and appreciated either in brief or at length. 128pp. 5⅜ x 8½.   0-486-44034-6

JOHNSON'S DICTIONARY: A Modern Selection, Samuel Johnson (E. L. McAdam and George Milne, eds.). This modern version reduces the original 1755 edition's 2,300 pages of definitions and literary examples to a more manageable length, retaining the verbal pleasure and historical curiosity of the original. 480pp. 5¾₁₆ x 8¼.   0-486-44089-3

ADVENTURES OF HUCKLEBERRY FINN, Mark Twain, Illustrated by E. W. Kemble. A work of eternal richness and complexity, a source of ongoing critical debate, and a literary landmark, Twain's 1885 masterpiece about a barefoot boy's journey of self-discovery has enthralled readers around the world. This handsome clothbound reproduction of the first edition features all 174 of the original black-and-white illustrations. 368pp. 5⅜ x 8½.   0-486-44322-1

HOW TO DO BEADWORK, Mary White. Fundamental book on craft from simple projects to five-bead chains and woven works. 106 illustrations. 142pp. 5⅜ x 8. 0-486-20697-1

THE 1912 AND 1915 GUSTAV STICKLEY FURNITURE CATALOGS, Gustav Stickley. With over 200 detailed illustrations and descriptions, these two catalogs are essential reading and reference materials and identification guides for Stickley furniture. Captions cite materials, dimensions and prices. 112pp. 6½ x 9¼. 0-486-26676-1

EARLY AMERICAN LOCOMOTIVES, John H. White, Jr. Finest locomotive engravings from early 19th century: historical (1804–74), main-line (after 1870), special, foreign, etc. 147 plates. 142pp. 11⅜ x 8¼. 0-486-22772-3

LITTLE BOOK OF EARLY AMERICAN CRAFTS AND TRADES, Peter Stockham (ed.). 1807 children's book explains crafts and trades: baker, hatter, cooper, potter, and many others. 23 copperplate illustrations. 140pp. 4⅝ x 6. 0-486-23336-7

VICTORIAN FASHIONS AND COSTUMES FROM HARPER'S BAZAR, 1867–1898, Stella Blum (ed.). Day costumes, evening wear, sports clothes, shoes, hats, other accessories in over 1,000 detailed engravings. 320pp. 9⅜ x 12¼. 0-486-22990-4

THE LONG ISLAND RAIL ROAD IN EARLY PHOTOGRAPHS, Ron Ziel. Over 220 rare photos, informative text document origin (1844) and development of rail service on Long Island. Vintage views of early trains, locomotives, stations, passengers, crews, much more. Captions. 8⅞ x 11¾. 0-486-26301-0

VOYAGE OF THE LIBERDADE, Joshua Slocum. Great 19th-century mariner's thrilling, first-hand account of the wreck of his ship off South America, the 35-foot boat he built from the wreckage, and its remarkable voyage home. 128pp. 5⅜ x 8½. 0-486-40022-0

TEN BOOKS ON ARCHITECTURE, Vitruvius. The most important book ever written on architecture. Early Roman aesthetics, technology, classical orders, site selection, all other aspects. Morgan translation. 331pp. 5⅜ x 8½. 0-486-20645-9

THE HUMAN FIGURE IN MOTION, Eadweard Muybridge. More than 4,500 stopped-action photos, in action series, showing undraped men, women, children jumping, lying down, throwing, sitting, wrestling, carrying, etc. 390pp. 7⅞ x 10⅝. 0-486-20204-6 Clothbd.

TREES OF THE EASTERN AND CENTRAL UNITED STATES AND CANADA, William M. Harlow. Best one-volume guide to 140 trees. Full descriptions, woodlore, range, etc. Over 600 illustrations. Handy size. 288pp. 4½ x 6⅜. 0-486-20395-6

GROWING AND USING HERBS AND SPICES, Milo Miloradovich. Versatile handbook provides all the information needed for cultivation and use of all the herbs and spices available in North America. 4 illustrations. Index. Glossary. 236pp. 5⅜ x 8½. 0-486-25058-X

BIG BOOK OF MAZES AND LABYRINTHS, Walter Shepherd. 50 mazes and labyrinths in all–classical, solid, ripple, and more–in one great volume. Perfect inexpensive puzzler for clever youngsters. Full solutions. 112pp. 8⅛ x 11. 0-486-22951-3

PIANO TUNING, J. Cree Fischer. Clearest, best book for beginner, amateur. Simple repairs, raising dropped notes, tuning by easy method of flattened fifths. No previous skills needed. 4 illustrations. 201pp. 5⅜ x 8½. 0-486-23267-0

HINTS TO SINGERS, Lillian Nordica. Selecting the right teacher, developing confidence, overcoming stage fright, and many other important skills receive thoughtful discussion in this indispensible guide, written by a world-famous diva of four decades' experience. 96pp. 5⅜ x 8½. 0-486-40094-8

THE COMPLETE NONSENSE OF EDWARD LEAR, Edward Lear. All nonsense limericks, zany alphabets, Owl and Pussycat, songs, nonsense botany, etc., illustrated by Lear. Total of 320pp. 5⅜ x 8½. (Available in U.S. only.) 0-486-20167-8

VICTORIAN PARLOUR POETRY: An Annotated Anthology, Michael R. Turner. 117 gems by Longfellow, Tennyson, Browning, many lesser-known poets. "The Village Blacksmith," "Curfew Must Not Ring Tonight," "Only a Baby Small," dozens more, often difficult to find elsewhere. Index of poets, titles, first lines. xxiii + 325pp. 5⅝ x 8¼. 0-486-27044-0

DUBLINERS, James Joyce. Fifteen stories offer vivid, tightly focused observations of the lives of Dublin's poorer classes. At least one, "The Dead," is considered a masterpiece. Reprinted complete and unabridged from standard edition. 160pp. 5³⁄₁₆ x 8¼. 0-486-26870-5

GREAT WEIRD TALES: 14 Stories by Lovecraft, Blackwood, Machen and Others, S. T. Joshi (ed.). 14 spellbinding tales, including "The Sin Eater," by Fiona McLeod, "The Eye Above the Mantel," by Frank Belknap Long, as well as renowned works by R. H. Barlow, Lord Dunsany, Arthur Machen, W. C. Morrow and eight other masters of the genre. 256pp. 5⅜ x 8½. (Available in U.S. only.) 0-486-40436-6

THE BOOK OF THE SACRED MAGIC OF ABRAMELIN THE MAGE, translated by S. MacGregor Mathers. Medieval manuscript of ceremonial magic. Basic document in Aleister Crowley, Golden Dawn groups. 268pp. 5⅜ x 8½. 0-486-23211-5

THE BATTLES THAT CHANGED HISTORY, Fletcher Pratt. Eminent historian profiles 16 crucial conflicts, ancient to modern, that changed the course of civilization. 352pp. 5⅜ x 8½. 0-486-41129-X

NEW RUSSIAN-ENGLISH AND ENGLISH-RUSSIAN DICTIONARY, M. A. O'Brien. This is a remarkably handy Russian dictionary, containing a surprising amount of information, including over 70,000 entries. 366pp. 4½ x 6⅛. 0-486-20208-9

NEW YORK IN THE FORTIES, Andreas Feininger. 162 brilliant photographs by the well-known photographer, formerly with *Life* magazine. Commuters, shoppers, Times Square at night, much else from city at its peak. Captions by John von Hartz. 181pp. 9¼ x 10¾. 0-486-23585-8

INDIAN SIGN LANGUAGE, William Tomkins. Over 525 signs developed by Sioux and other tribes. Written instructions and diagrams. Also 290 pictographs. 111pp. 6⅛ x 9¼. 0-486-22029-X

ANATOMY: A Complete Guide for Artists, Joseph Sheppard. A master of figure drawing shows artists how to render human anatomy convincingly. Over 460 illustrations. 224pp. 8⅜ x 11¼. 0-486-27279-6

MEDIEVAL CALLIGRAPHY: Its History and Technique, Marc Drogin. Spirited history, comprehensive instruction manual covers 13 styles (ca. 4th century through 15th). Excellent photographs; directions for duplicating medieval techniques with modern tools. 224pp. 8⅜ x 11¼. 0-486-26142-5

DRIED FLOWERS: How to Prepare Them, Sarah Whitlock and Martha Rankin. Complete instructions on how to use silica gel, meal and borax, perlite aggregate, sand and borax, glycerine and water to create attractive permanent flower arrangements. 12 illustrations. 32pp. 5⅜ x 8½. 0-486-21802-3

EASY-TO-MAKE BIRD FEEDERS FOR WOODWORKERS, Scott D. Campbell. Detailed, simple-to-use guide for designing, constructing, caring for and using feeders. Text, illustrations for 12 classic and contemporary designs. 96pp. 5⅜ x 8½. 0-486-25847-5

THE COMPLETE BOOK OF BIRDHOUSE CONSTRUCTION FOR WOODWORKERS, Scott D. Campbell. Detailed instructions, illustrations, tables. Also data on bird habitat and instinct patterns. Bibliography. 3 tables. 63 illustrations in 15 figures. 48pp. 5¼ x 8½. 0-486-24407-5

SCOTTISH WONDER TALES FROM MYTH AND LEGEND, Donald A. Mackenzie. 16 lively tales tell of giants rumbling down mountainsides, of a magic wand that turns stone pillars into warriors, of gods and goddesses, evil hags, powerful forces and more. 240pp. 5⅜ x 8½. 0-486-29677-6

THE HISTORY OF UNDERCLOTHES, C. Willett Cunnington and Phyllis Cunnington. Fascinating, well-documented survey covering six centuries of English undergarments, enhanced with over 100 illustrations: 12th-century laced-up bodice, footed long drawers (1795), 19th-century bustles, 19th-century corsets for men, Victorian "bust improvers," much more. 272pp. 5⅜ x 8¼. 0-486-27124-2

ARTS AND CRAFTS FURNITURE: The Complete Brooks Catalog of 1912, Brooks Manufacturing Co. Photos and detailed descriptions of more than 150 now very collectible furniture designs from the Arts and Crafts movement depict davenports, settees, buffets, desks, tables, chairs, bedsteads, dressers and more, all built of solid, quarter-sawed oak. Invaluable for students and enthusiasts of antiques, Americana and the decorative arts. 80pp. 6½ x 9¼. 0-486-27471-3

WILBUR AND ORVILLE: A Biography of the Wright Brothers, Fred Howard. Definitive, crisply written study tells the full story of the brothers' lives and work. A vividly written biography, unparalleled in scope and color, that also captures the spirit of an extraordinary era. 560pp. 6⅛ x 9¼. 0-486-40297-5

THE ARTS OF THE SAILOR: Knotting, Splicing and Ropework, Hervey Garrett Smith. Indispensable shipboard reference covers tools, basic knots and useful hitches; handsewing and canvas work, more. Over 100 illustrations. Delightful reading for sea lovers. 256pp. 5⅜ x 8½. 0-486-26440-8

FRANK LLOYD WRIGHT'S FALLINGWATER: The House and Its History, Second, Revised Edition, Donald Hoffmann. A total revision–both in text and illustrations–of the standard document on Fallingwater, the boldest, most personal architectural statement of Wright's mature years, updated with valuable new material from the recently opened Frank Lloyd Wright Archives. "Fascinating"–*The New York Times*. 116 illustrations. 128pp. 9¼ x 10¾. 0-486-27430-6

PHOTOGRAPHIC SKETCHBOOK OF THE CIVIL WAR, Alexander Gardner. 100 photos taken on field during the Civil War. Famous shots of Manassas Harper's Ferry, Lincoln, Richmond, slave pens, etc. 244pp. 10⅞ x 8¼. 0-486-22731-6

FIVE ACRES AND INDEPENDENCE, Maurice G. Kains. Great back-to-the-land classic explains basics of self-sufficient farming. The one book to get. 95 illustrations. 397pp. 5⅜ x 8½. 0-486-20974-1

A MODERN HERBAL, Margaret Grieve. Much the fullest, most exact, most useful compilation of herbal material. Gigantic alphabetical encyclopedia, from aconite to zedoary, gives botanical information, medical properties, folklore, economic uses, much else. Indispensable to serious reader. 161 illustrations. 888pp. 6½ x 9¼. 2-vol. set. (Available in U.S. only.) Vol. I: 0-486-22798-7 Vol. II: 0-486-22799-5

HIDDEN TREASURE MAZE BOOK, Dave Phillips. Solve 34 challenging mazes accompanied by heroic tales of adventure. Evil dragons, people-eating plants, blood-thirsty giants, many more dangerous adversaries lurk at every twist and turn. 34 mazes, stories, solutions. 48pp. 8¼ x 11. 0-486-24566-7

LETTERS OF W. A. MOZART, Wolfgang A. Mozart. Remarkable letters show bawdy wit, humor, imagination, musical insights, contemporary musical world; includes some letters from Leopold Mozart. 276pp. 5⅜ x 8½. 0-486-22859-2

BASIC PRINCIPLES OF CLASSICAL BALLET, Agrippina Vaganova. Great Russian theoretician, teacher explains methods for teaching classical ballet. 118 illustrations. 175pp. 5⅜ x 8½. 0-486-22036-2

THE JUMPING FROG, Mark Twain. Revenge edition. The original story of The Celebrated Jumping Frog of Calaveras County, a hapless French translation, and Twain's hilarious "retranslation" from the French. 12 illustrations. 66pp. 5⅜ x 8½. 0-486-22686-7

BEST REMEMBERED POEMS, Martin Gardner (ed.). The 126 poems in this superb collection of 19th- and 20th-century British and American verse range from Shelley's "To a Skylark" to the impassioned "Renascence" of Edna St. Vincent Millay and to Edward Lear's whimsical "The Owl and the Pussycat." 224pp. 5⅜ x 8½. 0-486-27165-X

COMPLETE SONNETS, William Shakespeare. Over 150 exquisite poems deal with love, friendship, the tyranny of time, beauty's evanescence, death and other themes in language of remarkable power, precision and beauty. Glossary of archaic terms. 80pp. 5$\frac{3}{16}$ x 8¼. 0-486-26686-9

HISTORIC HOMES OF THE AMERICAN PRESIDENTS, Second, Revised Edition, Irvin Haas. A traveler's guide to American Presidential homes, most open to the public, depicting and describing homes occupied by every American President from George Washington to George Bush. With visiting hours, admission charges, travel routes. 175 photographs. Index. 160pp. 8¼ x 11. 0-486-26751-2

THE WIT AND HUMOR OF OSCAR WILDE, Alvin Redman (ed.). More than 1,000 ripostes, paradoxes, wisecracks: Work is the curse of the drinking classes; I can resist everything except temptation; etc. 258pp. 5⅜ x 8½. 0-486-20602-5

SHAKESPEARE LEXICON AND QUOTATION DICTIONARY, Alexander Schmidt. Full definitions, locations, shades of meaning in every word in plays and poems. More than 50,000 exact quotations. 1,485pp. 6½ x 9¼. 2-vol. set. Vol. 1: 0-486-22726-X Vol. 2: 0-486-22727-8

SELECTED POEMS, Emily Dickinson. Over 100 best-known, best-loved poems by one of America's foremost poets, reprinted from authoritative early editions. No comparable edition at this price. Index of first lines. 64pp. 5$\frac{3}{16}$ x 8¼. 0-486-26466-1

THE INSIDIOUS DR. FU-MANCHU, Sax Rohmer. The first of the popular mystery series introduces a pair of English detectives to their archnemesis, the diabolical Dr. Fu-Manchu. Flavorful atmosphere, fast-paced action, and colorful characters enliven this classic of the genre. 208pp. 5$\frac{3}{16}$ x 8¼. 0-486-29898-1

LIGHT AND SHADE: A Classic Approach to Three-Dimensional Drawing, Mrs. Mary P. Merrifield. Handy reference clearly demonstrates principles of light and shade by revealing effects of common daylight, sunshine, and candle or artificial light on geometrical solids. 13 plates. 64pp. 5⅜ x 8½. 0-486-44143-1

ASTROLOGY AND ASTRONOMY: A Pictorial Archive of Signs and Symbols, Ernst and Johanna Lehner. Treasure trove of stories, lore, and myth, accompanied by more than 300 rare illustrations of planets, the Milky Way, signs of the zodiac, comets, meteors, and other astronomical phenomena. 192pp. 8⅜ x 11. 0-486-43981-X

JEWELRY MAKING: Techniques for Metal, Tim McCreight. Easy-to-follow instructions and carefully executed illustrations describe tools and techniques, use of gems and enamels, wire inlay, casting, and other topics. 72 line illustrations and diagrams. 176pp. 8¼ x 10⅞. 0-486-44043-5

MAKING BIRDHOUSES: Easy and Advanced Projects, Gladstone Califf. Easy-to-follow instructions include diagrams for everything from a one-room house for bluebirds to a forty-two-room structure for purple martins. 56 plates; 4 figures. 80pp. 8¾ x 6⅜. 0-486-44183-0

LITTLE BOOK OF LOG CABINS: How to Build and Furnish Them, William S. Wicks. Handy how-to manual, with instructions and illustrations for building cabins in the Adirondack style, fireplaces, stairways, furniture, beamed ceilings, and more. 102 line drawings. 96pp. 8¾ x 6⅜. 0-486-44259-4

THE SEASONS OF AMERICA PAST, Eric Sloane. From "sugaring time" and strawberry picking to Indian summer and fall harvest, a whole year's activities described in charming prose and enhanced with 79 of the author's own illustrations. 160pp. 8¼ x 11. 0-486-44220-9

THE METROPOLIS OF TOMORROW, Hugh Ferriss. Generous, prophetic vision of the metropolis of the future, as perceived in 1929. Powerful illustrations of towering structures, wide avenues, and rooftop parks–all features in many of today's modern cities. 59 illustrations. 144pp. 8¼ x 11. 0-486-43727-2

THE PATH TO ROME, Hilaire Belloc. This 1902 memoir abounds in lively vignettes from a vanished time, recounting a pilgrimage on foot across the Alps and Apennines in order to "see all Europe which the Christian Faith has saved." 77 of the author's original line drawings complement his sparkling prose. 272pp. 5⅜ x 8½. 0-486-44001-X

THE HISTORY OF RASSELAS: Prince of Abissinia, Samuel Johnson. Distinguished English writer attacks eighteenth-century optimism and man's unrealistic estimates of what life has to offer. 112pp. 5⅜ x 8½. 0-486-44094-X

A VOYAGE TO ARCTURUS, David Lindsay. A brilliant flight of pure fancy, where wild creatures crowd the fantastic landscape and demented torturers dominate victims with their bizarre mental powers. 272pp. 5⅜ x 8½. 0-486-44198-9

Paperbound unless otherwise indicated. Available at your book dealer, online at **www.doverpublications.com**, or by writing to Dept. GI, Dover Publications, Inc., 31 East 2nd Street, Mineola, NY 11501. For current price information or for free catalogs (please indicate field of interest), write to Dover Publications or log on to **www.doverpublications.com** and see every Dover book in print. Dover publishes more than 500 books each year on science, elementary and advanced mathematics, biology, music, art, literary history, social sciences, and other areas.